THE ECONOMY OF THE ROMAN EMPIRE: QUANTITATIVE STUDIES

CONTENTS

[vii]

PART 3: POPULATION AND DEMOGRAPHIC POLICY

APPENDICES

TABLES

PREFACE

This book owes much to the advice and encouragement of the late Professor A. H. M. Jones, who supervised the doctoral thesis on which chapters 3 and 4 are based. Three chapters were composed and the remainder rewritten after Professor Jones's death in 1970, but his many writings have remained an unfailing source of stimulus. Professor M. I Finley has also given me invaluable help and advice over a long period. Professor P. A. Brunt kindly read chapter 2 in draft and made many useful criticisms. Mr J. A. Crook gave most helpful comments on the doctoral thesis which he examined. Professor E. R. Birley and Dr H.-G. Pflaum kindly encouraged me to write this book. I should like to offer my warmest thanks to all of them.

I should also like to thank many others who have helped me, including Professor C. O. Brink, Lady Brogan, Professor T. R. S. Broughton, Mr. M. H. Crawford, Professor A. Gershenkron, Professor J. F. Gilliam, Professor P. Grierson, Professor J. Guey, Professor G. M. A. Hanfmann, Professor C. P. Jones, Professor M. Leglay, Dr W. D. Macpherson, Dr F. G. B. Millar, Professor A. D. Momigliano, Dr John Morris, Professor G. C. Picard, Monsieur Cl. Poinssot, Miss J. M. Reynolds, Professor D. R. Shackleton Bailey, Professor F. W. Walbank and Mr J. B. Ward Perkins.

I carried out the research on which the book is based while holding a Studentship at King's College, Cambridge, followed by a Fellowship at Gonville and Caius College, Cambridge. I should like to express my gratitude to both Colleges. I wrote part of the text in the United States, while enjoying the hospitality and research facilities of the Institute for Advanced Study at Princeton, of which I was a member during 1971-2.

Parts of the book have appeared in an earlier form in periodicals, chapters 1, 3, 4 and 7 in the *Papers of the British School at Rome*, and a fragment of chapter 6 in the *Journal of Roman Studies*. The chapters concerned are intended to supersede the earlier articles, from which they differ substantially.

Cambridge, November 1972   R.P.D.-J.

ABBREVIATIONS

For abbreviations used only in the lists of costs see p. 89 (Africa) and p. 156 (Italy).

Capital Roman numerals followed by Arabic numerals refer to volumes of the *Corpus Inscriptionum Latinarum*: thus VIII 23107 means *Corpus Inscriptionum Latinarum* volume VIII no.23107.

References in the form of an Arabic numeral preceded by 'no.' refer to entries in the list of costs on pp. 90 ff. and pp. 157 ff.

IX Censimento	*IX Censimento generale delle popolazioni* [*dell'Italia*]. *Dati sommari per comuni* (1955)
AAA	S. Gsell *Atlas archéologique de l'Algérie* (1911)
AAASH	*Acta antiqua academiae scientiarum Hungaricae*
ACSDIR	*Atti, Centro di Studi e Documentazione sull'Italia Romana*
AE	*Année épigraphique*
AESC	*Annales. Économies. Sociétés. Civilisations*
AJP	*American Journal of Philology*
Ant.afr.	*Antiquités africaines*
Apol.	Apuleius *Apologia*
BAC	*Bulletin archéologique du Comité des travaux historiques et scientifiques*
BCAR	*Bullettino della Commissione archeol. municipale (comunale) di Roma*
BCB	E. Boeswillwald, R. Cagnat, A. Ballu, *Timgad, une cité africaine sous l'empire romain* (1905)
Beloch	J. Beloch *Bevölkerung der griechisch-römischen Welt* (1886)
BGU	*Ägyptische Urkunden aus den Staatlichen Museen zu Berlin. Griechische Urkunden* (1895–)
Billeter	G. Billeter *Geschichte des Zinsfusses im griechisch-römischen Altertum bis auf Justinian* (1898)
Bourne	F. C. Bourne 'The Roman Alimentary Program and Italian Agriculture' *TAPHA* 91 (1960) 47–75
Brockmeyer	N. Brockmeyer *Arbeitsorganisation und ökonomisches Denken in der Gutswirtschaft des römischen Reiches* (1968)
Broughton	T. R. S. Broughton *The Romanization of Africa Proconsularis* (1929)
Brunt	P. A. Brunt *Italian manpower 225 B.C.–A.D. 14* (1971)
Buecheler	F. Buecheler *Carmina Latina epigraphica* (1895–7); supp. ed. Lommatzsch (1926)
C. no.	Numbered item in the list of costs on pp. 90 ff. and pp. 157 ff.
CAH	*Cambridge ancient history*

Carcopino — J. Carcopino [and H. T. Rowell] *Daily life in ancient Rome* (1941)

CG — R. Cagnat, F. Gauckler *Monuments historiques de la Tunisie* 1 (1898)

Chilver — G. E. F. Chilver *Cisalpine Gaul* (1941)

CIL — *Corpus Inscriptionum Latinarum*

Cod.Iust. — *Codex Iustinianus*

CP — *Classical Philology*

CRAI — *Comptes-Rendus de l'Académie des Inscriptions et Belles-Lettres*

CTh — *Codex Theodosianus*

Degrassi — A. Degrassi *I fasti consolari dell'impero romano* (1952)

de Pachtere — F. G. de Pachtere *La table hypothécaire de Veleia* (1920) (*Bibliothèque de l'École des Hautes Études*, fasc.228)

DS — Ch. Daremberg, E. Saglio, E. Pottier, G. Lafaye *Dictionnaire des antiquités* (1877–1919)

Dumont — R. Dumont *Types of rural economy; studies in world agriculture* (1957)

EcHR — *Economic History Review*

EE — *Ephemeris epigraphica* (1872–1913)

Enc.art.ant. — *Enciclopedia dell'arte antica* (1958–66)

Enc.it. — *Enciclopedia italiana* (1929–)

Ep. — Pliny *Epistulae*

ESAR — T. Frank (ed.) *Economic Survey of Ancient Rome* (1933–40)

FIRA — *Fontes Iuris Romani Antejustiniani* ed. S. Riccobono (1940–3)

Friedlaender — L. Friedlaender [and others] *Darstellungen aus der Sittengeschichte Roms*[10] (1921–2)

Fr.Vat. — *Fragmenta Vaticana*

Garnsey 1968 — P. Garnsey 'Trajan's alimenta. Some problems' *Historia* 17 (1968) 367–81

Garnsey 1971 (1) — P. Garnsey 'Honorarium decurionatus' *Historia* 20 (1971) 309–25

Garnsey 1971 (2) — P. Garnsey '*Taxatio* and *Pollicitatio* in Roman Africa' *JRS* 61 (1971) 116–29

Garzetti *Nerva* — A. Garzetti *Nerva* (1950)

Gascou — J. Gascou *La politique municipale de l'empire romain en Afrique proconsulaire de Trajan à Septime Sévère* (1972)

Gentile — I. Gentile 'Le Beneficenze di Plinio Cecilio Secondo ai Comensi' *RIL* ser.2, 14 (1881) 458–70

Gordon — A. E. & J. S. Gordon *Album of dated Latin inscriptions* (1958–65)

Gr.Texte — P. M. Meyer *Griechische Texte aus Ägypten* (1916)

Gsell *Monuments* — S. Gsell *Monuments antiques de l'Algérie* (1901)

Gsell–Joly — S. Gsell, C. A. Joly *Khamissa, Mdaourouch, Announa* (1914–22)

Gummerus — H. Gummerus *Der römische Gutsbetrieb als wirtschaftlicher Organismus nach den Werken des Cato, Varro und Columella* (*Klio* Beiheft 5) (1906)

HA — *Historia Augusta*

Henzen — G. Henzen 'De Tabula Alimentaria Baebianorum' *Annali dell'Istituto di corrispondenza archeologica* 16 (1844) 5–111

Hirschfeld *VW*²

O. Hirschfeld *Die kaiserliche Verwaltungsbeamten bis auf Diocletian*²
(1905)

Hörle   J. Hörle *Catos Hausbücher* (*Studien z. Gesch. u. Kultur d. Altertums*
15.3–4) (1929)

HS   Sestertii

HSCP   *Harvard Studies in Classical Philology*

Hultsch   F. Hultsch *Griechische und römische Metrologie*² (1882)

IG   *Inscriptiones Graecae*

IGRR   R. Cagnat, J. Toutain, P. Jouguet *Inscriptiones Graecae ad res Romanas
pertinentes* ([1901]–1927)

IIt   *Inscriptiones Italiae* (1931–   )

ILAF   R. Cagnat, A. Merlin, L. Chatelain *Inscriptions latines d'Afrique* (1923)

ILAlg   S. Gsell, H.-G. Pflaum *Inscriptions latines de l'Algérie* (1922 & 1957–   )

ILLRP   A. Degrassi *Inscriptiones Latinae Liberae Reipublicae* (1957–65)

ILM   L. Chatelain *Inscriptions latines du Maroc* fasc. 1 (1942)

ILS   H. Dessau *Inscriptiones Latinae Selectae* (1892–1916)

ILTun   A. Merlin *Inscriptions latines de la Tunisie* (1944)

Inst.   Justinian *Institutiones*

IRT   J. M. Reynolds and J. B. Ward Perkins *Inscriptions of Roman Tripolitania* (1952)

Jasny   N. Jasny 'Wheat prices and milling costs in classical Rome' *Wheat
Studies of the Food Research Institute* 20.4 (1944) 137–68

JOAI   *Jahreshefte des Österreichischen archäologischen Instituts in Wien*

Jones 1971   A. H. M. Jones 'Rome and the provincial cities' *Tijdschrift voor Rechts-
geschiedenis* 39 (1971) 513–51

JRS   *Journal of Roman Studies*

Kahrstedt   U. Kahrstedt *Die wirtschaftliche Lage Grossgriechenlands in der Kaiserzeit* (*Historia* Einzelschriften 4) (1960)

Kotula   T. Kotula *Les curies municipales en Afrique romaine* (*Prace Wrocław-
skiego Towarzystwa Naukowego* ser. A, 128) (1968)

Lauffer   S. Lauffer *Diokletians Preisedikt* (*Texte und Kommentare* 5) (1971)

Laum   B. Laum *Stiftungen in der griechischen und römischen Antike* (1914)

Leschi   L. Leschi *Études d'Épigraphie, d'Archéologie et d'Histoire africaines*
(1957)

Liebenam   W. Liebenam *Städteverwaltung im römischen Kaiserreiche* (1900)

LRE   A. H. M. Jones *The later Roman Empire 284–602* (1964)

MAF   *Mémoires de la Société nationale des antiquaires de France*

Marquardt *Staatsverwaltung*²

J. Marquardt *Römische Staatsverwaltung*² (1881–5)

Martin   R. Martin *Recherches sur les agronomes latins et leurs conceptions économiques et sociales* (1971)

Mattingly   H. Mattingly *Coins of the Roman Empire in the British Museum* (1923–   )

MEFR   *Mélanges d'archéologie et d'histoire* (*École française à Rome*)

Meiggs   R. Meiggs *Roman Ostia* (1960)

Mello–Voza   M. Mello, G. Voza *Le iscrizioni latine di Paestum* (1968)

Mommsen *Ges.Schr.*

Th. Mommsen *Gesammelte Schriften* (1905–13)

Moritz	L. A. Moritz *Grain-mills and flour in classical antiquity* (1958)
NAM	*Nouvelles archives des missions scientifiques et archéologiques*
Nissen	H. Nissen *Italische Landeskunde* (1883–1902)
NS	*Notizie degli Scavi dell'Antichità*
Otto	W. Otto 'Zur Lebensgeschichte des jüngeren Plinius' *Sitzungsberichte der Bayer. Akad. der Wiss.* (*Philos. philol. und hist. Klasse*) 10. Abhandlung (1919)
Pais	E. Pais *CIL Supplementa Italica…Additamenta ad vol. V Galliae Cisalpinae* (*Atti dei Lincei, Mem.class.sci.mor.stor. e filol.* ser. 4, 5 (1888)
P. Basel	E. Rabel *Papyrusurkunden der Öffentlichen Bibliothek der Universität zu Basel* (1917)
PBSR	*Papers of the British School at Rome*
Pflaum	H.-G. Pflaum *Carrières procuratoriennes équestres* (1960–1)
Picard *Civilisation*	
	G. C. Picard *La Civilisation de l'Afrique romaine* (1959)
Picard *Religions*	
	G. C. Picard *Les Religions de l'Afrique antique* (1954)
PIR	*Prosopographia Imperii Romani*
P.Lond.	*Greek Papyri in the British Museum* (1893–1917)
Poinssot *Dougga*	
	C. Poinssot *Les Ruines de Dougga* (1958)
POxy	B. P. Grenfell, A. S. Hunt and others *The Oxyrhynchus Papyri* (1898–)
PP	*Parola del Passato*
PSI	*Pubblicazioni della società italiana per la ricerca dei Papiri greci in Egitto* (1912–)
Radice *Pliny*	Pliny *Letters and Panegyricus* with trans. by B. Radice (1969)
RAf	*Revue africaine*
Ramsey	P. H. Ramsey (ed.) *The Price Revolution in Sixteenth-Century England* (1971)
Rangordnung	A. von Domaszewski (revised by B. Dobson) *Die Rangordnung des römischen Heeres* (1967)
RE	Pauly–Wissowa–Kroll *Real-Encyclopädie der classischen Altertumswissenschaft* (1894–)
REA	*Revue des études anciennes*
Recueil	*Recueil des notices et mémoires de la société archéologique du Département de Constantine*
REG	*Revue des études grecques*
REL	*Revue des études latines*
RHDFE	*Revue historique de droit français et étranger*
RIL	*Rendiconti del r. Istituto lombardo, cl. lett.sci.mor.*
Romanelli	P. Romanelli *Storia delle province romane dell'Africa* (1959)
RPAA	*Atti della Pontificia accademia romana di archeologia: Rendiconti*
RSI	*Rivista storica italiana*
Ruggiero	E. de Ruggiero *Dizionario epigrafico di antichità romane* (1895–)
Salomon	P. Salomon 'Essai sur les structures agraires de l'Italie centrale au IIe siècle avant J-C' in P. Salomon, G. Frêche, J. Boucher *Recherches*

	d'histoire économique (Trav. et recherches de la Fac. de droit et des sci.
	écon. de Paris, Sciences historiques 3) (1964) 1–68
SB	F. Preisigke, F. Bilabel *Sammelbuch griechischer Urkunden aus Ägypten* (1915–)
SDHI	*Studia et documenta historiae et iuris*
SEG	*Supplementum Epigraphicum Graecum*
*SEHRE*²	M. I. Rostovtzeff (revised by P. M. Fraser) *Social and economic history of the Roman Empire*² (1957)
Sherwin-White	
	A. N. Sherwin-White *The Letters of Pliny* (1966)
Sirago	V. A. Sirago *L'Italia agraria sotto Traiano* (1958)
SPP	C. Wessely *Studien zur Palaeographie und Papyruskunde* (1904–24)
Staatsrecht	Th. Mommsen *Römisches Staatsrecht*³ (1887)
Stone	L. Stone *The crisis of the aristocracy 1558–1641* (1965)
Strack	P. L. Strack *Untersuchungen zur römischen Reichsprägung des zweiten Jahrhunderts* (1931–37)
St.Vel.	*Terzo Convegno di Studi Veleiati, 31 maggio–2 giugno 1967* (1969)
Syme	R. Syme *Tacitus* (1958)
TAPHA	*Transactions of the American Philological Association*
Thirsk	J. Thirsk (ed.) *Agrarian history of England and Wales* 4 (1967)
Thomasson	B. E. Thomasson *Die Statthalter der römischen Provinzen Nordafrikas von Augustus bis Diocletianus (Skr. utg. av Svenska Inst. i Rom*, ser. in 8°, 9) (1960)
TLL	*Thesaurus linguae Latinae*
Toller	O. Toller *De spectaculis, cenis, distributionibus in municipiis Romanis occidentis Imperatorum aetate exhibitis* (1889)
Veyne 1957 & 1958	
	P. Veyne 'La Table des Ligures Baebiani et l'institution alimentaire de Trajan' *MEFR* 69 (1957) 81–135; 70 (1958) 177–241
Veyne 1964	P. Veyne 'Les "alimenta" de Trajan' in *Les Empereurs romains d'Espagne, Madrid-Italica 31 mars–6 avril 1964* (1965) 163–79
Wallace	S. L. Wallace *Taxation in Egypt from Augustus to Diocletian* (1938)
Walsh *Roman Novel*	
	P. G. Walsh *The Roman Novel* (1970)
Waltzing	J. P. Waltzing *Étude historique sur les corporations professionnelles chez les Romains* (1895–1900)
Weber	A. F. Weber *The Growth of Cities in the Nineteenth Century. A Study in Statistics* (New York 1899; reprinted Ithaca 1963)
White	K. D. White *Roman farming* (1970)
Yeo	C. A. Yeo 'The development of the Roman plantation and the marketing of farm products'; 'The economics of Roman and American slavery' *Finanzarchiv* 13 (1952) 321–42; 445–83

Introduction

Any general appraisal of the Roman economy of the Principate must be related to the Roman world as a political entity. Rome's Empire represented a prodigious achievement in sheer size. The Roman state acquired and held together for a number of centuries an enormous territory which included all the countries of the Mediterranean seaboard and a large part of northern Europe. No subsequent imperial expansion has succeeded in uniting the same areas. Rome ruled these lands as a series of provinces, imposing her institutions and her language wholesale in the West, while making piecemeal adaptations in the East, much of which already possessed institutions and culture of Greek type.[1] It is with the West that this book is mainly concerned.

The Roman economy however remained a primitive system which would today qualify the Roman Empire for recognition as a 'developing' country. Almost everywhere a large part of the population was engaged in agriculture at a relatively low level, while industry depended on a backward technology and was rarely organised in large units.[2] Despite the existence of a comprehensive network of trunk roads, land transport remained so costly and inefficient that it was often impossible to relieve inland famines from stocks of grain held elsewhere.[3] The creation of a very large area with uniform currency and low customs barriers probably encouraged the growth of sea-borne commerce. But the staples of long-distance trade were luxury goods and government supplies rather than

[1] Short recent surveys of the earlier Empire, or Principate: F. Millar in F. Millar, D. Berciu, R. N. Frye *The Roman Empire and its neighbours* (1967); P. Petit *La Paix romaine* (1967).

[2] For technology see M. I Finley *EcHR* 18 (1965) 29–45. Nevertheless within these limits standards of craftsmanship and engineering were often very high. The structural techniques employed in Roman ships can compare favourably with those used in some present day wooden vessels, while many surviving buildings show the remarkable durability of Roman concrete and mortar (for building see below, p.2 n.5; for ships, P. Throckmorton in G. F. Bass (ed.) *A History of Seafaring based on Underwater Archaeology* (1972) 69; cf. L. Casson *TAPHA* 81 (1950) 43–56; *Ships and seamanship in the ancient world* (1971)).

[3] Cf. *LRE* 2.844. For transport costs see Appendix 17; cf. A. Burford *EcHR* 13 (1960–1) 1–18.

low-priced goods intended for sale to a mass market.[1] Shipping was slow, and sailings were suspended in the winter.[2] No effective credit system was evolved, and banks were rarely more than small-scale and isolated institutions.[3] Judged in modern terms the gross national product is likely to have been extremely low for a country with a population of the order of 50 million.[4]

Yet these economic disadvantages did not preclude remarkable physical achievements. In Rome and other large cities buildings were constructed which exceeded in size anything built before the high Middle Ages; the magnificence of material and ornament of the finest buildings has few parallels in European architecture.[5] And under Roman rule, cities each with a substantial complement of public buildings constructed on Hellenistic models proliferated all over the Mediterranean. In the West immense areas were divided for purposes of land allocation by an efficient grid system whose remains are still visible today.[6] Thus Rome was able to muster and organise labour in a way that produced results on a scale not usually associated with primitive European economies. The absolute resources of the Empire in terms of land and men were sufficiently great to allow a centralised political system and a heavily stratified social hierarchy to create impressive achievements, notwithstanding the relatively low efficiency of the agriculture on which the Empire's wealth was mainly based.[7] Roman building activity owed its scale partly to a sizeable standing army whose peacetime pursuits included the construction of roads, frontier works and fortresses; and partly to city-authorities and landowners who financed civilian building which was carried out by contractors who sometimes controlled a large permanent labour

[1] Cf. A. H. M. Jones *Recueils de la Société Jean Bodin* 7.2 (1955) 161–7 (reprinted in A. H. M. Jones *The Roman Economy* (forthcoming)). For the organisation of trade, see J. Rougé *Recherches sur l'organisation du commerce maritime en Méditerranée sous l'empire romain* (1966); *SEHRE²*. Customs duties within the Empire usually varied between 2% and 5% (cf. S. J. de Laet *Portorium* (1949) 242).

[2] *LRE* 1.403; 2.843.

[3] Cf. p.300 n.3 below. Marquardt *Staatsverwaltung²* 2.64–9; Mommsen *Ges.Schr.* 3.221–74; B. Laum *RE* Supp. 4.71–82.

[4] For population cf. Beloch 507, estimating 54 million inhabitants of the Empire at the death of Augustus.

[5] For Roman building techniques, see M. E. Blake *Ancient Roman Construction in Italy* (1947–59); G. Lugli *La tecnica edilizia romana* (1957). For architecture, L. Crema *L'architettura romana* (G. B. Pighi ed. *Encic. classica* 12.1) (1959); A. Boethius and J. B. Ward Perkins *Etruscan and Roman architecture* (1969).

[6] Illustrations of centuriation in J. Bradford *Ancient landscapes* (1957) 145–216; F. Castagnoli *Le ricerche sui resti della centuriazione* (1958). Further literature in O. A. W. Dilke *The Roman land surveyors* (1971).

[7] Some parallel features can be seen in autocratic eastern societies; cf. K. A. Wittfogel *Oriental Despotism. A Comparative Study of Total Power* (1957).

force.[1] There is little doubt that the ready availability of slave and convict labour was important in determining the scale on which buildings could be constructed.[2] In addition, local free populations might occasionally be drafted into public building operations.[3]

Without the presence of large cash resources in a few hands, much of the adornment of the cities would have been impossible. But the Roman social system both permitted and encouraged extreme inequalities of private wealth. In the army, pay scales varied within the legion by a factor as high as 67.[4] In part these extremes reflected existing economic contrasts between the social strata from which different ranks were recruited; but they also created still wider disparities. Large private fortunes often represented the surplus from low efficiency agriculture accumulated over a number of generations and concentrated in fewer and fewer hands by social tendencies that reduced the birth-rate among the upper classes.[5] These fortunes also reflected a degree of economic disparity permitted by the widespread use of slaves, many of whom would retain little of what they produced beyond what was needed for subsistence.[6] Extreme inequalities of wealth were hardly unusual in ancient Mediterranean societies. But the explicit and active domination of Roman social structures by wealth and by wealth requirements is an integral feature that deserves special notice.[7]

The Roman state was firmly oligarchic and timocratic. The ownership of wealth was the essential prerequisite for all the high statuses of public life under the Principate. Entry to the Senate, the body of knights, the

[1] The most successful property developer of the late Republic had a labour force of more than 500 building workers (Plutarch *Crassus* 2.4–5). For permanent labour gangs see also Frontinus *de aquis* 2.96; 116. Claudius is said to have employed 30,000 men for 11 years in digging a channel to drain the Fucine lake (Suetonius *Claud.* 20.2). Another useful index of scale is provided by the huge budget figures for certain building projects (see p.318 n.4).

[2] Some notion of the importance of coercion is given by the fact that the employment of chained slaves was often an integral feature of the cultivation of large country estates in Italy (pp.323–4). For convict labour cf. P. Garnsey *Social status and legal privilege in the Roman Empire* (1970) index s.v. Opus Publicum.

[3] P.310 n.1 below. Cf. J. A. Crook *Law and life of Rome* (1967) 202–3.

[4] *Primi pili* probably received a salary of the order of HS60,000 at a time when legionaries were paid HS900 per year (P. A. Brunt *PBSR* 18 (1950) 50–71 at 71). The senator who commanded the legion, the *legatus legionis*, is likely to have received an even higher salary than a *primus pilus*.

[5] See p.318 nn.2–3. For restriction of family size, cf. K. Hopkins *Comparative Studies in Society and History* 8 (1965) 124–51.

[6] For slaves engaged in agriculture see pp.323–4; 53 below. Cf. M. I Finley in *International Encyclopedia of the Social Sciences* (1968) 14.310–11.

[7] Cf. W. S. Davis *The influence of wealth in ancient Rome* (1910) (a popular work without references).

judiciary, and the local town council was in each case controlled by a property qualification. Senators whose fortune fell below the necessary level could even hope for reimbursement from the Emperor.[1] The formal structure of civilian wealth qualifications represented ratios of $1:2:4:12$. The juryman must have double the wealth of the town-councillor, the knight twice the wealth of the juryman, and the senator three times the wealth of the knight.[2] The minima were often exceeded in practice. We hear of town-councillors whose fortunes were counted in millions;[3] jurymen could sometimes spend on public gifts during their lifetime sums which exceeded the minimum census for their class;[4] and equestrian administrators were paid annual salaries which much exceeded any annual revenue corresponding to the equestrian census figure.[5] When Emperors attempted to restore the finances of impoverished senators, their gifts usually ran at levels much higher than the minimum senatorial census.[6] Gifts that rewarded a senator who had four sons with only one and a half times the senatorial census could be considered shamefully inadequate.[7]

The scale of the largest private fortunes at Rome (sometimes swollen by the proceeds of extortion from provincials) was extremely high. The two largest fortunes in private hands in the first century A.D. (400 million sesterces) each had a value in real terms of the order of $\frac{3}{4}$–$1\frac{1}{2}$ million metric tons of wheat. A number of other Roman fortunes were of the same size.[8] By comparison, the largest private fortunes of England in the

[1] See p.18 n.7. A similar concern to maintain the standing of the aristocracy can be seen in Queen Elizabeth I's payments for the funerals of impoverished noblemen (Stone 578).

[2] Town-councillors: HS100,000 in some Italian towns (p.243 below). *Iudices*: HS200,000 for the lower *decuriae* (Suetonius *Aug.* 32.3). Knights: HS400,000 (Pliny *Ep.* 1.19). Senators: HS1,200,000 (rather than HS1 million: Suetonius *Aug.* 41.1 and Cassius Dio 55.13.6, against Cassius Dio 54.17.3). In A.D. 27 HS400,000 was made the minimum census-requirement for those giving gladiatorial shows (Tacitus *Ann.* 4.63). After the great fire of A.D. 64 Nero granted citizenship to Latins having at least HS200,000 who spent half their wealth on building a house in Rome (Gaius *Inst.* 1.33). Roman citizens worth HS100,000 or more could not inherit if they were childless and unmarried (*FIRA* 1.99 c.32).

[3] Appendix 7, nos.25–8.

[4] Two *iudices* at Thugga in Africa Proconsularis provided the town with its theatre and Capitol (R. Duncan-Jones *PBSR* 35 (1967) 147–88, nos.102, 103).

[5] At 6% (cf. p.33) a capital of HS400,000 would yield HS24,000. The salaries of equestrian procurators were HS60,000, 100,000, 200,000 and 300,000 (cf. H.-G. Pflaum *Les procurateurs équestres sous le Haut-Empire romain* (1950)).

[6] For grants of HS500,000 per year (corresponding to a capital in the region of HS8 million) see p.18 n.7.

[7] Tacitus *Ann.* 2.37–8. The total grant to M. Hortensius Hortalus from Augustus and Tiberius was HS1,800,000.

[8] See Appendix 7; for a wheat price of HS2–4 per modius see pp.144–6; the metric ton equals 0.985 British tons. Wheat equivalents are no more than an approximate index of real wealth,

mid-sixteenth and mid-seventeenth centuries appear to have been worth roughly 21,000–42,000 metric tons of wheat.[1] On the same reckoning an adequate basic capital for a Roman senator, 8 million sesterces, would be worth 14,000–29,000 metric tons.[2] The grandiose life-style of a senator of the Principate would today be thought appropriate to royalty; a modest illustration of its features is provided by Pliny's letters (see Chapter 1). The senator's minimum census would be worth between 2,100 and 4,300 metric tons of wheat, the knight's census between 700 and 1,400 and the juror's census between 350 and 700 metric tons. Private wealth was not subject to progressive taxation, and rates of tax under the Principate were not especially heavy.[3] Death-duty was only 5% until the early third century.[4] Thus there were few restraints on the aggregation of wealth, and wealth was a public necessity for men of any prominence or ambition. Tendencies for the richest families to die out also favoured progressive growth in the size of fortunes.[5]

since wheat prices may fluctuate substantially. But they offer a much better basis for comparisons between different societies than any monetary equations (see below p.11 and n.4).

[1] If this comparison has any validity, in real terms the biggest fortunes in first-century Rome exceeded those in England between the mid-fifteenth and the mid-sixteenth centuries by a factor between 18 and 72. But the total population probably differed by a factor of 18 or more (Roman population estimated as 54 million in A.D. 14, p.2 n.4 above; the population of England estimated as 3.75 million in 1603, J. Cornwall *EcHR* 23 (1970) 32–44). L. Stone estimates the annual income of the richest English aristocrat in 1559 as £6,000 and the income of the richest commoner in 1640 as £20,000 (Stone 760; 140). Land changed hands at a valuation of 16–20 years' income during this period (Stone 165). P. J. Bowden gives the price of wheat in 1640–9 as 45 shillings per quarter, and as roughly $(291 \div 615 \times 45s)$ in 1559 (in Thirsk 614; 815–21).

[2] For senatorial fortunes, see p.18 and Appendix 7.

[3] Private property in Italy remained exempt from tax until the end of the third century A.D. (cf. *LRE* 1.64). In the provinces basic tribute rates of 10% and 5% of the crop are known (Republican Sicily, Sardinia and Spain; Livy 42.31.8; 43.2.12). 12% was imposed on one provincial town exceptionally as a penal provision in place of 10% by Caesar (*Bell.Afr.* 98). Percentage rates of tribute payable in money are obscure, but presumably ran at comparable levels; the Three Gauls yielded HS40 million annually after Caesar's conquest (Suetonius *Iul.* 25). In Egypt (the only source of plentiful documentation) there is little evidence of any alteration in the basic rates of land tax during the Principate (Wallace 19; contrast Johnson *ESAR* 2.483 n.2). Nevertheless, tax-rates in some parts of the Empire were evidently increased in the first century A.D. by Vespasian, who is said to have doubled some payments (Suetonius *Vesp.* 16.1; cf. *PIR*[1] R 167). Hyginus writing early in the second century A.D. mentions rates of 20% and 14% (Lachmann ed. *Gromatici veteres* p.205). Cf. Marquardt *Staatsverwaltung*[2] 2.177–238; *RE* s.v. Tributum. For indirect taxes, cf. S. J. de Laet *Portorium* (1949).

[4] P.64 n.6 below. For Caracalla's increase to 10%, Cassius Dio 77.9.4; but cf. 78.12.2.

[5] P.3 n.5 above. Cf. M. I Finley *The ancient economy* (1973) chapter 4; also *LRE* 2.554–5. The largest figures come from the Julio-Claudian period, but there is little information about large fortunes at Rome during the Principate after the first century A.D. (Appendix 7).

This book is concerned with wealth in the Roman world, with its economic context, and with its social applications. Detailed study of these questions is impossible without quantification. Consequently much of the discussion is directed to questions of scale. The financial affairs of a senator are examined in detail in Chapter 1. Agriculture, the prime investment medium, and rates of profit from agriculture are considered in the second chapter. The size of large private fortunes, the area of landed estates, and the organisation of the agricultural labour force are discussed in separate appendices (Appendices 7, 1 and 2). The background of money and prices is considered next, in surveys of costs in Italy and the African provinces (Chapters 3 and 4 and Appendices 8–10 and 16–17). The evidence mainly comes from a substantial body of inscriptions. Efforts are made to present and analyse this scattered material systematically. The dating pattern, the size of the surviving sample, and the regional distribution of the inscriptions are examined in separate Appendices (Appendices 11–14). The fifth chapter considers prices from a different source, the Latin novelists. The frequency with which prices occur in fiction reflects the pervasiveness of monetary exchanges in urban life. In a society which, despite the prominence of the city unit, was primarily agrarian and lacked mechanical sources of power, the availability of manpower was of crucial importance. The level of local populations and the size of town-organisations are considered in Chapter 6. Here the technique first used by Beloch of employing gift inscriptions to reduce population sizes is applied on a larger scale than before. The final chapter examines the *alimenta*, a government attempt to encourage population growth in Italy by direct subsidy (Chapter 7 and Appendices 3–6).

It is clear that the Roman economy of the Principate was basically a money economy.[1] References to exchanges in kind are few. Where tribute-payments were made in corn, this may have been due at least in part to the absence of good transport facilities.[2] Since the government in any case needed corn for provisioning, and transport was slow and expensive, it was convenient to take payment from some provinces in kind. This reduced the number of transactions, and avoided the need to purchase corn on the open market. Surviving evidence for the use of money comes almost entirely from the cities, but there are few sources of information about typical conditions in the countryside. Columella, the one surviving agricultural writer of the Principate, thinks mainly in terms of a cash return, but he is concerned with the big estate belonging

[1] Cf. J.-P. Callu 'La fonction monétaire dans la société romaine sous l'Empire' Ve Congrès Internationale d'Histoire Économique, Leningrad, 1970.
[2] For tribute see p.5 n.3 above. For transport, Appendix 17.

to a wealthy owner.[1] Surviving rural coin-hoards come most often from well-to-do households, and need not indicate widespread peasant owner-ship of money. But the market function of the Roman town implies that most rural producers would have had some access to money through the market-place of the town on whose territory their land lay.[2] Rural populations were no less liable than city-dwellers to pay government taxes, which were often assessed in money.[3] Nevertheless, it remains possible on general grounds that money was less pervasive in the country-side than in the towns.[4]

The prices collected below come from large areas, and span a period of several centuries. Whether direct comparisons between different figures are legitimate depends both on the degree to which prices were stable and on how far they were consistent from one area to another. The fact that corn-prices from different parts of the Empire under the late Republic and early Principate are broadly comparable suggests that there was some consistency of prices for basic commodities between different areas.[5] In several different parts of Italy road-construction costs ran at roughly the same level.[6] And in the African provinces, statue prices were relatively consistent from one district to another.[7] Cicero suggests that corn prices were roughly the same all over Sicily in the first century B.C. But he also indicates that corn prices were subject to wide local variations in Asia, an observation echoed in more general terms by Gaius in the second century A.D.[8]

There are few statements by contemporaries about long-term price movements. The size and the silver content of successive Roman coin-issues are sometimes invoked today as a possible index of changes in price-levels.[9] There is abundant documentary evidence that inflation of prices on a staggering scale had taken place by the end of the third century A.D. Diocletian's Price Edict in A.D. 301 which attempted to stabilise

---

[1] For Columella, see Chapter 2 and Appendices 1 and 2.

[2] See Columella *de r.r.* 7.3.22; R. Macmullen *Phoenix* 24 (1970) 333–41.

[3] In the Arsinoite nome in Egypt under the Principate, registered inhabitants of the metro-polis paid poll-tax at half the rate paid by other inhabitants of the nome (Wallace 121–2). Under the Dominate, it was the city dwellers who more often possessed tax-immunities in the Empire as a whole (*LRE* 1.464).

[4] For rural self-sufficiency, Martial 4.66. Cf. M. H. Crawford *JRS* 60 (1970) 44.

[5] See pp.145–6.   [6] See pp.124–5 and p.153.

[7] See p.78 and nos.77–212.

[8] Cicero *Verr.* 2.3.191–2; *Digesta* 13.4.3; cf. Pliny *NH* 33.164. See also Appendix 8, p.345.

[9] Cf. Frank *ESAR* 5.90–3; G. Mickwitz in *RE* supp. 6.127–33; A. H. M. Jones *EcHR* 5 (1952–3) 293–318; T. Pékary *Historia* 8 (1959) 443–89. Recent analyses of the silver coinage: L. H. Cope in E. T. Hall & D. M. Metcalf (ed.) *Methods of chemical and metallurgical investigation of ancient coinage* (1972) 3–47. For objections to 'quantity' theories of inflation, see I. Hammarström, J. D. Gould and C. E. Challis in Ramsey 54–5; 101–6; 145–6.

prices by stipulating maximum levels that must not be exceeded shows enormously swollen values.[1] Wheat is tariffed at a level 50–100 times higher than a representative second-century price.[2] By contrast the 'price revolution' in England between the late fifteenth and the mid-seventeenth century only led to an increase in food costs by a factor of 4 or 5.[3] Rome's disastrous inflation brought a total reconstitution of the coinage on a new basis.[4] As a result prices from the fourth century onwards are in no way comparable with prices from the first three centuries of the Empire. The underlying causes of this inflation are usually taken to be the debasement of the coin issue and a related expansion of the money supply.[5] In certain areas population increase might also have influenced upward price movements.[6]

It would be unrealistic to suppose that the Roman world enjoyed stable prices for centuries, which then dissolved into uncontrollable inflation within a few years.[7] The worst period of price increase before the date

---

[1] For the Edict see Appendix 17. Fragments of the Edict survive from many towns; their distribution indicates that the Edict was published only in the eastern provinces (J. & L. Robert *REG* 77 (1964) 140–1).

[2] See p.66 n.4. But the Edict did not allow for regional price variations: when the fragments found in different cities refer to the same goods, they give the same prices. Yet there could be sharp variations between prices in town and country, as well as between those in large and small towns (see Appendix 8, pp.345–6). If the levels in the Edict were derived from local observation in the city at which the Emperor was resident at the time (perhaps Nicomedia), they might well be based on market prices higher than those obtaining in country areas or in smaller towns. Since the corn price from the Principate used in this calculation does not necessarily correspond with the price level in a large town, the factor of inflation implicit in the Edict's corn price may have been less than 50/100. But, since the Edict had the effect of driving goods off the market, the prices that it stipulated were evidently lower than those prevailing in free exchanges, as the preamble to the Edict clearly implies (see A. H. M. Jones *EcHR* 5 (1952–3) 293–318 at 299, citing Lactantius *de mort.pers.* 7.6).

[3] P. Mathias in Ramsey vii. J. D. Gould points out that a three-fold rise in 100 years, which entails a compound increase of 1.1% per year, is not a price revolution in any sense recognisable today (Ramsey 92).

[4] For prices and currency in the late Empire see *LRE* 1.438–48; 2.848–50; 1017–18; G. Mickwitz *Geld und Wirtschaft im römischen Reich des vierten Jahrhunderts n.Chr.* (1932) 195–232; A. C. Johnson, L. C. West *Byzantine Egypt: economic studies* (Princeton, 1949); A. H. M. Jones *JRS* 49 (1959) 34–8; L. Ruggini *Economia e società nell'Italia annonaria* (1961). Comparisons between prices in the two periods are extremely hazardous. Jones concluded from wheat figures which suggest that the purchasing power of gold remained constant that 'as far as gold prices went...there was no inflation' (*EcHR* 5 (1952–3) 293–318 at 304; see also *LRE* 2.822). But this could easily be controverted if HS4 were taken as the typical price for wheat per modius in the Principate instead of the figure of HS2 that Jones is using (for wheat prices see pp.145–6). On that basis prices in gold would show 'deflation' by the fourth century. For objections to such comparisons, see A. V. Judges (cited in p.11 n.4 below).   [5] See p.7 n.9.

[6] Cf. Tertullian *de anima* 30 (Africa). For the impact of population increase on price levels, I. Hammarström and Y. S. Brenner in Ramsey 66–7; 79–80.

[7] It is doubtful what importance should be given to the fact that 'there is no indication of a

of Diocletian's Price Edict probably belongs to the last three-quarters of
the third century A.D. But some inflation was evidently noticeable at an
earlier date. The one clear index comes from Egypt, the only plentiful
source of commodity prices. Unfortunately for the historian, Egypt was a
separate area with its own currency, whose prices contemporaries perhaps
considered low.[1] Nevertheless, Egypt enjoyed some trading contacts with
other provinces, and its economy probably followed a similar course to
that of other parts of the Empire.[2] Egyptian prices show a clear upward
trend from an early date. The median averages for corn increase from an
index level of 3 at the beginning of the first century A.D. to a level of 14 in
the mid-third century, a rise by a factor of 4.7. Egyptian land prices also
increased over this period. The pattern is less clearly marked, but the
land prices are vitiated as an economic index by the lack of any means of
compensating for variations in the quality of land.[3]

The costs from Italy and Africa collected below give little indication of
price movement during the first two centuries of the Principate. Since
neither sample contains any series of commodity prices or wage-rates,
this need not be significant. But where there are dated series of any kind,
they appear to show comparatively little price fluctuation. The average
cost of statues in the African provinces remained within the same broad
range throughout the period of a century for which evidence is
available. The same is true of the average rates of cash handout in Italy,
though these may be arbitrary stereotypes which would not respond to
inflation.[4] Neither series is sustained far into the third century; public

significant change in price level in the period covered by the parchments and papyri from
Dura' which extend to the mid-third century A.D. (they contain no series of prices for
measures of grain or other foodstuffs, and no long dated price-series for the same article;
A. Perkins (ed.) *The excavations at Dura-Europos: final report* (1959) 5.1.8). D. Sperber
discounts evidence for inflation in the mid-third century on the ground that if translated
into gold values prices reckoned in debased currency can be scaled down to a much lower
level (*Journ.Econ.Soc.Hist.Orient* 11 (1968) 237, cf. 13 (1970) 1; for weaknesses of this
approach cf. p.8 n.4 above).

During the first century A.D. there was a substantial drain of bullion to the East to pay for
imported luxuries: Pliny gives a figure of HS100 million per year (*NH* 12.84, cf. 6.101).
This might have had some deflationary effect while it lasted. But coin finds in India suggest
that export of coined bullion to the East had greatly diminished by the end of the first century
A.D. (see E. H. Warmington *The commerce between the Roman Empire and India* (1929) 272–
318).

[1] Diodorus 1.80.6 is not conclusive evidence. For Egyptian currency, see A. Segré *Circolazione monetaria e prezzi nel mondo antico ed in particolare in Egitto* (1922); Johnson *ESAR*
2.424–45. For commodity prices in Egypt, Johnson *ESAR* 2, and L. C. West, *CP* 11 (1916)
293–314.
[2] For comparability between Egypt and other provinces, cf. A. H. M. Jones in S. R. K.
Glanville (ed.) *The Legacy of Egypt*[1] (1942) 286–7; *EcHR* 5 (1952–3) 293–318 at 295.
[3] See Appendix 16.
[4] See Appendix 11.

gifts tend to disappear when economic conditions become adverse. But the three African statue prices belonging to the late third century show levels very much higher than the average for the second century.[1] This suggests that inflation was being directly reflected in the cost of building.

A possible crude reflection of inflation not limited to any one region is provided by military pay increases. The basic rate for the ordinary legionary was 900 sesterces from the reign of Augustus to the reign of Domitian (*c.* 31 B.C.–*c.* A.D. 85), and 1,200 sesterces from Domitian to Septimius Severus (*c.* A.D. 85–*c.* 200). Septimius Severus again increased the rate, probably to 1,800 or 2,000 sesterces.[2] The overall increase during the two centuries from Augustus to Septimius Severus is thus 122/100%, an average compound increase between 0.35 and 0.4% per year. The substantial level of these pay rises, together with the fact that they were given so rarely, may imply that the rate of military pay tended to lag behind inflation. The amount of the increases might thus provide a rough minimum index of the course of inflation during the first two centuries A.D.

The slow inflation during the second century suggested by the pattern of military pay is supported by figures from Egypt and Asia. Second-century prices for wheat in Egypt show an increase of roughly one quarter over first-century figures.[3] Bread tariffs at Ephesus in Asia Minor suggest a price-rise between the early second century and the early third century of about two-fold.[4] If by this date prices had roughly doubled since the early second century, most of the rise after the early second century suggested by Diocletian's Edict would lie within the third century. An increase of 25/50-fold in roughly eighty years would mean an average compound inflation of 4.0/4.9% per year. But the actual rate of increase cannot have been constant; and the speed of price movements is bound to have varied from one region to another.[5]

Most of the prices collected below evidently belong to the second century A.D. If it is fair to assess general inflation within this period as being of the order of two-fold, it will not be unreasonable to make internal

---

[1] See pp.66–7.

[2] For discussion and literature, see G. R. Watson *The Roman soldier* (1969) 91 and nn.231–2. The pay increases could perhaps be seen instead as representing successive gestures of favour towards the troops by pro-military rulers. This does not seem very plausible as a prime explanation; the Egyptian figures show that prices were going up steadily in one of the areas where legionaries were stationed. For imperial concern about the purchasing power of military pay, see the preamble to Diocletian's Price Edict (Lauffer 94–5 = *ESAR* 5.314).

[3] Appendix 16.

[4] Texts in Broughton *ESAR* 4.879–80; cf. N. Jasny *Agricultural History* 21 (1947) 190 ff.

[5] For a possible difference between the rate of inflation in Africa and that in Italy see pp.355–7 below.

comparisons between different undated prices within the sample. On the assumption that price-levels were relatively consistent, there will be a danger of serious discontinuity only in extreme cases when costs lie at opposite ends of the period.[1] Some scattered Italian building-costs for road-building show fair consistency despite the fact that one appears to be at least a century earlier than the remainder, which belong to the second century A.D.[2]

The interpretation of ancient prices as such remains difficult. It is extremely simple to render ancient prices into modern by a linear formula; and translations into modern currency in terms of metal content have often been made.[3] But the purchasing power of precious metals is not a constant, and there are many differences between ancient spending patterns and price structures and those of modern societies. The discontinuities are in fact so great as to make any linear translations of ancient currency into modern completely worthless.[4] The only valid index of the purchasing power of ancient money remains that provided by ancient prices and wages.

A useful index of relationships within the Roman price structure can be found in prices for food and for slaves related to personal resources. A basic allowance of 20 sesterces in cash and 5 modii in wheat per month paid to an urban slave represents a division of approximately 1 part in kind and 1–2 parts in cash.[5] The lowest wage in Diocletian's Price Edict, that of farm labourers and other unskilled workers, implies a distribution of roughly 1 part in kind and $1\frac{1}{2}$–3 parts in cash.[6] By comparison, a government order restricting prices in sixteenth-century England envisaged that maintenance would absorb at least half the wages of farm

---

1 For signs of regional price consistency see p.7 above.

2 See pp.124–5 and p.153. For relatively long periods of stable prices in other pre-industrial economies, cf. H. Antoniadis-Bibicou 'Démographie, salaires et prix à Byzance au XIe siècle' *AESC* 27 (1972) 215–46; E. Ashtor *Histoire des prix et des salaires dans l'Orient médiéval* (1969) 453 ff.

3 A. J. C. Dureau de la Malle's *Économie politique des Romains* published in 1840 was based throughout on the assumption that ancient currencies could be translated into modern. The same belief is apparent in the Italian volumes of Frank's *Economic Survey of Ancient Rome* written almost a century later (as in countless other modern works, including Rostovtzeff *SEHRE*[2] 470).

4 For one of the serious discontinuities that result from a linear formula see R. Duncan-Jones *PBSR* 30 (1962) 75. See also M. Giacchero *Studi Romani* 18 (1970) 149–62. Cf. A. V. Judges *RSI* 63 (1951) 162–79 at 162 (reprinted in R. Romano (ed.) *I prezzi in Europa dal XIII secolo a oggi* (1967) 521–37).

5 See p.208 no.1170. For a wheat price of HS2–4 per modius, see p.146.

6 The farm labourer received 25 denarii per day and food. Assuming the same allowance of 5 modii of wheat per month (see p.146), the cost of food from the price in the Edict per kastrensis modius (whose meaning is ambiguous, see p.66 n.4) would be 250–500 denarii per month (Lauffer 118, 98 = *ESAR* 5.337; 318).

workers hired by the day.[1] The Roman legionary received pay that allowed him a much larger proportion for items other than food, though this was somewhat offset by heavy compulsory charges for uniform and other items. Assuming the basic corn ration as his main staple diet, the second-century wage of 1,200 sesterces would permit the legionary to spend between 80 and 90% of his salary on items other than food (making no allowance for compulsory deductions).[2]

The ownership of wealth even on a small scale gave ready access to an abundant supply of labour. The legionary's pay for one year represented a sum large enough to purchase a cheap slave. The slave prices of 1,000 sesterces and less which are several times attested represent quite a low value, something of the order of 4–8 years' basic rations for one man.[3] They imply that slaves were not in short supply. The availability to most owners of large households of some slaves bred in the house or on the farm may have kept down the market price for slaves who lacked any special accomplishment or skill.[4] The minimum census of the town-councillor, 100,000 sesterces in some Italian towns, corresponds in value to the cost of a substantial troop of slaves, as many as fifty at the legal compensation price of 2,000 sesterces.[5] The fact that both town-councillors and slaves had a legally ordained 'value' illustrates the rigid regulation which lay behind the functioning of wealth in Roman society. The comparison also shows one of the ways in which an investigation of economic history can illuminate social structures.

To conclude, a prime feature of Roman society was extreme differentiation between social classes and groups. A number of economic differentials were explicitly incorporated in wealth requirements for particular ranks, whose minima were often exceeded. The cost of labour was relatively low, though some basic wage-rates seem to have allowed the employee more than bare subsistence. The economy of the cities was monetary, though the place of money in the countryside may have been less important. Rates of inflation appear to have been slow during the first two centuries of the Principate, and apart from short-term fluctuations it is likely that prices were relatively stable. But in the course of the third century a

---

[1] Elizabeth I's Statute for Rutland of 1563 allowed reapers 4*d* per day 'with meat', 8*d* 'without meat', and haymakers 3*d* 'with meat' but 6*d* 'without meat' (J. E. T. Rogers *A History of Agriculture and Prices in England* (1866–1902) 4.120–2).

[2] For a wheat price of HS2–4 per modius (see p.146). For stoppages against pay, G. R. Watson *The Roman Soldier* (1969) 102–8. In practice the legionary might eat better and so spend a larger proportion on food (cf. *LRE* 1.447 for details of actual rations in the sixth century).

[3] For slave-prices see Appendix 10 and literature cited there; for Egyptian slave-prices, Johnson *ESAR* 2.279–81, and O. Montevecchi *Aegyptus* 19 (1939) 14–16.

[4] See p.50.

[5] For town-councillors see p.243; for slaves, see Appendix 10.

much more drastic inflation took hold. This subverted the monetary system and the money economy as it had existed for a number of centuries. By the fourth century, payments in kind had assumed far greater importance in the running of the Empire,[1] and a new currency based on gold rather than on silver had replaced the currency of the Principate.[2]

[1] *LRE* 1.396; 2.623 p.237 below.   [2] See p.8 n.4 above.

PART 1

WEALTH AND ITS SOURCES

I

The finances of a senator

There is only one senator of the Principate about whose finances we have
any breadth of information. This is Pliny the younger, whose letters,
published by their author at the beginning of the second century A.D.,
provide a carefully rounded picture of the life of a senator and his circle.
Pliny also sought fame by his generosity, and possessed wealth which
allowed him to become one of the leading civic benefactors of the West.[1]
Chance has supplemented Pliny's writings by preserving most of a posthumous inscription that lists Pliny's gifts to his native town of Comum.

There is no contemporary assessment of the scale of Pliny's wealth,
apart from his own deprecating remarks. Despite implicit suggestions
about the size of his fortune in the Letters, his place in the senatorial
hierarchy of wealth is not immediately obvious. But it is clear that
Pliny was not among the proverbially rich senators of the early Empire,
men such as Cn. Cornelius Lentulus, Q. Vibius Crispus, L. Annaeus
Seneca and C. Passienus Crispus, who counted their wealth in hundreds
of millions.[2] It is unlikely that Pliny could vie with M. Aquillius Regulus,

---

[1] The massive benefactions and the publication of nine books of letters during his lifetime
were evidently both the product of Pliny's desire for public recognition (see *Ep.* 1.8; 7.20).
Citations by numeral alone in this chapter refer to Pliny's Letters. For general bibliography
of Pliny, see Sherwin-White xv, with R. Hanslik *Anzeiger für Altertumswissenschaft* 17
(1964) 1–16. The only extensive discussion of Pliny's public and private generosities together
with his resources appears in a popular work of limited value (E. Allain *Pline le Jeune et
ses héritiers* 1 (1901) 56–118). Friedlaender's brief account is more useful (Friedlaender
1.126–7). Pliny's resources are considered by Sirago (p.19 n.5, p.20 n.4 and p.23 n.6; Sirago
22–40): his account is more informative than that of Tissoni (G. G. Tissoni 'Nota sul
patrimonio immobiliare di Plinio il giovane' *RIL* 101 (1967) 161–83). Pliny's letters about
the management and condition of his estates have attracted more than one discussion (cf.
R. Martin 'Pline le Jeune et les problèmes économiques de son temps' *REA* 69 (1967)
62–97). Gentile's treatment of Pliny's gifts is somewhat out of date and deals fully only with
the gifts to Comum (I. Gentile *RIL* 14 (1881) 458–70). Mommsen gives a short account of
Pliny's main gifts, but does not deal with his resources (Mommsen *Ges.Schr.* 4. 366–468,
at 433–7).
[2] These men were reputed to have fortunes of HS400, 300, 300 and 200 million: Seneca *de
ben.* 2.27; Tacitus *Dial.* 8; Cassius Dio 61.10.3; Suetonius *v. Passieni Crispi.* Further examples
in Appendix 7 below.

a senator and advocate of his own day who expected to have HS60 million or more.[1] And Italian senators whose landholdings extended to the provinces might in general be richer than Pliny, whose only estates lay in Italy.[2]

Nevertheless, Pliny must not be judged a 'poor' senator.[3] A man who showed outstanding openhandedness during his lifetime, and who left phenomenally large public bequests cannot be regarded in this light. Pliny's own contention that his means were modest (put forward when writing off a bad debt) meant little or nothing in a man born to substantial wealth.[4] Although Pliny made public gifts that were quite exceptional by the standards of his time, they do not seem to have brought any diminution of the spacious and luxurious existence expected of a senator.[5] Pliny owned and maintained at least six houses, situated in four different parts of Italy. Pliny's frequent acts of generosity during his lifetime suggest a man in easy circumstances: the clearest single demonstration is his giving a sum as large as HS300,000 to a friend as part of a minor act of political patronage.[6] A close consideration of the Letters suggests that Pliny may have possessed at least twice the sum of HS8 million that contemporary sources sometimes indicate as an appropriate capital for a senator.[7] Pliny's family inheritances united in the hands of one man

[1] 2.20.13; for Regulus, cf. Syme 100–2 and *PIR*[2] A 1005. Regulus could afford two houses near Rome, compared with Pliny's one. Regulus owned a *rus* at the third milestone from Rome and a house at Tusculum, as well as estates in Umbria and Tuscany (Martial 7.31; 1.12).

[2] Compare for example two senators of the first century A.D., Sex. Pompeius, who owned estates in Sicily, Macedonia and Campania, and Rubellius Plautus, who owned estates in Asia and Latium (*PIR*[1] P 450 and R 85). Cf. Friedlaender 1.123–4. For provincial land as an investment, cf. Pliny *NH* 18.35; Petronius *Sat.* 117.

[3] Carcopino is inclined to take Pliny's remarks about his wealth at face value (Carcopino 67–8). Friedlaender calls Pliny 'ein nicht besonders reicher Senator' (Friedlaender 1.127). Sherwin-White says that Pliny 'was in the second grade of wealth' (Sherwin-White 150).

[4] 'Sunt quidem omnino nobis modicae facultates' 2.4.3. 'Pliny is not averse to explaining that the rich are not really well-off' (Syme 84). Pliny's father was sufficiently wealthy to donate a temple to Comum during his lifetime (Pais no.745; for the identification see below, p.27 n.3). Both his father and his mother bequeathed to Pliny estates near Lake Como (7.11.5) and Pliny was the adopted heir of his uncle, Pliny the elder, a ducenarian procurator (5.8.5).

[5] Pliny refers to his position as a 'dignitas sumptuosa' (2.4.3); cf. Seneca *Ep.* 50.3. Although some posts of the senatorial career were salaried (few details are known, cf. *Staatsrecht* 1.302–3), magistrates also had to contribute to the cost of highly expensive games at Rome. As a result, many career senators probably made an overall loss on their tenure of office; a minority indulged in peculation as provincial governors (3.9.12). For games and their cost *Staatsrecht* 2.137–8; 236–7; 534; Marquardt *Staatsverwaltung* 2.85–7; 3.487–9 (L. Friedlaender); W. M. Green *AJP* 51 (1930) 249–50.

[6] 1.19; 4.29.

[7] Imperial grants of revenues of HS500,000 to impoverished senators would imply a capital in the region of HS8 million at 6% (Tacitus *Ann.* 13.34; Suet. *Nero* 10; *Vesp.* 17; cf. Dio 60.29.2; Pliny *NH* 29.7). A friend for whom Pliny tried to obtain senatorial rank had not

one 'equestrian' fortune (inherited from his uncle) and two 'municipal' fortunes (from his father and mother).[1] Pliny's three marriages are bound to have increased his wealth further.[2]

Pliny, like most Roman magnates of high social standing, drew his main wealth from landed estates: 'sum quidem prope totus in praediis...'.[3] Pliny owned substantial estates in the region of his native town of Comum: one Letter shows that he had a number of *praedia* near Lake Como besides those inherited from his father and mother. When he inherited another property there, he chose to sell it to a friend at a reduced price.[4] There is no sound evidence that Pliny owned other estates in the north of Italy besides the bloc round Lake Como.[5] His other main property lay much further south, near Tifernum Tiberinum, a town in Umbria (the estate is called 'Tusci' in the Letters).[6] Pliny's ownership of this estate is not explained, but it is difficult to see that the estate can have come from any source but his uncle, Pliny the elder, whose heir the younger Pliny was. The elder Pliny, as a procurator of high rank, must have bequeathed substantial property to his nephew: the Tifernum estate is the only obviously large unit in the nephew's landholdings which is otherwise unaccounted for.[7] Pliny's property at Tifernum was bringing in more than HS400,000 per year early in the reign of Trajan.[8]

only received HS4 million from his mother, but had also inherited his father's estate (whose size is unspecified), and been adopted by his stepfather (10.4).

[1] See below, n.7 and p.27 n.3.
[2] Friedlaender 1.126. For Pliny's matrimonial history, Sherwin-White 71. For the custom of marriage dowries, see p.28 below.
[3] 3.19.8.
[4] 7.11.5–6; for the estates inherited from his mother see also 2.15.2.
[5] Sirago's distinction between Pliny's 'praedia circa Larium' and his 'praedia trans Padum' seems to be spurious (Sirago 27–8; also criticised by Sherwin-White 416). Pliny's mentions of Transpadana carry no topographical weight by themselves. Sirago is obliged to admit one instance where Pliny's use of 'trans Padum' is clearly generic, not precise (6.1.1, to which add 4.6.1). His case appears to rest merely on the proximity of lands owned by Pliny to lands owned by the Milanese L. Verginius Rufus (a point already made by Chilver 150; 2.1.8). This has no sure topographical significance, as Rufus may, like many senators, have owned estates in several districts (see Appendix 1).

Mommsen assigned an inscription found at Cantù in which Pliny is honoured as a municipal 'flamen divi Titi' to the territory of Milan (v 5667). This would argue that Pliny held office at Milan, perhaps as a consequence of landownership there (cf. 4.1.4), if Mommsen's identification of the site were correct. However, it is now thought that Cantù belonged to the territory of Comum (A. T. Sartori *ACSDIR* 1 (1967–8) 277, following Passerini). Mommsen himself concluded that the priesthood was held at Comum (Mommsen *Ges.Schr.* 4. 434).
[6] 4.1.3–5; 5.6.1, etc. For epigraphic record of Pliny's estate near Tifernum, XI 6689[171] and Mommsen *Ges.Schr.* 4. 442.
[7] His uncle's heir: 5.8.5. The elder Pliny's career: R. Syme *HSCP* 73 (1969) 201–36. Sherwin-White 322 also suggests that the Tifernum estate came from this source.
[8] 10.8.5.

Another estate, which we see Pliny on the verge of buying, was evidently also at Tifernum, though modern opinion has often placed it at Comum. Through neglect the property had depreciated in value from HS5 to HS3 million, at which price Pliny thought it an attractive proposition.[1] Pliny describes the estate as adjoining lands which he already owns, in a letter to Calvisius Rufus, a native and decurion of Comum.[2] Since Pliny thought it necessary to inform Rufus that no one used chained labour in the district to which the property belonged, the estate is unlikely to have lain near Comum. Furthermore, Pliny speaks of being able to practise economy by keeping up only one house in the district concerned, though he had at least three houses on his Comum estates.[3] The new property must thus have adjoined the estate at Tifernum, where there was a single house, since this was Pliny's only other substantial landholding.[4]

It is not clear that Pliny's estates near Tifernum Tiberinum were originally larger than those which he owned to the north of the Po. The Letters suggest that Pliny visited Tifernum more frequently than Comum, but this would be natural on grounds of convenience when Comum lay three times as far from the capital as Tifernum. Though unavoidably absent from them for most of the time, Pliny took an active part in running his estates in both districts when he had the opportunity.[5] The capital value of the Tifernum estate was approximately HS7 million before the new purchase (the income of over HS400,000 probably representing a return of about 6%).[6] If we assume a comparable figure for his Transpadane lands, and add the further property probably purchased at Tifernum for HS3 million, we reach a very rough estimate for the capital value of Pliny's landholdings of HS17 million.[7]

Pliny's immediate cash resources were evidently very much less than his holdings in land, at least at the time when he was planning to buy the new estate at Tifernum. At this juncture he also expected to be able to draw on the funds of his mother-in-law, which were freely available

---

[1] 3.19.7.

[2] 5.7.4; *PIR*² C 349.

[3] 3.19.2; 3.19.7; 9.7.2.

[4] 5.6.3; 4.6.1. See also Sherwin-White 254. The suggestion in Friedlaender 1.126 that the alimentary table from Ligures Baebiani shows Pliny as a landowner in southern Italy is groundless (see Sirago 35 n.1).

[5] Tifernum: 9.15; 9.16; 9.20; 10.8.5; 8.2 (because addressed to Calvisius Rufus, who lived at Comum p.20 n.2). Comum: 2.15.2 (cf. 7.11.5). 5.14.8, 7.30.3 and 9.37, which concern leasing arrangements, may refer to either area, though they recall 10.8.5 which refers to Tifernum.

[6] 10.8.5. See p.33.

[7] The only grounds attached to Pliny's Laurentine villa were a garden and a beach (4.6), though the house was probably grand enough to fetch a substantial price.

to him.[1] Nevertheless, Pliny appears to have enjoyed quite a high level of liquidity, judging by the gift during his lifetime alone of more than HS1,600,000 to public bodies, and more than HS740,000 to private individuals (the figures are discussed below). Despite the catalogue of adverse reports from his estates,[2] Pliny still had sufficient funds to allow him to invest part outside the land market: 'aliquid tamen fenero'.[3] This candid reference in a letter edited for publication is enough to show that no stigma attached to moneylending in the Senate of Pliny's day. We can compare Seneca's depiction of usury as an integral part of the economic activities of the man who enjoys good fortune.[4]

A ratio between income from rents and income from usury is suggested in Martial's description of the finances of the millionaire 'Afer'. Even if 'Afer's' loans were at rates as high as 12%, they would provide only about one-tenth of his income.[5] The income from Pliny's estates, using the provisional valuation of HS17 million estimated above, would have been about HS1 million per year, at 6%. If usury brought in about as much as one-tenth more his total income would be in the region of HS1,100,000 per year. But even this sum appears a little low to have been the basis for spontaneous lifetime gifts totalling well over HS2 million.

Here it is important to remember that substantial sums were frequently reaching Pliny from inheritances and legacies: those whose amount he mentions have a total value of HS1,450,000, while three further bequests are referred to without mention of their amount. The failure to quantify their value need not mean that these were always small. Pliny's disclosures in the Letters are sometimes random: benefactions as small as HS50,000 and HS40,000 may be mentioned explicitly, while the cost of much larger gifts such as the library at Comum and the temple at Tifernum is left to be guessed at.[6] Pliny indicates that he regularly received legacies as a literary celebrity, being mentioned in wills side by side with Cornelius Tacitus: the will of Dasumius made in A.D. 108 appears to bear him out.[7]

---

[1] 3.19.8.

[2] 2.4.3; 2.15.2; 4.6.1; 5.14.8; 7.30.3; 8.2; 9.15; 9.16; 9.20.2; 9.28.2; 9.37; 10.8.5.

[3] 3.19.8. Loans to relatives (2.4) may have been interest-free, cf. 3.11.2.

[4] 'Familiam formosam habet et domum pulchram, multum serit, multum fenerat' (*Ep.* 41.7). Cf. Martial 3.31. Tacitus implies that moneylending was universal in the Senate of Tiberius's reign (*Ann.* 6.16). Dio's patrimony included HS1,600,000 in loans and other investments (*Or.* 46.5).

[5] Martial 4.37 (the loan figures are capital, the rent figures income). For loans at high rates, p.307 n.1.

[6] 6.32; 6.25. 1.8.2; 4.1.5.

[7] 7.20.6; cf. 2.18.2; 9.11; 9.23; Martial 10.19; *FIRA* 3, no.48. The name of the author of this will, first identified as [Dasumius] by Borghesi (*Oeuvres* 6.429) has been the subject of further conjecture: 'L. Dasumius Tuscus?' (Mommsen *ad CIL* VI 10229, and B. Saria *JOAI* 26 (1930) 71, followed by Pflaum 636); 'P. Dasumius Tuscus' (Arangio-Ruiz *FIRA* 3, p.133);

Even if the legacies that Pliny received as a successful littérateur were quite small, other bequests that came his way were sometimes substantial. Revenue from this source cannot be ignored when seeking an explanation of Pliny's capacity for large-scale generosities during his lifetime and in his will.

Pliny owned a number of houses. The house in Rome, on the Esquiline Hill, may well have been the most valuable.[1] The house which Pliny visited most often for relaxation was his Laurentine villa near Ostia, which Pliny regarded as being within reach after a full working-day in Rome (the distance was 17 miles).[2] Pliny's detailed account of its amenities shows that it was a place of some size and splendour.[3] Pliny's pride in the location of the house may suggest that he purchased it (he did not build the house as a whole). If so, this was no doubt cheaper than buying a country house at one of the fashionable resorts in the hills near Rome. Pliny mentions that the upkeep of the Laurentum house was not expensive.[4]

Another letter refers ambiguously to three of the resorts near Rome. 'Habes causas cur ego Tuscos meos Tusculanis Tiburtinis Praenestinisque praeponam.'[5] This remark has been regarded as clearly indicating Pliny's ownership of villas at all four of the localities named,[6] especially since one of the manuscript sources gives the penultimate phrase as 'Pernestinisque meis'. But the support for this reading is inadequate.[7] Pliny in fact shows a quiet ostentation in revealing his possessions, however much of the tone of the Letters may seem to deny it. His connexion with Comum occurs in fourteen different letters;[8] the estates near Tifernum are mentioned nine times,[9] and the Laurentine villa occurs seven times.[10] If Pliny actually owned villas at Tibur, Praeneste and Tusculum, it would be very surprising that he should mention them only once, and then disparagingly. Furthermore, in a letter expressing

---

'L. Dasumius [Hadrianus?]' (A. Degrassi, *I fasti consolari dell'impero romano* (1952) 28; cf. Groag *PIR²* 3, p.xi no.14, and Syme 664).

[1] 3.21.5; Martial 10.19. For extremely high land and housing prices in Rome, see *PBSR* 33 (1965) 224–5.

[2] 9.40; 2.17.2; 2.17.24.

[3] 2.17. Sherwin-White 186–99.

[4] 2.17.20; 2.17.3.   [5] 5.6.45.

[6] That Pliny owned these further three villas is accepted by Gentile 470, n.1; Syme 84, n.5; Sirago 32–4; G. B. Ford *Helikon* 5 (1965) 381; Brockmeyer 386, n.38. The notion is rejected by Mrs Radice (Radice *Pliny* 1.354 n.1), and by Sherwin-White 329.

[7] Cf. edition by R. A. B. Mynors 1963.

[8] 1.3.1; 1.8.2; 2.8.1; 3.6.4; 4.6.1; 4.13.3; 4.30.1; 5.7.2–4; 5.11.2; 5.14.1 & 8; 6.1.1; 6.24.2; 7.11.5; 9.7.1.

[9] 3.4.2; 4.1.3; 4.6.1; 5.6; 5.18.2; 9.15; 9.36; 9.40.1; 10.8.5 (cf. 3.4.2).

[10] 1.9.4; 1.22.11; 2.17; 4.6; 5.2; 7.4.3; 9.40.

mock alarm at adverse news from both his estates, Pliny says that he has only Laurentum to fall back on as a support.[1] The three other villas near Rome should have been mentioned here if anywhere, had they existed. The remark is in fact a comparison between Pliny's summer refuge on his estates near Tifernum ('Tusci') and the conventional resorts close to Rome. Tusculum, Tibur, and Praeneste are also among the first four towns named in Martial's catalogue of possible rivals to the charms of Formiae.[2] The apparent reference in another letter to Pliny's staying a few days at Tusculum may indicate a visit to a friend or connexion there; Pliny certainly stayed with friends from time to time.[3] Mommsen's suggestion that 'Tusculano' here is merely a corruption of 'Tuscano', indicating another visit to the estate at Tifernum, is perhaps preferable, in view of the conciseness of the allusion.[4]

Pliny nevertheless owned other houses besides those at Rome and Laurentum. He possessed at least three villas on the shores of Lake Como; as noticed above, his property in this region came from at least three difference sources. These villas Pliny built in whole or in part, like most of his houses.[5] It has been suggested that Pliny owned a town-house in Comum, but the evidence is inconclusive.[6] On one of his visits to Comum, Pliny appears to have stayed with his wife's grandfather, L. Calpurnius Fabatus, who lived there.[7] There was also a villa on Pliny's estate at Tifernum Tiberinum, which he often visited. From his account it appears to have been quite large, if less elaborate than the Laurentum house. He used the Tifernum villa as a place of summer relaxation.[8] The purchase of a second estate at Tifernum brought with it the acquisition of a second house in that neighbourhood, assuming that the transaction proposed in *Ep.* 3.19 was carried out.

Thus in sum Pliny owned a town-house in Rome, a 'suburban' seaside villa 17 miles from Rome at Vicus Laurentium, one or two villas near Tifernum Tiberinum, and at least three villas on Lake Como, making a total of not less than six or seven houses in all. Unlike a number of sena-

---

[1] 4.6.1.

[2] Martial 10.30 (also noted by Sherwin-White 329).

[3] Pliny stays with Pompeia Celerina, one of his mothers-in-law: 1.4; 6.10; with Vestricius Spurinna: 3.1; with Iunius Mauricus at Formiae: 6.14; at the house of Pontius Allifanus in Campania: 6.28; stays frequently with Calestrius Tiro: 7.16.2; with Terentius Iunior: 7.25.3. Cf. 5.14.8 and 4.1.1, a visit to Calpurnius Fabatus, the grandfather of Pliny's third wife. Cf. Varro *r.r.* 3.2.15.

[4] Mommsen *Ges.Schr.* 4.388, n.3.

[5] 9.7; 2.17.20; 5.6.41.

[6] Sirago claims that 4.13.3; 4.30; 5.14; and 6.1 show that Pliny had a house in the town of Comum, but the letters do not support his inference (Sirago 28).

[7] 5.14.8; cf. 4.1.1.

[8] 5.6; 9.36; 9.40.

tors, Pliny did not own a villa in Campania.[1] When he mentions a visit to Campania he says that he stayed at the house of a friend, Pontius Allifanus.[2] But since his *suburbanum* was on the coast at Laurentum, it may have served some of the purposes of a Campanian villa.

Besides having landed estates, house property and liquid cash, Pliny, like all monied men of his time, owned slaves. In one letter we see Pliny buying slaves, using the advice of Plinius Paternus. In another letter to Paternus, Pliny sets out the principles on which he ran his household: he was very ready to manumit, and to allow slaves to make wills that were binding as long as the legatees were within the household.[3] The slaves referred to here were evidently all domestic employees of one sort or another. Pliny owned agricultural slaves as well, though none of them were chained; one of the necessities which he foresaw when contemplating the purchase of a new property was the equipping of the tenants with new rustic slaves (*mancipia*).[4] There would be nothing surprising for a man of Pliny's means in owning slaves by the hundred. Aemilia Pudentilla, a woman of equestrian family whose resources of HS4 million could hardly have been a quarter of those of Pliny, owned 400 slaves, most of whom worked on her estates in Tripolitania.[5] Whatever the relative importance of agricultural slavery in Italy and Africa in the second century, Pliny's slave-holding would probably have been considerably more than 400, if not several times as big, on this analogy. Since Pliny negotiated with wine-dealers on a large scale over the produce of his estates,[6] it is likely that a substantial area was under direct cultivation by slave labour.

Pliny made provision for the support of 100 freedmen in his will. This probably indicates the manumission of this number by will, a facility which the law only allowed to those who owned 500 slaves or more.[7] Despite his stated liberality in manumitting during his lifetime, it is unlikely that many agricultural slaves were freed, since this would have affected a large part of the labour-force available for working the estates. Manumission of agricultural slaves does not seem to have been a regular

---

[1] Cf. J. D'Arms *Romans on the Bay of Naples* (1970).

[2] 6.28. Sherwin-White's statement that Pliny the elder owned property in Campania appears to be based on a passage in the *Natural History* which mentions the time of day at which an eclipse in A.D. 59 was observed in Campania. This has little force, especially since Pliny does not claim to be making an eyewitness report (*NH* 2.180; Sherwin-White 70). 6.16.8 refers to a house at Misenum; but as commander of the fleet there, the elder Pliny was bound to have a house in the town whether he owned private property in Campania or not (6.16.4).

[3] 1.21.2; 8.16. [4] 3.19.7.

[5] Apuleius *Apol.* 77; 93. See Appendix 15.

[6] 8.2. The letter contains no suggestion that there were only half a dozen dealers, as conjectured by Sherwin-White 449.

[7] *ILS* 2927. W. W. Buckland *Textbook of Roman Law*[3] (1963) 78 and n.2. This is also the conclusion of Carcopino (Carcopino 70).

feature of Roman farm management, to judge from the absence of references to freedmen in the agrarian writers. The *liberti* who received
their freedom before Pliny's death would probably have been provided
for by separate viritim bequests.[1]

Pliny's resources were augmented during his lifetime by a number of
inheritances and legacies, even if his will was to deplete them by an even
greater amount. The biggest of the inheritances about which Pliny gives
details is described so casually that confusion has arisen over its size.[2]
Pliny explains that a certain Saturninus had made him his heir, having
first also made the city of Comum joint heir to one quarter of the estate.
Saturninus had then substituted for the city's fourth part a preliminary
legacy of HS400,000 to be paid to the city out of the estate. Since neither
procedure was legally admissible, this part of the will was evidently void.
Pliny proposed however to carry out Saturninus' intention, by donating
to the city HS400,000 from the estate, the whole of which had fallen to
him through the inadvertence of the testator. Then follows the sentence
which is variously interpreted: 'An cui [*sc.* communi patriae] de meo
sestertium sedecies contuli, huic quadringentorum milium paulo amplius
tertiam partem ex adventicio denegem?' Most editors until the late
nineteenth century construed 'tertiam partem' as applying to 'sedecies',
which they consequently emended to 'undecies' or 'decies' in order to
improve the arithmetic. Because this is not the only possible construction
of the sentence, and because the better manuscripts give 'sedecies', this
emendation must be rejected, as Mommsen made clear.[3]

Mommsen's own interpretation of the passage is based on what is
almost certainly a false premiss: that Calvisius Rufus, the decurion of
Comum to whom the letter was addressed, was Pliny's co-heir to the
estate of Saturninus. Mommsen consequently read 'paulo amplius tertiam
partem' as indicating the proportion of the estate which Pliny was to
inherit. This makes the passage very awkward: it would have been much
more natural in such circumstances to indicate the extent of Pliny's
liability towards the city directly, than to say that he would have to part
with slightly more than one-third of HS400,000, leaving it to be inferred
that this was the proportion of the estate which he stood to inherit.
Mommsen took Calvisius Rufus's share to have been the complement of
Pliny's, that is, slightly under two-thirds.[4]

But the evidence is against regarding Rufus as an heir at all. 'Satur-

---

[1] Compare the contemporary will of Dasumius *FIRA* 3, no.48, ll.36 ff.; Syme 603.

[2] 5.7.   [3] Mommsen *Ges.Schr.* 4.434, n.6.

[4] *Ibid.* Mommsen's position (accepted by Gentile 468–9) is set out in greater detail in *Zeit-
schrift für Rechtsgeschichte* 7 (1868) 314–18, though he is primarily concerned there with the
juridical point at issue, not with the details of Pliny's affairs.

ninus autem, qui nos reliquit heredes' at the opening of the letter, can
quite well be translated (with Mrs Radice) as 'but Saturninus, who has
made *me* his heir', since Pliny often refers to himself in the plural in the
Letters.[1] We see why Pliny feels it necessary to justify his procedure to
Rufus, when he later goes on to ask Rufus to do him the favour of raising
Pliny's proposed payment to the city before the town-council at Comum.[2]
If Pliny had been asking Rufus to accede to arrangements which would
deprive him of more than HS200,000, as Mommsen's interpretation
would entail, Pliny's oblique method of asking and his assumption that
Rufus would acquiesce would have been cavalier and out of keeping
with the tone of the Letters (especially since, on this view, Rufus would
have stood to lose more than Pliny himself). Furthermore, if Rufus had
been a fellow-heir of Saturninus, this rehearsal of elementary details
would have been superfluous: Rufus would already have been as con-
versant with them as Pliny.

The correct interpretation of the sentence in question is given by Mrs
Radice: 'I have given HS1,600,000 to the town out of my own money, so
surely I ought not to grudge it this 400,000, little more than a third of
my unexpected inheritance.'[3] The total amount of the estate would thus
have been about HS1,100,000, since HS400,000 formed slightly more
than one-third of the whole; after Pliny had paid HS400,000 to the city,
the amount that he kept would have been HS700,000 or so.

HS700,000 was also the effective value of an inheritance which Pliny
received in the form of lands adjoining Lake Como, perhaps at a slightly
later date. This constituted five-twelfths of the estate of a testator who is
not named. The lands could probably have fetched as much as HS900,000
if put up for sale on the open market, since this was the valuation on
which the *publicani* assessed the 5% death duty. But Pliny chose to sell
the property at once at the price of HS700,000 to Corellia, wife of
Minicius Iustus, to whom he wanted to do a favour (Corellia was left to
pay the inheritance tax of HS45,000).[4] Pliny was also part-heir to Acilianus
and to Sabina, though the size of the inheritances is not mentioned.[5]
He received legacies of HS50,000 and of an unstated amount, from

---

[1] Radice *Pliny* 1.355. For transitions between first person singular and first person plural
where the singular is intended throughout, see 1.8, where Pliny is again describing his public
generosities. Cf. S. Lilja *Eranos* 69 (1971) 89–103.

[2] 5.7.4.

[3] This translation should involve the substitution of 'quadringenta milia' for 'quadringentorum
milium' in 5.7.3. That raises little difficulty, as the figure may originally have appeared in the
neutral form 'CCCC', as was pointed out to the writer by Professor D. R. Shackleton Bailey.
'CCCC' for 400,000 appears in 10.8.5.

[4] 7.11; 7.14.

[5] 2.16; 4.10. Cf. 3.6.1.

Iulius Largus and Asudius Curianus.[1] Pliny's total increments from inheritances and bequests within the period of fifteen years or so covered by the Letters thus amounted to well over HS1,450,000.

We now come to Pliny's generosities. His public gifts must be seen in the context of the 'munificentia parentum nostrorum' which Pliny mentioned in his speech at the opening of the Comum library.[2] Pliny's father has been convincingly identified as the 'L. Ca[eciliu]s Secundus' who built a temple to *Aeternitas Romae et Augusti* at Comum, which was dedicated by his son '[...Caeci]lius Secundus'.[3] In view of the plural which Pliny uses, one of his other forebears probably also made a gift to the city of Comum. Pliny elsewhere suggests that his public munificence owed much of its impetus to the direct encouragement given to such activities by the Emperor Nerva, which is also mentioned by Martial.[4]

Three donations to Comum formed the largest of the gifts made during Pliny's lifetime. The alimentary fund was worth HS500,000, the fund for the maintenance of the library HS100,000, and the library itself HS1,000,000 (if Mommsen's subtraction of the first two figures from the total of HS1,600,000 for Pliny's lifetime gifts to Comum given in *Ep.* 5.7.3 is correct).[5] Pliny's fund for *alimenta* was 25% larger than the only previous alimentary gift whose size we know, the fund bequeathed to Atina Latii at least a generation earlier by T. Helvius Basila.[6] His fund is also larger than one of the two imperial alimentary funds of known size, that at Ligures Baebiani.[7] Later alimentary gifts for the support of children tended to be still larger, though none of the later donors is known to have been as generous in other directions as Pliny.[8] The number of children supported by Pliny's scheme was of the order of 175.[9] In accordance with the wishes of Saturninus, Pliny also gave to Comum the sum of HS400,000 which the law would have allowed him to keep (see above).

---

[1] 10.75; 5.1.1; cf. 7.20.6. [2] 1.8.5.

[3] Pais no.745, examined by Otto 5–16; the identification is accepted by Chilver, Syme and Sherwin-White (Chilver 106; Syme 60 and n.4; Sherwin-White 70). This conjecture is clearly preferable to the identification of Pliny's father as the L. Caecilius Cilo mentioned in v 5279 (who may nevertheless be a relation, perhaps one of the munificent forebears referred to in 1.8.5); Mommsen *Ges.Schr.* 4.394–5.

[4] 10.8.1; Martial 12.6.

[5] 7.18.2–4 (Pliny makes clear that he actually spent more than HS500,000 on his *alimenta*); *ILS* 2927, l.14; Mommsen *Ges.Schr.* 4.434 and n.6; 5.7.3.

[6] x5056 = *ILS* 977. For the date of this gift, M. Hammond *Mem.Amer.Acad. in Rome* 21 (1953) 147–51. Another apparent precursor is the alimentary gift at Florentia (xi 1602).

[7] This fund had a value of HS401,800; ix 1455 (selections in *ILS* 6509).

[8] See C. nos.248; 637; 641; 642; ii 1174 (discussed in *Historia* 13 (1964) 207).

[9] Perhaps 100 boys and 75 girls, *Historia* 13 (1964) 206; the conjecture was anticipated by Gentile 464.

Tifernum Tiberinum also received a building from Pliny, a temple to house the imperial statues which he presented to the town. This temple, promised under Nerva, was nominally given in return for the patronate which the town had voted him at an early age. Though the temple is mentioned in three letters, Pliny does not say what it cost. Pliny celebrated its dedication by giving a public feast at Tifernum at his own expense.[1] Pliny restored another temple, which lay on his estates, on religious advice; this was for the benefit of the country people round about who gathered there every September. This temple dedicated to Ceres, which was tetrastyle, was probably smaller than the temple at Tifernum. Pliny's public donations during his lifetime also included two minor gifts to Comum: a Corinthian bronze statue intended for the temple of Jupiter; and one-third of a teacher's salary, which Pliny offered to pay provided that the parents of Comum would find the remaining two-thirds.[2]

Private individuals also benefited from Pliny's gifts during his lifetime. The large sum of HS300,000 went to his contemporary Romatius Firmus of Comum, to enable him to achieve the equestrian census; Pliny evidently also obtained for Firmus membership of the *decuriae*, the jury-panels at Rome.[3] Martial implies that gifts endowing the recipient with equestrian wealth were a traditional form of munificence which had somewhat declined by this time.[4] Pliny gave a farm worth HS100,000 to his nurse, as a support for her old age.[5] He mentions the amounts of two dowries presented to daughters of his friends: HS100,000 for Calvina, and HS50,000 for the fiancée of Nonius Celer. More than a century earlier Cicero had commended the giving of dowries to the daughters of one's friends as a proper form of munificence.[6] In selling an estate to Corellia,

---

[1] 10.8.2–4; 4.1.4–5; 3.4.2; Mommsen *Ges.Schr.* 4.370, n.1.

[2] 9.39; 3.6; 4.13.5–6.

[3] 1.19; 4.29. Martial says that endowing those who lacked wealth was a fitting characteristic of the reign of Nerva. Since Pliny's munificence is known to have owed some of its impetus to Nerva's exhortation and example (10.8.1–2), his generosity towards Firmus may have been inspired by current imperial policy (most of the letters in book 1 are thought to belong to the reign of Nerva, Sherwin-White 27–8; 129). Martial 12.6.9–11:

> Largiri, praestare, breves extendere census
> et dare quae faciles vix tribuere dei,
> nunc licet et fas est.

[4]
> *Anuli*
> Ante frequens sed nunc rarus nos donat amicus.
> Felix cui comes est non alienus eques.

Martial 14.122; cf. Martial 5.19; 5.81; 4.67. For the decline in munificence cf. *Ep.* 3.21.3.

[5] 6.3.1.

[6] 2.4.2; 6.32.2. Cicero *de off.* 2.55. For gifts within the senatorial class, compare Seneca *de ben.* 2.21.5–6; this shows that a senator faced with the expense of games in honour of public office could expect contributions from a wide circle of acquaintances. The two consulars

the sister of Corellius Rufus, for HS700,000 when its market price was HS900,000, Pliny ceded the sum of HS155,000 (Corellia paid the tax of 5% levied on the market price).[1] The ill-fated Metilius Crispus of Comum was given HS40,000 to pay the expenses involved in taking up the centurionate that Pliny had obtained for him.[2] Pliny also gave travelling expenses to the poet Martial when he retired from Rome, and a large interest-free loan to the philosopher Artemidorus.[3]

At Pliny's death the town of Comum benefited from his generosity once again.[4] In the nature of the evidence, we know nothing of Pliny's bequests to individuals; it would be unrealistic to suppose that Pliny did not make many legacies to friends and relations.[5] His legal heirs, who were bound to receive not less than 25% of the whole estate,[6] probably received Pliny's main properties more or less intact.[7]

The biggest of the bequests to Comum whose value we know was in fact intended in the first place to provide income for the maintenance of 100 of Pliny's freedmen while they were living. The fund (of HS1,866,666) was then to be transferred to the provision of an annual dinner for the *plebs urbana* of Comum.[8] It is not known whether this fund was vested in land, like the alimentary foundation that Pliny gave to Comum during his lifetime. The income per head, while the foundation was being used for the support of the freedmen, would have been between HS70 and HS85

---

whose contributions Graecinus refused because he disapproved of their mode of life can hardly have been among his friends. Cf. Martial 4.67.

[1] 7.11; 7.14.

[2] Crispus was never seen again after his departure to take up the commission, 6.25.3.

[3] 3.21.2; 3.11.2. Martial writes as if he were himself an *eques*; though many of his poems in the first person contain invention, it is difficult to see that this could be fictitious (Martial 3.95; 9.97; 12.26). Cf. U. Scamuzzi *Rivista di Studi Classici* 14 (1966) 149–207.

[4] Carcopino's contention that most of the gifts mentioned in Pliny's inscription were made during his lifetime, and that his will was published before his death, is unconvincing (J. Carcopino *Rencontres de l'histoire et de la littérature romaines* (1963) 171–231).

[5] Cf. 2.20; 5.1.1; 7.20.6; Cicero *Phil.* 2.16.40; *FIRA* 3, no.48.

[6] W. W. Buckland *Textbook of Roman Law*[3] 342 ff.; *Digesta* 35.2.1 ff.

[7] Carcopino, who states that Pliny's will almost reached HS20 million, writes that 'Pliny produced no heir, and his fortune was divided at his death between pious foundations and his servants' (Carcopino 67; 91). There is no evidence that the Comum inscription records the disposition of the greater part of Pliny's wealth; the fact that the totals recorded there evidently amounted to a sum substantially less than the HS20 million that Pliny appears to have been worth argues against the contention. The inscription offers no suggestion that Pliny made the town of Comum his heir (though such arrangements were technically possible, cf. *ILS* 6729; 6723).

[8] *ILS* 2927 ll.11–12. Another alimentary gift transferred to a different purpose after the death of the recipients is mentioned in *Digesta* 33.2.34.pr. (Mommsen *Ges.Schr.* 4.437). Money for an annual feast was also given to Comum by Pliny's literary friend Caninius Rufus (7.18.1). Regarded as a provision for feasts, Pliny's fund is enormous, easily the biggest of the eight Italian feast-foundations whose size is known (C. nos.1079m ff.).

per head per month (the interest rate would hardly reach 6% when the
capital was so large).[1] Though this is very much more than the rates of
support for children in the Imperial scheme (the highest of which is
HS16 per month), some alimentary payments for adults mentioned in the
Digesta show comparable monthly average figures: HS83, HS42 and
HS40.[2] There is no direct evidence that alimentary payments to adults
were intended to contribute to the support of dependants, but a jurist of
Pliny's time defined *alimenta* left by will as meaning the provision of
clothing and housing as well as food.[3] Pliny's provision for the members
of his household appears to have been generous. The irregularity of the
capital sum is very unusual among Roman endowments.[4] It probably results
from Pliny's wanting to apply a particular rate of benefit per head for the
support of his freedmen.[5] Pliny's penchant for financial innovation is illustrated elsewhere in his account of the investment of his alimentary fund, and
in the system of rebates which he granted to wine-dealers in a bad year[6].

Pliny also bequeathed to Comum HS300,000 (or more, since the figure
may be incomplete) for the decoration of public baths, and a fund of
HS200,000 for the *tutela* of the baths (which meant their upkeep but not
their running costs).[7] The baths themselves appear to have been promised
while Pliny was still alive, since the fund for their decoration was an

---

[1] For the relation between the size of foundations and their interest-rate, see p. 134.

[2] XI 1147; *Digesta* 34.1.20.pr.; 34.1.20.3; 10.2.39.2. The jurists' figures may have been chosen
exempli gratia but they probably bore some resemblance to current practice. Illustrations
apparently drawn from actual bequests show monthly allowances of HS20 for food and HS42
for clothing for Attia Sempronia, and HS24 for food and HS8 for clothing for each of two
orphans named Arellius who were under 14 (34.4.30.pr.; 34.3.28.pr.). Cf. S. Mrozek *AAASH*
18 (1970) 353–60.

[3] Iavolenus Priscus, *Digesta* 34.1.6. However, bequests for clothing and housing as such were
considered under separate rubrics in a speech about alimentary gifts by Marcus Aurelius
(Ulpian in *Digesta* 2.15.8.12; 2.15.8.1).

[4] One of the few parallels is a foundation worth 3,333 drachmae at Tralles, *Papers Amer.
School. Class. Stud. Athens* I (1882–3) 98–9.

[5] A round figure monthly rate of HS70 would occur if interest were 4.5%. If instead the rate
of support was reckoned on an annual basis as in juristic examples (*Digesta* 34.1.20.pr.; 34.1.
20.3; 33.1.13.1) individual payments of HS1,000 would be possible if the interest-rate were
5.36%. Pliny can be seen to be using an interest-rate effectively below 6% in 7.18. Whether
financial provision for housing would have been included is uncertain; we hear of a testator
at Arles who allowed his freedmen and freedwomen to go on living on his property for the
rest of their lives (*Digesta* 33.2.34.pr.; cf. 32.41.1; 32.41.3).

[6] 7.18; 8.2. Cf. 9.37.3.

[7] *ILS* 2927, ll.10–11. C. nos.646 and 653 for the difference between 'tutela' and 'calefactio'.
Gentile argued that Pliny's gift provided no more than the enlargement of existing baths,
but there is no evidence for his assumption. Even if Comum already possessed public baths
at the time of Pliny's death (as is probable), it was quite usual for Roman towns to have
several sets of baths (cf. C. no.468; even the Laurentes near Pliny's seaside villa had three sets
of baths for hire, 2.17.26). Gentile 467 and n.2.

addition to the original sum. The figure for their basic cost is missing; it can hardly have been less than the HS300,000 allowed for decoration, and may have been considerably more, since Pliny appears to have been willing to spend as much as HS1 million on the library. Two sets of baths at Altinum for whose *tutela* a fund with the identical value of HS200,000 was established cost in all HS800,000 to restore.[1] Pliny also bequeathed a monument to Hispellum.[2]

When his lifetime gifts to Comum totalling HS1,600,000 are taken into account, it emerges that Pliny was easily the largest public donor in Italy among those the value of whose gifts is known. If we take only that part of Pliny's generosities which is known from inscriptions (to create an accurate basis for comparison with other epigraphic evidence) the total is still substantially higher than the next largest group of Italian gifts known from inscriptions, more than HS2,466,666 compared with HS1,600,000.[3] Our knowledge of the value of his public gifts is certainly incomplete, since no estimate of the basic cost of the Comum baths, of the temple at Tifernum or of the monument at Hispellum is possible. Pliny's public gifts of known value (using literary as well as epigraphic information) total HS3,966,666; but the three buildings whose cost is not known must have brought the total close to HS5 million, if not beyond this figure.

Pliny's main rival in public generosity in Italy (if the great-niece of an Emperor can be counted among private individuals) was the younger Matidia. Her alimentary foundation worth several millions (perhaps at Capua), which Fronto mentions, was accompanied by the gift of a library at Suessa Aurunca, in the later second century.[4] The Italian donations next in size were worth HS1,600,000, HS1,500,000 and HS1,300,000.[5] The provinces however offer instances of gifts which greatly exceed Pliny's public generosities. Massilia in Narbonensis received nearly HS10 million by the will of Crinas under Nero.[6] A donor at Aspendos in Pamphylia gave HS8 million towards the cost of an aqueduct there.[7] And the father of Herodes Atticus made up a deficit of HS16 million for

---

[1] C. nos.468; 653.

[2] XI 5272; Mommsen *Ges.Schr.* 4.444–6. Perhaps the monument was connected with the free public baths at Hispellum of which Pliny wrote appreciatively in 8.8.6.

[3] C. nos.468 + 646 + 653 + 654.

[4] C. no.637; X 4744–7.

[5] N.3 above; C. nos.639; 1197; 446 + 640 (joint gifts by two brothers).

[6] Pliny *NH* 29.9; *RE* 11.1865. For gifts of HS2 million and HS1¼ million in Gaul, see XIII 596–600 and *ILS* 2709. As transmitted, a Spanish inscription known only from a sixteenth-century copy states that a procurator of Baetica gave the town of Castulo HS10 million; the figure would be easier to credit if the stone survived (*ILS* 5513). To state the amount in words (as 'centies') instead of in figures is very unusual in Latin inscriptions.

[7] *IGRR* 3.804.

an aqueduct at Alexandreia Troas under Hadrian (if Philostratus' report is reliable). His bequest to the citizens of Athens was probably intended to be larger still.[1] Imposing though they are, these examples need not point to higher levels of wealth in the provinces, since a larger proportion of the wealthiest families in Italy were committed to the heavy expenditures required by senatorial rank and by residence at Rome.[2]

Pliny's generosities appear pre-eminent among gifts by private individuals in Italy. They are partly to be explained, no doubt, by Pliny's susceptibility to imperial example at a time when public munificence was being actively encouraged by the ruler.[3] It is also relevant that Pliny was a man of 'municipal' origin[4] and almost certainly felt local ties more strongly than did men of similar means who were born into senatorial families. And childlessness probably made it easier to commit large sums to local communities, though many other donors must also have been childless.[5] But Pliny's means do not seem to have been exceptionally large, especially judged by the standards of subsequent generations. By the time of Marcus Aurelius a fortune of HS20 million could be considered moderate, at any rate by Galen, whose practice lay among the highest circles in Rome.[6] Yet in spite of this, few if any subsequent benefactors in Italy appear to have rivalled Pliny either in the scope or in the scale of their munificence. Thus taking everything into account, it must be concluded that Pliny was outstanding in the extent of his public generosity.

[1] P. Graindor *Hérode Atticus* (1930) 32; 72 (Philostratus *VS* 548–9).

[2] For great fortunes in Italy, see above, p.17 n.2, and Appendix 7.

[3] See p.28 n.3.

[4] L. Caecilius Secundus, probably Pliny's father, was *praefectus fabrum*, and held a magistracy and a priesthood at Comum (Pais no.745, above, p.27 n.3).

[5] For the heavy financial impact of parenthood on a senator, see Tacitus *Ann.* 2.37–8.

[6] Galen vol.13.636 (Kühn) appears to suggest that there was a definite distinction between someone with HS20 million and a truly rich man. Jones pointed out tendencies towards the progressive increase in the size of large fortunes under the Empire (*LRE* 554–5). The possibility that Pliny's fortune was substantially larger than HS20 million cannot be excluded, since we do not know the size of his income from Transpadana. Nevertheless the fact that he evidently spent more time at Tifernum as an active landlord (p.20 n.5) offers some suggestion that the Comum holdings were not substantially greater than those at Tifernum.

2

Agricultural investment and agricultural profits

The overwhelming importance of agriculture in the Roman economy is generally recognised.[1] Most of the wealth of Roman society came from this source.[2] However, information about actual rates of profit is very sparse, though we know something of rates of interest on investment capital. The long-term yield on capital, almost certainly an agricultural dividend in most cases, was commonly of the order of 5–6% in Italy.[3]

Wine is the only crop about whose rate of profitability we have any explicit statements. The profits from other crops such as cereals and olives have sometimes been conjectured, but there is too little evidence to produce any firm conclusions.[4] The figures for wine-growing deserve closer scrutiny than they have so far been given, and a critical examination of them forms the main part of this chapter. It will be argued that the main set of figures (from Columella) is palpably inaccurate. Nevertheless, the construction of a framework within which to assess this evidence can provide a basis for some inferences about actual levels of profit.

[1] Cf. Jones *LRE* 769. This discussion has benefited from the general exposition provided by K. D. White's *Roman Farming* (1970) despite differences of interpretation.

[2] The cases of Pliny the younger and Martial's acquaintance 'Afer' illustrate the investment of private fortunes (Pliny *Ep.* 3.19.8; Martial 4.37, where the loans refer to capital, the dividends to income, meaning that the major part of 'Afer"s wealth was in property). Cf. Tacitus *Hist.* 2.78; Seneca *Ep.* 41.7.

[3] When Pliny set up a permanent foundation during his lifetime, he vested the fund in land, and nominally gave it an interest-rate of 6%. The foundations known from inscriptions were normally also invested in land, where the arrangements are known, and bore interest at 6% or 5% in most areas. When Columella recommends wine-growing, he first tries to convince the reader that a return of more than 6% was available, thus indicating that 6% was a normal level of return. (Pliny *Ep.* 7.18; *ILS* 3546; 3775; 6271; 6328a; 6469; 6663; 6664; 8370; 8376. Col. *de r.r.* 3.3.9–10. For interest rates on foundations, see pp. 132–6.) For mean agricultural dividends of 4–6% in late mediaeval Italy, see P. J. Jones *RSI* 76 (1964) 294.

[4] 8% profit is inferred from the 15-fold wheat yield mentioned by Varro for parts of Etruria by White (apparently assuming a land cost of HS2,500 per iugerum, and a wheat cost of HS3 per modius, cf. Frank *ESAR* 1.365; White 66). This crop yield is hardly typical (see below, p.49 n.4) and there is no indication that cereal land would normally have cost as much as HS2,500. For different calculations about cereals, see below, pp.48–52. Frank's reckoning of profits from olives has too few firm coordinates to be useful (we know only the planting-

[33]

THE PROFITABILITY OF DIFFERENT CROPS

The discussion must concentrate on Italy, because of our dependence on the agricultural writers for information. Varro speaks of Italy as a land planted with trees as though it were one vast orchard, while Columella contrasts the open corn fields of North Africa with the vineyards and olive-trees that cover Italian soil.[1] Although there were certainly parts of Italy to which these descriptions could not apply,[2] it is significant that the agricultural writers could speak in such terms. The cultivation of staple cereals was almost bound to be widespread in any economy which had no means of low-cost transport by land.[3] But in Italy the growing of cereals was frequently combined with arboriculture, and mixed cultivation was a common feature of the landscape.[4]

Vines are considered the most profitable crop in ancient assessments of Italian agriculture. Cato places vines first in his list of crops arranged in order of profit, provided that the wine produced is plentiful and of high quality.[5] Columella tries to show with figures that the profits of wine-growing were very large (he does not make a specific caveat about the quality of the crop). Pliny concludes, after producing details of exceptional profits obtained from vines on two estates within the last few years, that wine-growing can yield even greater profits than trade with the Far East.[6] There were nevertheless schools of thought which considered vines a doubtful proposition, partly at least because of the high level of investment which they required.[7] Clearly their profitability was not unfailing. Pliny quotes a case of a great fortune lost in a single generation, which was evidently invested in Italian vineyards in Picenum. The local wine was so cheap in some parts of Italy that profits could not have been

distance and the price of the oil). Frank's oil-yield (15–20 pounds per tree) is very much higher than the two modern Italian figures cited by Dumont (both about 3 Roman pounds per tree; Dumont 243; 246; Frank *ESAR* 1.171 and White 391).
[1] Varro *r.r.* 1.2.6; Columella *de r.r.* 2.2.24–5.
[2] Particularly the ranching lands of the south, C. A. Yeo *TAPHA* 79 (1948) 275–307.
[3] Cf. C. A. Yeo *TAPHA* 77 (1946) 221–44.
[4] See p.36 n.1.
[5] Cato 1.7. Cato's caveat about the wine crop is enough to show that his enumeration is a hierarchy in descending order (Salomon 46 states that it is not a hierarchy).
[6] Columella *de r.r.* 3.3; Pliny *NH* 14.47–52.
[7] Varro *r.r.* 1.7.9–1.8.1; Columella *de r.r.* 3.3.4–6, who cites Iulius Graecinus in support of his view. Saserna was opposed to *arbustum* (vines supported by trees); Col. *de r.r.* 3.3.2. Cicero speaks as though *silvae* or woodland might have been worth more than vines ('luxuriosus est nepos, qui prius silvas vendat quam vineas' *de leg. ag.* 2.18.48). Aymard builds large conclusions on this remark, but it can hardly override the favourable assessments of viticulture by Cato, Columella and Pliny (A. Aymard *AESC* 2 (1947) 257–65). *Silvae* were a standby which did not deteriorate rapidly, whose labour requirements were also much less than those of vines.

high: the wine of Aricia in Latium fetched so little that the cultivators could only afford to prune the vines in alternate years; while at Ravenna in Aemilia wine was cheaper than water, in Martial's scornful phrase.[1] A really good harvest could mean a glut and a serious drop in wine prices.[2] Wine-growing seems nonetheless to have expanded under the early Empire; there are indications of a growing overseas trade in wine, while Columella indicates that new vineyards were frequently being established under Nero in the part of central Italy in which his estates lay.[3] Local cheapness was possibly an index of excessive production of wine, granted that the market for such a staple product would have been reasonably constant. This could suggest that at some stage vineyards had been extended in anticipation of good profits. The edict limiting vine-growing passed by Domitian in A.D. 92 seems to have been based at least in part on the view that vineyards had grown dangerously far at the expense of cereals.[4]

There is little doubt that cereals were less profitable than vineyards; grain land ranks sixth in Cato's order of profitability, out of nine types of cultivation. Other explicit indications are few, but what is known of corn prices suggests that the profitability of cereals cannot ordinarily have been high in Italy, except in regions of exceptional fertility.[5] Much of the

---

[1] Pliny *NH* 18.37 (cf. Yeo 455; V 8112[78]; III 12010[30]); *NH* 17.213; Martial 3.56–7.

[2] Pliny *Ep.* 4.6.1; Martial 12.76.

[3] Martial 10.36; Petronius *Sat.* 76; in general Yeo 332 ff.; Columella *de r.r.* 3.3.13.

[4] Dated to 92 by Eusebius *Chronicon* ed. A. Schoene 2 (1875) 160. Suetonius states that Domitian's edict, passed at a time when a grain famine was accompanied by a glut of wine, prohibited the extension of Italian vineyards and ordered the destruction of half the vineyards in the provinces (*Dom.* 7.2; cf. 14.2). The edict was not the first legislation to restrict wine-growing in the provinces (Cicero *de repub.* 3.16), but Domitian's limitations on wine-growing in Italy as well imply that the purpose of his edict was not protectionist. (For differentials in favour of Italy in legislation intended for the Empire as a whole, cf. *Fr.Vat.* 247 = *Cod.Iust.* 5.66.1; *Inst.* 1.25.pr.). Statius praises Domitian's restoration of sobriety, and Philostratus says that the edict was intended to curb provincial unrest (*Silvae* 4.3.11–12; *VS* 521). The intention may have been partly that of modern licensing laws, in view of the bulk of Domitian's moral legislation (for which see S. Gsell *Essai sur le règne de l'empereur Domitien* (1894) 84–6. The view that Domitian had at heart the interests of wine-growing, and intervened by means of the edict to protect the industry from a crisis of over-production, is quite implausible (R. Dion *Histoire de la vigne et du vin en France des origines au XIXe siècle* (1959) 131).

Dumont's comments on wine-growing in Algeria, written in the early 1950s, are curiously interesting as a comparison. 'The vine has forced much of the cereal cultivation out of the fertile lowlands of Algeria, and while it has made fortunes for the settlers, it has also aggravated alcoholism in France...Moreover, it has seriously compromised the dietetic balance in Algeria. The vine is no doubt well suited to the dry hillsides, but it has also invaded the more humid lowlands. And although it employs more labour and makes larger profits than grain-growing, it is a heavy burden on the balance of payments of the France–North Africa group. Indeed its development has forced these countries to import both bread cereals and coarse grains, especially in recent years' (Dumont 169). Cf. L. Signorini *RSI* 84 (1972) 186–98.

[5] Cato 1.7. See below, p.51.

grain that was grown in Italy as a staple crop was probably intercultivated with olives and vines.[1] Prescriptions for the cultivation of an arable farm devoted to cereals and leguminous crops are nevertheless given by Columella.[2]

Olives appear to have offered a smaller gross return than vines, as well as taking longer to mature. They were however much less labour intensive, and the wide planting-distance between the trees made it especially easy to combine olives with cereals or legumes.[3] Nevertheless, olives do not seem to have been very highly regarded as a capitalist investment in Italy: Cato places them fourth in his list of nine types of cultivation in order of profitability. Columella shows little interest in olive-growing (the short section describing olive-cultivation is only a fraction of the space devoted to vines); while Pliny the elder says that it can be difficult to make a profit from olives.[4] In view of this evidence, it is impossible to accept that the statement, which appears in a Syrian fiscal document of the late Empire, that olive-land was worth 5 times as much as vineyard, has any relevance to economic reality in Italy.[5]

Varro, speaking partly from his own experience, says that large profits can be made from rearing specialised types of poultry on farms in the hinterland of big towns. He gives figures for the revenues that had been achieved by this means on some farms within reach of Rome.[6] Though they suggest profits which outstripped those of conventional farming,[7] it is clear that the presence of a large and specialised market nearby was all-important. Good profits could be made from the sale of other farm products such as lambs, sucking-pigs and roses, but only if the estate lay near a large town.[8]

---

[1] For intercultivation between vines (*arbustum* not *vinea*) see below, p.59 n.1. In Columella's longer work, very wide spacing of olive-trees (an average of 50 feet) is recommended unless the land is so poor that intercultivation is impossible, in which case the intervals should be 25 feet. In the *de arboribus* the only spacing envisaged is the wider one; this shows that intercultivation was envisaged as the norm for olives (*de arb.* 17.3; *de r.r.* 5.9.7; also 2.2.24; 2.9.6; 5.9.12; 11.2.82; *de arb.* 19.3).

[2] *de r.r.* 2.12. Cf. 1.7.6.

[3] See above, n.1.

[4] Cato 1.7; Columella *de r.r.* 5.8–9, though his section on treatment of the olive crop is longer, 12.49–54; Pliny *NH* 18.38.

[5] The 'Syro-Roman Lawbook' states that 1,000 *perticae* of vines is equal in value for tax-purposes to 220 *perticae* of olives (Leges saeculares 121, *FIRA*, 2.795–6). These figures deserve more critical attention than they have so far received.

[6] *r.r.* 3.2.7; 3.2.14; 3.2.15; 3.2.17; 3.6.1; 3.6.3; 3.6.6; 3.7.10; 3.16.10.

[7] L. Abuccius said that on his property at Alba, the *villa* brought in HS20,000, more than twice as much as the *fundus*; while the *villa* belonging to Varro's aunt on the via Salaria brought in HS60,000, twice as much as the 200 iugerum *fundus* at Reate which belonged to Q. Axius (*r.r.* 3.2.14–17).

[8] Col. *de r.r.* 7.3.13; 7.9.4; Varro *r.r.* 1.16.3. See Appendix 8 pp.345–6 below.

None of the agricultural writers specifically advocates complete monoculture (that is, concentration on a single crop to the exclusion of all others). Columella's synopsis of the ideal farm includes all the main crops as well as stock breeding; while Cato's provisions for a vineyard and an olive-farm include details which show that other crops would be farmed there as well.[1] Varro says briefly that there are properties which need supplies of grain or wine from outside, in contrast to the many which grow a surplus of such products. He also states that it may sometimes be profitable for the landowner to conduct a two-way trade with his neighbours, in such products as props, poles and reeds.[2] But Varro does not recommend the setting up of a farm to which staple crops have to be imported from outside, and his reference to their importation in certain cases may refer primarily to the specialised villa concerns around Rome on which Varro was an expert, or to farms in regions where land was not suited to the cultivation of all staples.[3] The belief that an estate should produce everything that was needed in the way of crops and livestock was clearly widespread. The self-sufficient estate is portrayed in glowing terms by Martial, while Pliny shows that his lands at Tifernum included vines, meadows, arable land and timber groves within the same boundaries.[4]

Although self-sufficiency almost acquired the status of an unassailable moral precept,[5] the concept was based on economic observation of a limited kind. Firstly, diversification of products could allow full utilisation of the labour force throughout the year on different tasks,[6] as well as providing cross-benefits, such as manure from animals with which to fertilise the fields, and fodder from arable land with which to feed cattle in the winter.[7] Secondly, the landowner who bought what he might have produced profitably conceded the profit on that article to another party. Thirdly, self-sufficiency meant that the farm was protected from the

---

[1] *de r.r.* 1.2.4–5; Cato 10–11. Varro's description of the farm buildings likewise assumes the presence of the main crops and some cattle (*r.r.* 1.13). Cf. Yeo 451 ff.

[2] *r.r.* 1.16.2–3. Dio Chrysostom, a substantial landowner at Prusa in Bithynia under Trajan, says that all his income came from wine and cattle and that his land almost never produced a surplus of grain (*Or.* 46.5; 46.7; 46.8). Cf. *Or.* 45.10; 47.21; pp.21 n.4; 88 n.6.

[3] Columella refers to regions where wine is in short supply (*de r.r.* 12.17.1).

[4] Martial 3.58; cf. 4.66; Pliny *Ep.* 5.6.

[5] Columella is able to say that the landowner who lacks ancillary groves of trees to supply vine props has no business to grow vines (*de r.r.* 4.30.1). This view is absurd in economic terms (for cost calculations see p.54). Varro's belief that vines would still pay if props could be obtained locally (by purchase) is far more realistic (*r.r.* 1.8.2; cf. 1.16.3). Cf. *Digesta* 8.3.3.1.

[6] For full utilisation of the labour force, cf. Col. *de r.r.* 1.8.8; 2.12.9; 2.21.3; 11.1.27–8; 11.2.1–101.

[7] Varro *r.r.* 2.pr.5; Col. *de r.r.* 6.pr.2; 8.1.2.

effects of shortage through the failure of any crop, insofar as it had its own reserves to fall back on.[1] The farm could weather a time of shortage without excessive inconvenience, and the capitalist owner, instead of having to pay inflated prices for essential foodstuffs and supplies, might even reap a handsome profit from selling the surplus part of his reserve at the highest possible price. Varro in effect advises him to do this, when he tells the owner to keep back crops which do not decay rapidly, for sale at a time when the price is high: it may be possible to double one's return by doing so. Varro lists grain, wine and honey as long-lasting crops, and commends price-speculation by the producer in honey and vintage wine.[2] The landowner who practised opportunism of this kind probably felt the need for protection against others who did the same: owning an estate which was self-sufficient for all its main needs was an effective safeguard. Shortages and famines were frequent, even in rich cereal-growing areas such as Africa, and there are sometimes indications of stockpiling by the wealthy.[3] The doctrine of self-sufficiency as applied in practice could thus have anti-social effects. Some cities found it expedient to make sale to the city of a proportion of crops a condition of owning land on their territory; and the landowner who spontaneously released grain stocks below the current price at a time of famine might receive permanent commemoration for doing so.[4] But local shortages and related insistence on self-sufficiency by the landowner also resulted from inadequate and expensive land-transport.[5] This was a serious physical discouragement to monoculture, at least in areas out of reach of water-borne transport. The self-sufficient estate thus owed part of its justification to the technological backwardness of the Roman economy.

[1] Cato allowed enough wine storage capacity for five vintages, with the evident intention of delaying sales until prices were high (Cato 11.1 with Varro *r.r.* 1.22.4). Varro explains the construction of storage pits in which wheat will keep for up to 50 years (*r.r.* 1.57.2). Grain prices might fluctuate heavily with the seasons (below, p.146 n.2).

[2] Varro *r.r.* 1.69; 1.22.4; 3.16.11. For wine marketing see also Columella *de r.r.* 3.21.6.

[3] For grain famines see Brunt 703–6; Rostovtzeff *SEHRE*[2] 599–601; R. Macmullen *Enemies of the Roman Order* (1967) 249–54; H. P. Kohns *Versorgungskrisen und Hungerrevolten im spätantiken Rom* (*Antiquitas* 6) (1961); *LRE* 445–6; 810–11; 853–4. An oil shortage at an Italian town, *ILS* 6643. Stockpiling: the edict issued at Pisidian Antioch under Domitian by one of the legates of Asia during a famine after a hard winter commands all private individuals who possess grain not needed for sowing or for the support of their *familiae* to release it within a month under severe penalties. The owners of grain were still conceded the right to sell it at nearly twice the normal market price by this edict (*AE* 1925, 126). See also Dio Chrys. *Or.* 46.8; L. Robert *Hellenica* 7 (1949) 74–81.

[4] *Digesta* 7.1.27.3; 50.4.18.25. XI 6117, etc. Cf. Ruggiero 3.237–8.

[5] Cf. Cicero *Verr.* 2.3.191; *LRE* 445; C. A. Yeo *TAPHA* 77 (1946) 221–44; Col. *de r.r.* 7.9.4.

THE NET YIELD ON VINES IMPLIED BY
COLUMELLA'S FIGURES

Viticulture[1] was both capital-intensive and labour-intensive. A new vineyard took several years to produce a crop, and demanded a substantial initial investment in plants and supports. The agricultural writers give manning ratios for vines of 1 man for every 7 to 10 iugera, compared with ratios for olives of 1 man to 30 and for arable of 1 man to 25 iugera (see Appendix 2).

Columella gives a calculation of the expense of establishing and running a small model vineyard; he allows for sizeable capital and labour costs, but still overlooks important overheads.[2] He assumes that a plot of 7 iugera, an area suitable for one vine-dresser, can be obtained at HS1,000 per iugerum for HS7,000. Columella apparently intended the purchase of virgin or uncultivated land (referred to as 'rudis terra' and 'silvestris ager'), though he gives no details of land-type in this brief passage.[3]

---

[1] In the present discussion 'viticulture' means the intensive type of vine-growing, which the Romans called *vinea*, where the vines were supported on artificial props, and were planted densely, normally at intervals of 3–10 feet (Columella *de r.r.* 5.3.1–9). There was a second common type, called *arbustum*, where the vines were supported on other trees, and planting densities were much lower (*op.cit.* 5.6.11; Frank *ESAR* 5.147–8). On Saserna's figures *arbustum* required 1 man for 18 iugera compared with 1 man for 25 iugera of arable. *Vinea* required 1 man for 7–10 iugera, on figures from four different writers, and was clearly much more labour-intensive (see Appendix 2). *Arbustum* ranks eighth in Cato's list of nine types of cultivation in order of profitability which is headed by *vinea* (Cato 1.7).

[2] Columella's figures are usually reproduced with the simple caveat that they are incomplete. J. Day *Yale Classical Studies* 3 (1932) 179; Frank *ESAR* 5.149–51; Yeo 475–7; White 268–9 (Frank's account reprinted). Frank does not make any deduction about net income, but his account is open to methodological objections. He excludes Columella's calculation of profits from nursery-plants; and continues to deduct from the income 6% interest on capital in the years after the vines have begun to yield. This deduction would be correct only if the capital outlay were a loan from another party (for other objections, Yeo 473 and nn.138–9). But Columella cannot be envisaging a loan, since his initial demonstration that a return of 6½% could be obtained from vines would have no force if all but ⅓% were returnable to a creditor. (Private loans were in any case often at rates higher than 6%; cf. Pliny *Ep.* 9.28.5; 10.54.1; L. Breglia in *Pompeiana. Raccolta di studi per il secondo centenario degli scavi di Pompei* (1950) 52; Billeter 163–7.) In fact Columella evidently takes as his starting point a reader with money of his own to invest, who wishes to be sure in the first place that he can get at least 6% from any investment. Frank argues against Columella's contentions about nursery-plants by pointing out that the equipping of Columella's model vineyard cost only HS2,000 per iugerum, whereas he expects HS3,000 per iugerum from future sales of his own nursery-plants. But this ignores the fact that nursery-plants grown between the rows exceeded vines grown in the vineyard by about 20 to 1 (*de r.r.* 3.3.13; 5.3.4–9). Equally, it ignores Columella's contention that the most fertile vines were so prolific that one plant could father a small vineyard by itself (*de r.r.* 3.9.6–7).

Mickwitz suggested technical reasons for Columella's omissions, arguing from the farm accounts in the Zeno papyri (*English Historical Review* 52 (1937) 586; cf. Yeo 477).

[3] Columella later makes clear that land previously sown with corn, as well as old vineyard,

He allows HS6,000–8,000 for the cost of the slave vine-dresser, preferring to pay the higher sum to get a man of proven capacity. Equipping the vineyard with vines and their stakes and osier ties will cost HS2,000 per iugerum, or HS14,000 in all, he says. This is the total capital expenditure that Columella takes into account: farm buildings, wine-presses, maintenance of labour force and amortisation of capital outlay are all omitted.[1] The total cost of the items that he considers is HS29,000, to which he adds HS3,840 for loss of income (interest at 6%) for the first two years after planting during which there is no return.[2] In fact it is preferable to keep this lost income under the heading of income and write it off against actual revenue, as is done in all the workings below.

In estimating the return Columella employs two different wine-yield figures. In his specimen calculation he uses a minimum yield taken from his predecessor Iulius Graecinus of 1 culleus (5.24 hectolitres) per iugerum (2,546 m²) (though he says when introducing the total that proper care should allow a yield of 1½–2 cullei). With a wine price that Columella considers an absolute minimum (HS300 per culleus is a 'minimum pretium'), the total annual return on the 7 iugerum holding is HS2,100. Columella emphasises that this already outstrips the normal 6% yield (true only if we are content to overlook the missing overheads).[3] Columella then rhetorically observes that the lowest yield which he considered acceptable was 3 cullei per iugerum, or three times the yield that he has just been using ('vineyards yielding less than 3 cullei should be uprooted').[4] Substitution of this figure increases the annual return to HS6,300, equal to a running yield from wine-sales of 21.7% after the third year, on the items considered by Columella.

Columella envisaged further substantial profits from the sale of nursery-plants, which would be enough to cover the cost of the land provided that the vineyard was in Italy.[5] He reckoned as a minimum to

whether supported by trees or on props, was undesirable as the site for a new vineyard. 'Rudis terra' is the best choice, even if using it means clearing wild bushes and shrubs from the ground first of all (*de r.r.* 3.11.1–3). ('Ager requietus' in *de arb.* 3.5.) For 'rudis terra' see also Varro *r.r.* 1.44.2. Nerva's assignment of HS60 million worth of land to the plebs perhaps implies that some of the *ager publicus* was unoccupied (Cassius Dio 68.2.1).

[1] Nevertheless, Columella was not unfamiliar with the idea that expenses should be assessed closely. He notes that the danger that expenses might balance income should be guarded against in keeping poultry (*de r.r.* 8.4.6). Cf. Varro *r.r.* 1.53.

[2] Martin suggests that two years is too short a period to allow development of the full wine-yield (Martin 372); Pliny also gives this figure, *NH* 17.173.

[3] *de r.r.* 3.3.7–10. Even on the basis employed by Columella, the excess over 6% is only 0.46%, which is too little to justify his statement that it far exceeds a 6% return ('ea porro summa excedit usuram semissium', 3.3.11).

[4] 3.3.11.

[5] 3.3.11. In the provinces there was no sale for nursery-plants: methods of vine-propagation were different there, and less sophisticated than in Italy (3.14.2). Though this is Columella's

plant 112,000 nursery-plants between the rows of vines on his 7 iugera, and to sell at least 70,000 survivors after two years, at a total price not less than HS21,000. It seems that nursery-plants would first have become available for sale eight years after the planting of the vineyards.[1] Thus a further bonus of HS3,000 per iugerum exactly equal to the expenditure on land and vine-planting at the outset accrues after eight years. The overall revenue for these eight years is thus HS55,320 (setting the loss of income at the outset against subsequent income). Columella's indications suggest that this income from nursery-plants could at least have been maintained with a further full crop at intervals of not more than six years.[2] The running yield on a six-year cycle starting after the first three years will thus be an average annual return of 33.8%.[3]

We should now look at the missing items. The most important omissions from Columella's calculation is probably the cost of related farm-buildings.[4] The only available indication of typical values is apparently Palladius's statement that it should be possible to restore them from one to two years' income in case of accident. It may be reasonable to take the higher figure as being sufficient to include the cost of farm equipment. This will give the farm buildings and equipment here a valuation on Columella's gross income figures of HS19,600.[5]

The major cost of maintaining the *vinitor* would be supplying him with bread, which would normally be made from wheat or wheat and

only concession in his profit reckoning to the possibility of different economic conditions in the two areas, the remark implies that his prescriptions were intended for the provinces as well as for Italy. (The calculation is usually taken to refer to Italy alone.)

[1] 3.3.12–13. It takes 4 vintages to decide whether a vine is a suitable source of *mallei* or nursery shoots (3.6.3–4; in *de arb.* 2.1 the time is 3 years or more). Once planted between the rows, *mallei* should be taken up in the second autumn (*de r.r.* 4.16.1). The *mallei* planted at the same time as the main vines (4.16.1) appear to have been planted as reserve stock to replace any vines that perished in the vineyard itself; they do not seem to have been intended for sale (4.15.1; cf. Pliny *NH* 17.172).

[2] For a six-year cycle see n.1 above.

[3] The total income for a clear six-year cycle starting with year 4 is HS58,800 (sales of wine and nursery-plants), and Columella's actual capital outlay is HS29,000.

[4] As Yeo pointed out, the 7 iugerum farm in Columella's calculation is too small to be a credible unit of capitalist exploitation (Yeo 477). But the figures are merely kept small for ease of reckoning, and it is doubtful whether any serious arithmetical error arises from this source (the omitted overheads of the *vilicus* and *vilica* would have been comparatively small in relation to one 7 iugerum fraction of a much larger estate).

[5] Palladius 1.8. For details of vineyard equipment, Cato 11.1–5. Columella advises the landlord to keep duplicates of all agricultural tools, to avoid having to borrow from neighbours (*de r.r.* 1.8.8; 11.1.20). The valuation here uses gross income, as Columella does in the passage under discussion. The income from nursery-plants is included here (averaged on a six-year basis) and the deduction for the first two years without revenue is disregarded. The resulting valuation is patently too high, but mainly because the underlying income figures are inflated, as can be seen below.

barley grown on the farm.[1] A normal ration would be about 51 modii per year. Wheat prices might be in the region of HS4 per modius.[2] Thus the landowner would need land which would produce about 50 modii of grain (probably wheat, since the *vinitor* was a valued employee) as part of the cost of running the 7 iugerum vineyard. If a fair selling price for wheat was in the region of HS4 per modius, we may take the arbitrary figure of HS2 as the net production cost of bread for the *vinitor*, allowing for the possibility that his bread would be partly barley. The land cost might thus be a rough capitalisation of HS102 at 6%, which equals HS1,700.[3] Other maintenance expenses (wine and clothing) might bring the annual cost of the vinitor to HS140; it is unsafe to speculate about the size of the *peculium*, which might have been very little.[4] A further HS30 should probably be allowed for the annual maintenance cost of the slaves who tended the cereals and the trees other than vines.[5]

Figures which Columella gives elsewhere argue that trees needed to supply the vineyard with stakes and ties would add 14% to the area of the vineyard itself.[6] If bought fully grown, their price would presumably exceed the minimum land price for uncultivated land indicated by Columella as HS1,000 per iugerum. It might be equal to a capitalisation of the income figure for woodlands and meadows of HS100 per iugerum which Columella cites.[7] If so, a further 0.98 iugera of woodland would add about HS1,670 to the initial capital investment. Last of the missing

---

[1] For bread, Cato 56 (only the chained slaves get their bread made for them; the others receive a ration of grain). Wheat and barley: Columella *de r.r.* 2.9.16.

[2] 51 modii is an average of the winter and summer rations for field hands laid down by Cato (assuming equal periods at each rate; 4 and 4½ modii per month, Cato 56; for other instances of rations at about this rate, p.146). For grain prices, see below, pp.145–6.

[3] The figure may be too high, since cereal land might be rated at a lower multiple of income than 16, in view of its low profitability. Columella's price for uncultivated land of HS1,000 per iugerum is hardly reliable (see below, pp.48–52). Consequently the present calculation has to be based on grain, not on land.

[4] Columella's profit-calculation makes no provision for payment to the *vinitor*, but neither does it allow for the cost of his subsistence. Columella's brief account of how to treat agricultural slaves does not refer to a *peculium*, though provision for clothes is mentioned (*de r.r.* 1.8.15–18; 11.1.21). Varro's account of general slave-management mentions *peculium* only in connection with the *praefecti mancipiorum* or slave foremen (*r.r.* 1.17.5). The transfer of *peculium* is provided for in his account of the acquisition of slave herdsmen, who may however include *magistri* or foremen (*r.r.* 2.10.5). An agricultural *peculium* is indicated by *ILS* 7367–8; cf. *Digesta* 34.1.15.1.

[5] Only a small percentage of the work of these slaves could have been carried out directly in connexion with the 7 iugera of vineyard. In fact it would have been uneconomic to employ them unless the total unit of exploitation were substantially larger, but this does not affect the present workings.

[6] The figure taken from Iulius Atticus gives 3½ iugera of groves to 25 iugera of vines (*de r.r.* 4.30.2).

[7] *de r.r.* 3.3.8; 3.3.3.

overheads are amortisation costs. The life of the vineyard can be reckoned as about thirty years.[1] The working life of the slaves can be reckoned as twenty years, and the life of the farm buildings and equipment as about thirty years.[2]

A revised version of Columella's calculations can thus read as follows (approximations for the missing items are in square brackets):

Capital outlay

	HS
Purchase of land for 7 iugerum vineyard	7,000
Purchase of *vinitor*	8,000
Purchase and planting of vines with supports, plus labour costs	14,000
[farm buildings and equipment	19,600]
[grain land	1,700]
[ancillary woodland	1,670]
[ancillary slave labour	400]
	52,370

Overhead expenses

Loss of income in first two years on [52,370] at 6%, divided by 8 to give average	[785]
[maintenance of *vinitor* and other slaves	170]
[amortisation of vines over 30 years	467]
[amortisation of farm building and equipment over 30 years	653]
[amortisation of *vinitor* over 20 years with HS118 for amortisation of other slaves	518]
	2,595

The net average income for the first eight years[3] is HS4,755 or

---

[1] Cf. A. J. Winkler *General Viticulture* (University of California Press, 1962) 614, describing modern practice in California. Columella was anxious to see that the reader avoided planting his vines on the site of an old vineyard (*de r.r.* 3.11.1–4; *de arb.* 3.5; cf. *de r.r.* 2.10.1).

[2] This purely notional figure assumes that the cost of repairs and renovations might amount to a figure equal to replacement at 30-year intervals. Alternative calculations based on a 50-year interval hardly influence the net yield. (6.73% instead of 6.85% as an average running yield, see Table 1, p.58 below.)

[3] The reasons for the time-spans chosen are as follows: since there is no crop for the first two years, and *mallei* may take six years more to produce (see above, p.41 n.1), it will be 8 years before the first account of available income can be produced in full. The running-

9.08%.[1] On a six-year cycle from year 4 onwards the net average income is HS7,990 or 15.3%.[2]

Thus on Columella's figures for income with such supplements as we can find, the net rate of yield, for income from wine and nursery-plants for the first eight years, is just over 9%, very much below the 25.3% implied by his figures taken at face value. The running yield is 15.3% instead of the 34% implied by Columella. But if we ignore the income from nursery-plants, as is preferable (see p.56), the running yield becomes 10.7%.[3]

THE NET YIELD FROM CORRECTED INCOME FIGURES

It might be held that this drastic scaling-down of Columella's figures is misleading, since his basic data are all described as minima. His wine price is a 'minimum pretium', and the initial wine-yield taken from Graecinus is one which even 'the worst vineyard' will provide. He uses a planting-figure for nursery-plants taken from Iulius Atticus which is one-fifth too low from his own experience (16,000 per iugerum, instead of 20,000). And the price which he uses for nursery-plants is only half the price at which he himself is able to sell them. Columella's own wine-yield is introduced in a way which paradoxically suggests that it too is minimal ('In my view, vineyards yielding less than 3 cullei per iugerum should be uprooted').[4]

To say that figures are minimal is another way of saying that they are below average. In order to find the average on these contentions, we should need to increase Columella's wine price, his yield figure for wine, and his planting and selling figures for nursery-plants. Taken literally, his indications should point to average figures for net profitability much higher than the minima arrived at above (perhaps a running yield of the order of 25% instead of 15%).

But comparisons with other data show on the contrary that Columella's 'minima' are sometimes very high. Columella's implied gross return from wine sales is HS900 per iugerum. Yet incomplete figures for

yield thereafter will be on a 6-year cycle because of the *mallei*, and this cycle will strictly begin in year 4, because the income in year 3 will be offset by the loss in years 1 and 2 when there was no income.

[1] Income over 6 years, of 58,800, less overheads over 8 years of 20,760.

[2] The deduction of HS785 for loss of income does not apply here; aggregate gross income is 58,800, and overheads are 10,860.

[3] 25.3%: HS7,350 (income for years 3–8 averaged over first 8 years, after deducting 6% for loss of income in years 1–2) as the return on HS29,000. 34%: HS9,800 (average annual income in years 3–8) as the return on HS29,000. For remaining figures, see Table 1 on p.58.

[4] *de r.r.* 3.3.

prodigious profits on wine given by Pliny the elder only suggest a return in the region of HS1,100 per iugerum, in a context of quite exceptional gains (p.47 below and n.3). A more clear-cut comparison is with modern Italian wine-yields. These show that Columella's minimum yield of 3 cullei per iugerum is nearly three times the average for Italian vineyards in the early twentieth century; Columella's figure therefore exceeds modern minimum yields by an even greater margin.[1] The average for Italy (areas with vine monoculture) in 1909–13 was 1.16 cullei per iugerum. The average for 1909–36 was 1.17 cullei per iugerum. In a province with especially low wine-yields, Calabria, the average was about 0.60 cullei per iugerum at a more recent date (1931–4).[2] Even if we conjecture some radical difference between the yield of ancient and modern methods of cultivation and vinification, it is very difficult to accept that this could lead to a three-fold difference in the size of yield, with the difference in favour of antiquity.[3] Writers of Columella's era such as Graecinus were prepared to take a much lower yield figure than 3 cullei as representative (see above). The annual yield on Cato's vineyard of 100 iugera was 160 cullei, on the face of it a yield of 1.6 cullei per iugerum. But we do not know what proportion was under vines,[4] and so

---

[1] The undocumented view that the Roman agronomists used liquid measures one-third of the standard size is a fantasy (Salomon 31, followed with reserve by Martin 371, n.1). For actual liquid measures, see Hultsch 115–16.

[2] Production figures for Italy 1906–36 from *International yearbook of agricultural statistics 1909–1921* (1922) table 89; *id. 1924–5* (1925) table 58; *id. 1926–7* (1927) table 62; *id. 1934–5* (1936) table 73; *id. 1935–7* (1937) table 79; *id. 1939–40* (1940) table 89. Figures for Calabria from *Enc.it.* 35 (1937) 389.

Bréhaut quotes a wine production figure for Italy in 1923–6 of 50.6 hectolitres per hectare (2.42 cullei per iugerum), citing *Encyclopaedia Britannica*[14] (1929) 12.774. The figure given there is actually 10.6 hectolitres per hectare (a useless statistic which takes no account of the predominance of mixed cultivation in Italy). (E. Bréhaut *Cato the Censor on Farming* (1933) 25, n.2.)

Columella's minimum of 3 cullei is accepted by R. Billiard *La vigne dans l'antiquité* (1913) 133–5; Frank *ESAR* 5.150; Yeo 376, 484; White 244. Billiard is alone in citing evidence for modern yields (an average in France of 0.89 cullei per iugerum in 1887–97), though this did not lead him to question Columella's data.

[3] Modern calculations based on Columella's minimum of 3 cullei, such as estimates of the size of farmholdings from the capacity of wine-storage jars, are thus extremely suspect (J. Day *Yale Classical Studies* 3 (1932) 180; Frank *ESAR* 5.264; Yeo 447). If the yield was only one-third of the figure taken from Columella, the implied farm areas at Pompeii would be three times as great as has been concluded. However, Day's assumption that it was normal to store only one vintage is itself quite uncertain (Cato allowed storage capacity for 5 vintages, Cato 11.1; Varro *r.r.* 1.22.4; 1.65; cf. Columella *de r.r.* 3.21.6; 3.21.10). This uncertainty vitiates any attempt to deduce farm sizes from wine storage capacity.

[4] Cato 11.1; there is considerable doubt about the value of Cato's figures for the *vinea*; see Appendix 2, p.327. White presents three hypotheses about the area under vines, which range from 30% to 70% of the total (White 373; 392–3). Hörle conjectured 80% (Hörle 205).

it is difficult to make any inference about actual yield per iugerum.[1] 1.6 cullei should at any rate be a minimum yield, but we should remember that Cato only recommends wine-growing subject to the caveat that the wine should be good, and plentiful; so the yield is not necessarily intended as a minimal or even an average figure.[2]

Columella's minimum wine price of HS15 per amphora (HS300 per culleus) is also open to doubt. Two Italian inscriptions of the early Empire suggest retail prices for wine lower than Columella's wholesale price. A colloquial graffito from Pompeii puts forward three prices for wine of different quality, of which the cheapest is 1 *as*. Other sources, including a similar bar-tariff from the nearby Herculaneum, indicate the sextarius as the normal unit of sale, which would result in a minimum price in the Pompeian tariff of HS12 per amphora retail, 20% below Columella's wholesale price of HS15 per amphora.[3] A curious inscription from Aesernia in Samnium contains a dialogue between an innkeeper and one of his guests about the bill for a night's stay. It begins with a series of items accepted willingly by the guest, who finally reaches exasperation on hearing the amount charged for fodder for his mule. Although the dialogue is comic in intention, the first two items may be more or less realistic charges that no one would baulk at. The first is a charge of 1 *as* for a sextarius of wine and bread (enough at least for an evening meal).[4] The price of a sextarius of wine here is evidently well below 1 *as*, and probably does not exceed two-thirds of this payment (for bread, cf. p.244). This would result in a price of HS8 per amphora, though the historical value of the inscription from which it comes is very uncertain.

A less explicit indication of a low wholesale price can be found in Pliny's account of Acilius Sthenelus, the wine entrepreneur who made spectacular improvements in two vineyards at Nomentum, near Rome.[5]

[1] Frank's inference of a yield of 8 cullei per iugerum from Cato 11.1 is based on a misinterpretation (Frank *ESAR* 1.163, followed by Yeo 475); see Varro *r.r.* 1.22.4.

[2] Cato 1.7. R. Goujard drastically emends Cato's figures (*Rev.Phil.* 46 (1972) 267).

[3] IV 1679 which colloquially sets out prices for different grades of wine, of 1, 2 and 4 *asses* (the most expensive is described as Falernian). Wine is sold by the sextarius at an inn in IX 2689, and in an unpublished wall-painting from a bar or inn at Herculaneum. This shows four glass wine jugs with contents of different colours, and reads 'AD CVCVMAS/ A.IIIIS A.IIIS A.IIIISS A.IIS'. Each price is immediately beneath one of the wine jugs (the prices are 4, 3, 4½ and 2 *asses* per sextarius). Wine prices are also reckoned by the sextarius in Diocletian's price edict (2.1 f. *ESAR* 5.320–2 = Lauffer 100–2). Reckoning in sesterces per amphora, the Pompeian prices are HS12, HS24 and HS48; those from Herculaneum are HS24, HS36, HS48 and HS54. For a wine price of HS61–88 per amphora at Rome under Antoninus Pius, see Appendix 15. For possible Spanish wine prices of HS8–12 per amphora (inferred from customs-dues) see T. Frank *AJP* 57 (1936) 87–90.

[4] IX 2689 = *ILS* 7478. The first price evidently refers to the cost of both bread and wine.

[5] Pliny *NH* 14.48–52.

Sthenelus improved one vineyard to a point where he could sell it for HS6,666 per iugerum, a price which Pliny indicates as being extremely high (the exploit was 'summa gloria'). Later, acting for Remmius Palaemon, Sthenelus did even better with another vineyard, for which Palaemon had paid HS600,000. By the eighth year a harvest had been achieved which was sold on the vine[1] for HS400,000; and within ten years of buying it, Palaemon was able to sell the estate to Seneca for four times the purchase price (or HS2,400,000). Pliny indicates that it was not unusual for this vineyard to reach yields of 7 cullei per iugerum even subsequently.[2] If the yield in the annus mirabilis when the harvest was sold for HS400,000 also reached 7 cullei per iugerum, and the final land price was no higher than the figure which Pliny regarded as phenomenal in the case of the earlier estate, the implied area would be not less than 360 iugera, and the wine price not more than HS7.94 per amphora. It is difficult to think that the yield was lower than 7 cullei in this year. The yield might in fact have been higher, but if it were, the wine price per amphora would fall to a still lower level.[3]

Thus Columella's minimum wholesale price for wine of HS15 per amphora appears to conflict with a retail price at Pompeii of HS12; a wholesale price for a sale on the vine at Nomentum of perhaps HS8, or less; and a retail price at Aesernia (which may be apocryphal) of about HS8. The price of wine was of course subject to variation and could fall if the vintage was too abundant (p.35 n.2). There were also no doubt regional variations: Campania, the source of one of the low wine prices, was the province with the highest wine-yield per hectare in Italy in the 1930s.[4] Nevertheless, Columella probably drew his minimum price from personal experience on his estates in the hinterland of Rome, where commodity prices were often significantly higher than in other regions (see Appendix 8). One of his estates was at Alba, where the quality of the local wine was very high (see below, p.55 n.4).

It is clearly worthwhile to see what results are obtained by substituting

---

[1] An arrangement where the landowner sold the hanging crop to a contractor who would either provide his own labour force to harvest the crop or would meet the bill for extra labour. Cf. *Digesta* 9.2.27.25. This saved the owner the trouble of recruiting extra labour for the harvest, although it must have meant accepting a somewhat lower price. (See Cato 144–8; the practice is also indicated in Pliny *Ep.* 8.2.)

[2] Columella, who also knew of this estate, says that it often yielded 8 cullei per iugerum (*de r.r.* 3.3.3). For Seneca's interest in vines cf. *Ep.* 86.20–1.

[3] If the land price were lower than in the earlier case, the crop would be greater, and the wine price even lower. If it had been substantially higher than in the later case, Pliny would probably have singled it out. The sale was of grapes on the vine, whose price would no doubt have been lower than that of wine as such (cf. Frank *ESAR* 5.152), but the crop was presumably one of reasonably high quality. For Nomentan wine see Martial 1.105; 10.48; 13.119.

[4] *Enc.it.* 35 (1937) 389.

a different wine-yield and selling-price for the figures offered by Columella. The yield from Calabria of 0.60 cullei per iugerum (p.45 n.2) may serve as a minimum wine-yield. A minimum wholesale wine price might be HS8.5 per amphora from our scanty evidence: this is an average of the lowest Pompeian retail figure (deducting one-quarter for the retail element) and the Nomentum wholesale figure deduced from Pliny (HS9 and HS8).[1] A reasonable average yield might be 1.17 cullei per iugerum (the figure for the period from 1909 to 1936). An *average* wine price can be taken as the median of the seven figures in the two tariffs from Pompeii and Herculaneum:[2] HS36 per amphora retail, which becomes HS27 wholesale (deducting one-quarter for the retail element). This is nearly double Columella's minimum wholesale price.[3]

If inserted into Columella's figures as expanded above, these new coordinates produce the following results (on a running yield basis for a 6-year cycle from year 4 onwards):

Minimum figures (income from wine sales only): minus 1.38%
Minimum figures (income from wine and nursery-plants): 6.85%
Average figures (income from wine sales only): 7.11%
Average figures (income from wine and nursery-plants): 12.32%

(See Table 1, p.58)

The income from minimum yield and minimum prices is so low that it suggests an excessive level of capital investment, or excessive running costs. We thus need to scrutinise the remaining estimates in Columella's calculation.

THE RELIABILITY OF COLUMELLA'S CAPITAL INVESTMENT FIGURES

We have seen that Columella's figures for minimum wine-yield and for the minimum price of wine are open to doubt. His calculation also depends on stated prices for land, slaves, nursery-plants, and for equipping land with vines.

The cost of land

The land price is HS1,000 per iugerum, a convenient round figure which Columella appears to employ both for Italy and for the provinces (p.40

---

[1] This is considerably more than the price at which it was unprofitable to sell wine given by Martial (HS5 per amphora, Martial 12.76).

[2] See above, p.45 n.2 and p.46 n.3.

[3] Martial mentions a retailer's profit-margin of more than 50% for booksellers: the book will be sold for HS4 but would make a profit even if sold for HS2, Martial 13.3; cf. 1.66; 1.117. Thus an assumed retail margin of 25% may be too little. 33% profit is repugnant to Juvenal, but the poet is opposed to commerce as such (Juvenal 14.200-1).

n.5). It evidently refers to uncultivated land, whose price was presumably lower than that of land already under cultivation.[1] If uncultivated land cost HS1,000 per iugerum, it should have been capable of providing a revenue which would broadly justify that price. We do not know the dividend return on the less profitable crops such as cereals. But if Columella's land price is taken literally, the percentage return on wheat that it implies is so low as to be implausible.[2] The sowing quantity for wheat (*triticum*) is given as 5 modii per iugerum by Varro, Columella and Pliny;[3] Columella's average maximum yield on cereals in Italy is four-fold (presumably a gross figure).[4] Columella and others recommend fallowing the land in alternate years.[5] Columella (perhaps using Saserna's calculations) reckons that a 200 iugerum farm will need 8 men (not including an overseer or housekeeper). Half will be under grain, half under legumes, it seems; the grain area will be fallowed so that only 50 iugera are under grain in a given year.[6] On this basis roughly 4 men

[1] Despite Columella's preference for virgin land for planting vines (p.39 n.3), it seems unlikely that uncultivated land could command any premium over cultivated land in normal circumstances; as a rule cultivated land would have fetched the higher price, *de r.r.* 3.3.8.

[2] Cf. Cato 1.7; Dio Chrysostom *Or.* 46.10. For the ensuing calculation cf. C. Clark, M. Haswell *The economics of subsistence agriculture*[4] (1970) 164: 'Land prices are a consequence of rents, not vice versa.'

[3] Varro *r.r.* 1.44.1; Columella *de r.r.* 2.9.1; Pliny *NH* 18.198. In *de r.r.* 11.2.75 Columella varies the figure, giving 4–5 modii as the sowing quantity for *triticum* and in 2.12.1 it is this quantity of *triticum* that he evidently considers appropriate for 1 iugerum.

[4] See *de r.r.* 3.3.4. Unfortunately there is no other contemporary average figure. The much higher yields reported at Leontini in Sicily and in Etruria by Cicero and Varro are taken as representative by White, but both seem to refer to regions of exceptional fertility: Leontini was the 'caput rei frumentariae' in Sicily, Cic. *Verr.* 2.3.47, while Etruria was Varro's exemplar of an area where the land was exceptionally good, *r.r.* 1.9.6; K. D. White *Antiquity* 37 (1963) 208. Some of the mediaeval European evidence collected by Slicher van Bath shows yields lower than 4-fold, though none of it comes from Italy. (B. H. Slicher van Bath *Yield ratios 810–1820* (*A. A. G. Bijdragen* 10) (1963) 60.) Yields of 4-, 5-, and 6-fold are recorded in sixteenth- and seventeenth-century Italy (A. de Maddalena, *RSI* 76 (1964) 425).

[5] Columella *de r.r.* 2.9.4; 2.9.15; 2.10.7; 2.12.7–10; cf. Pliny *NH* 18.187; Varro *r.r.* 1.44.2–3; 3.16.33. For fallowing see also Brunt 194; *Cambridge Econ. History of Europe* I[2] (1966) 97 (C. E. Stevens); 127 (C. Parain). Although Pliny *NH* 18.191 shows that fallowing was not universal, White's view that cropping the same land every year was common is difficult to substantiate. The existence of a Latin word to indicate land which was sown every year ('restibilis') need not mean that cereals were normally sown on such land (White 120). Pliny in the passage referring to annual cropping in Campania, which White takes as representative of particularly fertile areas, goes on to say that the Campanian plain surpassed all other lands ('universas terras campus Campanus antecedit' *NH* 18.111; White 47). Cf. Dion. Hal. 1.37.2; Strabo 5.4.3.

[6] *de r.r.* 2.12.7–9. Equal quantities of grain and leguminous crops are sown. Strictly this could mean a disproportion between the area under grain and the area under legumes, since the sowing quantities for legumes were mostly different from those for grain (some higher, others lower, 2.12.1–6). But Columella is evidently thinking in broad general terms, and can hardly be assuming a differential since he does not prescribe particular leguminous crops.

were needed to work a net 50 iugera of grain (that half of the grain area under cultivation at any one time). Hence 1 iugerum might carry $\frac{1}{12}$ of the maintenance cost of a slave. If his grain ration is 51 modii and its net cost is estimated as HS2 per modius, the annual cost would be HS102.[1] Other food and clothing might add a further HS40 to the bill. This produces an annual cost per iugerum of HS11.83. If the slave's capital cost were HS2,000[2] and his working life 20 years on average, the annual amortisation cost assignable to 1 iugerum would be HS8.5. But many agricultural slaves would typically have been *vernae*, bred on the farm and not bought. The agronomists' comments show that this was a more economical way of acquiring slaves than purchase.[3] A lower figure of HS5 can therefore be included for amortisation, making a cost of HS17 per iugerum for labour overheads. Calculating the value of farm-buildings as two years' gross income as before, the value of that part of the buildings assignable to 1 iugerum of grain, which (on an assumed overall 6% yield) already needs a gross income of HS77, will be not less than HS154. The annual charge is HS5–3 (amortisation over 30–50 years). Thus the overheads will be about HS20–22 per iugerum.

A controlled price of HS4 per modius, introduced by a benefactor at an Italian town at a time when a famine had pushed market prices to a higher level, may be representative of normal conditions in Italy.[4] This price can reasonably be reconciled with the alimentary rates laid down for the support of children at Italian towns under Trajan, whose maximum was HS16 per month, for boys of legitimate birth; the lowest rate was HS10 per month, for illegitimate girls.[5] Assuming that boys were entitled to a ration of not less than 3 modii per month (at a time when the adult ration was commonly 5 modii)[6] the implied corn-price works out at not more than HS5.33 per modius, assuming that the whole allowance was absorbed by corn. In fact alimentary provisions normally also included provision for other rations;[7] and so it can be assumed that not more than three-quarters of the allowance was absorbed by the price of corn.[8] This leads to a price for corn in Italy of about HS4 per modius, taking the ration of *legitimi* as 3 modii per month. Prices in Rome itself tended

---

[1] For the ration and its cost, see pp.145–6.

[2] This was the sum at which the value of a slave was reckoned for purposes of legal compensation (*Digesta* 4.4.31; 40.4.47; 5.2.8.17; 5.2.9; VIII 23956). For market slave prices see Appendix 10.

[3] Columella *de r.r.* 1.8.19 (rewards to slave-women for bearing children): Varro *r.r.* 2.1.26 (procreation by slave herdsmen makes ranching more profitable); 2.10.6–9. Cf. Martial 3.58.

[4] XI 6117 + p.1397. For grain prices see also Appendix 8 and pp.145–6.

[5] XI 1147.   [6] See p.146.

[7] *Digesta* 34.1.1; XIV 4450.

[8] For this view, see also A. Segré *Aegyptus* 30 (1950) 185 n.5.

to be higher (see Appendix 1). But corn prices in the provinces seem to have been lower than those in Italy: the normal figure in Sicily in the 70s B.C. was HS2–3 per modius; at Pisidian Antioch, an inland city in Asia, the normal figure was HS2.25 per modius at the end of the first century A.D. At Sicca Veneria, a large inland city in Africa, the alimentary rates introduced by a private benefactor in the late second century A.D. show a maximum of HS10 per month (for boys) and a minimum of HS8 (for girls).[1] On the assumption that three modii of corn could be purchased with three-quarters of the larger sum, the price per modius would be HS2.5.[2]

At the price of HS4 per modius of wheat, the cash value of an average annual production of $7\frac{1}{2}$ modii per iugerum will be HS30. Set against overheads of HS20–22 per iugerum, this means a net return of HS8–10 per iugerum, which is a dividend of 1% or less if uncultivated land really cost HS1,000 per iugerum. Rather than accept such a low dividend figure for wheat (when agricultural dividends in general might reach 6%),[3] it is reasonable to assume that Columella's land price is exaggerated. If for example we conjecture a net return of 3% on cereals, the projected land price on these Italian figures will be roughly HS260–330 per iugerum (33 × HS8–10). Alternatively, a 2% return would give a land price of HS400–500 (50 × HS8–10).

The one part of the Empire where numbers of actual land prices are known, the province of Egypt, shows a first-century average even lower than these projected costs, despite the fact that corn yields in this area were unusually high.[4] Egyptian averages work out at HS141 per iugerum for the first century and HS183 for the second. While Egyptian prices in general seem to have been lower than those elsewhere (and Egyptian interest-rates were often high),[5] in most instances these figures refer to land already under cultivation, where Columella's price refers to uncultivated land. Figures in Apuleius's *Apology* may point to a price of HS390–920 per iugerum for cultivated land in Tripolitania (see Appendix 9).

The calculations for Italy cannot claim any precision; they are in any case partly dependent on data drawn from Columella, whose land price they tend to undermine.[6] It is possible that some allowance should be

---

[1] Cicero *Verr.* 2.3.189; *AE* 1925, 126; VIII 1641 = *ILS* 6818.
[2] Corn prices in a given area could of course show drastic seasonal fluctuations. In Sicily (where corn prices were the same all over the island, according to Cicero, *Verr.* 2.3.192) the price in the spring of 74 B.C. (before the main harvest) was HS20 per modius, compared with a norm of HS2–3 (*Verr.* 2.3.214; 189).
[3] Cf. p. 33 n.3 above. [4] Jones *LRE* 767. [5] See Appendix 16.
[6] Jones sought to explain the high level of Columella's land price by arguing that purchases of land by senators and *equites* with wealth drawn from outside Italy were forcing Italian land prices artificially high (Pliny *Ep.* 6.19 shows that the Italian market was responsive to such

made for regular additional income from a crop of 3-month wheat, which would increase the estimated land price.[1] Nevertheless, the difference between Columella's stated land price and the price that appears justifiable by income from wheat in these provisional calculations is so great that it is very difficult to accept Columella's figure as a reliable guide to minimum land prices. Columella introduces his figure in a casual way,[2] the price itself is a remarkably round total and it is made to serve both for Italy and for the provinces. Since Columella can hardly have been unaware of current land values, we might think that he deliberately chose a high price, even though he does not specify that the price is high (in the preceding passage he criticises those who fail to make vines pay for using land of inadequate quality). But if so, it is curious that he later writes that 'rudis terra' is preferable for planting a new vineyard.[3] It is possible that he was influenced by the prices prevailing in the neighbourhood of his estates; since these were near Rome, and included land at Alba, famous for its wine, he may have been accustomed to higher prices than those for other parts of Italy (land was notoriously cheap in Apulia).[4] But it is not clear that Columella's figure is in any way a considered estimate.

pressures; *LRE* 822). But there is little indication, where detailed lists of Italian landholdings survive, as in the two alimentary tables of Trajan's reign, that landholding in Italy as a whole was dominated by senatorial and equestrian landowners (IX 1445; XI 1147).

[1] For *trimestre* Pliny *NH* 18.69–70; Cato 35.2; Columella *de r.r.* 2.12.9; 2.6.2; *ILS* 8745. Minor omitted items would tend to increase running costs: maintenance of the *vilicus* and *vilica*; and weighting for the fact that cereals absorbed more labour than legumes (from Columella's figures in *de r.r.* 2.12.7–9). But the yield of grain may sometimes have been more than the 4-fold taken from Columella (since he is denigrating alternatives to viticulture in the passage in question, *de r.r.* 3.3.4). A yield of 6-fold would increase the projected land price to *c.* HS930 on the basis of a 3% return. Frank's attempt to derive a land price of HS1,000 per iugerum from Cato 136–7 cannot be accepted (*ESAR* 1.168 and 365).

[2] 'cum ipsum solum septem iugerum totidem milibus nummorum partum' (3.3.8).

[3] (See above, p.39 n.3.) 3.3.5; 3.11.3.

[4] Juvenal 4.25–7, cf. Seneca *Ep.* 87.7. If there were many who felt the attractions of owning land within easy reach of Rome, as Columella did (*de r.r.* 1.1.19), prices in the territory of such cities as Alba and Carsioli where Columella owned land might have been higher than average (*de r.r.* 3.9.2). Alba was one of the select number of Italian cities famous for the quality of its wine (see below, p.55 n.4). Pliny's reference to the well-known cheapness of land in the 'suburban' regions around Rome goes against other evidence about price-levels in and around the capital (see Appendix 8). It even contradicts indications from Pliny himself such as the reference to there being many trees 'circa suburbana' which brought in annual returns of HS2,000 each (*NH* 14.50; 17.8). The statement is also contrary to what we might expect in the immediate hinterland of the largest city of antiquity. Although this reduces Pliny's remark to a statement of the obvious, it is perhaps conceivable that he is contrasting the cost of land in the city of Rome itself, and the cost of land in the 'suburbs' outside; that would at least explain the differential, since land values in the capital were enormous (see p.345). But the quality of some land near Rome was poor; cf. Varro *r.r.* 1.9.5; Col. *de r.r.* 1.4.3. Seneca nevertheless suggests that 'suburban' land was costly (*Ep.* 87.7).

The cost of slaves

Columella's slave price for a skilled *vinitor* (HS6,000–8,000) is more difficult to comment on. It is one of the highest prices known for Italian slaves who performed manual labour (see Appendix 10). But the comparative evidence is inexplicit, and it is possible that skilled agricultural workers did fetch relatively high prices. Nevertheless, if a vine-plantation were being set up on a realistic scale, it would hardly have been essential that all the labourers should already have first-class skills. It would surely have been possible to train some men adequately in the early years of the vineyard's life, and thus to use some workers obtained at a much lower price. HS8,000 per man may therefore be an overestimate of the average cost of obtaining slave labour of the necessary quality for a vineyard of economic size (cf. Appendix 2). The cost of the *vilicus* and *vilica*, which is not allowed for by Columella (and has been omitted here because of uncertainty about the likely size of the estate), would increase the staff costs, but probably by a lesser amount, unless the estate were very small.

The cost of preparing the vineyard

Columella's impressive figure for the cost of preparing vineyard on uncultivated land is HS2,000 per iugerum, including vines, stakes and labour. His figures for planting density, and his formula for calculating the layout, give an average density of 706 vines per iugerum.[1] The selling-price of nursery-plants is given in his main calculation as HS0.3–0.6 each.[2] Taking an average, the cost of equipping the vineyard with vines would thus be HS328 per iugerum.[3] Preparing the land for vines meant thorough trenching of the soil first of all (*pastinatio*); when nursery-plants were being grown on the same spot (as in this case) the trenching should reach a depth of 3 feet, and would take 80 man-days per iugerum. The vines would apparently be planted in planting-holes (*scrobae*) which could be dug at the rate of 15 per day, thus taking a further 47 man-days per iugerum in this instance.[4] The digging would have to be carried out

---

[1] *de r.r.* 5.3.1–9; planting formula 5.3.1–2. The planting intervals listed here range from 3 to 10 feet, giving an average interval of 6½ feet which is taken as the basis of the present calculation. (The less thorough enumeration in 3.15.1 gives the intervals as 5–7 feet.) The brief account in the *de arboribus* is similar, save that the minimum interval is 5 feet (*de arb.* 4.4).   [2] *de r.r.* 3.3.13.

[3] HS0.465 (the average price) × 706 = HS328. The speed with which the vineyard reaches its first vintage in Columella's cost calculation (two years) shows that he has in mind *viviradices* or nursery-plants (cf. Pliny *NH* 17.172–3; 183). Nevertheless, he says elsewhere that the true enthusiast should use *surculi* or vine-shoots in order to obtain the best results from his vines, although they take much longer to mature (an extra two years: Pliny *NH* 17.172, but cf. 17.182; Columella *de r.r.* 3.4.1; *de arb.* 1.3).

[4] *de arb.* 1.6; 4.2; *de r.r.* 11.2.17; 3.15.2; 11.2.28, cf. *de arb.* 4.3.

rapidly at the beginning of the first year, and so extra labour would be needed: the single *vinitor* would take more than two years to do all the digging himself for a seven-iugerum vineyard on Columella's figures.[1] The *vinitor* would almost certainly also need help in planting and staking the vines (of which there were nearly 5,000), as well as in cutting the vine-props. If we estimate a further 30 man-days per iugerum for the extra labour required for these operations (probably a generous estimate), the total of extra labour will be about 160 man-days per iugerum, or nearly half a year's work for one man. The *vinitor* himself would carry out normal vine maintenance once the vines were planted. Since a labourer at Rome could perhaps earn HS3 per day, the rural rate of remuneration was bound to be lower, not more than half at a guess.[2] This is still about the level of the pay and allowances of an urban slave, if Seneca's remark is reliable.

Thus a very rough estimate of the maximum cost of extra labour would make it approximately HS240 per iugerum. The total cost so far for vines and extra labour is HS568 per iugerum. The chief remaining item is supports for the vines (wooden props and ties). Columella followed Atticus in reckoning that a vineyard needed an ancillary area of woodland about 14% of the size of the vineyard itself. He says that HS100 per iugerum is a good income from meadows and woodland. Thus the income from the woodland associated with one iugerum of vineyard would bring in only HS14 or thereabouts. Though this does not tell us the price of the props and stakes required for a iugerum of vines, it suggests that the cost cannot have been more than a few hundred sesterces at most. Work-rates for cutting and shaping wood are given as 100 stakes (*palus*) or 60 props (*ridica*) per man-day.[3]

Thus it seems difficult to account for even half the total of HS2,000 allowed for preparing 1 iugerum of land with vines and props. This appears to be another case where Columella has chosen a convenient round figure without considering its plausibility in detail.

---

[1] Columella's reference to a trenching contractor is a further demonstration that outside labour was needed for *pastinatio* (*de r.r.* 3.13.12, cf. Gummerus 81). Also *ILS* 6469.

[2] For Rome Cicero *pro Rosc. com.* 28. In Cato 22.3, HS2 will buy one man's labour together with the hire of (one?) yoke of oxen for a day. The wage of a farm worker in Diocletian's Edict was half that of various skilled workers (Frank *ESAR* 5.336–9 = Lauffer 118). Seneca wrote 'servus est, quinque modios accipit et quinque denarios' (*Ep.* 80.7). It is a little difficult to see why his brief imaginary example should contain figures at all, unless they represented some standard rate of support.

[3] *de r.r.* 4.30.2; 3.3.3; 11.2.12.

CONCLUSION

Examination of its details shows that Columella's calculation does not provide a sound example of typical wine-profits. Although the omissions and distortions partly reflect the shortcomings of ancient accounting practice,[1] Columella also appears to have been careless in his choice of figures with which to show the potentialities of wine-investment.[2] Documenting his own experience in detail would probably have been easier than looking for typical figures, and it would no doubt have been more valuable to the historian, who has only Pliny's short account of two estates at Nomentum as a case-history of profitable vine-growing. But negative inferences from Columella's short passage about wine-profits can be carried too far. The unreliability of this section does not necessarily throw doubt on the rest of Columella's work. Elsewhere Columella's narrative is less partisan than in this passage, where he is attempting to convince an apparently sceptical reader that vines can be made to pay handsomely. But his manpower figures are also open to criticism (Appendix 2).

Columella urges that large profits are available from selling nursery-plants (as well as from wine). But it is doubtful whether this can be accepted as a general statement. Income from this source was not available in the provinces (p.40 n.5). And the entrepreneurial activity which provided a steady market for nursery-plants in central Italy near Rome was not necessarily found in other parts of the Italian peninsula. This source of income is not mentioned by other writers such as Varro or Pliny. Columella himself was apparently a very proficient cultivator, whose plants were especially sought after.[3] One of the districts in which Columella farmed (Alba) was actually famous for the quality of its wine: Pliny and Strabo indicate that Alban wine was the equivalent of a 'grand cru classé'.[4] Moreover, Columella's figures for profits from nursery-plants are so encouraging (an increased dividend of at least 4% per year,

---

[1] Mickwitz (cited in n.2, p.39 above); G. E. M. de Sainte Croix in A. C. Littleton and B. S. Yamey (ed.) *Studies in the history of accounting* (1956) 14–74.

[2] Serious errors occur in another important practical treatise of the early Empire. The reckonings of water output in Frontinus's *de aquis* fail to take sufficient account of the effect of the velocity of the current and the differences in the size of the channel, among other things. 'All that can be said for the methods (of calculation) which he used is that they were still employed in Paris, both in practice and in theory…up to the middle of the nineteenth century' (T. Ashby *The Aqueducts of ancient Rome* (1935) 29; 28).

[3] *de r.r.* 3.3.3; 3.9.2; 3.9.6; 3.16.3.

[4] *de r.r.* 3.9.2. Pliny *NH* 14.64; Strabo 5.3.6. Cf. Martial 13.109. (Frank's view that the Italian wines listed by Martial in 13.108 ff. are mentioned in order of preference is evidently unfounded, as Setian and Caecuban appear elsewhere on a par with Falernian: Martial 13.111; 112; 115; cf. 4.69; 9.22; 10.36; 3.49. Frank *ESAR* 5.128.)

see Table 1, p.58) that if the market was really as strong as he claims, it would have been profitable to set up a separate nursery operation to cultivate them as a cash crop.[1] Columella nowhere suggests this under-taking, and he is not explicit in indicating whether more than one crop of nursery-plants should be grown. Although we must accept that Columella, and presumably other landowners of his region, were able to add handsomely to their profits from this source, nursery-plants should probably be dis-counted in a calculation of typical running-profits from vine-cultivation.[2]

The figures for profits from wine sales put forward by Columella are transformed by compensations for missing overheads.[3] Columella first indicates that if we are needlessly cautious and accept Graecinus's figure for minimum wine-yields of 1 culleus per iugerum, the running income from wine sales will be 6.46% (7.25% from the fourth year if the initial loss is carried by income, as is preferable). But when further overheads are taken into consideration, the Graecinus income falls to 2.06%. Thus Columella's demonstration that even this yield will produce a satisfactory profit is unconvincing.

When Columella gives 3 cullei per iugerum as a minimum acceptable yield based on his own observation, it is probably safe to conclude that he at least was able to obtain such a yield on his estates. After compensating for the overheads that he omits, this suggests a return from wine sales of 10 or 11%[4] (given his minimum price of HS15 per amphora).[5] This is very satisfactory, although much lower than the 21.7% implicit in Colu-mella's figures as they stand. But 3 cullei was hardly a normal yield (p.45 above). Taking instead a wine-yield corresponding to recent Italian averages, and an average wine price of HS27 per amphora, the average return for wine of medium quality was probably closer to 7% than to the 10–11% based on Columella's figures.[6]

---

[1] Taken at their face value, Columella's figures indicate an average annual gross revenue not less than HS1,250 per iugerum from a nursery planted with young vines. (Planting total 24,000 per iugerum, *de r.r.* 3.5.4; wastage 37%, 3.3.13; lowest selling price HS0.30 each, 3.3.13; slowest rate of turnover of complete crop 4 years, 4.16.1.)

[2] For the sake of completeness, calculations that include nursery-plants have nevertheless been given in Table 1, p.58.

[3] For references and arguments, see above, pp.41–4. For arithmetical data, see Table 1, p.58.

[4] White's inference of a 13.3% yield (based on Frank's résumé, *ESAR* 5.150) is not very different (White 244); but the present analysis suggests that such high figures were the exception rather than the norm.

[5] This assumes that Columella's estates would have yielded 3 cullei in good years. A plentiful harvest however tended to mean low prices (Pliny *Ep.* 4.6.1). Some at least of Columella's wine was probably of high quality (p.44 and p.55 n.4); no doubt profits here would have been greater.

[6] This assumes that the level of land-investment mentioned in Columella's calculation (HS3,000 per iugerum), which is certainly too high for a context of minimum returns, might be roughly appropriate for the production of medium quality wine. Presumably land

Columella's prices for land and for the preparation of the vineyard do not seem appropriate to the calculation of minimum profits that he puts forward. This inference is partly based on working times taken from other sections of his writings which may be unreliable in ways that cannot be determined. But Columella's investment figure of HS3,000 per iugerum for the purchase and preparation of average or minimum value land as vineyard is suspiciously close to the ceiling price of HS6,666 per iugerum for prodigiously fertile vineyard given by his contemporary Pliny.[1] Thus actual minimum profits are difficult to surmise because the basic level of investment assumed in Columella's calculation is almost certainly too high for a context of minimum returns. But even if we halve Columella's land investment, a minimum wine-yield and a minimum wine price will still apparently mean that the vineyard is run at a loss (Table 1, p.58). This is not especially surprising, granted that Roman viticulture was labour-intensive and required relatively heavy initial investment. But it is very different from the message of encouragement that Columella tries to convey to those contemplating an investment in vines.

The owner who like Columella had vines which yielded as much as 3 cullei to the iugerum could expect profits well above the usual agricultural dividend in good years, especially if his wine was of good enough quality to fetch one of the higher attested selling prices.[2] But the proprietor who had no good vine-land, and was forced to use an unsuitable site where the yield was much lower, would still if he followed Columella's methods have to face heavy overheads, which might absorb the whole of his profit and create a loss. In such cases, the landlord could either refrain from growing wine as a cash crop, though local demand might make this inexpedient in a district where there was no soil that produced good wine; or he could reduce operating expenses by cultivating in a less elaborate way. This is illustrated by the practice at Aricia of pruning only in alternate years, because wine fetched so little that the proceeds would not cover the cost of annual pruning. Wine was evidently grown there as a cash crop nonetheless.[3] Enough of the Italian wine output was produced at a low profit, or at a loss, to have given viticulture a bad name in some quarters (see p.34 n.2). A third expedient was to rely on *arbustum*, vines planted irregularly between trees which were used as their supports; the soil between the trees could be used to grow

---

costs in areas where good wine was grown would normally reflect that potential. But if the scale of investment is still unrealistically high, the implied return should be more than 7%.

[1] *NH* 14.48.

[2] See p.46 n.3 with p.48 n.3 above.

[3] Pliny *NH* 17.213. Aricia had the added problem that its vines were exceptionally tall, *NH* 14.12.

TABLE I. *The return from wine-growing*

	Compensated Graecinus figures as given by Columella, running yield[1] (no mallei)	Compensated Columella figures, first 8 years (no mallei)	Compensated Columella figures, first 8 years with mallei	Compensated Columella figures, running yield (no mallei)	Compensated Columella figures, running yield with mallei
Net percentage yield	2.06% (3.55%)[2]	5.21%	9.08%	10.70%	15.26%
Capital outlay (HS)	39,970 (26,470)	45,370	52,370	45,370	52,370
Net income (HS)	823 (940)	2,363	4,755	4,853	7,990
Gross income (HS) (annual average)	2,100	4,725	7,350	6,300	9,800
Overheads (HS)[3]	1,277	2,362	2,595	1,447	1,810
Wine price per amphora (wholesale)	15	15	15	15	15
Wine yield (cullei per iugerum)	1	3	3	3	3
House and equipment valuation[4]	4,200	12,600	19,600	12,600	19,600

	Actual minimum[5] running yield[1] (no mallei)	Actual minimum[5] running yield with mallei	Average running yield (no mallei)	Average running yield with mallei
Net percentage yield	−1.38% (−1.49%)[2]	6.85% (9.61%)	7.11%	12.32%
Capital outlay (HS)	34,198 (23,698)	40,798 (30,298)	42,056	50,816
Net income (HS)	−471 (−354)	2,796 (2,913)	2,991	6,258
Gross income (HS) (annual average)	714	4,214	4,423	7,923
Overheads (HS)[3]	1,185	1,418	1,432	1,665
Wine price per amphora (wholesale)	8.5	8.5	27	27
Wine yield (cullei per iugerum)	0.60	0.60	1.17	1.17
House and equipment valuation[4]	1,428	8,428	8,846	15,846

NOTES (All totals are based on a cultivated area of 7 iugera.)

[1] Running yield is the yield from year 4 onwards, calculated, where income from *mallei* is included, on a 6-year cycle. (Income in year 3 must absorb loss from no crop in years 1–2: for *mallei* on a 6-year cycle, see above, p.41 n.1).

[2] Figures in round brackets are alternative calculations based on a land investment half that drawn from Columella (HS10,500 instead of HS21,000); vineyard amortisation is consequently reduced by HS117 p.a. (See p.43.)

[3] Overheads are calculated on the basis described in the text (pp.41 ff.); they vary with the house amortisation figure (see n.4) and they include, in the case of calculations for the first eight years, loss of income at 6% during first two years, averaged over the whole period.

[4] The house and equipment valuation depends in each case on gross income (see p.41).

[5] Minimum yield from modern figure for Calabria (p.45 n.2).

other crops on a reasonably large scale. This practice was clearly wide-spread in Italy.[1] Although *arbustum* could not produce maximum profit from vines, it allowed the chance to supplement the return from vines with sales of other crops grown on the same soil. This must have been a strong recommendation in areas where the land was not suited to the production of good or abundant wine; it allowed the added advantage of lower labour costs than pure viticulture.[2]

The figures considered here leave the impression that wine-growing was potentially more profitable than most other forms of cultivation, as Cato maintained. However, profits depended crucially, as Cato implies, on the suitability of the land. Nevertheless, it appears that provided that the quality of the wine was reasonably good, an average yield could suffice to give profits of the order of 7–10%.[3] This is higher than ordinary dividends of 5–6% and compares favourably with what we can see of likely profits from ordinary arable land (see above, p.51). The profits of poultry rearing could evidently be higher still, to judge from Varro's incomplete descriptions.[4] This luxury market had evidently grown still more profitable by Columella's time.[5] But Varro describes villas which served the needs of the capital; these profits would hardly have been attainable in the provinces or in the parts of Italy out of reach of Rome. Thus wine-growing was a more representative form of high-return investment. There must have been a steady market for wine wherever Roman or Mediterranean civilisation flourished. The action of an unsympathetic ruler in attempting to restrict wine-growing throughout the Empire[6] illustrates the extent to which this type of cultivation had spread by the end of the first century A.D.

[1] Columella *de r.r.* 2.2.24; 5.6.11; Frank *ESAR* 5.148, n.14.
[2] 1 man to 18 iugera for *arbustum*, 1 man to 10 iugera (or less) for *vinea*, see Appendix 2, p.327.
[3] Profit-levels would presumably depend to some degree on the distance of the estate from the market, and the efficiency of transport. But wine kept well enough and had a high enough cost:weight ratio to be a profitable commodity for long-distance trade (cf. Yeo 332 ff.).
[4] See above, p.36 nn.6–7.
[5] Columella *de r.r.* 8.8.9–10.
[6] See above, p.35 n.4.

PART 2

PRICES AND PRICE-LEVELS

3
Prices in the African provinces[1]

Africa Proconsularis, including Numidia, later a separate province,[2] is the one western province that has left extensive information about costs.[3] This is partly the result of a relatively high local rate of inscription-survival.[4] Much of the evidence has been revealed by excavation, and the amount of information is thus growing steadily.[5] The quantity of African cost evidence does not rival that from Italy, but it is considerably more abundant than the material from the other western Mediterranean provinces in Spain and Gaul. The most valuable single feature of the African evidence is information about the level of the *summae honorariae*, the fixed charges for local office; there is very little evidence from other areas, and the thirty-six figures from Africa form the bulk of our information about these charges in the Empire as a whole. Africa is also especially prolific in prices of monuments, both buildings and statues. The number of perpetual foundations is sizeable, and there are prices for games, feasts and distributions. Explicit commodity prices are lacking, though an exceptional corn price prevailing during a famine is attested at one town. But the provisions of an alimentary scheme for child-support suggest approximate normal levels of grain prices in the later second century

[1] A preliminary version of this chapter appeared in *PBSR* 30 (1962) 47–115. References by number refer to items in the list of costs below.

[2] Numidia remained part of Africa Proconsularis until the reign of Septimius Severus. The earliest certain evidence for Numidia as a separate province belongs to A.D. 208/10 (*ILS* 9488; cf. Thomasson 2.203–4). The modern contention that the province was formed in 197/8 rests on disputed ground; see M. Speidel *JRS* 60 (1970) 145.

[3] The present survey is concerned with the Principate and omits the few post-Diocletianic costs from Africa (see p.8 n.4 and p.367). The provisions of the Severan military colleges at Lambaesis, whose local relevance is limited, are not reproduced here. They are collected in *ILS* 2354; 2438; 2445; 9096–100.

[4] See Appendix 13.

[5] For costs not available in 1961 when this survey was first compiled, see nos.10a; 20a; 24a; 32a; 37; 67a; 69a; 69b; 171a; 211a; 282a; 295; 323a; 332a; 332b; 333a; 334a; 336a; 339a; 339b; 339c; 366a; 370a. Other addenda: nos.19a; 37a; 37b; 151a; 322a; 386a; 386b; 400b; 408a; 427–38. Funerary costs of a given amount conflated under a single heading in the earlier list have been given individual entries here (see nos.228–44).

The earlier survey of Bourgarel-Musso published in 1934 was incomplete, and did not

A.D.[1] Some of the foundations are also useful in suggesting the size of town-organisations and even the level of local populations. The evidence from the Mauretanias has been included here; but costs are few and a single foundation and a *summa honoraria* are the only important examples from this area.[2]

The information about costs given by inscriptions is usually the by-product of munificence. Many African magistrates made public gifts in honour of their tenure of local office, and saw that the details (sometimes including the cost) were inscribed on a monument. There were contexts in which the publication of such details was a legal requirement; for example, if a man contributed privately to the construction of a building paid for from civic funds, his name and the amount of his contribution were supposed to be inscribed on the building.[3] There were also certain types of gift, especially foundations, any record of which was likely to include mention of their value. But in most cases in Africa, the publication of costs seems to have been a matter of individual pride or local custom. Mention of statue prices for instance is especially common in certain Numidian towns, but virtually unknown in towns in Zeugitana and Byzacena where inscribed statue-bases have survived equally well.[4] Not all the gifts whose cost is known were made in the lifetime of the donor; about one-sixth were testamentary. These include many of the larger gifts: five of the six gifts over HS500,000 are testamentary, as well as five of the fourteen gifts between HS500,000 and HS200,000.[5] In two instances deduction of the 5% inheritance tax from the value of the gift is mentioned (two statues bequeathed at Thamugadi under Trajan and money bequeathed to Thugga at about the same date). In other cases testamentary gifts were perhaps bequeathed net of tax.[6]

Most of the cost inscriptions probably belong to the period of a century and a half between the accession of Trajan in A.D. 98 and the death of

always reach an acceptable standard of accuracy. The present study is based on an independent scrutiny of the African inscriptions, but owes a small number of costs that would otherwise have been overlooked to Bourgarel-Musso (A. Bourgarel-Musso *Revue africaine* 75 (1934) 354–414; 491–520).

[1] Famine price: no.389 (see also p.252 n.3). Alimentary gift: no.248 (see p.145).
[2] Nos.258 and 351. Also nos.6; 87; 118; 133; 134; 149; 219; 239b; 287; 297; 300; 397; 400a.
[3] *Digesta* 50.10.7.1 (Callistratus). Cf. no.64.
[4] Compare Thamugadi and Cuicul with Thugga, Sufetula and Mactar (see pp.70–3 below).
[5] See tabulation in R. Duncan-Jones *PBSR* 31 (1963) 174–5 (which lacks the addenda listed in n.5 p.63 above). Legacies administered by the city: nos.1; 5; 32a; 38; 63; 67. Administered by heirs: nos.4; 6a; 11; 15; 19a; 32; 36; 41; 54; 77; 82; 95; 101; 104; 137; 152; 154; 177; 180; 196; 248; 249; 250; 251; 252; 254; 258; 259; 261; 262; 263; 265; 322a; 323a; 342; 343; 344; 382; 390; 9; 79; 97; 109.
[6] Nos.138a; 323a; cf. no.469. See no.1329, where payment of the gross amount is stipulated For the inheritance tax, *RE* 2. Reihe, 8.2471–7. See also p. 5 n. 4.

Gordian III in A.D. 244, though less than a quarter are explicitly dated. The concentrations of dated African inscriptions as a whole outside this period are relatively small, apart from post-Diocletianic inscriptions, most of which are easily recognised as such.[1] Costs from the period after Diocletian (of which there are relatively few) have been excluded from this survey as far as possible, since they belong to a period when costs, as well as the currency, had changed beyond recognition.[2] In terms of the annual average the number of African inscriptions dated to the first century A.D. is almost negligible compared with the number from the second century.[3] Among the cities whose inscriptions survive well, only Lepcis Magna, which was already a town of considerable wealth at the end of the Republic, shows any substantial concentration of municipal building activity in the first century.[4] This does not necessarily mean that there was correspondingly little building in African cities as a whole during the first century; but if there was, the traces have mainly been erased by later activity on a more ambitious scale. In the reign of Trajan fourteen dated public buildings are attested in Africa as a whole; they include at least six which were privately financed. Forty dedications to Trajan, mainly statues, appear in the African volume of the *Corpus Inscriptionum Latinarum*. After Trajan's time, the number of privately financed public buildings went on increasing until the time of Caracalla almost without a break (assessed in terms of the annual average). Imperial dedications as a whole also increase steadily throughout this period (allowing for the destruction of most statues of Commodus after 192 because of his *damnatio memoriae*).[5]

Dated costs[6] are not available in sufficient numbers to overcome the distortions created by differences in the size and wealth of the towns from which the evidence comes. A shortage of available correlations with archaeology makes it difficult to assess any variations in purchasing power that might be indicated by dated expenditures on buildings. But the dated gifts broadly suggest continued spending by individuals from the time of Hadrian onwards at an impressive level that was sustained into the

---

[1] In terms of imperial dedications (other than milestones) listed in VIII, the highest number of dedications per year in the first century (1.3 under Vespasian and Titus) is well below the lowest figure recorded in the second century (2.1 under Trajan). The highest rate at any point is 41.3 under Caracalla. The rate under Gordian III is 6.6. The highest rate in the period between Gordian III and Diocletian is 2.8 in the reigns from Valerian to Aurelian. (See Appendix 11.)

[2] For prices and currency in the period from Diocletian, see p.8 n.4 and p.66 n.4 below.

[3] See n.1.

[4] *Bell. Africanum* 97.3; *IRT* p. 252, including nos.3 and 7 of the present survey.

[5] See Appendix 11.

[6] Tabulated in Appendix 11.

3   D J E

early Severan period. Spending in other provinces had begun to decline before the end of the second century (Appendix 11).

The ten African building costs from the later third century provide evidence for continued urban development in Africa at a time when such evidence is very rare in most other parts of the Empire. Under Gallienus HS200,000 was spent on a building at Abbir Cella, HS67,500 on a temple of Pluto at Macomades, HS50,000 was given to the town by a donor at Thugga, and decurions subscribed HS41,200 for the mosaics of baths being constructed from public funds at Thibursicum Bure.[1] Under Probus HS28,000 was spent on a building (or statue) at Tichilla, while, under Diocletian, buildings costing at least HS350,000 and HS61,000 were put up at Calama and Thugga.[2] A statue costing HS16,000 was put up at Membressa under Tacitus in A.D. 275, while statue outlays of HS50,000 at Vallis and HS32,200 at Abthugni also appear to belong to the late third century.[3] The figures are large enough to suggest that they refer to substantial outlays, but the likelihood of acute inflation at this period makes them difficult to interpret. If the statue outlays refer to statues of the same type as those whose median cost in the second and early third century was HS5,000, the figures could imply cost inflation by a factor between three-fold and ten-fold in the late third century.[4] But the simple fact that public building was going on in Africa at all should indicate that inflation was not as yet having the crippling effect suggested by the virtual cessation of activity in other parts of the Empire. The late third-century evidence mainly comes from inland towns where costs might have been affected less rapidly than elsewhere by changes in the currency of the Empire. Since Africa and Numidia constituted a large and thickly populated area which contained only one legion, one of the prime agencies for the diffusion of current coin in the provinces, military pay, may have had a relatively slight effect there. It is perhaps significant that the costs mainly come from towns in Zeugitana which were relatively distant from Lambaesis, the legionary base;[5] whereas Lambaesis and the towns surrounding it, although still fertile in costs in the Severan period, produce none in the late third century. It is also

[1] Nos. 398a; 10; 323; 64.

[2] Nos. 403; 2; 63a.

[3] Nos. 99; 91; 92.

[4] Even a factor of 10 is slight in comparison with the degree of inflation suggested by Dio-cletian's Price Edict (published at the end of A.D. 301, J. Lafaurie *CRAI* (1965) 192–210). The 'kastrensis modius' was equal to either one or two 'Italian' modii (cf. Lauffer 213). On the face of it, the Edict's price of 100 denarii per kastrensis modius of wheat (Lauffer 98) thus represents an increase of 50/100-fold on a representative second-century price of HS4 per 'Italian' modius (see p.50). But see also p.8 n.2.

[5] Macomades was only 90 km from Lambaesis in a straight line; Calama 150 km. Of the other seven towns, the nearest (Thugga) was 275 km from Lambaesis in a straight line.

interesting that four of the ten costs come from towns which succeeded in obtaining new civic status in the mid-third century; two of these towns put up public baths at about the time of their promotion in rank.[1] Nevertheless, the expenditures implied by the late third-century costs as a whole are bound to be less than those that the same figures would imply if they belonged to the second century.

REGIONAL DISTRIBUTION

Prices have survived from a wide range of African cities, including the most important centres. But with one exception, the cities of greatest political importance, Carthage, Cirta, Hadrumetum, Hippo Regius and Lepcis Magna have not left records of spontaneous outlays which correspond with their standing. The highest surviving price for a building, HS600,000, comes from Lambaesis, the station of the African legion in the second and third centuries;[2] while the remaining building costs above HS300,000 mainly come from cities of secondary importance which include Calama, Madauros, Thagura and Thamugadi. This lack of imposing expenditures in the most important towns is mainly a random consequence of the poor survival of evidence from these towns. The towns whose prices survive in bulk tend to be mainly remote places whose sites have not been extensively built over or thoroughly plundered since antiquity. The material from Lepcis gives some indication of the scale of outlays that probably also took place at Carthage, Cirta, Hadrumetum and perhaps Utica. The *summae honorariae*, which are discussed separately below (pp.82ff.), sometimes provide a better index of the relative importance of different towns than records of gifts.

Carthage, by far the largest city in Africa, has left some considerable prices, though they do not always reflect its importance.[3] The *summa honoraria* for the *quinquennalitas* was extremely high (HS38,000);[4] and a price for games in the amphitheatre with gladiators and panthers

---

[1] Abbir Cella became a *municipium* under Philip, while Thugga (which contributes two of these costs) and its neighbour Thibursicum Bure became colonies under Gallienus (*ILS* 508; 541; *MAF* (1912) 109). Baths: *BAC* (1925) xxix–xxxiv; *ILAf* 506 (no.64 below).

[2] For geographical distribution see also Appendix 12. The earliest evidence for legionary activity at Lambaesis belongs to A.D. 81 (Romanelli 300–1). But the construction of a camp may not imply transfer of the whole legion at this early date (cf. M. Leglay *MEFR* 80 (1968) 218–19).

[3] By the early third century Carthage was considered second or third largest city of the Empire as a whole (Herodian 7.6.1). This implies a population of 300,000 or more (see p.260 n.4). The 'pertica Carthaginiensis' evidently comprised a large part of northern Zeugitana, though the precise limits are not known (*AE* 1963, 94; Cl. Poinssot *CRAI* (1962) 55–76; T. R. S. Broughton *REL* 47.2 (1969) 265–75; H.-G. Pflaum *Ant.afr.* 4 (1970) 75–118; Gascou 158–61).

[4] No.360.

from the same Hadrianic inscription is also quite exceptional. The cost
(more than HS200,000 for a four-day *munus*) even exceeds the highest
price-category for gladiatorial *munera* in the *senatus consultum* passed
forty years later in A.D. 177/80.[1] Carthage has left two massive building
outlays, HS300,000 and HS200,000, though they are exceeded by some
expenditures recorded in secondary towns of the province.[2] The voluntary
payments in honour of office (which may include the amount of substantial *summae honorariae* as well) are higher than those at any other
town except Rusicade: HS90,000 is once recorded as a payment of the
aedileship, and HS50,000 is recorded twice, in one case as a payment for
the aedileship.[3] (Other costs from Carthage: HS50,000–10,000; 42,000,
1,200; 600–300; 120–49.5.)[4]

Lepcis Magna, capital of the Diocletianic province of Tripolitania, has
left prices as impressive as those from Carthage (with the exception of the
summa honoraria, about which there is no information).[5] The ruins are
much better preserved than those of Carthage, and more of the important
public inscriptions have survived. A bequest of one million sesterces at
Lepcis to pay for sixteen statues is not only the second largest cost
attested in Africa, but also implies a statue price of startling size, over
HS65,000 per statue. The stage of the theatre at Lepcis, renewed under
Antoninus Pius, cost HS500,000, more than any other building component attested in Africa; the statues and marbles that survive show that
the money purchased work of very high quality. An individual silver
statue given at Lepcis in the mid-second century is the most expensive
statue of any material attested in Africa; only the weight of bullion is
indicated (144 pounds), but the total cost was probably not less than
HS100,000.[6] (The gift is still dwarfed by the cost of a statue at Beneventum
given under Hadrian which contained more than ten times as much
silver.)[7] Costs for individual buildings include three large figures, which
can however be paralleled in less important towns: HS272,500, HS200,000
and over HS120,000.[8] Lepcis also provides the most expensive tomb
whose cost is known in Africa; its cost was more than HS80,000.[9] But
Italy again has higher costs than this. (Other costs from Lepcis: HS80,000,
40,000, 20,000, 36,020, 460, 10,000.)[10]

No.281; *ILS* 5163 and 9340 (the highest category that is specified is that of *munera* which
cost between HS150,000 and HS200,000).

[2] Nos.40; 43.   [3] Nos.324; 327; 328.

[4] Nos. 401; 402; 230; 423; 424.

[5] *Enc.art.ant.* s.v. Leptis Magna; *IRT* pp.73–86.

[6] 16 statues: no.77; stage: no.63; silver statue: no.82.

[7] No.513 below.

[8] Nos.41; 3; 32a.   [9] No.213.

[10] Nos.7; 51; 56; 79; 212; 411.

Hadrumetum (the modern Sousse), capital of the Diocletianic province of Byzacena, another town of considerable size and importance, has left very few inscriptions of any kind.[1] A small quinquennial foundation provides the only cost of any note (HS11,000).[2] Hippo Regius, seat of one of the proconsular legates,[3] has left record of the most costly African statue after those recorded at Lepcis; its cost was HS51,335.44. Another statue cost HS17,000.[4] The *summa honoraria* of HS10,000 is not especially high for a leading town, being equalled at Diana Veteranorum in the interior of Numidia, and exceeded at Uchi Maius, a smaller town in Zeugitana.[5] A foundation of HS100,000 is also no larger than others recorded at less important towns. A sportula distribution of HS200 is recorded at Hippo.[6]

Cirta (the modern Constantine), leading city of Numidia and capital of the Diocletianic province, was linked until the later third century in a political federation with three other important towns, Rusicade, Milev and Chullu.[7] The joint territory of the federation was vast, most belonging to Cirta.[8] Of the four towns, only Cirta and Rusicade have left large numbers of inscriptions. The most notable cost is the record of seven charges for office, of which five are from Cirta and two from Rusicade. The six secular charges all show a level of HS20,000, while the one priesthood about which there is evidence cost HS10,000.[9] A full career of municipal office in the Cirtan confederacy thus entailed minimum payments of HS60,000–HS80,000. The magistrates of the confederacy were almost bound to be drawn from men who possessed wealth which approached the equestrian census of HS400,000.[10] Cirtan construction prices include the relatively high figure of HS200,000. The gold and silver plate stored in the town's Capitol was valued at HS312,000. Distributions made at Cirta were at rates of HS12, HS8 and HS4 per head.[11] (Other costs from Cirta: HS100,000; 47,000; 10,000; 12,000; 6,000; 140; 200.)[12]

Rusicade, a coastal town like Milev and Chullu, has also left two very large voluntary payments to the city (probably including a *summa*

---

[1] L. Foucher *Hadrumetum* (1964); VIII pp.14–15; *RE* 7.2178; *Enc.art.ant.* s.v. Hadrumetum.

[2] No.264; also no.240, a tomb cost of HS400.

[3] *ILAlg* 1, p.1. [4] Nos.83; 84.

[5] Nos.363; 367; 366. [6] Nos.252; 310.

[7] *ILS* 439; 440; *ILAlg* 2, pp.1; 40–1; VIII pp.618–19. The confederacy was still in existence in A.D. 251 (*AE* 1946, 61).

[8] *ILAlg* 2, p.40.

[9] Nos.345; 349; 357; 361; 379; 345a; 350.

[10] Many Cirtan magistrates in fact obtained formal equestrian rank, and there were a number of men from Cirta in the Senate in the mid-second century (R. Duncan-Jones *PBSR* 35 (1967) 147–88 at 154, nn.39–41).

[11] Construction price: no.398; plate: no.381; distributions: nos.294; 298; 304.

[12] Nos.49; 50a; 61; 102; 129; 247; 394.

honoraria as a component): HS82,000 in honour of the flaminate, and HS55,000 for the pontificate.[1] Two prices for statues with tetrastyles, HS33,000 and HS30,000, are the only explicit costs for this type of monument from Africa.[2] There are four payments towards the cost of public buildings at Rusicade, which suggest that joint-financing was a custom at this town, though it is rarely attested elsewhere in Africa: HS30,000; 10,000; 4,000; 2,000.[3] There is also a price for games of HS6,000 for a single day, very much lower than the rate of over HS50,000 per day attested for a gladiatorial *munus* at Carthage.[4]

Lambaesis in southern Numidia, base of the legion in Africa from the start of the second century or earlier (p. 67 n. 2), has left 49 costs, more than any other African city. Two-thirds of these figures refer to the cost of burial and funerary monuments; they range between HS26,000 and HS96, varying by a factor of 270.[5] One of the prices for a mausoleum refers to a surviving building.[6] The cost of one of the temples at Lambaesis, HS600,000, is the highest price for a building specifically attested in Africa. The *summa honoraria* for the flaminate, HS12,000, is the third highest of which there is record in Africa (though it is equalled at Uchi Maius).[7] The sportula of HS100 attested in a distribution at Lambaesis is the highest figure known in Africa.[8] Of the seven statue prices ranging from HS14,000 to HS3,000, four are at or above the median level of HS5,000 for African statues as a whole, and three are below it.[9] (Other costs from Lambaesis: HS10,000; 8,000; 10,000.)[10]

Four more Numidian towns have yielded substantial numbers of prices. Like Lambaesis they were all towns of military origin: Thamugadi and Cuicul were both veteran colonies;[11] Diana Veteranorum was a *municipium* whose name indicates its origin;[12] and Verecunda was a veteran *vicus* which eventually reached municipal status.[13] Verecunda was only 4 km from Lambaesis, Thamugadi 20 km, Diana 35 km, and Cuicul, much further away, 100 km. At all four towns the most numerous prices are those for statues. At Thamugadi, where the fourteen statue prices range between HS22,000 and HS1,000, eight reach or exceed the median level of HS5,000 for Africa as a whole, and six fall below it.[14] The library

[1] Nos.325; 326 cf. 329.
[2] Nos.93; 94.
[3] Nos.65; 69; 74; 75.
[4] Nos.284; 281.
[5] Nos.217–44 *passim*.
[6] No.221.
[7] Nos.1; 365; 366.
[8] No.290.
[9] Nos.86; 132; 143; 146; 170; 171; 171a; 194.
[10] Nos.68; 336; 409.
[11] Thamugadi founded by Trajan (*ILS* 6841); Cuicul founded by Nerva or Trajan (R. Cagnat *Musée belge* 27 (1923) 114–16; Gascou 109–10).
[12] Diana had a large territory (Broughton 136–7).
[13] Broughton 137; 202.
[14] Nos.78; 95; 98; 100; 125; 138a; 150; 151; 151a; 160; 161; 179; 183; 207; 209.

built from money bequeathed to Thamugadi by a senator provides one
of the highest African building costs, HS400,000, but in view of its date
(probably third century) the cost may be somewhat inflationary. The
ruins show that the building was not very large, despite its cost.[1] The
two *summae honorariae* from Thamugadi (one discovered very recently)
show widely differing amounts: HS10,000 for the flaminate, which is
quite high, and HS2,000 for the duovirate, which is relatively low. One
of the voluntary payments for office (probably including a *summa honoraria*) reaches a high level, HS21,000.[2] (Other costs from Thamugadi:
HS64,500; 32,348; 4,400; 12,080; 6,000; 4,000; 80.)[3]

At Cuicul, the one *summa honoraria* that is known, HS4,000 for the
duovirate, is relatively low.[4] Of the 17 statue prices ranging from HS12,000
to HS1,220 (?), nine exceed or equal the median level of HS5,000, and
eight fall below it.[5] The highest building price is HS70,000.[6] (Other
costs from Cuicul: HS30,000 (twice); 10,000; 1,000.)[7] The one *summa
honoraria* from Diana is very much higher, HS10,000 for the flaminate;[8]
but if the differential between the charge for the flaminate and that for
the duovirate at Cuicul approached the Thamugadi ratio of 5 to 1, the
difference between charges at the two towns would be illusory. Nevertheless, Diana was evidently large to judge from the extent of its remains.[9]
The nine statue prices at Diana range between HS10,000 + and HS3,000;
four reach or exceed the median of HS5,000, and five fall below it.[10]
At Verecunda the *summa honoraria* for the flaminate, the highest office,
was only HS2,000 (the town began as no more than a *vicus*, and one of
the records of this charge certainly belongs to the period when the town
had advanced no further).[11] Of the ten statue prices from Verecunda,
ranging from HS9,000 to HS3,700, four exceed or equal the median of
HS5,000, while six fall below it.[12] (Other costs from Verecunda: HS20,000;
4,000; 1,000; 120.)[13]

Theveste on the border of Numidia Proconsularis adjoining Byzacena
was a town of some importance, at which the African legion was stationed
for a time under the Flavians.[14] The town's twelve prices are the most

[1] No.38 and note.   [2] Nos.366a; 356; 330.
[3] Nos.10a; 52; 73; 407; 337; 339; 312.
[4] No.355.
[5] Nos. 80; 81; 104; 112; 121; 126; 130; 141; 142; 162; 166; 167; 176; 189; 191; 192; 208.
[6] No.50.
[7] Nos.36; 53; 410; 245.   [8] No.367.
[9] The territory was also extensive. *AAA* fe.27.62; Broughton 136–7.
[10] Nos.107; 108; 131; 145; 159; 169; 177; 178; 193.
[11] No.375: *ILS* 6852. For the meaning of 'vicus', Broughton 198–204.
[12] Nos.109; 124; 136; 158; 163; 172; 173; 181; 182; 184.
[13] Nos.19a; 416; 341; 311.
[14] Romanelli 293; 300–1.

varied range surviving from a single city. They include three foundations (the largest is the third biggest foundation attested in Africa): the figures are HS250,000, 50,000 and 2,400.[1] A quadrifrontal arch that still stands cost (together with two tetrastyles) HS250,000.[2] The *summa honoraria* for the aedileship was HS4,000, not a high figure, though the charge for more important offices may have been greater. A spontaneous payment to the city reached the much higher level of HS20,000.[3] A temple at Theveste cost HS63,000, rather more than the median cost for complete buildings in Africa as a whole, HS43,500. One of the two statue prices is very high, HS50,000; another statue cost HS7,000.[4] A substantial gift of plate to the Capitol, together with the largest foundation and the arch and tetrastyles were the product of a single legacy, made by a *praefectus legionis* in A.D. 214; they formed the fourth largest gift recorded in Africa, with a value of over HS700,000.[5]

Two other sizeable towns in Numidia Proconsularis, Calama and Thubursicu Numidarum, have left a number of costs.[6] Calama has left one of the highest building prices, more than HS350,000 for a temple of Apollo. But since it belongs to the time of Diocletian, the figure is bound to be very inflationary.[7] The sum promised for the Calama theatre at least a century earlier, HS400,000, is probably substantially less than the final building cost. A much smaller theatre at Madauros whose remains also survive cost HS375,000, almost as much, in the early third century.[8] The three statue prices from Calama, ranging from HS7,340 to 5,640, are all somewhat higher than the median level of HS5,000.[9] (Other costs from Calama: HS30,000; 5,000.)[10] Three *summae honorariae* are attested at Thubursicu Numidarum: HS6,000 for the flaminate and HS4,000 for the aedileship and the decurionate.[11] The differential of 3:2 is much smaller than the ratio of 5:1 for different *summae honorariae* attested at Thamugadi, and is also less than the 2:1 ratio at Cirta. The one building cost, HS77,000 for the arch, is considerably higher than the median building cost of HS43,500. The two statue prices both fall at the median level, HS5,000.[12]

Madauros, a veteran colony planted at an existing town,[13] has left prices for two important buildings whose remains survive: HS375,000 for the theatre, and HS200,000 for the forum and its portico.[14] Two other

[1] Nos.250; 257; 268.
[2] No.32.
[3] Nos.352; 331.
[4] Nos.11; 85; 122.
[5] Nos.382; 32; 250.
[6] Calama: *ILAlg* 1 p.20; *RE* 3.1328–9. Thubursicu: Gsell–Joly 'Khamissa' (1914).
[7] No.2.
[8] Nos.27; 28; see p.77 below.
[9] Nos.119; 128; 137.
[10] Nos.54; 413.
[11] Nos.370; 353; 346.
[12] Nos.33; 155; 156.
[13] Gsell–Joly 'Mdaourouch' (1922).
[14] Nos.28; 42.

buildings cost HS40,000 each. A mausoleum costing HS30,000 is the fourth most costly known in Africa.[1] The two statue costs fall on either side of the median of HS5,000.[2] A duovir of the town in the mid-second century (the father of Apuleius) was worth about HS2 million, a fortune half of which the novelist inherited.[3]

Thugga, a minor hill-town which lay in the 'pertica Carthaginiensis', was a double community containing a Roman *pagus* and a native *civitas*, until it became a *municipium* under Septimius Severus.[4] Though the town's area was relatively small,[5] a great many inscriptions survive, and give details of more building prices than are known at any other town in Africa. The highest is HS150,000 for a building whose remains survive, though its function is uncertain.[6] The cost of the theatre is not known, but is almost certain to have been higher than HS150,000, to judge from its size and from the parallels at Calama and Madauros.[7] Six of the seven prices for complete buildings exceed the median of HS43,500; but since the monuments are not large they do not imply that the town was especially wealthy.[8] This evidence effectively shows that the surviving building costs from Africa do not include many costs for large buildings. Two colossal statues of the Emperors cost HS15,000 each; the only other published statue price is probably incomplete.[9] The many statue-bases at Thugga usually say nothing about the cost of the statues. The foundations cover a respectable but unremarkable range; HS100,000 and HS25,000 (two examples).[10] The one sportula, HS12 paid to the decurions, is relatively high for Africa.[11] (Other costs from Thugga: HS61,000; 60,000 and 30,000; 50,000.)[12]

Mustis, a small town in central Zeugitana which evidently received Roman settlement at an early date, has left a series of fifteen costs which mainly come from inscriptions excavated recently.[13] They show a series

---

[1] Nos.14; 35; 216.

[2] HS7,100; 3,600, nos.120; 185.

[3] Nos.385–6. A benefactor also left the members of a fraternity 12 modii (of grain) per year (no.390).

[4] Thugga's inclusion in the 'pertica Carthaginiensis': *AE* 1963, 94; double community: *ILS* 9404; 9399; *municipium*: *ILS* 6796. Description: Poinssot *Dougga*. The profusion of inscriptions from Thugga, many recording substantial gifts, has sometimes led modern scholars to consider Thugga as a town of outstanding wealth and importance. In fact the town was small and very slow to achieve political recognition (cf. R. Duncan-Jones *PBSR* 30 (1962) 59, n.34.)

[5] 20–25 hectares of urban area; plan in Poinssot *Dougga*.

[6] No.45.   [7] Poinssot p.28. See p.77 below.

[8] Nos.4; 5; 12; 15; 8; 6a. Also no.15 (HS30,000).

[9] No.101; statue price HS600 + (no.211a).

[10] Nos.253; 260; 261.   [11] No.295.

[12] Nos.63a; 400; 323.

[13] A. Beschaouch *Karthago* 14 (1968).

of variations on a theme: a *summa honoraria* of HS5,000 payable for the flaminate is frequently doubled to HS10,000 at the discretion of the individual but is spent in a number of different ways.[1] The expenditure twice assessed in parallel for the duovirate, HS2,000, may represent another doubled *summa honoraria*.[2] If so, the ratio between the payments for the flaminate and duovirate would be 5:1 at Mustis as at Thamugadi, where the amounts were HS10,000 and HS2,000. But the differential need not be so great, as can be seen at Thubursicu Numidarum (above, p.72). HS1,000 is a small and rare payment for office in Africa.[3] Alternatively, HS2,000 may represent the amount of the *summa honoraria* for the duovirate at Mustis. The temple of Fortuna at Mustis cost HS70,000, substantially more than the median of HS43,500.[4] An arch cost HS50,000. (Other costs: HS12,000+; 9,000+; 5,000; 3,000; 2,000.)[5]

The remaining costs come from a wide variety of towns which produce less than eight figures each; the majority are in Zeugitana. There are some regional peculiarities in the distribution of the evidence as a whole. Most of the funerary costs come from Numidia, which also contributes a much higher percentage of the statue costs than the relatively small number of cities there would suggest. Perpetual foundations by contrast come almost entirely from Proconsularis: thirty are from Proconsularis (including Numidia Proconsularis) while only two foundations (both of minute size) come from Numidia proper[6] (there is also one from Auzia in Mauretania Caesariensis).[7] The reasons for these configurations are uncertain. Mention of the prices of monuments seems to have been especially common in the Numidian towns which had a military origin and a partly veteran population. The same social background failed to produce many costs in the inscriptions of military zones north of the Mediterranean; but soldiers in Numidia were mainly recruited from the African provinces, whose customs they consequently shared.[8] Perpetual foundations were evidently not a type of gift that exercised an appeal in Numidia, even in the centres of great wealth such as Cirta and Rusicade.

Summa honoraria: no.370a; doubling: nos.67a; 332a; 332b; 333; 333a; 334a. There appear to be no grounds for the inference that the assessment ran to HS15,000 rather than HS10,000 in the inscription referred to under no.24a (Garnsey 1971 (2) 124–5). The assessment evidently included the *summa honoraria* for the office, a common practice (cf. nos.329; 324–35).

[2] No.339b–c.

[3] HS1,000 for the flaminate at Sarra; HS800 for the sufeteship at Themetra (nos.377; 359).

[4] No.9 (the cost is interpreted as HS40,000 by Garnsey 1971 (2) 125, n.51).

[5] Nos.37; 69b; 20a; 24a; 339a; 269.

[6] One of the Numidian foundations provided 'parentalia' in memory of a legionary veteran at Lambaesis, the other an annual dinner for a group of temple priests at Macomades (VIII 3284; *AE* 1905, 35).

[7] No.258.   [8] R. Cagnat *L'armée romaine d'Afrique*[2] (1913) 287–308.

Building costs (nos. 1–76)

The highest cost is HS600,000 for a temple at Lambaesis; the lowest complete figure for an identifiable building is HS8,000 for a temple with effigies of five local deities at Magifa in Numidia Proconsularis. What appears to have been another small shrine cost HS5,000 at Celtianis in Numidia, no more than a medium-priced statue.[1] The range of variation is thus at least a factor of 100. But the biggest temples at towns such as Carthage and Lepcis are bound to have cost more than the highest attested figure of HS600,000. The only price for a complete theatre refers to a small theatre at Madauros.[2] There are no prices for amphitheatres, which because of their size were almost certainly the most costly of all town monuments. Probably amphitheatres were not built from private resources as a rule, since there are so few references to them in the inscriptions of local benefactors. The majority of costs for buildings whose function is identifiable refer to temples, whose size could vary enormously.

The distribution of the prices for complete buildings is as follows (the figures followed by a plus refer to buildings whose original financing was increased by an amount which the inscription does not specify).

HS600,000–200,000 +	10 buildings	(15.2%)
200,000–100,000	15	(22.7%)
80,000–50,000 +	9	(13.6%)
50,000–20,000	18	(27.3%)
14,000–3,000 +	14	(21.2%)
	66	

The median cost is HS43,500.

The majority of the complete costs for buildings are in round figures, even when the building is large and elaborate and the cost is correspondingly high. Thus a temple with a large surrounding portico at Lambaesis was built from a bequest of HS600,000; a temple of Mater Magna at Lepcis Magna was constructed at a cost of HS200,000 by a living donor; and the stage of the theatre at Lepcis Magna was built at a cost of HS500,000, derived from separate legacies of HS300,000 and HS200,000.[3] Where the building was bequeathed, the round figure clearly results from the amount of the legacy.

The practice of allotting building contracts by competitive tender was

---

[1] Nos.1; 23; 62.   [2] No.28.   [3] Nos.1; 3; 63.

normal at Rome in the late Republic.[1] In a similar way, contracts for the provision of town sacrifices were leased out in the charter of Caesar's colony at Urso in Spain; and the building of a wall was leased to contractors at Puteoli at the end of the second century B.C.[2] It is reasonable to think that there would have been similar procedures in provinces where as much public building took place as in Africa. Whether sureties would have been demanded in land from the contractors as is attested in Italy is uncertain. But in one case it emerges from an African inscription that the author of a promise at an African city had a guarantor (*fideiussor*).[3] Probably the spending of public funds on town building projects would also have been backed by financial precautions or guarantees in some form.

It is likely that the majority of the round-figure building costs result from the acceptance by contractors of fixed-price contracts.[4] This was evidently the practice in the early contract at Puteoli, where half the money allocated for the project was to be paid over once the contractors had given sufficient security, before the building was started.[5] But a different practice is suggested by Columella, who says that architects scorn to cost buildings for themselves, and leave this to separate cost-surveyors who base their calculations on the dimensions of the completed building.[6] The same practice may be implied when Gellius shows an architect giving Fronto an approximate quotation for the cost of a set of baths (whose plan they were looking at), which is immediately contradicted by one of his client's friends.[7] The increases that sometimes occur in the financing of African buildings and statues might result from discrepancy between an original estimate and calculations based on the completed monument.[8] Over-runs might also occur irrespective of any

---

[1] Cicero *Verr.* 2.1.143–6; *ILS* 6085, 29–49.

[2] *ILS* 6087, 69; 5317, 1.6–1.8.

[3] *ILS* 5476.

[4] If the price was fixed, any competition would presumably take the form of offering better value for money, in the form of a bigger or better appointed monument for the same price. For a fixed price, cf. Seneca *de ben.* 6.15.7: 'Certo tamen et levi pretio fultura conducitur.'

[5] *ILS* 5317, 3.13–3.15.

[6] *de r.r.* 5.1.3. Cf. *Digesta* 19.2.36 (J. A. Crook *Law and life of Rome* (1967) 222).

[7] A. Gellius 19.10.2–4 (no.444 below).

[8] For example at Thamugadi an augur promised HS3,000 for a statue on which he finally spent HS4,800 (no.160). Since it is not a round figure the sum added, HS1,800, does not appear a likely total for a deliberate increase. Similarly a *duovir quinquennalis* designate promised a statue for HS4,000 and built it for HS4,500 (no.161). The amount of the increase seems too insignificant to be a deliberate display of generosity. Increases in the financing of buildings were sometimes very substantial: in the case of a small temple at Gigthis whose financing was promised as HS6,000 but finally cost HS21,000 the increase (250%) seems too spectacular to be a contractor's over-run. Perhaps the donor deliberately decided to spend more (no.18). (For contractors who exceed their estimates, see Vitruvius 10.1–2.)

change in the final construction cost, if the lowest price that any contractor would quote for a suitable monument was more than the amount that the donor had originally promised. The few irregular totals for the price of monuments, for example HS32,348 spent on a fountain donated at Thamugadi, were probably based on calculations from the completed monument.[1]

Some of these costs refer to buildings whose size is known from existing remains. They thus offer considerable scope for investigations of actual building costs in different towns.[2] But detailed reconstructions based on full surveys of the buildings in question are needed before this evidence can be utilised effectively.[3] Sometimes the archaeological evidence usefully modifies the interpretation of a building cost. The HS400,000 promised for a theatre at Calama between 161 and 209, is a large sum which might be thought to indicate the rough cost of the theatre, whose remains survive. But a theatre at Madauros whose remains are much smaller cost almost as much, HS375,000, in the early third century.[4] From rough comparisons with other costed building remains, it appears unlikely that the Madauros expenditure is seriously inflationary. Unless there were enormous variations between construction costs in the two towns, which belong to the same part of Africa (inland Numidia Proconsularis), the Calama theatre is likely to have cost substantially more than the HS400,000 originally promised for its construction. A figure of HS10 million for the cost of an unfinished theatre at Nicaea in Bithynia quoted by Pliny, though based only on hearsay, was plausible enough to be worth transmitting to the Emperor.[5] But the area of the Nicaea theatre is more than twice the area of the theatre at Calama.[6] And

[1] No.52; see also nos.10; 10a; 20; 41 (HS67,500; 64,500; 13,180; 272,500). Statues: nos.83; 92; 119; 123; 124; 125; 137; 138; 139; 198; 208 (HS51,335.44; 33,200; 7,340; 6,661; 6,140; 6,040; 5,640; 5,525; 10,407; 2,642; 1,220). No irregular totals occur in the African prices for tombs (nos.213–44). Irregular figures for public monuments or building works in Italy: nos.460; 475; 480; 484; 485; 490; 500 (HS53,608; 29,300; 8,841.5+; 5,250; 4,936; 672.5; 3,055). A few of the Italian tomb-costs are irregular: nos.580, 611; 635 (HS18,300; 3,400; 260).

[2] See nos.1; 3; 4; 5; 6; 10a; 12; 15; 16; 17; 18; 21; 26; 27; 28; 32; 38; 42; 45; 52; 53; 63; 221 and notes (not all of the costs in question are complete).

[3] Unpublished work by the writer (based in the case of buildings at Thugga and Lepcis on scrutiny of the remains) suggests some degree of consistency between a number of the building-costs when related to their remains; but in most cases published building-plans of adequate size are not available. The road prices related to specific lengths of road provide comparable evidence from Italy; see p.124 below. An Italian price for a tomb whose remains survive: no.600 (Ostia).

[4] Nos.27; 28. The area of the Madauros theatre is about 900 m², that of the Calama theatre about 3,050 m². Gsell–Joly 'Mdaourouch' 80–9; Gsell *Monuments* 1.194–7.

[5] *Ep.* 10.39.1.

[6] Calama theatre, n.4 above. A plan of the theatre at Nicaea with commentary is given by

allowance for the fact that the Nicaea theatre is free standing, while the Calama theatre is hollowed from a hillside, as well as for the proportionately greater height of a larger structure, would probably make the difference in the amount of masonry at least four- or five-fold. Thus the cost of the Calama building could not be expected to approach the cost of the theatre at Nicaea, even if that were not the example of wasteful and extravagant expenditure that Pliny suggests.

Statue costs (*nos.77–212*)

There are 138 prices for statues or groups of statues. Total outlays range from a gift of HS1 million for sixteen statues to HS460 for a single statue (both from Lepcis Magna).[1] The highest individual statue price is roughly HS66,666, but such a level was quite exceptional.[2] The next highest prices for marble statues, HS50,000 and HS33,200, both appear to be inflationary.[3] Although there are seventeen costs for marble statues between HS33,000 and HS9,000 the highest figure found more than once is HS8,000. The distribution of costs between HS8,000 and HS2,000 is as follows:

HS	Examples	%	HS	Examples	%
8,000	9	8.6	4,000–4,999	17	16.2
7,000–7,999	4	3.8	3,000–3,999	13	12.4
6,000–6,999	13	12.4	2,000–2,999	6	5.7
5,000–5,999	19	18.1			

The median average price is HS5,000. The 81 complete costs between HS8,000 and HS2,000 form 77% of the 105 complete statue costs. Of the statues whose final cost is unknown, the largest concentration (eight in all) had an original budget of HS4,000. The cost of a statue normally included its base, but the cost of the base is specified separately in one instance. At Sigus in Numidia a statue of Baliddir built after the death of Caracalla cost HS3,200 and its limestone base HS400.[4] The total cost is relatively low, well below the median of HS5,000, despite its fairly late date. The base is of a more or less standard size: its frontal dimensions are 1 × 0.60 metres, and the inscription of fourteen lines is about the usual

---

A. M. Schneider in *Istanbuler Forschungen* 16 (1943) 8–9. The area of the theatre at Nicaea is about 6,600 m²; if its proportions were the same as those of the building at Calama, the height would have been nearly half as much again as the height of the Calama theatre (the stage-widths are respectively 85 and 58 m). Some other African theatres were about the same size as the building at Calama; at Cuicul the stage-width is 62 m; at Thubursicu Numidarum 56.80 m; at Thamugadi 63.60 m; and at Thugga 63.50 m (Gsell–Joly 'Khamissa' 99). The theatre at Carthage was approximately 110 m wide (L. Foucher *Hadrumetum* (1964) 166).

[1] Nos.77; 212.   [2] No.77.
[3] Nos.91; 92.   [4] Nos.186; 393.

length. Its cost makes up nearly 12% of the total outlay. Bases of marble might have cost more, but the combined sum spent on a statue and its base was usually higher than the total found here.

Tombs and funerary monuments (nos.213–44)

There are effectively two types of monument here, imposing mausolea whose price could run to more than HS80,000, and much simpler monuments costing HS2,000 or HS1,000. Five of the large-scale monuments cost between HS32,000 and HS24,000; nine between HS12,000 and HS2,500; eight cost exactly HS2,000; and seventeen between HS1,500 and HS1,000; eleven cost less than HS1,000.[1] A large number of the tombs belonged to soldiers and veterans of the legio III Augusta stationed at Lambaesis.

Information about the rank of the deceased allows a number of comparisons between earnings and the amount spent on the tomb (not all of it always provided by the deceased himself).[2]

TABLE 2. *Expenditure on tombs in Africa related to salaries*

Final rank	Tomb outlay	Conjectured rate of pay	Number of years' pay spent	Reference
Centurio	26,000	20,000/33,000	1.3–0.78	217
Praef. leg.	12,000	80,000/134,000	0.15–0.09	221
Centurio	9,200	20,000/33,000	0.46–0.27	222
Imaginifer	2,000	2,400/4,000	0.83–0.50	228
Centurio	2,000	20,000/33,000	0.10–0.06	228a
Centurio	2,000	20,000/33,000	0.10–0.06	228b
Signifer	1,200	2,400–4,000	0.50–0.30	231
Centurio	1,200	20,000/33,000	0.06–0.04	231a
Centurio	1,000	20,000/33,000	0.05–0.03	234c
Miles	800	1,200/2,000	0.67–0.40	237
Miles	400	1,200/2,000	0.33–0.20	242

The figures in Table 2 show that the level of expenditure on tombs was very much a matter of personal preference among soldiers and veterans at Lambaesis. Centurions might sometimes spend less on a tomb than *principales* whose earnings were only a fraction of the salary of a centurion. There were evidently a number of veterans who felt no need to make any social display in this direction that was commensurate with their wealth and standing. The highest multiple, expenditure on a tomb which more or less approximated to one year's salary (no.217, at

[1] Nos.215–19; 220–7; 228–228g; 229–36; 237–44.
[2] Pay-scales from P. A. Brunt *PBSR* 18 (1950) 71; pay of *principales* from D. J. Breeze *JRS* 61 (1971) 134.

the top of the list in Table 2), is not far short of the highest multiple attested for legionaries and praetorians in Italy (1.66–1.25 years' pay, nos.555 etc.). But the normal level of expenditure at Lambaesis seems to have been lower than in Italy.[1] This is also consistent with the much higher maximum level of tomb costs in Italy in general, where ten tomb costs exceed the highest figure explicitly attested in Africa (nos.550–9). The median averages are respectively HS10,000 for Italy and HS1,380 for Africa.

The actual level of outlay was often standardised for the smaller tombs. The allowance for burial for deceased members of the college of *cornicines* at Lambaesis was HS2,000.[2] The same payment is four times attested as the funerary grant made by the city to distinguished citizens at Pompeii in the first century.[3] The frequent expenditures of HS2,000 and HS1,000 at Lambaesis (eight and ten instances respectively)[4] may both correspond with the provisions of funerary colleges. The centurions who spent such small amounts on burial may have relied on the insurance that such organisations afforded, without going to the trouble of making more ambitious arrangements. Standardisation is also visible in a civilian context when a man builds a tomb at Lamiggiga of the exact design and dimensions of an existing tomb whose occupants he mentions by name (no.232). The same practice is also attested in Italy: Alfenus mentions a testator at Rome who insisted under heavy penalties that the tomb built after his death should be an exact copy of an existing tomb, but perplexed his heirs by omitting to identify the model clearly.[5]

Foundations and ephemeral outlays (nos.248–320)

There are twenty-two African foundations of known size, and a further twelve whose financial details are not known.[6] Their capital yielded interest which paid for entertainments, distributions or subsistence allowance. The largest foundation whose size is known provided for the support of 600 children, boys and girls in equal numbers. The capital of HS1,300,000 which constitutes the largest gift of any kind recorded in Africa, was bequeathed by a procurator under Marcus Aurelius at Sicca

---

[1] See p.128 below for a tabulation of the Italian figures.

[2] *ILS* 2354. Civilian colleges in Italy also made burial grants to their members; see p.131 below.

[3] Nos.620–3.

[4] Nos.228–228g; 233–6.

[5] *Digesta* 35.1.27 (mentioned by Dessau under *ILS* 8074).

[6] Nos.248–69. Foundations whose financial details are not known: *Zeugitana*, *ILS* 9407, Curubis; VIII 26281, Uchi Maius; VIII 26458, Thugga; *ILAf* 527, Thugga; *Byzacena*, *AE* 1968, 588, Mustis; VIII 22856 Thysdrus; VIII 22904, Leptis Minor; *Tripolitania*, *IRT* 140, Sabratha; *Numidia Proconsularis*, *Libyca* 2 (1954) 394, Hippo Regius; *Numidia* VIII 3284, Lambaesis; *AE* 1905, 35, Macomades.

Veneria.[1] Alimentary gifts whose financial details are unknown were also made at Curubis on the coast of Zeugitana and Leptis Minor on the coast of Byzacena. At Gigthis in Tripolitania a senator gave private *alimenta* for the support of members of his own *familia*.[2] The remaining thirty foundations, which often had more than one application, were not devoted to charitable purposes. Thirteen included provisions for cash-handouts (sportulae);[3] twelve provided dinners;[4] nine provided games;[5] four provided oil-distributions (known in Africa as 'gymnasia');[6] and one provided commemorative rites for its donor.[7] The smallest foundation whose capital is definitely known was a fund of HS2,400 at Theveste which provided a dinner for members of a single *curia*. A fund intended for a dinner for the members of a single *classis* or subdivision of a *curia* at Mustis is likely to have been still smaller.[8]

The occasions provided vary in frequency between once every seven years and sixty-four times per year: the foundations concerned are a fund at Abthugni for the construction of a series of new statues of its donor with accompanying festivities every seven years, and a large fund for oil-distributions at Theveste on sixty-four days of the year.[9] The interest-rate is occasionally mentioned: in the giant alimentary fund at Sicca the rate was 5%; in a foundation of HS4,000 at Gor 6%; and in a foundation of HS2,400 at Theveste 12%. The septennial foundation of HS22,000 at Abthugni is likely to have had a rate of 5%, to judge from its financial details.[10] These four examples fit the pattern of inverse correlation between interest-rates and foundation-sizes that is more fully attested in Italy; the same three interest-rates were also the norm there. The lowest rate, 5%, and probably the intermediate rate, 6%, appear to be versions of a land-dividend; the highest (12%) may represent interest on money which was placed out at loan, to judge from analogies in the East.[11] About half of the foundations are testamentary gifts, a much higher proportion than that found in the African costs as a whole, where testamentary gifts form about one-sixth of the total.

The sixteen cash-handouts whose rate is attested range between HS100

---

[1] No.248.

[2] *ILS* 9407; VIII 22904; *ILS* 8978.

[3] Nos.249; 251; 253; 256; 258; 260; 261; 262; 263; 265; VIII 22856; 26458; *Libyca* 2 (1954) 394.

[4] Nos.252; 253; 254; 255; 266; 267; 268; 269; *ILAf* 527; *Libyca* 2 (1954) 394; *AE* 1905, 35; VIII 22856.

[5] Nos.249; 251; 253; 258; 259; 265; VIII 22856; 26281; 26458.

[6] Nos.250; 253; 263; 267. For the meaning of 'gymnasium' in Africa, Friedlaender 4.282–3 and S. Lancel *Libyca* 6 (1958) 143–51.

[7] VIII 3284 (Lambaesis).

[8] No.268; *AE* 1968, 588.   [9] Nos.250; 262.

[10] Nos.248; 267; 268; 262.

[11] See p.133 below.

and HS1 per head. The highest rate was paid to a restricted group, the *flamines perpetui* or highest office-holders at Lambaesis; the lowest rate went to all the citizens at Siagu in Zeugitana.[1] The commonest rate in Africa, as in Italy, where evidence is far more plentiful, was HS4 or one denarius per head; this is found in five or one-third of the examples. This rate was also the maximum recorded in African distributions to the citizens as distinct from more privileged groups; in Italy the much higher maximum for such distributions is HS20.[2]

Explicit prices for feasts or dinners for the *curiae* range from a possible HS500 per *curia* at (Zawiet-el-Laâla) to HS240 per *curia* at Abthugni.[3] The range of variation is relatively narrow, and four prices (one of which is not stated directly) are closely grouped in the range from HS300 to HS240 per *curia*, though they come from four different towns, Uthina, Theveste, Mactar and Abthugni. The figure from (Zawiet-el-Laâla) appears to belong to the third century from the form of the numeral, and may be inflationary.

The prices for games range from a price for a *munus* with gladiators and panthers in the amphitheatre at Carthage of more than HS200,000 (over HS50,000 per day) to a price for boxing displays at Gor of less than HS240.[4] But the entertainments in question differed greatly in type. The other cost that explicitly belongs to the amphitheatre is a payment of HS16,000 for a *munus* at which four leopards were killed at (Smirat). The one explicit price for circus-races is surprisingly low: HS540 for races provided by a foundation at Auzia in Mauretania.[5]

Summae honorariae and other civic payments (nos.321–79)

The holders of magistracies as well as the holders of civic priesthoods and simple town-councillors were expected to pay specified amounts to the city in virtue of their office. The bulk of the African evidence for payments of these *summae honorariae* belongs to the second and early third centuries. How far the payments were already widespread at an earlier period is not always clear. Progressive Romanisation and the acquisition of Roman constitutions by previously native communities may have introduced the *summa honoraria* to towns where it was previously unknown.[6] But the payments are found even in communities of non-Roman type during the second century; in the absence of extensive

---

[1] Nos.290–305. [2] See p.142 below.
[3] Nos.271; 272; 273; 275; 276; 277.
[4] Nos.281–9. [5] Nos.282a; 287.
[6] Tacitus suggests that compulsory payments for office had been introduced at the colony of Camulodunum less than twenty years after the Claudian invasion of Britain: 'delectique sacerdotes specie religionis omnis fortunas effundebant' (a reason for local animus against Rome in A.D. 61); *Ann.* 14.31.

first-century epigraphy of any kind it is difficult to gauge whether this was a recent development. We know the amount of the *summa honoraria* payable for the sufeteship at Themetra in A.D. 146 (HS800, the lowest figure attested for any magistracy in Africa), and the amount payable for the undecimprimate at (Henchir Debbik) in A.D. 182 (HS4,000).[1] Towns of Roman type would evidently have had *summae honorariae* for magistrates at least, from an early date, since such payments are attested in Italy even under the Republic.[2] The same may be true of payments for the decurionate.[3]

There were enormous differences in the amount of the *summa honoraria* between one town and another. The total factor of variation was more than 47: the extremes that are known are payments of HS38,000 for the *quinquennalitas* at Carthage and HS800 for the sufeteship at Themetra.[4] It would be interesting to know how such wide modulation was achieved, and who made the economic appraisal of each town on which the figure was based. There are too many different figures to suggest that the rates of payment generally derived from a standard constitution or even from a range of standard constitutions.[5]

Antoninus Pius when called on to fix the *summa honoraria* payable by the decurions at a town in Macedonia (perhaps Parthicopolis) chose the round figure of HS2,000.[6] His enactment does not suggest that the government seriously tried to assess the economic potential of the town's ruling class. HS2,000 was something of a standard figure, found as the expenditure required of magistrates in Caesar's colony at Urso, and in Octavian's colony at Cnossus, as well as in four African secondary towns. The same payment was made by Augustales at Lacippo in Baetica, and probably also by Augustales in different Italian towns.[7] Where the amounts vary from such obvious norms, the initiative in setting the rate may sometimes

---

[1] Nos.359; 358. For the undecimprimate cf. T. Kotula *Eos* 55 (1965) 347–65.

[2] The *duoviri* of the Sullan colony at Pompeii were obliged to spend a certain sum either on games or on a monument (*ILS* 5706; x p.89). Some of the mentions of money spent 'pro ludis' at other Italian towns may also belong to the late Republic (see p.149). Each duovir and aedile of Caesar's colony at Urso in Spain had to spend HS2,000 on games (*ILS* 6087, 70–1). The same payment for games was expected of magistrates at the Julian colony of Cnossus (*ILS* 7210).

[3] See below, p.148 n.2.

[4] Nos.360; 359. The cost of the decurionate at Muzuc is uncertain, but may have been as little as HS400 (no.348).

[5] Twelve different levels are recorded: HS800; 1,000; 1,600; 2,000; 3,000; 4,000; 5,000; 6,000; 10,000; 12,000; 20,000; 38,000 (see nos.345–79).

[6] Not HS200 as indicated by Garnsey 1971 (1) 312. Pius also stipulated that the town should have 80 decurions. Text in *SEG* 14 (1957) no.479, re-edited by J. H. Oliver *AJP* 79 (1958) 52–60. Commentary, with suggested identification of Sveti Vrač as Parthicopolis, by J. and L. Robert *REG* 69 (1956) 138–9.

[7] *ILS* 6087, 70–1; 7210; below nos.356; 374; 375; 376; II 1934; below nos. 1313–15.

have come from the city concerned rather than from the central government. Pliny's correspondence shows that the recent additions to the size of town councils in Bithynia had been made with Trajan's consent rather than at Trajan's instigation. The Emperor's comments on constitutional arrangements in Bithynian cities show no desire on his part to make innovations.[1] Equally, Dio, speaking for one of the cities in question, shows that the 100 extra councillors at Prusa were a concession obtained from the Emperor by an express initiative of the city, in this case acting through Dio himself.[2] The cities of Bithynia wanted the *summae honorariae* paid by the new councillors as a source of revenue. At Claudiopolis the payments were used to finance the construction of town baths. And at Prusa an envious rumour briefly circulated to the effect that a rival city had been granted permission to create 10,000 new councillors, who would fill that city's coffers with gold.[3] The same desire for revenue might also lead cities to ask permission to levy a higher *summa honoraria*; thus the frequent variations in the *summa honoraria* from one African town to another may sometimes have reflected local wishes.

Some variation was also allowed in Bithynia. Pliny briefly mentions sums of one and two thousand denarii (HS4,000 and HS8,000), payable to cities by the supernumerary decurions who had been admitted by Trajan's permission. The decurions who were adlected every five years by the censors in the normal course of things now also made some payment in a very few cities, by order of another Trajanic governor, which varied from place to place.[4] Pliny's résumé is too compact to indicate whether the second group paid at different rates from the first; they did not necessarily belong to the same cities.

The variations in the *summa honoraria* very broadly reflect the wealth of the towns from which they come. It is no surprise that Carthage, the capital of Africa Proconsularis and a very large city by ancient standards, leaves record of a *summa honoraria* almost twice as high as any other of which there is evidence (HS38,000 for the *quinquennalitas*).[5] The Cirtan confederacy, an aggregation of four early colonies which had a vast territory, was evidently the largest agglomeration in Africa after the pertica Carthaginiensis.[6] The position of the Cirtan *summae honorariae*, next in size after that at Carthage, is no less appropriate. The payment for six civil functions was HS20,000, while one of the priesthoods cost HS10,000.[7] No information is available from Hadrumetum or Lepcis

[1] Pliny refers to 'ii, quos indulgentia tua quibusdam civitatibus super legitimum numerum adicere permisit', *Ep.* 10.112. Trajan's reply in 10.113; see also 10.39.5 and 10.79–80.
[2] *Or.* 45.7–10; 48.11.
[3] Pliny *Ep.* 10.39.5; Dio *Or.* 40.14.   [4] Pliny *Ep.* 10.112.1–2.
[5] No.360: see p. 67 n.3.   [6] See above, p. 69 n.7.
[7] Nos. 345; 349; 357; 361; 379; 345a; 350.

Magna, though the *summae honorariae* at these towns may have approached the figure known at Cirta. But correspondence between the size of city and the known level of the *summa honoraria* is not unfailing. The charge for the flaminate at Uchi Maius was HS12,000 under Septimius Severus, somewhat more than the charge for the *quinquennalitas* at Hippo Regius, HS10,000 under Hadrian.[1] Yet Hippo, the centre of a tax-district, and seat of one of the governor's legates, was much more important than Uchi as well as being considerably larger.[2] A marked difference between the payments might have been expected in the opposite direction. And the flaminate at Diana Veteranorum cost the same as the flaminate or *quinquennalitas* at Ammaedara and the augurate at Sabratha, both more notable towns than Diana.[3]

Comparisons between different towns cannot always be pressed very hard, because changes may sometimes have occurred in the charges for office during the period covered by the inscriptions.[4] There were undoubted variations between the charges for different offices at the same town. At Cirta, one of the priesthoods, the pontificate, cost only half as much as the secular functions.[5] At Thamugadi, a much smaller Numidian town, the flaminate cost HS10,000 under Marcus Aurelius (from a recently discovered inscription), but the duovirate cost only HS2,000, in an undated inscription of the second century.[6] If the charges were contemporary, they indicate a five-fold difference between the payments for different offices. At Thubursicu Numidarum in Numidia Proconsularis, the flaminate cost HS6,000, or half as much again as the aedileship and the decurionate (HS4,000), from the figures in a single third-century inscription.[7] The flaminate appears as the most important single function in many African towns, and could have been expected to cost more than other offices where any modulation of charges existed. At Mustis the *summa honoraria* for the duovirate was probably either one-fifth or two-fifths of the payment for the flaminate, which was HS5,000.[8] In cases where the cost of the flaminate is the only *summa honoraria* that survives from a town, charges for the magistracies may have been on a smaller scale. Conversely, where the only available information concerns a magistracy, the charge for the flaminate may have been somewhat higher. The five-fold variation at Thamugadi makes local comparisons which are

---

[1] Nos.366; 363.

[2] *ILAlg* i, p.i. The respective areas are roughly 60 hectares (Hippo) and 20 hectares (Uchi) (E. Marec *Hippone la royale* (1954) 43; *Notes et Documents de la Tunisie* 2 (1908) 127).

[3] Nos.367; 362; 378.

[4] There is no explicit evidence for changes in the level of the *summa honoraria* at a given town; cf. R. Duncan-Jones *PBSR* 30 (1962) 66–7.

[5] See above, p. 84 n.7.   [6] Nos.366a; 356.

[7] Nos.346; 353; 370.   [8] See above p.74.

not based on information about the same office somewhat uncertain. But the narrower degree of variation in the charges at Cirta and Thubursicu Numidarum shows that the degree of modulation found at Thamugadi was not universal.[1]

In African cities the *summae honorariae* appear to have been originally intended as direct cash-payments to the city. But they were sometimes devoted to monuments built by the magistrate for the adornment of the town.[2] In towns in Bithynia and Italy we see *summae honorariae* being used en masse for the construction of public baths.[3] The city occasionally also received cash donations which were not connected with office: in Africa gifts of this kind range in size from HS200,000 to HS9,500.[4] But revenue from office-holders is much more widely attested. Often the magistrate would add to the *summa honoraria* as a gesture of generosity, and either pay the city a sum larger than the mandatory amount, or apply funds to a building work in honour of his tenure of office.[5]

When his outlay exceeded the *summa honoraria*, the magistrate still as a rule related his payments to the office, and described the expenditure as being made 'ob honorem'. Sometimes the *summa honoraria* recedes from view behind a larger payment which is made 'ob honorem'. The reason was partly the individual's natural desire to emphasise his own generosity. One consequence of this practice is that payments described only as 'ob honorem' are an uncertain guide by themselves to the level of the fixed charges for office (for which the term 'legitima' or 'summa legitima' is sometimes used as an alternative to 'summa honoraria'). It is almost always necessary to discard expenditures made simply 'ob honorem' as indications of fixed payments for office, though the two types have often been confused.[6] The 'ob honorem' payments run as

---

[1] The payments for games asked of the *duoviri* and the *aediles* at Urso was HS2,000 in both cases (*ILS* 6087, 70–1).

[2] Some instances: VIII 14370 (no.127 Avedda); VIII 26255 = *ILS* 9401 (no.103 Uchi Maius); *ILAf* 119 (Sufetula); *AE* 1946, 234 (no.211 Themetra). Normal expenditure of the *summa honoraria* by the magistrate on a monument or on games is attested at Pompeii, colonised by Sulla (*ILS* 5706; see also *ILS* 6086, 36–8 and examples on pp. 149–53). Thus it is not clear whether transfers of the *summa honoraria* to a monument built by the magistrate in Africa constituted an abuse (as suggested by the writer in *PBSR* 30 (1962) 69).

[3] Pliny *Ep.* 10.39.5 (Claudiopolis); *ILS* 5686 (Lanuvium, under Septimius Severus).

[4] Nos.321–23a.

[5] Nos.324–41.

[6] The distinction was pointed out by Hirschfeld in *Annali del Inst. di Corrisp. Arch.* 38 (1866) 62, though most subsequent lists of African *summae honorariae* ignore it (DS s.v. Honoraria summa (Cagnat); Liebenam 57–65; Ruggiero 3.951–2 (Campanile); A. Bourgarel-Musso *Revue africaine* 75 (1934) 513–16; Haywood *ESAR* 4.76–8). In one case an *ob honorem* payment of HS20,000 was twice made at Rusicade, without mention of its being a *summa honoraria*; it appears to be a *summa honoraria* nevertheless, since an identical charge was made for the decurionate at Cirta, which belonged to the same confederacy (nos.345a,

high as HS90,000, which is far more than the amount of the highest attested *summa honoraria*, HS38,000 (nos.324, 360, both from Carthage). Four other 'ob honorem' payments also exceed the highest known *summa honoraria* HS82,000–50,000 (nos.325–8, from Rusicade and Carthage). Most of the 'ob honorem' payments bear no obvious relation to the amount of the *summa honoraria* at the town in question. But at Mustis in central Byzacena, where the *summa honoraria* for the flaminate was HS5,000, five individuals assessed their obligations for this office at HS10,000, or twice the mandatory figure (usually employing the word 'taxare'). A sixth donor at Mustis who paid the *summa honoraria* and promised a further HS5,000, evidently followed the same pattern.[1]

Promises in honour of office were especially widespread in Africa. Their origin seems to lie in competition for elective office, combined with the fact that the object of the promise was usually a gift such as a monument which could not be produced immediately.[2] In practice the institution sometimes led to abuses in the form of civic undertakings whose fulfilment was long delayed.[3] The slowness with which municipal benefactors could go about their work is illustrated by another inscription from Mustis. A military tribune bequeathed HS30,000 for the construction of a small temple of Fortuna. A cousin who was the tribune's heir increased the financing by HS40,000, and supervised the beginning of the construction, in collaboration with his sister and two brothers. But the building was completed and dedicated by yet further members of the family, apparently the nephew and great-nephew of the second donor. The dedication took place in A.D. 164/5, probably decades after the original

345). Most other *ob honorem* payments cannot be interpreted in this way: see R. Duncan-Jones *PBSR* 30 (1962) 66. The present list of *summae honorariae* thus excludes some payments listed under this heading elsewhere, re-classifying them as 'ob honorem' payments (see nos.324 ff.).

[1] No.37. See above, p. 74 n.1. 'Taxatio' in the municipal context was little more than a peculiarity of local terminology, found mainly at Mustis in Zeugitana and at Cuicul in Numidia. In effect 'cum ob honorem...HS...taxasset' had the same meaning as 'cum ob honorem...HS...promisisset', though 'promittere' could be used without mention of a specific sum of money. For a detailed discussion of 'taxatio' see Garnsey 1971 (2). The mistaken view that 'taxatio' referred to a sliding scale of *summae honorariae* depending on the individual was first put forward by Schmidt (VIII 12018). For objections, R. Duncan-Jones *PBSR* 30 (1962) 66–7, n.53, and Garnsey 1971 (2).

[2] A recent interpretation of the promise as a device whose inherent delays allowed men who could not afford to make instantaneous gifts to participate in civic munificence, thus widening the class that took an active part in municipal life, seems to be artificial (Garnsey 1971 (2) 117). It is doubtful whether the promise beckoned into municipal activities those who would otherwise have abstained from them; men whose resources were so restricted that office was a burden would try to avoid spontaneous expenditures of this kind. For promises to cities, cf. R. Villers *RHDFE* 18 (1939) 1–38.

[3] For extended delays in fulfilling promises, see inscriptions mentioned under nos.14; 21; 22; 24; 36; 37; 181.

bequest.[1] At Muzuc the promise of a tiny temple of Apollo was fulfilled by the granddaughter of the decurion who had made the promise.[2] Antoninus Pius was evidently concerned about delays in the fulfilment of civic undertakings, since he authorised cities to charge interest to heirs who failed to carry out bequests of monuments to the city within a reasonable time; at the end of his reign a legate of Numidia was active in calling in outstanding promises to the city.[3] Despite these pitfalls, the promise was also used outside the context of normal local office by the most opulent benefactors. The Emperor Hadrian promised baths of Neptune costing HS2 million to Ostia, a promise which it was left to Antoninus Pius to complete.[4] Pliny the younger promised *alimenta* to Comum in a speech at the dedication of the library which he had previously given to the city.[5] And Dio Chrysostom pledged a building to Prusa without holding any local office to provoke the undertaking.[6]

The system of *summae honorariae* indicates that voluntary munificence was not enough by itself to meet the financial needs of cities. But the presence of both forms of payment also shows that for a time at least, the compulsory demands of local office did not deter the private donor from continuing his voluntary efforts to benefit the city.

[1] No.9, cf. p. 74 n.4.

[2] No.21.

[3] *Digesta* 50.10.5 pr.; *ILS* 5476; *AE* 1964, 225.

[4] Since Hadrian was twice duovir at Ostia while Emperor, the baths were perhaps promised in honour of this office. His second tenure took place in A.D. 126 (Meiggs 175), though the structure of the baths was not begun until the last years of his reign (Meiggs 409), and the building was still unfinished when Pius succeeded him as Emperor in A.D. 138 (*ILS* 334).

[5] Pliny *Ep.*1.8.10. Pliny's relative, L. Calpurnius Fabatus, who held three offices at Comum, followed the same practice of attaching the promise of a new gift to the completion of its predecessor. His promise of money for the decoration of doors was made on the day following the dedication of the portico that he had given to the city (Pliny *Ep.* 5.11; *ILS* 2721).

[6] Dio *Or.* 40.5; 40.8–9; 45.12; 46.9; 47.11–20; *Ep.* 10.81.

THE ECONOMY OF THE
ROMAN EMPIRE

QUANTITATIVE STUDIES

RICHARD DUNCAN-JONES

Fellow of Gonville and Caius College
Cambridge

CAMBRIDGE
AT THE UNIVERSITY PRESS
1974

Published by the Syndics of the Cambridge University Press
Bentley House, 200 Euston Road, London NW1 2DB
American Branch: 32 East 57th Street, New York, N.Y.10022

© Cambridge University Press 1974

Library of Congress Catalogue Card Number: 72–93146

ISBN: 0 521 20165 9

Printed in Great Britain
at the University Printing House, Cambridge
(Brooke Crutchley, University Printer)

TO MY PARENTS

African costs

CONTENTS
Numbers refer to items in the list

ABBREVIATIONS
Entries numbered in italics in the list are the subject of notes on pp.114–19.

MC	Mauretania Caesariensis	PZ	Proconsularis (Zeugitana)
MT	Mauretania Tingitana	D	Costs given in denarii
N	Numidia	PR	Promise fulfilled by heir or descendant
NP	Numidia Proconsularis	*	Testamentary outlay
PB	Proconsularis (Byzacena)	**	Public outlay
PT	Proconsularis (Tripolitania)	***	Private bequest administered by a city

Round brackets indicate a town or site whose ancient name is not known.

Square brackets enclose sections of an ancient text that have been restored.

+ after a figure indicates that some increase in the amount is referred to in the inscription
  without being specified.

Other abbreviations are listed on pp.x–xiv.

BUILDING COSTS

	Identification	Price (HS)	Town	Date	Reference
	TEMPLES				
***1.	Genius Lambaesis	600,000	Lambaesis N	(190/235)	VIII 18226–7
2.	Apollo	350,000+	Calama NP	286/305	*ILAlg* 1.250; cf. VIII 5333, 17487
3.	Mater Magna	200,000	Lepcis Magna PT	72	*IRT* 300; cf. VIII 22671c
*4.	Mercurius	120,000+	Thugga PZ	(185/92)	VIII 26482, cf. 26485, 26595a, 26631, 26635; *ILAf* 517
***5.	Saturn	100,000 (?+)	Thugga PZ	194/5	VIII 26498; cf. *ILTun* 1400
**6.	(Capitol)	100,000 (?+)	Volubilis MT	217	*Hespéris* 7 (1927) 367; cf. *ILM* 45
*6a.	—	100,000	Thugga PZ	214	*ILAf* 527+unpub. section; cf. VIII 26546
7.	—	80,000 (?+)	Lepcis Magna PT	93/4	*IRT* 348
8.	Fortuna	70,000+	Thugga PZ	119/38	VIII 26471; cf. *ILTun* 1392; *AE* 1951, 75
*9.	Fortuna	70,000	Mustis PZ	164/5	VIII 15576
10.	Pluto	67,500	Macomades N	265	*AE* 1905, 35
10a.	Genius coloniae	64,500	Thamugadi N	167/9 (?)	*AE* 1968, 647
*11.	Saturnus	63,000 (?+50,000)	Theveste NP	163/5	Leschi 117
12.	Concordia	50,000+	Thugga PZ	117/38	VIII 26467; cf. *ILAf* 515; *ILTun* 1389; *AE* 1951, 75
13.	(Capitol)	50,000 (?+)	(Hr. Duamis-es-Slitnia) PZ	198/209	VIII 25484
14.	Concordia	40,000	Madauros NP	(post-180)	*ILAlg* 1.2035
*15.	Pietas	30,000	Thugga PZ	(80/130)	VIII 26493; cf. *AE* 1951, 75
16.	—	26,300+	(Bir-el-Faouera) PZ	—	VIII 912 = 11182
17.	(Capitol)	24,000+	Numluli PZ	170	VIII 26121
18.	Concordia	21,000	Gigthis PT	(100/180)	VIII 22693+ *ILTun* 19
19.	—	20,000+	Thibursicum Bure PZ	(post-200)	VIII 1463; cf. pp.938, 1473; *ILTun* 1332
*19a.	Genius patriae	20,000	Verecunda N	193/5	VIII 4192; cf. p.1769 = *ILS* 6851

	Identification	Price (HS)	Town	Date	Reference
**20.	Saturnus	13,180	Civitas Pop-thensis NP	—	*ILAlg* 1.1109
20a.	Aesculapius	12,000+	Mustis PZ	117 (?)	*AE* 1968, 586
21.	Apollo	12,000	Muzuc PB	(post-200)	VIII 12058
22.	Aedes	10,000+	Muzuc PB	—	VIII 12067
23.	Dii Magifae	8,000	Magifa NP	198/ 211 (?)	*ILAlg* 1.2977; cf. VIII 16749
24.	Fortuna Redux	7,000+	(Hr. Sidi Navi) PB	196	VIII 23107
24a.	Mercurius	5,000+	Mustis PZ	217/18	*AE* 1968, 591
25.	Fortuna Redux	5,000+	Sutunurca PZ	—	*ILAf* 304
26.	Mercurius Sobrius	3,000+	Sarra PB	211/12	VIII 12006, 12007, cf. p.2397
	THEATRES				
27.	Promise of a theatre	400,000 (?+)	Calama NP	(161/209)	*ILAlg* 1.286; cf. VIII 5365; 17495
28.	Theatre	375,000	Madauros NP	—	*ILAlg* 1.2121
	PUBLIC BATHS				
29.	Thermae	400,0co	Thagura NP	—	VIII 28065; cf. *ILAlg* 1.1033
**30.	Genio balineo	100,000	Mastar N	228/30	*AE* 1908, 244–5
**31.	(Baths?)	100,000	Gibba N	194 & 195	VIII 18547–8
	ARCHES				
*32.	Quadrifrontal arch (+2 separate statues and tetrastyles)	250,000	Theveste NP	214	*ILAlg* 1.3040; cf. VIII 1858 + p.939, 16504
***32a.	Quadrifrontal arch	120,000+	Lepcis Magna PT	173/4	*AE* 1967, 536; cf. *IRT* 633
33.	Arch of forum novum	77,000	Thubursicu Numidarum NP	198	*ILAlg* 1.1255
34.	Arch with statue of Hadrian and quadriga	42,600+	Capsa PB	119/38	VIII 98, cf. pp.1172, 2349
35.	Arch with statue	40,000	Madauros NP	—	*ILAlg* 1.2130
PR*36.	Arch with three statues	30,000	Cuicul N	160/1	*AE* 1949, 40; *AE* 1925, 23–4
PR37.	Arch and statues	50,000+	Mustis PZ	239	*Bull.Soc.Nat. Ant.Fr.* (1967) 273
37a.	Arch	3,000	Celtianis N	—	*ILAlg* 2.2095; cf. VIII 19695

MISCELLANEOUS AND UNCLASSIFIED BUILDINGS

37b.	Fons...quadrato lapide novo et signino opere...instructus	600,000 (?)	Caputamsaga N	(post-180)	*BAC* (1914) 562
***38.	Bibliotheca	400,000	Thamugadi N	(post-180)	*ILS* 9362
39.	Building with portico	300,000	Thagaste NP	(post-180)	*ILAlg* 1.877; cf. VIII 5147–8

	Identification	Price (HS)	Town	Date	Reference
40.	—	300,000	Karthago PZ	—	VIII 12533
*41.	Arcaded enclosure dedicated to Apollo	272,500	Lepcis Magna PT	(pre-180)	*PBSR* 23 (1955) 133; cf. *IRT* 707
42.	Rebuilding of forum with new portico and paving	200,000	Madauros NP	—	*ILAlg* 1.2120
43–4.	Restoration of building with porticoes	200,000	Karthago PZ	(post-180)	*ILAf* 403
45.	('Dar-el-Acheb')	150,000	Thugga PZ	164/6	VIII 26527; cf. *ILTun* 1404
46.	—	110,000	Lares PZ	—	VIII 16322
47.	—	100,000	(Schuhud-el-Batel) PZ	—	*ILAf* 489
48.	—	100,000	Thuburbo Maius PZ	213	*ILAf* 274
49.	… novum	100,000	Cirta N	—	*ILAlg* 2.501; cf. VIII 6958 + p.1847 = *ILS* 6860
50.	—	70,000 (? +)	Cuicul N	—	*PBSR* 30 (1962) 109 n.114
50a.	—	47,000	Cirta N	—	*ILAlg* 2.717
51.	—	40,000 +	Lepcis Magna PT	—	*IRT* 788
52.	Octagonal fountain	32,348	Thamugadi N	(post-180)	BCB 318
53.	Market	30,000 +	Cuicul N	(*c.* 138/61)	*AE* 1916, 36
*54.	(Fountain?)	30,000 (? +)	Calama NP	—	*ILAlg* 1.298
55.	—	30,000 (? +)	(Schuhud-el-Batel) PZ	—	VIII 25847
56.	—	20,000 (? +)	Lepcis Magna PT	101/2	*IRT* 352
57.	Laet(it)iae	20,000	(Zawiet-el-Laâla) PZ	(post-180)	VIII 12434, cf. p.2434; cf. 25935; *ILS* 6623
58.	Porticus ascensus fori cum spiritis et gradibus et capitibus et [epistyliis]	12,000	(Hr. Udeka) PZ	225	VIII 15497 = *ILS* 5553
59.	—	11,000	Celtianis N	—	*ILAlg* 2.2101 = VIII 19698
60.	—	10,000 +	Mustis PZ	222/35 (?)	VIII 1578
61.	—	10,000 (? +)	Cirta N	180/95	*ILAlg* 2.558; cf. VIII 6993; 19417
62.	—	5,000	Celtianis N	—	*ILAlg* 2.2106

SECTIONS OF BUILDINGS AND MISCELLANEOUS CONTRIBUTIONS

	Identification	Price (HS)	Town	Date	Reference
***63.	Rebuilding of proscaenium and scaenae frons of	500,000	Lepcis Magna PT	157/8	*IRT* 534

	Identification	Price (HS)	Town	Date	Reference
	theatre in Greek marble, and adding marble statues				
63a.	To improvement of templum Genii patriae	61,000 (? +)	Thugga PZ	293/305	VIII 26472
64.	Musaeum (thermarum)	41,200	Thibursicum Bure PZ	260/2	*ILAf* 506
65.	[Ad opus] amphitheatri	30,000	Rusicade N	—	*ILAlg* 2.34; cf. VIII 7983, 7984 + p.1879
66.	Ad ornamenta (arcus)	25,000	Seressi PZ	—	VIII 11216, cf. p.2340
***67.	(? +4) cancelli aerei [ad] ornamentum rostrorum	20,000 +	Thugga PZ	(post-205)	VIII 26593, cf. *ILAf* 534
67a.	Porticus media	10,000 +	Mustis PZ	116	*AE* 1968, 599
68.	Ad opus curiae	10,000	Lambaesis N	—	*AE* 1914, 40
69.	In opus cultumque theatri	10,000	Rusicade N	(post-193)	*ILAlg* 2.5 = VIII 7960 = *ILS* 5077
69a.	Portico with 4 columns in temple of Caelestis	(part of 9,000 +)	Mustis PZ	138/45	*AE* 1968, 595
70.	Restoration	8,000 (? +)	Mateur PZ	—	VIII 25430
71.	Pronaos templi Mercurii, cum ornamentis	6,000 (? +)	Furnos Maius PB	183/5	VIII 12030; 12039 = *ILS* 6812
72.	Ad opus theatri	5,000	Ammaedara PB	198/211	*ILTun* 460
73.	Aedes for statue (*v.* 95)	4,400	Thamugadi N	(pre-200)	VIII 17831 = *ILS* 5400
D74.	Ad opus theatri	4,000	Rusicade N	225	*ILAlg* 2.37 = VIII 7988 + p.1879 = *ILS* 5648
75.	[Ad per]fectionem operis tea[tri] (*sic*)	2,000(? +)	Rusicade N	—	*ILAlg* 2.34; cf. VIII 7983, 7984 + p.1879
D76.	Ad ampliationem templi (Caelestis) et gradus	500	Tuccabor PZ	(post-180)	VIII 14850 = *ILS* 5422a

STATUES

MULTIPLE STATUE GIFTS

	Identification	Price (HS)	Town	Date	Reference
*77.	16 statues	1,000,000 (66,666)	Lepcis Magna PT	—	*IRT* 706
78.	5 statues	50,000 (10,000)	Thamugadi N	196/211	*AE* 1941, 46
*D79.	4 statues	36,020 (9,005)	Lepcis Magna PT	(post-180)	*IRT* 700
80.	(Some statues)	30,000	Cuicul N	(*c.* 160)	*AE* 1920, 114
81.	3 statues without bases	21,000 + (7,000 +)	Cuicul N	—	*AE* 1916, 12 & 16

	Identification	Price (HS)	Town	Date	Reference
	SILVER STATUES				
*82.	Aunt of Emperor Septimius Severus	$144\frac{7}{8}$ Roman pounds (HS115,000 +)	Lepcis Magna PT	(before 170)	*IRT* 607
83.	Deity with gold crown	HS51,335$\frac{7}{16}$	Hippo Regius NP	117/38	*ILAlg* 1.10 = VIII 17408; *BAC* 1938/40, 135; cf. *ILS* 5474
84.	Imagines argent. Imp. Caes. Traiani Hadriani	17,000?	Hippo Regius NP	117/38	v. 83
85.	Signum [argent.?]	50,000	Theveste NP	—	VIII 1887 + 16510 = *ILAlg* 1.3066
86.	Statuncula Mercurii	14,000	Lambaesis N	—	VIII 18233
87.	Imago argentea of Septimius Severus	3 Roman pounds (HS2,400 +)	Safar MC	198/210	VIII 9797
88.	Imago argentea Faustinae	1,593	Cillium PB	139/61	*AE* 1957, 77
	BRONZE STATUES				
D89.	Baliddir	4,000	Sigus N	post-217	VIII 19121 = *ILS* 4479
90.	Marcus non regnans	2,000 (? +)	Thuburbo Maius PZ	139/46	*ILTun* 714

MARBLE STATUES (The use of marble can generally be assumed where nothing is known to the contrary)

	Identification	Price (HS)	Town	Date	Reference
91.	—	50,000	Vallis PZ	(post-250)	*ILTun* 1282
D92.	—	33,200	Abthugni PZ	(post-250)	VIII 11207
93.	Hercules cum tetrastylo	33,000	Rusicade N	—	*ILAlg* 2.34; cf. VIII 7983, 7984 + p.1879
94.	Victoria...cum tetrastylo	30,000	Rusicade N	218/22 (?)	*ILAlg* 2.10; cf. VIII 7963; 19849 + p.967
*95–6.	Fortuna	22,000	Thamugadi N	(pre-200)	VIII 17831 = *ILS* 5400
97.	Marcus & Verus	(19,000)–38,000	Sabratha PT	169/70	*IRT* 22
98.	Concordia & (?)	(17,500)–35,000	Thamugadi N	198/211	VIII 17829 = *ILS* 434
99.	Victoriae Aug.	16,000 +	Membressa PZ	275/6	VIII 25836 = *ILS* 8926
100.	Fortuna Redux	16,000	Thamugadi N	(post-180)	VIII 2344, cf. 17812

	Identification	Price (HS)	Town	Date	Reference
*101.	Marcus & Verus (colossi)	(15,000)–30,000	Thugga PZ	173	*ILAf* 561 + *ILTun* 1406
*102.	Caracalla	12,000+	Cirta N	213/17	VIII 7001 + p.1847; cf. *ILAlg* 2.570
103.	Septimius (equestrian statue without base)	12,000+	Uchi Maius PZ 197		VIII 26255 = *ILS* 9401; *v.* 366
*104–5.	Divus M. Antoninus	12,000	Cuicul N	180/92	*PBSR* 30 (1962) 109 n.114
106.	Iulia Domna	10,000+	Ammaedara PB 198/211		*ILTun* 460
107.	Divus Commodus	10,000+	Diana N	199/200	VIII 4596, cf. 18650
108.	Septimius	10,000+	Diana N	196/7	VIII 4594, cf. 18649
*109.	Victoria Germanica	9,000	Verecunda N	213	VIII 4202, cf. 18494
110.	—	8,000	(Hr. Bou Cha) PZ	—	*ILTun* 746
111.	Genius Celtianis	8,000	Celtianis N	—	*ILAlg* 2.2086; cf. VIII 19688
112.	Virtus divi M. Antonini	8,000	Cuicul N	180/3	*BAC* (1911) 116
113.	Genius kastell. Elefant.	8,000	Kastellum Elephantum N	(post-180)	*ILS* 6865
114.	Apollo	8,000	Giufi PZ	—	VIII 858 = *ILS* 5073
115.	Victoria	8,000	Giufi PZ	—	VIII 862 = 12382 = *ILS* 6821
116.	Victoria	8,000	Giufi PZ	—	VIII 863, cf. p.1273
117.	M. Aurelius	8,000	Sutunurca PZ	146	VIII 24003
118.	Septimius	8,000	Tupusuctu MC	194/5	VIII 8835, cf. p.1950
119.	Neptunus	7,340	Calama NP	—	VIII 5298; cf. *ILAlg* 1.185
120.	—	7,100 (? +)	Madauros NP	(post-180)	*ILAlg* 1.2152
121.	Divus M. Antoninus Pius	7,000	Cuicul N	176/92	*AE* 1916, 14
121a.	Signum Marsyae	7,000	Furnos Minus PZ	(*c.* 214?)	*AE* 1961, 53; *v.* Kotula 34
122.	Mercurius	7,000	Theveste NP	—	*ILAlg* 1.3007; cf. VIII 1842
123.	Q. Fl. Lappianus	6,661	Thabarbusi NP	—	*AE* 1960, 214
124.	Minerva	6,140	Verecunda N	—	VIII 4198, cf. p.1769
125.	Victoria	6,040	Thamugadi N	160/3	VIII 2353, cf. p.1693 = *ILS* 5476
126.	Victoria	6,000+	Cuicul N	—	VIII 8310 = 20148
127.	Septimius & (?) (equestrian)	(6,000)–12,000	Avedda PZ	196	VIII 14370

	Identification	Price (HS)	Town	Date	Reference
128.	Hercules	6,000	Calama NP	—	*ILAlg* 1.181; cf. VIII 5292
129.	Genius populi	6,000	Cirta N	180/92?	*ILAlg* 2.479; cf. VIII 6948 + p.1847 = *ILS* 6858
130.	Genius populi Cuiculitanor(um)	6,000	Cuicul N	—	*AE* 1914, 44
131.	Iuppiter Victor	6,000	Diana N	—	VIII 4577
132.	Marsyas	6,000 (?)	Lambaesis N	—	*AE* 1914, 40
133.	Antoninus Pius	6,000	Sitifis MC	155/6	VIII 8466, cf. p.1920
134.	Sex. Lucretius Rogatus	6,000	Tupusuctu MC	—	VIII 8840, cf. p.1950
135.	Minerva (?)	6,000	Tichilla PZ	—	VIII 25861
136.	—	6,000	Verecunda N	—	VIII 4243 cf. 18502
*137.	Apollo	5,640	Calama NP	—	*ILAlg* 1.177; cf. VIII 5299; 17479
138.	Divus Hadrianus & L. Verus	5,525	Sutunurca PZ	146	*ILAf* 300
138a.	Victoria(e) Parthica(e) (duae)	(5,300)– 10,600	Thamugadi N	116	VIII 2354, cf. p.1693, = *ILS* 305
139.	Pius & L. (Verus)	(5,203)– 10,407	Cillium PB	139/61	*AE* 1957, 77
140.	Mars	5,200	Sigus N	222/35	VIII 19124
141.	Victoria & Mercurius	(5,000 +)– 10,000 +	Cuicul N	—	*AE* 1911, 105
142.	Iup(p)iter Omnipotens	5,000 +	Cuicul N	182	*AE* 1908, 242
143.	Caracalla	5,000 +	Lambaesis N	208	VIII 2711, cf. p.1739
144.	Fortuna	5,000 +	Agbia PZ	138/61	VIII 1548, cf. 15550 = *ILS* 6827
145.	Mercurius	5,000	Diana N	—	VIII 4579 = *ILS* 5355
146.	Victoria	5,000	Lambaesis N	—	VIII 18241 = *ILS* 6847a
147.	Neptunus, cum ostiis	5,000	Pheradi Maius PB	138/61	*ILTun* 246
148.	Mercurius	5,000	Sarra PB	—	VIII 12001 = *ILS* 5470
149.	—	5,000	Sitifis MC	—	VIII 8497, cf. pp.972, 1920
150.	Pius & M. Aurelius	(5,000)– 10,000	Thamugadi N	139/61	VIII 2362, 17864; cf. *AE* 1941, 45
151.	Sol	5,000	Thamugadi N	—	VIII 2350, cf. 17815
151a.	Genius coloniae Thamugadis	5,000	Thamugadi N	—	VIII 17913 + *AE* 1954, 147

	Identification	Price (HS)	Town	Date	Reference
*152.	Bonus Eventus	5,000	Thibilis N	—	VIII 18890 = *ILS* 3751
153.	Mercurius	5,000	Thignica PZ	—	VIII 1400, cf. 14904
*154.	Genius municipii	5,000	Thuburbo Maius PZ	(160/92)	*ILAf* 240
155.	Minerva	5,000	Thubursicu Numidarum NP	—	*ILAlg* 1.1236
156.	Fortuna Redux	5,000	Thubursicu Numidarum NP	—	VIII 4874; cf. *ILAlg* 1.1223
157.	Karthago Aug. (without base)	5,000	Uchi Maius PZ	(post-200)	VIII 26239 = *ILS* 9398
158.	Sanctissimus genius ordinis	5,000	Verecunda N	—	VIII 4187, cf. p.1769
159.	Septimius Severus	4,800	Diana N	195/6	*AE* 1933, 67
160.	Victoria Victrix	4,800	Thamugadi N	198/211	*AE* 1941, 49
161.	[Genius] ordinis	4,500	Thamugadi N	—	VIII 2341, cf. 17811
162.	Hercules	4,400+	Cuicul N	—	*AE* 1914, 236
163.	—	4,400	Verecunda N	—	VIII 4235, cf. 18501
164.	Iuno	4(?),200	Thuburnica PZ	—	VIII 25702
165.	Caracalla	4,200	(Hr. Kudiat Setieh) NP	201/10	*ILAlg* 1.951; cf. VIII 17258
166.	Aesculapius	4,000+	Cuicul N	(post-200)	*BAC* (1919) 97
167.	Concordia Augg.	4,000+	Cuicul N	166/9	VIII 8300, cf. p.1896
168.	Apollo	4,000+	(Hr. Debbik) PZ	181/2	VIII 14791; cf. *ILTun* 1283 = *ILS* 6808
169.	Victoria Parthica	4,000+	Diana N	198	VIII 4583
170.	Minerva	4,000+	Lambaesis N	147/8	VIII 18234
171.	Fortuna	4,000+	Lambaesis N	147/8	VIII 18214
171a.	Mercurius	[4],000+	Lambaesis N	(post-117)	*AE* 1968, 646 = *Ant.af.* 5 (1971) 133
172.	Iuppiter Conservator	4,000+	Verecunda N	212	VIII 4196, cf. 18491
173.	Iuno	4,000+	Verecunda N	212	VIII 4197, cf. 18492 = *ILS* 450
174.	Genius curiae	4,000	Agbia PZ	138/61	VIII 1548, cf. 15550 = *ILS* 6827
175.	Iuppiter Optimus Maximus	4,000	Chidibbia PZ	—	VIII 14875
176.	Genius Senatus	4,000	Cuicul N	—	*AE* 1908, 241
*177.	Victoria Augg.	4,000	Diana N	160/3	VIII 4582
178.	(Septimius?)	4,000	Diana N	193	Leschi 274

	Identification	Price (HS)	Town	Date	Reference
179.	Fortuna Redux Auggg.	[4],000	Thamugadi N	198/211	*AE* 1901, 191
*180.	Genius populi	4,000	Tiddis N	214	*ILAlg* 2.3575
181.	Genius populi	4,000	Verecunda N	—	VIII 4193
182.	—	4,000	Verecunda N	—	VIII 4250, cf. 18504
183.	Victoria	3,900	Thamugadi N	—	VIII 17838
184.	Genius vici	3,700	Verecunda N	—	VIII 4194, cf. 18490 = *ILS* 6852
185.	—	3,600	Madauros NP	—	*ILAlg* 1.2151
186.	Baliddir cum base (*v.* 393)	3,600	Sigus N	(post-217)	VIII 19122
187.	Septimius Severus	3,400	(Hr. Kudiat Setieh) NP	197/8	VIII 10833, cf. 17257; *ILAlg* 1.950
188.	L. Sisenna Bassus	3,200	Abthugni PZ	—	VIII 11201 + p.2338 = *ILS* 5494; cf. *ILTun* 783
189.	Marcus & divus Verus	(3,000+)–6,000+	Cuicul N	169/70	VIII 8318–19, cf. pp.1896–7; cf. also *ILS* 5533; *AE* 1913, 21; 1920, 114.
190.	Serapis	3,000+	(Hr. Debbik) PZ	185/91	VIII 14792
191.	Mercurius	3,000	Cuicul N	—	*AE* 1914, 237
192.	Fides publica	3,000	Cuicul N	—	*AE* 1914, 43
193.	(Signum)	3,000	Diana N	—	VIII 4601
194.	Genius leg. III Aug.	3,000	Lambaesis N	198	VIII 2527, cf. 18039 & p.954
195.	Iulia Domna	3,000	Medeli PZ	198/211	VIII 885, cf. 12387 & p. 2427 = *ILS* 6803
*196.	L. Cornelius Saturninus	3,000	Numluli PZ	—	VIII 15392
197.	L. Verus	3,000	Sutunurca PZ	162	*ILAf* 303
198.	—	2,642+	Thubba PZ	—	VIII 14296
199.	Signum Marsyae	2,400+	Althiburos PB	—	VIII 27771
**200.	Caracalla	2,400	(Hr. Kudiat Setieh) NP	202/10	VIII 17259 = *ILS* 449; cf. *ILAlg* 1.952
201.	Septimius	2,400	(Hr. Kudiat Setieh) NP	198	*ILAlg* 1.950 cf. VIII 10833 = 17257
202.	Divus Hadrianus	2,400	Vina PZ	138/61	*AE* 1961, 199
202a.	—	2,000+	(Hr. es-Shorr) PB	—	VIII 11998 = *ILS* 5072; cf. *ILTun* 610
203.	Commodus	2,000+	(Biniana) PB	186	VIII 76

	Identification	Price (HS)	Town	Date	Reference
204.	[Geta?] Caesar	2,000+	Thignica PZ	(pre-209)	VIII 15202
205.	Pluto & (?)	(2,000+)–4,000+	Zama Regia PB	post-138	VIII 12018 = *ILS* 4454; cf. *ILTun* 603
206.	Genius coloniae Milevensis	2,000	Milev N	—	VIII 19980
207.	Mercurius	2,000	Thamugadi N	—	*AE* 1954, 144
208.	Signum Herculis	[1?]220	Cuicul N	—	*AE* 1913, 154
209.	Mars	1,000 (?+)	Thamugadi N	—	*BAC* (1893) 157, n.27
210.	Minerva	900	(Hr. Bedjar)	—	VIII 14349
211.	Antoninus Pius	800 (?+)	Themetra PB	139/61	*AE* 1946, 234
211a.	Antoninus Pius	600+	Thugga PZ	156/7	*AE* 1968, 585
D212.	Liber Pater	460	Lepcis Magna PT	—	*IRT* 294

SEPULCHRAL AND BURIAL COSTS

	Identification	Price (HS)	Town	Date	Reference
213.	P. Lucretius Rogatianus & son	(?)+ 80,000	Lepcis Magna PT	—	VIII 21, cf. 10995 +p.979 = *IRT* 721; cf. also VIII 22682 = *IRT* 720
214.	C. Iunius Victor (centurio) leg. III Aug. (vivus)	63,000	Mascula N	(140/238)	VIII 2224, cf. 17618
215.	Pinarius Processianus, aed. IIvir. et augur, dec(urio)	32,000 (?+)	Saltus Aurasius N	(post-100)	VIII 2451, cf. 17945 & p.952
216.	...Saturninus, praesidis ben...	30,000	Madauros NP	(post-200)	*ILAlg* 1.2203
217.	C. Cornelius Florentinus (centurio) leg. III Aug.	26,000	Lambaesis N	(post-81)	VIII 2851
218.	C. Iul(ius) Martialis vet(eran.)	26,000	Zarai N	—	VIII 4524
219.	Q. Gargilius Campanus	24,000	Auzia MC	233	VIII 9109 = *ILS* 8096
220.	Fabricia Silvana	12,000	(Ksar Ouled Zid) N	(post-180)	Leschi 296
221.	T. Flavius Maximus, praef. leg. III Aug.	12,000	Lambaesis N	222/37	VIII 2764, cf. p.954; cf. also VIII 2624
222.	...(centurio) of 5 legions	9,200	Lambaesis N	(post-81)	VIII 3005, cf. p.1740
D223.	Thanubdau byn Enasif	8,400 (?+4,000)	(Wadi Umm el-Agerem) PT	(post-180)	*PBSR* 23 (1955) 141–2; cf. *IRT* 906
224.	Martis	5,000	Aquae Caesaris NP	(post-140)	VIII 2185, cf. *ILAlg* 1.2957 = Buecheler no.2166

	Identification	Price (HS)	Town	Date	Reference
224a.	Octavia Rogata et Masupius Rogatianus	5,000	Avitta Bibba PZ	—	VIII 811 cf. 12270
225.	C. Aemilius Victor, veteranus	4,000	Lambaesis N	(post-81)	VIII 3025, cf. p.1740
226.	L. Apuleius Felix, veteran.	3,000	Lambaesis N	(post-81)	*BAC* (1916) 210
227.	P. Cerennius P.f. Quir. Severus, vet. leg. III Aug.	2,500	Lambaesis N	(81/200)	VIII 3079, cf. p.1740
228.	. . .imag[inifer] leg. III Aug.	2,000	Lambaesis N	(post-117)	VIII 2783, cf. p.1739
228a.	Aurelius A[man]dus (centurio) leg. III A[ug.]	2,000	Lambaesis N	(post-180)	VIII 2817 = *ILS* 2212
228b.	M. Furius M.f. Pap. Candidus, Thevest(inus), (centurio) leg. III Aug.	2,000	Lambaesis N	*c.* 212/38	VIII 2878, cf. p.1740
228c.	C. Iulius C.f. Col. Atticus, Tar(entinus?), optio leg. III Aug.	2,000	Lambaesis N	(post-81)	VIII 2886, cf. p.1740
228d.	Nonia Manliana, virgo ablata, (centurionis filia)	2,000	Lambaesis N	(post-200)	VIII 2953, cf. p.1740
228e.	Sergia Marcia Bassilla	2,000	Lambaesis N	(post-81)	VIII 4055, cf. p.1743
228f.	—	2,000	Lambaesis N	—	VIII 4180
228g.	C. Domitius Secundus vet.	2,000	Lambaesis N	(post-81)	VIII 18297
229.	Aur(elius) Hermias, b(ene)f(iciarius) leg(ionis)	1,500	Lambaesis N	(post-200)	VIII 2823, cf. p.1740
D230.	M' Iulius Dativus	1,260	Karthago PZ	—	VIII 24934
231.	P. Aufidius Felix, sig(nifer) leg. III Aug.	1,200	Lambaesis N	—	VIII 2815, cf. p.1739
231a.	T. Fl. Virilis, (centurio) leg. III Aug. (& 5 other legions), stip(endia 45)	1,200	Lambaesis N	—	VIII 2877, cf. p.1740 = *ILS* 2653; cf. also *AE* 1914, 24
231b.	P. Aelius Maior, vet. leg. III Aug.	1,200	Lambaesis N	(post-200)	VIII 3016, cf. p.1740
231c.	Ann[ius?]	1,200	Lambaesis N	(post-81)	VIII 3654
232.	T. Caninius Sa[turnin(us)]	1,200	Lamiggiga N	(post-200)	VIII 4387, cf. 18555 = *ILS* 8074
233.	L. Sentius Valerianus, ex adiutore princ(ipis) leg. III Aug.	1,000	Casa N	*c.* 150/8	VIII 4332, cf. p.1772 = *ILS* 2448; cf. also VIII 4330

	Identification	Price (HS)	Town	Date	Reference
234.	Clodius Honoratus, optio leg. III Aug.	1,000	Lambaesis N	(post-81)	VIII 2845
234a.	Iul(ius) Marcius Saecularis, (centurio) leg. III Aug.	1,000	Lambaesis N	(post-200)	VIII 2896, cf. p.1740
234b.	Cn. Tannonius Maior, adiutor	1,000	Lambaesis N	(post-81)	VIII 2981
234c.	T. Vitellius Atillianus T.fil., Viminac(ensis), (centurio) leg. III Aug. (and 9 other legions), milit(avit) ann(is) (48)	1,000	Lambaesis N	—	VIII 3001, cf. p.1740
234d.	Valeria Manilia, coniunx...vet(erani)	1,000	Lambaesis N	—	VIII 3109
234e.	L. Aelius L.f. Pap. Macer, Hadrimeto(nensis)	1,000	Lambaesis N	(post-81)	VIII 3334, cf. p.1741
234f.	—	1,000	Lambaesis N	—	*Musée de Lambèse* I, 216
235.	T. Flavius Rog[atus], vet.	1,000	Lamiggiga N	—	*AE* 1938, 44
D236.	L. Domitius Aumura	1,000	Matmata PT	(post-180)	*ILTun* 52
237.	Val(erius) Faustus, mil(es) leg. III Aug.	800	Lambaesis N	—	VIII 3254, cf. pp. 955, 1741
238.	Aurel(ius) Marcianus [mil.] leg. III	600(? +)	Lambaesis N	—	VIII 3055
D238a.	—	600	Matmata PT	(post-180)	*ILTun* 53
239.	Demetria Polla	500	Lambaesis N	—	VIII 3572
239a.	T. Gargiliu[s F]lorus	500	Lambaesis N	—	VIII 3668, cf. 18195
239b.	Q. Aselius	500	Safar MC	(50/100)	VIII 9801, cf. p.2054
D240.	L. Calpurnius Furnarius, ad funus eius erogatis *C	400	Hadrumetum PB	(post-180)	VIII 22944
D241.	M. Mauc[..v]et. leg(ionis)...ex testam...fieri mo[numentum] *C et in patria[...]	400	Lambaesis N	—	VIII 3006
242.	A[...] Maritimus (?), mil(es) leg(ionis)	400	Lambaesis N	(post-200)	VIII 3191
243.	P. Aelius Securus, Nap(ocensis?), dec(urio) coh(ortis) II His(panorum)	200	Lambaesis N	(post-117)	VIII 2787, cf. p.1739
D244.	Caecilia Sa[..] vet(erani) uxor	96	Lambaesis N	(post-180)	VIII 3042, cf. 18162

ALTARS

	Identification	Price (HS)	Town	Date	Reference
245.	Hercules	1,000	Cuicul N	(post-200)	VIII 20145 = *ILS* 5460
246.	Marcus and Commodus	500	Tuccabor PZ	176/80	VIII 14853
247.	Numen Silvani	140	Cirta N	—	VIII 6963 = *ILAlg* 2.2046

PERPETUAL FOUNDATIONS

	Identification	Price (HS)	Town	Date	Reference
*248.	Alimenta for 300 boys aged 3–15 at HS10 per month, [3]oo girls aged 3–13 at HS8 per month	1,300,000 at 5% (annual residue HS200)	Sicca PZ	175/80	VIII 1641, cf. pp.1523 & 2707 = *ILS* 6818
*249.	For sportulae to citizens, and ludi	1,000,000	Oea PT	183/5	*IRT* 230
*250.	Ut [certis diebus gy]mnasia populo publice in thermis prae[berentur] (64 days per year)	250,000	Theveste NP	214	*ILAlg* 1.3040, cf. VIII 1858, 16504 & p.939
*251.	Ludi scaenici quodannis natali eius...et decurio[nib]us sing. sportulae [denarii qu]ini (HS20)	200,000	Thisi PZ	—	VIII 25428 + *ILTun* 1190
*252.	Decurio[nibus item curiis omnibus?] et Augustalibus epula[to]ria	100,000	Hippo Regius NP	—	*AE* 1958, 144
253.	[Decurionibus] utriusq. ordinis sportulae, curiis e[pulum et universo] populo gymnasia, ludiq[ue scaenici]	100,000	Thugga PZ	193/205	VIII 26590–1; cf. *ILTun* 1427
D*254.	Cur(i)is singulis annui (HS300) ut natali eius in publico vescantur	(50,000–60,000 if 6–5% & 10 curiae)	Uthina PZ	117/38	VIII 24017
255.	Epulaticium curialibus quodannis	50,000	Mactar PB	*c.* 180/92	VIII 11813, cf. p.2372 = *ILS* 1410
256.	Divisiones dec(urionibus) quodannis die	50,000	Sufes PB	(post-150)	VIII 262 = 11430 = *ILS* 6835

	Identification	Price (HS)	Town	Date	Reference
	natali dei Herculis genii patriae				
257.	Cur[iis...ut ex] usuris...q[uodannis epularentur]	50,000	Theveste NP	—	VIII 1887; cf. 16510 & *ILAlg* 1.3066
*258.	Semestrial circuenses (*sic*) ce[ler]es, sportulae to decurions & 3 others, decoration of 2 statues	(40,000?) 1968 p.a.	Auzia MC	—	VIII 9052, cf. p.1960
D*259.	[Ex us]uris ludi et sp[ectacula] omnibus annis die X[...] Ianuar. edantur	(40,000? if 5% (2,000? p.a.)	Siagu PZ	(post-180)	VIII 967, cf. 12448
260.	Promise of foundation for sportulae to decurions of civitas only	25,000	Thugga PZ	185/92	VIII 26482; cf. *ILAf* 516
*261.	Sportulae [decurionibus pagi?]	25,000	Thugga PZ	(pre-205)	VIII 26623
D*262.	Septimo quoque anno statua ex HS3,200 et epulationis nomine decurionibus sportulae (HS20) et curialibus (*sic*) (HS240)	22,000 (if 5% HS7,700 at each septennial yield)	Abthugni PZ	(post-180)	VIII 11201 + p.2338 = *ILS* 5494; cf. *ILTun* 783
*263.	Decurionibus sportulae...et gymnasium universis civibus	12,000	Gor PZ	—	VIII 12422, cf. p.2432
264.	Quinsto (*sic*) qu[oque an]no semper uni...	11,000	Hadrumetum PB	—	*ILAf* 58
*265.	Decurionibus sportulae et populo ludi	10,000	Uchi Maius PZ	(post-230)	VIII 26275 = *ILS* 9405; cf. *AE* 1951, 81
D266.	[...] pugile[...] [gymnasium] et epulum decurionibus	4,000	Gor PZ	(post-180)	*ILTun* 769
267.	Pugiles et gymnasium, itemque decurionibus epulum	4,000 at 6%	Gor PZ	(post-180)	VIII 12421, cf. p.2432 = *ILS* 5071; cf. *ILTun* 766 & *AE* 1941, 157
D268.	Ex...usuris centesim. concuriales epulentur	2,400 at 12%	Theveste NP	(post-180)	*ILAlg* 1.3017, cf. VIII 1845, 16501 = *ILS* 6837
269.	Quodannis ob diem dedicationis epulum et [gymnasium populo?]	2,000 (? +)	Mustis PZ	—	VIII 15578, cf. p.2698

FEASTS

	Identification	Price (HS)	Town	Date	Reference
270.	Decurio[nibus item curiis omnibus?] et Augustalibus epula[to]ria	(5,000 p.a. if 5%)	Hippo Regius NP	—	= 252
271.	Epulum universis cur(i)is	5,000 (500 per curia if 10)	(Zawiet-el-Laâla) PZ	(post-200)	VIII 12434, cf. p.2434
272.	Cur(i)is singulis... ut natali eius in publico vescantur	300 per curia p.a.	Uthina PZ	117/38	= 254
273–4.	To a single curia for annual feast	288 p.a.	Theveste NP	(post-180)	= 268
275.	Epulum (universis) curialib(us), annually	(250 to each curia if 10 curiae & 5%)	Mactar PB	c. 180/92	= 255
276.	To (curiae), epulationis nomine	240 each septennially	Abthugni PZ	(post-180)	v. 262
277.	Cur[iis ut...] q[uodannis epularentur]	(225 to each of 11 curiae if 5%; HS25 annual surplus	Theveste NP	—	= 257; see p.282
278.	Curiis e[pulum]	(part of 5,000? p.a.)	Thugga PZ	193/205	v. 253
279.	In epu[lationem]	2,000 +	Uchi Maius PZ	(post-200)	VIII 26239 = *ILS* 9398
280.	Epulum decurionibus	(part of 240 p.a.)	Gor PZ	(post-180)	v. 267; cf. 266

GAMES

	Identification	Price (HS)	Town	Date	Reference
281.	Gladiators and panthers in amphitheatre	200,000 + for 4 days	Karthago PZ	c. 133/8	*ILAf* 390 = *ILS* 9406
282.	Ludi	(part of 50,000? p.a.)	Oea PT	183/5	v. 249
282a.	'Munus' (venatio at which 4 leopards were killed)	16,000	(Smirat) PB	(post-200)	*AE* 1967, 549
283.	Ludi scaenici	(8,000? for one day p.a.)	Thisi PZ	—	v. 251
284.	Ludi	6,000 for a single day	Rusicade N	—	*ILAlg* 2.42–3, cf. VIII 7990, 7991 & p.1879
285.	Ludi scaenici	(part of 5,000? p.a.)	Thugga PZ	(post-205)	v. 253
286.	Ludi	6,000 for 3 days	Siagu PZ	(post-180)	VIII 967, cf. 12448

	Identification	Price (HS)	Town	Date	Reference
287.	Circuenses (*sic*) ce[ler]es	540 semestrially	Auzia MC	—	*v.* 258
288.	Pugiles	(part of 240 p.a.)	Gor PZ	(post-180)	*v.* 267
289.	Ludi	(200–100? p.a.)	Uchi Maius PZ	(post-230)	*v.* 265

SPORTULAE

SPORTULAE AT SPECIFIED RATES PER HEAD

	Identification	Price (HS)	Town	Date	Reference
290.	Fl(amini)b(us) p(er)p(etuis) aurei singuli	100	Lambaesis N	—	*AE* 1914, 40
D291.	Denarii quini to each decurion	20 p.a.	Thisi PZ	(post-180)	*v.* 251
D292.	Denarii quini to decurions	20	Theveste NP	(post-180)	*ILAlg* 1.3072; cf. VIII 1889 & p.1576
D293.	(Denarii quini) to each decurion 'epulationis nomine'	20 septennially	Abthugni PZ	(post-180)	*v.* 262
D294.	Denarii terni to each decurion	12	Cirta N	(post-180)	VIII 19513; cf. *ILAlg* 2.688
295.	3 denarii to each decurion	12	Thugga PZ	—	Cl. Poinssot, *Mélanges J. Carcopino* (1966) 777, no.2
*296.	To wife and 2 nieces	8 semestrially	Auzia MC	—	*v.* 258
297.	Dec(urionibus) et eq(uitibus) R(omanis) victoriati terni	6	Saldae MC	(post-161)	VIII 8938, cf. p.1953 = *ILS* 5078
D298.	Sportulae denarii singuli secundum matricem public(am) civibus	4	Cirta N	(180/92?)	*ILAlg* 2.479; cf. VIII 6948 & p.1847 = *ILS* 6858
D299.	Sportulae denarii singuli	4	Kastellum Elephantum N		*ILS* 6865
D300.	To decurions and 2 clerks	4 semestrially	Auzia MC	(post-180)	*v.* 258
D301.	To decurions	4	Thuburbo Maius PZ	225	*ILAf* 271
D302.	[Epul?]onib(us) n(umero) CCC CCC denarii sing[uli]	4	Thuburbo Maius PZ	186/9	*ILAf* 266 + *AE* 1964, 44
303.	To decurions	2 on 2 occasions	Agbia PZ	138/61	*v.* 144, 174
304.	To citizens	2	Cirta N	—	*ILAlg* 2.688; cf. VIII 19513

	Identification	Price (HS)	Town	Date	Reference
*D305.	Reliquis (HS4,000) omnibus civibus n(ummum) HS dividi volo	1	Siagu PZ	(post-180)	VIII 967, cf. 12448

OTHER SPORTULA DISTRIBUTIONS

	Identification	Price (HS)	Town	Date	Reference
306.	Pudentilla…in populum expunxisset	50,000	Oea PT	154/5	*Apol.* 87
D307.	Curiis denarii quingeni	2,000 per curia	Thagaste NP	(post-180)	*ILAlg* 1.876; cf. VIII 5146 & p.1634
D308.	Curiis singulis denarii quinquageni	200 to each of 11 curiae	Thuburbo Maius PZ	225	v. 301 (cf. *ILTun* 728)
309.	Sportul(ae) decurionib. et lib(ertis) Caes(aris) N(ostri) itemq. forensibus et amicis curiis quoque et Augustalibus aurei bini	200 to each group (?)	Theveste NP	—	*ILAlg* 1.3064; cf. VIII 16556 = *ILS* 6839
310.	Corpori quoque Augustalium ad sportulas aurei bini	200	Hippo Regius NP	—	*Libyca* 2 (1954) 394
311.	To each curia	120	Verecunda N	213	v. 109
D312.	Curiis item dendrophoris denarii XX	80	Thamugadi N	(post-180)	*AE* 1954, 154
313.	Bequest for sportulae to citizens	(part of 50,000? p.a.)	Oea PT	183/5	v. 249
314.	Divisiones decurionibus	(2,500 p.a.)	Sufes PB	(post-150)	v. 256
315.	To decurions	(part of 5,000? p.a.)	Thugga PZ	193/205	v. 253
316.	(To decurions of pagus?)	(1,250? p.a.)	Thugga PZ	(pre-205)	v. 261
317.	To decurions of civitas	(1,250? p.a.)	Thugga PZ	185/92	v. 260
318.	To decurions	(400? p.a.)	Uchi Maius PZ	(post-230)	v. 265
319-20.	To decurions	(part of 600? p.a.)	Gor PZ	—	v. 263

CAPITAL PAYMENTS TO CITIES

	Identification	Price (HS)	Town	Date	Reference
321.	Ad tutelam aquae	200,000	Sabratha PT	(112/17)	*IRT* 117; *Libya antiqua* 1 (1964) 21–42
322.	Ad opus munificentiae	100,000	Thagaste NP	(post-180)	*ILAlg* 1.876; cf. VIII 5146 & p.1634

	Identification	Price (HS)	Town	Date	Reference
*322a.	[In]ter cetera municipio...[le]gavit	100,000 (?)	Thibiuca PZ	—	VIII 14293
323.	[Reipu]bl. praesentibus	50,000	Thugga PZ	264	*ILTun* 1416
*323a.	Bequest of HS10,000 (gross)	9,500 (net)	Thugga PZ	*c.* 83/110	Cl. Poinssot, *BAC* n.s.5 (1969) 239; 230

INDIVIDUAL SUMS PAID OR SPENT IN HONOUR OF OFFICE

	Identification	Price (HS)	Town	Date	Reference
324.	Ob honor. aed(ilitatis)	90,000	Karthago PZ	114	*ILAf* 384
325.	Ob honor. flam(onii) ...praesentia	82,000	Rusicade N	(217/22?)	*ILAlg* 2.10; cf. VIII 7963, 19849 & p.967 = *ILS* 5473
326.	Ob honorem pont[ificatus]	55,000	Rusicade N	—	*ILAlg* 2.34; cf. VIII 7983–4 & p.1879
327.	Ob honor. aedilitat(is)	50,000	Karthago PZ	(post-161)	VIII 24640
328.	[Ob ho]norem...	50,000	Karthago PZ	—	VIII 24644
329.	...inib(i) legitim(a) ob honor. augurat(us)	34,000	Rusicade N	—	*ILAlg* 2.42–3; cf. VIII 7990 = *ILS* 6861; VIII 7991 & p.1879
330.	Ob honorem auguratus	21,200	Thamugadi N	198/211	VIII 17837
331.	[Inlati]s aerario (ob. honor. decurionatus?)	20,000	Theveste NP	180/2	*ILAlg* 1.3032; cf. VIII 16530 & p.2731
332.	[Prae]ter HS XX quae[...]	20,000	Cirta N	—	*BAC* (1905) cxcv n.4
332a.	Pro honore flamon(i)i perp...(taxavit)	10,000	Mustis PZ	138/45	*AE* 1968, 595
332b.	Ob [honor. flam. perp.] in opus munificentiae (promisit)	10,000	Mustis PZ	117	*AE* 1968, 586
333.	Ob honorem flam(onii) (put towards the cost of a privately financed temple)	10,000	Mustis PZ	164/5	VIII 15576; *v.* 9 above
333a.	Ob honorem fl. perp... (taxavit)	10,000	Mustis PZ	217/18	*AE* 1968, 591
334.	Ob honorem flamon(i)i (put towards the cost of a privately financed arch)	10,000	Capsa PB	119/38	VIII 98, cf. pp.1172 & 2349; *v.* 34 above
334a.	Ob honorem flam. perp. taxatis	10,000	Mustis PZ	116	*AE* 1968, 599

	Identification	Price (HS)	Town	Date	Reference
335.	[Ob ho]norem flam(onii)	10,000	Thuburbo Maius PZ	138/65	VIII 853 & 12370; cf. *AE* 1942/3, 102 & *ILTun* 692
336.	Honoraria summa et eo amplius r(ei) p(ublicae) inlatis	8,000	Lambaesis N	208	VIII 2711, cf. p.1739
336a.	Ob honorem q(uin)q(uennalitatis)	6,000	Bulla Regia PZ	198/9	Unpublished
337.	Ob honorem auguratus inlatis super legitimam	6,000	Thamugadi N	202/11	*AE* 1941, 49
338.	Ob honorem flamon(i)i (put towards the cost of a privately financed temple)	4,000	Numluli PZ	170	VIII 26121; *v.* 17 above
339.	Legitimam pollicitationemve	4,000	Thamugadi N	198/211	*AE* 1901, 191
339a.	Inlatis aerario	3,000	Mustis PZ	138/45	*AE* 1968, 595
339b.	Et ob honor(em) IIvir(atus)	2,000	Mustis PZ	138/45	*AE* 1968, 595
339c.	Et ob honor(em) IIvir(atus)	2,000	Mustis PZ	117	*AE* 1968, 586
340.	Ob [hon]orem flamon(i)i	1,000	Sutunurca PZ	162	*ILAf* 303
341.	Amplius	1,000	Verecunda N	—	VIII 4194, cf. 18490 = *ILS* 6852

LEGACIES TO SINGLE CURIAE

	Identification	Price (HS)	Town	Date	Reference
*342.	Ad remunerandos curiales curiae Aeliae	10,000	Neapolis PZ	(post-180)	VIII 974, cf. p.1282 = *ILS* 6828
*343.	Curiae [Caeles]tiae	10,000	Simitthus PZ	—	VIII 14613 = *ILS* 6825
D*344.	To 2 curiae, divided equally, for celebration of commemorative rites annually for not less than 5 years	2,000	Simitthus PZ	—	*AE* 1955, 126

SUMMAE HONORARIAE

	Identification	Price (HS)	Town	Date	Reference
345.	Decurionate	[2]0,000	Cirta N	—	*ILAlg* 2.529; cf. VIII 19489
345a.	Decurionate	20,000	Rusicade N	—	*ILAlg* 2.10; 34; cf. VIII 7963, 19849, 7983, 7984 & pp.967, 1879; cf. *ILS* 5473

	Identification	Price (HS)	Town	Date	Reference
346.	Decurionate	4,000	Thubursicu Numidarum NP	(post-180)	*ILAlg* 1.1236
347.	Decurionate	1,600	Muzuc PB	(post-180)	VIII 12058
348.	Decurionate	400 (? +)	(Munchar) PZ	161/9	VIII 25468; cf. *ILTun* 1221
349.	Aedileship	20,000	Cirta N	—	*ILAlg* 2.473; 562; cf. VIII 6944, 6996 & p.1847
350.	Aedileship	20,000	Rusicade N	—	*ILAlg* 2.42–3; cf. VIII 7990 = *ILS* 6861; VIII 7991 & p.1879
351.	Aedileship	5,000	Auzia MC	194/6	VIII 9024, cf. p.1960
352.	Aedileship	4,000	Theveste NP	—	*ILAlg* 1.3007; cf. VIII 1842
353.	Aedileship	4,000	Thubursicu Numidarum NP	(post-180)	*ILAlg* 1.1223; cf. VIII 4874 = *ILS* 2116; *ILAlg* 1.1236
354.	IIvirate	5,000	Bulla Regia PZ	208/10	*ILAf* 451
355.	IIvirate	4,000	Cuicul N	—	*AE* 1914, 237
356.	IIvirate	2,000	Thamugadi N	—	*BAC* (1893) 157, no.27
357.	IIIvirate	20,000	Cirta N	203, 210, 212	*ILAlg* 2.562; 569; 473; cf. VIII 6996, 7000, 19418, 6944 & p.1847
358.	Undecimprimate	4,000	(Hr. Debbik) PZ	182	VIII 14791 = *ILS* 6808; cf. *ILTun* 1283
359.	Sufeteship	800	Themetra PB	138/61	*AE* 1946, 234
360.	Quinquennalitas	38,000	Karthago PZ	133/8	*ILAf* 390 = *ILS* 9406
361.	Quinquennalitas	20,000	Cirta N	212/17	*ILAlg* 2.675; cf. VIII 7095, 19435 = *ILS* 2933
362.	Quinquennalitas (or flaminate?)	10,000	Ammaedara PB	193/211	*ILTun* 460
363.	Quinquennalitas	10,000	Hippo Regius NP	117/38	*ILAlg* 1.10; cf. VIII 17408
364.	Quinquennalitas	3,000	Thuburbo Maius PZ	139/46	*ILTun* 714
365.	Flaminate	12,000	Lambaesis N	208, etc.	VIII 2711, cf. p.1739; *AE* 1914, 40. *PBSR* 30 (1962) 67

	Identification	Price (HS)	Town	Date	Reference
366.	Flaminate	12,000	Uchi Maius PZ	197	VIII 26255 = *ILS* 9401
366a.	Flaminate	10,000	Thamugadi N	167/9 (?)	*AE* 1968, 647
367.	Flaminate	10,000	Diana N	164/5, 197	VIII 4588; 4594, cf. 18649
368.	Flaminate	6,000	(Hr. Sidi Navi) PB	196	VIII 23107
369.	Flaminate	6,000	Avedda PZ	196	VIII 14370
370.	Flaminate	6,000	Thubursicum Numidarum NP	(post-180)	*ILAlg* 1.1236
370a.	Flaminate	5,000	Mustis PZ	217/18	*AE* 1968, 591
371–3.	Flaminate	4,000	Sutunurca PZ	146	*ILAf* 300 cf. 303
374.	Flaminate	2,000	Medeli PZ	195/211	VIII 885, cf. 12387 & p.2427 = *ILS* 6803
375.	Flaminate	2,000	Verecunda N	213, etc.	VIII 4187; 4202, cf. 18494; 4193; 4243; 4194, cf. 18490 = *ILS* 6852
376.	Flaminate	2,000	(Hr. es-Shorr) PB	(post-180)	VIII 11998 = *ILS* 5072; cf. *ILTun* 610
377.	Flaminate	1,000	Sarra PB	211/12	VIII 12006, cf. p.2397
378.	Augurate	10,000	Sabratha PT	230/1	*IRT* 43
379–80.	Pontificate	10,000	Cirta N	88/139	*ILAlg* 2.671, cf. VIII 7079 & p.1848 = *ILS* 5549

BULLION

381.	Argenteum in kapitolio	312,000	Cirta N	—	*ILAlg* 2.538, VIII 6983–4 and pp.965, 1847
*382.	[Datasque a]d kapitol(ium) arg(enti) lib(ras) CLXX... auri lib(ras) XIIII (in the form of dishes and vessels)	(206,000 bullion value)	Theveste NP	214	*v.* 32 & 250

FORTUNE SIZES

383.	Aemilia Pudentilla, a widow	4 million	Oea PT	*c.* 158/9	*Apol.* 77
384.	Herennius Rufinus, father-in-law of elder son of preceding; a knight	3 million	Oea PT	*c.* 158/9	*Apol.* 75

	Identification	Price (HS)	Town	Date	Reference
385.	Father of Apuleius 'duumviralem cunctis honoribus perfunctum'	2 million (?+)	Madauros NP	*c.* 120/50	*Apol.* 23–4
386.	Apuleius	1 million	Madauros NP	*c.* 150/7	*Apol.* 23
386a.	Dowry of daughter of Herennius Rufinus (no.384)	400,000	Oea PT	*c.* 158/9	*Apol.* 92
386b.	Dowry of Pudentilla when re-marrying (no.383)	300,000	Oea PT	*c.* 158/9	*Apol.* 92

LAND COSTS

	Identification	Price (HS)	Town	Date	Reference
387.	At oasis whose soil supported olives, figs, vines, pomegranates, corn, pulse & vegetables, yielding twice-yearly	16 per square of 4 short cubits (approx. 50,000 per iugerum)	Tacape PT	pre-79	Pliny *NH* 18.188
388.	Exiguum herediolum	60,000	Oea PT	*c.* 150/9	*Apol.* 101

GRAIN

	Identification	Price (HS)	Town	Date	Reference
D389.	10,000 modii of wheat as a gift to the city at a time of famine	40 per modius	Thuburnica PZ	(post-180)	VIII 25703–4; cf. *AE* 1951, 81
*390.	Sodalibus suis posterisque eorum	12 modii per man p.a.	Madauros NP	—	*ILAlg* 1.2233

MINOR OBJECTS AND OUTLAYS

	Identification	Price (HS)	Town	Date	Reference
391.	Dextri (*sic*) duo	4,000+	Rusicade N	—	*ILAlg* 2.42–3; cf. VIII 7990–1 & p.1879
392.	(Statue base)	500	Tiddis N	(pre-200)	*ILAlg* 2.3606
393.	Statue base	400	Sigus N	(post-217)	*v.* 186
394.	Marble vat measuring 1.04 × 0.81 × 0.51m	200	Cirta N	—	*ILAlg* 2.491; cf. VIII 6970 (Louvre no.2020)
D395.	Palma argentea	100	Thuburbo Maius PZ	—	*ILAf* 256
D396.	Palma argentea	40	Thuburbo Maius PZ	—	*ILTun* 709
D397.	Ad custod(em) ita ut statuam meam et (statuam) uxoris meae tergeat et unguat et coronet et cer(eos) II accendat	12 on 2 days per year	Auzia MC	—	*v.* 258

FRAGMENTS AND UNIDENTIFIED OUTLAYS

	Identification	Price (HS)	Town	Date	Reference
398.	—	200,000	Cirta N	—	*ILAlg* 2.681; cf. VIII 7135
398a.	—	200,000	Abbir Cella PZ	264/8	*ILAf* 222
399.	Iuppiter Maximus	100,000 (? +) 226,(000?)	Utica PZ	—	*ILTun* 1176
400.	(From portico of temple of Caelestis)	60,000 & 30,000	Thugga PZ	222/35	VIII 26458; cf. *ILAf* 514
400a.	Genius municipii	50,000	Satafi MC	—	VIII 8389, cf. p.1909
400b.	Gift by Attidius	50,000	Althiburos PB	(post-180)	VIII 27784; cf. 16474
401.	List of nine sums	50,000–5,000	Karthago PZ	—	*ILTun* 1070
402.	—	42,000(? +)	Karthago PZ	Jan. 98	*ILAf* 363
D403.	—	28,000	Tichilla PZ	276/82	VIII 14891
404–5.	—	23,500	Sabratha PT	—	*IRT* 116
406.	—	16,000	Althiburos PB	—	VIII 1830, cf. 16468
407.	—	12,080	Thamugadi N	—	VIII 17914
D408.	...ad quod opus sola *tria milia a fisco accepta sunt (cf. nos.1336a–38)	12,000 +	Simitthus PZ	—	VIII 14590
409.	—	10,000	Lambaesis N	—	*BAC* (1954) 168
410.	—	10,000 (? +)	Cuicul N	—	*PBSR* 30 (1962) 109 n.114
411–12.	—	10,000	Lepcis Magna PT	—	*IRT* 789
413.	—	5,000	Calama NP	—	VIII 17531; cf. *ILAlg* 1.309
414.	—	4,000 +	Chidibbia PZ	—	VIII 1344, cf. 14872
415.	—	4,000 +	Sicilibba PZ	—	VIII 25823
416.	—	4,000	Verecunda N	—	VIII 4253, cf. p.1769
417–18.	—	3,200	Celtianis N	—	*ILAlg* 2.2109
419.	(Connected with baths built by Memmia...Fidiana)	3,000?	Bulla Regia PZ	193/211	*ILAf* 454b
420.	List of figures	2,272/21	Simitthus PZ	—	VIII 25643
421–2.	List of figures	2,000	Lambaesis N	—	*Musée de Lambèse* I 123
423.	List of payments	600/300 (?000)	Karthago PZ	—	VIII 24615
424–5.	List of payments	120/49.5	Karthago PZ	—	*ILTun* 896
426.	List of at least 31 payments	8/0.5	Tiddis N	—	*ILAlg* 2.3624

COLLEGE PROVISIONS AND STIPULATIONS

	Identification	Price (HS)	Town	Date	Reference
	LEX CURIAE IOVIS				
D427.	Si quis pro patre et matre pro socrum [pr]o socra[m], [d](are) d(ebebit)	20	Simitthus PZ	185	VIII 14683 = *ILS* 6824
D428.	I[t]em qu[i] propin[q](u)us decesserit, d(are) d(ebebit)	16	Simitthus PZ	185	VIII 14683 = *ILS* 6824
D429.	Si quis flamini male dixerit aut manus iniecerit, d(are) d(ebebit)	[12]	Simitthus PZ	185	VIII 14683 = *ILS* 6824
D430.	[Si quis quaestor (esse voluerit), d(are)] d(ebebit)	8	Simitthus PZ	185	VIII 14683 = *ILS* 6824
D431.	[S]i quis de propinquis decesserit at miliarium VI et cui nuntiatur non ierit, d(are) d(ebebit)	8	Simitthus PZ	185	VIII 14683 = *ILS* 6824
D432.	Si qu(a)estor alicui non n[u]ntiaverit, d(are) d(ebebit)	4	Simitthus PZ	185	VIII 14683 = *ILS* 6824
433.	Si quis flam[en e]sse volue[rit], d(are) d(ebebit)	3 amphorae of wine (78 litres) 'p[raeterea] pane et sale et ci[baria]'	Simitthus PZ	185	VIII 14683 = *ILS* 6824
434.	Si quis magister [esse voluerit, d(are) d(ebebit)]	2 amphorae of wine (52 litres)	Simitthus PZ	185	VIII 14683 = *ILS* 6824
435.	Si magister questori imp[e]raverit et non fecerit, d(are) d(ebebit)	1 amphora of wine	Simitthus PZ	185	VIII 14683 = *ILS* 6824
436.	Si in concilium pr(a)esens non venerit, d(are) d(ebebit) c(ongium?) [Schmidt]	1/40th? of an amphora of wine (0.64 litres)	Simitthus PZ	185	VIII 14683 = *ILS* 6824

Identification	Price (HS)	Town	Date	Reference
LEX COLLEGII INCERTI				
D437. [D]at vini	HS4	Karthago PZ	—	VIII 12574
438. Dat vini (bis)	1 amphora (25.79 litres)	Karthago PZ	—	VIII 12574

NOTES

1. For this temple see *AAA* fe.27, 222–4, no.21; Gsell *Monuments* 1.145 (the peribolos measures 75 by 35 metres).

3. The temple (excluding peribolos) measures 7.9 × 15.3 metres (unpublished survey by L. Catanuso, 1946, kindly communicated by M. H. Ballance).

4. Dated to 185/92 by L. Poinssot *NAM* 18 (1910) 95. Poinssot *Dougga* no.5.

5. The cost of the temple was first assessed as HS50,000, and finally reached a sum not less than HS100,000 (the inscription contains a lacuna). CG 82–5+pl.25–7; Poinssot *Dougga* no.26+pl.18; Picard *Religions* 158.

6. For the building see R. Thouvenot *Volubilis* (1949) 37–8. The figure which is incomplete consists of a $\overline{C}$ with space for three more digits (photograph in *Hespéris* 7 (1927) 367). The total might thus have been as much as HS400,000 (rather than the maximum of HS300,000 suggested by Chatelain in *ILM* 45). The larger figure might not be disproportionate as the cost of the Capitol of an important town, but the actual total is quite uncertain.

10. The figure refers to the cost of extensive rebuilding on the site of an earlier and smaller temple: 'templum modicum antiqua vet[ust]ate dilapsum ampliato spatio columnis et regiis duabus picturis ornatum pecunia sua ex HS $\overline{\text{LXVII}}$ mil. $\overline{\text{D}}$ n. a solo coeptum perfecit...'.

10a. For identification and photographs of the temple, S. Tourrenc *Ant.afr.* 2 (1968) 199–209.

11. Leschi's restorations of this inscription are not altogether satisfactory, but the temple cost which they suggest (HS63,000 or HS113,000) appears to be correct.

12. A series of additions to this temple whose cost is not known were made at a slightly later date, and the basic construction cost must have been substantially more than HS50,000. VIII 26470+*ILTun* 1391; Poinssot *Dougga* no.16; Picard *Religions* 160. One of the donors, A. Gabinius Datus filius, was an *eques* and *iudex* (R. Duncan-Jones *PBSR* 35 (1967) 173, no.96).

14. The promise of this temple was executed by T. Iulius Sabinus [Victorianus], procurator of the regio Leptiminensis (Pflaum 950 and nn.13–16).

15. Since the temple of Fortune (no.8) built in 119/38 slightly infringes its entrance, the temple of Pietas is probably somewhat earlier, Trajanic or even Flavian (photograph *NAM* 12 (1904) 408; L. Poinssot *loc. cit.* 408 suggests a possible Hadrianic date). Poinssot *Dougga* no.3+pl.6; F. Benoit *L'Afrique méditerranéenne* (1931) pl.29.

16. This temple was built by subscription, an unusual arrangement for public buildings; most of the contributions were between HS2,000 and HS2,400, though the list is incomplete. CG 104–5+pl.28–9. A more explicit account of a temple built by subscription in *ILS* 5466 (Philippi). Cf. also notes on nos.443 and 493.

17. CG 6–8+pl.5–6; F. Benoit *L'Afrique méditerrané enne*(1931) pl.56. The Numluli temple is the smallest of the 11 Capitolia whose dimensions are given by Cagiano de Azevedo (M. Cagiano de Azevedo *Atti Pont. Acc. Rom. Arch.: Mem.* 5 (1941) 1–76 at 74; for 'lungh. m.4.14' read 'lungh. m.14.14').

18. L. A. Constans *NAM* 14 (1916) 48–51 + pl.2 & 7. This study was reprinted as *Gigthis. Études d'histoire et d'archéologie sur un emporium de la petite Syrte* (1916).
20. The temple is circular, and measures 7 metres in diameter (S. Gsell *BAC* (1917) 314). For other circular temples of Saturn in Africa, J. Toutain *BAC* (1919) 221–4.
21. CG 19–20.
26. CG 66–9 + pl.19–21. The temple is quite sizeable despite the small sum originally promised (HS3,000), which is the only information about its cost.
27. See above pp.77–8.
30. The two inscriptions referring to these baths appear to be respectively foundation stone and final dedication; if so their dates indicate a construction time of 17½ months. No remains are known, but Mastar, one of the castella of Cirta, was probably a small community. The total area of remains extant at the beginning of the century (without excavation) was 6 hectares (*Recueil* 40 (1907) 258–9).
31. The two inscriptions here are similar to those in no.30: they are dated to adjacent years, they show an outlay of HS100,000, and they come from a small community in Numidia. It has been tentatively conjectured here that they also indicate the construction of a set of baths financed by the town. No deity is mentioned in the inscriptions.
32. This quadrifrontal arch together with two tetrastyles cost HS250,000. If the tetrastyles cost HS30,000 each (see nos.93 and 94) the arch by itself would have cost HS190,000. A quadrifrontal arch at Lepcis (no.32a) cost more than HS120,000. For the inscription, S. Accame *Epigraphica* 3 (1941) 237–43. For the building, Gsell *Monuments* 1.180–5 + pl.43; J. Meunier *RAf* 82 (1938) 84–107; V. Ciotti *BCAR* App. 15 (1946/8) 21–42.
38. BCB 297–304 + figs.140–2 + pl.38; H. Pfeiffer *Mem.Amer.Acad.Rome* 9 (1931) 157–66 + pl.16–19 (giving restorations of the building). The ground plan measures roughly 25 by 30 metres. The donor, who bequeathed funds for the building, was a senator, M. Iulius Quintianus Flavius Rogatianus (*PIR*² I 510; cf. *PIR*¹ I 339 for a possible mention in an inscription from Ionia). For city libraries, R. Cagnat *Mém.Inst.Acad.Insc.* 38 (1909) 1–26
42. Gsell–Joly 'Mdaourouch' 57–73 + figs.9–12 + pl.1, 17.
45. L. Carton *Recueil* 39 (1906) 61–5 with 4 plates; Poinssot *Dougga* no.11 + pl.6. Poinssot suggests that the building (whose function is uncertain) was a temple.
52. The inscription and an account of the building in BCB 317–19 + figs.148–50. For the donor, P. Iulius Liberalis, a priest of the province, see R. Duncan-Jones *Epigraphische Studien* 5 (1968) 157.
53. Picard *Civilisation* pl.19.
61. The donor, M. Coculnius Quintillianus, was adlected to the Senate by Septimius Severus *c.* A.D. 195, after holding all the municipal *honores* at Cirta (*ILS* 6857; *PIR*² C 1234).
63. G. Caputo *Il Teatro di Sabratha* (1959) tav.90; G. Caputo in *Enciclopedia dello Spettacolo* (S. d'Amico ed.) 6.1410–11 + tav.191.
64. HS41,200 was subscribed for mosaics by some of the decurions; the remainder of the restoration cost was contributed from town funds. The size of these baths is not known. Public baths built nearby at Thugga, also under Gallienus, contained roughly 600–700 square metres of mosaic (cf. Poinssot *Dougga* no.15 + pl.11, 12, 13 + fig.5; L. Poinssot, R. Lantier *BAC* (1925) xxix–xxxi). If the two buildings were of comparable size, the mosaic cost might be of the order of HS70 per square metre.
66. The city added a quadriga whose cost is not known to the decorations of the arch contributed by the relations of the original donor, which cost HS25,000. For the weight of a silver quadriga, see no.513.
78. Leschi points out that the dedication to the Genius coloniae from which this gift is known is not itself mentioned as part of the outlay (Leschi 229). But since the base on which it is engraved is too shallow to have been used as the support for a statue, its cost was probably a negligible part of the total outlay, recorded as HS50,000 (statue bases cost sums of the order of HS400 and 500; see nos.392–3).

80. These statues worth HS30,000, two statues worth over HS6,000 (no.189), the basilica Iulia at Cuicul whose price is not known, and half of the price of an arch costing HS30,000 (no.36) were given by the same donor: C. Iulius Crescens Didius Crescentianus, an *eques* of the reign of Marcus Aurelius who served one of the *militiae* (R. Duncan-Jones *PBSR* 35 (1967) 170 no.57).

82. For the cost of workmanship as a proportion of the cost of a silver statue, see p.126.

92. HS12,000 of the cost of the statue was provided by the city, the remainder by the private donor (cf. nos.1335–8; 408).

109. This statue costing HS9,000 was given by three donors, who perhaps contributed equal amounts of HS3,000 (cf. no.138a). At the dedication the decurions received 'sportulae duplae', a phrase which implies that there was a standard rate (perhaps HS4 per head, the commonest single rate in both Africa and Italy, nos.290–305; 818–1051). The *curiae* were also given payments of HS120 each. This low payment perhaps points to *curiae* at Verecunda, a former *vicus*, of smaller size than those attested at more important towns; a *curia* at Thamugadi had fifty-two members in A.D. 211/12 (see pp.281–2).

124. A false duplicate of this inscription appears as VIII 5295 (rescinded in VIII p.1685). Liebenam inferred a payment of over 600,000 from the figure, which is stated as $\overline{VICXL}$ (Liebenam 57), but the context, the construction of a statue in celebration of office makes clear that the figure is only 6,000 odd. Confusion arose in the use of the supralineate bar for numerals, because it could either indicate that the numeral was multiplied by one thousand, or that the symbol below it was a numeral and not a letter (as in '$\overline{II}$VIRO' *ILAlg* 1.1295). Other ambiguities: '$\overline{IIID}$' where the context indicates a relatively small sum, which must be read as 3,500 (no.404); '$\overline{IDCCC}$' as part of the cost of an ordinary statue must mean 1,800, not 799,000 (no.160). Cf. A. E. Gordon *Univ.Calif. Publications in Class. Archaeology* 2.3 (1948) 111–12.

138a. This statue was erected from a bequest of HS8,000, from which the 5% inheritance tax was subtracted, leaving 7,600, to which 3,000 was added by three freedmen of the donor, presumably each contributing 1,000.

221. For this tomb, whose ground plan measures 3 metres square, see L. Renier *Revue archéologique* 7 (1850) 186–7.

248. Given by P. Licinius Papirianus, *a rationibus* under Marcus Aurelius (*PIR²* L 229).

249. Part of a bequest under Commodus by L. Aemilius Frontinus, proconsul of Asia, which also included a temple dedicated to the Genius of Oea, which would have brought the value of his gift to well over HS1 million. *PIR²* A 348.

250. The total value of this gift was probably more than HS700,000, its other components being nos.32 and 382. It was bequeathed by C. Cornelius Egrilianus, *praef. legionis*, in A.D. 214. See note on no.263.

251. The main figure is stated thus: '...[HS]...IN LEGAVIT ITA VT EX[usuri]s SESTERTI-ORVM DVGENTORVM MIL...' Mommsen's inference (*CIL ad loc.*) that the second figure represents the income results in a capital sum (*c*. HS4 million) which is unparalleled for perpetual foundations in the West; moreover Thisi is not known to have been an important town. Schmidt's interpretation (*CIL ad loc.*) which makes 200,000 the amount of the capital is clearly correct. His view can be supported by the wording of an Italian inscription: '...qui decies centena millia num. dedit ita ut per sing. annos ex sestertiorum cccc usuris populo epulum natali...divideretur...' (nos.643; 648). The Thisi gift was evidently worth more than HS200,000, but its total is not clear.

258. The amount of the capital is not stated in the surviving part of the inscription, but a series of charges are listed which may give a complete account of the disposition of the income (see nos.296; 300; 287; 397; total HS1,968 per year if there were 100 decurions). The statement of the interest-rate is eccentric: '...quae s[u]mm(ae) fenerantur n(ummis) xx menses quosque asses octonos'. The interest refers to the payment due on a notional capital of 100 denarii or HS400, but the two coordinates are out of line: HS20 per year

equals only 6.66 asses per month, while 8 asses per month equals 24 sesterces per year. Billeter avoided the difficulty by simply emending the figure for sesterces to 24 (thus assuming with little plausibility that four symbols had dropped out of the text, since 4 was usually depicted as 'IIII'; Billeter 226). Mommsen preferred to accept the coordinates as they stood, deducing that a notional 10-month year was being employed, for which there is evidence in the early Republic (*CIL ad loc.*) This at least has the merit of bringing the coordinates as stated into line with each other. Billeter's interpretation (followed by Gsell *ILAlg* 1.3017 and Haywood *ESAR* 4.80) gives an interest-rate of 6%, Mommsen's a rate of 5%. A third possibility (for which the writer is indebted to Mr M. H. Crawford) would be to infer that the coinages were in fact out of line with each other, and that at Auzia HS20 equalled 96 asses (8 × 12) instead of 80 asses as the normal relationship (HS1 = 4 asses) would entail. This would give a relationship of 19.2 asses to the denarius. There are examples in Asia of the denarius being worth as much as 18 or 17 asses in market exchanges of bronze for silver (cf. M. H. Crawford *JRS* 60 (1970) 43). There is no clear parallel for a valuation of the denarius as high as 19.2 asses (cf. J. R. Melville Jones *Bull.Inst.Class.Stud.* 18 (1971) 99–105). The second and third interpretations both point to an interest-rate of 5%, which seems the most likely rate. However the coordinates are reconciled, the notation in sesterces ('nummi') can probably be taken at face value, indicating a rate of 5%. On this basis, the implied capital value is HS39,360, suggesting an actual capital of HS40,000, which left a small residue. (Alternatively, some minor provision might be lacking from the surviving text.)

259. The amount of the capital is missing, but the revenue was intended to provide a single day of games each year. At the dedication of the monument from which the text comes, three days of games costing HS6,000 in all were to be celebrated, the residue of HS4,000 being distributed among the citizens at the rate per HS1 per head. If the cost of the annual games were the same, the revenue needed would be HS2,000 per year, which would require a capital of HS40,000 if the interest were 5% (cf. no.258, a similar capital sum whose interest was evidently 5%). The total value of the gift on this basis would be HS50,000 (not including the cost of the monument from which the inscription comes, which is unknown).

260. See note on no.261.

261. This fragmentary inscription seems to show a foundation of HS25,000 for the distribution of sportulae to the decurions of the *pagus* at Thugga. If so, it may be a companion donation to no.260, a foundation of the same value for sportulae for the decurions of the *pagus* at Thugga, given by Q. Pacuvius Saturus and Nahania Victoria. These donors gave sportulae to the decurions of both communities at the dedication of their temple of Mercury (no.4). For the double community at Thugga, cf. p.73 n.4.

262. According to the inscription the foundation had a capital of HS22,000 which was intended to provide in every seventh or sixth year ('septimo quoque anno' is ambiguous, see note on no.264) a new statue of the donor costing HS3,200, together with sportulae of HS20 each for the decurions, and HS240 each for the *curiales*. The last figure is far too high to be credible as the text stands. The highest popular sportula attested in Africa is only HS4 per head (no.298); while Mommsen's suggestion that the donor was favouring members of the single *curia* to which he himself belonged is not supported by the text, and there are no parallels for subversion of precedence on such a massive scale. But HS240 is close to the amount allowed per *curia* for benefits at other towns: HS300 at Uthina, HS288 and HS225 at Theveste, probably HS250 at Mactar (see p.281). If the Abthugni text is emended to read '*curiis*', almost all the income can be accounted for effectively. If the interest-rate were 5%, the yield septennial, the number of *curiae* 10 (cf. p.282) and the number of decurions 100 (cf. p.283) the terms would work out as follows. The income is HS7,700, of which the statue absorbs HS3,200, the decurions HS2,000, and the *curiae* HS2,400. This accounts for all but HS100 of the income, a

residue of 1.3%. None of the other possible permutations of frequency, interest-rate and *ordo*-size produces a number of *curiae* that is attested elsewhere, or such a small residue. (Toller conjectured that the distribution was annual, and that only the statue was septennial; but on this basis even if the interest were 12% and the *ordo* as small as 30 (see p.284) there would still only be enough money for 6.6 curiae, an implausible total; Toller 28 and 98.)

263. Another foundation at Gor provided HS240 per year to cover a feast for the decurions. boxing and an oil-distribution (to the citizens) (no.267). Such a meagre provision for three purposes suggests that there was a miniature *ordo* at Gor, probably 30 decurions (cf. p.284). The present provision for sportulae for the decurions and oil for all the citizens would have amounted to HS720 at the interest-rate of 6% (attested at Gor in no.267). If 30 decurions received HS4 per head, the sportula most often attested for this rank in Africa (nos. 290–305), the residue for oil-distribution would be HS600. This is considerably higher than the daily average provided by a foundation at Theveste, a much larger town in Numidia Proconsularis (no.250). The daily allowance at Theveste was probably only HS195 per day, if the interest was 5% (almost inevitable in a foundation as large as HS250,000, cf. pp.134–5); but this fund provided for 64 distributions per year, compared with only one distribution from the fund at Gor. (For 'gymnasium' meaning oil-distribution cf. S. Lancel *Libyca* 6 (1958) 143–52.)

264. 'Quinto quoque anno' may mean either every 4 or every 5 years, in literary sources (cf. C. L. Howard *Classical Quarterly* 52 (1958) 1–11). For present purposes, it has been assumed that the higher figure should be inferred in the few cases where such a usage occurs in inscriptions (nos.262, 264, 643). The present foundation evidently provided for a distribution of some kind to 'univ[ersis civibus]' or 'univ[ersis curiis]'. Since the yield was only every 5 (or 4) years the capital is comparable with a normal capital of HS55,000–44,000 (cf. nos.255 and 257). Nevertheless, the total HS11,000 ('$\overline{\text{XI}}$') remains irregular and unusual. It is possible (subject to re-reading of the inscription) that the true total was '$\overline{\text{XL}}$' or 40,000.

281. The cost of gladiatorial *munera* was sometimes offset by box-office returns: see p.149 n.7. Figures quoted for expenditure probably represent the gross and not the net cost, in cases where there was any difference between the two.

282a. The price actually paid for the *venatio* was HS16,000, though the sum asked by the herald on behalf of the *venatores* was only half of this amount (500 denarii per leopard killed).

286. The same budgeting for games is found in the Caesarian charter at Urso in Spain (HS2,000 per day, *ILS* 6087, 70). The Siagu gift probably belongs to the second century A.D.

290. The account of the sportulae in this distribution is: 'fl(aminibus) p(er)p(etuis) aureis singulis et honor(ibus) functis duplis et cond(ecurionibus) sed et curial(ibus) sportulis datis'. Another Lambaesis inscription contains part of the same formula: 'datis sportulis condecurionibus suis et honorib(us) functis duplis' (VIII 2711, reign of Severus). An inscription of the reign of Caracalla from the nearby town of Verecunda mentions 'sportulae duplae' (no.109 and note). When referred to in this way, the 'sportula' might be HS4, the commonest rate in Africa and Italy, and the double rate would thus be HS8 (cf. nos.290–305; 818–1051).

302. See p.283 n.7.

305. For the demographic implications of this gift, see pp.264–5.

307. M. Amullius Optatus Crementianus, an *eques*, paid for a building costing HS300,000 at Thagaste (no.39), as well as giving the *curiae* the large sum of HS2,000 each (for smaller payments to the *curiae* see nos.271–8; 308; 311).

330. For arguments against reading this payment as a *summa honoraria*, see R. Duncan-Jones *PBSR* 30 (1962) 66; 112, n.152.

345a. See p.86 n.6.

381. The figure of HS412,000 may be a valuation of the treasure in the incomplete list from Cirta which starts 'Synopsis Iovis Victor in kapitolio' (*ILAlg* 2.483); or it may refer to other bullion in the Cirta Capitol.

394. The volume of marble used for this vat if equal to its maximum dimensions would have been about $\frac{2}{3}$ of a cubic metre. Ordinary statues would hardly have used more than three times this quantity of rough marble. The normal cost of raw material would have been not more than HS600 on this basis. Since statues often cost something between HS4,000 and HS7,000 (see nos.121–82), the cost of workmanship was evidently the major ingredient. Statue bases by themselves cost HS500 or HS400 (nos.392–3). For the cost of workmanship, see also p.126.

4
Prices in Italy

The present survey provides about twice as many costs from Italy as from Africa.[1] The totals are 893 and 464. Italy has far more figures for foundations, sportulae and tombs. The two sets of Italian land valuations in the alimentary tables are without parallel in Africa. But there are many fewer prices for public buildings and statues than in Africa, and very few explicit *summae honorariae*. Thus the costs from the two areas to a large extent complement each other, though neither includes extensive information about commodity prices. Italy has however left some indication of wheat prices in the two sets of alimentary benefits; these can usefully be compared with the lower alimentary rates known in Africa.[2] Bequests form a higher proportion of the gifts recorded here, approximately 26%, compared with approximately 16% in Africa.[3] As in Africa,

---

[1] A preliminary version of this chapter appeared in *PBSR* 33 (1965) 189–306. Additional costs: nos.445a; 467; (467d); 479a; 500a; (511a); 645a; 676a; 758a; 759a; 843a; 864b; 896a; 970a; 1075a; 1075b; 1077a; 1179a; 1181a; 1255a; 1323a; 1336a; 1336b; 1348a; 1357a. The survey includes 12 costs from Sicily and 6 from Alpes Maritimae in addition to the 895 costs from Italy. The list is based on a survey of Italian inscriptions, the following categories being omitted: costs from the city of Rome (see Appendices 8 and 15 for selective discussion); financial penalties for tomb-rifling (see Liebenam 49–53 and F. De Visscher *Le droit des tombeaux romains* (1963) 112–23); and the majority of costs from the wax tablets and graffiti of Pompeii and Herculaneum. For the material from Pompeii and Herculaneum see IV 3340; V. Arangio-Ruiz and G. Pugliese Carratelli in *PP* 1 (1946) 379–85; 3 (1948) 165–84; 8 (1953) 455–63; 9 (1954) 54–74; 10 (1955) 448–77; 16 (1961) 66–73; *FIRA* 3, no.134; *AE* 1969–70, 94–105; C. Giordano *Rend.Acc.Arch.Nap.* 45 (1970) 211–31; 46 (1971) 173–97. Cf. L. Breglia in *Pompeiana* (1950) 50–3.

The epigraphic material has been supplemented by literary evidence, especially the works of the two Plinys, Martial and Suetonius. No attempt has been made to incorporate all costs from literary sources, but they are much less numerous than those in inscriptions. For costs in the novelists, see pp.238–56 below.

Laum collected about three-quarters of the available evidence for Italian foundations, and Bang about half of the tomb costs; neither list precluded the need for a separate scrutiny of all the epigraphic material (Laum 2.166–86; M. Bang in Friedlaender 4, Appendix 25). Toller made a thorough collection of the evidence for sportulae, games and feasts in the West as it stood in 1889 (Toller 5–34). None of the collections of inscriptions indexes costs systematically.

[2] See pp.144–5.

[3] Bequests are marked with a single asterisk in the list of costs.

a number of foundations can be used to make inferences about the size of towns and town-organisations.[1]

The proportion of the Italian costs that have any explicit date is relatively low. The concentrations of the dated material and the distribution of indirect dating indications suggest that the evidence is mainly concentrated in the first and second centuries A.D. But there are also a few costs from the second and first centuries B.C., for which Africa has no parallel.[2] Most of the tomb costs appear to be no later than the end of the first century A.D. The concentrations of foundations and sportulae suggest that munificence in Italy had begun to decline somewhat by the last two decades of the second century A.D.[3] However Italian dated inscriptions as a whole continue to be plentiful under the Severi. The dated evidence is analysed in detail below (Appendix 11).

REGIONAL DISTRIBUTION

The survival of costs from the different regions of Italy broadly reflects the regional distribution of inscriptions as a whole. Where there are exceptions they can usually be traced to a local preponderance of one type of cost (see Appendix 12). The single town that has left the largest amount of evidence (Rome excluded) is Ostia, which provides a total of fifty-one costs and twenty specified weights of gold and silver objects.[4] Ostia was large and prosperous, though as the port which served Rome, Ostia was not a typical Italian town. Its costs do not directly reflect the town's importance.[5] The HS2 million promised by Hadrian for the construction of baths of Neptune is not an indication of local wealth, though the figure (which is incomplete) is interesting because it refers to a building whose size is known.[6] The perpetual foundation of HS1 million given by a consul's daughter, which is the largest private cost at Ostia, is paralleled at Tarracina and Pisaurum, while being exceeded at Comum and Spoletium.[7] There are three other sizeable foundations from

---

[1] See pp.264–86 above.

[2] Nos.455; 457; 460; 466; 480; 500; 585; 1189.

[3] Discussions of munificence in the West: Toller (see abbreviations); J. C. Rockwell *Private Baustiftungen für die Stadtgemeinde auf Inschriften der Kaiserzeit im Westen des römischen Reiches* (1909); Laum vol.1; A. Lussana *Epigraphica* 12 (1950) 116–23; 14 (1952) 100–13; 18 (1956) 77–93; E. Magaldi *Lucania romana* 1 (1947) 270 ff.; J. F. Ferguson *Class. Journal* 13 (1917/18) 513–20; T. Loposko *Meander* 17 (1962) 207–14; R. Duncan-Jones *PBSR* 31 (1963) 159–77; S. Mrozek *Epigraphica* 30 (1968) 156–71; 33 (1971) 60–9; 34 (1972) 30–54; *Meander* 25 (1970) 15–31; *Athenaeum* 60 (1972) 274–300.

[4] Index s.v. Ostia.

[5] Meiggs *passim*.

[6] No.439; the baths of Neptune measured 67 × 67 m (Meiggs 410).

[7] No.641. Cf. nos.642; 643 + 648; 638; 639.

Ostia,[1] but most of the town's surviving costs are quite small. They include a series of small foundations which bore interest at 12%, a much higher rate than those normally found in Italian foundations. The commercial opportunities of a large port probably allowed small sums to be invested as loan capital. 12% per year (1% per month) was a conventional rate of interest for loans.[2]

Capua and Puteoli, two other leading Italian towns, have left more than ten figures each.[3] Capua's largest surviving cost is a foundation of HS1 million, given by two senators; this is no larger than gifts found at a number of other Italian towns. A fund of several million given by a member of the imperial family, the younger Matidia, under Marcus Aurelius may also belong to Capua, though it is no index of local wealth.[4] The other costs include four relatively low tomb prices.[5] Puteoli has left a remarkable decree setting out the conditions under which the town leased the contract for the construction of a wall within the town at the end of the second century B.C. The cost of the wall was probably no more than HS7,500. There is also a letter giving the rental of one of the offices of a foreign trading corporation, the statio Tyrensium. The rental was HS100,000 per year in A.D. 174. Other costs from Puteoli include a multiple distribution of sportulae.[6]

Three other substantial Italian towns have each left more than ten costs: Comum, Brixia and Pisaurum.[7] The evidence from Comum is dominated by the public gifts of the younger Pliny, a consular senator. They include foundations worth HS1,866,666, HS500,000, HS200,000 and HS100,000, and buildings which cost HS1 million and more than HS300,000.[8] The next largest cost at Comum is a gift of two foundations by one man worth HS105,000.[9] Brixia's largest figure is the restoration of a temple of Minerva at a cost of HS150,000. There are also eleven small foundations ranging in value from HS10,000 to HS400.[10] The costs from Pisaurum include two foundations given by the same donor, with a joint value of HS1 million. There are also eight sportula rates.[11]

The large cities of the far north have usually left rather few costs. Aquileia has a price of HS1 million for a building, which is well above the

[1] Worth HS50,000, 50,000 and 40,000 (nos.672; 674; 675).
[2] See p.133 below.
[3] Index s.v. Capua and Puteoli.   [4] Nos.640; 637.
[5] They range from HS11,000 to HS2,000 (nos.586; 603; 608a; 618a).
[6] Nos.480a; 1187; 757.
[7] Index s.v. Comum, Brixia, Pisaurum.
[8] For Pliny see pp.17–32 above. Nos.638; 644; 655; 661; 441; 469a.
[9] Nos.668 + 677.
[10] Nos.470a; 690; 717; 719; 733; 734; 735; 736; 746; 748.
[11] Nos.643 + 648; 760; 776; 830; 833.

usual levels attested in Italy, though it is paralleled at Comum and exceeded at Ostia.[1] Patavium has left record of a very large outlay on statues of HS550,000, as well as record of an even larger expenditure of HS1,051,000 in honour of a magistracy. The largest figure from Mediolanum is a relatively high tomb cost of HS100,000. The only figure from Tergeste is a tomb cost of HS20,000. Cremona has left record of an expenditure of HS20,000 on roads in honour of the aedileship.[2] If this indicates the amount of the *summa honoraria* for the office, the level is very high, equal to the second highest of the thirty-six figures from the African provinces.[3] But the inference is uncertain.

Six remaining towns which have left more than ten costs each are all relatively minor. The most prolific are the obscure towns of Veleia in Aemilia and Ligures Baebiani in Samnium, which provide an alimentary table containing many details of land-valuations and loans.[4] Single inscriptions from Lanuvium and Trebula Mutuesca each provide sizeable numbers of costs. They are both sets of rules belonging to plebeian dining and funeral clubs: the college of Diana and Antinous at Lanuvium and the *familia* of Silvanus at Trebula Mutuesca.[5] The costs from Aeclanum and Ameria come from a series of different sources.[6] The figures from Aeclanum include the large outlays of HS250,000 and 200,000 and a relatively large payment of HS50,000 in honour of a priesthood. There is also a multiple distribution of sportulae.[7] The figures from Ameria include four tomb costs, the largest of which reaches the high level of HS100,000. The five sportulae include the very high level of HS100.[8]

Many of the Italian costs come from a long series of towns which contribute little material individually, but which taken together provide a widely spaced cross-section of the area as a whole. The Italian evidence is not so dependent as the evidence from Africa on the survival of many costs from a few secondary inland towns. There are, as usual, random discontinuities between the political importance of towns and the level of their surviving costs. But the bigger towns as a whole are better represented in the Italian sample than they are in the sample from Africa.[9]

[1] Nos.440; 441; 439.
[2] Nos.491; 1339; 556; 579; 464a. [3] P.84 below.
[4] Nos.1197–1305 *passim*; 639a; 645a. [5] Nos.1377–98.
[6] Index s.v. Aeclanum, Ameria.
[7] Nos.1346; 1075; 1318; 779.
[8] Nos.553; 583; 601; 629; 700; 823; 831; 837; 845.
[9] Cf. p.67 above.

TYPES OF COST

Construction costs (nos.439–90)

The types of building cost mainly found in Italy do not allow many direct comparisons with the African material.[1] There are few prices for temples, and the most conspicuous types are prices of public baths and roads. The number of Italian temple costs is less than one-quarter of the number from Africa, despite there being many more costs from Italy.

The six Italian prices for baths range from over HS2 million, for baths at Ostia promised by Hadrian and completed by Antoninus Pius, to HS60,000 for a set of baths purchased by the city at Teanum Sidicinum.[2] Three of the costs lie in the region of HS350,000–300,000, which is close to the level of one of the African bath prices, HS400,000. The sixteen Italian road-costs include two explicit prices for road construction. 414 Roman feet of road built at Cereatae Marianae perhaps in the late Republic cost HS20.75 per foot of length. And the re-building of 15.75 Roman miles of the Via Appia near Beneventum cost HS21.79 per foot of length in A.D. 123. Two expenditures on roads by seviri Augustales at Forum Sempronii may point to a similar cost of road-construction.[3] Both inscriptions probably belong to the second century A.D. In three towns in Italy and one town in Baetica, Augustales or seviri appear to have made a mandatory payment of HS2,000 in honour of their office.[4] If the same amount is conjectured at Forum Sempronii, the road-costs that ensue are very close to the two explicit road prices. The 1,165 feet paved by 13 seviri Augustales would have cost HS22.32 per foot, and the 248 feet paved by another 3 seviri Augustales would have cost HS24.2 per foot.[5] A fifth inscription (probably of the Republican period) from Tarquinii refers to the paving of 3,000 feet of road from a bequest of HS200,000. As it stands, this gives a construction cost of HS66.7 per foot, a very high cost which it is difficult to credit at such an early date. But the inscription is incomplete and some of the money may well have been used for another purpose.[6]

---

[1] Nos.439–90 (cf. also nos.1339 ff.).   [2] Nos.439 and 450; also nos.443–5 and 447.

[3] Nos.466; 454; 463; 467. Liebenam was the first to notice this implication of one of the Forum Sempronii inscriptions (Liebenam 150). For road costs, see also T. Pekáry *Untersuchungen zu den römischen Reichsstrassen* (*Antiquitas* 17) (1968) 94–5.

[4] Pp. 152–3 below.

[5] It has been suggested that the abbreviation 'P' (used in the inscriptions from Cereatae Marianae and Forum Sempronii) should normally be read as 'P(assus)' in this context and not as 'P(edes)' (S. Panciera *Epigraphica* 29 (1967) 53). But road-measurements are explicitly stated in 'pedes' in a number of inscriptions dealing with road-building: *ILS* 5387; 5881; XI 3384; 6128; IX 968; 6259; *AE* 1899, 144.

[6] No.456. The last line may contain a reference to surplus funds: 'quae [s]upe[r]fui[t]' (see XI p.1337).

The four complete prices for road construction (if the interpretation of the Forum Sempronii inscriptions is accepted) are quite close together: the prices per foot are HS20.75, 21.79, 22.32 and 24.2. They offer some suggestion of standardised or at least consistent construction costs. Seneca's remark about structural repairs may also suggest fixed prices: 'Certo tamen et levi pretio fultura conducitur.'[1] The primitive method of reckoning building costs described by Cato explicitly assumes a stereotyped level. Cato says that the owner, who is to provide materials, should pay the builder of the farm villa HS1 per roof-tile.[2] And Columella's statement that the cost of a building was calculated from measurements taken after the structure had been completed seems to imply that there were set prices at which individual features would be assessed.[3] Presumably columns were reckoned to cost so much for a given size,[4] walls so much for a given area and thickness, and foundations so much for a given depth. Actual rates on which calculations were based would naturally depend on quality of materials and quality of workmanship. But the rates might still take the form of a limited series of stereotypes, analogous to those implied in the simple classifications of Diocletian's price edict. Here goods were divided into three different qualities each of which directly corresponded with a price category.[5]

Taken as a whole the distribution of the Italian building outlays is as follows:

HS2,000,000 +−700,000	5 (11.6%)	80,000–50,000 +	3 (7.0%)
600,000–200,000 +	10 (23.2%)	50,000–20,000	11 (25.6%)
200,000–100,000	11 (25.6%)	19,000–6,500	3 (7.0%)

The highest outlays, extending to HS2 million or more, are much greater than the largest building outlay in Africa (HS600,000).[6] But the donors of the largest Italian gifts include the Emperor, and a number of senators.[7] Only one senatorial outlay occurs among the large African building costs

[1] *de ben.* 6.15.7. See also pp. 76–7.
[2] Cato 14.3. The same index of building size is used in the late Republican lex municipii Tarentini, which states that every decurion must occupy a house in the town with a minimum of 1,500 roof-tiles (*ILS* 6086, 28).
[3] *de r.r.* 5.1.3.
[4] Cicero quotes a price for columns related to size alone: HS20,000 each for columns in a private house, whose size equalled that of the columns of the temple of Castor (*Verr.* 2.1.147).
[5] Text of the Edict in Lauffer. Nevertheless, Roman systems of costing were not so rigid that they failed to take into account the expense of transporting materials (no.465; Cicero *Verr.* 2.1.147; Cato 22.3; cf. Strabo 5.3.11; 5.4.8; Pliny *Ep.* 5.6.12).
[6] Nos.439 and 1.
[7] The Emperor (or in his name): nos.439; 454 (partly private funds); 506; 639b; 645b. Senators: nos.443; 445; 446; 514; 641; 650; p. 122 n.8 above.

(HS400,000 spent on the library at Thamugadi),[1] and there are no African buildings provided by the Emperor. Thus the higher level of the maxima in Italy does not necessarily suggest that building costs were higher there than in Africa.

Statue costs and weights (nos.491–549a)

The fifteen Italian statue costs form too small and uneven a sample to point to average prices for statues in this area.[2] But the municipal statue was a relatively standard article; it is reasonable to suppose that the norms in Italy would not have been very different from those in Africa, where the heaviest concentration of statue prices lies in the range from HS4,000 to HS7,000. The highest of the Italian prices for single statues, *c.* HS1 million at Beneventum, greatly exceeds the maximum in Africa, where the highest level is approximately HS67,000.[3] But the highest multiple statue outlay, HS550,000 at Patavium, is exceeded in Africa by a gift of statues worth HS1 million.[4]

A silver chariot constructed from 100 pounds of silver at Formiae cost HS100,000.[5] This indicates roughly what proportion of the cost of metal statues was taken up by the expense of workmanship. The gift being roughly mid-second century, the metal would cost HS42,000–55,000. Assuming the earlier date, the ratio of metal cost to the cost of working the statue would have been roughly 42:58.[6] Manufacture would thus amount to about 58% of the total cost. The relative cost of workmanship of a small silver plaque from Asia Minor was the same, 58%.[7] There are cases where manufacture absorbed an even larger proportion of the total cost. The bronze for a statuette found in Lincolnshire cost HS12, and the statuette itself HS112 in all. Manufacture thus formed 93% of the cost.[8] And Martial refers to a pound of worked silver which cost HS5,000.[9] Workmanship here would have accounted for about 91% of the cost, at silver values of the time of Domitian. However Martial implies that the price was exceptionally high. Workmanship probably also accounted for at least 90% of the cost of the average marble statue.[10]

The statue weights from Italy form a larger and more homogeneous sample than the statue prices; there are fifty examples in all.[11] Seven of

---

[1] No.38.
[2] Nos.491–504.
[3] Nos.513; 77.
[4] Nos.491; 77.
[5] No.492.
[6] *PBSR* 30 (1962) 78, Table III.
[7] P. Jacobsthal & A. H. M. Jones *JRS* 30 (1940) 29.
[8] VII 180; J. M. C. Toynbee *Art in Roman Britain* (1962) 131, no.16, dating the statuette to the second or third century.
[9] Martial 3.62.
[10] See note on no.394, p.119.
[11] Nos.505–49a.

the offerings are gold, the remainder silver. The largest of the gold statues, golden dragons weighing five pounds, would have been worth HS21,000 in terms of bullion value alone.[1] But the cost of workmanship would have been relatively low, because of the enormously high basic cost of gold, about twelve times greater than the cost of silver.[2]

The concentrations of the silver statue weights are as follows:

100 Roman pounds and over	4 (9.3%)
99–30 pounds	4 (9.3%)
29–10 pounds	6 (14%)
9–6 pounds	2 (4.6%)
5–2 pounds	14 (32.6%)
less than 2 pounds	13 (30.2%)
	43

The largest gift is a statue of Hadrian in a chariot at Beneventum whose donor bequeathed over half a ton of silver for its construction (1,567.17 Roman pounds).[3] The bullion value would have been about HS730,000. When the statue was so large, workmanship probably absorbed a much smaller proportion of the total cost than in the case of the smaller examples quoted above. The total cost might thus have been not more than HS1 million. The majority of the remaining offerings are very small, five pounds of silver or less. More than half come from Ostia.

Tombs and funerals (nos.550–636)

The Italian burial costs are more numerous and more widely distributed than those from Africa.[4] There are ninety-one in all (compared with an African sample of fifty-one, the majority of which come from one town, Lambaesis). Although few of the Italian burial costs are explicitly dated, most of them are probably no later than the first century A.D. As in Africa, only a small minority of the tombstones as a whole give cost details, and in Italy the practice was starting to vanish altogether by the beginning of the second century A.D.

The commonest burial costs in Italy were, in order of frequency,

HS20,000	11 instances	5,000	6 instances
2,000	10 instances	50,000	6 instances
10,000	7 instances	3,000	5 instances
100,000	7 instances		

There is some suggestion of standardisation at HS20,000, since more than half of the tombs in the range between HS99,000 and HS20,000

---

[1] No.505. [2] H. Mattingly *Roman coins*[2] 122–3.
[3] No.513. [4] Nos.550–636.

in fact cost HS20,000 (11 out of the 21 that fall within this range). The 10 duplications of HS2,000 may have the same implication. HS2,000 was the amount of a standard funerary grant made to distinguished citizens of Pompeii.[1] This sum was also the burial allowance in the college of *cornicines* at Lambaesis. HS2,000 occurs eight times in the African burial costs.[2]

The highest tomb cost recorded in Italy, HS500,000 at Fabrateria Nova, appears relatively isolated, the next highest cost being HS100,100.[3] But other substantial figures are recorded. A freedman who died in 8 B.C. leaving HS60 million in cash and over a quarter of a million herd animals, intended HS1 million to be spent on his burial.[4] The cost of burying Vespasian was anticipated as HS10 million, according to a jocular anecdote in Suetonius.[5] The tomb of Sulpicius Similis at Rome cost HS400,000.[6] And the burial of Nero, now a fugitive, cost HS200,000.[7]

The distribution of burial costs from Italy and Africa is as follows.

	Italy	*Africa*
HS500,000–100,000	10 (11%)	—
99,000–50,000	7 (7.7%)	2 (3.9%)
49,000–20,000	13 (14.3%)	5 (9.8%)
19,000–10,000	17 (18.7%)	2 (3.9%)
9,000–5,000	13 (14.3%)	4 (7.9%)
4,000 and below	31 (34.0%)	38 (74.5%)
	91 (100.0)	51 (100.0)

The median average for Italy is HS10,000, compared with a much lower African median of HS1,380. The distribution of the two samples is decisively different. Africa has nothing to correspond with the ten Italian costs of HS100,000 or more; and almost three-quarters of the African material falls in the lowest range between HS4,000 and HS96. Little more than one third of the Italian evidence belongs to this range. The differences are partly accounted for by social variants.[8]

There are more indications of high rank in the Italian sample than in the costs from Africa. The African evidence offers only one tomb explicitly belonging to a local magistrate; its cost was HS32,000.[9] The remainder of those whose social identity is indicated were all veterans, the highest being ex-centurions, whose tombs ranged in expense between

[1] Nos.620–3.   [2] P.79 above.
[3] Nos.550; 552.   [4] Pliny *NH* 33.135.
Suetonius *Vesp.* 19.2.
[5,6] VI 31865. Not the praetorian prefect of Hadrian's time, according to Stein (*RE* 2. Reihe 4.872).   [7] Suetonius *Nero* 50.
[8] The tomb was intended to reflect the 'substantia et dignitas' of the deceased (*Digesta* 35.127)
[9] No.215.

HS63,000 and HS1,000.[1] The Italian sample includes one career senator, whose tomb cost HS10,000 or more; eight town magistrates, whose tombs range between HS100,000 and HS4,000; and six freedmen, whose tombs cost between HS100,000 (the tomb of a merchant from Spain) and HS3,000.[2] The highest military ranks represented are *primipili* and holders of the *tres militiae*, of whom there are three and four respectively.[3] Two of the *primipili* spent the very large sum of HS100,000 on their tombs, while the holders of the *militiae* spent smaller sums ranging from HS50,000 to HS10,000. This may well reflect the enormous size of the retirement bonus paid to *primipili*, if Suetonius's information about this payment is reliable.[4] The *primipili* had also spent a lifetime of salaried service in the legions, latterly at very high rates of pay, whereas holders of the *militiae*, though likewise highly paid, usually served only for a few years. Insofar as either category was dependent on a salary rather than on private wealth, former *primipili* would have been better placed at retirement, whatever the size of their retirement bonus.

The Italian sample also includes a major municipal benefactor, a lady who gave the towns of Minturnae and Casinum HS100,000 each, and spent a further HS100,000 on her family tomb.[5] The tomb of a functionary from Rome, a *scriba aedilis curulis*, cost HS15,000 at Ameria.[6] The four funerary grants to important local figures at Pompeii and the two such grants at Surrentum appear to be standard amounts covering the funeral as such, which should be added to the actual cost of the tomb. The allowance was HS2,000 at Pompeii, but HS5,000, more than twice as much, at Surrentum.[7] One of the Pompeian magistrates who received the grant was buried in a fortress-like tomb whose cost must have been much more than HS2,000.[8]

As in Africa, the tombs of soldiers allow some comparisons between the size of the funerary outlay and the level of pay (Table 3).[9] The highest rate of outlay (not less than $1\frac{1}{4}$ years' pay) is found in the inscriptions of the two *primipilares* and one of the praetorian *milites*. The lowest rate of outlay, about one-fifth of a year's pay, is found in the case of one of the *tribuni militum* and the *optio praetorianorum*. As is the case in

---

[1] Nos.214; 234c.

[2] Nos.588; 555, 610, 560, 578, 590, 592, 593, 608; 557, 615, 569, 570, 581, 587.

[3] Nos.555, 556, 561a; 564, 575, 586, 592.

[4] Suetonius *Gaius* 44 suggests a figure of HS600,000; cf. *Rangordnung* 118. See also B. Dobson *Ancient Society* 3 (1972) 193–207.

[5] No.558 (cf. nos.665–6).

[6] No.583. [7] Nos.605–6; 620–3.

[8] No.622; see p.170 for reference to a description of the tomb.

[9] Pay-scales from Brunt (cited on p.79 n.2) 71. For discussion of individual examples, R. Duncan-Jones *PBSR* 33 (1965) 199–201.

TABLE 3. *Expenditure on tombs in Italy related to salaries*

Final rank	Conjectured rate of pay	Tomb outlay	Number of years' pay	Reference
Primipilaris	HS60,000/ 80,000 p.a.	100,000 +	1.66/1.25 +	no.555
Primipilaris	60,000/80,000	100,000	1.66/1.25	no.556
Praef. equitum	60,000	50,000	0.83	no.564
Trib. mil. (angusticlavius)	50,000	20,000	0.40	no.575
Trib. mil. (angusticlavius)	50,000	10,000	0.20	no.592
Centurio legionis	15,000	4,000	0.27	no.590
Optio (praet.)	9,000	2,000	0.22	no.624
Miles (praet.)	4,000	4,000	1.00	no.609
Miles (praet.)	4,000	2,000	0.50	no.618
Miles (praet.)	3,000/4,000	5,000	1.66/1.25	no.604

Africa, there is no clear correlation between military rank and the sum allotted for burial. But there is, as might be expected, some tendency for the percentage of salary spent on the tomb to be highest at the top of the social scale. In a society without progressive taxation, the percentage of income that is freely disposable is likely to increase with the degree of wealth.

A few other comparisons can be made between individual resources and the size of the funerary outlay. A *praefectus cohortis* at Rome was buried at a cost of HS12,000, probably about $\frac{1}{5}$ of his annual military salary.[1] This is as low as any of the relationships found in Italy. The millionaire freedman of the Augustan period whose burial expenditure of HS1 million is the highest figure recorded for any private individual, might have been worth HS100 million.[2] If he was able to obtain an overall return of 6% on his capital, his funerary outlay would have been approximately 0.17 of his annual income.[3] When compared with the statistics for soldiers, this is a low proportionate outlay, but in absolute terms the order of size is entirely different. HS1 million was probably enough to build a tomb as large as the biggest private tombs whose size is known from the Roman period.[4] Scaevola mentions a testator who proposed to

[1] VI 3504.

[2] He bequeathed HS60 million in cash. The estimate assumes that the 257,000 herd animals might have been worth something more than HS100 per head (for cattle at HS115, *FIRA* 3, no.137); Pliny *NH* 33.135.

[3] Stock-raising may have yielded less than 6%, usury rather more. The figure is used here as an arbitrary mean.

[4] Examples in L. Crema *L'architettura romana* (G. B. Pighi ed. *Encic. classica* 12.1) (1959) 242 ff.

spend HS40,000 on his tomb, out of an estate whose value was anticipated as HS500,000.[1] If his income were not more than 6%, the tomb outlay would represent at least $1\frac{1}{3}$ years' income.

It is clear from their amounts that the tomb costs from both areas mainly belong to economically privileged classes. Some general information is also available about expenditure on burial at lower levels of society. In the Hadrianic college of Diana and Antinous at Lanuvium, whose members included slaves, the burial grant to members was a net HS250, a further HS50 being spent on the distribution at the funeral.[2] The same grant of HS250 was instituted as a burial allowance for members of the Roman plebs by the Emperor Nerva.[3] Any new member of the college of Aesculapius and Hygia on the Via Appia near Rome under Antoninus Pius had to pay the college half of the 'funeraticium'. Since the membership was restricted to sixty and new members were only recruited to take the place of members who had died, this probably refers to the funerary payment accruing under Nerva's scheme for the plebs of Rome.[4] If so, the entry fee was HS125, slightly more than the HS100 payable by new members of the Neronian 'familia Silvani' at Trebula Mutuesca, but possibly less than the HS100 and one amphora of good wine asked of new members of the college of Diana and Antinous at Lanuvium.[5] The 'familia Silvani' was rather more generous in its funeral grant. The payment was HS560, a sum which evidently depended on the college's having at least seventy members, each of whom would contribute HS8 for this purpose.[6] But these two levels of funerary grant are very low in comparison with most of the costs recorded in inscriptions. Only four of the ninety-one tombs recorded individually in Italy cost less than HS600, and only two cost as little as the HS250 paid to members of the college at Lanuvium.[7] The most modest Roman burials usually leave little trace in archaeology. But burials of the poor in the form of ashes in pottery amphorae placed upright in the ground have been uncovered in the cemetery by the Via Domitiana at Isola Sacra near Ostia.[8]

---

[1] *Digesta* 32.42.

[2] No.1390.

[3] 'Funeraticium plebi urbanae instituit *LXIIS.' Mommsen ed. *Chron.Min.* 1.146, with A. Degrassi *Scritti vari di antichità* 1 (1962) 697–702. 'Funeraticium' could evidently refer to the monument as well as to the funeral ceremony; see XII 736; 4159; *ILS* 7215a.

[4] *ILS* 7213, 5–7.

[5] Nos.1382; 1391.

[6] Nos.1377; 1368 and n. For a funeral college which was wound up in A.D. 167 after its membership had shrunk from 54 to 17, see *ILS* 7215a (the college of Iuppiter Cernenus at Alburnum in Dacia).

[7] Nos.634–6.

[8] See G. Calza *La necropoli del Porto di Roma nell'Isola Sacra* (1940) 44–6 and fig.9–10.

Perpetual foundations and interest-rates (nos.637–755)

(i) Italy has left record of at least 121 perpetual foundations or groups of foundations whose financial details are explicit. None of the western provinces can rival this total. From Laum's figures (which are incomplete) private foundations in the main areas of the West are distributed as follows: Italy 73.5%, Spanish provinces 5.1%, Gallic provinces 11.1%, African provinces 10.2%.[1] Investment opportunities thus appear to have been good in Italy, though foundations are not merely grouped in the commercial centres. The concentration of foundations varied widely between different districts. To take the most extreme contrast, the concentration is much higher in the prosperous northern regions, VIII, X and XI, than in the southern regions, II, III and IV. The first group produce 66 or 48.7% of the foundations, but only 29% of the inscriptions from Italy as a whole (not counting Ostia); while the second group produces 18.1% of the inscriptions, but only 10 or 7.3% of the foundations from Italy as a whole.[2]

Nevertheless, the foundations are spread over the whole of Italy, and they were to a greater or lesser extent a typical form of gift all over the country. Most of the foundations of known date belong to the second century A.D.[3] The majority are thus later than the time of Trajan, in whose reign an elaborate system of government child-support grants (the *alimenta*) was established in many towns of Italy. These government funds were invested locally as perpetual foundations whose capital was underwritten in land; the income was paid by the owners of the land who held the original capital sums.[4] The wide diffusion of these government sponsored investments may have encouraged the foundation as a type of gift favoured in Italian towns. The same spur never existed in the provinces.

Most of the private gifts were probably invested in land, like the government *alimenta*. There are nine instances of Italian private foundations whose capital was explicitly invested in this way.[5] The evidence about typical rates of private dividend income is not very clear. But in a heavily agrarian society, most investment capital must have been invested in land

---

[1] Laum 2, pp.166–97 The total sample is 117 (Italy 86, Spain 6, Gaul 13, Africa 12). Laum listed only 78 of the 112 or more costed foundations from Italy known in 1914; his total of African foundations is 12 compared with the 34 collected above (some discovered after 1914). Some figures in Laum's lists are distorted beyond recognition.

[2] For the distribution of foundations see Appendix 12; for the number of inscriptions from Italy see Appendix 5.

[3] See Appendix 11.

[4] For the *alimenta*, see pp.288–319 and Appendices 3–6.

[5] *ILS* 3546; 3775; 6271; 6328a; 6663; 6664; 8370; 8376. Pliny *Ep.* 7.18.

whatever purpose it served. Columella indicates 6% as an adequate return on capital, and Pliny shows that his own alimentary fund bore nominal interest of 6% while being invested in land. 6% thus seems to have been a typical rate of land dividend.[1] It is also the rate found in the only other private foundation explicitly invested in land whose interest-rate is known.[2] In the government alimentary foundations vested in land the interest-rate was 5%. But the circumstances in which the funds were set up were unusual, involving cooperation between the government and private landowners; the interest-rate may have been somewhat preferential. Nevertheless, the scheme was evidently based on the assumption that landowners all over Italy would normally be able to achieve a return of not less than 5%.[3] This rate is also found in several Italian private foundations.[4]

The much higher interest-rate of 12% is found in a number of small foundations at Ostia and Rome, as well as in a single foundation at Opitergium, an inland town in region x.[5] It is most unlikely that this rate also refers to an agricultural dividend. Rome and Ostia were both important commercial centres, unlike the majority of Italian towns. The high rate of interest found there evidently corresponds with the availability of investment opportunities which were not so widespread elsewhere. Direct investment of perpetual funds in a commercial enterprise would hardly have been a reliable expedient under the informal conditions of Roman commerce. Furthermore if foundations were invested in this way, we might expect to see more than one high rate of return. But the stereotyped figure of 12% in fact embodies one of the traditional loan-rates: 12% resulted from the crude calculation of interest at 1% per month.[6] The foundations which bore interest at 12% in Italy were almost certainly based on loans. The loaning of perpetual funds provided by a private gift to borrowers who would pay interest at a specified rate of interest is explicitly attested at Ephesus under Trajan. However hazardous an expedient this might seem, the inscription makes clear that it was acceptable both to the city and to the benefactor in this instance.[7]

---

[1] See p.33 n.3 above.   [2] No.669.

[3] It could be objected that the interest-rate may have been different in units of the scheme for which there is no specific evidence. The one certainty is that interest was 5% per year at Veleia; the payments of 2½% at Ligures Baebiani were construed by Mommsen as being made every six months, thus representing 5% per year (a convincing interpretation; IX p.129, cf. Billeter 191–3). But it is very unlikely that the terms of the scheme would have been varied from place to place in any radical way once the final working basis of the *alimenta* (shown by the main scheme at Veleia and the scheme at Ligures Baebiani) had been evolved.

[4] Nos.637; 672; 685. Cf. no.248; II 4511.

[5] See p.135 below.   [6] Cf. Billeter 199.

[7] See p.307 n.2. The fact that the rate is 9% and not 12% only reflects normal loan-rates of the province of Asia: a notional calculation based on the Rhodian drachma worth HS3 instead

The jurists explicitly state that interest-rates varied widely from one region to another.[1] But this does not necessarily mean that only one interest-rate was characteristic of a given district. Comum for example offers instances of foundations bearing interest at 6.66% and at a rate below 6%.[2] Both 5% and 12% are found at Ostia; while at Barcino in Hispania Tarraconensis, 5% and 6% are both found in perpetual foundations.[3] Apart from the concentration of high rates at commercial towns the epigraphic evidence gives little sign of rates peculiar to particular areas. The variations mentioned by the jurists may in fact refer primarily to loan-rates, rather than to the land-dividends which mainly determined the yield on perpetual foundations.

The modulations of interest-rate in the foundations can be partly explained by the size of the funds in question. There is a broad inverse correlation between fund-size and level of interest-rate: large funds have low interest-rates, and the highest interest rates occur only when the funds are relatively small.

The highest common rate, 12%, occurs in no foundation larger than HS20,000, while the only other rates above 6% (15% and 6.66%) occur only once, in small funds with values of HS30,000 and HS80.

In the intermediate ranges there is considerable overlap between 5% and 6%. But their extremes correspond with the pattern of inverse correlation. For 5% the range is HS2,000,000–16,000, while the range for 6% is HS100,000–4,000. The lowest interest-rate, 4.33%, belongs to the second largest of the 24 foundations with explicit interest-rates. Its capital is HS1 million.

These examples suggest that in Italy larger perpetual foundations never had interest-rates of more than 6%; that the rate of 12% was confined to funds of HS20,000 or less, and that foundations of HS100,000 or more generally had interest-rates of 5%, or occasionally less. There was evidently a strong tendency for large sums given in perpetuity to be safeguarded by being invested at conservative rates of interest. But this did not prevent smaller sums from being also invested with a relatively low rate of return in some cases. Investment at a really high interest-rate, almost certainly entailing loans, was largely confined to commercial

---

of the denarius worth HS4 as the monthly interest on 100 denarii led to an annual interest rate of 9% instead of 12% (cf. E. L. Hicks in C. T. Newton (ed.) *The Collection of ancient Greek inscriptions in the British Museum* 3.2 (1890) 139; Broughton *ESAR* 4.900; p.307 n.2 below).

[1] *Digesta* 13.4.3; 17.1.10.3; 22.1.pr; 22.1.37; 26.7.7.10; 27.4.3.1; 30.39.1; 33.1.21 (Billeter 103–9; 179–81).

[2] Nos.677; 644. Pliny's larger alimentary foundation may offer a third rate, 4.5% or 5.37% (see p.30 n.5).

[3] See p.135.

TABLE 4. *The relationship between interest-rates
and the size of perpetual foundations*

		Italy		
HS2,000,000 +	5%	(Capua?) I	161/70	no.637
1,000,000	4.33%	Tarracina I	(100/90)	no.642
500,000 +	less than 6%	Comum XI	96/108	no.644
100,000	6%	Petelia III	138/61	no.664
70,000	6%	Ferentinum I	(post-100)	no.669
50,000	5%	Ostia I	(160/200)	no.672
30,000	6.66%	Comum XI	—	no.677
20,000	12%	Opitergium X	—	no.680
16,000	5%	Lanuvium I	136	no.685
10,000	6%	Croto III	—	no.691
10,000	6%	Petelia III	138/61	no.694
6,000 (2 funds)	12%	Ostia I	*c.* 190/200	no.698
5,000	6%	Capena VII	172	no.701
3,000	12%	Ostia I	*c.* 190/200	no.715
2,000 (7 funds)	12%	Ostia I	*c.* 190/200	nos.723–26c
80	15%	Bergomum XI	—	no.754
		Africa		
1,300,000	5%	Sicca Veneria PZ	175/80	no.248
4,000	6%	Gor PZ	—	no.267
2,400	12%	Theveste NP	(post-180)	no.268
		The remainder of the West		
100,000	5%	Barcino	II 4511	
30,000	6%	Barcino	*ILS* 6957	
20,000	12%	Roma	*ILS* 7244	
16,000	6%	Narbo	*ILS* 7259	
5,000	12%	Roma	VI 10297	

centres as far as we can tell. Where interest-rates need to be conjectured below, 6% has been suggested for foundations of HS100,000 and less, 5% for foundations above HS100,000.

There are too few dated examples to show any chronological trend in the interest-rates of perpetual funds. The dominant influences determining which rate was adopted seem to have been the size of the fund and the type of investment. The view of Billeter, followed by Rostovtzeff, that interest-rates in general had fallen heavily by the time of Severus Alexander, seems to have little application here.[1] There is explicit evidence for the simultaneous existence of widely different rates of interest for perpetual funds in the second century. Rates as high as 12% were still a familiar feature of financial life in the fourth century: Constantine renewed the traditional prohibition on levying interest at any higher rate.

[1] Billeter 211–19; *SEHRE*[2] 473.

An Italian foundation of his reign bore interest at 12%; the fund was worth 500,000 denarii.[1]

(ii) The distribution of foundation sizes can be summarised as follows:

HS2,000,000–1,000,000	6 (5.4%)
999,999–500,000	2 (1.8%)
499,999–250,000	9 (8.0%)
249,999–100,000	14 (12.5%)
99,999–50,000	7 (6.3%)
49,999–20,000	11 (9.8%)
19,999–10,000	10 (8.9%)
9,999–32	53 (47.3%)
	112

The median average is HS10,000, which compares with a much higher median for Africa of HS40,000. But the Italian sample is five times larger, and contains foundations bigger than the largest from Africa as well as foundations smaller than the smallest of those from Africa. The numerous dwarf foundations, of which the smallest were worth less than HS100, are very rare outside Italy. They are largely concentrated in the north of Italy, and only one of the forty-seven foundations of HS3,000 and below comes from a town south of Rome.[2]

The most conspicuous type of large-scale foundation was the alimentary gift, usually inspired by the example of the imperial *alimenta*. Alimentary schemes provide five of the eight largest private foundations in Italy, including the two largest foundations of all, worth HS2,000,000 and HS1,866,666.[3] The next largest foundation, HS1,500,000, provided income for public feasts at Spoletium; thirty-one other costed foundations were intended for feasts or a similar purpose.[4] The median of the twenty-five feast foundations whose capital value is known is HS16,000. The next highest foundation devoted to a single purpose (HS1 million) provided for the upkeep of roads at Capua. There are a further twenty-four costed foundations for the upkeep of monuments and public works. Their median is HS2,000, and the smallest had a capital value of HS400.[5]

Next in order of maximum size are the provisions for games, the

[1] *Cod.Theod.* 2.33.1.2; *ILS* 9420 (Feltria, region x).
[2] No.721, HS2,000 (Fabrateria Vetus, region i).
[3] Nos.637; 638; 641; 642; 644; 650.
[4] Nos.1079m–1105; see also nos.639 ff.
[5] Nos.1143a–60; see also nos.640 ff. Funds for *tutela* are discussed by S. Mrozek *AAASH* 16 (1968) 283–8.

largest of which was worth HS600,000.[1] There are only three such foundations, but official attempts were made to divert bequests for games and
shows to more useful public purposes. The small number of foundations
suggests that the legislation had some effect.[2] Then follow the foundations
for sportulae, whose size ranges from HS504,000 to HS2,000, with a
median of HS25,000.[3] There are twenty-six examples in all. In the first
century A.D. Rustius Caepio had attempted to leave money for the
regular distribution of sportulae to the senators of Rome; but Domitian
quashed the bequest.[4] The rates of sportulae are not usually stated in
these inscriptions, but there is copious evidence from other distributions
about the most frequent rates per head.[5]

The cash foundations for the maintenance of public baths have values
of HS400,000 and HS30,000; a fourth foundation without financial
details provided 400 cartloads of hard wood per year.[6] Heating the
furnaces was probably the main running expense. Finally there is a group
of foundations which provided for commemorative rites and votive
offerings. There are 33 costed examples, whose capital value ranges from
HS60,000 to HS80, with a low median average of HS1,600.[7] In sum 5
Italian costed foundations provided *alimenta*, 32 feasts and refreshments,
25 upkeep of monuments and public works, 3 games, 26 sportulae, 2
maintenance of public baths, and 33 commemorative rites and votive
offerings.[8] This distribution does not support the view that perpetual
foundations were primarily intended for religious purposes.[9] Only 33 out
of an effective sample of 121 Italian foundations mentioning sums of
money were ostensibly religious in intention.

The occasions provided for vary in frequency from monthly intervals
in the alimentary foundations, to four- or five-year intervals in a foundation that provided gladiatorial games at Pisaurum.[10] A high proportion of
the foundations are testamentary. The proportion is 46 out of 123 or
37%, compared with a proportion in Africa of 12 out of 22 or 55%.[11] The
African sample is very small, and does not contain small foundations

---

[1] Nos.641; 643; 651. For the cost of games cf. Toller 57–8; Friedlaender 4.258–67 (F. Drexel).

[2] *Digesta* 50.8.6; Cassius Dio 52.30.3–8 (Jones 1971, 542). Lifetime *munera* given by special
   permission of the Emperor: *ILS* 5058; 5186; 5878; *AE* 1888, 126 (cf. Mommsen *Ges.Schr.*
   8.513 n.3). Diversion of games money: p.149; nos.191; 459; 1052.

[3] Nos.1052–74; see also nos.645 ff.

[4] Suetonius *Dom.* 9.2.

[5] Pp.140–3 below.

[6] Nos.1308–9.   [7] Nos.1108–43.

[8] A few foundations provided for more than one purpose and have thus been counted more
   than once. Groups of identical foundations are counted as one.

[9] Suggested by G. Le Bras *Studi in onore di S. Riccobono* 3 (1936) 23–67, at 28.

[10] Nos.642; 643.

[11] See entries marked with a single asterisk in the list of costs.

worth less than HS3,000 which tended more often to be made during the donor's lifetime. Only 8 of the 46 foundations below HS3,000 in Italy were testamentary. By contrast the 7 largest Italian foundations, ranging from HS2,000,000 to HS600,000, were all testamentary, as were 27 of the 31 Italian private foundations of HS100,000 or more. Where very large sums were concerned, financial inconvenience to the donor was obviously minimised when the gift was made by will. The 5% inheritance tax was not enough in itself to make large-scale lifetime munificence attractive.[1]

Sportulae and feasts (nos.756–1107)

In the reign of Domitian Martial shows private patrons at Rome giving clients who called on them sums of 100 quadrantes (HS6¼) for each daily visit.[2] The visits were made at dawn at the patron's house and in the early evening at the public baths.[3] Domitian tried to suppress these payments by patrons, presumably as part of his campaign to improve public morals.[4] He also quashed a bequest of money for sportula distributions for senators made by Rustius Caepio,[5] and revived the public dinners at Rome that Nero had suppressed in favour of sportula distributions.[6] But Domitian's efforts to discourage the sportula seem to have been ineffective. The client's sportula recurs in the later poems of Martial as well as in the poems of Juvenal.[7] Cash handouts in general seem to have become increasingly widespread during the second century. Pliny reported from Bithynia late in Trajan's reign that cash payments of HS4 and HS8 were regularly made to the town-councillors and to a sizeable part of the town population at marriages, at coming-of-age ceremonies, at the induction of new magistrates, and at the dedication of public buildings. Distributions of sportulae to the citizens of a town at marriages and coming-of-age ceremonies were also a regular feature of urban life in Tripolitania under Antoninus Pius.[8]

The inscriptions illustrate in great detail the practice of giving sportulae at the dedication of monuments. They also show a further category of sportula, the commemorative distribution made each year from the income of a capital fund, to preserve the memory of the benefactor whose birthday

---

[1] For this tax see p.64 n.6.

[2] Martial 1.59; 3.7; 4.68; 6.88; 10.70; 10.74; 10.75. For a parallel discussion of sportulae, see now A. Pasqualini *Helikon* 9–10 (1969–70) 265–312.

[3] Martial 3.36; 10.70; 10.74; 3.7; Juvenal 1.127–8.

[4] Martial 3.7; 3.14; 3.30; 3.60. For official suspicion of the municipal sportula, Pliny *Ep.* 10.116. Domitian and public morality, p.35 n.4 above.

[5] Suetonius *Dom.* 9.2.

[6] Suetonius *Nero* 16.2; *Dom.* 7.1; Martial 8.50 (which shows Domitian entertaining senators, knights and plebs with a dinner).

[7] Martial 10.70; 10.74; Juvenal 1.117–28.   [8] Pliny *Ep.* 10.116; Apuleius *Apol.* 87.

it celebrated. The evidence for both types of gift mainly belongs to the second and third centuries.[1] The rates of these distributions are very well attested in Italy, and to a lesser extent in the western provinces.[2] The distributions show a clear pattern of social discrimination in favour of politically important groups. It must be recognised that the sportula belonged to a society in which munificence and exchanges of gifts occupied a place of great importance. The distributions to the citizens of secondary towns represent no more than an extension of the motive that impelled Emperors to reward their councillors with presents, and private hosts to make cash gifts to their senatorial guests at dinner.[3] Thus the municipal sportula was not intended as a dole for the relief of poverty.[4] In so far as it had a utilitarian purpose, it was intended to glorify the donor, who wished to publicise the monument which he had given to the city. By giving a sportula he performed a further act of generosity which would ensure the attendance of as many spectators as possible at the dedication ceremony. Each man received a payment according to the deserts of his social rank, town-councillors so much, Augustales rather less and ordinary citizens less still.

An alternative means of ensuring wide recognition for the gift of a monument was to give a public feast instead of a cash handout. This needed more organisation, but was evidently an earlier practice than the cash distribution. Early examples include an 'epulum trichilinis CCXVII colonis' given at Ostia probably under Augustus, and two municipal *epula* at rates of HS8 per head mentioned in Petronius's novel of the time of Nero.[5] Pliny also gave a public feast to celebrate the dedication of his temple at Tifernum Tiberinum.[6] Sometimes donors combined the two practices by providing a dinner as well as a cash hand-out. The evidence is occasionally ambiguous, and leaves it uncertain whether a figure refers to a cash gift made on the occasion of a feast or to the cost per head of the feast itself.[7] The cash sportula could evidently sometimes be used for a

[1] See Appendix 11.
[2] For Africa see nos.290–319. Distributions in other parts of the west: II 1276; 2011; 4511; XII 3306; 4354; XIII 1921; *EE* 2.314 (see Toller 5–34).
[3] Pliny *Ep.* 6.31.14. Martial 10.27, cf. *ILS* 9522; 5040.
[4] Suggested by A. R. Hands *Charities and social aid in Greece and Rome* (1968) 92. Martial's derision of an acquaintance who depended for subsistence entirely on his sportula as a client seems to imply that the sportula was not intended as a dole even in the context of daily distributions by patrons at Rome (Martial 3.30).
[5] *ILS* 6147, cf. Meiggs 493–500; Petronius *Sat.* 45; 71. Tiberius gave a 'prandium' for the people of Rome at 1,000 tables shortly before his accession (Suetonius *Tib.* 20). For feasts as an earlier custom than sportulae cf. also Toller 82–3; 86.   [6] *Ep.* 4.1.5–6.
[7] The following appear to be cash gifts provided in addition to a dinner: nos.834; 841; 862; 879; 923; 960; 976; 992; 994; 1000; 1036. Nos.1079b–k appear to show the cost of dinners themselves. For a detailed discussion, see Toller 77–90.

feast. The Arval Brothers, a small religious college composed of senators, recorded in A.D. 118 '[hoc a]nno sportulis cenatum est denar(i)is cente-[nis]'.[1] A donor at an African city bequeathed funds for the distribution of five denarii to the decurions 'epulationis nomine'.[2] In an early work Mommsen argued from such evidence that the municipal sportula was invariably intended for feasting, and was never a separate cash donative.[3] This entailed some strained interpretations of other evidence, and it is specifically contradicted by Italian inscriptions which distinguish the dinner from the cash handout. A donor at Forum Clodii for example gave the citizens an 'epulum cum sportulis' in A.D. 165 and an 'epulum... et viritim HS vicenos' in A.D. 174.[4]

Sportulae are recorded as payments which could be diverted and subscribed for building purposes both in Africa and in Italy.[5] In Italy provisions for feasts were also encashed and used to pay for buildings. There are records of monuments paid for 'ex collatione legativi epuli', 'ex epulis suis' and 'ex divisione epularum'.[6]

There are few references to the cost of feasts per head, but such figures as there are show expenditures very similar to the amounts of the sportulae. In separate passages of the *Satyricon* Petronius credits two of his characters with giving feasts at rates of HS8 per head. The same outlay for a feast is found in an inscription from Fagifulae.[7] The other nine feast prices in Italian inscriptions range from HS30 to HS2 per head, while the 277 sportula rates range from HS400 to HS1 per head.[8] Martial mentions dinners at Rome that cost HS20, HS12 and HS8; HS6¼ (the amount of the client's sportula) was too little for a good dinner.[9] Martial also refers to a sportula rate, at a dinner at which senators and knights were present, of HS30 per head, implying however that this rate was exceptionally high.[10] The regular expenditure per head at the celebrations of the Arval Brothers was HS400, a rate which is recorded as a municipal sportula only once. HS400 is recorded as the sportula given to the Arval Brothers

---

[1] VI 32374, 2.20–1.   [2] No.293.

[3] *De collegiis* (1843) 109–111.

[4] *ILS* 6584 (no.859 below). The distinction is elaborated in the detailed account of entertainments for a college on the Via Appia (*ILS* 7213). See also nos.758; 774; 775; 781; 788; 791; 813; 836; 841; 857; 859; 898; 1026.

[5] VIII 883; *ILS* 5590; 6595 (Toller 78). For subscription financing in general, see J. F. Ferguson 'Aere conlato' *Class. Journal* 13 (1917/18) 515–20.

[6] *ILS* 6295; 6642; XI 6369.

[7] *Sat.* 45; 71; no.1079 f.

[8] Nos.1079b–k; 818–1051. Nevertheless the sportula, which depended on spontaneous generosity, cannot be treated as an index of living costs (J. Szilagyi *AAASH* 11 (1963) 325–89 at 369–70; see R. Duncan-Jones *PBSR* 33 (1965) 306).

[9] Martial 12.26; 9.100; 2.57; 4.68. For collegiate dinners see p. 281.

[10] Martial 10.27.

in isolation, as the sportula given to them after a feast, and as the actual cost of a feast.[1]

The 277 sportula rates in Italy contain many duplications. More than a quarter, 26.5%, show the distribution of HS4 per head. This is sometimes explicitly referred to as a rate of 1 denarius, and was clearly chosen in preference to HS3 or HS5 because it corresponded to a single silver coin. The next most frequent rates also equal whole numbers of denarii: HS8 (19.1%), HS12 (13.7%) and HS20 (13.0%). Between them these four rates provide over 72% of all examples. The next most frequent rate, HS6, accounts for only 5.1% of the total. Choice of a rate thus appears to have generally envisaged a distribution in whole numbers of denarii, though only 93 (33.6%) of the rates are explicitly stated in denarii.[2]

The Italian sportula rates (including four examples from Sicily) are distributed as shown in Table 5 (p. 142). Women mentioned as a separate group are included under E. Where two groups are included in the same distribution at the same rate this is registered twice, under the name of each group. But 'utriusque sexus', 'collegia' and 'municipes et incolae' are counted as single units.

The distributions reveal a clear social pattern. There is a wide range of variation in the size of expenditures from town to town, as well as between one distribution and another.[3] But despite this, the figures as a whole consistently show financial discrimination in favour of the socially powerful.[4] On median average the decurions receive HS12, the Augustales HS8 and the people HS4 per head. The figures are the same on modal average, except that the sportula of the decurions rises to HS20. On mean average (inflated by a single bequest of immense size at one town)[5] the figures are: decurions HS24.4, Augustales HS17 and people HS8.

In keeping with this pattern of discrimination the decurions are the only recipients who invariably figure in the distributions to multiple groups. Their rate of benefit was also the highest, with only two exceptions.[6] By contrast the Augustales were sometimes omitted from the distributions given to several groups, even at towns where their organisa-

---

[1] No.818. *ILS* 9522; 5040; VI 32374.

[2] For this peculiarity, cf. M. H. Crawford *JRS* 60 (1970) 41 n.10. The present survey shows that sesterces remained the dominant monetary notation in Italy and Africa under the Principate. See also S. Mrozek *Eos* 57 (1967/8) 288–95.

[3] See tabulation in *PBSR* 33 (1965) 219: at 9 out of 17 towns there are inconsistencies of rate between different distributions to the same group at the same town. Only 2 towns of the 10 that have relevant information for more than one group show consistency throughout.

[4] Cf. Toller 58 ff.

[5] No.756, Mons Fereter, with rates of HS400, 300 and 200. For this relatively obscure community, see *Enc.art.ant.* s.v. San Leo. Higher rates in Greece: p.32 n.1; Lucian *Navig.* 24.

[6] In no.772 the donor (himself a freedman) gave the Augustales HS20 and the decurions HS12 per head. In no.780 the d[uovirales?] received HS20 per head and the decurions HS8.

TABLE 5. *Italian sportula rates*

Rates (HS)	A	B	C	D	E*	Total
400	1	—	—	—	—	1 (0.4%)
300	—	1	—	—	—	1 (0.4%)
200	1	—	—	1	—	2 (0.7%)
100	3	1	1	—	4	9 (3.2%)
70	1	—	—	—	—	1 (0.4%)
50	—	1	2	—	1	4 (1.4%)
40	2	—	1	—	1	4 (1.4%)
32	—	—	1	—	—	1 (0.4%)
30	3	—	1	—	2	6 (2.2%)
24	2	1	—	—	1	4 (1.4%)
20	20	8	3	2	3	36 (13.0%)
16	2	1	1	—	1	5 (1.8%)
12	17	8	5	3	5	38 (13.7%)
11	—	—	—	—	1	1 (0.4%)
10	1	1	1	—	—	3 (1.1%)
9	2	—	—	—	—	2 (0.7%)
8	14	14	8	8	9	53 (19.1%)
6	3	3	1	2	5	14 (5.1%)
5	1	1	1	—	1	4 (1.4%)
4	6	6	10	38	14	74 (26.7%)
2	—	1	3	6	1	11 (4.0%)
1	—	—	—	2	1	3 (1.1%)
Totals	79	47	39	62	50	277

* A = decurions; B = (Augustales and seviri); C = other colleges; D = people; E = others.

tion is known to have existed. They are absent from 13 of the 58 Italian distributions at multiple rates, even though there were Augustales at eight of the towns in question.[1] Since the bulk of the distributions belong to the second century, it is unlikely that the distributions in question are earlier than the formation of the body of Augustales at the towns concerned. When the Augustales appear side by side with the decurions, their sportula is most often about two-thirds of the sportula of the decurions.[2] The sportula of the citizens was separated by a wider differential. The popular sportula was rarely more than HS12;[3] and 60% of

[1] Firmum Picenum no.765 (Ruggiero 1.865.1); Pisaurum no.776 (Ruggiero 1.866.1); Forum Flaminiae Fulginiae no.781 (XI p. 755,2); Auximum nos.792 and 803 (cf. no.791, where Augustales were included); Atina Latii no.794 (Ruggiero 1.857.2); Lupiae, nos.795 and 805 (Ruggiero 1.862.1); Perusia nos.806 and 816 (Ruggiero 1.867.1); Sestinum no.807 (XI p.884,2).

[2] In roughly 70% of the cases, the sportula of the Augustales is between 50% and 80% of the sportula of the decurions. See tabulations of relative amounts under nos.756–816.

[3] The three exceptions are nos.820 (HS200 bequeathed at Mons Fereter); 851 (HS20 bequeathed at Auximum); 852a (HS20 given at (Ostia?)).

the distributions in which the people were included allowed them the rate of HS4, a single denarius per head. The Augustales typically received at least twice as much, and the decurions three times as much. Of the three groups, the citizens were the only category whose size was unrestricted.[1] This meant that giving large sportulae to the decurions and Augustales was much less costly than giving the same amounts to the citizens. But decurions and Augustales normally received substantial sportulae whether the total cost of the distribution was large or small. Even when the donor economised by excluding the people, he still normally rewarded the decurions at a relatively high rate. The modulation of rate in favour of exclusive groups was thus a deliberate recognition of their higher social status.

Another social feature illustrated by the sportula distributions is the position of women in Italian towns. At one town whose size was obviously small, women were regularly included in popular distributions on equal terms with men (at Tuficum in Umbria).[2] Equal rates for women are also found at Compsa and Petelia, though both these towns also have distributions to the male plebs alone.[3] But at most towns where women are mentioned as participants in popular distributions, they received smaller sums than the men. This is the case at Firmum Picenum, Puteoli, Volcei, Croto and Tuder.[4] Similarly in distributions at Bovillae and Volcei the wives of the privileged citizens received smaller sums than their husbands.[5] This discrimination of rate in distributions that explicitly included women argues that women did not normally benefit in popular distributions. The majority contain no statement about the sex of the beneficiaries and no indication of dual rates of benefit. The highest rate that women received in popular distributions was HS4, compared with a maximum of HS20 for the (male) plebs.[6] With few exceptions, the towns at which women were included in popular distributions were small. Obviously when the town population was low, it would be financially easier for the donor to include a wider section of the population in his distribution.

The status of the donor is known in 83 of the 117 Italian distributions

---

[1] For numbers of decurions and Augustales see pp.283–7. Popular distributions were sometimes restricted to the *plebs urbana* or those living within the walls of the town (*PBSR* 33 (1965) 217).

[2] Nos.1026, 1027, 1028.

[3] Both sexes: nos.991, 991a, 1014; men alone: nos.989, 1049.

[4] Nos.995, 1017, 1033, 1039, 1051.

[5] Nos.759, 762. Cf. *ILS* 6271, where the only women who benefit from a distribution in kind at Ferentinum are married.

[6] Nos.995, 1014, 851, 852a (the freak bequest of HS200 to the male plebs of Mons Fereter, no.820, is atypical).

of sportulae at specified rates. 29 or 35% belong to the highest reaches of the municipal class: patrons, curators of cities and *equites*.[1] A further 22 or 27% had held at least one of the highest local magistracies, the *quinquennalitas*, the IIIIvirate or IIvirate.[2] 16 or 19% were freedmen, including 3 *biselliarii*, 7 honorary members of the town council and 6 plain Augustales.[3] The remaining 15 donors included 2 patrons of municipal colleges, 3 army veterans, 6 women and one public slave.[4] The cross-section as a whole contains a higher proportion of men of relatively high rank than might have been foreseen. But considering its ephemeral nature, the sportula distribution was a type of gift whose financial demands were heavy. To give sportulae at the dedication of a statue could easily double the cost of the statue; while any commitment to give sportulae to the citizens at a sizeable town was potentially a source of heavy expense. Apuleius's excuse for holding his marriage in the country was that he wanted to escape a further demand for sportulae from the townspeople of Oea who had already cost his wife HS50,000 in this way. This shows that at a large town the drain threatened by the sportula was potentially great enough to discourage even the wealthiest members of the municipal class. Apuleius and his wife both came from millionaire families.[5]

Subsistence costs and allowances (nos.1161–83)

There are two sets of alimentary rates for children in Italy, one belonging to the government scheme of the time of Trajan, and one to a private scheme set up at Tarracina during the second century. The Trajanic allowances varied from HS16 per month for legitimate boys to HS10 per month for illegitimate girls, the one intermediate rate being HS12. The private scheme was more generous: boys were allowed HS20 per month and girls HS16.[6] The donor may have consciously tried to outdo the provisions of the government scheme; or she may have recognised

---

[1] The totals allow for any duplications of role. Patrons: nos.766, 767, 771, 774, 778, 781, 784, 790, 794, 806, 827, 833, 841, 843a, 864b, 977, 1014, 1040. *Curatores rei publicae/curatores kalendarii*: nos.763, 778, 784, 790, 793, 806, 822, 828, 831, 977, 980, 1040. *Equites*: nos.767, 783, 790, 793, 794, 800, 806, 827, 977.

[2] *Quinquennales*: nos.758, 760, 783, 786, 798, 803, 989, 991, 991a. *IIIIviri* and *IIviri*: nos.787, 813, 816, 837, 892, 893, 896a, 924, 972, 992, 1004, 1047.

[3] *Biselliarii* (cf. Ruggiero 1.1007): nos.796, 815, 858. Recipients of *ornamenta decurionalia*, etc.: nos. 776, 788, 809, 830, 858, 872, 898, 942. Augustales: nos.791, 801–2, 808, 812, 863, 880.

[4] Patrons of colleges: nos.936, 1041. Veterans: nos.761, 999, 1026. Women: nos.775 ('Marcia, stolata femina', perhaps the concubine of Commodus, Mommsen *ILS* 406, n.1); 777; 799; 805; 807; 978. Slave: no.849 (a *dispensator arcae summarum*, who was also chief contributor to the cost of a temple whose dedication the distribution celebrated).

[5] *Apol.* 87; nos.385; 383.   [6] Nos.1171–6.

that subsistence costs were higher at her town (Tarracina on the coast of Latium) than those allowed for in the government rates. The one alimentary scheme in Africa, given in the late 170s at Sicca Veneria, provided monthly amounts of HS10 and HS8 per head for the two sexes.[1]

The prescriptions of the jurists imply that alimentary schemes were intended to provide all the necessities of life, including for instance water in regions where the supply was so short that water was a marketable commodity.[2] The alimentary schemes for children evidently provided only the bare minimum. Rich men who wanted to provide for personal dependants from their own household might be much more generous. Pliny's freedmen evidently received between HS70 and HS85 per month, while similar cases mentioned in the Digest suggest monthly averages which range between HS83, HS42 and HS40.[3] Since the child alimentary allowances are so low, their main component was probably payment for the cost of grain. They may suggest norms of not more than HS4 per modius in Italy and HS2.5 per modius in Africa (pp. 50–1 above).

Wheat sometimes cost less than HS2 per modius in Egypt, one of the main producing areas, under the early Principate.[4] In Sicily in the 70s B.C. wheat normally cost HS2–3 per modius. The normal figure at Pisidian Antioch at the end of the first century A.D. was HS2.25 per modius. HS3 per modius was imposed as a controlled price at Rome after the fire in A.D. 64;[5] but the circumstances were unusual, and ordinary wheat prices at Rome may well have been as high as HS6–8.[6] Tiberius allowed a subsidy of HS2 per modius in order to keep prices at Rome down during a shortage in A.D. 19. HS4 was introduced as a controlled price by a benefactor at Forum Sempronii in Italy during a famine in the second century A.D.[7] Graffiti from Pompeii appear to mention wheat

---

[1] No.248.

[2] 'Si alimenta fuerint legata, dici potest etiam aquam legato inesse, si in ea regione fuerint legata, ubi venumdari aqua solet' (Ulpian *Digesta* 34.1.1; cf. 34.1.14.3). Iavolenus carried the application further: 'Legatis alimentis cibaria et vestitus et habitatio debebitur, quia sine his ali corpus non potest' (*Digesta* 34.1.6; for Iavolenus cf. Syme 52 and 91). However Ulpian apparently separates provision for clothes and lodging from alimentary provisions proper in *Digesta* 2.15.8.12, cf. 2.15.8.1. The crux is considered by Paulus in *Digesta* 34.1.23.

[3] See p.30 n.2.

[4] Egyptian wheat prices listed by Johnson include the following (translated from drachmae per artaba into sesterces per modius): HS1 in 18 B.C.; HS1.2 in 13 B.C.; HS0.75 in 10 and 9 B.C.; HS0.58 in 5 B.C.; HS1 in 4 B.C.: HS0.9 in A.D. 3; HS1.3 in A.D. 45/6 and in A.D. 56; HS0.65 in A.D. 65; HS1.8 in A.D. 138/61 (*ESAR* 2.310–11).

[5] Cicero *Verr.* 2.3.189; 2.3.194. *AE* 1925, 126b. Tacitus *Ann.* 15.39.

[6] For ordinary wheat prices at Rome see Appendix 8. Hirschfeld's suggestion of a norm at Rome of HS4 per modius on the basis of Augustus's congiaria of 5 and 2 B.C. is unconvincing (*PBSR* 33 (1965) 222).

[7] Tacitus *Ann.* 2.87; no.1178.

prices of HS3 and HS7.5 per modius. Martial indicates that when a glut forced wheat prices as low as HS1 per modius, the farmer could no longer make a decent profit.[1] The price of wheat was so volatile that seasonal fluctuations might force it as high as HS20 per modius in the months just before the new harvest in a region where the normal price was only HS2–3.[2] Some very high prices during famines and shortages are known: HS400 in Africa, HS48 in Asia; HS50, 44 and 40 in Italy and Africa; HS32 in Asia; HS23–27 at Sparta; HS24 in Greece; HS22 at Rome.[3] But despite the fluctuations, contemporaries had a clear concept of what wheat prices were normal.[4] The basic level seems most often to have been between HS2 and HS4 per modius.[5]

Cato provides a glimpse of the basic subsistence diet in antiquity.[6] His slaves were allowed wine, olives, oil and salt in addition to bread or grain. Unchained field slaves received 4–4½ modii of wheat per month depending on the time of the year. Slaves whose manual tasks were lighter, such as the *vilicus* and *vilica*, received only 3 modii per month. The chain gang, who were evidently unable to grind their own flour, received their allowance in bread at the high rates of 120–150 pounds per month, depending on the time of year. This was roughly equal to 4.8–6 modii of wheat, apparently a recognition of the heavier dietary requirements of men employed in hard labour. A comparable differential occurs in Cato's wine rations, where the basic ration is 7 quadrantals per year, but 10 quadrantals for the chain-gang (180 and 260 litres).

Later evidence shows comparable grain allowances. 5 modii per month was the ration of members of the *plebs frumentaria* at Rome from the end of the Republic. Seneca suggests that 5 modii was a normal ration for an urban slave who also received a cash wage. Gardeners employed at Lingones Galli in Germania Superior received the same ration. At Nemausus in Gallia Narbonensis corn seems to have been available to the privileged under Tiberius in rations of 50 modii per year, 4.2 modii per month.[7] According to Polybius the corn-ration of the footsoldier of the mid-Republic was 3 modii.[8] The military ration would not necessarily have been so low at a later date when the plebs of Rome was receiving a substantially higher ration. The single artaba per month (3.33 modii) attested

---

[1] E. Diehl *Pompeianische Wandinschriften* (1930) nos.391–2. Martial 12.76.

[2] Cicero *Verr.* 2.3.214. It is far from certain that seasonal fluctuations were normally so extreme.

[3] See pp.252 and 38 with comparative literature.

[4] Cicero *Verr.* 2.3.227, cf. 2.3.189, 2.3.194; *AE* 1925, 126b. Cf. Petronius *Sat.* 44.

[5] Cf. also A. H. M. Jones *EcHR* ser.2, 5 (1952–3) 295–6.

[6] Cato 56–8.

[7] Nos.1176b; 1170; *ILS* 8379; 2267.

[8] Polybius 6.39.13, cf. F. W. Walbank *A Commentary on Polybius* I (1957) 722.

for Egyptian legionaries under the Principate does not necessarily represent the position in the legions as whole.[1]

In dietetic terms a ration of 5 modii per month may have been equivalent to 3,000–3,500 calories per day, which is close to modern ideals of 3,300 calories per day for male adults.[2]

Summae honorariae and other payments to cities (nos.1310–38)

Although the Italian inscriptions do not offer the profusion of *summae honorariae* recorded in Africa, there is interesting evidence about qualifications for the town-council and about the nature of early magisterial obligations.

A property-qualification for civic dignitaries is first found in the constitutions which Rome imposed in Greece in the second century B.C.[3] Cicero mentions a property-qualification for decurions at Sicilian towns in the first century B.C. The late Republican Lex Tarentina shows a version of this requirement in Italy: each decurion has to own a house within the town having not less than 1,500 roof-tiles.[4] A property-qualification of HS100,000 for the decurionate at Comum is mentioned in one of Pliny's letters written at the end of the first century A.D. The same qualification for this rank is referred to less explicitly by Petronius, also speaking of Italy, and perhaps by Catullus.[5] A decree passed at Tergeste under Antoninus Pius implies that entry to the *ordo* there was likewise regulated by a property-qualification.[6] Jones concludes that a property-qualification for the *ordo* was 'probably a universal rule'.[7]

The qualifying figure of HS100,000 appears relatively high, although the reference in Petronius seems to indicate that it was not an unusual level for Italian towns. Taken in conjunction with the total of 100 elsewhere indicated as a normal level of membership for the town-council,[8] this qualification would require the availability at all times of 100 men with the necessary social qualifications and wealth of HS100,000 at each

---

[1] The Egyptian legionary was apparently less privileged than his colleagues elsewhere. Johnson *ESAR* 2.301 and n.10; 670–1; P. A. Brunt *PBSR* 18 (1950) 59.

[2] Pliny indicates the bread yield of one modius as 25–6 Roman pounds (*NH* 18.66–8; cf. Moritz 186, 202–7). An Egyptian source makes the yield 24 pounds (*POxy* 1920, cf. Jones *LRE* 3.217 n.23). The Roman pound was roughly 327.45 grams (Ruggiero s.v. Libra). The calorific value of modern bread ranges from about 3.03 to 2.47 calories per gram (R. Hutchison & V. H. Mottram *Food and the Principles of Dietetics*[11] (1956) 24). If the calorific value of Roman bread was the same, these coordinates would suggest that 5 modii per month represented 3,200–3,700 calories per day; but the calorific value of Roman bread may have been less than that of modern bread. For ideal rations, *loc. cit.* 48 and 53.

[3] Livy 34.51.6; Pausanias 7.16.9.

[4] *Verr.* 2.2.120; 2.2.122. *ILS* 6086, 28.

[5] See p.243 n.4.

[6] *ILS* 6680, 2.2.5.

[7] Jones 1971, 524.

[8] See p.283.

town concerned. It is likely that only the larger towns could have met
such a requirement fully. If both stipulations were found at many Italian
towns, they can hardly have been effective in all cases. At a group of
African towns an even higher level of wealth was required: decurions
of the four towns of the Cirtan confederacy in the second century A.D.
were expected to pay a *summa honoraria* of HS20,000.[1] They were thus
almost certainly drawn from men whose fortunes were substantially
greater than HS100,000. But the Cirtan confederacy was a centre of
great wealth and it does not represent the situation in African towns at
large. There are few towns in Italy for which it could provide an analogy.
There is no explicit evidence about the level of any fixed payment for the
decurionate in Italy. But a cash *summa honoraria* was evidently levied,
since a number of adlections of distinguished men to the *ordo* were
singled out as being made without charge to the individual concerned.[2]
At Iguvium an office-holder of the reign of Augustus paid the city
HS6,000 'decurionatus nomine'.[3]

The statutory obligation of the main magistrates in Roman towns in

---

[1] See p.69.

[2] *ILS* 2071; 2748; 5698; 5371; 6135; 6147; 6296; 6367; 6447; *AE* 1919, 64; 1954, 162;
1959, 254. Garnsey puts forward the interesting hypothesis that these inscriptions refer to
exceptional procedures and that payment for the decurionate remained abnormal in Italian
towns under the early Principate (some of the inscriptions belong to the first century A.D.
ILS 6147, 6367, etc.) (Garnsey 1971 (1)). He argues that since the Lex Pompeia in Bithynia
prescribed no payment for the decurionate (cf. Pliny *Ep.* 10.112), the early Italian references
to a charge for this position (in the form of inscriptions mentioning exemption from payment
in specific cases) may well be unusual. The fact that only 'supernumerary' decurions adlected
by recent dispensation of Trajan (Pliny *Ep.* 10.112; 39) were liable to payment at the Bithynian towns which Pliny mentions could offer an analogy from which to infer that distinctions
may have been drawn in Italy between the financial liabilities of decurions recruited under
different headings. Garnsey therefore distinguishes in Italy between those who entered
through adlection (or through adlection by the decurions) who were liable to a charge, from
the evidence of the inscriptions, and those decurions who first served as magistrates, or who
entered the *ordo* through enrolment by the censors, who (from the analogy of the Lex
Pompeia) were not liable to a charge.
But there are several objections to this view. First, there is no *a priori* reason to consider
the Lex Pompeia in Bithynia an accurate index of municipal procedures in Italy, whose
towns owed their constitutions to other sources. Second, if as Pliny indicates (*Ep.* 10.112.1)
there was no charge for the decurionate under the Lex Pompeia in Bithynia, Bithynia's
institutions differed in this respect from those of Italian towns, where the inscriptions show
decurions who were liable to pay for their position. The Lex Pompeia is thus visibly unsatis-
factory as a basis for inference about the financial liabilities of decurions in Italy. Third, the
fact that the men exempted from payment in Italy were typically adlected 'by decree of the
decurions' does not necessarily distinguish them from decurions enrolled by the censors
from whom no payment was expected under the Lex Pompeia (Garnsey 319–20). Gratuitous
adlection was a special concession for which a vote of the decurions as a whole would have
been needed in any case.

[3] No.1325.

Italy seems originally to have taken the form of payments for games.[1] When the payment for a magistracy was devoted to building, it was sometimes described as a commutation for games. For example a statue of Mars was dedicated by an aedile at Ferentinum in Etruria 'ex d(ecreto) d(ecurionum) pro ludis sua pecunia'.[2] The practice was broadened when the possibility of spending on a monument was introduced as a formal alternative: an inscription of the Sullan period from Pompeii (which Sulla colonised) refers to the 'pecunia quod (*sic*) eos (*sc.* IIviri iure dicundo) e lege in ludos aut in monumento (*sic*) consumere oportuit'.[3] The same dichotomy between games and building appears in the roughly contemporary Lex Tarentina.[4] But fixed obligations in the form of payment for games alone were still being promulgated as late as the date of the foundation of the Caesarian colony at Urso in Spain. At Urso each duovir and each aedile had to subscribe HS2,000 towards the cost of public games; each duovir was given a further HS2,000 as a public subvention, while each aedile received HS1,000.[5] It is not certain however that there was not also a cash *summa honoraria*, since the lex Ursonensis is seriously incomplete.[6] Most of the payments for office mentioned in inscriptions were spent on monuments not on games. But games, unless so splendid that a statue of the donor commemorated them, tended to leave no memorial.[7] The use of the phrase 'pro ludis' to describe expenditure on monuments by magistrates still persisted in some Italian towns under the Empire.[8] A third type of obligation, the provision of a dinner by a magistrate, attested at Aesernia, does not seem to have been widespread.[9]

---

[1] But the phrase 'venatio legitima' attested at certain towns may refer to the nature of the entertainment rather than to its origin (*ILS* 5145; 5057; *AE* 1951, 19; cf. de Visscher & de Ruyt in *Antiquité classique* 20 (1951) 57).

[2] *AE* 1909, 59. Cf. also examples from Antium, Telesia, Hispellum, Pompeii, Beneventum, Volsinii and Tarquinii (*ILS* 160; 5328; 5377; 5653a–e: IX 1643; XI 7301: *NS* (1948) 258). At some towns the Augustales were expected to give games, which in certain cases they commuted for monuments: Luceria, Falerii (Augustan), Veii (A.D. 34) and Castel di Sangro (IX 808; XI 3083; 3781; *AE* 1933, 152).

[3] *ILS* 5706. The 'ministri' or city employees at Pompeii were expected to put up a 'signum' which they could commute for a small monument by arrangement (*ILS* 6385, A.D. 45). Claudius substituted expenditure on games for expenditure on roads as the obligation of the quaestors at Rome (Suet. *Claud.* 24.2).   [4] *ILS* 6086, 36–8.

[5] *ILS* 6087, 70–1. The same obligation in the Julian colony at Cnossus: *ILS* 7210, cf. Ruggiero 2.1274.2.

[6] The surviving chapters run from 61–106 and from 123–34 (*ILS* 6087).

[7] Statues were occasionally erected from the proceeds of a specific *munus*, indicating that there were admission charges: *ILS* 3316; 3589; *AE* 1969/70, 134 (all from Canusium); *ILS* 6208 (Tusculum). Charges for admission to the amphitheatre are explicit in a Cirtan inscription of the reign of Severus referring to the erection of a statue 'ex reditibus locorum amphitheatri diei muneris quem...edidit' (*ILS* 411).

[8] See above, n.2.

[9] Repairs made 'pro cena IIIvira[li]' at Aesernia, *AE* 1951, 185.

Taking the magistracies in turn, there is no evidence for the payment of a *summa honoraria* for the quaestorship.[1] Monuments built in honour of the aedileship are attested at Cremona, Falerii and Lilybaeum.[2] At Cremona the sum of HS20,000 was spent 'in viam', while at Falerii HS29,300 was spent on a portico. The second figure is too irregular to suggest the amount of a *summa honoraria*. But HS20,000 is attested as a *summa honoraria* at Cirta and its confederate cities in Numidia; and Cremona was a substantial town.[3] Though the level is high it may represent a *summa honoraria* here. At Lanuvium a father and son contributed HS15,000 to the restoration of public baths, the son 'pro honore aed(ilitatis)', the father 'pro honore flamon(i)i'.[4] To judge from the plentifu African evidence, the two *summae honorariae* would have been round figures; the obvious values suggested by this total are HS10,000 and HS5,000. African analogies would make the payment for the flaminate the larger of the two;[5] but the flaminate did not occupy the same pre-eminent position in the normal institutions of Italian cities. The aedileship is mentioned first in the Lanuvium inscription, in which case it may correspond to the larger payment. On this basis the aedileship would have cost HS10,000 at Lanuvium, half of the amount tentatively inferred at Cremona.

A duovir at Pompeii under Augustus paid the city HS10,000 'pro duomviratu', besides giving copious and varied games.[6] The account of his second and third tenures of the same office lists no further payment, though he continued to give games for the citizens. Repetition of office would seem to require repeated payment of the *summa honoraria*, although there are no explicit records of repeated payment under this heading. Thus it is not clear that the initial cash payment at Pompeii constituted a mandatory payment which had to be made to the city in that form.[7] It might nevertheless indicate the minimum expenditure required of duoviri, who were normally expected to spend it on games rather than pay it to the city. On this interpretation the magistrate discharged his formal obligation in cash during his first tenure, leaving his elaborate celebrations of games as a spontaneous gesture.

Other payments for the duovirate took the form of a statue of the genius (?) of Beneventum, two towers built jointly by duoviri at Telesia, and a sphaeristerium at Centuripae in Sicily.[8] The gift of a large equestrian

---

[1] Liebenam 57.

[2] Nos.464a; 475; 525; cf. nos.1322; 1324.

[3] No.345 etc. Strabo 5.1.11; Plutarch *Otho* 7; Tacitus *Hist.* 3.30–4; Cassius Dio 65.15 (v p.414; Nissen 2.199–202). Cf. no. 459 (Hispellum).

[4] *ILS* 6198 = no.479.

[5] Cf. nos.349–53; 365–77.

[6] No.1324a.

[7] Cf. Garnsey 1971 (1) 324.

[8] IX 1645; 2235; X 7004.

statue accompanied by sportulae at Nuceria before A.D. 62 was rewarded by remission of the *summa honoraria* for the duovirate.[1] An equestrian priest at another town in southern Italy was honoured for his willingness to hold the duovirate in spite of being exempt from public office: 'ad honorem quoque duumviratus ad cumulanda munera patriae suae libenter accessit'.[2]

A holder of the *quinquennalitas* at Fagifulae in Samnium spent HS4,000 on a statue of the Emperor which he dedicated 'ob honor(em) quinquenn(alitatis)' under Antoninus Pius.[3] Since the text refers to no other discharge of obligations for this office, the expenditure may have corresponded to the statutory payment for the *quinquennalitas*. The other expenditure, a feast given at the dedication, did not fall into any of the usual categories for expenditures in honour of office.[4] HS4,000 is attested as a *summa honoraria* in five African towns.[5] At Ausculum in Apulia another *quinquennalis* paved 44 passus (220 Roman feet) of road 'ob [honorem quin]quennalitatis' (also under Antoninus Pius).[6] If the construction cost was close to the range from HS20.75–24.2 per foot which is attested at four other Italian towns, the outlay would have been roughly HS4,565–5,324.[7] Since the road length was both short and irregular, it was probably determined by a fixed financial obligation. *Summae honorariae* were normally in round figures. Thus the payment suggested here by the analogies for road construction cost is HS5,000 (corresponding with a construction cost of HS22.72 per foot). A *summa honoraria* of HS5,000 is attested at three African towns.[8]

At Aeclanum one *quinquennalis* appears to have spent HS200,000 in honour of his office, while another tenure of this office was celebrated by the paving of 3 Roman miles of road.[9] The cost of the road works can have been little less than HS300,000.[10] It is inconceivable that such large payments can have been mandatory. They exceed the highest known *summa honoraria* (HS38,000 at Carthage)[11] by factors of 5 and 7. Both gifts represent spontaneous generosity on the grand scale. Another payment at Aeclanum, HS50,000 paid to the city 'ob honorem sacerdotii' by a 'flam(inica) div[ae] Iuliae Piae [A]ug(ustae)' must also refer mainly to spontaneous generosity.[12] The only direct suggestion of the amount of the

---

[1] *ILS* 6446 (no.1004 below).
[2] *ILS* 5054 (the town has not been identified).
[3] No.498, with nos.1079f, 1079i, 1079k.
[4] But cf. above, p.149 n.9.
[5] Nos.346; 352; 355; 358; 371.
[6] No.467h. [7] P.125 above.
[8] Nos.351; 354; 370a.
[9] Nos.1075; 467a. [10] Cf. p.125 above.
[11] No.360. [12] No.1318.

summa honoraria for a municipal priesthood in Italy is the HS5,000 inferred above as payment for a flaminate at Lanuvium. It is interesting to note in contrast that at Rome under Caligula Claudius was forced to pay HS8 million 'pro introitu novi sacerdotii'.[1] A gold statuette weighing one pound was dedicated at Brundisium in recognition of an augurate awarded without charge to the holder. The statuette probably cost HS5,000–6,000.[2] But the spontaneous reciprocation would not necessarily match the amount of the charge, especially when it took the form of an effigy of stereotyped size.

Evidence for the *summae honorariae* paid by the freedmen Augustales is more explicit. HS2,000 was paid to Asisium 'pro seviratu' by a first-century Augustalis.[3] The same amount is indicated as the charge for the sevirate at Lacippo (?) in Baetica.[4] An inscription from the region of Puteoli shows an Augustalis spending HS2,000 on re-paving a road or street by decree of the decurions. And an inscription from Cereatae Marianae describing expenditure on a bridge in honour of the Augustalitas isolates the sum of HS2,000 from the larger amount actually spent.[5] The charge for the sevirate was probably HS2,000 at Forum Sempronii in Umbria.[6] These five examples drawn from a wide area suggest that the charge of HS2,000 for the Augustalitas or sevirate was quite common. Three inscriptions show that the charge for the curatorship of the Augustales at Ostia at the end of the second century was HS10,000; they date from A.D. 182, 193 and 200. The charge for the Augustalitas proper seems to have been HS10,000 at Teanum Sidicinum. In the first century A.D. a set of baths was purchased by the city for HS60,000, which represented the 'pecunia Augustal(itatis)' paid by six individuals.[7] Five or more sevirales each contributed HS3,000 to the restoration of a bath at Cures Sabini. The stereotyped contribution suggests that HS3,000 was the fixed charge for their office.[8]

Individual Augustales paved 800 and 880 feet of road (*platea*) at Aquilonia in the Hirpini.[9] The amounts appear close enough together to suggest the fulfilment of a fixed charge translated into differing construction costs. If the figures are read as lengths of road of standard width, the implied

---

[1] Suetonius *Claud.* 9.2; cf. *Gaius* 22.3; Dio 59.5.

[2] No.509. For the value cf. p.126 above.

[3] No.1313.

[4] II 1934: 'Fortunae Aug... ob honorem seviratus sui...ex (HS3,000) remissis sibi ab ordine (HS2,000).'

[5] Nos.1314; 1315. The recent rediscovery of the Cereatae Marianae inscription confirms the writer's earlier conjecture that the figure was II and not IL as transmitted (*PBSR* 33 (1965) 294; cf. S. Panciera *Epigraphica* 29 (1967) 53 and fig.8; 49).

[6] P.124 above.   [7] Nos.1311; 1312.

[8] No.478.   [9] Nos.467d; 467e.

outlay would be considerable, of the order of HS16,000 in each case.[1] This seems implausible as the amount of a fixed charge for the Augustalitas at Aquilonia when set against the HS10,000 paid for the highest office of the Augustales at Ostia.[2] Aquilonia was an extremely obscure town which can scarcely have had high charges for office.[3] An alternative would be to see the totals as a square measure; on this basis, the longitudinal road distance notionally represented would be 89 and 98 feet for the two expenditures at Aquilonia.[4] These lengths are quite compatible with the familiar charge for the Augustalitas of HS2,000. The construction costs that would be implied are HS22.4 and HS20.4 per longitudinal foot; both figures are very close to the attested examples ranging from HS20.7 to HS24.2.[5]

Finally there are some payments made 'pro magi(stratu)' within the Imperial household at Antium, one of the villas of the Julio-Claudians. The calendar shows seven magistrates holding office each year, a minority of whom make payments for their office by decree of the town's decurions. Most of the holders are freedmen and slaves, whose functions in the household are sometimes mentioned by name. Since four of the figures are identical, they seem to represent a fixed charge. HS1,600 was paid by different individuals in A.D. 40, 41 (twice) and 44. Other payments made for the same function were HS1,000 in A.D. 37 and HS2,000 in A.D. 48. These figures as a whole show a cumulative tendency.[6] (The figures are summarised in Table 6.)

Uncertain though some of these figures are, they seem to point to a pattern of charges for municipal office in Italy that was not very different from the pattern in Africa. Taking all 16 Italian figures listed in Table 6, including those that are conjectured, the median average is HS4,500. In Africa, where there are 36 firmly attested *summae honorariae*, the median is HS5,500. The discrepancy is hardly significant in view of the disparity between the effective size of the two samples. But the repeated charge of HS2,000 for the sevirate and Augustalitas might suggest that payments for office were somewhat more stereotyped in Italy than in Africa, where municipal institutions developed in a piecemeal fashion during the Principate.

Some more information about the budgets of Italian towns is provided by the public subventions paid to magistrates for different expenses that they had to meet.[7] At Aeclanum the town paid HS62,000 to a magistrate

[1] At an assumed HS20 per foot of road (see pp.124-5).
[2] No.1311. [3] Cf. IX p.88; Nissen 2.820.
[4] This assumes a road width of 9 feet, for which see no.467g.
[5] See p.125.
[6] Nos.1316; 1317. The payment of HS1,500 in A.D. 39 may be incomplete.
[7] The town of Amisus in Bithynia paid HS160,000 to one of its magistrates (Pliny *Ep.* 10.110).

TABLE 6. *Italian summae honorariae*

Aedileship	HS20,000 (?)	Cremona x	—	no.464a
Aedileship	10,000 (?)	Lanuvium I	—	no.479
Duovirate	10,000 (?)	Pompeii I	c. 10 B.C.	no.1324a
Quinquennalitas	4,000 (?)	Fagifulae IV	140	no.498
Quinquennalitas	5,000 (?)	Ausculum II	161/180	no.467h
Flaminate	5,000 (?)	Lanuvium I	—	no.479
Augurate	5,000–6,000 (?)	Brundisium II	—	no.509
Sevirate	2,000	Asisium VI	(pre-100)	no.1313
Sevirate	2,000	Forum Sempronii IV	—	no.463; 463a
(Sevirate)	2,000	Lacippo BAETICA	—	II 1934
Augustalitas	2,000	(regio I)	—	no.1314
Augustalitas	2,000	Cereatae Marianae I	—	no.1315
Augustalitas	2,000 (?)	Aquilonia II	—	nos.467d; 467e
Augustalitas	3,000	Cures Sabini IV	—	no.478
Augustalitas	10,000	Teanum Sidicinum I	—	no.1312
Curator Augustalium	10,000	Ostia I	182 etc.	no.1311
Magister collegii	1,600 (?)	Antium I	40–4	no.1316

for a show which he re-paid as an act of generosity. The town of Paestum on two occasions paid HS25,000 to magistrates to meet the cost of gladiatorial shows.[1] The plebs of Formiae offered a magistrate the same sum in order to double the value of the *munus* that he was about to give. At Allifae, a magistrate received HS13,000 from the city for gladiators and *venationes*. And at Velitrae a magistrate engaged in road building received HS14,000 from the city to cover transport costs.[2] These five examples all come from towns south of Rome. The local funds that provided these payments may have been accumulated from *summae honorariae*. Although most records of payments for magistracies in Italy show them being made in kind rather than in cash, this is not necessarily significant, since cash payments need not leave any epigraphic record. There were also sometimes substantial cash gifts to the city. Six legacies for this purpose range in value from HS400,000 at Mantua to HS100,000 at Petelia.[3] It was not unknown for funds given to the city for one purpose to be diverted to another; fear of such practices made Pliny discourage his friends from making cash payments to cities.[4] Most foundations seem to have taken the form of cash payments to the city nevertheless. These

[1] Nos.1335; 1336a; 1336b.
[2] Nos.1336; 1338; 1337.   [3] Nos.1328–33.
[4] *Ep.* 7.18. Technically towns needed government permission to transfer funds from one purpose to another; see Suetonius *Tib.* 31.1; *IRT* 396 (Commodus). Cf. also above p.137 n.2.

endowments must have added to the administrative problems of local government. Many Italian cities had substantial funds at their disposal. Aquileia for instance was able to spend HS500,000 of public money on a town building project.[1] Whether or not the government saw financial maladministration as a growing problem, the appointment of *curatores reipublicae* in Italy from Trajan onwards represents an attempt by the central government to regulate civic spending.[2]

---

[1] No.440 and note. Other costed outlays by cities in Italy (marked with a double asterisk) have the following values: HS53,608 (no.460); HS30,000 (no.452); HS25,000 (no.496); HS22,600 (no.464); HS8,590.5 (no. 466); (7,500?) (no.480a); 7,000+ (no.481); HS5,250 (no.484); HS4,936 (no.485); HS672.5 (no.490). The transfers of funds to building purposes mentioned in the preceding account of *summae honorariae* also represent the expenditure of civic funds.

[2] Cf. *ILS* 5918a; 6190. Ruggiero 2.1345–77; *Staatsrecht* 2.1082–4; R. Duncan-Jones *PBSR* 33 (1965) 206–7; Jones 1971, 543.

Italian costs

CONTENTS
Numbers refer to items in the list

ABBREVIATIONS
Entries numbered in italics in the list are the subject of notes on pp. 224–37.

The Roman numeral in capitals after each place name indicates the region of Italy to which the town belongs.

AM   Alpes Maritimae
D   Cost given in denarii
PR   Promise fulfilled by heir or descendant
*   Testamentary outlay

**   Public outlay
***   Private bequest administered by the city

Round brackets indicate a town or site whose ancient name is not known.

Square brackets enclose sections of an ancient text that have been restored.

+ after a figure indicates that some increases in the amount is referred to in the inscription without being specified.

Other abbreviations are listed on pp. x–xiv above.

I. CONSTRUCTION COSTS

	Identification	Price (HS)	Town	Date	Reference
	BUILDINGS				
439.	Thermae (Neptuni), promised by Hadrian, built by Pius	2,000,000+	Ostia I	139	XIV 98, cf. p.481 =*ILS* 334
**440.*	In hoc opus res p(ublica)...erogavit	1,000,000	Aquileia X	—	V 969; cf. *Aquileia Nostra* 8–9 (1937–8) 42, fig.1
441.	[Bibliotheca] given by the younger Pliny	[1,000,000]	Comum XI	96/108	Mommsen *Ges.Schr.*4. 434 and n.6; *Ep.* 5.7; *Ep.* 7.18; V 5262 = *ILS* 2927
442.	In aquam... testamento dedit	600,000	Verona X	(pre-100)	*NS* (1893) 11; *ILS* 5757, cf. V 3402; V 3447
443.	Balineum solo suo... aedificavit	352,000+	Corfinium IV	122/50	IX 3152 = *ILS* 5676; cf. IX 3153
444.	Balnea projected by Fronto	350,000/ 300,000	—	140/80	A. Gellius 19.10.2–4
445.	[T]hermae municipi...	330,000+	Tarquinii VII	161/70	XI 3366
445a.	Imp...Antonino Aug. Pio...indulgentissimo patrono	300,000	Neapolis I	139/61	*NS* (1892) 480
446.	Ex qua pecunia templum exstructum et forum stratum est	300,000	Sinuessa I	pre-69	*AE* 1926, 143; *v.* no.640
446a.	—	300,000 (?)	Tarracina I	(100/90)	X 6328 = *ILS* 6278
447.	Reliquit ad balinei fabrica(m)	150,000	Tifernum Tiberinum VI	*c.* 170	XI 5939 = *ILS* 5678
448.	(fragment of epistylium)	120,000 (?+)	Pola X	—	V 62; cf. *IIt* 10.1.93
449.	[Aqu]a Virgin...	100,000	Perusia VII	(pre-100)	XI 1946
450–1.	Balneum Clodianum emptum cum suis aedificiis	60,000	Teanum Sidicinum I	(pre-100)	X 4792 = *ILS* 5677
**452–3.*	—	30,000	Praeneste I	(pre-100)	XIV 3016 = I² 1474
	ROADS				
454.	Imp...Hadrianus ...viam Appiam per millia passus (15.75) longa vetustate amissam ...fecit	1,726,100 (HS21.79 per foot)	Beneventum-Aeclanum II	123	IX 6075 = *ILS* 5875; IX 6072; *NS* (1897) 160; *AE* 1930, 122; cf. Liebenam 150

	Identification	Price (HS)	Town	Date	Reference
**455.	[Via a(b)] mil(iario) LXX[XXV]III ad mil(iarium) CX...la Interamnium vo[rsus ad mil(iarium) C]XX	600,000 (? +)	(Interamnia Praetuttiano- rum V)	pre-50 B.C.	VI 3824+31603, cf. *NS* (1896) 87 ff. = *ILS* 5799 = *ILLRP* 465
*456.	Et m(ilia) p(edum) (3) (stravit)	200,000 (or less)	Tarquinii VII	(pre-100)	XI 3384+p.1337
**457.	[Via gla]rea sternenda a(b) mil(iario) [LXXVIII et per A]p[e]nninum muunien[da per mil. pass.] XX	150,000 (? +)	(*regiones* VIII/ VI)	(pre-50 B.C.)	*v.* 455
457a.	Viam Augustam a porta Cimina usque ad Anniam et viam Sacram a Chalcidico ad lucum Iunon. Curritis vetustate consumptas a novo restituerunt	100,000	Falerii VII	(pre-200)	XI 3126 cf. p.1323 = *ILS* 5374
458.	[Via] faciunda	100,000 (?)	Florentia VII	(pre-200)	XI 1601
**459.	Viae latitudin(em) adiecer(unt), substruction(es) et erismas fac(iundum) loc(averunt); in id opus ex d(ecreto) d(ecurionum) pecu[n](ia) lud(orum)	80,000 (? +)	Hispellum VI	(pre-100)	XI 5276 = *ILS* 5377
**460.	P(ecunia) p(ublica) ...ad [f]orum pecuari[um] viam sternund[am] coer(averunt)	53,608	Atina Latii I	—	X 5074 = *ILS* 5367 = *ILLRP* 551
461.	In vias sternendas in publicum dedit	37,000	Asisium VI	(pre-100)	XI 5400 = *ILS* 7812; XI 5399 = *ILS* 5369; *v.* 494, 1313, 1341, 1354
*462.	Testamento viam sterni iussit	30,000	Concordia X	—	V 1894
463.	(13) Augustales (se)viri...viam long(am) p(edum) (1165)...ob honorem sexviratus sua pecunia silice sternen(dam) curarunt	(26,000, if summa honoraria of HS2,000; cost per foot HS 22.32?)	Forum Sempronii VI	(pre-200)	Liebenam 150; XI 6126; cf. 1313 and 467 below
**464.	Via facta	22,600	(vallis Ossolae) XI	196	*ILS* 5884, cf. V 6649

Identification	Price (HS)	Town	Date	Reference
464a. Aed(ilis), ob honorem, in viam	20,000	Cremona X	(pre-100)	V 4097
(**)465. Viam Mactorinam longa vetustate rescis(am)... restituit, acceptis ab r.p. in [ve]ctui (*sic*) silicis HS $\overline{XIIII}$	14,000+	Velitrae I	(pre-200)	*AE* 1919, 64
**466. Viam lapide ster(nendam) p(edum) (414) ex d(ecreto) d(ecurionum) p(ecunia) p(ublica), pr(etio) (denariorum 5, assium 3)	(8,590.5) at HS20.75 (per foot)	Cereatae Marianae I	(pre-100)	I² 2537 = *ILLRP* 466; cf. *NS* (1921) 69 ff.
466a. Viam plostralem fecit de sua pecunia	[6,500]	Atina I	(pre-200)	*AE* 1922, 127
467. (3) Augustales (se)viri viam long. p(edes) (248) ...ob honorem sexviratus sua pecunia silice sternendam curarunt	(6,000?; cost per foot HS24.2?)	Forum Sempronii VI	(pre-200)	XI 6127; *v.* 463
467a. 3 miles of road, 'ob honorem (quinquennalitatis)'	—	Aeclanum II	138/61	IX 1156 = *ILS* 5878
467b. Curator viarum sternendarum pedum decem millia viam sua pecunia fecit [i.e. 2 miles of road]	—	Allifae IV	(pre-200)	IX 2345 = *ILS* 5881
467c. Hic permissu... Hadriani Aug. viam per passuum duum milium euntibus in Apuliam (stravit) [2 miles]	—	Trivicum II	117/38	IX 1414 = *ILS* 5877
467d. Aug(ustalis) plateam stravit ped(es) (880)	—	Aquilonia II	—	IX 968; see p.152
467e. Aug(ustalis) plateam stravit ped(es) 800	—	Aquilonia II	—	IX 6259; see p.152
467f. Augustales straverunt [pedes] (800) [almost 1/6th mile]	—	Aquilonia II	161/80	IX 6258
467g. Impensa mea clivom stravi lapide ab imo susum longum pedes (340) latum cum marginibus pedes (9)	—	Ficulea I	41/69	XIV 4012, cf. *EE* IX, p.488 = *ILS* 5387; *AE* 1964, 115
467h. Ob [honorem quin]quennalitat(is) per (44) passuum [ex indulgen]tia divi Pii ...stravit [220 feet]	—	Ausculum II	161/80	IX 670

Identification	Price (HS)	Town	Date	Reference
467i. Mag(ister) Aug(ustalis) viam stravit long(am) p(edum) (58)	—	(Frigento) near Aeclanum II	(pre-200)	IX 1048 = *ILS* 5879

MISCELLANEOUS BUILDING WORKS AND RESTORATIONS

Identification	Price (HS)	Town	Date	Reference
*468. ...[Dedit] ita ut balinea Sergium et Put[inium]...refecta in usu mu[nicip(um)] essent	800,000	Altinum X	(post-100)	*NS* (1928) 283
*469. In opus ornament(a) HS $\overline{CCCC}$, ded(ucta) (vigesima) p(opuli) R(omani) d(edit)	380,000	Concordia X	—	V 1895
469a. Adiectis in ornatum (thermarum) (Pliny the younger)	300,000 (? +)	Comum XI	111/13	V 5262 = *ILS* 2927
470. Balineum quod vi consumptum fuerat ampliatis solo et operibus, intra biennium pecunia sua restituit...in quod opus legata quoque rei p. testamento...uxoris suae HS CC consensu ordinis amplius erogavit	(?) + 200,000	Novaria XI	(138/61)	V 6513
470a. ...et aedem Mi[nervae ex] HS $\overline{CL}$ restituit	150,000	Brixia X	(pre-200)	Pais no.682
*471. [Temple dedicated to Tiberius] Testamento suo ex HS C refici iussit	100,000	Tarracina I	—	X 6309 + p.1015
*472. Hic HS $\overline{C}$ in opus amphithe[atri...] in annos decem	100,000 (? +)	Luca VII	(50/200)	XI 1527
*473. Et ad schol(am) exornandam HS $\overline{C}$ (legavit)	100,000	Mantua X	(50/200)	V 4059 = *ILS* 5012; *v.* 1328
*474. Legavit ad exornandam aedem Pomonis, ex qua summa factum est fastigium inauratum, podium, pavimenta marm(orea), opus tectorium	50,000	Salernum I	—	X 531, cf. p.965 = *ILS* 3593
475. Hic ob honorem aedilitat(is) hanc [po]rticum vetustate dilapsam [refecit]	29,300	Falerii VII	—	XI 3123 + p.1323 = *ILS* 6587

	Identification	Price (HS)	Town	Date	Reference
476.	Ad aedem [Fortunae] Melioris [in] pavimen[t](um) [dedit]	20,000	Interamna Nahars VI	(pre-100)	XI 4216
477.	Ad amphitheatri dedicationem... p(ollicitus?) [e(st)?]	20,000	Tibur IV	(pre-100)	XIV 4259 = *ILS* 5630; cf. *IIt* 4.1.202
478.	[B]alneum refectum pe[c(unia) pu]blica et ex HS ternis milli[bus q]uae contulerunt sevirales (5?+)	(?)+ 15,000 (?+)	Cures Sabini X	(pre-200)	IX 4978 = *ILS* 5670
479.	In refectionem balinei intulerunt	15,000	Lanuvium I	(pre-200)	XIV 2115 = *ILS* 6198
479a.	In straturam plateae Cererum sacrae	13,000	Lilybaeum SICILY	169/72	*AE* 1964, 181
480.	[Thermas?] reficiundas	8,841.5+	Tegianum III	(pre-100)	X 290 = *ILLRP* 674
480a.	Lex parieti faciendo in area quae est ante aedem Serapi trans viam	[7,500] (?)	Puteoli I	104 B.C.	X 1781+p.1009 = *ILS* 5317 = *ILLRP* 518
**481.	Ponte[m] d(e) s(enatus) s(ententia) f(aciendum) c(uraverunt)	7,000+	Ager Beneventanus II	(pre-100)	IX 2121
482.	Et dedit...in aedem Dianae restituendam	6,200	Iguvium VI	27 B.C./ A.D. 14	XI 5820+p.1395 = *ILS* 5531; *v.* 1079, 1325, 1364a
483.	HS VI n. coll(egio) f(abrum) quae... avus eius...ad exornandam scholam pollicitus erat, dedit	6,000	Ostra VI	—	XI 6191
**484.	Labrum...ex p(ecunia) p(ublica) f(aciendum) c(uraverunt)	5,250	Pompeii I	3/4 A.D.	X 817+p.967 = *ILS* 5726
**485.	Turrim ex s(enatus) c(onsulto) refici[end(am)] curarunt	4,936	Pinna IV	(pre-100)	IX 3354 = *ILS* 5327
*486.	Porticum testamento p[oni]...fieri iussit	4,000	Abellinum I	—	X 1136
487.	Porticus...	3,600 (?+)	Mediolanum XI	(pre-100)	Pais no.1297
488.	Ad stratam refic(iendam)	2,000	(regio I)	—	X 1885 = *ILS* 5882 (IX 664 is a false copy, cf. *Epigraphica* 10 (1948) 15–16)

6

	Identification	Price (HS)	Town	Date	Reference
489.	Ob honorem Augustali(tatis) collabentem pontem pecunia publica restitutum, in cujus restitutionem HS$\overline{II}$ contulerat, adiecta pecunia	2,000 +	Cereatae Marianae I	(pre-200)	*NS* (1921) 70
**490.	—	672.5	Pompeii I	pre-80	x 803 (cf. 804) = *ILS* 6357

STATUE COSTS

	Identification	Price (HS)	Town	Date	Reference
491.	Statuas...fieri ...iussit	550,000 (?)	Patavium x	(pre-100)	v 2861, 2862
492.	Is...HS $\overline{C}$ m.n. legaverit, ex qua summa tensae Minervae ex argenti libris (100) cum parergis suis to[tis fierent]	100,000	Formiae I	(pre-200)	x 6102 = *ILS* 6282
493.	[Plebs urbana die ab] excessu eius XXXIII beneficior(um) eius [memor ex aere co]nlato...(statuam?) posuit	43,000	Mons Fereter VI	148	XI 6481
494.	Hic in statuas ponendas in aedem Herculis dedit	30,000	Asisium VI	(pre-100)	XI 5400 = *ILS* 7812; *v.* 461, 1313, 1341, 1354
495.	[Statuas s]ibi et fil(io) suo... poni iussit	(30,000)–60,000	Tifernum Tiberinum VI	*c.* 170	XI 5939 = *ILS* 5678
**496.	[Municipes e]t incolae in statuam ...in comitio ponendam censuer(unt)	25,000	Perusia VII	(pre-100)	XI 1946
496a.	C. Sentius C.f. Fab. Marianus, equo pub.	20,000	Brixia x	—	v 4472
497.	(Statuam) Iovi(s) Aug(usti)... test(amento) poni iussit	10,000	Augusta Taurinorum XI	(pre-200)	v 6955
498.	[Statue of Pius] ob honor. quinquen-(nalitatis)	4,000	Fagifulae IV	140	IX 2553

	Identification	Price (HS)	Town	Date	Reference
499.	Geminiae P. fil. Maximae statua (cum ornamentis?)	4,000	Parma VIII	(pre-200)	XI 1088
500.	[Mentei Bo]nae	3,055 (? +)	Cora I	pre-1 B.C.	X 6514 = *ILS* 3819 = *ILLRP* 225
500a.	Hercules	(?) + 2,200	Mantua X	—	Pais no.669
*501.	Genio Dom(i)nor(um), Cereri...imagines argent. (2)	2,000	Patavium X	—	V 2795 = *ILS* 3625
*502.	Iovi Felvenni	800	Pagus Arusnatium X	(pre-200)	V 3904 = *ILS* 4899
503.	Signum Proserpinae reficiundum statuendumque arasque reficiundas...curarunt	770	Vibo III	(pre-100)	X 39 = *ILS* 3974
504.	(Statuam?), acceptis ex arca (HS 500), reliq(ua) sua pec(unia) fec(it)	500 +	Volsinii VII	(pre-200)	XI 7302

STATUE WEIGHTS

(Weights are given in the Roman pound, which equalled approximately 327.45 gms, or 72% of the pound avoirdupois)

	A. GOLD				
505.	Mercurio...ex voto don(o) ded(it) dracones aureos... adiectis ornament. [e]t cortina	5 pounds of gold	Mediolanum XI	(pre-200)	*ILS* 3192
506.	Imp...Hadrianus... I(unoni) S(ospiti) M(atri) R(eginae) statuam ex donis aureis et arg(enteis) vetustate corruptis fieri et consecrari iussit	3.08 pounds of gold; 206.17 pounds of silver (bullion value about HS110,000)	Lanuvium I	136	XIV 2088 = *ILS* 316
*507.	Imago	2 pounds of gold	Ariminum VIII	—	XI 364 = *ILS* 5471a
508.	Dracon(em)... Deae don(o) posuit	1 pound of gold	Augusta Taurinorum XI	—	V 6965
509.	Genius decurion(um) et populi in auguratu gratuit. sibi delato	1 pound of gold	Brundisium II	(pre-200)	IX 32
*509a.	Fortunae Primig(eniae) corona aurea	1 pound of gold	Praeneste I	(pre-100)	XIV 3015 cf. *ILS* 6256

	Identification	Price (HS)	Town	Date	Reference
510.	Luna, voto suscepto	½ pound of gold	Luna VII	—	*AE* 1931, 94
*511.	Cor(ona) aur(ea)	0.26 of a pound of gold	Ostia I	—	XIV 21 + p.481 = *ILS* 4373
511a.	Fortuna	0.20 of a pound of gold	Arna VI	—	XI 5607
*512.	(Liber Pater,) cum redimiculo aur(eo)	0.01 of a pound of gold	Ariminum VIII	—	XI 358 = *ILS* 3363
	B. SILVER (see also no.506 above)				
*513.	Opus quadrigae cum effigie Imp. Hadriani Aug.	1,567.17 pounds of silver (HS730,000 bullion value)	Beneventum II	120/38	IX 1619 = *ILS* 5502
513a.	Scyphos	[150.37 (?)] pounds of silver	Neapolis I	(96/130)	*IGRR* 1.432
*514.	Aesculapius	100 pounds of silver	Ager Amiternus IV	153/79	IX 4512
515.	Clipeo posito in curia	100 pounds of silver	Mons Fereter VI	*c*. 120/48	XI 6481
*516.	I(uppiter) O(ptimus) M(aximus)	30.52 pounds (of silver?)	(Ferrara) X	(pre-200)	V 2381
517.	Deus Patrius	15.03 pounds of silver	Ostia I	(pre-200)	XIV 3 = *ILS* 3299
518.	Fortuna Primigenia	11.06 pounds of silver	Praeneste I	54/69	XIV 2861
**519.	Fortuna Redux	10.42 pounds of silver	Cures Sabini IV	128/38	IX 4952 = *ILS* 3702
520.	'Tunni Iovis'	10 pounds of silver	Florentia VII	—	XI 1593
521.	Genius coloniae Ostiensium	10 pounds of silver	Ostia I	141	XIV 8 = *ILS* 6154
522.	Tiberius	10 pounds of silver	Teate Marrucinorum IV	36/7	*AE* 1941, 105
523.	Fortuna	6.16 pounds of silver	Praeneste I	—	XIV 2869
524.	Imago Gen(i)i praef(ecturae) Claudiae	6 pounds of silver	Forum Clodii VII	165	XI 7556 = *ILS* 6584

	Identification	Price (HS)	Town	Date	Reference
525.	Imago Genii municip(i)i Lilybitanorum	5 pounds of silver	Lilybaeum SICILY	(pre-193)	X 7223 = *ILS* 6768
526.	I(uppiter)... Dol(ichenus)	4½ pounds of silver	Puteoli I	—	X 1577
527.	—	3 pounds of silver	Ostia I	196	XIV 71
528.	[Im]ag(o) Crispinae	3 pounds of silver	Ostia I	177/88	*AE* 1948, 24
*529.	Trulla argentea anaglypta	2.92 pounds of silver	Regium Iulium III	(pre-200)	X 6 = *ILS* 5471
*530.	Lares argentei (7)	2.66 pounds of silver	Regium Iulium III	(pre-200)	X 6 = *ILS* 5471
*531.	Liber Pater	2½ pounds of silver	Ariminum VIII	—	XI 358 = *ILS* 3363
532.	[Im]ag(o)	2½ pounds of silver	Ostia I	166	XIV 4554
533.	[Imago?]	2½ pounds of silver	Ostia I	169/76	XIV 4556
533a.	Spei Aug. gabat⟨h⟩a	2.01 pounds of silver	Concordia x	—	*ILS* 3774
534.	Typus Matris deus	2 pounds of silver	Ostia I	—	XIV 36 = *ILS* 4113
535.	Virtus dendrop(horum)	2 pounds of silver	Ostia I	—	XIV 69
536.	Imago Antonini Aug.	2 pounds of silver	Ostia I	143/61	*AE* 1940, 62; *v.* 539, 540, 545–8, 1006, 1010
537.	Minerva Aug(usta)	2 pounds of silver	Placentia VIII	(pre-200)	XI 1295 = *ILS* 3136
537a.	Bonae Deae phiala	1.58 pounds of silver	Aquileia x	—	V 8242 = *ILS* 3769
*538.	Isis Bubastis Venus	1½ pounds of silver	Ostia I	—	XIV 21 + p.481 = *ILS* 4373
539.	Imago Concordiae	1½ pounds of silver	Ostia I	143/61	*AE* 1940, 62
540.	Imago Verissimi Caesar(is)	1½ pounds of silver	Ostia I	143/61	*AE* 1940, 62
541.	Caracalla	1.03 pounds of silver	Ostia I	212	XIV 119 + p.481
542.	—	1 pound of silver	Florentia VII	—	XI 1586
543.	Imago Matris Deum	1 pound of silver	Ostia I	—	XIV 34 = *ILS* 4111
544.	Imago Attis	1 pound of silver	Ostia I	—	XIV 35 = *ILS* 4112
545.	Imago...Antonini Aug.	1 pound of silver	Ostia I	143/61	*AE* 1940, 62
546.	Imago Ael(i) Caesaris	1 pound of silver	Ostia I	143/61	*AE* 1940, 62

	Identification	Price (HS)	Town	Date	Reference
547.	Imag(o) Antonini Aug.	1 pound of silver	Ostia I	143/61	*AE* 1940, 62
548.	Imag(o) Verissimi Caes(aris)	1 pound of silver	Ostia I	143/61	*AE* 1940, 62
549.	[Man]telum arg(enteum)	0.25 pounds of silver	Puteoli I	—	X 1598
549a.	Luna argentea	0.17 pounds of silver	Corfinium IV	—	IX 3146 = *ILS* 4107

SEPULCHRAL AND BURIAL COSTS

	Identification	Price (HS)	Town	Date	Reference
550.	..st.Popillius Theo...	500,000 (? +)	Fabrateria Nova I	(pre-100)	X 5624
551.	Valerius Ianuarius, [ex libris argen?]ti	500 [pounds of silver?]	Verona X	—	V 3801
552.	Usonia Mu. f(ilia)...	100,100	Praeneste I	(pre-100)	XIV 3399
553.	...alvi...	100,000 (? +)	Ameria VI	—	XI 4518
554.	L. Polem...	100,000 (? +)	Brixia X	—	V 4677
555.	C. Apidius P.f. Qui. Bassus, prim(ipilaris) leg XI, (octo) vir Amiterni	100,000 (excluding cost of site)	(Lunghezza) I	—	XIV 3906 = *ILS* 6544
556.	C. Asinius C.f. Ani. Severus, p(rimi)-p(ilaris)	100,000	Mediolanum XI	—	V 5820
557.	L. Numisius L. lib. Agathemerus, sevir Augustalis, negotiator ex Hispania citeriore	100,000	Ostia I	(pre-200)	XIV 397
558.	Corellia C.f. Galla Papiana, uxor C. Corelli N.f. Fab	100,000	(San Cesareo), near Praeneste I	(pre-100)	XIV 2827 = X, p.979 = *ILS* 6294; *v.* 665 and 666
559.	...Nonius L.f. Ter. L..	100,000?	Venafrum I	—	X 4967
560.	M. Doius M.[f]. Ro[m]. Clemens, decur. adl(ectus), quaest(or) (bis), flamen Augustalis	76,000	Ateste X	(pre-200)	V 2524
561.	P. Manlius Ti.f. Pal. Ligus	60,000	(Ausonia) I	—	X 5377
561a.	C. Tifanus C.f. Clu. Cilo, pr. pil.	50,000	Carsulae VI	(pre-100)	XI 4573
562.	—	50,000 (? +)	Formiae I	—	X 6210
563.	Socrates Astomachi, natus in egregiis Trallibus ex Asia	50,000	Ostia I	(pre-200)	XIV 480
564.	...T.f. Libo, praef. equit...	50,000	Spoletium VI	—	*AE* 1954, 47

	Identification	Price (HS)	Town	Date	Reference
565.	...inius...	50,000	Trea V	(pre-100)	IX 5675
D566.	Aurelius Flavinus, optio leg. XI Claudiae	40,000	Aquileia X	(post-200)	v 895; cf. *Aquileia Nostra* 4–5 (1933–4) 30, fig.49
567.	...N.l. Philomusus	30,000	Suessa Aurunca I	(pre-100)	*EE* VIII, p.143, n.569
568.	L. Casienus A.f. Cla.	20,000	Aequiculi IV	(pre-100)	IX 4142
569.	...s Serviliae l. Pylad[es],... Aug(ustalitate) Allif(ensibus) honorat(us)	20,000	Allifae IV	(pre-100)	IX 2365
570–1.	L. Valeri[us] Firmi f. St[el.] Firminu[s], (se)vir Aug(ustalis)	20,000	Augusta Taurinorum XI	—	v 7036
572.	L. Vibius Varus	20,000	Capena VII	—	XI 4009
573.	—	20,000	Carsioli IV	(pre-100)	IX 4102
573a.	M. Attius	20,000	Corfinium IV	(pre-100)	*Epigraphica* 20 (1958) 17
574.	—	20,000	Forum Novum IV	(pre-100)	IX 6358 = 4844
575.	Q. Veturius Q.f. Pom. Pexsus, trib. mil. (bis), praefectus fabrum	20,000	Nepet VII	(pre-100)	XI 3205 = *ILS* 4948
576.	P. Fabius P.l. Menodotus	20,000	Puteoli	(pre-100)	X 2402
577.	Pompeia Axiothea	20,000	Reate IV	(pre-200)	IX 4731 + p.685
578.	...Nasica quinq(uennalis)	20,000	Teanum Sidicinum I	(pre-100)	X 4795
579.	C. Vibius Valens, (se)vir Aug.	20,000	Tergeste X	(post-100)	v 560; cf. *IIt* 10.4.74
580.	C. Marcius Volson. f. Serg. Maximus, tr(ierarchus)	18,300	Misenum I	(pre-100)	X 3361 = *ILS* 2844
581.	M. Staius M. et Ɔ. lib. Lygdamus... Aug(ustalis)	15,000	Luceria II	(pre-200)	IX 816 = *ILS* 6479
582.	Fadius Dexter (dendrophorus)	15,000+	(vallis Silari superior) III	—	X 445
583.	.Sallustius T.f. Pup. Virgula, scrib(a) aed(ilis) cur(ulis)	15,000	Ameria VI	(pre-100)	XI 4358
584.	—	15,000	Blera VII	(pre-100)	XI 3352
585.	L. Papius L.f. Fal.	12,000	Ager Falernus I	(pre-100)	X 4727 = *ILS* 6297 = *ILLRP* 667

	Identification	Price (HS)	Town	Date	Reference
586.	...M.f. Fal... [tr.mil. a] populo	11,000	Capua I	37 B.C./ A.D. 14	X 3888
587.	P. Publilius Anthus, (se)vir Augustalis	(?)+ 10,000	Cures Sabini IV	54/68	IX 4977 = *ILS* 6558
587a.	[P]et[r]onius P.f. Fa[l]. Flac[cus]	10,000	Atella I	(pre-100)	X 3749
588.	...[leg(atus) leg(ionis)] I Adiutricis, quaest(or), [tri]bunus mili[t.] legionis X Geminae, in omnibus honoribus candidato Caesarum	[10,000] (?+)	Atina Lucaniae III	(pre-100)	X 336
589.	...et Pollentiae Iphidi et lib. libertabusq. suis	10,000	(Chioggia) X	—	V 2309
590.	L. Aemilius L.f. Vot. Proculus, (centurio) veteranus, pr(aetor) Cumis	10,000	Cumae I	(pre-100)	*ILS* 8269
591.	L. Valerius C.f. Ouf. Broccus	10,000	Mediolanum XI	(pre-100)	V 6110; cf. *Epigraphica* I (1939) 184
592.	P. Aufidius L.f., (quattuor)vir, (duo)vir, tr(ibunus) milit(um), praef(ectus) fab(rum)	10,000	Placentia VIII	(pre-100)	XI 1217
593.	...lius C.l. Philomus(us) mag(ister) pagi Felicis Suburbani	10,000	Pompeii I	pre-80	*ILS* 6377
594.	—	(?)+ 10,000	Saepinum IV	(pre-100)	IX 2497
595.	M. Seppius M.l. Philoxsenus	10,000	Teanum Sidicinum I	(pre-100)	X 4815
596.	L. Vilius C.f.	8,000	Spoletium VI	(pre-100)	XI 4938
597.	L. Vedius Q.f.	8,000	Tuder VI	(pre-100)	XI 4721
598.	[V]etilia L.f.	6,000	Asculum Picenum V	(pre-100)	*NS* (1958) 76, IX
599.	C. Iulius Her[a]clida tr(ierarchus)	6,000	Misenum I	—	X 3359
600.	T. Manlius Alexsa, Labicia M.f.	[6],000	Ostia I	(pre-100)	XIV 1307; *NS* (1938) 52; *Scavi di Ostia* 3.1 (1958) 74–7; 147–9
601.	...C.l. Priamus	6,000	Ameria VI	(pre-100)	XI 4504
602.	—	5,000	Abellinum I	(pre-100)	X 1166

	Identification	Price (HS)	Town	Date	Reference
603.	—	5,000	Capua I	(pre-100)	X 4450
604.	...nus Alpinus, miles coh(ortis) VIIII [p]r(aetoriae) speculator(um)	5,000	Ager Novariensis XI	(pre-200)	V 6597
605.	M. Sittius C.f. Fab. Fronto Saufeius Proculus [related to praef. fab., tribunus mil.] Huic decurion(es) locum sepulturae et in funere HS(5,000) decr(everunt)	5,000	Surrentum I	(pre-100)	X 680
606.	L. Cornelius L.f. Men. M... flamen Romae Ti. C[aes. Aug.], augur, aed., IIvir qu[inquenn.], praef. fabr. bis. Huic decurion. publice locum [sepulturae et in] funer(e) HS(5,000) ...[decreverunt]	5,000	Surrentum I	(pre-100)	X 688
607.	C. Arrius, Arria C.f. Bassa	5,000	Teanum Apulum II	(pre-100)	IX 707
608.	...Aquillius... [Se?]cundus, (quattuor)v[ir]	(?)+ 5,000	Vercellae XI	(pre-100)	V 6661
608a.	—	4,000	Capua I	(pre-100)	X 4444
609.	L. Gallius Silvester mil(es) c(o)hort. II praet(oriae), sibi et parentibus	4,000	Piquentum X	—	V 430; cf. *IIt* 10.3.124
610.	P. Sextilius P.f. Fal. Rufus, aed(ilis) iterum, (duo)vir quinq(uennalis) Pompeis, decurio adlectus ex veterib(us) Nola	4,000	Nola I	pre-80	X 1273 = *ILS* 6344
611.	Corn[elia] D.f. Maxima	3,400	Ager Compsinus II	—	IX 1077
612.	...T.l. Licinus	3,000(? +)	Amiternum IV	(pre-100)	IX 4269
613.	Tittia L.l. Daphne	3,000	Formiae I	(pre-100)	X 6186
614.	A. Sempronius A.l. Lucrio Gallus	3,000	Nola I	—	X 1327
615.	P. Aemilius P.f. Vopiscus, sevir	3,000	Perusia VII	—	XI 1939
616.	M. Tadius L.f. Rom.	3,000	Sora I	(pre-100)	X 5753
617.	Sex. Turuenus C.f. Ouf.	2,000	Aquinum I	(pre-100)	X 5530

	Identification	Price (HS)	Town	Date	Reference
618.	Q. Gracchius Rufus, mil(es) coh(ortis) II pr(aetoriae)	2,000	(Bagnacavallo) VIII	—	*AE* 1964, 209
618a.	C. Prosius M.f. Fal. Rufus	2,000	Capua I	(pre-100)	X 4306
619.	C. Iulius Postumus, miles ex class(e) pr(aetoria) Miseniens(i)	2,000	Misenum I	—	X 3360
620.	T. Terentius T.f. Men. Felix Maior, aedil(is). Huic publice locus datus et HS(2,000)	2,000 (? +)	Pompeii I	pre-80	X 1019 + p.967
621.	A. Umbricius A.f. Men. Scaurus, (duo)vir i(ure) d(icundo). Huic decuriones locum monum(enti) et HS(2,000) in funere...censuerunt	2,000 (? +)	Pompeii I	pre-80	X 1024 + p.967 = *ILS* 6366
622.	C. Vestorius Priscus, aedil(is)... locus sepulturae datus et in funere HS(2,000), d(ecreto) d(ecurionum)	2,000	Pompeii I	pre-80	*AE* 1911, 72 = *AE* 1913, 70. Cf. G. Spano *Mem.Lincei* ser. 7, 3 (1943) 237–315
623.	Septumia L.f. D(ecreto) d(ecurionum) locus sepulturae publice datus et in funere HS(2,000)	2,000	Pompeii I	pre-80	*AE* 1913, 71
624.	C. Lucilius C.f. Vel. Vindex, miles c(o)hor(tis) VI praet(oriae)..., principalis, beneficiarius tribuni, deinde optio in centuria	2,000	Potentia V	—	IX 5809 = *ILS* 2078
625.	C. Surenus T.f. Ani. Seneca, mil(es) coh(ortis) VII [c(ivium)] R(omanorum) volunt[ar(iorum)]... Hic reliquit sodalib(us) Martensibus in ossa sua tuenda HS(2,000). Collegius (*sic*) iumentariorum huic cippo locum dedit.	2,000	Vicus Martis Tudertium VI	—	XI 4749

	Identification	Price (HS)	Town	Date	Reference
626.	D. Haterius Priscus	1,500	Ager Atinas III	—	X 380
D627.	Memmia Fortunata, n(atione) Picenesis... c(oniunx) manuplarii n(atione) Alexandrini	1,200	Misenum I	—	X 3608 = *ILS* 2903
628.	...Calvina	1,000	Alba Fucens IV	—	*EE* VIII, p.46 n.188
629.	Ter. Valerius Ter.l. Felix	1,000 (? +)	Ameria VI	—	XI 4532
630.	T. Venuleius T.f. Pom. Priscus (et) Sex. Venuleius T.f. Pom. Fuscus	1,000	Volsinii VII	—	XI 2803
631.	L. Volcacius Optatus	800	Telesia IV	—	IX 2309
632.	—	700 (? +)	Aquileia X	—	V 8345 + Pais no.127
633.	L. Berienus L.f.	600	Venafrum I	(pre-100)	X 4929
D634.	Teiedia Fortunata et L. Cornelius Firmus	480	Beneventum II	—	IX 1986
634a.	L. Petronius C.f. Fab.	400	Alba Fucens IV	pre-100	IX 4017
635.	Sex. Ninnius M.f. Buticus	260 (? +)	Ortona IV	—	IX 6315
D636.	Aur(elius) Super, circit(or) sub cura Iusti, coniugi... fecit Aur. Quintina: in funus et memoria erog(avit) *XXX	120	Cremona X	(post-200)	V 4100 = *ILS* 2795. Cf. XIV 3649

FOUNDATIONS

	Identification	Price (HS)	Town	Date	Reference
*637.	Et (Matidia iunior) Varianis alumnis masculis feminisque sestertium deciens singulis reliquit usurarium potius quam propri[um]: nam quinquagena annua ab Augusta singulis dari iussit.	2 million + yielding 100,000 + p.a. (5% interest)	(Capua? I)	161/70	Fronto *Ad Amicos* 1.14.1 (Naber, p.183; van den Hout I, p.173; cf. p.98)
*638.	[In alimenta] libertor(um) suor(um) homin(um) (100)... rei [p. legavit; quorum inc]rement(a) postea ad epulum [pl]eb. urban. voluit pertin[ere] (Pliny the younger)	1,866,666	Comum XI	111/13	V 5262 = *ILS* 2927; cf. *AE* 1947, 65

	Identification	Price (HS)	Town	Date	Reference
*639.	Trib. mil. (legionum) (2)... Hic legavit... municip(ibus) suis... ut ex reditu...quotannis ...natale (*sic*) suo municipib(us) aepulum et crust(ulum) et mulsum daretur	1,500,000	Spoletium VI	—	XI 4789
639a.	Government alimentary foundation for the support of 264 boys and 36 girls; boys to receive HS16, girls HS12 per month (HS12 & HS10 if illegitimate)	1,116,000 yielding 55,800 at 5%	Veleia VIII	98/102 & 103/13	XI 1147, cf. *ILS* 6675
*640.	Ex reditu...legato a Clod(i)is...viae tutela praestatur	1,000,000	Capua I	pre-69	X 3851 = *ILS* 5890; *v.* no.446
*641.	[Ut ex]...usu[ris p]uellae [alime]ntar[iae] (100) alerentu[r e]t... quodannis ludi eder[entur in] memori[am]...[matris?] suae, [et t]er in ann[o] decurio[nes c]enar[ent]	1,000,000 (?)	Ostia I	148/*c.* 180	XIV 4450, cf. 350
*642.	Alimenta for 100 boys up to age of 16 at HS20 per month; 100 girls up to age of 14 at HS16 per month	1,000,000 (income required = 43,200; probably 4.33% interest)	Tarracina I	(100/90)	X 6328 = *ILS* 6278
*643.	(Ut) quinto quoque anno munus gladiatorium ederetur [i.e. once every 4/5 years]	600,000	Pisaurum VI	(post-100)	XI 6377; cf. 6369
644.	[Vivu]s dedit in aliment(a) pueror. et puellar. pleb(is) urban(ae) (Pliny the younger)	500,000 (+) with income of 30,000	Comum XI	96/108	V 5262 = *ILS* 2927 + *Ep.* 7.18; cf. *AE* 1947, 65
*D645.	Decurion(ibus) et vicanis vicor(um) (7) sing(ulis) in annos (HS12) in perpet(uum) re[l(iquit) et in eam rem fundos (21) obligari iussit;	(504,000 if 5%)	Ariminum VIII	70/100	XI 419 = *ILS* 6663; cf. XI 390 & no.681

	Identification	Price (HS)	Town	Date	Reference
	quorum partem VI legis Falc(idiae) nomin(e) deductam... Lepidi[a] Septimina populo concessit				
645a.	...mag(istris) vicor(um)	450,000 (?)	Spoletium VI	—	*BCAR* App. 16 (1949–50) 52–3 +fig.5; XI 7872; *v.* 676a, 1179a
645b.	Government alimentary foundation for the support of (120/110) children	(401,800) yielding annually (20,090) (5% inferred; *v.* 639a)	Ligures Baebiani II	101	IX 1455, cf. *ILS* 6509
*646.	Ut ex...reditu (balinea Sergium et Putinium) cale[fier]ent	400,000	Altinum X	(post-100)	*NS* (1928) 283
*647.	Ut ex reditu...in perpetuum viri et impuberes utriusq(ue) sexsus gratis laventur	400,000	Bononia VIII	38/41	XI 720 = *ILS* 5674
*648.	Ut per sing(ulos) annos...populo epulum die natali...fili eius divideretur	400,000	Pisaurum VI	(post-100)	XI 6377
649.	In tutela (aquae quam in superiorem partem coloniae et in inferiorem inpensa sua perduxit) dedit	400,000	Pola X	(post-100)	V 47 = *ILS* 5755: cf. *IIt* 10.1.70 & fig.
*650.	Atinatibus...legavit, ut liberis eorum ex reditu, dum in aetate[m] pervenirent frumentu[m] et postea (HS1,000) darentur	400,000	Atina Latii I	54/68	X 5056 = *ILS* 977
*651.	...August(alis). Hi[c...in] lud[os] et in c[enam?] et in epulum...dari iussit	300,000	Concordia X	—	V 8664, cf. 1897–900
652.	(Ut) decuriones in publico cenarent et municipes praesentes acciperent aeris octonos (on 1 day per year)	250,000	Spoletium VI	(post-100)	XI 4815 = *ILS* 6638

	Identification	Price (HS)	Town	Date	Reference
*653.	[In perp(etuam)] tutelam (balineorum Sergii et Putinii)	200,000	Altinum x	(post-100)	NS (1928) 283; v. 646
*654.	Ut...natali ipsius et...natali... ma[tris] suae (et)... natali...patris sui decurio[nes, Au]g(ustales) et seviri sportulas acci[perent]	200,000	Altinum x	(post-100)	NS (1928) 283
*655.	[Et...] in tutela[m (thermarum)...(Pliny the younger)	200,000	Comum xi	111/13	v 5262 = ILS 2927
*656.	[Ad divisi]onem epularum	200,000	Mons Fereter vi	148	xi 6481
*657.	Ex cuius reditu... die natalis sui [distributio fiat]	130,000	Suasa vi	—	xi 6173
*658.	In epulum quod XVII K. Germanicas daretur ...legavit	120,000	Sentinum vi	84/96	xi 5745 = ILS 6644
659.	Item dedit (se)viris Aug(ustalibus) et compit(alibus) Larum Aug. et mag(istris) vicorum...ut...eodem die in publico vescerentur	120,000	Spoletium vi	(post-100)	xi 4815 = ILS 6638; AE 1937, 134; v. 652
*660.	In [t]uit[ionem] (statuarum)	105,000 + (200,000 in all?)	Patavium x	(pre-100)	v 2861-2; v. 491
661.	In tutelam bybliothecae (Pliny the younger)	100,000	Comum xi	96/108	v 5262 = ILS 2927; cf. AE 1947, 65
*662.	Ut...[natali] patris ...decurio[nibus singulis HS X[X?]-IIII et [una vescentibus?] sexsus femin[ei] singuli[s] HS IIII n. [darentur; item na]tal[i] matris suae...decurio[nibus]...	100,000	Firmum Picenum v	—	ix 5376; v. 765
*663.	Divisio mulsa[rum et crustulorum? suff]icientium	100,000	Mons Fereter vi	148	xi 6481
*664.	Ut ex usuris semissibus...die natalis mei... distributio fiat	100,000 at 6%	Petelia iii	138/61	ILS 6468

	Identification	Price (HS)	Town	Date	Reference
	decurionibus epulantibus (HS1,200), deducto ex his sumptu strationis; reliqui inter eos qui praesentes ea hora erunt dividantur; item Augustalibus eadem condicione (HS600) et municipibus... utriusque sexus ex more loci (HS4)..., item in cena parentalicia (HS200)				
*665.	Dedit coloniae Menturnensi HS C̄... ita uti...natali suo quodannis crustulum et mulsum detur	100,000	(Minturnae I)	(pre-100)	XIV 2827 = X p.979 = *ILS* 6294
*666.	Dedit...municipio Casini HS C̄...ita uti ...natali suo quodannis crustulum et mulsum detur	100,000	(Casinum I)	(pre-100)	XIV 2827 = X p.979 = *ILS* 6294
667.	Promisit...HS L̄X̄X̄X̄ n. ut ex reditu... die natalis fili sui ...viscerationis nomine dividatur decur. sing. HS (20), Augustalibus HS (12), Mercurialib. HS (10), item populo viritim HS (8)	80,000	Rudiae II	117/38	IX 23 = *ILS* 6472
D668.	Colleg(io) (fabrum centonariorum) de[dit ...ex c]uius summae red[itu magistri coll(egii)...] die natal. eius... sportul(as) ex (HS800) in[ter praesentes arbit]r(atu) suo divid(ant), oleum et propin(ationem) ex (HS3,000) praebeant; item lectisternium tempore parentalior(um) ex (HS800)...quodannis ponatur et parentetur; item coronae...ex (HS200) (bis) profundantur	(75,000 if 6.66% interest as in allied gift, no.677 below)	Comum XI		V 5272

	Identification	Price (HS)	Town	Date	Reference
669.	Hic...fundos (4)... ab r(e) p(ublica) redem(it) HSLXX̄ m.n. et in avit(um) r(ei) p(ublicae) reddid(it), ex quor(um) reditu de HSĪV m. CC...die natal. suo...daretur praesent. municipib. et incol. et mulierib. nuptis (refreshments & sportulae at several rates)	70,000 with income of 4,200 (6% interest)	Ferentinum Latii I	(post-100)	X 5853 cf. p.1013 = *ILS* 6271; *v.* 798, 1106, 1107
670.	In memoriam (mariti et filii) et sui coll(egio) n(autarum) B(rixianorum) ad rosas et profusiones q(uot)a(nnis) fac(iendas)...dedit	60,000	(Riva) X	—	V 4990
671.	HS(50,000) et fundum ...[et praedia duo] ...ex quo(rum) reditu quot[annis epulum?] daretur, hostiaque... inmol(etur)	50,000 +	Auximum V	(pre-100)	IX 5845 + p.689 = *ILS* 3775
672.	Dedit, ex quorum usuris quincunci[bus quod]annis...die natali eius dec[urionibus si]ngulis (HS20) dentur et decuri[alibus scribis ce]raris (HS150), libraris (HS50)... lic[tor]ibus (HS100)	50,000 at 5% interest	Ostia I	(160/200)	XIV 353 = *ILS* 6148; XIV 4642
673.	Obtulit decurionibus et universo populo HS(50,000) quae Mammiana vocentur, ex cuius summae usuris die natalis eius...divisionem percipere possint	50,000	Corfinium IV	(post-200)	IX 3160 = *ILS* 6530; IX 3180
674.	Arcae (ordinis Augustalium) [intulit] excepta stipulatione ut ex usuris M. II (?) ...quodannis...natali suo in [c]onventu inter	50,000	Ostia I	*c.* 230/40	XIV 431 + p.482

	Identification	Price (HS)	Town	Date	Reference
	praesentes hora II usque ad asse(m) dividatur, deducta ornatione statuae HS(100)				
675.	Arcae (ordinis Augustalium)...dedit ...excepta stipulatione (ut) ex usuris semissibus et M. II (?)...quodannis ...natali suo inter praesentes hora II usque ad asse(m) dividiatur (*sic*), deducta ornatione statu(a)e et familiae Augustal(ium) HS(100)	40,000 (6%)	Ostia I	182	XIV 367 = *ILS* 6164
*676.	Ex...reditu quotannis per Neptunalia oleum in campo et in thermis et balineis omnibus quae sunt Comi populo praeberetur	40,000	Comum XI	(pre-100)	V 5279 = *ILS* 6728
*676a.	For [decuriae IIII scamillar. operae veteres] a scaena	30,000 (?+)	Spoletium VI	—	*BCAR* App.16 (1949–50) 52–3 + fig.5; XI 7872
677.	Ex...reditu...die... natalis eius ante statuam lectist(ernium) ex (HS1,000) ponant, sport(ulas) (HS1,000) inter praesent(es) sibi divid(ant), oleum et propin(ationem) per rosam praebeant	30,000 yielding 2,000 (6.66% interest)	Comum XI	—	V 5272; *v*. 668
678.	Ex quor(um) reditu quodannis decurionib(us) coll(egii) fabr(um) ...die Neptunaliorum praesentibus sport(ulae) (HS8) dividerentur; et dec(uriae) XXVIII suae (HS600) quodannis darentur ut...arca(s) (duas)...rosis exornent de (HS100), sacrificientque ex (HS50) et de reliq(uis) ibi epulentur	30,000	Ravenna VIII	—	XI 126, cf. 127, + p.1228

	Identification	Price (HS)	Town	Date	Reference
679.	...Ord(ini) dec(urionum) et populo donavit ut diae (*sic*) natalis eius...sportul(a)e dividantur	25,000	Fabrateria Vetus I	(post-200)	X 5654
680.	[Con]fero vobis HS(20,000)... [cu]m usuris centesimi[s]... sportulis vestr... [d]ie natalis mei...	20,000 at 12%	Opitergium X	—	V 1978, cf. *ILS* 6690
681.	Singulis vicis...ad emptionem possessionis cuius de reditu die natalis sui sportular(um) divisio semper celebretur	7 foundations of 20,000 each	Ariminum VIII	(post-200)	XI 379 = *ILS* 6664
682.	In tutelam statuae	20,000	Pisaurum VI	—	XI 6371
683.	Arcae Augustalium se vivo...dedit ut... die natali...prae- sentes vescerentur	20,000	Reate IV	(post-100)	IX 4691
*684.	In tutelam (templi Suasae Felicis quod testamento suo fieri iussit)	20,000	Suasa VI	(post-100)	XI 6173
685.	[D]aturum eis... HS(1[6],000) usum, die [natali]s Dianae ...HS(400) et die natalis Antinoi... HS(400)	1[6],000 with 800 income (5% interest)	Lanuvium I	136	XIV 2112 = *ILS* 7212; *v.* 1389– 98
686.	Ut...rosal(ia) et parent(alia)...in perpetuom procur- (entur)	12,000	Arilica X	—	V 4016 = *ILS* 8373
687.	Quoius (*sic*) ex reditu ...natali suo (seviri Augustales) vescerentur	10,000	Aletrium I	(pre-100)	X 5809
*688.	Iubeo [...] dari col(oniae) Benev[ent.]	10,000 (? +)	Beneventum II	(post-200)	IX 1670
*D689.	In perpetuum...die natale (*sic*)... epulantib(us) hic paganis annuos (HS500) dari iusserunt	(10,000 if 5%)	Beneventum II	—	IX 1618 = *ILS* 6507
D 690.	Agellus made over by mancipatio to yield HS600 for rites com- memorating donor	(10,000 if 6%)	Brixia X	—	V 4489 = *ILS* 8370

	Identification	Price (HS)	Town	Date	Reference
691.	Ut...natale (*sic*) filiae meae (decuriones) epulantes confrequentetis HS(400) et in profusionibus HS(200)	10,000 yielding 600 (6% interest)	Croto III	—	X 107 = *ILS* 6466
692.	Ut...die natalis... filiae suae decur(iones) et (se)vir(i) Aug(ustales) publice in triclini(i)s suis epulentur	10,000	Gabii I	168	XIV 2793 = *ILS* 5449
693.	Ut...natale (*sic*) Domitiae praesentibus decurionib(us) et sevir(is) discumbentibus in publico aequis portionibus fieret divisio	10,000	Gabii I	140	XIV 2795 + p.493 = *ILS* 272
*694.	Fund given to city, whose income was to be applied to improving the amenities of the Augustales	10,000 at 6%	Petelia III	138/61	X 114 = *ILS* 6469
695.	Ex...redit(u)...die natalis sui (coll. fabr. tig.) epulentur	10,000	Tolentinum V	—	IX 5568 = *ILS* 7256
696.	Ut...natali eius... (dendrophori) confrequentent	8,000	Eburum III	(post-100)	X 451
697.	Dotem eis dedit... ex cuius usuris... natali eius Aug(ustales) et plebs urb(ana) confreq(uentatione) et spor(tulatione) [f]ungan[t]ur	8,000	Saturnia VII	234	XI 2650
698.	(2 identical funds for annual feast for sodality on donor's birthday)	6,000 yielding HS720 (12% interest)	Ostia I	*c.* 190/200	XIV 326 + p.615
699.	(To colleges of dendrophori, fabri & centonarii) Uti... die natalis mei oleum singulis vobis (ex reditu HS4,000) dividatur, e[t] ex reditu HS(2,000) manes meos cola[t]is	6,000	Sassina VI	post-112	XI 6520 = *ILS* 6647

	Identification	Price (HS)	Town	Date	Reference
700.	Arkae (collegii centonariorum) intul(it)...ut die natalis sui... epulantes imperpetuum (*sic*) divider(entur)	5,000	Ameria VI	—	XI 4391
701.	Ut...die natalis sui ...decurionibus et August(alibus) et vicanis dividatur praesentibus et ex ea divisione iubeo statuae meae coronas emi (HS12)	5,000 with 300 income (6% interest)	Capena VII	172	*AE* 1954, 168
702.	Amplius in tutela et ornationibus templi	5,000	Gabii I	140	XIV 2795 + p.493 = *ILS* 272; *v.* 693
*703.	Inpendi volo in ornationem sepulchri et sacrific(i)is die parentaliorum HS(100), violae HS(100), rosae HS(100)	(5,000 if 6%; 6,000 if 5%)	Ostia I	—	*AE* 1940, 94
704.	In annonam perpetuo dedit	5,000	Ager Sorrinensium Novensium VII	—	XI 3009 + p.1313 = *ILS* 6595
D*705.*	Item *ĪL (dedit) ut ...die natal(i)... sacrificium facerent ans(e)re et libo et in templo...epularentur et rosas suo tempore deducerent et statuam tergerent et coronarent	4,200 (?)	Cemenelum AM	—	V 7906 = *ILS* 8374
706.	Annui Ƨ II(200) for feast	(4,000 if 5%)	Truentum? V	98/102	*ILS* 7215
707.	Dederunt coll(egio) n(autarum) V(eronensium) A(rilicae) consist(entium)... ut...rosas eis (deducant)...et cibos (ponant) secus veterem consuetudinem	4,000	Arilica X	—	V 4017 = *ILS* 8372
708.	Ut...natale (*sic*) eius sportul(a)e dividant(ur) (cultoribus antistitibus deae Cereris)	4,000	Fabrateria Vetus I	(post-200)	X 5654; *v.* 828 and 679

	Identification	Price (HS)	Town	Date	Reference
709.	Funds given to 5 colleges	5 foundations of 4,000 each	Mediolanum XI	—	V 5840
*710.	Uti...(natali eius) dec(uriones ordinis corporatorum?) omnibus annis epulentur	4,000	Ostia I	(140/80)	XIV 246 + p.482
*711.	Coll(egio) fabr(um) naval(ium) Pis(anorum)...ex cuius reditu parental(ia) et rosar(ia) quotann(is) at sepulchrum suum celebrent	4,000	Pisa VII	(post-150)	XI 1436 = *ILS* 7258
712.	Item...amplius...ex [quorum reditu (tetrastylum)...] si quando [necesse esset] reficeretur	4,000	Pitinum Mergens VI	—	XI 5963
713.	Quam summam ita donata habeb(unt ut)... die natali ...sportulas pr(a)esentib(us) dividant	4,000	Setia I	(post-200)	X 6465
*D714.	Domum meam...qu(a)m reliq(ui)...ut de(n)tur decuriae meae (HS60), ma(t?)ron(is) colleg(ii) fabr(um) (HS100), ad parentalia (HS50)	(3,500 if 6%)	Aquileia X	—	Pais no.181
715.	(Fund for annual feast for sodality on donor's birthday)	3,000 yielding (HS360) (i.e. 12%)	Ostia I	*c.* 190/200	XIV 326 + p.615
*716.	At sollemnia cibu[m] et rosarum (*sic*)	2,000	Arilica X	(post-200)	V 4015 = *ILS* 6711
D717.	Ut no[bis...] [rosalib.] et parentalib(us)	2,000	Brixia X	—	V 4440
718.	[In tuiti]onem	2,000	Concordia X	—	V 8655, cf. 8654
*719.	Fund for profusiones given to centonarii, together with tabernae cum cenaculis	2,000 +	Brixia X	—	V 4488
720.	In...tutel(am)	2,000	Comum XI	—	V 5287

	Identification	Price (HS)	Town	Date	Reference
721.	Ut e[x] usuris...die natali [e]ius... [s]portulae divid[ant]ur iuvenibus Herculanis	2,000	Fabrateria Vetus I	(post-200)	x 5657 = *ILS* 6287
722.	In tutelam (statuae)	2,000	Ager Mediolanensis XI	—	v 5658 + p.1085
723.	(Fund for annual feast for sodality on donor's birthday)	2,000 yielding (240) (i.e. 12% interest)	Ostia I	*c.* 190/200	XIV 326 + p.615
724.	(Fund for annual feast for sodality on donor's birthday)	2,000 yielding (240) (i.e. 12% interest)	Ostia I	*c.* 190/200	XIV 326 + p.615
725.	(Fund for annual feast for sodality on donor's birthday)	2,000 yielding (240) (i.e. 12% interest)	Ostia I	*c.* 190/200	XIV 326 + p.615
726–26c.	(4 funds for annual feast for sodality on donor's birthday)	2,000 yielding (240) (i.e. 12% interest)	Ostia I	*c.* 190/200	XIV 326 + p.615
727.	(Fund for annual feast for sodality on donor's birthday)	2,000	Ostia I	*c.* 190/200	XIV 326 + p.615
728–28a.	(2 funds for annual feast for sodality on donor's birthday)	2,000	Ostia I	*c.* 190/200	XIV 326 + p.615
729.	(In) tuition(em) (frontis templi)	2,000	Patavium x	(pre-100)	v 2864 = *ILS* 5406
*D730.	...ur (HS100), ut de eis sacrificiu[m ...quodannis faciant]	(2,000 if 5%)	Carsulae VI	—	XI 4593
731.	Donavi(t) Ciarne(nsibus?)... ut facerent...na(talia) tuc(eto) vin(o)	1,600	Feltria x	—	v 2072
D732.	Ex quor(um) reditu quodann(is) tempore parentalior(um) quam et rosae coronas ternas ponerentur et profus(iones) suo quoq(ue) anno fieri	1,600	Mediolanum XI	—	v 5907
733.	In tut(elam)...ex quorum usur(is) ...sacr(ificium) extis celebretur	1,000	Brixia x	—	v 4203 = *ILS* 6718

	Identification	Price (HS)	Town	Date	Reference
734.	Coll(egio) (se)vir(um) soccior. (*sic*)...ut... profus(iones) aei (*sic*) tan parent(alia) tan ros(aria)... celebrent(ur)	1,000	Brixia x	—	V 4410 = *ILS* 6719
735.	Coll(egio) dendr(ophorum)...et in tutelam dedit...	1,000	Brixia x	—	V 4418
736.	2 funds for sacrificium; 1 for profusio	3 foundations of 1,000 each	Brixia x	(post-100)	V 4449
737.	In cuius tutel(am) dederunt	1,000	Comum XI	—	V 5282
738.	In tutelam (statuae) dedit	1,000	Comum XI	—	*AE* 1951, 94
739.	In tutel(am) dedit	1,000	Ager Comensis XI	—	V 5447 = *ILS* 7253
*740.	Collegio fabr(um) Laud(is) in utrumq(ue) florem perpetuo sibi deducend(um)	1,000	Laus Pompeia XI	(post-50)	V 6363
*741.	Collegio suo centonariorum legavit ...ex cuius reditu quodannis die parentaliorum ne minus homines (12) ad rogum suum vescerentur	1,000	Mevania VI	—	XI 5047 + p.1380
742.	Ut...rosas ad monumentum ei spargant et ibi (decuria VII collegii fabrum) epulentur	1,000	Ravenna VIII	—	*NS* (1932) 425; XI 132 + p.1228 = *ILS* 7235
*743.	Ex cuius summ(a)e reditu rosam ne minus ex HS(16) posuisse ...et reliquum quot est ex usuris escas rosales et vindemiales...poni ...voluit	800	Acelum x	—	V 2090 + p.1068 = *ILS* 8371
744.	Ut monumentum remund(etur)	600	Arilica x	—	V 4016 = *ILS* 8373
745.	Ut...rosal(ia) et parent(alia)... procurent	600	(Toscolano ad lacum Benacum) x	—	V 4871 = *ILS* 6710
746.	In tut(elam) (statuae)	500	Brixia x	—	V 4416 + p.1079

	Identification	Price (HS)	Town	Date	Reference
747.	Ad rosas et escas ducendas	400	Atria X	—	V 2315
748.	In tutel(am)... ded(it) coll(egio) iument(ariorum) (statue or altar dedicated to Vulcan)	400	Brixia X	—	V 4294, cf. 4288
749.	Donavit...ut facerent mul(ieres) rosas	400	Feltria X	—	V 2072
750.	Donavi(t)...(ut facerent) Her(clanenses) par(entalia)	400	Feltria X	—	V 2072
*751.	In herm(am) tuend(um) et rosa quodannis ornandam (sic)	400	Mediolanum XI	—	V 5878 = *ILS* 6735
752.	Ut...rosam ponant parentibus et sibi	400	Vardagate IX	—	V 7450
753.	In tutela (tegurii)	200 (annually ?)	(Riva) X	189/200	V 5005 = *ILS* 3761, cf. V 4339, 4318
*D754.	Dedit (HS80) et profundi de usuris (HS12)	80 yielding 12 (15%)	Bergomum XI	—	V 5134; Billeter 227
D755.	Ut...die n(ostro) festo sollemne oleum in lucerna quem dedi d(e?) p(roprio?) ex usuris praestetur	32 (?+)	(Montalcino) VII	—	XI 2596 = *ILS* 8368

MULTIPLE DISTRIBUTIONS

	756	757	758	758a	759	759a	760–1	762	763–4	765
Patroni	—	—	100	—	—	—	—	—	—	—
Decuriones	400	200	100	100	20	?	40	30	30	[24]
Adlecti scaenicorum	—	—	—	—	100	—	—	—	—	—
Liberi decurionum	—	—	—	—	—	?	—	—	30	—
(Seviri et) Augustales	300	8	—	100	12	50	20	20	20	—
Ministri publici	—	—	50	—	—	—	—	—	—	—
Mulieres honoratorum	—	—	—	—	4	—	—	—	—	—
Uxores decurionum	—	—	—	—	—	—	—	16	—	4
Uxores Augustalium	—	—	—	—	—	—	—	8	—	—
Populus	—	—	—	—	4	4	—	—	—	—
Plebs	200	—	—	—	—	—	12	—	8	—
Coloni	—	4	—	—	—	—	—	—	—	—
Municipes	—	—	—	20	—	—	—	—	—	—
Vicani	—	—	—	—	—	—	—	12	—	—
Uxores vicanorum	—	—	—	—	—	—	—	4	—	—
...	—	4	—	—	—	—	—	—	—	—

	766	767	768–9	770	771	772	773	774	775
[Patroni]	—	—	—	—	20	—	—	—	—
Decuriones	20	20	20	20	?	12	20	20	20
(Seviri et) Augustales	—	12	12	12	12	20	10	8	8
Mercuriales	—	10	—	—	—	—	—	—	—
Collegia omnia	16	—	—	—	—	—	—	—	—
Honore usi	12	—	—	—	—	—	—	—	—
Tabernarii intra murum negotiantes	—	—	—	4	—	—	—	—	—
Populus	—	—	—	—	—	—	—	4	4
Plebs	12	—	8	—	?	—	4	—	—
Populus viritim	—	8	—	—	—	—	—	—	—

	776	777	778	779	780	781	782	783	784	785
D[uovirales?]	—	—	—	—	20	—	—	—	—	
Decuriones	20	20	20	?	8	20	20	16	16	12
Filii decurionum	—	8	—	—	—	—	—	—	—	
Liberi decurionum	—	—	—	—	8	20	—	8	—	—
(Seviri et) Augustales	—	—	8	20	—	—	—	12	16	8
Dendrophori	—	—	—	—	—	—	—	—	12	—
Collegia	8	—	—	—	—	—	—	—	—	
Liberi Augustalium	—	—	—	—	—	—	—	6	—	—
Populares	—	—	—	—	8	—	—	—	—	—
Liberi popularium	—	—	—	—	8	—	—	—	—	—
Populus intra murum morantes	—	—	—	—	—	—	4	—	—	—
Plebs intra murum habitantes	—	—	—	—	—	—	—	8	—	—
Populus	—	—	—	—	—	—	—	—	4	—
Plebs	4	4	2	8	—	—	—	—	—	—
Municipes	—	—	—	—	—	4	—	—	—	—
Liberi plebis intra murum habitantium	—	—	—	—	—	—	—	4	—	—

	786	787	788	789	790	791	792	793	794	795
Decuriones	12	8	12	12	12	12	12	12	12	12
(Seviri et) Augustales	[4?]	6	8	8	8	8	—	8	—	—
Dendrophori	—	12	—	—	—	—	—	—	—	—
Ingenui et veterani corporati	—	—	6	—	—	—	—	—	—	—
Iuvenes	12	—	—	—	—	—	—	—	—	—
Plebs urbana	—	4	—	—	—	—	—	—	6	—
Populus	—	—	—	4	4	—	—	—	—	—
Plebs	—	—	—	—	—	—	—	8	—	—
Coloni	—	—	—	—	—	—	8	—	—	—
Municipes	—	—	4	—	—	—	—	—	—	4
Incolae	—	—	—	—	—	—	—	—	—	4

Prices and price-levels

	796	797	798	799	800	801	802	803	804	805
Decuriones	?	12	10	8	8	8	4	8	8	8
Decuriones triclinii mei	—	—	11	—	—	—	—	—	—	—
Pueri decurionum	—	—	8	—	—	—	—	—	—	—
Liberi decurionum	—	—	—	8	—	—	—	—	—	—
Seviri Aug. urbani	—	—	—	—	—	—	—	—	8	—
(Seviri et) Augustales	12	?	8	6	6	4	4	—	—	—
Liberi Augustalium	—	—	—	6	—	—	—	—	—	—
Officiales	—	—	—	—	—	—	—	—	8	—
Collegia	—	—	—	—	—	—	—	—	4	—
Populus viritim	—	—	—	4	4	—	—	—	—	—
Populus virilis sexus	—	[2?]	—	—	—	—	—	—	—	—
Populus	1?	—	—	—	—	6?	4	—	—	—
Coloni	—	—	—	—	—	—	—	4	—	—
Municipes	—	—	—	—	—	—	—	—	—	[4]
Incolae	—	—	—	—	—	—	—	—	—	[4]
Feminae (populi)	—	1	—	2	—	—	—	—	—	—

	806	807	808	809–10	811	812	813–14	815	816
Patroni	—	[8]	—	—	—	—	—	—	—
Decuriones	8	[8]	?	8	6	6	6	4	4
Liberi decurionum	—	—	—	—	6	—	—	—	—
(Seviri et) Augustales	—	—	[8?]	—	4	4	—	2	—
Collegium incertum	—	4	—	—	—	—	—	—	—
Scribae	—	—	—	—	4	—	—	—	—
Liberi scribarum	—	—	—	—	4	—	—	—	—
Populus viritim	—	—	—	—	—	—	—	1	—
Populus	—	—	4	—	—	—	—	—	—
Plebs viritim	—	—	—	—	—	2	—	—	—
Plebs	4	—	—	—	—	—	—	—	2
Municipes	—	—	—	—	2	—	—	—	—
Plebs utriusque xesus (*sic*)	—	—	—	—	—	—	[4]	—	—
Ceteri utriusque sexus (*sc.* plebs)	—	—	—	4	—	—	—	—	—

Town	Date	Reference
*756. Mons Fereter VI	148	XI 6481
757. Puteoli I	(pre-200)	X 1839
758. Forum Clodii VII	165	XI 7556 = *ILS* 6584
D758a. (Ostia?) I	193	VI 1173c
D759. Bovillae I	169	XIV 2408 = *ILS* 5196
759a. Locri III	—	*Epigraphica* 26 (1964) 68–70
760–1. Pisaurum VI	(100/200)	XI 6360
762. Volcei III	(100/200)	X 415
763–4. Corfinium IV	(post-200)	IX 3160 = *ILS* 6530
765. Firmum Picenum V	—	IX 5376; *v.* 662
D766. Urvinum Mataurense VI	180/92	XI 6053
767. Rudiae II	117/38	IX 23 = *ILS* 6472
*D768–9. Tifernum Tiberinum VI	*c.* 170	XI 5939 = *ILS* 5678
D770. Gabii I	168	XIV 2793 = *ILS* 5449
771. Eburum III	(post-100)	X 451; *v.* 1062
D772. Ostia I	*c.* 230/240	XIV 431 + p.482; *v.* 674
773. Interamnia Praetuttianorum V	(post-100)	IX 5085 + *NS* (1893) 354
*D774. Anagnia I	180/95	X 5917 = *ILS* 1909
D775. Anagnia I	180/95	X 5918 = *ILS* 406
D776. Pisaurum VI	—	XI 6378
D777. Thermae Himeraeae SICILY	—	X 7352 + p.993
778. Antinum Marsorum IV	(post-100)	IX 3838
*779. Aeclanum II	—	IX 1177; *v.* 1353, 1362
780. Telesia I	(post-200)	IX 2243
781. Forum Flaminiae Fulginiae VI	(post-200)	XI 5215 = *ILS* 2650
D782. Compsa II	—	IX 982 = *ILS* 6483
*D783. Ager Sorrinensium Novensium VII	—	XI 3013
D784. Verulae I	197	X 5796 = *ILS* 6268
785. Salernum I	(post-100)	X 544
786. Carsulae VI	—	XI 4580 = *ILS* 6634
787. Antinum Marsorum IV	—	IX 3842
788. Misenum I	165	X 1881 = *ILS* 6328
D789. Anagnia I	—	X 5923 = *ILS* 6262a
D790. Volcei III	161/80	X 416
D791. Auximum V	159	IX 5823 = *ILS* 6048
D792. Auximum V	(169/90)	IX 5828
D793. Sestinum VI	198/211	XI 6014 + p.1396 *bis* = *ILS* 6645
794. Atina Latii I	208	X 5064 = *ILS* 2667
795. Lupiae II	(post-100)	*AE* 1958, 178, cf. *NS* (1957) 193 & fig. (cf. also *AE* 1948, 84)
796. Potentia III	(post-100)	X 141
797. Tuder VI	—	XI 4663
798. Ferentinum Latii I	(post-100)	X 5853, cf. p.1013 = *ILS* 6271
799. Croto III	(pre-200)	X 109; Kahrstedt 78
800. Vibo III	138/61	X 53; Kahrstedt 35
D801. Carsulae VI	—	XI 4582
D802. Carsulae VI	—	XI 4582
803. Auximum V	(161/9)	IX 5843

	Town	Date	Reference
D804.	Cemenelum AM	—	V 7920
805.	Lupiae II	(pre-200)	IX 22 + p.651
D806.	Perusia VII	205	XI 1926 + p.1276 = *ILS* 6616
807.	Sestinum VI	—	XI 6017, cf. 6018
808.	Trebula Balliensis I	(pre-200)	X 4563
809–10.	Tuficum VI	180/92	XI 5716
811.	Cales I	—	X 4643
812.	Saepinum IV	(pre-200)	IX 2440
813–14.	Tuficum VI	(post-200)	XI 5717 + p.1393 = *ILS* 6643
815.	Petelia III	102/13	X 112 = *ILS* 6467
*816–17.	Perusia VII	166	XI 1924 = *ILS* 5503

SPORTULAE AT SPECIFIED RATES

	Identification	Price (HS)	Town	Date	Reference
*818.	Legat(is) iis quos test(amento) non no[minavisset, decurio]nibus	400	Mons Fereter VI	148	v. 756
*819.	Legat(is) iis quos test(amento) non no[minavisset,...] ...(se)viris et Augustal(ibus)	300	Mons Fereter VI	148	v. 756
*820.	Legat(is) iis quos test(amento) non no[minavisset...]... [ple]beis	200	Mons Fereter VI	148	v. 756
821.	[Decurionibus?...]ris nomine sing(ulos)... [dedit]	200	Puteoli I	—	v. 757
822.	Dedicatione singulis universisq(ue ingenuorum honoratorum et Augustalium)...dedit	100	Acerrae I	—	X 3759 = *ILS* 6340
823.	Ob dedic(ationem) ded(it)	100	Ameria VI	—	XI 4405 + p.1368
D824.	Ob dedication(em) sportulas dedit adlectis (scaenicorum)	100	Bovillae I	169	v. 759
D824a.	Decuriones...Augustales	100	(Ostia?) I	193	v. 758a
825.	Dec(urionibus) sing(ulis)	100	Florentia VII	(pre-200)	XI 1601
826.	Patronis et decurionibus singulis	100	Forum Clodii VII	165	v. 758
827.	(Decurionibus) singulis ...sportulas dedit	70	Forum Sempronii VII	(100/200)	XI 6123
828.	Cultoribus antistitibus Cereris discunbentibus	50	Fabrateria Vetus I	(post-200)	X 5654; v. 708

	Identification	Price (HS)	Town	Date	Reference
829.	Item ministeriis (*sic*) publicis	50	Forum Clodii VII	165	*v.* 758
829a.	Seviris Aug[ustalibus] sing(ulis)	50	Locri III	—	*v.* 759a
830.	Singulis (collegii fabrum)...adiecto pane et vin(o)	50	Pisaurum VI	180/92	XI 6358 = *ILS* 6654
831.	(Singulis collegii fabrum tignuariorum?)	40	Ameria VI	(post-100)	XI 4404
832.	Decurionibus singul(is)	40	Pisaurum VI	(100/200)	*v.* 760
833.	To 9 'cives amici et amatores eius' 'adiecto pane et vino cum epu(lo)'	40	Pisaurum VI	post-180	XI 6362 = *ILS* 7364
D834–5.	Decurionibus pane(m et) vinu(m)...dedit	40	Ager Sorrinensium Novensium VII	—	XI 3009 = *ILS* 6595
836.	Sing(ulis collegii dendrofororum)...et epulum	32	Signia I	(post-200)	X 5968 + p.982 = *ILS* 6272
837.	Iuvenibus (Augustalibus) s(ingulis)..., adiecto pane et vino epulantibus	30	Ameria VI	—	XI 4395 = *ILS* 6632
*838.	[Decuri]onib(us) sing(ulis)	30	Capua IV	(pre-200)	X 3927; *v.* 853
839–40.	Decurionibus discumbentibus et liberis eorum singul(is)	30	Corfinium IV	post-200	*v.* 763-4
841.	Singulis (amatoribus Romuliorum) discumbentibus et epul(antibus)	30	Ocriculum VI	247/8	XI 7805 = *ILS* 7365; cf. 833; *v.* 1358
842.	[Decurionibus]	30	Volcei III	(100/200)	*v.* 762
843.	Decurio[nibus]	[2]4	Firmum Picenum V	—	*v.* 765
843a.	Viritim divisit decurionibus et Augustalibus et cur(i)is	24	Lanuvium I	—	XIV 2120 = *ILS* 6199. See p.278 n.1
*844.	[Sevi]r(is) et Aug(ustalibus)	20	Aeclanum II	—	*v.* 779
845.	Singulis (collegii centonariorum)	20	Ameria VI	—	XI 4391
*D846.	Decur(ionibus)	20	Anagnia I	180/95	*v.* 774
D847.	Decurionibus	20	Anagnia I	180/95	*v.* 775
848.	Dec(urionibus)	20	Antinum Marsorum IV	(post-100)	*v.* 778
849–50.	Singulis in collegio	20	Asculum Picenum V	172	IX 5177 = *ILS* 5450

	Identification	Price (HS)	Town	Date	Reference
*851.	[L]egavit colonis Auximatibus singulis [. . .] et decurionibus singulis HS XX	20	Auximum V	(pre-100)	IX 5855; *v.* 1330
D852.	Decur(ionibus) Bovill(ensium)	20	Bovillae I	169	*v.* 759
D852a.	Municipes	20	(Ostia?) I	193	*v.* 758a
*853.	[A]ugustalibus	20	Capua I	(pre-200)	X 3927; *v.* 838
D854.	Decurionibus singulis	20	Compsa II	—	*v.* 782
855.	Sevir(is) Augustal(ibus) vescent(ibus) sing(ulis)	20	Corfinium IV	(post-200)	*v.* 763–4
856.	Coll(egii patronis?)	20	Eburum III	(post-100)	*v.* 771
857.	Decur(ionibus) in luc(o) publice vescentib(us) sing(ulis)	20	Formiae I	(pre-200)	X 6073 = *ILS* 6284
D858.	Pavit in Capitol(io) pane et vino promiscue posito et dedit sportulas dec(urionibus), Aug(ustalibus), Regal(ibus) sing(ulis)	20	Formiae I	—	*AE* 1927, 124; *v.* 1077, 1323; cf. *ILS* 6283
859.	Epulum dedit et viritim HS vicenos	20	Forum Clodii VII	174	XI 7556 = *ILS* 6584
860.	Decurionibus et liberis eorum panem et vinum et ~~SS~~ XX n.	20	Forum Flaminiae Fulginiae VI	(post-200)	*v.* 781
D861.	Decurionibus sing(ulis)	20	Gabii I	168	*v.* 770
862.	Epul. [s]ing(ulis) dec(urionibus) HS XX n.	20	Interamnia Praetuttianorum V	(post-100)	*v.* 773
D*863*.	Decurionibus (HS 20) et Augustalibus (HS20)	20	Ostia I	182	XIV 367 = *ILS* 6164
D864.	Dec[urionibus si]ngulis (annually)	20	Ostia I	(160/200)	*v.* 672
D864a.	Augustalib(us)	20	Ostia I	*c.* 230/40	*v.* 772
864b.	Decurionibus	20	Paestum III	(post-180)	Mello–Voza no.92
865.	Augustal(ibus)	20	Pisaurum VI	(100/200)	*v.* 760
D866.	Sportulae decur(ionibus)	20	Pisaurum VI	—	*v.* 776
867.	Ut. . .omnibus annis viscerationis nomine dividatur decur(ionibus)	20	Rudiae II	117/38	*v.* 767
868.	D[uoviralib(us)?]	20	Telesia I	(post-200)	*v.* 780

	Identification	Price (HS)	Town	Date	Reference
D869.	Decurioni[bus]	20	Thermae Himeraeae SICILY	—	v. 777
*D870.	Dec(urionibus)	20	Tifernum Tiberinum VI	c. 170	v. 768
871.	Augustalibus	20	Volcei III	(100/200)	v. 762
872.	Decurion[ibus]	20	Volturnum I	198 (?)	X 8215 = *ILS* 2842
D873.	Decurion(ibus)	20	Urvinum Mataurense VI	180/92	v. 766
D874.	Decur(ionibus) et (se)vir(is) et Augus(talibus)... adiecto pane et vino	16	Verulae I	197	v. 784
*D875.	Decurionibus sing(ulis)	16	Ager Sorrinensium Novensium VII	—	v. 783
876.	Uxoribus decurionum	16	Volcei III	(100/200)	v. 762
D877.	Collegiis omnibus	16	Urvinum Mataurense VI	180/92	v. 766
D878.	Decurionib(us)	12	Anagnia I	—	v. 789
879.	Collegio (dendrophororum)... aepul(antibus) sing(ulis)	12	Antinum Marsorum IV	(post-150)	v. 787
D880-1.	Decurion(ibus vicorum) et vicanis (annually)	12	Ariminum VIII	—	v. 645
882.	Sportulae dec(urionibus)	12	Atina Latii I	208	v. 794
883.	[O]b [d]edicationem... [p]o[p]ulo	1[2]	Attidium IV	—	XI 5678a
D884.	Singulis decurionibus	12	Auximum V	159	v. 791
D885.	Decurionibus	12	Auximum V	(169/90)	v. 792
D886.	Sportulae... Augustal(ibus) sing(ulis)	12	Bovillae I	169	v. 759
887.	Iuven(ibus) sing(ulis) ...decur(ionibus)	12	Carsulae VI	—	v. 786
888-9.	Augustalib(us)	12	Eburum III	(post-100)	v. 771
D890.	Divisit...(se)vir(is) Aug(ustalibus)	12	Gabii I	168	v. 770
891.	Decurionib(us)	12	Lupiae II	(post-100)	v. 795
D892.	Dec(urionibus)	12	Minturnae I	249	X 6012 = *ILS* 5062
D893.	Decurionibus	12	Ostia I	251	XIV 352 = *ILS* 6149
D894.	Decurionib(us)	12?	Ostia I	c. 230/40	v. 772
D895.	—	12 (?+)	Ostia I	194	XIV p.614, 2, cf. XIV 325
D896.	Sing(ulis)	12	Ostia I	129	XIV 4743
*896a.	Dec[uri]onibus	12	Paestum III	—	Mello–Voza no.90

	Identification	Price (HS)	Town	Date	Reference
897.	Plebei...adiecto pane et vino	12	Pisaurum VI	(100/200)	v. 760
898.	Decurioni[bus]	12	Pitinum Mergens VI	—	XI 5965
899.	Au[g(ustalibus)]	12	Potentia III	(post-100)	v. 796
900.	Decurionibus sing(ulis) HS XII...et epulum...item...die pervigilii Dei Patrii alterum tantum dedit (2 identical distributions)	12	Misenum I	165	v. 788
901.	Ut...omnibus annis viscerationis nomine dividatur... Augustalibus	12	Rudiae II	117/38	v. 767
902.	De[c(urionibus)]	12	Salernum I	(post-100)	v. 785
903.	Augustalib(us)	12	Salernum I	(post-100)	X 544
D904.	Dec(urionibus)... cum pane et vino	12	Sestinum VI	198/211	v. 793
*D905.	(Se)vir(is)	12	Tifernum Tiberinum VI	c. 170	v. 768–9
906.	Decurionibus...	12	Tuder VI	—	v. 797
D907.	Dendrophor(is)... adiecto pane et vino	12	Verulae I	197	v. 784
*D908.	Augustal[ibus]	12	Ager Sorrinensium Novensium VII	—	v. 783
909.	Vicanis	12	Volcei III	(100/200)	v. 762
D910.	Dec(urionibus)	12	Volcei III	161/80	v. 790
D911.	Plebei et honore usis	12	Urvinum Mataurense VI	180/92	v. 766
912.	(Decurionibus triclinii mei) (at annual feast)	11	Ferentinum I	(post-100)	v. 798
913.	Et circa triclin(ia) decurionib(us) mulsum et crust(ulum) et sportul(ae) HS X n., (annually)	10	Ferentinum I	(post-100)	v. 798
914.	Epul. [s]ing(ulis) se[v]ir(is) et Aug(ustalibus)	10	Interamnia Praetuttianorum V	(post-100)	v. 773
915.	Ut...omnibus annis viscerationis nomine dividatur... Mercurialib(us)	10	Rudiae II	117/38	v. 767
916.	Ordin[i decuri]onum sing(ulis)	9	Bovillae I	158	XIV 2410 = *ILS* 6190
917.	Decurionibus aepulantibus	9	Antinum Marsorum IV	—	v. 787
918.	[Plebei (?)]	8	Aeclanum II	—	v. 779

	Identification	Price (HS)	Town	Date	Reference
*D919.	Sexv(iris)	8	Anagnia I	180/95	v. 774
D920.	Sivir(is) (sic)	8	Anagnia I	180/95	v. 775
D921.	Sexvir(is)	8	Anagnia I	—	v. 789
922–3.	Sexvir(is) epul.	8	Antinum Marsorum IV	(post-100)	v. 778
924–5.	Singul(is) (vicanis vici Velabri)	8	Ariminum VIII	(post-100)	XI 417 = *ILS* 6661
D926.	Singulis... Augustalibus	8	Auximum V	159	v. 791
D927.	Colonis	8	Auximum V	(169/90)	v. 792
928.	Decurionibus sing(ulis)	8	Auximum V	(161/9)	v. 803
D929.	Decurion(ibus)... adiecto pane et vino	8	Carsulae VI	—	v. 801
D930.	Decurionib(us) et (se)vir(is) Aug(ustalibus) u[rb]anis [e]t of[fi]cialib(us) sportulas	8	Cemenelum AM	—	v. 804
931.	Plebei universae epulantibus singulis	8	Corfinium IV	(post-200)	v. 763–4
932–3.	Decurionibus liberi[sque] eorum singulis	8	Croto III	(pre-200)	v. 799
934.	Item puer(is) curiae increment(a) et (se)vir(is) Aug(ustalibus) crust(ulum) mulsum et HS VIII n. (annually)	8	Ferentinum Latii I	(post-100)	v. 798
935.	Decurionibus	8	Lupiae II	(pre-200)	v. 805
D936.	Sportul(ae)... singul(is collegii centonariorum municipii Mevaniolae)	8	Mevaniola VI	—	XI 6605
D937.	[Corpori t]raiectus [Rusti]celi... [spor]tulae sing(ulis) (on 2 occasions)	8	Ostia I	166	XIV 4554
D938.	Decurionibus	8	Perusia VII	205	v. 806
D939.	Collegiis (fabrum, centonariorum, dendrophororum, naviculariūm)	8	Pisaurum VI	—	v. 776
940.	[August]al(ibus)	8	Puteoli I	(pre-200)	v. 757
941.	Augustalib(us) HS(8) ...et epulum (on 2 occasions)	8	Misenum I	165	v. 788

	Identification	Price (HS)	Town	Date	Reference
D942.	Decurionib(us) coll(egii) fabr(um) m(unicipii) R(avennatium) in aede Nept(uni)... praesentibus	8	Ravenna VIII	—	v. 678
943.	Ut...omnibus annis viscerationis nomine dividatur...populo viritim	8	Rudiae II	117/38	v. 767
944.	Aug(ustalibus) sing(ulis)	8	Salernum I	(post-100)	v. 785
D945.	Sevir(is) et pleb(i) ...cum pane et vino	8	Sestinum VI	198/211	v. 793
946.	Patronis colleg(ii) et decur(ionibus)	[8]	Sestinum VI	—	v. 807
*D947.	Plebei intra murum habitantibus	8	Ager Sorrinensium Novensium VII	—	v. 783
*D948.	Liberis (decurionum) dimidium	8	Ager Sorrinensium Novensium VII	—	v. 783
949.	Decurionibus [et] popularibus liberisque eorum	8	Telesia I	(post-200)	v. 780
D950.	Decu[ri]onum fil(i)is	8	Thermae Himeraeae SICILY	—	v. 777
*D951.	Pleb(i)	8	Tifernum Tiberinum VI	c. 170	v. 768
952.	Augustalibus	[8]	Trebula Balliensis I	(pre-200)	v. 808
953.	Decurion(ibus) sing(ulis)	8	Tuficum VI	180/92	v. 809–10
954.	Iterum decurionibus... dedit (2 distributions)	8	Vibo III	138/61	v. 800
955.	[Decuri]onibus sing(ulis)	8	Vibo III	(pre-200)	X 54
956.	Uxoribus... Augustalium	8	Volcei III	(100–200)	v. 762
D957.	Aug(ustalibus)	8	Volcei III	161/80	v. 790
D958.	[Decurio]nib(us) (annually?)	8	Volsinii VII	—	XI 7299
D959.	...es	8	Urvinum Mataurense VI	—	XI 6070
960–1.	Seviris Aug(ustalibus) aepulan(tibus) sing(ulis)	6	Antinum Marsorum IV	(post-150)	v. 787
962.	Sportulae...plebei urb(anae)	6	Atina Latii I	208	v. 794

	Identification	Price (HS)	Town	Date	Reference
963.	Nobis (*sc.* decurionibus) liberisq(ue) n(ostris) vic(toriatos) n.III (annually)	6	Cales I	—	*v.* 811
D964.	Populo...adiecto pane et vino	6	Carsulae VI	—	*v.* 801
965.	[Augusta]lib(us) liberisque eorum [sin]gul(is)	6	Croto III	(pre-200)	*v.* 799
966.	Ingenuis et veteran(is) corp(oratis) (on 2 occasions)	6	Misenum I	165	*v.* 788
967.	Decurion[i]bus sing(ulis)	6	Saepinum IV	(pre-200)	*v.* 812
*D968.	Liberis (Augustalium) dimidium	6	Ager Sorrinensium Novensium VII	—	*v.* 783
969.	Decur(ionibus)	6	Tuficum VI	(post-200)	*v.* 813
970.	Augustalibus	6	Vibo III	138/61	*v.* 800
970a.	[De]curionibus, [pleb]eis, [mul]ieribus	5 +	Reate IV	181	IX 4697
971.	P[atronis?]..., decurio[nibus]..., Augus[talibus]..., iuveni[bus]	5?	Alsium VII	(post-100)	XI 3723
972.	—	4	Alba Fucens IV	168	IX 3950
*D973.	Popul(o)...et epul(um) suff(iciens)	4	Anagnia I	180/95	*v.* 774
D974.	Popul(o)...et epulum sufficiens omnib(us)	4	Anagnia I	180/95	*v.* 775
D975.	Populo	4	Anagnia I	—	*v.* 789
976.	Plebi urbanae aepul(antibus) sing(ulis)	4	Antinum Marsorum IV	—	*v.* 787
977.	Vicanis (vicorum VII)	4	Ariminum VIII	(post-200)	XI 379 = *ILS* 6664; *v.* 681
978.	Sing(ulis) (collegii fabrum)	4	Ariminum VIII	169 (?)	XI 405
979.	Colonis sing(ulis)	4	Auximum V	(161/9)	*v.* 803
*D980.	Viritim populo	4	Beneventum II	120/38	IX 1619 = *ILS* 5502; *v.* 513
D981.	Sportulae...mulier(ibus) honorat(orum) et populo sing(ulis)	4	Bovillae I	169	*v.* 759
D982.	Dec(urionibus) et Aug(ustalibus)	4	Bovillae I	138/75	XIV 2416
983.	Scrib(is) liber[isq(ue) eorum]...Aug(ustalibus) vic(toriatos) n.II (annually)	4	Cales I	—	*v.* 811

	Identification	Price (HS)	Town	Date	Reference
D984.	Decurionib(us)..., Augustal(ibus)..., populo	4	Carsulae VI	—	v. 802 + 801
D985.	Augustalib(us)... adiecto pane et vino	4	Carsulae VI	—	v. 801
986.	(Se)vir(is)	[4?]	Carsulae VI	—	v. 786
D987.	Dendrophoris...[e]t vinum passim	4	Cemenelum AM	(100/200)	V 7904
D988.	Collegiis	4	Cemenelum AM	—	v. 804
D989.	[Popul]o viriti[m]	4	Compsa II	(100/200)	IX 976 + NS (1938) 103
D990.	Populo intra murum morantibus	4	Compsa II	—	v. 782
D991.	Decurioni[bus et] populo utriusq(ue) [se]xus (at the dedication of a statue financed by the plebs urbana)	4	Compsa II	—	IX 977
D991a.	Populo utrius[que] sexsus	4	Compsa II	—	IX 981
992.	Decurionibus...ut natale (sic) filiae meae epulantes confrequentetis HS(400)	(4)?	Croto III	—	v. 691
993.	Populo viritim	4	Croto III	(pre-200)	v. 799
994.	Ep...	4	Cupra Montana V	—	IX 5708
995.	Sexsus femini. singuli[s] (annually)	4	Firmum Picenum V	—	v. 662
996–7.	Municipibus	4	Forum Flaminiae Fulginiae VI	(post-200)	v. 781
D998.	Item tabernar(i)is intra murum negotiantibus	4	Gabii I	168	v. 770
*999.	Municipibus singulis	4	Herculaneum I	48/9	X 1416
1000.	Epul. sing(ulis)... plebei	4	Interamnia Praetuttianorum V	(post-100)	v. 773
1000a.	Po[pulo viri]tim	4	Locri III	—	v. 759a
1001.	Municipibus et incolis sing(ulis)	[4]	Lupiae II	(pre-200)	v. 805
1002.	Municip(ibus) et incolis	4	Lupiae II	(post-100)	v. 795
D1003.	[Den]arios divisit	4	Messina SICILY	(pre-200)	NS (1920) 340
1003a.	[Mu]nicipes	4	Misenum I	—	X 1840

Identification	Price (HS)	Town	Date	Reference
D1004. Populo	4	Nuceria Alfaterna I	pre-62	X 1081 = *ILS* 6446; cf. X p.124, 2
D1005. (Sportulae?)	4	Opitergium X	—	*v.* 680
1006. Viritim (to members of a college)	4	Ostia I	143/61	*AE* 1940, 62
D1007. Viritim	4	Ostia I	141	XIV 8 = *ILS* 6154
D1008. (Kannophoris) pan(em), vin(um) et (HS4)	4	Ostia I	212	XIV 119 + p.481
D1009. Virit(im corpori traiectus Rusticeli)	4	Ostia I	169/80	XIV 4556
1010. Viritim (to members of a college)	4	Ostia I	143/61	*AE* 1940, 62
D1011. Dend(rophoris)	4	Ostia I	177/88	*AE* 1948, 24; *v.* 528
D1012. Plebi	4	Perusia VII	205	*v.* 806
*1013. Decurionib(us)	4	Perusia VII	166	*v.* 816
*D1014. Municipibus Petelinis utriusque sexus ex more loci...omnibus annis	4	Petelia III	138/61	*v.* 664
1015. Dec(urionibus)	4	Petelia III	102/13	*v.* 815
D1016. Plebi	4	Pisaurum VI	—	*v.* 776
1017. Colon(is)..., [femini?]s...	4	Puteoli I	(pre-200)	*v.* 757
1018. Municipib(us) (on 2 occasions)	4	Misenum I	165	*v.* 788
D1018a. [Uni]versae plebei	4	Reate IV	184	IX 4686
1019. Augustalib(us)	4	Saepinum IV	pre-200	*v.* 812
1020. Colonis sing(ulis)	4	Salernum I	122/7	X 514
D1021. [Po]pulo sportulae	4	Saturnia VII	234	XI 2650; *v.* 697
1022. (Singulis collegii incerti)	4	Sestinum VI	—	*v.* 807
*D1023. Liberis (plebis intra murum habitantium)... dimidium	4	Ager Sorrinensium Novensium VII	—	*v.* 783
D1024. Ple[bis]	4	Thermae Himeraeae SICILY	—	*v.* 777
1025. Populo	4	Trebula Balliensis I	(pre-200)	*v.* 808
1026. Municipibus et incolis utriusq(ue) sexus epulum et HS(4)	4	Tuficum VI	141	XI 5693 = *ILS* 2666; cf. *ILS* 2666a
1027. Ceteris utriusque sexus	4	Tuficum VI	180/92	*v.* 809
1028. Plebeis utriusque xesu[s s]ing(ulis) (*sic*)	4	Tuficum VI	(post-200)	*v.* 813
D1029. (Sportulae?)	4	Tusculum I	—	XIV 2643

	Identification	Price (HS)	Town	Date	Reference
D1030.	Populo	4	Verulae I	197	*v.* 784
1031.	Populo viritim	4	Vibo III	138/61	*v.* 800
D1032.	Pop(ulo)	4	Volcei III	161/80	*v.* 790
1033–5.	Uxoribus…vicanorum	4	Volcei III	(100/200)	*v.* 762
1036.	Plebi epul. sing(ulis)	2	Antinum Marsorum IV	(post-100)	*v.* 778
1037–8.	Munic[ipibus] vic(toriatum) n.I (annually)	2	Cales I	—	*v.* 811
1039.	[Fe]minis	2	Croto III	(pre-200)	*v.* 799
1040–1.	Iuvenes Herculani	2	Fabrateria Vetus I	(post-200)	X 5657 = *ILS* 6287; *v.* 721
*1042.	Plebi	2	Perusia VII	166	*v.* 816
1043.	Aug(ustalibus)	2	Petelia III	102/13	*v.* 815
D*1044.*	(Cultoribus Iovis Latii) pane(m) et vinu(m) et (HS2) (between 38 & 44 recipients)	2	Pisaurum VI	—	XI 6310 = *ILS* 3082
D*1045.*	Populo	2	Praeneste I	195 (?)	XIV 3005
1046.	Plebi viritim	2	Saepinum IV	(pre-200)	*v.* 812
1047.	Ut…municipes praesentes acciperent aeris octonos (annually)	2	Spoletium VI	(post-100)	*v.* 652
1048.	Univer(so) numero (collegii) sing(ulis)	2	Volsinii VII	(pre-200)	XI 7302
1049.	Populo virit(im)	1	Petelia III	102/13	*v.* 815
1050.	Popul[o]	1	Potentia III	(post-100)	*v.* 796
1051.	[Feminis singu]los nummos	1	Tuder VI	—	*v.* 797

SPORTULAE WITHOUT SPECIFIED RATES

1052.	Ob promiss(am) venat(ionem) ph(r)etris divisit quina mil(ia) num.	5,000 per phretria	Neapolis I	(post-100)	X 1491 = *ILS* 6456; cf. *SDHI* 5 (1939) 543
1053.	HS200,000 for 3 annual distributions of sportulae to decurions, Augustales & seviri	(3,333 per occasion if 5%)	Altinum X	(post-100)	= 654
1054.	HS50,000 for annual divisio decurionibus et universo populo	(3,000 if 6%)	Corfinium IV	(post-200)	= 673
1055.	HS50,000 for annual distribution 'inter (Augustales) praesentes'	(3,000 if 6%)	Ostia I	*c.* 230/40	= 674

	Identification	Price (HS)	Town	Date	Reference
1056.	HS20,000 at 12% for sportulae	2,400 p.a.	Opitergium X	—	= 680
1057.	HS40,000 for annual distribution to Augustales, less HS100 per year	(2,300 if 6%)	Ostia I	182	= 675
1058.	HS25,000 for annual sportulae for decurions & people	(1,500 if 6%)	Fabrateria Vetus I	(post-200)	= 679
1059.	HS20,000 to each of 7 vici for purchase of possessio whose income will provide annual sportulae for the vicani	(1,200 each if 6%)	Ariminum VIII	(post-200)	= 681
1060.	Distributio... decurionibus epulantibus...deducto ...sumptu strationis	Less than 1200 p.a.	Petelia III	138/61	v. 664
1061.	Sport(ulae)...inter praesent(es)	1,000 p.a.	Comum XI	—	v. 677
1062.	Coll(egiis) dend[r]ophor(orum) et fab(rum) sing(ulis)	1,000 each	Eburum III	(post-100)	X 451; v. 696 & 771
1063.	Sportul(ae)...in[ter praesentes] (collegii fabrum centonarior.)	800 p.a.	Comum XI	—	v. 668
1064.	Ut...praesentibus decurionib(us) et sevir(is) discumbentibus in publico aequis portionibus fieret divisio (annually)	(600 if 6%)	Gabii I	140	= 693
1065.	Annual distribution and feast for Augustales	600 p.a.	Petelia III	138/61	v. 664
1066.	HS8,000 for annual confrequentatio & sportulae for Augustales & plebs urbana	(480 p.a. if 6%)	Saturnia VII	234	= 697
1067.	HS5,000 for annual divisio to members of collegium centonariorum 'epulantes'	(300 p.a. if 6%)	Ameria VI	—	= 700
1068.	Ut...decurionibus et August(alibus) et vicanis dividatur praesentibus	288 p.a.	Capena VII	172	v. 701
1069.	HS4,000 for annual sportulae for cultores antistites deae Cereris	(240 p.a. if 6%)	Fabrateria Vetus I	(post-200)	= 708
1070.	HS4,000 for sportulae for praesentes	(240 p.a. if 6%)	Setia I	(post-200)	v. 713

	Identification	Price (HS)	Town	Date	Reference
1071.	Distribution to decuriales scribae cerarii	150 p.a.	Ostia I	(160/200)	v. 672
1072.	HS2,000 for sportulae for iuvenes Herculani	(120 p.a. if 6%)	Fabrateria Vetus I	(post-200)	= 721
1073.	Distribution to lictores	100 p.a.	Ostia I	(160/200)	v. 672
D1073a.	Ma(t)ronis collegii fabrum	100 p.a.	Aquileia X	—	v. 714
D1073b.	Decuriae meae (collegii fabrum)	60 p.a.	Aquileia X	—	v. 714
1074.	Distribution to librarii	50 p.a.	Ostia I	(160/200)	v. 672

GAMES (See also no.1338)

	Identification	Price (HS)	Town	Date	Reference
1074a.	HS600,000, ut quinto quoque anno munus gladiatorium ederetur	(150,000 if 5%)	Pisaurum VI	(post-100)	=643
1075.	Cum ex HS(100,000) bidui [munus populo promisisset, impendio] suo alis HS(100,000) tertium d[iem ediderit et viam...] straverit per milia pass[uum...]	200,000 (?)	Aeclanum II	(161/9?)	IX 1175
1075a.	HS(25,000) acceptis at conparationem familiae gladiatoriae maiorem quantitatem auxerit	50,000 +	Paestum III	—	Mello–Voza no.91
1075b.	Familiam gladiatoriam ...primus ediderit... acceptis HS(25,000)... a re[pu]blica alium d[iem?]...[cu]raverit	50,000 (?)	Paestum III	—	Mello–Voza no.88
*1076.	[Test]amento... colonis...ad ludos [legavit?]	50,000	Ostia I	(pre-100)	XIV 4693
1077.	Munus	50,000	Formiae I	—	*AE* 1927, 124; v. 858 and 1323
1077a.	Ob promissam venationem (sportulae given instead)	40,000/ 45,000	Neapolis I	—	v. 1052 & note
**1078*.	Ludos...per dies (5) fieri iussit	40,000 (?) (8,000 per day)	Praeneste I	(pre-100)	XIV 3015, cf. *ILS* 6256
1078a.	[Ut]...quodannis ludi eder[entur in] memori[am matris?] suae	c. 20,000/ 25,000	Ostia I	148/80	v. 641

	Identification	Price (HS)	Town	Date	Reference
1079.	In ludos victoriae Caesaris Augusti	7,750	Iguvium VI	27 B.C./ A.D. 14	XI 5820 + p.1395 = *ILS* 5531; *v.* 482, 1325, 1364a
1079a.	Annual ludi	(Part of income of 300,000)	Concordia X	—	*v.* 651

FEASTS, REFRESHMENTS AND OIL-DISTRIBUTIONS

A. AT SPECIFIED RATE PER HEAD

1079b.	Epulum...decurionib. singul.	30	Forum Sempronii VI	—	XI 6117 + p.1397
D1079c.	Epulum decurionibus sing.	20	Asisium VI	(100/200)	XI 5372 + p.1388 = *ILS* 3398. *RE* (2) 5. 1100–1
D1079d.	Epulum...sexvir(is)	12	Asisium VI	(100/200)	*v.* 1079c
1079e.	Epulum...sexviris et Augustalib. sing.	12	Forum Sempronii VI	—	*v.* 1079b
1079f.	Epulum...decur(ionibus) et Augustal(ibus) sing(ulis)	8	Fagifulae IV	140	IX 2553; *v.* 498
D1079g.	Epulum...plebei	6	Asisium VI	(100/200)	*v.* 1079c
1079h.	(Epulum)...plebi sing.	4	Forum Sempronii VI	—	*v.* 1079b
1079i.	Epulum...Mart(ialibus)	3	Fagifulae IV	140	*v.* 1079f
D*1079j*.	Epul(um)...mulierib(us) sing(ulis)	2	Corfinium IV	—	IX 3171
1079k.	Epulum...plebei	2	Fagifulae IV	140	*v.* 1079f

B. GROUP COSTS

1079m.	Postea ad epulum [pl]eb(is) urban(ae)	(84,000 p.a. if 4½%)	Comum XI	111/13	*v.* 638 & note
1080.	Annual aepulum et crust(ulum) et mulsum for citizens	(75,000 p.a. if 5%)	Spoletium VI	—	= 639
1081.	Epulum populo	(20,000 p.a. if 5%)	Pisaurum VI	(post-100)	= 648
1082.	[Ad divisi]onem epularum	(10,000 p.a. if 5%)	Mons Fereter VI	148	= 656
1083.	Epulum for municipes	(6,000 p.a. if 5%)	Sentinum VI	84/96	= 658

	Identification	Price (HS)	Town	Date	Reference
1084.	(Ut) (se)viri Aug(ustales) et compit(ales) Larum Aug. et mag(istri) vicorum...in publico vescerentur	(6,000 p.a. if 5%)	Spoletium VI	(post-100)	= 659
1085.	Divisio mulsa[rum et crustulorum? suff]icientium	(6,000 p.a. if 6%)	Mons Fereter VI	148	= 663
1086.	Crustulum et mulsum	(6,000 p.a. if 6%)	(Casinum I)	(pre-100)	= 666
1087.	Crustulum et mulsum	(6,000 p.a. if 6%)	(Minturnae I)	(pre-100)	= 665
1088.	(Ut) per Neptunalia oleum in campo et in thermis et balineis omnibus quae sunt Comi populo praeberetur	(2,400 if 6%)	Comum XI	(pre-100)	= 676
1089.	Ut...natali suo... (Augustales) praesentes vescerentur	(1,200 p.a. if 6%)	Reate IV	(post-100)	= 683
1090.	Feast for sodality on donor's birthday	720 p.a. (12%)	Ostia I	*c.* 190/200	= 698
1091.	Natali suo...(seviri Augustales) vescerentur	(600 p.a. if 6%)	Aletrium I	(pre-100)	= 687
1092.	Ut decur(iones) et (se)vir(i) Aug(ustales) publice in triclin(i)is suis epulentur	(600 p.a. if 6%)	Gabii I	168	= 692
1093.	(Ut) ex...reditu (coll. fab. tig.) epulentur	(600 p.a. if 6%)	Tolentinum V	—	= 695
1094.	Ut...pagum lustrent et sequentibus diebus ex consuetudine sua cenent, item...die natale...epulentur	500 p.a.	Beneventum II	—	= 689
1095.	Ut (decuria XXVIII sua collegii fabrum)... (in aedem Neptuni) epulentur	450 p.a.	Ravenna VIII	—	= 678
1096.	2 annual feasts for the cultores Dianae et Antinoi	400 on each occasion	Lanuvium I	136	= 685
1097.	Feast for sodality on donor's birthday	360 p.a. (12%)	Ostia I	*c.* 190/200	= 715
1098.	To colleges of dendrophori, fabri & centonarii 'uti die natalis mei oleum singulis vobis dividatur'	(240 p.a. if 6%)	Sassina VI	post-112	= 699

	Identification	Price (HS)	Town	Date	Reference
1099.	7 funds for feasts for sodality on their donors' birthdays	240 p.a. in each case	Ostia I	*c.* 190/200	= 723–26c
1100.	3 funds for feasts for sodality on their donors' birthdays	(240 p.a. each, if 12% as in 1099)	Ostia I	*c.* 190/200	= 727–28a
1101.	Uti...(collegium) epulentur	(240 p.a. if 6%; 480 p.a. if 12%)	Ostia I	140/80	= 710
1102.	Uti (cultores Herculis)...natale (*sic*)...vescerentur	200 (?) p.a.	Truentum (?) V	98/102	= 706
1103.	3 cenae for decurions, (together with ludi & alimenta for 100 girls)	(part of 50,000 p.a. if 5%)	Ostia I	148/*c.* 180	*v.* 641
1104.	C[ena?] & epulum	(part of 15,000 p.a. if 5%)	Concordia X	—	*v.* 651
1105.	Cena for decurions	(part of 12,500 p.a. if 5%)	Spoletium VI	(post-100)	*v.* 652
1106.	(Ut) natal(i) suo ...daretur praesent(ibus) municipib(us) et incol(is) et mulierib(us) nuptis crustul(i) p(ondo) I, mulsi hemin(a)	1 pound of pastry & ½ pint of mead per head p.a.	Ferentinum I	(post-100)	X 5853, cf. p.1013 = *ILS* 6271; *v.* 669, 798
1107.	Plebeis sine distinctione libertatis nucum sparsion(em) mod(iorum) XXX	7.2 bushels of nuts p.a.	Ferentinum I	(post-100)	X 5853, cf. p.1013, = *ILS* 6271; *v.* 669, 798

COMMEMORATIVE RITES AND VOTIVE OFFERINGS

	Identification	Price (HS)	Town	Date	Reference
1108.	Ad rosas et profusiones ...fac(iendas in memoriam)	(3,600 p.a. if 6%)	(Riva) X	—	= 670
1108a.	Ut...rosal(ia) et parent(alia)...in perpetuom procur[entur]	(720 p.a. if 6%)	Arilica X	—	= 686
1109.	Coll(egio dendrophororum)...ut...natali eius... confrequentent	(480 p.a. if 6%)	Eburum III	(post-100)	= 696
1110.	(Decurionibus) ut... natale (*sic*)... epulantes confrequentetis	400 p.a.	Croto III	—	= 691

	Identification	Price (HS)	Town	Date	Reference
1111.	Commemorative feasts on birthdays of donor & wife at HS200 each & 2 days of parentalia & rosalia at HS100 each	600 p.a.	Brixia x	—	= 690
1112.	Ut...die natal(i)... sacrificium facerent ans(e)re et libo et in templo...epularentur et rosas suo tempore deducerent et statuam tergerent et coronarent	(260 p.a. if 6%)	Cemenelum AM	—	= 705
1113.	Ut (collegium nautarum) ...rosas eis deducant ...et cibos (ponant) secus veterem consuetudinem	(240 p.a. if 6%)	Arilica x	—	= 707
1114.	Ex cuius reditu (collegium fabrum navalium) parental(ia) et rosar(ia)...at sepulchrum suum celebrent	(240 p.a. if 6%)	Pisa VII	(post-150)	= 711
1115.	Et in profusionibus	200 p.a.	Croto III	—	*v.* 691; cf. 1110
1116.	In cena parentalicia	200 p.a.	Petelia III	138/61	*v.* 664
1117.	Ut...arcas duas... rosis exornent de (HS100) sacrificientque ex (HS50)	150 p.a.	Ravenna VIII	—	*v.* 678
1118.	At sollemnia cibu[m] et rosarum sibi et coniu[gi]	(120 p.a. if 6%)	Arilica x	(post-200)	= 716
1119.	HS2,000 ut no[bis... rosalib(us)] et parentalib(us)	(120 p.a. if 6%)	Brixia x	—	= 717
1120.	To 3 bodies '(ut) ex reditu...manes meos cola[t]is'	(120 p.a. if 6%)	Sassina VI	post-112	*v.* 699; cf. 1098
1121.	Ut de eis sacrificiu[m parentaliorum tempore quodannis faciant]	100 p.a.	Carsulae VI	—	*v.* 730
1122.	Inpendi volo in ornationem sepulchri et sacrific(i)is die parentaliorum	100 p.a.	Ostia I	—	*v.* 703
1123.	Violae	100 p.a.	Ostia I	—	*v.* 703
1124.	Rosae	100 p.a.	Ostia I	—	*v.* 703
1125.	Ut Ciarne(nses?) facerent...na(talia) tuc(eto) vin(o)	(96 p.a. if 6%)	Feltria x	—	= 731

	Identification	Price (HS)	Town	Date	Reference
1126.	Coronae ternae and profusiones	(96 p.a. if 6%)	Mediolanum XI	—	= 732
1127.	In tutelam (statuae)... ex quorum usur(is) ...sacr(ificium) extis celebretur	(60 p.a. if 6%)	Brixia x	—	= 733
1128.	Ut profus(iones) aei (*sic*) tan parent(alia) tan ros(aria)... celebrent(ur)	(60 p.a. if 6%)	Brixia x	—	= 734
1129.	Et in profusione(m)	(60 p.a. if 6%)	Brixia x	(post-100)	*v.* 736
1130.	In tutel(am)...ut... sacrif(icetur)	(60 p.a. if 6%)	Brixia x	(post-100)	*v.* 736
1131.	In tutelam...ut...per officiales sacrificetur	(60 p.a. if 6%)	Brixia x	(post-100)	*v.* 736
1132.	Collegio fabr(um)... in utrumq(ue) florem perpetuo sibi deducend(um)	(60 p.a. if 6%)	Laus Pompeia XI	—	= 740
1133.	Collegio suo centonariorum legavit HS(1,000), ex cuius reditu...die parentaliorum ne minus homines (12) ad rogum suum vescerentur	(60 p.a. if 6%)	Mevania VI	—	= 741
1134.	Ut...rosas ad monumentum ei spargant et ibi (decuria VII collegii fabrum) epulentur	(60 p.a. if 6%)	Ravenna VIII	—	= 742
1135.	Ad parentalia	50 p.a.	Aquileia x	—	*v.* 714
1136.	Ex cuius summ(a)e reditu rosam ne minus ex HS(16) posuisse ...et reliquum quot est ex usuris escas rosales et vinde-miales...poni...voluit	(48 p.a. if 6%)	Acelum x	—	= 743
1137.	Ut rosal(ia) et parent(alia)... procurent	(36 p.a. if 6%)	(Toscolano ad lacum Benacum) x	—	= 745
1138.	Ad rosas et escas ducendas	(24 p.a. if 6%)	Atria x	—	= 747
1139.	Ut profusio nobis fiat	(24 p.a. if 6%)	Brixia x	—	*v.* 719
1140.	(Ut facerent) Her(clanenses) par(entalia)	(24 p.a. if 6%)	Feltria x	—	= 750

	Identification	Price (HS)	Town	Date	Reference
1141.	Ut facerent mul(ieres) rosas	(24 p.a. if 6%)	Feltria x	—	= 749
1142.	Ut...rosam ponant parentibus et sibi	(24 p.a. if 6%)	Vardagate IX	—	= 752
1142a.	Hostiaque inmol(etur)	(Part of income of 50,000+ fundus)	Auximum V	(pre-100)	*v.* 671
1143.	Et profundi	12 p.a.	Bergomum XI	—	= 754

FUNDS FOR UPKEEP AND MAINTENANCE

	Identification	Price (HS)	Town	Date	Reference
1143a.	(Ut)...viae tutela praestetur	(50,000 p.a. if 5%)	Capua I	pre-69	= 640
1143b.	In tutelam (aquae)	(20,000 p.a. if 5%)	Pola x	(post-100)	= 649
1143c.	[In perp(etuam)] tutelam (balineorum Sergii et Putinii)	(10,000 p.a. if 5%)	Altinum x	(post-100)	= 653
1143d.	In tutela[m thermarum]	(10,000 p.a. if 5%)	Comum XI	111/13	= 655
1143e.	In [t]uit[ionem] (statuarum)	(5,250+ p.a. if 5%)	Patavium x	(pre-100)	= 660
1143f.	In tutelam bybliothecae	(6,000 p.a.)	Comum XI	96/108	= 661
1143g.	In tutelam (templi)	(1,200 p.a. if 6%)	Suasa VI	(post-100)	= 684
1144.	In tutelam statuae	(1,200 p.a. if 6%)	Pisaurum VI	—	= 682
1145.	Amplius in tutela et ornationibus templi	(300 p.a. if 6%)	Gabii I	140	= 702
1146.	Ex [quorum reditu (tetrastylum)...] si quando [necesse esset] reficeretur	(240 p.a. if 6%)	Pitinum Mergens VI	—	= 712
1147.	In...tutel(am)	(120 p.a. if 6%)	Comum XI	—	= 720
1148.	[In tuiti]onem	(120 p.a. if 6%)	Concordia x	—	= 718
1149.	In tutelam (statuae)	(120 p.a. if 6%)	Ager Mediolanensis XI	—	= 722
1150.	(In) tuition(em) (frontis templi)	(120 p.a. if 6%)	Patavium x	(pre-100)	= 729
1151.	Ornatio statuae	100 p.a.	Ostia I	*c.* 230/40	= 674
1152.	In tutelam	(60 p.a. if 6%)	Brixia x	—	= 735
1153.	In tutel(am)	(60 p.a. if 6%)	Comum XI	—	= 737
1154.	In tutelam (statuae)	(60 p.a. if 6%)	Comum XI	—	= 738

	Identification	Price (HS)	Town	Date	Reference
1155.	In tutel(am)	(60 p.a. if 6%)	Ager Comensis XI	—	= 739
1155a.	Ut monumentum remund(etur)	(36 p.a. if 6%)	Arilica X	—	= 744
1156.	In tut(elam) (statuae)	(30 p.a. if 6%)	Brixia X	—	= 746
1157.	In orn(ationem) statuae et imag(inum) mear(um)	30 p.a.	Ferentinum I	(post-100)	v. 669
1158.	In tutel(am)	(24 p.a. if 6%)	Brixia X	—	= 748
1159.	Tutel[a] taber[nar]um	(24 p.a. if 6%)	Brixia X	—	v. 719
1160.	In herm(am) tuend(um) et rosa quodannis ornandam (*sic*)	(24 p.a. if 6%)	Mediolanum XI	—	= 751

FUNDS FOR SUBSISTENCE

	Identification	Price (HS)	Town	Date	Reference
1161.	Bequest for the benefit of children already supported by a previous alimentary gift, divided equally between the sexes	2 million + yielding 100,000 + p.a.	(Capua?) I	161/70	= 637
1162.	Bequest by the younger Pliny for the support of 100 freedmen	1,866,666	Comum XI	111/13	= 638
1163.	Bequest for the maintenance of 100 boys & 100 girls, boys until 16, girls until 14	1 million (probably at 4.33%)	Tarracina I	(100/90)	= 642
1164.	Government foundation for the support of 264 boys and 36 girls	1,116,000	Veleia VIII	98/102 & 102/13	= 639a
1165.	Gift by the younger Pliny for the support of 'pueri et puellae pleb(is) urban(ae)'	500,000 (+) (at 6%)	Comum XI	96/108	= 644
1166.	Bequest for the support of 100 girls	(part of income of 1 million)	Ostia I	148/c. 180	v. 641
1167.	Government foundation for the support of (120/110) children	(401,800 at 5%)	Ligures Baebiani II	101	= 645b
1168.	Bequest for frumentum for the liberi Atinatium, with HS1,000 per head 'dum in aetate[m] pervenirent'	400,000	Atina Latii I	54/68	= 650

RATIONS AND SUBSISTENCE ALLOWANCES

	Identification	Price (HS)	Town	Date	Reference
1169.	In Pliny's gift for the support of 100 freedmen	(HS70 per month if 4½%)	Comum XI	111/13	*v.* 638 & note; cf. 1162
D*1170.*	Servus est, quinque modios accipit et quinque denarios	HS20 & 5 modii of grain (per month)	(Rome)	*c.* 60/5	Seneca *Ep.Mor.* 80.7
1171.	For the boys in a private alimentary gift	HS20 per month	Tarracina I	(100/90)	*v.* 642; cf. 1163 & 1173
1172.	For the legitimate boys in a government alimentary scheme	HS16 per month	Veleia VIII	98/102 & 102/13	*v.* 639a; cf. 1164
1173.	For the girls in a private alimentary gift	HS16 per month	Tarracina I	(100/90)	*v.* 642; cf. 1163 & 1171
1174.	For the legitimate girls in a government alimentary scheme	HS12 per month	Veleia VIII	98/102 & 102/13	*v.* 639a; cf. 1164
1175.	For the illegitimate boys in a government alimentary scheme	HS12 per month	Veleia VIII	98/102 & 102/13	*v.* 639a; cf. 1164
1176.	For the illegitimate girls in a government alimentary scheme	HS10 per month	Veleia VIII	98/102 & 102/13	*v.* 639a; cf. 1164
1176a.	Familiae cibaria... conpeditis per hiemem panis (P.IIII), ubi vineam fodere coeperint panis (P.V), usque adeo dum ficos esse coeperint, deinde ad P.IIII redito	(120/150) pounds of bread per month (39–49 kilograms)	[regio I]	*c.* 160 B.C.	Cato *de agri cult.* 56
1176b.	Corn dole	5 modii per month	Rome	73 B.C.	Granius Licinianus 34 F; Sall. *Hist.* 3.48.19
1176c.	Familiae cibaria. Qui opus facient per hiemem tritici modios (4), per aestatem modios (4½)	4/4½ modii of wheat (per month)	(regio I)	*c.* 160 B.C.	Cato *de agri cult.* 56
1176d.	Familiae cibaria... vilico, vilicae, epistatae, opilioni modios (3)	3 modii of wheat (per month)	[regio I]	*c.* 160 B.C.	Cato *de agri cult.* 56

	Identification	Price (HS)	Town	Date	Reference
1176e.	Habes vini (sextarium) (1), pane(m) a(ssem) (1), pulmentar. a(sses) (2) ...Puell(am) a(sses) (8)...Faenum mulo a(sses) (2)...	HS3.25 for a night's stay at an inn	Aesernia IV	—	IX 2689 = *ILS* 7478
1177.	...[in] caritat(e) ann[onae cum frume]nti copia non e[sset et HS] L modios sin[g(ulos) emerent]	50 (?) per modius of wheat	Histonium IV	(pre-180)	IX 2861
D*1178.*	Quod annona kara frument. denario modium praestitit	4 per modius of wheat	Forum Sempronii VI	(100/50)	XI 6117 + p.1397
1179.	Quod...tempore magist(ratus) sui in karitate olei civib(us) suis quattus libr. pr. p. et epulum dedit	1 (?) per pound of oil	Tuficum VI	(post-200)	XI 5717 + p.1393 = *ILS* 6643
1179a.	I[n] annon[a]m (?)	690,000	Spoletium VI	—	*BCAR* App. 16 (1949/50) 52–3 + XI 7872
1180.	Quod is primus omnium HS C̄...ad annonae comparationem...dedit	100,000	Reate IV	184	IX 4686
1181.	In subsidium annonae frument(i) HS L m.n. ...donavit	50,000	Corfinium IV	(post-100)	*AE* 1961, 109; *v.* 1308a
*1181a.	Populo in annonam... ab herede suo dari iusserit	25,000	Paestum III	—	Mello–Voza no.90
1182.	Quod auxerit ex suo ad annonariam pecuniam	10,000	Abella I	(post-100)	X 1217 = *ILS* 5651
1182a.	In annonam perpetuo	(300 p.a. if 6%)	Ager Sorrinensium Novensium VII	—	= 704
1183.	Idem populo Ca[puensi?] modios binos ded[it]	2 modii per head	Capua I	—	X 3925 + *Atti dei Lincei, Cl. Sci.Mor., Stor. e Filol., Mem.* (1901) 108

LAND RENTS AND VALUATIONS

A. RENTS

1184.	A normal rate of return on land	6% per year	(Italy)	—	*Ep.* 7.18; Columella *de re rust.*

	Identification	Price (HS)	Town	Date	Reference
					3.3.9–10; cf. Pliny *NH* 14.56; Cic. *ad fam.* 5.6.2; *Digesta* 22.1.17.6; 50.10.5; nos.644 664, 669, 691, 694, 701 above. See also pp.132–3 above.
1185.	The rental of some lands belonging to the younger Pliny	400,000 +	(Tifernum Tiberinum VI	98	*Ep.* 10.8.5; Otto 82–5 & Syme 658
1186.	Payment to Neapolis for the collis Leucogaeus by the fiscus from Augustus onwards	200,000 p.a.	Neapolis I	24 B.C./ A.D. 14	Pliny *NH* 18.114
D*1187.*	Annual rent of the statio Tyrensium	100,000	Puteoli I	174	*IG* 14.830
1188.	Revenue of a fundus 200 iugera in extent belonging to the senator Q. Axius	30,000 p.a.	Reate IV	before 37 B.C.	Varro *re rust.* 3.2.15
1189.	Pro eo agro vectigal Langenses Veiturii in poplicum Genuam dent in anos singulos vic(toriatos) n(ummos) CCCC	1,200 p.a.	Genua IX	117 B.C.	V 7749 = *ILS* 5946 = *ILLRP* 517. Cf. C. Castello *Synteleia V. Arangio-Ruiz* (1964) 1124–35

B. LAND VALUATIONS

	Identification	Price (HS)	Town	Date	Reference
1190.	Vineyard of 60 iugera improved by Acilius Sthenelus	6,666 per iugerum	Ager Nomentanus I	50/60	Pliny *NH* 14.48
1191.	Fundus of 200 iugera belonging to the senator Q. Axius which yielded HS30,000	(2,500 per iugerum, if income equal to 6% of capital value)	Reate IV	before 37 B.C.	Varro *re rust.* 3.2.15
1192–3.	Conventional price for unimproved land	1,000 per iugerum	(Italy)	*c.* 60	Columella *de re rust.* 3.3.8. See pp.48–52 above.
1194.	L. Tarius Rufus... usque ad detractationem heredis exhausit agros in Piceno coemendo colendoque in gloriam	100 million	[regio V]	*c.* 30 B.C./ A.D. 10	Pliny *NH* 18.37
1195.	Praedia agris meis vicina...quanti	3–5 million	(Tifernum Tiberinum) VI	96/108	*Ep.* 3.19

	Identification	Price (HS)	Town	Date	Reference
	videantur posse emi: Sestertio triciens, non quia non aliquando quinquagies fuerint				
1196.	Estate bought less than 10 years before for HS600,000, now purchased by Seneca, after spectacular improvements by Acilius Sthenelus	2,400,000	Ager Nomentanus I	50/65	Pliny *NH* 14.49–51
1197.	Coloni Lucenses... deductis reliquis colonorum et usuris pecuniae et pret(i)is mancipiorum quae in ⟨in⟩emptione eis cesserunt habita ratione etiam vectigalium	1,600,000 net (2,500,000 gross)	(Veleia) VIII	102/13	XI 1147, *oblig.* 43
1198.	L. Cornelius Severus/ Cornelia Severa	1,508,150	(Veleia) VIII	98/113	XI 1147, *oblig.* 31 & 48
1199.	M. Mommeius Persicus	1,240,600	(Veleia) VIII	98/113	XI 1147, *oblig.* 13 & 51
1200.	L. Annius Rufinus et C. Annius Verus	1,014,090	(Veleia) VIII	102/13	XI 1147, *oblig.* 17
1200a.	C. Coelius Verus	993,879	(Veleia) VIII	98/113	XI 1147, *oblig.* 16 and 47
1201.	Taxable value of property inherited by Pliny	900,000	(Comum) XI	96/108	*Ep.* 7.14 and 11
1202.	C. Vibius Severus	733,660	(Veleia) VIII	98/113	XI 1147, *oblig.* 30, 49 and 50
1203.	Cn. Marcius Rufinus	[501,000]	(Ligures Baebiani) II	101	IX 1455.2.29
1204.	Sulpicia Priscilla	490,000	(Veleia) VIII	102/13	XI 1147, *oblig.* 9
1205.	Annius Rufus	451,000	(Ligures Baebiani) II	101	IX 1455.2.50
1206.	P. Afranius Apthorus	425,000	(Veleia) VIII	102/13	XI 1147, *oblig.* 6
1207.	L. Maelius Severus	420,110	(Veleia) VIII	102/13	XI 1147, *oblig.* 24
1208.	C. Volumnius Epaphroditus	418,250	(Veleia) VIII	102/13	XI 1147, *oblig.* 22
1209.	Estate of 60 iugera planted with vines by Acilius Sthenelus	400,000	Ager Nomentanus I	*c.* 50	Pliny *NH* 14.48
1210.	Cn. Antonius Priscus	351,633	(Veleia) VIII	102/13	XI 1147, *oblig.* 28
1211.	M. Virius Nepos	310,545	(Veleia) VIII	102/13	XI 1147, *oblig.* 2
1212.	C. Dellius Proculus	292,820	(Veleia) VIII	102/13	XI 1147, *oblig.* 15
1213.	P. Publicius Senex	271,100	(Veleia) VIII	102/13	XI 1147, *oblig.* 45
1214.	L. Virius Fuscus	269,000	(Veleia) VIII	102/13	XI 1147, *oblig.* 46
1215–16.	T. Valius Verus	246,842	(Veleia) VIII	102/13	XI 1147, *oblig.* 44

	Identification	Price (HS)	Town	Date	Reference
1217.	C. Calidius Proculus	233,530	(Veleia) VIII	102/13	XI 1147, *oblig.* 21
1218.	M. Antonius Priscus	233,080	(Veleia) VIII	102/13	XI 1147, *oblig.* 5
1219.	Antonia Vera	210,866	(Veleia) VIII	102/13	XI 1147, *oblig.* 25
1220.	Stenius Felix	200,000	(Ligures Baebiani) II	101	IX 1455.3.78
1221.	—	172,000	(Ligures Baebiani) II	101	IX 1455.1.2
1222.	Q. Accaeus Aebutius Saturninus	158,800	(Veleia) VIII	102/13	XI 1147, *oblig.* 41
1223.	Q. Vibius C.f.	155,842	(Veleia) VIII	102/13	XI 1147, *oblig.* 26
1224.	P. Albius Secundus	151,200	(Veleia) VIII	102/13	XI 1147, *oblig.* 14
1225.	L. Tettius Etruscianus	150,000	(Ligures Baebiani) II	101	IX 1455.2.33
1226.	L. Granius Priscus	148,420	(Veleia) VIII	102/13	XI 1147, *oblig.* 19
1227.	C. Valerius Verus et L. Valerius et P. Valerius Ligurinus	[137,703]	(Veleia) VIII	102/13	XI 1147, *oblig.* 4
1228.	Ceius Vestigator	133,000	(Ligures Baebiani) II	101	IX 1455.3.27
1229.	P. Antonius Sabinus	132,450	(Veleia) VIII	102/13	XI 1147, *oblig.* 20
1230.	—	125,000	(Ligures Baebiani) II	101	IX 1455.2.3
1231.	Vibbius Modestus	122,000	(Ligures Baebiani) II	101	IX 1455.3.55
1232.	C. Naevius Firmus et pupillus Naevius Memor	113,600	(Veleia) VIII	102/13	XI 1147, *oblig.* 42
1233.	Clodius Conveniens	109,000	(Ligures Baebiani) II	101	IX 1455.2.68
1234.	C. Volumnius Memor	108,000	(Veleia) VIII	102/13	XI 1147, *oblig.* 1
1235.	Trebonius Primus	100,000	(Ligures Baebiani) II	101	IX 1455.2.64
1236.	Res publica Baebianorum	100,000	(Ligures Baebiani) II	101	IX 1455.3.23
1237.	Octavius Lybicus (*sic*)	100,000	(Ligures Baebiani) II	101	IX 1455.3.34
1238.	Antius Gamus	100,000	(Ligures Baebiani) II	101	IX 1455.3.36
1239.	M. Septicius Crescens	100,000	(Ligures Baebiani) II	101	IX 1455.3.69
1240.	Glitia Marcella	100,000	(Veleia) VIII	102/13	XI 1147, *oblig.* 39
1241.	Vibia Sabina	100,000	(Veleia) VIII	98/102	XI 1147, *oblig.* 52
1242.	Agellus (cum arboribus) quem nutrici meae donaveram	100,000	[regio VI or regio XI]	96/108	*Ep.* 6.3
1243.	L. Valerius Parra	98,000	(Veleia) VIII	102/13	XI 1147, *oblig.* 37
1244.	Q. Octavius Martialis	92,000	(Ligures Baebiani) II	101	IX 1455.3.12
1245.	Betutia Fusca	90,200	(Veleia) VIII	102/13	XI 1147, *oblig.* 38
1246.	—	86,000	(Ligures Baebiani) II	101	IX 1455.1.34

	Identification	Price (HS)	Town	Date	Reference
1247.	C. Iulius Saturninus	80,000	(Ligures Baebiani) II	101	IX 1455.2.52
1248.	P. Camurius Fortunatus	80,000	(Ligures Baebiani) II	101	IX 1455.2.61
1249.	M. Vibius Q.f.	80,000	(Veleia) VIII	102/13	XI 1147, *oblig.* 10
1250.	T. Naevius Verus	77,192	(Veleia) VIII	102/13	XI 1147, *oblig.* 3
1251.	L. Lucilius Collinus	75,975	(Veleia) VIII	102/13	XI 1147, *oblig.* 18
1252.	M. Caelius Flaccus	75,000	(Ligures Baebiani) II	101	IX 1455.3.16
1253.	L. Sulpicius Verus	71,522	(Veleia) VIII	102/13	XI 1147, *oblig.* 11
1254.	Petronius Epimeles	71,256	(Veleia) VIII	102/13	XI 1147, *oblig.* 40
1255.	A sale of praedia	70,000	(Anticoli) I	(14/37)	XIV 3471
1255a.	Fundus Licitallinus Granianus (sale price)	70,000	Herculaneum I	before 80	Tab. Herc. 64 (*PP* 9 (1954) 58)
1256.	Ceius Venator	70,000	(Ligures Baebiani) II	101	IX 1455.3.32
1257.	Valeria Ingenua	69,260	(Veleia) VIII	102/13	XI 1147, *oblig.* 35
1258.	—	69,000	(Ligures Baebiani) II	101	IX 1455.1.27
1259.	Naevius Vitalis	[67,000]	(Ligures Baebiani) II	101	IX 1455.2.79
1260.	—	66,000	(Ligures Baebiani) II	101	IX 1455.1.40
1261.	Minicia Polla	65,400	(Veleia) VIII	102/13	XI 1147, *oblig.* 32
1262.	C. Pontius Ligus	62,920	(Veleia) VIII	102/13	XI 1147, *oblig.* 34
1263.	—	60,000	(Ligures Baebiani) II	101	IX 1455.1.68
1264.	Badius Saturninus	60,000	(Ligures Baebiani) II	101	IX 1455.3.80
1265.	Afinius Cogitatus	60,000	(Ligures Baebiani) II	101	IX 1455.3.83
1266.	C. Vibius Probus	58,800	(Veleia) VIII	102/13	XI 1147, *oblig.* 12
1267.	M. Varius Felix	58,350	(Veleia) VIII	102/13	XI 1147, *oblig.* 27
1268.	L. Veturius Severus	55,800	(Veleia) VIII	102/13	XI 1147, *oblig.* 36
1269.	Sosius Secundus	55,000	(Ligures Baebiani) II	101	IX 1455.3.52
1270.	T. Naevius Titulius	53,900	(Veleia) VIII	102/13	XI 1147, *oblig.* 33
1271.	Iulia Hecate	52,000	(Ligures Baebiani) II	101	IX 1455.2.57
1272.	L. Cornelius Onesimus	51,000	(Veleia) VIII	102/13	XI 1147, *oblig.* 7
1273.	L. Licinius L.f.	50,350	(Veleia) VIII	102/13	XI 1147, *oblig.* 23
1274.	—	50,000	(Ligures Baebiani) II	101	IX 1455.1.17
1275.	Crispia Restituta	50,000	(Ligures Baebiani) II	101	IX 1455.2.7
1276.	...us Ferox	50,000	(Ligures Baebiani) II	101	IX 1455.3.3
1277.	Turselius Pudens	50,000	(Ligures Baebiani) II	101	IX 1455.3.40

	Identification	Price (HS)	Town	Date	Reference
1278.	Stafonius Secundus	50,000	(Ligures Baebiani) II	101	IX 1455.3.42
1279.	Nonius Restitutus	50,000	(Ligures Baebiani) II	101	IX 1455.3.71
1280.	Cosinius Cosmus	50,000	(Ligures Baebiani) II	101	IX 1455.3.73
1281.	Trebius Ampliatus	50,000	(Ligures Baebiani) II	101	IX 1455.3.76
1282.	P. Atilius Saturninus	50,000	(Veleia) VIII	102/13	XI 1147, *oblig.* 8
1283.	L. Cornelius Helius	50,000	(Veleia) VIII	102/13	XI 1147, *oblig.* 29
1284.	Valgia Secunda	48,000	(Ligures Baebiani) II	101	IX 1455.2.42
1285.	T. Amunius Silvanus	46,000	(Ligures Baebiani) II	101	IX 1455.2.13
1286.	—	44,200	(Ligures Baebiani) II	101	IX 1455.1.45
1287.	Helvius Modestus	42,000	(Ligures Baebiani) II	101	IX 1455.3.57
1288.	C. Valerius Pietas	40,000	(Ligures Baebiani) II	101	IX 1455.3.20
1289.	Statoria Prisca et Statorius Pudens	40,000	(Ligures Baebiani) II	101	IX 1455.3.46
1290.	P. Tintorius Felicio	35,000	(Ligures Baebiani) II	101	IX 1455.3.10
1291.	L. Naeratius Diadumenus	34,000	(Ligures Baebiani II	101	IX 1455.2.10
1292.	L. Vibbius Anencletus	30,000	(Ligures Baebiani) II	101	IX 1455.2.74
1293.	. . . tronius Primigenius	30,000	(Ligures Baebiani) II	101	IX 1455.3.5
1294.	Betulenus Priscus	30,000	(Ligures Baebiani) II	101	IX 1455.3.44
1295–6.	Antistius Iustus et Antistius Priscus	30,000	(Ligures Baebiani) II	101	IX 1455.3.64
1297.	Licinius Liberalis	27,000	(Ligures Baebiani) II	101	IX 1455.3.61
1298.	L. Statorius Restitutus	25,000	(Ligures Baebiani) II	101	IX 1455.2.71
1299.	Neratius Corellius	22,000	(Ligures Baebiani) II	101	IX 1455.2.16
1300.	L. Longius Pyramus	20,000	(Ligures Baebiani) II	101	IX 1455.2.45
1301.	Vergilius Proculus	20,000	(Ligures Baebiani) II	101	IX 1455.3.38
1302.	Bebbius Ferox	20,000	(Ligures Baebiani) II	101	IX 1455.3.48
1303.	Livinius Proculus	20,000	(Ligures Baebiani) II	101	IX 1455.3.50
1304.	A. Plotius Optatus	19,000	(Ligures Baebiani) II	101	IX 1455.3.8

	Identification	Price (HS)	Town	Date	Reference
1305.	P. Titius Aiax	14,000	(Ligures Baebiani) II	101	IX 1455.2.36
1306.	Cost of site for tomb of 12-year-old boy	[2]00	Teanum Sidicinum I	—	X 4811

FUNDS FOR HEATING AND RUNNING THE PUBLIC BATHS

	Identification	Price (HS)	Town	Date	Reference
1307.	Ut ex...reditu (balinea Sergium et Putinium) cale[fier]ent	(20,000 p.a. if 5%)	Altinum X	(post-100)	= 646
1308.	Ut ex reditu, in perpetuum viri et impuberes utriusq(ue) sexsus gratis laventur	(20,000 p.a. if 5%)	Bononia VIII	38/41	= 647
1308a.	Balineum...muliebre cum HS(30,000) donavit	(1,800 p.a. if 6%)	Corfinium IV	post-180	*AE* 1961, 109
1309.	Ad lavacrum balnear(um) publicar(um) ligni duri vehes n(umero) CCCC enthecae nomine in perpetuum obtulit, ita tamen ut magistratuus (*sic*) quodannis successorib(us) suis tradant	400 cartloads of hard wood p.a.	Misenum I	(post-160)	X 3678 = *ILS* 5689

SUMMAE HONORARIAE

	Identification	Price (HS)	Town	Date	Reference
1310–11.	Is arcae (Augustalium) HS(50,000) ded(it), ex qua summa HS(10,000) ob honorem curae / Ob h(onorem) c(urae) / Ob h/onorem) c(urae)	10,000	Ostia I	182; 193; 201	XIV 367 = *ILS* 6164; XIV 4560 (*bis*)
1312.	Summa honoraria? 'Balneum...emptum...ex pecunia Augustal(ium) HS(60,000) [6 names]'	(10,000)	Teanum Sidicinum I	(pre-100)	X 4792 = *ILS* 5677; *v.* 450
1313.	Hic pro seviratu in rem p. dedit	2,000	Asisium VI	(pre-100)	XI 5400 = *ILS* 7812; cf. nos.1314–15; II 1934
1314.	Aug(ustalis) ex d(ecreto) d(ecurionum) ad stratam refic(iendam)	2,000	(regio I)	(pre-200)	*v.* 488

	Identification	Price (HS)	Town	Date	Reference
1315.	Ob honorem Augustali(tatis) collabentem pontem pecunia publica restitutum, in cuius restitutionem HS $\overline{\text{II}}$ contulerat, adiecta pecunia	2,000	Cereatae Marianae I	(pre-200)	*v.* 489 and note
1315a.	Aed(ilis) viam et crepidin(em) ob honorem str(avit)...p(edes) (100)	(2,000 if HS20 per foot; cf. nos.454, 463, 466)	Venusia II	—	IX 442
1316.	Pro magi(stratu) (a college of the Imperial household)	1,600	Antium I	(39?); 40; 41 (twice); 44	X 6638 = I¹ pp.327 ff. = *IIt* 13.1 pp.320 ff.
1317.	Pro mag(istratu) (a college of the Imperial household)	2,000	Antium I	48	X 6638 = I¹ pp.327 ff. = *IIt* 13.1 pp.320 ff.
1317a.	Pro mag(istratu) (a college of the Imperial household)	1,000	Antium I	37	X 6638 = I¹ pp.327 ff.

INDIVIDUAL PAYMENTS IN HONOUR OF OFFICE

	Identification	Price (HS)	Town	Date	Reference
1318.	Sacerdos, flam(inica) div[ae] Iuliae Piae [A]ug...ob honorem sacerd(otii)	50,000	Aeclanum II	*c.* 81/96	IX 1153 = *ILS* 6487
1319.	Decurionatus ornamentis honoratus et biselliarius in primis constitutus inlatis reipublicae sestert(i)is (50,000)	50,000	Ostia I	*c.* 198	XIV 374+p.482 = *ILS* 6165
1320.	Ob honore(m) bisell(i)i HS(50,000) rei p. Pisanor. dedit	50,000	Pisa VII	(post-100)	XI 1441+p.1264 = *ILS* 6599; cf. *IIt* 7.1.23 & fig.
1321.	Huic [ordo Aug(ustalium) statu]am decrevit et in[ter biselliari?]os adlegit isque hono[re... accepto] HS(50,000) arcae eorum [intulit]	50,000	Ostia I	*c.* 230/40	XIV 431+p.482; *v.* 674
1322.	Hic ob honorem aedilitat(is)... [po]rticum...[refecit]	29,300	Falerii VII	—	*v.* 475

	Identification	Price (HS)	Town	Date	Reference
1323.	Bisell(i)arius cui ordo conscript(orum) ornamenta decur(ionatus) dedit quod is ob honor(em) bisell(i)i HS(25,000) rei p. obtulerit	25,000	Formiae I	—	*AE* 1927, 124; cf. 1077, 858
1323a.	Ob honorem aedilitatis promi[s(it)]	25,000	Lilybaeum SICILY	169/72	*AE* 1964, 181
1324.	Aed(ilis) ob honorem in viam	20,000	Cremona X	(pre-100)	V 4097 (*v.* 464a)
1324a.	In publicum pro duomviratu	10,000	Pompeii I	*c.* 10 B.C.	X 1074+pp.967 and 1006 = *ILS* 5053
1325.	Decurionatus nomine	6,000	Iguvium VI	27 B.C./ A.D. 14	XI 5820+p.1395 = *ILS* 5531
1326.	Viam...a novo restituerunt...pater ...et...filius ob honores et immunitates omnes in se constitutas	(50,000 per head)	Falerii VII	(pre-200)	XI 3126, cf. p.1323 = *ILS* 5374; *v.* 457ᵃ
1327.	Pater qui ob honores ei habitos...(rei publicae) dedit	50,000	Ostia I	(160/200)	XIV 353 = *ILS* 6148; XIV 4642; *v.* 672

CAPITAL PAYMENTS AND LEGACIES TO CITIES

	Identification	Price (HS)	Town	Date	Reference
*1328.	Hic rei p(ublicae) suae...legavit	400,000	Mantua X	(50/200)	V 4059 = *ILS* 5012; *v.* 473
*1329.	Caput ex [testame]nto colonis coloni[ae V]enusin(orum) HS(250,000) integra sine deduct(ione) vicesim(ae) ea condic(ione) ut hered(es) mei summ[...]	250,000	Venusia II	—	IX 449
*1330.	Legavit colonis coloniae Auximati(um)	100,000	Auximum V	(pre-100)	IX 5855; *v.* 851
*1331.	Reipublica[e] (legavit)	100,000	Capua I	(pre-200)	X 3927; *v.* 853 & 838
*1332.	In memoriam (uxoris?) ...rei p....legavit	100,000	Petelia III	138/61	*ILS* 6470; *v.* 664, 694, 1333
*1333.	In memoriam (matris) ...rei p....legavit	100,000	Petelia III	138/61	*ILS* 6471; *v.* 664, 694, 1332
1334.	Cum res publica praedia sua venderet ob pol[l]icitationem belli navalis...rei p...donavit	15,200	Ostia I	38/6 B.C.?	XIV 375+p.482, = *ILS* 6147; Meiggs 493–500

PUBLIC SUBVENTIONS ADDED TO OUTLAYS FROM PRIVATE SOURCES

	Identification	Price (HS)	Town	Date	Reference
1335.	Intra [tempus] anni HS LXII [reprae]-sentavit (repayment of sum subscribed by city to entertainment offered by magistrate)	62,[000]	Aeclanum II	(post-100)	IX 1178; cf. IX 1156
1336.	Quod is ob honor(em) bisell(i)i HS(25,000) rei p. obtulerit ex quib(us) familia glad(iatorum) ex postulatu universor(um) per ipsum edita est; ad cuius impensas insuper universa plebs ad ampliandam muneris eius famam HS(25,000) (obtulit)	25,000	Formiae I	—	*AE* 1927, 124; *v.* 858, 1077, 1323
1336a.	HS(25,000) acceptis at conparationem familiae gladiatoriae maiorem quantitatem auxit	25,000	Paestum III	—	*v.* 1075a
1336b.	Familiam gladiatoriam …primus edidit… acceptis HS(25,000) …a re[pu]blica alium d[iem?]…[cu]ravit	25,000	Paestum III	—	*v.* 1075b
1337.	Viam…restituit, acceptis ab r.p. in [ve]ctui (*sic*) silicis HS(14,000)	14,000	Velitrae I	(pre-200)	*v.* 465 & note; cf. 408
1338.	Duumviratu suo, acceptis a re p. (HS13,000), venation(es) plenas et gladiatorum paria (21) dedit	13,000	Allifae I	(post-100)	IX 2350 = *ILS* 5059; IX 2351; cf. 408

MISCELLANEOUS AND UNCLASSIFIED COSTS

1339.	In (quattuor)vi[ratu …de]dit idem […]	1,051,000	Patavium X	—	V 2878
1340.	4 sums of money	1,050, 000 10[000] 1,000 1,000	Ameria VI	—	XI 4418 + p.1368 n.1

	Identification	Price (HS)	Town	Date	Reference
*1341.	Hic pridie quam mortuus est reliquit patrimoni HSQ...	[800,000?]	Asisium VI	(pre-100)	XI 5400 = *ILS* 7812; *v.* 461 & note
1341a.	Net sum inherited from Saturninus by Pliny	*c.* 700,000	Comum XI	96/108	*Ep.* 5.7
*1342.	...or...cavit	5c0(,000?)	(Pedemontanae incertae) XI	—	V 7173
*1343.	[Ex H]S Q t(estamento) f(ieri) i(ussit)	500,000	Verona X	—	V 3867; *v.* 442
1343a.	Saturninus's bequest to Comum	400,000	Comum XI	96/108	*Ep.* 5.7
1344.	—	304,000	Vercellae XI	—	V 6667
1345.	...trecentoru[m]	300,000	Catina SICILY	*c.* 164	*AE* 1960, 202, cf. X 7024 & Manganaro in *Kokalos* 5 (1959) 145–58
1345a.	Gift by Pliny to Romatius Firmus	300,000	Comum XI	96/108	*Ep.* 1.19.2
1346.	Decurione[s] [de]crevissent uti [...] proque ea re [...] (205,000)	205,000	Aeclanum II	(pre-100)	IX 1146 = I² 1724
1347.	Summis[...]	250,000	Catina SICILY	*c.* 164	*v.* 1345
1348.	In...pu[bl]ica consum[ere]	250,000	Puteoli I	—	X 1788
1348a.	Dedit	200,000	Pisaurum VI	—	XI 6379
1349.	[P]raef(ectus) co[h(ortis)...] HS(200,000) ti[...]	200,000	Iguvium VI	—	XI 5810
1350.	—	100,000	Catina SICILY	*c.* 164	*v.* 1345
1350a.	Dowry given by Pliny to Calvina	100,000	(Comum XI)	96/108	*Ep.* 2.4.2
1351.	—	100,000	Fabrateria Nova I	(pre-100)	X 5644
1352.	[E]q(ues) R(omanus) eq(uo) p(ublico) [...] largit(us) est [...A]ug. c(reatus) d(ecreto) [d(ecurionum)]	100,000	Mediolanum XI	—	V 8922; cf. V 1198
*1353.	[...]st HS(50,000) lega[vit]	50,000	Aeclanum II	—	IX 1177; *v.* 779, 1362
1354.	Hic pro libertate dedit	50,000	Asisium VI	(pre-100)	XI 5400 = *ILS* 7812; *v.* 461 & note
1354a.	Dowry given by Pliny to fiancée of Nonius Celer	50,000	(Comum XI)	96/108	*Ep.* 6.32.2
*1355.	[Te]st(amento)	50,000	Spoletium VI	—	XI 4801

	Identification	Price (HS)	Town	Date	Reference
1356.	—	42,500 (? +)	Ameria VI	(pre-100)	XI 4417
1356a.	Gift by Pliny to Metilius Crispus	40,000	Comum XI	96/108	*Ep.* 6.25.3
1357.	Lacum purgatum operis [*sc.* laboribus] paganorum n(ostrorum). O(pus) c(onstat)...	15,000	Uscosium IV	139	IX 2828
1357a.	Reliqui HS XII m.n. (ob hon. aedil.)	12,000	Lilybaeum SICILY	169/72	*AE* 1964, 181
1358.	Ad roburandum consensum amatorum suorum donavit eis	10,000	Ocriculum VI	247/8	XI 7805 = *ILS* 7365; *v.* 841
1358a.	Arcae (collegii fabrum)	10,000	Pisaurum VI	—	XI 6371
D1359.	Figures belonging to a statue or building	9,814.5 8,800 1,050.5	Regium Lepidum VIII	—	XI 978
1360-1.	—	7,000 (? +)	Thermae Himeraeae SICILY	(pre-100)	X 7361
1362.	Dis[tribuit?]	4,000	Aeclanum II	—	IX 1177; *v.* 779 & 1353
D1363.	Don(avit) c(ollegio) f(abrum), se vivo	4,000	Aquileia X	—	Pais no.194
1364.	12 or more payments of the same amount by different individuals	4,000 in each case	Ostia I	—	XIV 276
1364a.	In commeatum legionibus	3,450	Iguvium VI	27 B.C./ A.D. 14	XI 5820 + p.1395 = *ILS* 5531; *v.* 482
1365.	D(uoviri) ex d(ecreto) d(ecurionum) ius luminum opstruendorum HS(3,000) redemerunt parietemque privatum col(oniae)...(Pompeianorum) usque a(d) tegulas faciundum coerarunt	3,000	Pompeii I	*c.* 2/1 B.C.	X 787 + p.967 = *ILS* 5915
1366.	Item praece[dentibus in] memoriam mari[ti sui et filia]e suae...dedit	2,000	Aquileia X	—	V 1019
1367.	Quod opus expensarum diur(narum) (various individuals)	1,330 700? 1,150?, 140	Placentia VIII	—	XI 1233
1368.	—	1,000 (? +)	Amiternum IV	(post-200)	IX 4305
1369.	Tr(ibunus) mil(itum) [...] praef(ectus) [coh(ortis)...] Hic HS(1,000? +) [...]	1,000 (? +)	Peltuinum IV	—	IX 3428
*1370.	[Le]gavit prata Maeci[...] a HS(330) et...	330	Spoletium VI	—	XI 7873

	Identification	Price (HS)	Town	Date	Reference
1371.	—	200	(Ripa lacus Benaci ad orientem) x	—	V 4006
D1372.	'M.f.*III *VIIII' (on lower part of funerary stele)	48?	Aesernia IV	—	IX 2749
D1373.	Et ex ea divisione iubeo statuae meae coronas emi *III	12 p.a.	Capena VII	172	*v.* 701
1374.	[Argen]ti libr(ae) C	100 pounds of silver	Aeclanum II	—	IX 1150
1375.	[Clipe?]os duos p(ondo) c(entum?)	100? pounds (of silver)	Ameria VI	—	XI 4417; cf. 515 above
*1376.	Speculum arg(enti)	0.83 pounds of silver	Sentinum VI	—	*AE* 1941, 96
1376a.	[Man]telum	0.25 pounds of silver	Puteoli I	—	X 1598

COLLEGE PROVISIONS AND STIPULATIONS

A. LEX FAMILIAE SILVANI

1377.	Item qui ex eo corpore decesserit sequi eum debeat aut heredem eius	560	Trebula Mutuesca IV	*c.* 60	*AE* 1929, 161, 16–17; cf. *NS* (1928) tav. v, p.394
1378.	Ad sacrum faciendum	400	Trebula Mutuesca IV	*c.* 60	*AE* 1929, 161. 3–5
1379.	If a magister fails to contribute HS200 towards the sum needed 'ad sacrum faciendum', he must pay a fine	300	Trebula Mutuesca IV	*c.* 60	*AE* 1929, 161.6
1380.	The magisterial contribution 'ad sacrum faciendum'	200	Trebula Mutuesca IV	*c.* 60	*AE* 1929, 161.4–5
1381.	The sum payable by the arca, 'ad sacrum faciendum'	200	Trebula Mutuesca IV	*c.* 60	*AE* 1929, 161.2–4
1382.	Et locus eius (qui ex eo corpore decesserit) HS C (veneat), si tamen testamento suo nominarit; si minus caducum erit	100	Trebula Mutuesca IV	*c.* 60	*AE* 1929, 161.17–19
1383.	Hoc amplius dare legare debeat familiae HS(50) (possibly a condition of receiving funerary benefits in full)	50	Trebula Mutuesca IV	*c.* 60	*AE* 1929, 161.19–20

	Identification	Price (HS)	Town	Date	Reference
1384.	Cum ad sacrum ventum erit ne quis litiget neve rixam faciat neve extraneum invitet ea die; si ita fecerit d(are) d(ebeat)	20	Trebula Mutuesca IV	*c.* 60	*AE* 1929, 161.6–9
1385.	The fine for not paying the contribution to the funeral expenses of another member (*v.* 1387) within 3 days; or for failing to attend the funeral without good cause	20	Trebula Mutuesca IV	*c.* 60	*AE* 1929, 161.11–14
1386.	If a member of a decuria of the familia dies, it shall be the responsibility of the members of that decuria to bury him; if they fail to do so, there will be a (per capita) fine	10	Trebula Mutuesca IV	*c.* 60	*AE* 1929, 161.14–15
1387.	Qui ex ea familia decesserit, ut ei conferant singuli HS(8)	8	Trebula Mutuesca IV	*c.* 60	*AE* 1929, 161.10–11
1388.	Quisquis decuriae suae (mortem decurialis alicuius) non denuntiarit d(are) d(ebeat)...in singulos homin(es)	5	Trebula Mutuesca IV	*c.* 60	*AE* 1929, 161.21–2

B. LEXS COLLEG(I)I CULTORUM DIANAE ET ANTINOI
(see also no.685)

1389.	If they embezzle the sum allowed for burial of a member who died beyond the 20th milestone (HS300), the 3 individuals concerned are liable to a 4-fold fine (quadruplum)	1,200	Lanuvium I	136	Gordon 2.61–8; XIV 2112 = *ILS* 7212 I.25 ff.
1390.	(When a member dies fully paid up) eum sequentur ex arca HS(300); ex qua summa decedent exequiari nomine HS(50), qui ad rogu(m) dividentur; exequiae autem pedibus fungentur	300	Lanuvium I	136	XIV 2112 = *ILS* 7212 I.23 ff.

	Identification	Price (HS)	Town	Date	Reference
1391.	Ut quisquis in hoc collegium intrare voluerit, dabit kapitulari nomine HS(100) et vi[ni] boni amphoram; item in menses sing(ulos) a(sses) (5)	100 + 1 amphora of good wine; HS1.25 per month thereafter	Lanuvium I	136	XIV 2112 = *ILS* 7212 1.20 ff.
1392.	Fine payable by a magister cenarum (4 were appointed at a time) who fails to contribute to a feast for which he has responsibility	30	Lanuvium I	136	XIV 2112 = *ILS* 7212 2.8–9
1393.	Viaticum payable to each of the 3 members to whom the task of burying a member who dies beyond the 20th milestone is delegated	20	Lanuvium I	136	XIV 2112 = *ILS* 7212 1.25 ff.
1394.	Si quis quinquennali inter epulas obprobrium aut quid contumeliose dixerit, ei multa esto	20	Lanuvium I	136	XIV 2112 = *ILS* 7212 1.27–8
1395.	Si quis autem in obprobrium alter alterius dixerit, aut tu[mul]tuatus fuerit, ei multa esto	12	Lanuvium I	136	XIV 2112 = *ILS* 7212 2.26–7
1396.	Placuit, ut quisquis siditionis causa de loco in alium locum transierit, ei multa esto	4	Lanuvium I	136	XIV 2112 = *ILS* 7212 2.25–6
1397.	Magistri cenarum ex ordine albi facti qu[oqu]o ordine homines quaterni [*scr.* quaternos] ponere debeb[unt]: vini boni amphoras singulas et panes a(ssium) II qui numerus colleg(i)i fuerit, et sardas n[u]mero (4), strationem, caldam cum ministerio	For each man, loaf costing HS½, 4 sardines and some wine	Lanuvium I	136	XIV 2112 = *ILS* 7212 2.14–16
1398.	Placuit ut quisquis servus ex hoc collegio liber factus fuerit, is dare debebit vini [bo]ni amphoram	1 amphora (26 litres) of good wine	Lanuvium I	136	XIV 2112 = *ILS* 7212 2.7–8

NOTES

439. For the remains of these baths, Meiggs 409-12, with fig.28; the brickstamps suggest that the foundations were laid in the last years of Hadrian. For the chronology see also p.88 n.4. For other imperial outlays in Italy, nos.454, 506, 639a, 645a; in the provinces, R. Macmullen *HSCP* 64 (1959) 207-35.

440. Half of this outlay was made by the city from its own resources, the remaining HS500,000 coming from a bequest by M. Antistius Nereus. For another public building work dependent on large private bequests see no.63, the stage of the theatre at Lepcis Magna which was financed by legacies of HS300,000 and 200,000.

441. The figure of HS1 million was inferred by Mommsen, who subtracted the cost of Pliny's first alimentary gift (HS500,000, no.644) and the cost of the upkeep of the library (HS100,000, no.661) from the sum of HS1,600,000 that Pliny said that he had spent on lifetime gifts to Comum (*Ep.* 5.7.3; Mommsen *Ges.Schr.* 4.434, n.6). The dating used for Pliny's gifts follows Syme and Sherwin-White in assigning books I-IX to A.D. 96-108, and Syme in assigning Pliny's death to 111/13 (Sherwin-White 41; Syme 660; 81 and 659).

443. The inscription begins by stating that the baths were built and roofed by Ser. Cornelius Ser.f. Dolabella Metilianus from his own resources (Metilianus was consul in A.D. 113 and patron of Corfinium, *PIR²* C 1350). It then states that two more consuls, M. Atilius (Metilius) Bradua (consul in A.D. 108, *PIR²* A 1302) and M'. Acilius Aviola (consul in A.D. 122, *PIR²* A 50), who were the 'bonor(um) possessor(es) Dolabellae Metiliani', each gave HS100,000 to its construction. Finally, the 'res p(ublica) et populus Corfiniensis' completed the building at a further cost of HS152,000. It thus appears that Metilianus began the baths, though the amount of his expenditure on them is not recorded. His effective heirs contributed a further HS200,000 from his estate, no doubt in accordance with Metilianus's wishes. This was not enough to complete the baths, which needed a further HS152,000 which was contributed partly from civic funds and partly by subscription (from the reference to the 'populus Corfiniensis'). For building projects whose cost overran the original budget, cf. pp.76-7. The decoration of Pliny's baths at Comum cost HS300,000 (no.469a).

444. There is little reason to suppose that these baths were intended as a public gift. For private baths costing HS600,000, Juvenal 7.178 ff. Though Fronto was a native of Cirta (*PIR²* C 1364) his career as senator and courtier must have meant his domicile in Italy from an early stage. Fronto's son-in-law, C. Aufidius Victorinus, came from Pisaurum in Umbria (*PIR²* A 1393, cf. A 1386). The baths in question are likely to have been built in Italy, if not in Rome.

445. Money for these baths was bequeathed by P. Tullius Varro, consul in A.D. 127 (Degrassi 37). They were built from the bequest, with additional funds, by L. Dasumius Tullius Tuscus, consul in A.D. 152, probably after his cooption as *sodalis Antoninianus* in A.D. 161 (*PIR²* D 16, cf. Bormann *ad* XI 3366, 3368). The inscription gives the amount of the bequest as '[s]estertio ter et tr…'. Bormann's restoration 'tr[icies]' makes the bequest HS3,300,000, a prodigious cost for a building in a secondary town. It is preferable to read 'ter et tr[icenis]' or 330,000 (suggested by Professor A. H. M. Jones). The testator appears to be named in the will of Dasumius in A.D. 108 (VI 10229.22, cf. *PIR¹* T 284). The names suggest that the consul who carried out the promise was Varro's natural son, whom Dasumius had adopted as his heir (Mommsen, VI p. 1349).

445a. This building, whose purpose is uncertain, was built with HS300,000 bequeathed by an imperial freedman named Fortunatus, who dedicated it to the reigning Emperor, Antoninus Pius 'optimo et indulgentissimo patrono'.

446. C. Clodius Adiutor and [Clodius Cap]ito, who both reached the praetorship, jointly bequeathed HS1 million to Capua for the upkeep of roads (no.640). Adiutor separately

bequeathed HS300,000 to Sinuessa for the construction of a temple and the paving of the forum (no.446). Groag dates their careers to the beginning of the Principate (*PIR*² C 1158 and 1156).

446a. The purpose of this building costing HS300,000 is not known. The donor, Caelia Macrina, also left HS1 million for the support of 200 children (no.642); the typology of this gift suggests an Antonine date.

447. The HS150,000 bequeathed here for the fabric of baths was paid to the city by the heirs of the donor (apparently Arruntius Granianus) only after successive hearings before 'Aemilius Fronto cl(arissimus) vir' and 'Arrius Antoninus cl(arissimus) vir' in the reign of Marcus Aurelius. (The senators were evidently successive *iuridici* for the zone of Italy in which Tifernum lay; cf. *PIR*² A 349 and A 1088, where the less likely alternative that the senators were *curatores rei publicae* of Tifernum is also suggested.) The donor also bequeathed the large sum of HS60,000 for statues of himself and his son (no.495), whose dedication the heirs were to celebrate with a distribution of sportulae at rates of HS20, HS12 and HS8 (no.768).

454. HS569,100 was subscribed by the 'possessores agrorum' of the district through which the road ran, and the residue of HS1,147,000 was made up by the Emperor or in his name. Another inscription records Hadrian's building a road to Suessa in the previous year (A.D. 122; X 4756).

455. T. Vibius Temudinus, the *quaestor urbis* named in the inscription as *curator viarum*, is dated to the Sullan period (T. R. S. Broughton *Magistrates of the Roman Republic* 2 (1952) 477).

457a. For the location of the roads named, M. W. Frederiksen & J. B. Ward Perkins *PBSR* 25 (1957) 145–6, 190–1.

458. The equestrian donor, whose name is missing, was a member of the *quinque decuriae*, who served as *praefectus fabrum*, duovir and augur. As well as spending HS100,000 (?) on road construction he gave sportulae to the decurions at the very high rate of HS100 (no.825).

459. Part of the figure is missing; the highest cost allowed by the notation is approximately HS95,000.

461. The donor P. Decimius P.l. Eros Merula, 'medicus, clinicus, chirurgus, ocularius, (se)vir', gave HS50,000 *pro libertate* (no.1354); HS2,000 *pro seviratu in rem p(ublicam)* (no.1313, evidently a *summa honoraria*); HS30,000 for statues in the temple of Hercules (no.494); HS37,000 *in vias sternendas in publicum* (no.461); and bequeathed HS[800,000?] the day before his death (no.1341). The archaic numerals suggest that the inscription is not later than the end of the first century A.D.

463. For the interpretation of this inscription see pp.124–5.

466. Piganiol's suggestion that 'pr.' should be read as 'pr(aestant)' and not as 'pr(etio)' (with Mancini) leads to a road-cost of HS0.05 per foot, which is quite implausible (see pp.124–5; A. Piganiol *Les documents cadastraux de la colonie romaine d'Orange, Gallia* supp. 16 (1962) 59n.).

467. See pp. 124–5 above.

468. The donor, whose nomen was Fabius, bequeathed altogether HS1,600,000 to Altinum. HS800,000 was assigned to the restoration of two public baths evidently given at an earlier date by other private individuals ('balinea Sergium et Puti[nium]', no.468). HS400,000 was to provide a perpetual fund for heating the baths (no.646); HS200,000 was to provide a perpetual fund for their upkeep (no.653); and HS200,000 was to provide income for three annual distributions on the birthdays of the donor, his father and his mother (no.654). The donor's parents were L. Fabius St[ell.] Amminianus, and Petronia Magna. The gift is the third largest whose size is explicitly recorded in Italy, after the gifts of Pliny (see pp.27–31) and Matidia (no.637 and note); cf. also no.1197 and note.

470. The donor was C. Valerius Pansa, procurator of Britain in the mid-second century (Pflaum 314; *PIR*[1] V 102).

472. It appears that the donor, whose name is missing, belonged to the *quinque decuriae* and served at least two of the equestrian *militiae*. He gave a specified amount over a period of ten years, and a further sum for the completion of the amphitheatre. It is not clear whether the annual payment was HS10,000 (HS100,000 spread over ten years) or HS100,000; but if the overall total were more than HS100,000 it would probably have been stated explicitly. Dimensions of the amphitheatre: *RE* 13.1540

473. M. Fabius Praesens bequeathed HS100,000 to Mantua for the adornment of a *schola*, together with HS400,000 whose purpose was unspecified (no.1328). Praesens was *sacerdos Caeninensis*, a holder of the *equus publicus* and a member of the *quinque decuriae*, besides holding local magistracies at Mantua.

477. M. Tullius Rufus made this payment in the fulfilment of a promise by his father M. Tullius Blaesus. Dessau identifies the latter with the M. Tullius Blaesus who appears in an inscription from Tibur of the reign of Pius (*ILS* 5630; 1061), but the archaic numerals of the present inscription argue that it is no later than the end of the first century A.D.

480. The inscription is an incomplete subscription list, showing seventeen contributions ranging from HS1,587 to HS250, with eight instances of the last figure. Half of the eight surviving names lack cognomina, and the sums are stated as 'N CCL' instead of the more usual 'HS CCL N'. Degrassi classifies the text as Republican.

480a. The inscription describes in remarkable detail the procedure laid down by the town council of Puteoli for building a wall in the town in 104 B.C. The wall's dimensions and the site are described in detail. The account of the financing reads: 'Dies pequn(iae): pars dimidia dabitur, ubei praedia satis subsignata erunt; altera pars dimidia solvetur opere effecto probatoque. C. Blossius Q.f. HS(1,500), idem praes'; four more names follow. The five persons named had evidently each underwritten the outlay with *praedia* of their own, whose value was either HS1,500 in each case or HS1,500 in all. The sum underwritten was presumably the total cost of the wall. For a full discussion, Th. Wiegand *Jahrb.f.class.Phil.* Supp.Bd.20 (1894) 661–778. Also A. Calderini *Studi Romani* 2 (1954) 649–62.

482. In addition to other generosities whose amount is not specified the donor, Cn. Satrius Rufus, gave the following sums: HS6,000 'decurionatus nomine' (no.1325); HS3,450 'in commeatum legionibus' (no.1364a); HS6,200 'in aedem Dianae restituendam' (no.482); and HS7,750 'in ludos Victoriae Caesaris August(i)' (no.1079). His only recorded office was the quattuorvirate at Iguvium. The inscription, whose numerals are archaic, belongs to the reign of Augustus.

489. In 1965 the writer conjectured that the figure transmitted as HS $\overline{\text{IL}}$ was in fact HS $\overline{\text{II}}$, on the basis of other evidence for the payment of HS2,000 by Augustales (*PBSR* 33 (1965) 294). The subsequent rediscovery of the stone has now confirmed this hypothesis (S. Panciera *Epigraphica* 29 (1967) 53 and fig.8; 49).

491. For large-scale outlays on statues see also nos.513; 77; 82; II 5523 (HS400,000 at Corduba). The present donor also bequeathed a fund of more than HS100,000 'in [t]uit[ionem] (statuarum)' (no.660).

493. In addition to generosities whose details are lacking, the donor, whose name is lost, gave a silver *clipeus* in the *curia* weighing 100 pounds (no.515, a lifetime gift); HS200,000 to provide income for annual feasts (no.656); HS100,000 to provide income for annual distributions of mead and pastry (no.663; cf. nos.665 and 666); and per capita bequests to persons not named in his will at rates of HS400 for decurions, HS300 for Augustales, and HS200 for the plebs (no.756). In return for these remarkable generosities, the donor received a monument costing HS43,000 (evidently a statue) erected by public subscription 33 days after his death. (This account follows the extensive but convincing restora-

tions of Bormann and Mommsen in *CIL*.) Mons Fereter was a small and obscure town (cf. *Enc.art.ant.* s.v. San Leo). Although the rates of the per capita legacies appear to indicate an outlay of prodigious size, the number of recipients may have been relatively few. The town would not necessarily have had more than 30 decurions and 20 Augustales (cf. pp.283–7). Another small Italian town Saturnia seems to have had an urban male population of as little as 500 overall (see p.272). The HS43,000 spent on the donor's statue by public subscription is also imposing. But it does not necessarily represent more than the re-transmission of part of the legacy bestowed by the donor's per capita legacies (for these exchanges, cf. p.302). For per capita cash bequests, elsewhere usually at much lower rates, see nos.838, 853, 779, 774, 851, 768, 783, 980, 999 and 816. An inscription from Narbonensis shows a bequest to the decurions of HS300 per head, still a lower rate than at Mons Fereter (XII 1115).

498. An epulum at rates of HS8, HS3 and HS2 was given at the dedication of this statue (nos.1079f, 1079i, 1079k).

504. This monument was erected by the *decurio* of the ninth *decuria* of an unidentified college, who gave sportulae of HS2 to all the members at its dedication (no.1048).

506. The Emperor's munificence lay only in paying for bullion that already existed to be reworked into a new statue.

513. The donor C. Oclatius Modestus held magistracies at Beneventum, followed by the *tres militiae* and the curatorships of the Aecani and of Canusium under Trajan and Hadrian. Sportulae of HS4 were to be given to the citizens at the dedication of the statue (no.980).

514. The statue was bequeathed by Laberia Hostilia Crispina, the wife of C. Bruttius Praesens (consul *c.* 121 and cos.ord. in 139) and mother of C. Bruttius Praesens (cos.ord. in 153 and again, after the date of this gift, in 180). *PIR²* B 164–5. Crispina was patroness of the 'mulieres Trebulanae' (*AE* 1964, 106).

521. HS4 per head was distributed (to the Augustales) by the curator Augustalium who gave this statuette (no.1007).

522. This statuette, bequeathed by a centurion, M. Pulfennius Sex.f., was dedicated by C. Herennius Capito, a notorious procurator under Tiberius (*RE* 8.666; *PIR²* H 103; P. Fraccaro *Opuscula* 3 (1957) 263–71).

524. L. Cascellius Probus gave this six pound silver statue to celebrate his adlection to the *ordo* as *quinquennalis*, and gave sportulae of HS100 and HS50 at its dedication in A.D. 165. Nine years later in A.D. 174 (by which time he had also served as *quaestor alimentorum* and *curator annonae*), he gave sportulae of HS20 at the dedication of a public statue of himself (nos.758, 859).

526. The inscription, whose text (derived from a single manuscript source) is corrupt, appears to indicate that four persons contributed silver for the statuette.

528. Sportulae of HS4 were distributed to the *dendrophori* at the dedication (no.1011).

533. At the dedication sportulae of HS4 were distributed to the members of the 'corpus traiectus Rusticelii' (a private ferry guild, Meiggs 195; no.1009).

541. Sportulae of HS4 together with bread and wine were distributed to the *kannophori* at the dedication (no.1008).

550. The inscribed stone is curved indicating that it belonged to a circular mausoleum (cf. Crema, cited p.130 n.4).

551. The inscription appears to be no earlier than the second century A.D. If dated before Marcus Aurelius, the bullion value is about HS226,000; if dated between Marcus and Severus, about HS265,000.

563. The price is incorporated in a metrical epitaph, whose relevant lines read: 'cuius honorificae vitae non immemor heres / quinquaginta meis millibus, ut volui / hanc aedem posuit struxidque novissima templa / manibus et cineri posteriisque meis.'

582. The college of *dendrophori* made a further contribution to the cost of the tomb, the amount of which has perished. The wife of the deceased bore the main expense.

585. Papius has the tribe of Sinuessa (Teretina); his father belonged to Falerna. He had given 'mulsum et crustum colonis Senuisanis et Caedicianeis omnibus', a 'munus gladiatorium', and a 'cenam colonis Senuisanis et Papieis'. Degrassi dates the inscription to the first century B.C.

635. Six men all bearing the *tria nomina* subscribed amounts between HS80 and HS20 to this burial. For burial by subscription cf. nos.1387; 1390. The abbreviation for sesterces here is the unusual 'SE'.

637. Since six of the nine alimentary gifts the status of whose donor is known came from senators, it is quite likely that the founder of the 'Variani alumni' was of senatorial family (nos.638, 641, 644, 650; II 1174; VIII 22721). It is not clear whether the name refers to the donor's nomen or to his cognomen: for the use of the nomen, compare 'pueri Ulpiani' at Ameria (XI 4351); for use of the cognomen, 'ingenui Iuncini' at Hispalis (II 1174). ('...ianus' was the standard ending for funds named after private individuals, cf. *PBSR* 33 (1965) 206 n.65). If the cognomen is the source, as suggested by Marquardt (*Staatsverwaltung*[2] 2.144 n.4), there is little purpose in conjecturing the donor's identity, since by itself the cognomen Varus can give little hint as to the family name. But if the source is the nomen, a possible donor is L. Varius Ambibullus, consul in 132 or 133 (Degrassi 38; *PIR*[1] V 183). Ambibullus apparently came from Capua, where his freedmen buried their families (X 3864; 4390; cf. 4391–2). Matidia, who augmented the benefits of the 'Variani alumni', also had Campanian connexions: she donated a library to Suessa Aurunca, which has left record of four statues of Matidia (X 4744–7). Thus it is conceivable that the 'Variani alumni' were the beneficiaries of a gift made at Capua by Ambibullus or a member of his family, which Matidia added to in her will. For another supplementary alimentary gift, see II 1174 (Hispalis). Matidia's decision to give the city income rather than capital is paralleled in some other foundations; Pliny explains and justifies the procedure in *Ep.* 7.18; see also nos.645; 669; 685; 689; *Digesta* 50.12.10; no.254. A donor at Ephesus explicitly vested a foundation in his estates (see J. H. Oliver *Hesperia* supp.6 (1941) 56–85, l.305).

638. Pliny indicates that the interest-rate in the foundation mentioned in his letters was effectively less than 6%, since the revenue was HS30,000 and the capital was in fact worth more than its nominal value of HS500,000 (*Ep.* 7.18). The parallels suggest that a provision in round figures would have underlain the terms of the present foundation at some point. If the monthly subsidy were a round figure, the amount would probably have been HS70 (HS840 per year per man), pointing to interest of $4\frac{1}{2}$%. If the annual subsidy were a round figure, say of HS1,000 per man, a figure paralleled in the *Digesta*, interest would be 5.36% per year (see p.30 n.5). Another very large Italian foundation had a low and irregular interest-rate, $4\frac{1}{3}$% (no.642, Tarracina, HS1 million).

639. The donor was twice *tribunus militum*. For possible demographic implications of the gift see pp.267–8.

639a. For the *alimenta*, see pp.288–319.

640. See note on no.446.

641. See also note on no.1078a below. The donor was a daughter of C. Fabius Agrippinus, consul in A.D. 148 (*PIR*[2] F 20). For other female donors of *alimenta*, see nos.637; 642; II 1174. The gift may have imitated one or other of the successive orders of *puellae Faustinianae* set up at Rome in memory of the elder and the younger Faustina (see p.319 n.1). The mention of a *quaestor alimentorum* in an Ostian inscription (XIV 298) may refer to this scheme (although some mention of the donor might well have been incorporated in the name of her alimentary fund; cf. note on no.637). More probably it indicates that Ostia had received an endowment under the government alimentary

scheme. Towns near Rome (such as Ostia) had a somewhat better chance of receiving government *alimenta* than towns distant from Rome (Appendix 5, p.337). There is no difficulty in reconciling Fabia's endowment with the presence of a government scheme already founded at Ostia. There are two instances of supplementary private alimentary schemes (no.637; II 1174); if the Table of Veleia is any index, the beneficiaries of the government *alimenta* tended to be mainly boys (no.639a), leaving scope for feminists to add further benefactions; and the fact that Fabia devoted only part of her endowment to *alimenta* could suggest that the need for such provisions at Ostia had in part been met already.

642. See note on no.446a. For the interest-rate, cf. Billeter 224.

643. The bequest was made up of two large foundations, one of HS600,000 for a *munus* every fourth or fifth year (cf. note on no.264), the other of HS400,000 for an annual *epulum* for the people (nos.643; 648). For possible demographic implications of the second gift, see p.268. The donor C. Titius Valentinus was a local magistrate who did not hold equestrian rank. The larger component of his bequest led to the appointment at Pisaurum of a special 'curator calendar. pecuniae Valentini n(ummorum) HS $\overline{DC}$' (XI 6369).

644. In setting up this foundation Pliny took pains to see that only the income and not the capital of the fund was given to the city to administer, because it was an unreliable trustee (*Ep.* 7.18, cf. note on no.637). The numbers who benefited may have been 100 boys and 75 girls (I. Gentile *RIL* ser.2, 14 (1881) 458–70; R. Duncan-Jones *Historia* 13 (1964) 206).

645. The gift was intended to provide the distribution of HS12 to each of the *vicani* of the seven *vici* of Ariminum. If there were 300 *vicani* per *vicus* (see p.283), the capital needed at the interest of 5% likely with a large-scale foundation would be HS504,000. The average value of the 21 *fundi* in which the gift was invested would be exactly HS24,000. The alternative possibility that the membership was 250 per *vicus* (see p.283) would result in a total capital of HS420,000, with an average valuation per *fundus* of HS20,000. The donor, L. Septimius Liberalis, was a *sevir Augustalis*. The Lex Falcidia entitled the legal heir(s) to a minimum of 25% of a man's estate (cf. *Digesta* 35.2.1 ff.). Since only one heir is referred to in this inscription, the figure VI given for the Falcidian share may be an error for IV. For heirs who were less complaisant, and refused to waive their legal rights under the Lex Falcidia in favour of the city, see *Digesta* 22.6.9.5; in this instance the testator, Gargilianus, had left most of his fortune to pay for an aqueduct at Cirta under Septimius Severus. (For immense expenditures on aqueducts cf. pp.31; 318 n.4)

645a. This fragmentary inscription was first reported by Bracceschi in the sixteenth century (whence XI 7872). It falls into two parts, the longer of which was rediscovered by Rambaldi, who provides a photograph (*BCAR loc. cit.*). The photograph shows that Bracceschi's accuracy was not perfect, but he remains a useful source for the sections that no longer survive. There is no obvious reason to reject the smaller fragment of the text known only from Bracceschi's copy; thus Rambaldi's restoration ignoring this fragment is less than adequate. Rambaldi's reading of the title 'curat. viar.' at the top of the surviving fragment does not appear reliable from the photograph.

The gifts which can be distinguished were a contribution of HS690,000 probably to the city, whose purpose is uncertain (no.1179a; the figure survives complete); a sum of HS450,000 given to the mag(istri) vicor(um) and no doubt other groups as well (cf. no.659), probably for annual feasts and distributions (the figure is from Bracceschi; the total that survives is only HS200,000, no.645a); and a sum of HS30,000 or more given apparently to the 'decuriae IIII scamillar(iorum) operae veteres a scaena' (cf. XI 4813), again probably for feasts or distributions (no.676a; cf. nos.652, 659). The gifts also included a building whose details are unknown. Their size suggests that they were almost certainly testamentary (see p.138); one of the occasions celebrated was the birth-day of the donor.

The section attested only by Bracceschi refers to 'Succoniae fi[liae]' (cf. XI 7873). The donor was therefore evidently a Succonius. The name is very rare and is not attested anywhere in Umbria outside Spoletium (XI index). The scale of municipal involvement implied by these gifts is so great that the donor was probably a municipal figure rather than a senator or procurator. He can be tentatively identified as L. Succonius Priscus. Bormann assigned Priscus's inscription to Mevania (XI 5054 = *ILS* 5271), but the 'decuriae IIII scabillar. veteres a scaena' who made this dedication were an organisation at Spoletium (from XI 4813 = *ILS* 5272 and the present gift inscription). Furthermore Priscus is recorded as 'q.a.' or *quaestor aerarii*, a post attested at Spoletium but not at Mevania (XI 5006). (For the wide extent of territory belonging to Spoletium, see p.268.) The inscription thus shows that Priscus served as magistrate both at Spoletium and at Trebia, as well as being patron of Spoletium (the highest of all civic honours) and patron of all its guilds. Priscus appears to have been a wealthy magnate from a small town whose ownership of land in the territory of its wealthy neighbour Spoletium gave him entry to the *ordo* there. By great acts of munificence (see also no. 1370), his family evidently became established among the leading families of Spoletium; and one of the Succonii attained high office as a procurator. L.Suc[conius...], after holding local office at Spoletium, followed an equestrian career and achieved ducenarian rank as 'proc. d[ucenar. Alexandriae ad] idios lo[gos]' (XI 7868, Pflaum no.269; the career is probably no earlier than the reign of Marcus Aurelius).

645b. For the *alimenta* see pp.288–319.

646. See note on no.468.

647. The inscription states that the baths at Bononia were built by Augustus and restored by Caligula. Under Caligula, T. Aviasius Servandus bequeathed in his son's name the present fund to provide free bathing for both sexes in perpetuity. For other endowments for this purpose, see *ILS* 5671–3; 6256; V 376; 6522; 6668; Pliny *Ep.* 8.8.6.

648. See note on no.643.

649. The donor, L. Menacius Priscus, was a holder of the *equus publicus* and *tribunus militum*; he was also magistrate and patron of Pola.

650. [T.] Helvius Basila held a proconsulship, possibly under Tiberius (*PIR*² H 67) and seems to have predeceased Nero (cf. M. Hammond *Mem.Amer.Acad.Rome* 21 (1953) 147–51). His endowment is the first recorded private alimentary gift.

652. The donor, C. Torasius Severus, who held a magistracy also gave a smaller foundation of HS120,000 (no.659). Either Severus or another member of his family also gave Spoletium a set of baths, mentioned by Cassiodorus as 'Turasii thermae' (*Var.* 4.24). For demographic implications of the present foundation, see pp.267–8.

653. See note on no.468.

654. See note on no.468.

655. See note on no.441.

656. See note on no.493.

657. The donor, [.A]etrius [De]xter, who held the *equus publicus*, bequeathed Suasa a founda-tion of HS130,000 (no.657); a fund for building a temple to Suasa Felix whose figure is missing; and a foundation of HS20,000 for the upkeep of the temple (no.684). He may have been a connexion of another equestrian, C. Aetrius Naso, who bequeathed HS120,000 to the nearby town of Sentinum under Domitian (no.658).

658. See note on no.657. The inscription is dated to 88/96 by the mention of the month 'Germanicus' (Suetonius *Domitian* 13, J. Janssen ed., (1913)).

659. See note on no.652 and p.285.

660. See no.491 and note.

661. See note on no.441.

662. See note on no.843 and p.284.
663. See note on no.493.
664. See Kahrstedt 83–4. The donor M'. Megonius M'.f. M'.n. M'.pron. Leo was patron of Petelia and held magistracies there. Under Antoninus Pius he bequeathed a foundation of HS100,000 promised during his lifetime for annual distributions to the decurions, Augustales and the citizens of both sexes (no.664; for the numbers implied, see pp.269–70; the interest is stated as 6%); capital sums of HS100,000 each, bequeathed in memory of his wife and mother (nos.1332 and 1333); a foundation of HS10,000 (bearing interest at 6%) to improve the amenities of the Augustales, the capital being confided to the city (no.694); and a vine and part of a *fundus* likewise for the purposes of the Augustales (x 114 = *ILS* 6469).
665. The donor, Corellia Galla Papiana, bequeathed identical foundations of HS100,000 to Minturnae and Casinum to provide annual distributions of mead and pastry on her birthday (nos.665, 666). These two towns, which are close to each other, are more than 100 km from San Cesareo (between Labici and Praeneste) where the donor was buried. Evidently she possessed property in the south of Latium as well as in the environs of Rome. She was buried in a circular tomb which cost a further HS100,000 (no.558). Her husband, C. Corellius, lacks a cognomen, and so the gifts are probably pre-Trajanic.
666. See note on no.665.
669. For details of the distribution and refreshments provided by this foundation see nos.798, 1106 and 1107. The donor retained the capital of HS70,000 (cf. note on no.637) which was invested in three *fundi* and a *pratum* or meadow. The average valuation of the *fundi* appears to have been similar to that of the twenty-one *fundi* bequeathed for a gift at Ariminum, where the average was either HS24,000 or HS20,000 (see note on no.645). Some of the *fundi* at Veleia were worth as little as HS12,000 (Appendix 3, p.335). The foundation bore interest at 6%.
671. The donor, whose name is missing, held at least one of the equestrian *militiae*.
672. The donor was the father of an equestrian, C. Domitius Fabius Hermogenes, who predeceased him. For the implications of this foundation about the number of decurions at Ostia, see p.284.
673. The donor, whose nomen was Mammius, was *curator kalendarii* and holder of magistracies at Corfinium. He had sons of equestrian rank. The equestrian P. Mammius Aufidius Priscinus whom Mommsen identified as the donor was probably one of the sons, and not the donor himself (IX 3180). The *ordo* made the donor patron, whereupon he gave a lavish public feast for the decurions and their wives, as well as for the people. The *ordo* and people reciprocated in their turn with a statue, to which the donor replied with the present foundation worth HS50,000. He celebrated the gift with a distribution of sportulae (no.763); the foundation had an escape clause in favour of the town of Sulmo if its provisions were not observed. The gift probably belongs to the third century A.D.
674. This Ostian foundation, which is dated prosopographically, appears to be a close imitation (in every detail except its size) of a gift made half a century earlier at the same town (no.675). There was an escape clause in both cases making the capital forfeit to the city if the Augustales failed to observe the terms. There was a slight difference in the sportulae given at the dedication: on the earlier occasion, decurions and Augustales both received HS20; on the later, the decurions again received HS20 but the decurions received only HS12 (nos.863, 772). This subversion of precedence is explained by the fact that the gift concerned was made by a freedman donor within the *ordo Augustalium*, and the inclusion of the decurions in the dedicatory ceremony was only a matter of courtesy. The later foundation is the larger of the two (HS40,000 in A.D. 182, HS50,000 in *c.* A.D. 230/40). This does not correspond with the general tendencies of munificence in Italy in this period; but Ostia whose economy was closely linked to that of Rome may have been in a more favourable position than other towns in Italy. The statement of

the interest-rate as 'ex usuris semissibus et ṁ.II' appears to indicate a rate close to 6% (Billeter 204, n.2; the Gordons suggest that the rate may be 6.4%, A. E. & J. S Gordon *Album of dated Latin inscriptions* 2 (1964) 141).

675. See note on no.674. The donor also paid HS10,000 to the treasury of the Augustales, fulfilling a fixed charge payable for the curatorship of his son (no.1311).

678. The number of decurions of the college of *fabri* at Ravenna who received sportulae o HS8 under the foundation would have been at least 112, unless the interest were less than 5%, which is unlikely with a capital of only HS30,000. Parallels suggest that 6% would be equally likely, in which case there would be 150 decurions. The inscription explicitly indicates that the college had at least 28 decuriae. The foundation apparently shows that the college contained 112–50 decuriae, which would point to a minimum membership (if the decuriae were up to strength) of 1,120–1,500 in all. For colleges with decuriae of 10 members, see VI 10396; 631; 30983 = *ILS* 3840 (see also Columella *de r.r.* 1.9.7, referring to the organisation of household slaves). This would imply that the college of *fabri* at Ravenna was one of the biggest colleges in Italy (see p.283; cf. Brunt 201, n.4). The donor also built a temple of Neptune in which the distribution to the decurions of the college was to take place.

679. The donor [.] Fl(avius) Proculeianus was 'curator kalendarii novi' at Fabrateria Vetus, and 'curator Formianorum'. His gifts were the present foundation of HS25,000 and a smaller foundation of HS4,000 (no.708), together with sportulae of HS50 (no.828). The inscription is dated to the third century by the use of the SS-symbol for sesterces. For demographic implications of the gift, see pp. 271–2.

680. The donor was patron of the college which he benefited, and held town magistracies at Opitergium. The text is seriously incomplete.

681. See note on no.645. The donor, C. Faesellius Rufio, *signo* Proserius, held the *equus publicus* and was 'cur. reip. Forodruentinorum'. Sportulae of HS4 were distributed to the *vicani* at the dedication of his statue (no.977). The *signum* and the use of the SS symbol point to a third-century date.

682. This fund was given by an augur and patron of the *collegium fabrum*, who also made a payment of HS10,000, apparently to the college treasury (no.1358a).

684. See note on no.657.

685. Eck emended the capital from XV to XVI, converting the interest-rate from 5⅓% to 5% (accepted by Mommsen; cf. Billeter 196 and n.2). The foundation seems to have covered the cost of only two of the six annual feasts that had been included in the calendar of the *cultores Dianae et Antinoi* by the time that its laws were codified (XIV 2112.2.11–13). The other occasions were presumably paid for by the four annually elected *magistri cenarum* (2.14–16). Cf. nos.1389–98 and especially no.1397.

686. This foundation of HS12,000 given to the *collegium nautarum* for the celebration of rites in memory of the donor was accompanied by a foundation of HS600 for the cleaning of the donor's tomb (no.744).

687. For the number of Augustales at Aletrium suggested by this foundation, see p.286. Compare no.683, a foundation twice as large set up at Reate for the same purpose.

689. The donors were M. Nasellius Sabinus, who had served one of the equestrian *militiae*, and his father, who held magistracies, presumably at Beneventum. The foundation was to provide annual commemoration of a portico which the Nasellii had built for the pagus Lucullanus. Only the income and not the capital was made over to the *pagus* (see note on no.637). There was an escape clause in favour of the *collegium medicorum* if the terms of the foundation were not properly observed.

690. For lifetime *mancipatio* of property to provide the basis for a foundation, see also no.644.

691. For the interest-rate see Billeter 225. Cf. Kahrstedt 78.

692. The donor, A. Plutius Epaphroditus, a silk dealer (also *accensus velatus*) gave a temple with various adornments to Gabii, together with sportulae at different rates at its dedica-

tion in A.D. 168 (no.770). He gave the present foundation of HS10,000 for an annual feast on his daughter's birthday (with an escape clause in favour of the town of Tusculum if its provisions were not properly observed).

693. The donors 'Domitii Polycarpus et Europe' dedicated their gifts to the memory of the wife of Domitian. The donors were evidently freedmen of the dowager Empress, since they bore her name and were assiduous in cultivating her memory (cf. Dessau *ad* XIV 2795); she apparently died not earlier than A.D. 129 (XV 552 with Syme 780). At some previous date the donors had built a temple in her honour at Gabii, and now in A.D. 140 they set up a foundation of HS10,000 to pay for distributions of equal amounts to the decurions and *seviri Augustales* on her birthday. They gave a further fund of HS5,000 for the upkeep of the temple that they had already built (no.702). The giving of sportulae at equal rates to decurions and Augustales is rare but not unique (see nos.784, 802, 824a and 863). It should be noted that the donors were freedmen.

694. See note on no.664.

695. This foundation celebrated the construction of the *schola* of the *collegium fabrorum tignuariorum*, the land for which came from the same donor.

696. The donor of this foundation of HS8,000 also gave sportulae at several rates at the dedication of his statue (no.771), together with lump sums of HS1,000 to the colleges of *dendrophori* and *fabri* (no.1062).

697. This foundation was one of two gifts made by the donor at the dedication of his statue; the other was a distribution of sportulae of HS4 to the people (no.1021). Since the 'confrequentatio' is contrasted with a 'sportulatio', it probably indicates a feast on the analogy of other Italian commemorative foundations (*TLL* does not clarify this point).

698. This foundation of HS6,000 belongs to a calendar of funds for feasting bequeathed by different members of an unidentified college (see also nos.715, 723–28a). The interest-rate was 12% in all cases where capital and income have survived (cf. Billeter 206–7).

700. At the dedication of his statue the donor, a *quattuorvir*, gave sportulae of HS20 to the *collegium centonariorum* (no.845), together with the present foundation of HS5,000, which had an escape clause in favour of the *familia publica* if its provisions were not properly carried out.

701. This foundation of HS5,000 was given by a *sevir Augustalis* in gratitude for a statue erected publicly. Since statues themselves could cost HS5,000, the gift may have been no more than a *quid pro quo* (cf. nos.141–58).

702. See note on no.693.

703. See F. De Visscher in *Studi S. Solazzi* (1948) 542–53.

704. The foundation of HS5,000 was accompanied by sportulae of HS40 with bread and wine given at the dedication of the donor's statue (no.834).

705. A fund which provided an annual feast for the *collegium centonariorum* would hardly have been less than several thousand. The figure *IL̄ which Mommsen transcribed as 'denarios...L' has therefore been read literally, as 1,050 denarii.

708. See note on no.679.

709. The terms of the foundation are missing in all five cases. Parallels suggest that they were probably intended for commemorative feasts or distributions on the birthday of the donor, Albucia Magna.

710. The inscription describing this foundation is inserted inconsequentially in a corner of a face of stone the remainder of which lists the members of the 'ordo corporatorum qui pecuniam ad ampliandum templum contulerunt'. The stone also lists the *quinquennales* of the *ordo* running from A.D. 140 to 172.

715. See note on no.698 above.

721. The donor, a *curator kalendarii arcae* and holder of all the *munera* at Fabrateria Vetus, gave at the dedication of his statue sportulae of HS2 per head to the *iuvenes Herculani* (no.1040), together with the present foundation of HS2,000 for annual sportulae for the

same body. For the number of members that is implied, see p.271 n.6. The use of the symbol SS for sesterces implies a third-century date.

723. See note on no.698.

724. See note on no.698.

725. See note on no.698.

726–26c. See note on no.698.

727. See note on no.698.

728–28a. See note on no.698.

742. This foundation had an escape clause in favour of the 8th *decuria* of the same college if the seventh *decuria* failed to carry out its provisions.

744. See note on no.686.

749. See no.731.

750. See no.731.

755. The foundation was only intended to pay for an annual offering of oil to Mithras. '*VIII should therefore be read as eight denarii, not as 8,000 (as in *ILS* 8368; for the ambiguity of the superscript bar, see note on no.124). The deity is clearly 'D(eo) I(invicto) M(ithrae)' (parallels in *ILS* 3 p.545) and not 'D(is) I(nferis) M(anibus)' as in *ILS* 8368.

758a. The stone was found in Rome, having been re-utilised for another dedication at a later date. The rare name Turellius is found at Ostia (XIV 1691); the stone may have been shipped as building material by river from Ostia, having been displaced after the *damnatio* of Commodus.

760–1. IX 5189 (showing rates of HS32 and HS8 at Asculum Picenum), which previously appeared as no.760 was shown by Dessau to be a forgery (IX p.699). The forgery was imitated from IX 5843 (no.803) with some deliberate alterations.

818. See note on no.493.

819. See note on no.493.

820. See note on no.493.

823. The authenticity of this text is questioned by Huelsen (XI p.1368).

827. The donor, C. Hedius Verus, held the *equus publicus* and served the three equestrian *militiae*. He held magistracies at Forum Sempronii, where he was also patron, and at Pitinum Mergens.

833. T. Caedius Atilius Crescens, *signo* Zminthius, held the *equus publicus*, served as magistrate at Pisaurum, and was patron of the city and various local bodies. He gave the sportula to his 9 'amici' at the dedication of his statue which they had financed. His total outlay appears to have been lower than theirs, since distributions of HS40 to 9 men together with bread, wine and an epulum for the same number would hardly cost more than HS600 in all. Statues on the other hand usually cost several thousand (nos.91–212). No.841, a distribution to the 'amatores Romuliorum' at Ocriculum, which is closely similar to this inscription, is dated to A.D. 247/8. For dedications by 'amici' compare also the statue of a quaestor of Africa financed by 23 'amici' at Hadrumetum (VIII 60).

838. No.853 comes from the same will but was not distributed on the same occasion.

841. See notes on nos.1358 and 833.

843. The inscription is transmitted only in a corrupt manuscript copy, which gives the decurions' sportula as XVIIII. There is no parallel for a sportula of HS19, a figure whose irregularity makes it implausible. The figure has therefore been emended to HS X[X]IIII or HS24. This is paralleled in one instance (no.843a, Lanuvium), and corresponds to a whole number of denarii (see p.141).

863. For sportulae given at equal rates to decurions and Augustales, see also nos.693, 784, 802 and 824a. The restoration 'HS XX [m(ilia) n(ummos)]' (*ILS* 2842) is unjustified, since per capita sportulae in thousands of sesterces are unknown in the west.

952. The figure reads 'V...'; but the spacing indicates that three numerals are missing. The figure is therefore restored as 'V[III]'.

978. Aurelia Calligenia, wife of Titius Sabinianus, *eques Romanus*, gave this sportula at the dedication of her statue financed by the *collegium fabrum*. The inscription is preserved only in copies. A text on the side of the base apparently dates it to A.D. 169, but the absence of tribe, filiation and praenomen, together with the phrasing of the text, would agree better with a third-century date. Compare IX 4894, a very similar text dated to A.D. 243. The main text may thus have been re-engraved over an earlier text of A.D. 169.

991a. The sportula rate of HS400 which Mommsen's reading entails is prodigious and unparalleled for a distribution to the people. It is preferable to read the rate as a single denarius, a rate of which there are three undoubted instances at this town (Compsa, nos.989–91). (The difficulty of Mommsen's reading was also noticed by Toller 94 n.3.)

992. The rate of distribution would have been HS4 per head if there were 100 decurions at Croto (cf. p.283). HS4 per head is explicitly attested as a sportula paid to decurions in Magna Graecia (no.1015, Petelia). Cf. Kahrstedt 78.

999. The donor of this sportula bequeathed money for a bronze statue of Claudius whose dedication the distribution celebrated. The statue is preserved in the Naples Museum.

1026. The donor, Sex. Aetrius Ferox, who was promoted centurion by Antoninus Pius, gave the sportula at the dedication of a statue voted him by the town. He had obtained permission from the Emperor for the town to levy a special tax to meet the cost of paving roads.

1044. For the figure see note on no.1079j.

1045. For the figure see note on no.1079j. The donor C. Sulpicius... held the *equus publicus*. He also gave sportulae to the decurions at a rate that has not survived. The text is garbled and is known only from a copy.

1052. There were at least eight and by the death of Hadrian at least nine *phretriae* at Neapolis (Kaibel *IG* XIV p.191,1). This distribution would thus have cost not less than HS40,000–45,000, a very large sum by the standards of ephemeral outlays on sportulae. The distribution was made in commutation for a promised beast-show that did not take place ('ob promiss(am) venat(ionem)'); the expenditure may thus have approximated to the cost of a *venatio*. Gladiatorial *munera* (perhaps more costly than *venationes*) which cost HS50,000 are attested at Formiae and Paestum (nos.1075a, 1075b, 1077). A *munus* which took place at Pisaurum once every five (or four) years cost roughly HS150,000 (no.1074a). A small *venatio* at an African town at which four leopards were killed cost HS16,000, though the price asked of the donor was only HS8,000 (no.282a).

1077. Cf. nos.1323 and 1336 below.

1078. The *CIL* text giving the total as HS40,000 has been followed here (*ILS* gives HS20,000, though Dessau was editor in both cases). The freedman donor also gave 'lavatio populo gratis per triennium' (cf. note on no.647), ten pairs of gladiators and a corona aurea weighing one pound dedicated to Fortuna Primigenia (no.509a).

1078a. At the rate of HS16 per month attested for girls in another Italian alimentary gift (no.1173) and at the commonest of the sportula rates for decurions (HS20, twice attested for decurions at Ostia, nos.863–4) the *alimenta* and *cenae* would absorb HS25,800 annually, there being apparently 110 decurions at Ostia (see p.284). The interest was probably 5% in such a large foundation, which would mean an income of HS50,000, out of which HS24,200 would remain for games on this hypothesis.

1079j. '*S' evidently means one-half of a denarius, 'S' standing for 'S(emis)'. A whole denarius was usually indicated as '*I' (cf. nos.973–1032). For '*IS' meaning 1½ denarii see nos.1079g and 801.

1169. See note on no.638.

1170. For this passage see p.54 n.2.

1176e. Polybius in the second century B.C. refers to the inns in Transpadana where one could stay for HS$\frac{1}{8}$ per night as being cheap (Polybius 2.15).

1178. The donor, L. Maesius Rufus, a procurator, also gave an *epulum* at several rates (nos. 1079b, 1079e, 1079h).

1182. *IIt* 7.1.22 which its editor accepts as being based on a genuine text from Pisa is undoubtedly a forgery (see Bormann, XI 194*). It is evidently modelled on the present text from Abella, which it follows closely in phraseology with deliberate changes in the name, the sum of money and the lineation. An authentic Pisan text mentioning the *bisellium* (no.1320) may have influenced the choice of model. (Compare the note on no.760–1.)

1187. The reading of the numeral as 25,000 denarii (Kaibel and others) is followed in preference to Mommsen's reading as 100,000 denarii, which assumes the use of Latin numerals in a Greek text. Cf. editor's note in Mommsen *Ges.Schr.* 8.13 n.1.

1189. If the Langenses defaulted on their annual payment of 400 victoriati (HS1,200), they were liable to pay in kind 1/20th of their grain crop and 1/6th of their wine. On the assumption that the money tribute represented a valuation of these fractions, the implied annual valuation of the two crops would have been HS18,400, if we conjecture that the grain rent had twice the value of the wine rent. But since the rent in kind was only payable under a penalty clause, it was almost certainly higher than that asked in money. Hence the true value of the crop was probably well over HS20,000. The implied valuation is still low, and it suggests that the Langenses were quite a small community, even though prices in the late second century B.C. were almost certainly lower than those of the Principate (cf. no.1176e and note).

1194. Seneca also represents Rufus (one of Augustus' admirals) as possessing great wealth (*de clem.* 1.15.4; *PIR*[1] T 14).

1196. For this estate see above p.47.

1197. This estate was evidently bequeathed to Luca by C. Attius Nepos (XI p.222). Its original valuation (HS2,500,000) dwarfs all the cash payments and legacies to cities known in Italy (see nos. 1328–34, where the highest amount is HS400,000). However the net value of the estate was only HS1,600,000. Bormann pointed out (XI p.222) that the phrase 'deducta parte quarta' could indicate the subtraction of the 25% due to the legal heir under the Lex Falcidia. There were also other explicit deductions.

1198. For the declarations of the Cornelii, see *PBSR* 32 (1964) 141, n.104.

1203. Mommsen restored this figure as 501,000 in place of the 466,000 given in the text, pointing out an error in addition (IX p.127,2).

1227. This follows de Pachtere's emendation: his substitution of the arithmetical total of the component valuations produces a loan rate of 8.88%, compared with a loan rate of 11.4% for the total given in the text. For normal rates of loan, see p.39 n.2; 133.

1307. For bath admission as HS$\frac{1}{16}$ (a quadrans): Martial 3.30; 8.42; Juvenal 6.445–7; Horace *Sat.* 1.3.137; Seneca *Ep.* 86.9; as HS$\frac{1}{4}$ (an as): Juvenal 2.152. The baths in government-run mines in Spain cost half an as for men and an as for women (*ILS* 6891.22–3). Cf. Frank *ESAR* 5.104.

1326. The donors were the 'duo Publii Nigrini Martialis pater et Dexter filius'. The inscription gives no detail of their offices.

1328. See note on no.473.

1354. For slave prices, see Appendix 10.

1358. M. Iulius Ulpius Cleopater, *signo* Romuli, gave this fund of HS10,000 to the 'amatores Romuliorum' in return for a statue which they had financed. The recompense was more impressive than that provided in a parallel case at Pisaurum (no.833 and note). Cleopater was patron of the town, of the *collegium centonariorum* and of the *amatores* themselves. The *amatores* received sportulae of HS30 at the dedication (no.841). The gift is dated to A.D. 247/8.

1377. R. Paribeni provides a useful commentary and good photographs of the stone (*NS* (1928) 387–97).

1387. This sentence states that a contribution towards funeral expenses of HS8 was payable by all members on the decease of a colleague. A later sentence (no.1377) states that the benefit accruing to a member or his heir at his decease was HS560. This sum would be made up if as many as 70 members subscribed HS8 each; the album engraved at about the same time as the laws of the college shows a total membership under Nero of either 78 or 80 members, divided into 4 decuriae of about 20 members each, a standard complement (cf. III 633; VI 9405; XI 1449; XIV 4569).

1389. The size of this college cannot be deduced from the financial provisions; although the outlay on the death of a member was fixed at HS300/360 (nos.1390, 1393), this evidently derived from the entrance fee (HS100) and the monthly subscription (HS1.25, no.1391). The revenue thus available would have varied with the number of members, but so would the frequency of deaths.

1393. Travel allowances at a more exalted level are shown in an African inscription of the fourth century. In A.D. 361/3, *principes* were entitled to an allowance of 5 modii of Italian wheat for local journeys, with an additional 2 modii for every further 10 miles. For an overseas journey they received 100 modii. Their immediate inferiors received half of these rates. (VIII 17896 with *EE* 5 p.640.)

5
The use of prices in the Latin novel

Roman novelists and poets are sometimes brought into use as sources for the economic history of their time, in the hope of supplementing deficiencies in the evidence of the surviving historians. There is no doubt that Roman poetry and fiction can yield useful historical information about a social milieu and about social conditions.[1] The reliability of the figures and particularly the prices that they supply is less certain. Prices found in the novelists are nevertheless sometimes cited on an equal footing with prices from contemporary historical, epigraphic and papyrological sources.[2] It is reasonable to question the validity of this literalminded use of works whose evident purpose was to entertain rather than to record or instruct. While considering prices in the Roman world it therefore seems worthwhile to examine the figures offered by the Latin novelists in conjunction with evidence from elsewhere in order to decide whether anything can be learnt from them.[3] The conclusions may help in assessing the usefulness for economic history of other comparable literary sources.

PETRONIUS

Petronius, the earliest and most gifted of the Latin novelists whose work survives, seems to mention sums of money or quantities for two main

---

[1] For the social relevance of the *Satyricon*, cf. P. Veyne 'Vie de Trimalcion' *Annales. Économies. Sociétés. Civilisations* 16 (1961) 213–47.

[2] For example, a slave price of HS1,200 from Petronius (*Sat.* 68) is reproduced beside prices from historians, inscriptions and papyri in a standard modern work on slavery (W. L. Westermann *Slave systems of Greek and Roman antiquity* (1955) 100). Figures from novels by Apuleius and Ps.-Lucian are cited in isolation as evidence of actual prices for donkeys under the Empire, in Frank *ESAR* 5.279.

[3] The prices in Martial and Juvenal mainly refer to the city of Rome, and are thus less immediately relevant to the concerns of the present volume. Another attempt at a price-analysis of Petronius has been made by P. Moreno, to whose work this chapter is occasionally indebted for parallels (*Istituto italiano di numismatica. Annali* 9–11 (1962–4) 53–73). Moreno's study is hampered by numerical errors, and generally draws on a restricted range of comparative evidence. Some obvious limitations of the prices in Latin comedy are noted by G. Duckworth *The nature of Roman comedy* (1952) 276 (cf. M. Delcourt *Antiquité classique* 17 (1948) 123–32).

A price-analysis of Lucian (12 prices listed): S. Mrozek *Eos* 59 (1971) 231–9.

reasons: either in order to suggest the exaggeration to which his characters are prone; or, more simply, to illustrate their vulgar insistence on frequently bringing sums of money into their conversation. In the *Cena* he chooses amounts which could well have been given in conversation at a freedman's dinner-party; he is probably not attempting literal accuracy, which might even conflict with his literary purposes. Insofar as Petronius aims at plausibility here it seems to be mainly plausibility of an oblique kind. If this is accepted, it ceases to be surprising that no coherent picture of the framework of wealth within which his characters move emerges despite the many financial details. For example, the fact that Trimalchio claims a fortune of HS30 million (71)[1] is scarcely reconcilable with the statement that no less than HS10 million in ready cash is lying idle on a single day[2] on one of his estates (53). The second amount was chosen in order to amuse by exaggeration (in a way familiar to readers of Rabelais),[3] as is shown by its conjunction with the absurd figure of seventy children for a single day's births to the slaves working on the same estate.[4]

[1] Numbers in brackets refer to chapters of the novel in question.

[2] Modern opinion is divided between seeing the period covered by the bulletin as a single day and seeing it as a six-month period. The first interpretation is evidently correct. Were the period as long as a semester, plausibility would require that the six events in the part of the bulletin whose words are reported verbatim (which include a fire and a crucifixion) belong to different points within the 180 day period. However the first three entries are dated by the initial phrase 'VII kalendas sextiles' and the last three by the phrase 'eodem die', showing that all six items belong to the same day. The contention about a longer period would have been surprising in any case if true, since Petronius describes the gazette as being read 'tanquam urbis acta', and the *acta urbis* were not six-monthly bulletins. (A six-month period was suggested by Bücheler, editio maior (1862) 61, followed by L. Friedlaender *Petronii Cena Trimalchionis*[2] (1906) 283, Frank *ESAR* 5.24 n.42, and E. Marmorale *La questione petroniana* (1948) 113. Goesius in P. Burmann (ed.) *Petronius*[2] (1743) 1.340 was already certain that the bulletin could not refer to a single day. A single day is assumed by: E. Paratore *Il Satyricon di Petronio* 2 (1933) 161; Rose *TAPHA* 93 (1962) 406; Walsh *Roman Novel* 130.)

[3] Cf. also Delcourt (*loc. cit.* 126) speaking of Plautus: 'La seule mention d'un prix offert ou demandé était, pour les auditeurs, une indication psychologique qui provoquait le rire.'

[4] The harvest is equally Gargantuan: 500,000 modii, or enough to feed two legions for a year. Rose's suggestion that Petronius intended the reader to see the estate bulletin in (53) as fraudulent, while meaning him to regard details elsewhere in the novel as 'genuine' is not persuasive (K. F. C. Rose *CP* 62 (1967) 258–9). Rose argues that the exchanges between Trimalchio and his *actuarius* do not make sense. But the dialogue is only intended to show that Trimalchio's agents were buying estates on their master's behalf at such a rate that they did not always keep him up-to-date about his possessions. When reproached with this, the *actuarius* lamely pleads that Trimalchio has not been notified of the purchase in question because he has not yet seen the accounts (*rationes*) for the period in which the purchase took place. Trimalchio then insists, understandably, that he must be given direct notification of any purchase within six months, and not have to wait for the accounts (which were presumably always well n arrear, whatever their periodicity) in order to find out where he stood.

It is not the case that the figures in the bulletin are rounded off in order to single out their spurious character (Rose 259): the totals for children (30 boys and 40 girls) are relatively exact, and round totals like the HS10 million in idle cash are in fact found throughout the novel.

There are other clear discontinuities, which betray the fantasy underlying much of Petronius's brilliant invention. One occurs in the account
of Trimalchio's life-style. His house is not especially large by luxury
standards, but in terms of household slaves, Trimalchio seems to boast
an establishment which would do credit to a consular senator. 400 or
more household slaves are implied by the allusion to a fortieth *decuria*
in one passage (47.12); this was the number in the household of Pedanius
Secundus, the prefect of the city murdered in A.D. 61 (from Tacitus's
account).[1] Even in terms of the slaves whose functions are named, the
number ascribed to Trimalchio is evidently still too large for his house.[2]
Comparison with the figure of seventy children born on Trimalchio's
Cumaean estate shows that Petronius deliberately credits Trimalchio
with a fabulous number of slaves. It would be pointless to attempt to
justify the allusion to a fortieth *decuria* by suggesting that the number
could have included agricultural slaves (whose total could run into six
figures at Cumae alone, if we extrapolated from the stated birth-rate!),
or by supposing that many of the slaves could have belonged to other
houses owned by Trimalchio which are not mentioned in the novel.[3]
The fact that some internal dating indications mutually conflict may again
suggest that the author wished to create a deliberate fantasy-area in which
most things are larger than life, and few things make literal sense.[4] As
Marmorale pointed out, the indications of the time of year of the *Cena*

---

[1] *Ann.* 14.43.

[2] P. G. Walsh *The Roman Novel* (1970) 129; 128; 117. A detailed discussion of the house by
G. Bagnani *AJP* 75 (1954) 16–39.

[3] If Trimalchio is meant to have owned other houses, there is no apparent reason why his
encomia of his wealth and possessions at successive points in the evening should ignore them
(cf. especially the account of the amenities of the house of the *Cena* in 77.4–6).

[4] The careful analysis of H. T. Rowell *TAPHA* 89 (1958) 14–24 is concerned only to establish
a Neronian date of composition for the novel, which it does convincingly. Rose gives a
résumé of some of the internal dating criteria (*TAPHA* 93 (1962) 407–8). But his attempt to
show the dramatic date of the novel as decisively Neronian is not convincing. The use of the
name 'Maecenatianus' (with its possible allusion to the time of Augustus) in Trimalchio's
epitaph (71) cannot be discounted on the grounds that it is lacking from the household dedication in c.30 (Rose 407, from Haley). For incomplete nomenclature in household dedications
we can compare the dedication to the banker L. Caecilius Iucundus as 'L(ucius) noster'
by one of his freedmen which is inscribed below a bronze bust discovered in his house at
Pompeii (x 860 cf. also *ILS* 4841; 3594). Also unconvincing is the view that the 'Scaurus'
in 77.5 was a magistrate at Pompeii (known to modern scholars, though hardly to Petronius's
metropolitan audience, from inscriptions at that town), rather than a member of the re-
nowned senatorial family which became extinct in A.D. 34 (Rose 408, following Maiuri;
the present writer is publishing a note on this point in *Latomus*). The month of August is
given in the Republican form as 'sextilis' (53). The Tiberian anecdote about unbreakable
glass (*Sat.* 51; Rose 408) is a further ingredient that may conflict with the Neronian allusions
in the novel collected by Rowell (Rowell *loc. cit.*). Now see also K. F. C. Rose *The date and
author of the Satyricon* (1971) (*Mnemosyne*, supp. 16).

conflict (despite the July date of the bulletin in c.53), and there is almost no season for which no case can be made.[1] Parts of the *Cena* almost belong to the same world of burlesque as the anonymous *Testamentum porcelli*,[2] and are as little susceptible to any literal interpretation.

Some of Petronius's mentions of sums of money show a lack of inventiveness which might seem surprising in a novelist of such striking imaginative strength. At five different points in the surviving narrative, he chooses to specify a figure with which to denote great personal wealth, and in every instance uses the sum of HS30 million. This sum is first ascribed to T...Mammaea, a municipal figure who is said to have inherited HS30 million, and is consequently thought capable of devoting HS400,000 to a three-day *munus* in the amphitheatre (45). Next, Trimalchio says that he will record on his tombstone that he bequeathed the sum of HS30 million (a certainty that apparently conflicts with his information that he has another thirty years to live) (71; 77). Later in the evening Trimalchio is made to say when describing his early commercial enterprises that he had lost HS30 million through shipwreck in a single voyage (76). When lamenting modern decadence, Eumolpus (who was not present at the dinner) cites as one of a range of common human aspirations the wish to make a fortune of HS30 million (88). Lastly, when Eumolpus is about to masquerade as a Croesus before the citizens of Croto, he proposes to his fellow-conspirators that he should pretend to be a childless man with HS30 million invested in Africa (117). It is difficult to see why Eumolpus should have specified a figure at all when moralising unless the amount were proverbial. 'Si ad trecenties sestertium salvus pervenerit' might then have the force of '(another man promises an offering) if he safely makes his million' (88). But evidence for HS30 million as a proverbial fortune is apparently not found elsewhere. The total sometimes occurs here in conjunction with other financial details which have a more circumstantial air. Trimalchio's loss of HS30 million at sea is followed by the information that his wife provided her husband with one hundred aurei (HS10,000) in his hour of need (76). In the account of Eumolpus's assumption of millionaire status, the familiar total is preceded by the invented information that the pseudo-Eumolpus had lost over HS2 million by shipwreck (117).

A further series of duplications involve the more obvious round total of HS10 million. This is used successively as the sum for which no investment can be found on Trimalchio's Cumaean estate (53); as the dowry of a lady whom Trimalchio might have married (74); as the amount of Trimalchio's profit from a single voyage (76); and as the

---

[1] E. V. Marmorale *La questione petroniana* (Bari, 1948) 116.

[2] This comic vignette is reproduced in Bücheler's editions of Petronius.

amount which those who eat the flesh of Eumolpus should think they are eating (141). Doubling occurs again in the only details of feasts given by benefactors at the town of the *Cena*: Trimalchio gave, and it is hoped that Mammaea may give, an 'epulum binos denarios', a feast costing HS8 per head (71; 45).

Assuming that they are not the mere product of scribal error, these repetitions suggest that Petronius did not attempt realism to the extent of working out economic descriptions in any detail (though since most of the examples occur in dialogue they may be explained as belonging to the characterisation of the different individuals concerned). Figures that are more or less apt to the situation being described seem to be arbitrarily repeated as it suits the author. Because they appear so un-studied, little can be read into the amounts themselves. But we can notice that HS8 is a possible figure for a municipal *epulum* or *sportulatio*, to judge from copious epigraphic evidence.[1] The figure of HS30 million is less easily placed (unless it is simply proverbial).[2] Taken literally, its connotations in the municipal context to which the *Satyricon* belongs seem to be those of fabulous wealth. To ascribe wealth of this order to an Augustalis and to a magistrate[3] at the same town is evidently hyperbolic (45; 77). HS8 million or so was an adequate fortune for a senator;[4] and the younger Pliny, a senator in easy circumstances who could afford very large public and private generosities, seems to have been worth about HS20 million.[5] Three large municipal fortunes attested in Africa in the mid-second century ranged from HS4 to HS2 million.[6] Martial regarded the squandering of an inheritance of HS1 million by a man who lived at a *municipium* as a notable achievement (4.66).

Another numerical index of Trimalchio's wealth may be suggested in the episode in which he claims to be wearing a bracelet weighing ten pounds made from dedications of one-thousandth made to Mercury (67). Though the interpretation of this passage is not entirely clear, some index of the scale of Trimalchio's transactions as a businessman is evidently

---

[1] C. nos.1079b ff.; 918–59.

[2] As suggested by G. Bagnani *Studies in honour of G. Norwood* (Toronto, 1952) 223, n.12.

[3] Mammaea's gift of a three-day *munus* clearly suggests that he was a city magistrate. For a tradesman to give *munera* was piquant enough for Martial to celebrate such events in three epigrams (3.16; 59; 99).

[4] See p.18 n.7.

[5] See pp.20–1.

[6] Apuleius *Apol.* 77; 75; 23–4. The fact that they are large fortunes for members of the local aristocracy can be seen from a comparison with Pliny *Ep.* 10.4, where a would-be senator is described by his sponsor as having current resources of HS4 million. Bagnani's attempt to document his view that Trimalchio's HS30 million was not exceptional 'even in the pro-vinces' by pointing out that Petronius ascribes an equal fortune to T…Mammaea is merely circular (*loc. cit.* n.2, 220).

intended. The sum implied is in the region of HS42–45 million (translating in terms of the gold–silver ratios then current).[1]

Private fortunes of more modest size are also mentioned in the dialogue at the *Cena*. C. Iulius Proculus, a former undertaker who was present, had once made a fortune of HS1 million, but was now mortgaged up to the hilt, owing to difficulties caused by his freedmen (38). Another more successful friend (who shared the names C. Pompeius with Trimalchio) possessed a fortune of HS800,000 (38); while a third, Chrysanthus, who owned vineyards, was thought notable by another speaker for having bequeathed HS100,000 in cash (43). Since they occur in dialogue these figures may be intended to contain deliberate exaggeration. But the upper limits which they indicate effectively suggest the type of guest whom Trimalchio entertained: well-to-do local business men and landowners, whose fortunes were nevertheless dwarfed by that of their host.

One of the figures now widely construed as another fortune-size[2] almost certainly refers in fact to the standard property-qualification for membership of the town-council. The sentence 'Iam scio, unde acceperit denarios mille aureos', follows an account of a certain aedile's corruption while in office. It is evidently meant to convey the sense 'Now I know where he got (the wherewithal for office)', and is rightly rendered by Ehlers as 'Ich weiss schon, wie er zu seinen tausend Goldstücken gekommen ist' (44).[3] The same eligibility level (HS100,000) is found explicitly as the property-qualification for the decurionate at Comum in one of Pliny's letters a few decades later.[4] The figure provides a revealing instance in which Petronius shows a technical knowledge of municipal institutions.

The other main category of intelligible prices in Petronius is the prices referring to slaves. Four prices are given. The favourite slave freed by Scissa at his death was valued at HS50,000. He received a very lavish funeral and was thus clearly an important household figure (65–6). Hermeros, a freedman at the dinner who now boasted a household of his own of twenty, had paid HS4,000 for his freedom (57). Habinnas, the supplier of monuments patronised by Trimalchio, had acquired a versatile male slave for HS1,200; the slave figures in the narrative mainly in order

[1] It seems clear that the bracelet was made of gold, since the passage contains two references to Fortunata's gold ornaments, and Trimalchio was not likely to be outdone by his wife. (L. Friedlaender *Petronii Cena Trimalchionis*[2] 332 suggests gold or silver as possibilities.)

[2] J. P. Sullivan *The Satyricon of Petronius* (1968) 144. A. Ernout (ed.) *Petronius* (1922) *ad loc.* Moreno (*loc. cit.* p.238 n.3 above) 67. M. Heseltine and E. H. Warmington *Petronius* (revised Loeb ed., 1969) *ad loc.*

[3] K. Müller and W. Ehlers *Petronius, Satyrica* (1965) 81–3.

[4] Pliny *Ep.* 1.19. The implication of this passage in Petronius was pointed out by Huschke (E. Huschke *Über den Census und die Steuerverfassung der frühern Kaiserzeit* (1847) 94 n.194 followed by Marquardt, *Römische Staatsverwaltung* I[2] 180, n.4), who cited as possible ancillary confirmation Catullus 23.26–7. See also Cassius Dio 72.16.3.

to allow Petronius to describe the vulgarity of his accomplishments (68). Finally, the reward offered by Ascyltus when Giton, one of the central figures in the story, was lost, was HS1,000 (97).

Actual slave prices and valuations which are closely parallel can be found in Italian epigraphic evidence. A slave doctor paid HS50,000 'pro libertate' at Asisium in the first century A.D. A male slave was sold at Herculaneum in May 63 for HS4,050 (cf. 57). A pair of slave-boys cost HS1,450 at Pompeii in 61, or about HS700 each.[1] The slave prices given by Petronius thus appear possible from available comparative evidence. But the range of actual prices known is so wide that it remains doubtful whether the similarities show that the author was aiming at graphic realism here. The slave-prices are however heavily modulated, in contrast to the stereotypes listed above.

A price for bread is given in the nostalgic remarks of Ganymede at the *Cena* about the easier economic conditions of his town in former years: a loaf too big for two people to eat at one sitting had cost as little as 1 *as*, or HS$\frac{1}{4}$ (44). Reflections on the price of bread may have had some contemporary relevance for readers in Rome who had recently suffered the famine of 64.[2] But bread prices must have been a constant subject of interest in Roman towns everywhere. A loaf for one man costing 2 *asses* was part of the provision at the regular dinners of a relatively humble funeral club at Lanuvium in the time of Hadrian.[3] A loaf costing 2 *asses* also seems to figure in some personal accounts for one week (eight days) given in a graffito from Pompeii. On three of the eight days the graffitist bought 'pane(m) puero', bread for his boy-slave, at 2 *asses* each time. Presumably this was a standard-sized loaf thought to be enough to last a young slave for two days or so. On a fourth day the payment for 'pane(m) puero' was 4 *asses*, suggesting the purchase of two loaves. (Bread was also bought on the main account to a value of 8 *asses* on each of the first four days, though conceivably for more than one person.)[4] Thus the evidence from Lanuvium and Pompeii confirms the implication that one *as* for a loaf too large for two people was a very

---

[1] *ILS* 7812; Tabulae Herculanenses LXI (*Parola del Passato* 9 (1954) 54–74); IV 3340, 154–5 = *FIRA* 3, no.91.

[2] Tacitus *Ann.* 15.39.

[3] Moreno (*loc. cit.* p. 238 n. 3, above) 65, n.56: the club's members included slaves, *ILS* 7212.

[4] IV 5380 = E. Diehl *Pompeianische Wandinschriften*[2] no. 390. The daily totals for expenditure worked out by L. Breglia in *Pompeiana* (Naples, 1950) 53 ignore the fact that the dates indicate the eight days of a Roman week; the assumed nine-day period results in faulty calculations. The graffitist's total expenditure ranged between 3 and 8 sesterces for the first four days; after the fifth day, when he spent HS28 (mainly on comparative luxuries), his daily total dropped to an average of less than 2 sesterces per day for the remaining three days of the week.

low price. Whether in fact it was so low as to be a deliberate exaggeration for comic effect we cannot tell, though nothing excludes the possibility. The price of 2 *asses* for some lupins (and chickpeas?) for two people which occurs in a partly corrupt passage is not securely quantified, though it can be compared with Martial's colloquial 'asse cicer tepidum constat'.[1]

The price of HS10,000 for Fortunata's clothes and jewels at the end of her husband's first period of affluence does not seem especially high, though well above the level at which women's wardrobes had incurred supertax under Cato's legislation in the early second century B.C.[2] But 100 aurei is a convenient round figure. There is little reason to think that the amount was intended to convey a satirical point (this lies rather in the vulgarity of Trimalchio's making the allusion at all), or that it can show us how much the wives of freedmen normally spent on their jewels and wardrobe.

Two more figures can be compared with costs from elsewhere: one is for a *munus* in the amphitheatre, and the other for offerings of gold in Rome. Echion, the clothes-dealer at Trimalchio's dinner, hopefully anticipated that HS400,000 would be spent on a forthcoming gladiatorial *munus* lasting three days (45). Our other evidence suggests that such a figure for a gladiatorial show at a secondary town must be wildly exaggerated.[3] The highest level of expenditure specifically mentioned in the *Senatus consultum de gladiatorum sumptibus minuendis* which prescribed upper limits for *munera* a century later was HS200,000.[4] The five ranges envisaged were: up to HS30,000; HS30,000–60,000; 60,000–100,000; 100,000–150,000; 150,000–200,000 and beyond. The *Senatus consultum* also seems to indicate that the average cost of municipal *munera* was well below the highest of the specified limits. The tax on *munera* was between $\frac{1}{3}$ and $\frac{1}{4}$, and its revenue was between HS20 and HS30 million per year, which implies an annual outlay by the donors of *munera* in the Empire as a whole in the region of HS90 million.[5] Had the average outlay been as high as HS200,000, the total number of *munera* per year would be little more than 450, or only one per year for each town in Italy, leaving none for the provinces. Even though some towns were not equipped with amphitheatres, it is still likely that the annual number of *munera* would have been very much higher than 450 in an Empire of several thousand

---

[1] Moreno (*loc. cit.* p.238 n.3, above) 63; Martial 1.103.10; *Sat.* 14.3, a partly corrupt passage.

[2] Livy 39.44; Frank *ESAR* 1.194.

[3] Cf. also J. P. V. D. Balsdon *Life and leisure in ancient Rome* (1969) 333.

[4] II 6278 = *ILS* 5163; *ILS* 9340; commentary by Mommsen in *Ges.Schr.* 8.499–531; new publication by J. H. Oliver and R. E. A. Palmer *Hesperia* 24 (1955) 320–49. Restrictions on the giving of *munera* were already being imposed in the time of Augustus and Tiberius (Dio 54.2; Tacitus *Ann.* 4.63).

[5] The *Senatus consultum* excluded Rome (Friedlaender 2.64).

cities.[1] This places the implied average level of outlay lower than
HS200,000 per *munus* (probably a good deal lower). The few scattered
prices for individual *munera* support this calculation. A four-day *munus*
in the amphitheatre at Carthage under Hadrian cost something more
than HS200,000. A *munus* held at Pisaurum every four or five years under
a second-century bequest cost approximately HS150,000. This was
probably also the cost of a single three-day *munus* at Aeclanum. The other
figures known for *ludi* and *munera* in Italy and Africa are all considerably
lower.[2] Thus Echion's suggestion of a *munus* for HS400,000 shows
conversational exaggeration at its most extreme; probably the town would
have done well to get a *munus* costing HS100,000 at this date (the epigraphic prices are mainly second century).

The reference to the Senate's making dedications on the Capitol of
gold offerings weighing 1,000 pounds included in Eumolpus's indictment
of modern decadence need not be pure invention (88). The dedication of a
gold statue weighing 25 pounds apparently by decree of the Senate is
recorded in an inscription; and the depositing of gold in the Capitol is
attested by Suetonius, who records that Augustus gave 16,000 pounds of
gold (and pearls and gems) as a single donation to the temple of Jupiter
Capitolinus.[3] Similar though more modest deposits of bullion in the
Capitolia of provincial cities are recorded in inscriptions. The actual vote
of a 1,000-pound gold statue of the Emperor which was made in Nero's
reign may have some oblique relevance to Eumolpus's remark, assuming
that the vote took place before the composition of this section of the
Satyricon.[4] Petronius's invention here is closer to the practice of his time
than we might have expected, though one cannot claim that it adds to our
knowledge of Roman financial history.

No direct parallel is available for the charge of 1 *as* for the use of a room
(without services) in a brothel (8). In Martial's poems a 'plebeia Venus'
cost 2 *asses* (a mean man might give 1 *as*); the commonest figure for the
services of prostitutes in the Pompeian graffiti is likewise 2 *asses*.[5] This
is no more than the cost of a loaf of bread, but it is possible that some of
the graffiti represent abuse rather than advertisement. The Pompeian
charge could also be as high as 16 *asses* or HS4.[6]

---

[1] For the total number of cities in the Empire, cf. Mommsen, *Ges.Schr.* 5.559–60.
[2] C. nos.281–9; 1074a–9.
[3] *ILS* 153 and n. (Tac. *Ann.* 2.32); Suetonius *Aug.* 30.2.
[4] Dio 63.18.3; Dio also records the construction of such a statue of Commodus (72.15).
See K. Scott 'The significance of statues in precious metals in Emperor worship' *TAPHA*
62 (1931) 101–23.
[5] Martial 2.53.7; 1.103.10, a passage of heavy caricature; E. Diehl *Pompeianische Wandinschriften*² 455; 456; 460; 461; 462 (*bis*); 463; 1021.
[6] IV 2193.

Three more sums of money are mentioned in the *Satyricon*: HS400 and HS800 for breaches of the compact arrived at on Lichas's ship and HS200 as the *ad hoc* fine for killing a sacred goose (109; 137). But these figures only have dramatic significance and cannot be thought to have any wider importance.

In sum, the only main area of Petronius's prices that seems broadly plausible is the prices for slaves. Even here it must be noted that the range of slave prices firmly attested elsewhere is enormous (a factor of more than 100).[1] Thus it is difficult for any figure for slave costs quoted in a work of fiction not to coincide with some point in the historical scale.

It has been suggested elsewhere[2] that an important stratum of direct realism can be found in Petronius, if we discriminate accurately between the different strands in his narrative; but this does not seem to be true of the prices to any significant extent. In fact comparatively little in the novel can be shown to correspond with any exact reality, although deliberate fantasies like those mentioned at the beginning of this chapter are easy to find.[3] The question of the location of the *Cena* is revealing in this respect. After centuries of discussion some agreement seems to have been reached that Puteoli was the town concerned (from the mention of the *vigiles* and the eventual embarkation in a large sea-going vessel).[4] But if Puteoli is meant, Petronius does not trouble to reproduce accurately the name of the town-magistrates (the references to local 'praetores' which led Mommsen to decide on Cumae as the location might represent imprecision dictated by a stylistic preference for 'praetores' over 'duoviri iure dicundo'—the actual title at Puteoli).[5] Furthermore, if Puteoli is in question Petronius does not take many pains to render the talk of commerce and trade which could be expected at this town, as Bücheler pointed out.[6] Although Trimalchio himself had been a mercantile entrepreneur, the conversation of his guests at dinner is mainly stock small-town gossip, brilliantly evoked, of a kind which could as easily belong to an inland town as to the biggest port in Italy. It remains likely that the town of the *Cena* was named at some point in the lost sections of the novel, but the modern quest for its identity is probably delusive. In the one case in which the surviving narrative combines the name of a town with an

---

[1] Pliny *NH* 7.128 gives HS700,000 as the highest price paid for a slave. See Appendix 10.

[2] K. F. C. Rose *TAPHA* 93 (1962), 402; *CP* 62 (1967) 258; cf. Sullivan *Satyricon* 46–7.

[3] Cf. in general P. G. Walsh *The Roman Novel* (1970).

[4] Rose (1962) (*loc. cit.* n.2) 405; Sullivan *loc. cit.* (n.2); J. D'Arms *Romans on the Bay of Naples* (1970) 220.

[5] Th. Mommsen *Ges.Schr.* 7.191–205; for praetors at Cumae, references in *RE* s.v. Kyme 2. Rose (*TAPHA* 93 (1962) 404) confuses the functions of the aediles with those of the senior magistrates of the town (whether these were *duoviri* or praetors).

[6] F. Bücheler ed. *Petronii Arbitri Satirarum Reliquiae* ed. maior (1862) VIIII.

account of action set in that town (the Croto episode) Petronius includes nothing that could seriously count as local reportage.[1]

To say that the prices in the *Satyricon* as a whole are subject to fantasy is not in any way to criticise its author. It seems that in general actual circumstances were only reproduced in order that they might be parodied. Any educated Roman writing of his own times would have found no difficulty in inserting figures in his narrative which roughly made sense. The fact that Petronius so often did not do so in a work which shows every sign of being highly polished suggests that the reluctance was deliberate. The allusions to the property-qualification for the decurionate, and to gold offerings on the Capitol, as well as the mentions of the gladiator Petraites[2] show nevertheless that Petronius was fully capable of inserting accurate naturalistic details when he chose. But the achieving of undiluted naturalism was evidently not his aim in writing a work intended to amuse.

The use of sums of money for burlesque effect (53) will be seen again in the discussion of Apuleius.

APULEIUS

Apuleius in the *Metamorphoses* is much less concerned than Petronius with satire in the modern sense, and is not interested in evoking any social milieu in great detail. The main outlines of his novel were determined by his dependence on a lost earlier version of the story.[3] To judge from the parallel version of Ps.-Lucian, Apuleius's most substantial additions seem to have been the episodes which lie furthest from the world of everyday life (the story of Cupid and Psyche; the redemption by Isis).

Prosaically naturalistic details such as prices are less common in the *Metamorphoses* than in the *Satyricon*, taking into account the relative lengths of the works as they survive. There is even less indication in Apuleius's novel that the author transmits or seeks to transmit accurate economic information. Sometimes the intention is openly comic, as when Jupiter imposes a fine of HS10,000 on any gods who fail to attend a meeting on Olympus, in the story of Cupid and Psyche.[4] Although most of the prices in the *Metamorphoses* belong to the main narrative, the only

---

[1] The characterisation of Croto as a resort of legacy-hunters does not appear to be a genuine local allusion. Pliny *Ep.* 8.18 and frequent references in Martial and Juvenal suggest that the practice was very common in Rome. While the topographical indications that occur in the account of the town of the *Cena* are numerous, there is little real suggestion that they refer to one maritime town rather than another. For the town as a composite creation, cf. Walsh *Roman Novel* 75–6 (also citing Paratore and Marmorale).

[2] Rowell (*loc. cit.* p.240 n.4).

[3] Cf. B. E. Perry *The Ancient Romances* (1967) 211 ff.

[4] *Met.* 6.23.

statement about costs which is clearly historical is the reference in the final book to the much higher cost of living in Rome than in the provinces (11.28).[1]

The *Metamorphoses* offers prices for five commodities: an ass (five different figures); some fish (enough for one man's supper); a bear; a large wooden cask; and some poison (two different figures). The prices for the ass have been reproduced as though they had some value as market indications;[2] but comparative evidence does not support this view. The prices paid for Apuleius's ass, which range from HS44 to HS176, work out at an average of HS81 (8.25; 9.10; 31; 10.13; 17). In Egypt, where prices in general were clearly lower than in other parts of the Empire, six second-century prices for male donkeys average 247 drachmas, roughly HS250.[3] We should expect prices in Greece (or Africa) to be noticeably higher than in Egypt if anything, yet the Apuleian average price is only a third of that attested in Egypt. Prices for asses as high as HS40,000, 60,000, 100,000, 300,000 and even 400,000 are cited by Varro and Pliny, showing how highly prized the animal could be, especially for breeding mules. A price of HS520 for a mule at Pompeii in A.D. 15 is also worth noticing.[4]

It seems that Apuleius's prices for his ass were pitched very low indeed. No doubt this was done deliberately, for comic or dramatic effect, to add to the hero's humiliations in his animal form. The same seems to be true in the "Ονος of Ps.-Lucian, where the ass changes hands for HS100 and HS120 on two occasions (35; 46).[5] The invention may thus derive from the lost original.

Distortion in the opposite direction is apparent in the two prices for fish bought for the hero's supper. Lucius beat the fishmonger in the market at Hypata down from HS100 to HS80, but afterwards lost the fish in a quarrel begun by an officious friend who was town aedile (1.24-5). Though Lucius did not take the initiative in complaining about the price, the figure was clearly exorbitant. Egypt again offers the main comparative evidence: prices per fish under the Principate range from 4 Egyptian drachmas (about HS4) to 1/20th of a drachma or HS0.05.[6] A completely different range of prices at Rome are given by literary sources: HS1,200

---

[1] See Appendix 8. See also Martial 4.66; 10.96; Juvenal 3.223-5.
[2] Frank *ESAR* 5.279.
[3] Papyri collected by Johnson in Frank *ESAR* 2.230-1: *PSI* 38 (306 dr.); *Gr. Texte* 13 (340 dr.); *P. Basel* 4 (148 dr.); *SB* 6001 (160 dr.); *BGU* 527 (300 dr.); *SPP* xxii, 29 (230 dr.).
[4] *r.r.* 3.2.7; 2.8.3; 2.1.14; Pliny *NH* 8.167; 170; iv 3340, i. For high prices cf. Martial 3.62.
[5] McLeod's suggestion that the drachmas in the second figure should be understood as being different from the Attic drachmas of the first figure seems to have little force (Loeb edition, *ad loc.*).
[6] Papyri cited by Johnson in Frank *ESAR* 2.317.

and 1,600 for jars of smoked fish under the Republic; prices for mullets under the Principate of HS10,000 and 8,000 each, and HS1,111, HS1,000 and HS300 per pound; and a price for garum or fish-sauce of HS500 per congius (= 3.27 litres).[1] But these figures from Rome refer to exorbitant or maximal prices, usually cited to shock or amaze the reader; and even normal market prices at Rome were higher than those elsewhere (see Appendix 8). The Egyptian evidence must be used as the basis for comparison. Even if we compensate for regional variants by assuming for the sake of argument that prices in Egypt were no more than half those in other provinces, the price in Apuleius of HS80 for a single meal still bears no resemblance to even the highest of the Egyptian figures of HS4 per fish. Once again the author evidently chose a figure for the sake of effect, pitching it high in order to add to the hero's discomfiture at losing his supper through his friend's intervention. It would be unrealistic to think that the fish concerned could have been luxury articles for which a very high price would have been appropriate, when the text offers no suggestion that this was so. It should be noticed incidentally that Lucius was not travelling through Thessaly in any style, and had to do his own shopping.[2]

The price for a bear occurs in a story where a local magistrate who was about to give a *munus* in the amphitheatre, but had lost all the bears he had originally collected, is deceived into buying a robber dressed in a bearskin (4.16). The price, ten aurei or HS1,000, may have been pitched high in order to reinforce the irony of the transaction, though any price would have been advantageous in the circumstances. In an African town in the third century the price asked for a leopard, together with the services of the *venator* who fought against it in the arena, was only HS2,000.[3]

The price of a large barrel is given as HS20–28 in an anecdote which provided Boccaccio with one of the livelier tales in the Decameron (9.7; cf. *Dec.* VII, 2). Comparative evidence does not seem to be available; but the point of the story need not involve a distorted price. The evident implication was that the sum eventually paid, HS28, was small recompense for the act of adultery which the sale entailed, even if it was a good price for the barrel.

---

[1] Polybius 31.25.5–6; Diodorus 37.3.5; Suetonius *Tib.* 34; Pliny *NH* 9.67; 31.94; Seneca *Ep.* 95.42; Martial 10.31. The price of the mullet bought under Caligula by Asinius Celer which Pliny gives as HS8,000 (*NH* 9.67) is given as HS7,000 by Macrobius (*Sat.* 2.12) and as HS6,000 by Tertullian (*de pall.* 5). (The last four references are owed to A. C. Andrews *Class. Weekly* 42 (1948–9) 186–8.) The figure for a mullet in Juvenal 4.15–16 is HS1,000 per pound, and not HS1 per pound as stated by Scramuzza, *ESAR* 3.352; cf. P. Labriolle, F. Villeneuve ed. *Juvenal* (1921) 37, 40.

[2] The real Apuleius of course travelled with a sizeable retinue, like any well-to-do Roman (*Apol.* 17).

[3] *AE* 1967, 549; the *munerarius* from whose house the mosaic record comes actually paid HS4,000 in each case, or twice the sum asked.

The two prices for poison, in different stories in the *Metamorphoses*, are both very high: HS10,000 and HS50,000 (10.9; 10.25). Comparative evidence seems to be lacking, but the payments clearly incorporated bribes for the doctors concerned, and do not simply refer to the cost of ingredients.

Payments to astrologers must have been a regular feature of life in the Empire, and the example provided by Apuleius is thus of some interest. A merchant offers HS400 to an astrologer as payment for a prediction about a suitable date for a commercial voyage (2.13). But the story turns on the revelation of the astrologer's incompetence from his own lips; and the sum offered may thus have been pitched high in order to emphasise his fraudulence.

Finally, the *Metamorphoses* contain five prices which are only of internal interest: HS1,000 for watching a corpse against witches; HS2,000 and 1,000 as amatory bribes for a mistress and her slave; HS100,000 as the savings of a bandit; and HS200,000 as the purchase price for the captaincy of a robber band (2.23, cf. 2.21; 9.18; 7.4; 7.8).

Apuleius's commodity prices no doubt had a point for contemporaries, who would have been readily aware of the author's deliberate exaggerations and minimisations. But they are only of marginal value to the economic historian. Like Petronius, Apuleius contributes one concrete piece of economic observation: the information that prices in Rome were higher than elsewhere.

Both novelists evidently sometimes used prices for comic effect. Where this is so their figures have little positive value for economic history. It is equally difficult to show that they sought to achieve realism by choosing a plausible amount even when the context was quite neutral.

THE 'HISTORIA APOLLONII TYRIENSIS'

In the form in which it has reached us, this short novel is a naive work whose literary merits are slight. It survives only in late versions, both Latin and vernacular, of which the earliest is a Latin text (evidently abbreviated) whose language suggests a sixth-century date. The monetary indications however clearly imply that the original can have been written no later than the third century A.D. They also suggest that the immediate antecedent of the earliest surviving text was also written in Latin, despite the Hellenistic locale of the story. Greek writers did not normally employ as a unit of reckoning the sesterces which occur throughout the *Historia*.[1]

---

[1] E. Klebs *Die Erzählung von Apollonius aus Tyrus* (1899); Schanz–Hosius–Krüger *Gesch. der röm. Lit.* IV, 2 (1920) 87–92. A recent discussion in B. E. Perry *The Ancient Romances* (1967) 294–324. The novel was an important source for Shakespeare's *Pericles, Prince of Tyre*.

A date of composition not later than the second or third quarter of the third century is suggested by the monetary value of gold indicated at one point in the novel. An exchange between the heroine and one of her visitors in c.34 indicates that 40 aurei was somewhat less, but perhaps not much less, than a pound of gold. This might correspond with the coin-issue of Alexander Severus (222/35) in which the aureus was struck at approximately 54 to the pound. By the 240s, the aureus was being struck at the much lower weight of approximately 69 to the pound. By the reigns of Valerian and Gallienus (253–67) the aureus was being struck at about 100 to the pound.[1] The exchange in c.34 would thus begin to seem anachronistic in terms of the coinage of the period after 250. If coin with high bullion content disappeared from circulation rapidly at this period, as seems likely when shrinkage of weight was so rapid, these figures could suggest a date of composition for the novel within the period 230–60. A final *terminus ante quem* is provided by the frequent use of the sestertius, which is last attested at the end of the third century.[2]

Figures that have dramatic meaning but no external significance predominate among the prices. There are however a few commodity prices. The most notable are the corn prices given in the account of Apollonius's benefaction to Tarsus (9–10). Apollonius found the city in a state of dire famine: corn had risen to a price of 1 aureus, or HS100 per modius. Apollonius earned the lasting gratitude of the citizens by selling 100,000 modii of corn to the town at the much lower price of HS2 per modius ('octo aereis', c.10). Such episodes are a familiar feature of town-life in the Principate, and even the prices given in the novel are not beyond recognition. As early as the first century B.C. we hear of a famine price for corn of HS48 per modius in Asia. Under the Principate prices of HS40, HS44 and HS50 are attested during famines in Africa and Italy; another famine price from Asia mentioned in the Apocalypse is HS32 per modius; and a famine price at Sparta is between HS23 and HS27 per modius.[3] The inflation that had taken place by the mid-third century

---

[1] Cf. tables (compiled by L. C. West) in S. Bolin *State and Currency in the Roman Empire* (1958) 252–3.

[2] Cf. *RE* s.v. Sestertius.

[3] Cicero *ad fam.* 12.13.4 indicates a famine price of HS48 (per modius) in 43 B.C. Rostovtzeff's suggestion that *medimnoi* rather than *modii* should be understood as the unit of measurement here is implausible, since the figure comes from correspondence between two Roman senators about conditions in a Roman army-camp (*RE* 7.147; for the omission of the unit of measurement in another context where 'modius' should be understood, compare Pliny *NH* 18.16). The other costs: VIII 25703–4; IX 2861; *Apocalypse* 6; *Ann. Brit. Sch. Athens* 27 (1925–6) 228 = *SEG* XI 492 = *AE* 1929, 20. The price of HS400 per modius said to have been extorted from his colleagues by a soldier on an expedition in Africa is hardly typical, though it shows to what extent corn prices could soar under really extreme conditions (Suetonius *Galba* 7.2). The chronicles which give famine prices for Rome in A.D. 6 and for

could well have produced a famine level of HS100 per modius. The concessionary price of HS2 which Apollonius charged for his supply can be compared with a controlled price of HS4 imposed during a famine at Pisidian Antioch in A.D. 93/4.[1] The *biga*, or statue with chariot, that Apollonius received from the town of Tarsus as a token of gratitude is again characteristic of the practices of the Principate. It does not obviously belong to the context of the later Empire, when economic difficulties had made such large civic gestures a rarity.[2]

The other clear-cut commodity price refers to a burial. Apollonius allotted HS10,000 in gold for the funeral of his wife, who was thought to have died while they were at sea. Apollonius was not short of funds at this point, having set out on the voyage 'cum multa familia multoque apparatu atque copia' (25). The money was placed in the coffin, which was set adrift for superstitious reasons (a total of HS20,000, half being a reward for the finder); but since it was in gold, the weight would only be three or four pounds. There is little reason to think that the funeral cost, which is repeated, is intended as a low figure (unless it is corrupt). It nevertheless seems very low when set against the epigraphic tomb prices, which range up to HS500,000 in Italy. HS10,000 is only the median average of the Italian tomb costs, all of which refer to commoners. Although Nero was utterly disgraced and buried privately, his funeral still cost HS200,000.[3] Thus it does not seem that the author attempted a realistic evaluation here of an appropriate figure for the burial of a king's wife, even in pre-inflationary terms. He may have been led to fix a low sum in order to achieve a pathetic effect, in view of the obvious uncertainties of the funeral ever taking place.

The economic details of Tharsia's pretended sojourn as a prostitute seem to lack explicit parallels: the price for which she was eventually sold to the brothel-keeper after an auction whose successive bids (starting at HS10,000) are described, was HS100,000.[4] This was comparable to the sums paid at Rome under the early Principate for slaves of the highest

Greece in A.D. 49 seriously contradict each other (R. Corsetti 'Sul prezzo dei grani nel-l'antichità classica' *Studi di storia antica pubb. da G. Beloch* 2 (1893) 90–1). If we follow St Jerome (whose figure for the earlier famine is clearly the more plausible) the respective prices were HS22 and HS24 per modius (sources in A. Schoene (ed.) *Eusebius, Chronicon* II (1866) 146–7; 152–3).

[1] *AE* 1925, 126b.

[2] Apollonius's other gifts to Tarsus are by contrast of a 'late' type: his restoration of the ramparts, fortifications and public baths of Tarsus is more characteristic of the munificence of the late Empire than of gifts of the second century, when new buildings *ab initio* would have been typical (51).

[3] Suetonius *Nero* 50.

[4] For a 'Dutch' auction in which a prostitute reduces her price by successive stages, Martial 10.75, where the highest figure is HS20,000.

accomplishments.[1] Tharsia's official 'price' was half a pound of gold (*c.* HS3,000?), in the first instance, and one aureus (HS100) thereafter (33); her actual 'earnings' included amounts of 40 aurei (HS4,000) and a pound of gold (*c.* HS6,000?) (34).

When called on to give figures for large fortunes, the author shows a lack of inventiveness that recalls corresponding statements in Petronius. The figure of 200 talents (nominally HS4,800,000) occurs as the cash sum with which Apollonius is rewarded by the king of Pentapolis (17); as the cash sum with which the *vilicus* of the brothel is rewarded at the end of the novel (46); and as the reward offered by his enemy Antiochus for the murder of Apollonius near the beginning of the story (7). The figure may also be echoed in the fortune of HS200,000 in gold with which a beneficent fisherman is endowed in c.51. In such cases the author appears to be supplying an arbitrary figure with which to quantify the notion of a princely fortune or a princely gift. There is probably little purpose in comparing fortune-sizes from this explicitly fantastic context with those attested in historical sources, though gifts amounting to millions of sesterces are certainly attested under the Principate.[2]

Seven remaining costs in the novel may be mentioned briefly. Tharsia's fee when she sang before Apollonius was 200 aurei, and she was offered 400 aurei for a repeat performance (40–1).[3] The sailors of Apollonius were given 10 aurei each with which to celebrate the feast of Neptune when they were anchored at Mytilene (39). The interloper Athenagoras tried to bribe them with offers of 10 aurei to let him share the table of Apollonius, and then 2 aurei to take a message to Apollonius (39). When Apollonius was being hounded by his enemy Antiochus early in the story, Antiochus offered 100 gold talents for his capture alive (and 200 for his murder, see above) (7). On learning of this Apollonius rewarded his informant with 100 talents in gold (8). None of these payments tell us

[1] Cf. Pliny *NH* 7.128; Appendix 10.

[2] For grants of fortunes in the form of an annual revenue of HS500,000 per year (or roughly HS8 million at 6% interest) by Claudius, Nero and Vespasian (Pliny *NH* 29.7; Tac. *Ann.* 13.34; Suetonius *Nero* 10; *Vesp.* 17). For Augustus's gift of HS10 million to Virgil, who is said to have received an equal amount from other friends, Suetonius *v. Verg.* 13; *vita Probiana* 16 (OCT); *v. Donati* 13 (42–3); cf. Martial 5.16. For grants of a revenue of HS100,000 per year (*c.* HS1,600,000 capital) to grammarians and rhetors by Augustus and Vespasian, Suetonius *de gramm.* 17; *Vesp.* 18. For testamentary receipts of wealth, cf. the HS20 million inherited by Cicero, and the HS1½ million (and more) inherited by Pliny the younger (Cicero *Phil.* 2.16.40; p.27 above).

[3] The fee first offered to Tharsia for singing before Apollonius is uncertain (c.40 'decem sestertia auri' Teubner text A; 'ducenta sestertia et XX aureos', Teubner text B). If we follow A, the sum can be construed as HS10,000 in gold, which makes Apollonius's actual payment of 200 aurei (HS20,000) a conventional doubling of the amount first offered (41), like that made later on when offering an increased fee for a second performance (*ibid.*). Cf. above, p.250 n.3.

any more than what notion the author had of princely munificence in different contexts.

It is striking that the sums of money are almost always in units of aurei (or equally high values reckoned in sestertii). It is tempting to regard this as a direct indication of inflation at the time when the *Historia* was written, when we compare the occurrence of sums as small as a single *as* in Petronius's novel of two centuries earlier (*Sat.* 8; 44). This inference may be legitimate, but it is blurred by the fact that the *Historia* is a tale of kings and princesses, whereas the *Satyricon* and *Metamorphoses* rarely rise above the bourgeoisie, and include many scenes of low life. The social settings partly converge in the brothel episode of the *Historia*; but the tariff given here (33) refers to a most exceptional acquisition, a princess in disguise, and could hardly be considered on the same basis as the first-century prices for street prostitutes (see above, p. 246 n. 5). The most realistic episode in the novel, the relief of famine at Tarsus, includes a subsidised price for corn which is as low as any that we hear of under the Principate. If the episode were pure fantasy, it is difficult to see why the author made Apollonius charge a price for the corn at all; his generosity would have been all the greater if he had given it for nothing. This makes it less easy to conclude that the novel's prices are necessarily the product of an inflationary age. Nevertheless, the emphasis on payments in gold is characteristic of a period when the silver currency was failing, and price-inflation was on the increase.[1]

The *Historia* is set in a world of small Hellenistic kingdoms, of a kind that had disappeared from the shores of the Mediterranean centuries before. Thus there is no obvious reason to suppose that its author intended to use his economic indications as an aid to direct realism (the work is hardly an 'historical novel'). Nevertheless, he frequently quantifies payments, and appears to use current monetary terms. In one instance he introduces a type of monetary benefaction (cheap corn at Tarsus) which aptly, though perhaps incongruously, recalls the practice of municipal benefactors of the Principate. In the frequent appearance of sums of money in a fabulous narrative, the story in some ways appears closer in spirit to the *Arabian Nights* than to the other novels of classical antiquity. The political background of the *Satyricon* and *Metamorphoses* is of course one of orthodox Roman rule by an Emperor. The author of the *Historia* however has no real dealings with the supernatural, and his work is in this respect less fantastic than that of Apuleius.

Our conclusion about the usefulness of prices in the Latin novel must be chiefly negative. Although this is no criticism of the novelists, it appears

[1] Cf. XIII 3162.

that, as a matter of deliberate intention, they did not mainly use sums of money as a means of reinforcing the literal accuracy of their narratives. Their narratives aimed rather at intermittent realism of tone, which the mention of any sum of money sometimes helped to strengthen. This conclusion must incidentally be disappointing for the economic historian. Nevertheless, the comparative material needed to assess these figures has some interest in itself, and the analysis of parts of the novels from an unaccustomed point of view may also contribute to our knowledge of their authors' intentions as a whole.

PART 3

POPULATION AND DEMOGRAPHIC POLICY

6
The size of cities

In modern usage city population usually means those who live within a built-up area called a city, and perhaps includes those living in a narrow adjoining periphery. The typical situation in the Roman world was radically different. Most of the countryside as a whole belonged to the territory of one city or another. City territories were thus of substantial size, and their native inhabitants normally counted among the inhabitants of each city. Juridically, though not always in practice, they were as much local citizens as were the urban residents.[1] The ordinary secondary town was not necessarily an important residential centre in itself.[2] It was a civilised nucleus for those who were able to live away from the soil, which also offered its facilities to the inhabitants living outside the town.[3] It was the main centre of worship and many of its public buildings were temples and shrines; it was the centre of administration and the source of legal decisions; the commercial centre; the centre of hygiene and medicine;

---

[1] Ulpian *Digesta* 50.1.30. Dio Chrysostom cites as proof that a poor peasant living on a city-territory possessed local citizenship the fact that he was able to benefit from a *sportulatio* that happened to be taking place when he visited the city (*Or.* 7.49). However, distributions might be confined to those living within the walls (cf. C. nos.947; 962; 976; 990; 998). At Veii the outlying citizens appear as a collective unit ('municipes extramurani' *ILS* 6581). This is unusual, though the converse in the form of dedications by the 'plebs urbana', 'intramurani', or 'urbani' is quite common (cf. *ILS* 3, p.680). For the size of city-territories in Italy, cf. J. Beloch *Italische Bund* (1880) 149–50; Chilver 45–50; Appendix 5 below.

[2] For town areas in Italy, cf. J. Beloch *Atene e Roma* 1 (1898) 257–78; Nissen 2.36–9. Some town plans are reproduced in *Enc.art.ant.* in articles on particular towns. For Africa cf. p.265 n.4 below.

[3] Because local citizenship depended primarily on descent not on residence (*Cod.Iust.* 10.40.7 pr.), any local residents whose 'origo' lay elsewhere were not citizens but *incolae* as far as the town was concerned. It was evidently quite common for men to live or at least to own property outside their ancestral town: in Cicero's time most of the land in the territory of the town of Aetna belonged to citizens of Centuripae; at Leontini only one family of local citizens cultivated any land there; while there were few districts in Sicily as a whole whose farmers did not include citizens of Centuripae (Cicero *Verr.* 2.3.108–9). *Incolae* occasionally shared in civic benefits or distributions (C. nos.248; 1001; 1002; 1026). By the mid-second century A.D. *incolae* had become liable to tenure of local magistracies and *munera* as though they were local citizens (Gaius *Digesta* 50.1.29), although this had not been the general situation at the start of the second century (*ILS* 1374).

the centre of social life; and the place where entertainments were held. To some extent the proliferation of town monuments was the result of Roman liking for the grandiose, rather than the fulfilment of genuine social needs.[1] Nevertheless, the abundance of large public buildings in a Roman town and the high proportion of the built-up area that they often occupied also suggest that the urban unit existed for the use of a community larger than could be contained in the houses within the built-up area. Similarly, the wealth needed to construct these buildings was typically drawn from sources extending well beyond the city walls.

The phenomenon of agricultural workers who live in towns and go out to work in the fields each day existed in Roman times at Capua, one of the biggest towns in southern Italy, and was still common in the south of the peninsula in the 1930s.[2] But it is difficult to conceive that most agricultural workers can have lived in cities, even in antiquity. Urban centres were fewer and thus further apart in Roman times than they are in modern Italy, and transport was greatly inferior. In antiquity the percentage of the Italian working population engaged in agriculture is bound to have been much higher than the 51% recorded in the Italy of 1931. Yet even at this date over 50% of the local population was still living on the land and outside towns in Umbria and Marche; in Emilia the proportion was 45%, in Veneto 33%, and in Toscana 31%.[3]

Explicit ancient allusions to the total population of cities will normally refer to a sizeable rural territory as well as to the built-up area. This has its disadvantages for the historian. It may mean that the implications of an ancient figure in terms of population density are uncertain, the size of ancient city-territories normally being a matter of conjecture. In such cases, comparisons with modern population figures for the town in question will be equally uncertain. Nevertheless, even ancient figures for indeterminate areas can be useful in showing the demographic importance of one city against another. They may also offer clues to the population of larger areas.

Because there are so few explicit ancient figures,[4] more general

---

[1] Pliny thought it necessary to re-build a temple on his estate (on religious advice), for the benefit of the crowd from the whole district that assembled at the shrine on one day each year (*Ep.* 9.39).

[2] Cicero *de leg.ag.* 2.88; cf. Brunt 345. R. Almagià in *Enc.it.* 19.744.

[3] These are the percentages of 'popolazione sparsa' as distinct from 'popolazione agglomerata' (*Enc.it.* 19.744). The modern divisions correspond roughly with the ancient Umbria, Picenum, Aemilia, Venetia and Etruria.

[4] The main explicit population figures for cities (as distinct from units such as tribes) under the late Republic and Empire can be listed briefly. Alexandria in Egypt had more than 300,000 free inhabitants at the end of the Republic (Diodorus 17.52.6). Carthage came to rival Alexandria, perhaps exceeding it in size in the early third century (Herodian 7.6.1); apparently Carthage had more than overtaken Alexandria by the fourth century (Ausonius *Ord.urb.nob.*

approaches have often been made to the problem of local population sizes, directed as a rule to estimating the population of the built-up area of a city or cities. In the African provinces, for example, modern assessments of city population have been based on estimates of the numbers that a given area of land is likely to have supported;[1] on estimates of the size of the piped water-supply;[2] on comparisons between ancient and modern city areas;[3] and on inferences from the density of surviving Roman remains.[4] Reference has also sometimes been made to the seating capacity of theatres or amphitheatres.[5] While some of these methods have an ancillary value, none of them provide firm or precise information.

Deductions from the maximum agricultural potential can be applied only to the few cities the extent of whose territory is known; even in these cases there are large residual uncertainties about types of cultivation, the size of the cultivated zone, and about the efficiency of ancient agriculture in the area concerned. Estimates of the size of the piped water-supply have little relevance to demography, as there is no reliable way of estimating the amount of water used per person; supplying public baths (and sometimes fountains) was at least as important a purpose of aqueducts as the provision of drinking water, some of which came from separate wells and rainwater cisterns. Comparisons of ancient and modern

2 and 5). Antioch in Syria was nearly equal to Alexandria under Augustus, and was still its rival in the fourth century (Strabo 16.2.5; Auson. *Ord.urb.nob.* 4). Pergamum in the second century A.D. had a free adult population of about 80,000, and about 40,000 slaves, implying a total population of about 180,000 including children (for the ratio see p.264 n.4 below) (Galen 5.49 (Kuhn)). Ephesus had at least 40,000 male citizens, and thus a population probably no smaller than that of Pergamum, from the terms of a gift made in the second or early third century A.D. (*JOAI* 26 (1930) Beibl. 57 ff.). Apamea in Syria had 117,000 free inhabitants in a census taken under Augustus (*ILS* 2683; cf. R. Duncan-Jones *JRS* 53 (1963) 90). The civitas Aeduorum in Gaul was assessed as having 32,000 'libera capita' under Constantine, probably adult citizens of both sexes, and thus a free population of 50,000–55,000 (*Panegyricus* VIII.2; cf. Jones *LRE* 3.339, n.15). Centuripae in Sicily had 10,000 male citizens, and thus perhaps 35,000 free inhabitants c. 70 B.C. (Cicero *Verr.* 2.2.163).

[1] Gsell–Joly 'Mdaourouch' (1922) 18 ff.
[2] P. Grimal *MEFR* 54 (1937) 117 ff.
[3] C. Courtois *Les Vandales et l'Afrique* (1955) 104 ff. A. Lézine *Antiquités africaines* 3 (1969) 69–82.
[4] Picard *Civilisation* 44–59.
[5] Cf. R. M. Haywood *ESAR* 4.112. J. C. Russell uses *summae honorariae* as a basis for linear estimates of the population of different cities. But the relationship between population and wealth is hardly linear; and *summae honorariae* are not necessarily a sensitive index of actual wealth (*Trans.Amer.Philos.Soc.* 48.3 (1958) 67; 76). On this yardstick, if Carthage had a population of 300,000 (see above, p.260 n.4), Uchi Maius should have had 100,000 inhabitants, since the respective *summae honorariae* that are attested are HS38,000 and HS12,000 (C. nos.360; 366). The archaeology of Uchi shows that the conjecture is patently absurd (cf. plan and text in *Notes et Documents (de la Tunisie)* 2 (1908) 127, etc.). There were many towns close together in the part of Africa Proconsularis in which Uchi stood, and the town territory cannot have been very large.

city areas tell us little about numbers, as the density of ancient settlement is uncertain; such comparisons must also omit the inhabitants living on the territory of the city outside the walls. Arguments from the overall density of ancient remains rest on assumptions about the relationship between human numbers and material remains that are no easier to verify; they are also at the mercy of the chances affecting the survival of monuments over a period of two millennia. And the proportion of the population that theatres and amphitheatres were intended to seat on a single occasion is not known. Questions of local wealth and local rivalry may be as important in determining their size as demographic requirements.[1]

Rather than attempt further demographic conjectures from archaeology alone, it seems more profitable to consider the epigraphic evidence in detail. Beloch showed the potential value of using large-scale gifts for feasts or distributions as a means of estimating town population.[2] Deductions of this kind can usefully be applied to a wider range of evidence than that utilised by Beloch. At least a dozen inscriptions from Italy and Africa can be put to some use as a guide to population.

In most cases, some details have to be restored using comparative evidence. From the explicit evidence, interest-rates in foundations were relatively standardised, and their pattern, related to the size of foundation, follows an intelligible form.[3] Rates of benefit in distributions are very well attested in Italy, less well in Africa. As with interest-rates, there is much repetition at a few common levels.[4] Outlays on feasts seem to have followed the same pattern as outlays on cash sportulae, with which they are to some extent interchangeable.[5] Where the amounts of provisions within foundations are known, they seem to repeat the details of the single ephemeral outlays for which evidence is more plentiful.[6] It appears that the benefits would not normally be higher in a foundation than they

---

[1] The amphitheatre at Pompeii was large enough to seat a large number of visitors from the nearby Nuceria as well as local citizens on the occasion of a notorious riot in A.D. 59 (Tacitus *Ann.* 14.17). A jurist mentions 'aemulatio alterius civitatis' as one of the common motivations behind new building works (Macer *Digesta* 50.10.3.pr). The rivalry of neighbouring cities is shown in an acute form by the local war which broke out between Oea and Lepcis Magna in A.D. 69 (Tacitus *Hist.* 4.50). Less virulent rivalries between cities are portrayed in Dio Chrysostom's speeches about Apamea and Prusa (*Or.* 40; 41).

[2] Beloch 441-2. Beloch briefly conjectured 6,000-7,000 male adult citizens for Spoletium (p.267 below) and 500 for Rudiae (p.271 below). His estimate for Ferentinum is based on a mis-reading of the inscription: no cash payment was made to the body of citizens, and consequently no inference about their numbers seems to be possible (*ILS* 6271).

[3] See pp.134-5.   [4] See pp.140-1.   [5] See pp.139-41.

[6] The decurions received HS20 in the terms of a late-second-century foundation at Ostia (C. no.864). At Petelia and Spoletium the citizens received HS4 and HS2 under the terms of foundations (C. nos.1014; 1047). The payment to the decurions at Ostia is repeated in the

were in single donations. We might guess that they could well be lower in certain cases, the cost of a foundation to the donor being 17 or 20 times greater than that of an individual distribution providing the same benefits. This view is supported in two examples: in one case a donor gave three days of games to inaugurate a foundation that provided for only one day of games; in another, a donor gave cash sportulae at the inauguration that were too high to have been repeated in the terms of the foundation itself.[1] It is often impossible to elicit a single firm estimate of the number of beneficiaries in a foundation, despite the abundance of comparative evidence from which to supply missing coordinates. Where this is so, two estimates are given below, the lower of which is the minimum number of recipients allowed on the assumption that the rate of benefit was the highest that is likely from the parallel evidence.

The beneficiaries of foundations for feasts and cash-handouts are usually described as the 'plebs' or 'populus'. We know that women were occasionally included among the recipients of cash-handouts, and also (more rarely) among the participants at public feasts.[2] But the evidence strongly implies that their inclusion was a minority practice, common only at certain small towns in Italy; the practice appears to have been signalised by explicit references to the inclusion of women, when it took place. In the majority of gifts, where there is no reference to women, it is legitimate to conclude that the beneficiaries of a gift to 'populus' or 'plebs' were only the male adult citizens of the town. The inclusion of both sexes would double the number of recipients, and double the size of the outlay, thus enhancing the donor's generosity to a degree which he was not likely to leave unmentioned. The feasts themselves were usually modest affairs, as might be expected when the numbers were so large: in a number of cases the provisions seem to have consisted of bread and wine.[3] It is not always clear whether the citizens who took

---

amount of an ephemeral payment to the same group at this town (C. no.863). The rates of HS4 and HS2 are among the lower rates attested for single distributions to the people (see p.142). In Africa the payment of HS20 to the decurions in two foundations is paralleled by one ephemeral payment of the same amount (C. nos.291–3). The payment of HS4 to the decurions in another foundation is also paralleled in the payment of this amount in an ephemeral distribution (C. nos.300–1).

[1] VIII 967 + 12448; C. nos.673; 763.

[2] For sportulae given to women, see p.143. At Lanuvium (whose citizen organisations were abnormal) a donor gave the 'curia mulierum' an 'epulum duplum' on the occasion of a cash-distribution paid to male recipients (*ILS* 6199). At Veii, a lady whose husband was giving an *epulum* for the male citizens provided a parallel occasion for the women of the town (*ILS* 6583). At Corfinium the wives of the decurions took part in an *epulum* with their husbands (*ILS* 6530).

[3] The menu at the regular dinners (*cenae*) of the college of Diana and Antinous at Lanuvium under Hadrian consisted of bread, sardines and wine (*ILS* 7212; cf. 7214). In the college of

part came from the whole territory, or merely from the urban centre. The inscriptions rarely specify that the recipients were to include all citizens (however that is defined territorially). But if the purpose of the donors was to gratify rather than to tantalise, it is reasonable to assume that in most cases the scope of the foundations was more or less comprehensive (whether in terms of the urban unit alone, or in terms of the whole territory).[1] In cases where this assumption is incorrect, the population estimate is likely to be too low.

The more explicit of the two African examples comes from Siagu in Zeugitana, a town now largely buried under olive groves, which lies 4 km inland on the north-eastern coast of Tunisia.[2] The donor of a foundation for games bequeathed a residue of HS10,000, of which HS6,000 was to be spent on an inaugural celebration of games lasting three days. The balance of HS4,000 was to be spent on a distribution to all citizens at the rate of HS1 per head ('et reliquis *∞ omnibus civibus N HS dividi volo').[3] No reconstruction of the number of recipients is needed here, the details being stated in full. The inscription tells us that the free population of Siagu was little less than 4,000 in all. If, as is likely, the recipients were all adult, the total free population actually implied is not less than 7,000. But parallels would further imply that the recipients were only the male citizens. If so the overall free total would be about 14,000.[4] However, this figure produces a surprisingly high population density when related to any reasonable estimate of the size of Siagu's territory. The coast lay 4 km away from the town centre to the east.

Aesculapius and Hygia on the via Appia near Rome under Antoninus Pius, the members who consumed bread and wine were described as having assembled 'ad epulandum'; hence the bread and wine was evidently an 'epulum' (the officials of the college received cash as well, *ILS* 7213, l.16). For bread and wine at municipal distributions see for example *ILS* 2650; 3082; 4174; 6268; 6595; 6632; 6645; 6654 (also Toller 90–2).

[1] See below pp.274–5. For the restriction of sportulae to urban inhabitants, C. nos.962, 976, 990. For the inclusion of *incolae*, examples p.259 n.3 above. Comprehensive distributions: VIII 23880; *ILS* 6858; 7196; X 4727; nos. 820; 931; 974; 1018a.

[2] Notices of Siagu: V. Guérin *Voyage en Tunisie* (1862) 2.259–61; C. Tissot *Géographie comparée de la province romaine d'Afrique* 2 (1888) 129–31; E. Babelon, R. Cagnat, S. Reinach *Atlas archéologique de la Tunisie* (1893–1926) fe.37.3 (map-reference; commentary under 37.4); P. Gauckler *Enquête sur les installations hydrauliques romaines en Tunisie* (1897–1902) 233–8, plan 234; L. Poinssot in *Atlas historique, géographique, économique et touristique de la Tunisie* (ed. C. Leconte, J. Despois, G. Garbe, F. Gérard) (1936) 34.

[3] VIII 967 + 12448 (C. nos.259; 286; 305). The sportula is extremely low, and very little attested. Hence parallels may not be relevant here. Women given sportulae in Italy usually received less than men (see p.143).

[4] The ratio assumed throughout in interpreting figures for the free male population is adult males = $\frac{2}{7}$ (28.6%) of the free population. This is based on the analogy of age-distribution for India in 1901 (*United Nations Population Studies* 26 (1956) 112). Cf. R. Duncan-Jones *JRS* 53 (1963) 87, n.24. The proportion assumed by Brunt varies between 28% (Italy in 225 B.C. and Flavian Spain) and 35% (Augustan Italy) (Brunt 59; 117; 261 n.4).

$4\frac{1}{2}$ km away to the SW lay Pupput, which had its own territory of about 40 km². Neapolis lay 13 km NW of Siagu, Vina 10 km N by W. Thinissut was 4 km away N by E. Only to the west is there a clear expanse of territory of any considerable distance without any other city as neighbour. The territory of Siagu may have spread 15 km or more in this direction, although part of the terrain is the arid foothills of Djebel Zit.[1] It seems unlikely that Siagu can have had a fertile territory of more than 60–70 km², at most. If a free population of 14,000 presupposes a further body of slaves numbering 4,000 or so,[2] the implied overall density would be between 257 and 300 inhabitants per km². This is a relatively high density even by modern standards.[3] Since Siagu was a minor town which never attained any higher political status than that of *civitas* as far as we know, it is unlikely that its size can have been especially great. Thus the estimate which places its size between 4,000 and 7,000 in terms of free inhabitants is the more plausible. The area of the town centre may have been relatively large, 50 or 60 hectares, although built-up area need not be a reliable index of the demographic importance of the town. We know of a number of African towns with areas as little as 20 hectares, although the larger towns ran to more than 100 hectares.[4]

In Africa there are also two references to the size of sportula-distributions at one of the bigger towns, Oea in Tripolitania (modern Tripoli). Apuleius claims in his *Apology* that the distribution of sportulae which his wife Pudentilla held at their house in Oea to celebrate her son's coming of age cost HS50,000. A generation later, under Commodus, a

[1] Territory of Pupput, W. Seston *BAC* (1946/9) 309–11. Neapolis, Pupput and Vina were all politically more important than Siagu, the first two being colonies, the third a *municipium*. For locations see inset 'Les grands carrefours de la région de Carthage' in the map in P. Salama *Les Voies romaines de l'Afrique* (1951).

[2] See p.273 n.1 below.

[3] The overall population density in modern Tunisia was 27 inhabitants per km² in 1966; in Algeria 35 inhabitants per km² (J. Paxton *The statesman's yearbook 1971–1972* (1971) 1378; 736). There is little doubt that population was heavier in antiquity than it is today in some parts of North Africa (cf. J. Bradford *Ancient landscapes* (1957) 203). But in 1931 when the total population of mainland Italy was 36,306,780, only 6 of the 92 Italian provinces had a population density exceeding 270 inhabitants per km² (*Enc.it.* 19.739).

[4] For Siagu, see above, p.264 n.2. There is little doubt that the figures alleged for the built-up area of large African towns by early archaeologists are exaggerated (Thelepte 500 hectares; Diana Veteranorum 400 hectares; Althiburos 200 hectares; Gauckler (cited in p.264 n.2) 154; Tissot (cited *ibid.*) 2.484; Gauckler 144–6). Figures which appear more reliable (some inferred from town-plans) are Leptis Minor 120 hectares; Thaenae over 100 hectares; Thubursicu Numidarum 65 hectares; Thamugadi 50 hectares; Mactar 30 hectares; Thugga 20 hectares; Madauros 20 hectares; Muzuc (Henchir Khachoun) 15 hectares; Cuicul 12 hectares or more (plan in Babelon (cited in p.264 n.2) fe.66.7); plan in Gauckler (cited *ibid.*) 259; Gsell–Joly 'Khamissa' 26; C. Courtois *Timgad, antique Thamugadi* (1951) 19; G. C. Picard *Enc.art.ant.* s.v. Mactar; plan in Poinssot *Dougga*; Gsell–Joly (cited in p.261 n.1); Tissot (*op. cit.* p.264 n.2) 603; plan in L. Leschi *Djemila, antique Cuicul* (1953)).

consul bequeathed a capital of HS1 million to the town, whose income was to provide games and sportulae for the citizens.[1] The income at the interest-rate of 5% likely with a foundation of such size would be HS50,000.[2] If the games absorbed not more than half of the income, as parallels might reasonably suggest, the income available for sportulae would be HS25,000. The sportula-rates attested in Africa are no higher than those in Italy, where information is much more abundant; the highest popular rate specifically attested in Africa is HS4 per head, but there are only three examples of popular sportulae from these provinces.[3] In Italy the highest popular rate attested more than once is HS20, but the most frequent rate by far is HS4 per head.[4] This was a natural amount, since it corresponded with a single silver coin, the denarius.

If the consular gift was intended to provide for all male citizens, the total at a rate of HS4 per head might have been in the region of 6,250. In this case, the rate of distribution adopted by Pudentilla would have been higher than HS4 per head (if Apuleius's report is accurate). A total of 6,250 recipients would suggest a total free population of 21,900, which is quite conceivable for a major city such as Oea. 100 decurions and their relatives would raise the projected total to 22,250. The higher popular sportula rates attested in Italy are less likely in Africa, where the giving of sportulae does not seem to have become so much engrained in social practice. The free population figures which they would suggest are 11,600 (HS8) and 7,650 (HS12), including the decurions in each case.

The first of the Italian examples (in descending order of size) is Pliny's enormous gift which provided for the support of 100 of his freedmen at Comum late in Trajan's reign. The money was to be transferred in due course to the provision of an 'epulum' for the 'plebs urbana' at Comum, after the death of the original beneficiaries. The capital of HS1,866,666 represents an annual revenue between HS84,000 and HS100,000.[5] Since the prime purpose was the support of Pliny's dependants, the size of the gift can hardly have been calculated with close reference to the size of the *plebs urbana* at Comum. The gift appears to have been a generous provision for the feast which was its secondary objective. At the highest rate

---

[1] C. nos.249; 306. Oea has been almost entirely erased by the buildings of Tripoli. Though Tacitus records that the town was smaller than its neighbour Lepcis Magna (one of the biggest towns of Africa), the presence of municipal families with fortunes of HS4 and HS3 million in the mid-second century suggests that Oea was a place of importance (Tacitus *Hist.* 4.50; C. nos.383–4). Oea, Lepcis and Sabratha were the three coastal cities which gave Tripolitania its name; between them they controlled a substantial area whose agriculture was probably more extensive than it is today (for archaeological studies cf. R. G. Goodchild *PBSR* 19 (1951) 43–77; D. Oates *PBSR* 21 (1953) 81–117).

[2] See p.134. [3] C. nos.298; 304; 305.

[4] See p.142. [5] C. no.638 and note.

of popular benefit attested more than once (HS20), the number of beneficiaries would have been between 4,200 and 5,000.[1] On this basis the
citizen population of the urban centre might have been 14,700–17,500.
The population of the urban centre of Como recorded in the census of
1921 was 37,537 (56,937 in 1951).[2] Trajanic Comum must have been a
town of some size overall (including its considerable territory); Comum
had received three instalments of colonists, including 3,000 planted in the
early first century B.C., and 4,500 more from Caesar.[3] Although the totals
should not necessarily be combined, the Caesarian figure by itself implies
a free colonial population for Comum and its territory of roughly 15,700,
a total which must have been considerably increased by the earlier
colonists and the original inhabitants. A substantial town in a prosperous
part of Italy such as Comum is likely to have grown substantially larger
by the time of Trajan.

Two foundations allow some inferences about the number of citizens
at Spoletium in Umbria (modern Spoleto).[4] The larger gift (perhaps
Flavian) had a capital of HS1,500,000, which even approaches the size
of Pliny's foundation. At 5%, the rate of interest most likely with a fund
of this size, the income would be HS75,000.[5] It was to provide the
citizens ('municipes') with a dinner, accompanied or preceded by mead
and pastries, on the birthday of the equestrian donor ('aepulum et
crust(ulum) et mulsum'). Assuming that the cost of the feast lay within
the popular rates of benefit that are frequently attested,[6] and that the
mead and pastries cost no more than HS4 per head, the number of
recipients would be between 4,700 and 9,400 (the cost per head being
HS16–HS8).[6] The implied citizen population, men, women and children,
would reach 16,450–32,900.[7] In the second foundation at Spoletium
(which is probably Antonine in date), HS250,000 was given by a donor
during his lifetime to provide a dinner on his son's birthday for the
decurions ('ex...reditu...cenarent') together with the distribution of
sums of HS2 per head to the citizens ('municipes'). If there were the
usual 100 decurions and they received the highest of the common rates
of benefit for their class (HS20), the share of a 5% income remaining for
the distribution would suffice for 5,250 citizen recipients. If alternatively
the decurions received the higher rate of HS30, the number of popular
recipients would be only 4,750. The two foundations thus offer similar
possibilities in the region of 4,700 citizens. It is likely that the free

[1] See p.142.
[2] *Enc.it.* s.v. Como; Appendice 3 s.v. Como.
[3] Strabo 5.1.6. For territory of Comum cf. Chilver 46.
[4] C. nos. 639; 652. Bibliography of Spoletium in *Enc.art.ant.* s.v. Spoleto.
[5] See p.134. [6] HS4–HS12, see p.142.
[7] See p.264 n.4 above.

plebeian population thus indicated is not less than 16,450. From the details of another foundation given by the second donor, there appear to have been not less than 300 'seviri Augustales et compitales Larum Augustorum et magistri vicorum' at Spoletium.[1] If these are added to the decurions, the total free population, men, women and children, rises to 17,850, or nearly 18,000. If the territory of Spoletium extended to 800 km² as Beloch suggested, it is possible that not all of the inhabitants would have been in a position to benefit from distributions and meals held in the town centre on a certain day.[2] Thus it is not clear that the population figure need be complete. In 1951, the town of Spoleto had 13,729 inhabitants, and its surrounding *comune* of 349 km² a further 25,426 inhabitants.[3]

At Pisaurum, a port in Umbria (the modern Pesaro), a donor bequeathed HS400,000 to pay for an annual dinner for the citizens on his son's birthday ('ut...populo epulum...divideretur').[4] Since it was the *plebs urbana* who honoured the donor with the statue from whose base the inscription comes, it is conceivable that the benefit was restricted to this body (as at Comum). At the likely 5%, the income would have been HS20,000, sufficient for 1,666 shares at HS12, almost the highest popular rate of benefit.[5] At HS8 there would be 2,500 beneficiaries; at HS4, the most frequent rate, there would have been 5,000 beneficiaries. Pisaurum seems to have been a sizeable town with its own colleges of craftsmen (*fabri*), clothes dealers (*centonarii*), and shippers (*navicularii*).[6] One of the two higher totals is thus more plausible, implying a free plebeian population in the region of 8,750/18,550. The total may refer only to the urban centre (above); if it does, the lower figure is the more likely of the two. In 1951 the urban centre of Pesaro contained 34,647 inhabitants, and the surrounding *comune* of 127 km² a further 19,466 inhabitants.[7]

An equestrian donor at Sentinum in Umbria bequeathed HS120,000 under Domitian for a feast for the citizens on his birthday ('municipibus ...epulum').[8] At 5% the income would have been HS6,000.[9] This would suffice for 1,500 recipients at the lowest of the common popular rates.

[1] C. no.659: HS120,000 was given to these three groups collectively 'ut...eodem die in publico vescerentur'. At 5% (p.134) the income would be HS6,000. At the highest common rate of benefit, HS20, the income would provide for 300 diners (assuming that there was no differentiation between them). C. no.645a, which is fragmentary, appears to be a much larger foundation (HS450,000) of which the *magistri vicorum* were one of the beneficiaries.

[2] J. Beloch *Italische Bund* (1880) 145.

[3] *IX Censimento* s.v. Spoleto (prov. Perugia).

[4] C. no.648. Bibliography of Pisaurum, *Enc.art.ant.* s.v. Pesaro.

[5] See p.142.   [6] XI p.941.

[7] *IX Censimento* s.v. Pesaro (prov. Pesaro).

[8] C. no.658. Bibliography of Sentinum *Enc.art.ant.* s.v. Sentino.

[9] See p.134.

The other common rates would reduce the number of recipients to 750 (HS8) or 500 (HS12).[1] The free population is thus unlikely to have been more than 5,250 in all. Decurions and their families would presumably add another 100–300, depending on the size of the *ordo*; this would lead to a maximum free population of 5,550, though the actual total may have been only half this number. There is no modern town on the site of Sentinum. Sassoferrato, which has grown up nearby in the period since antiquity, had 3,598 inhabitants in 1951, with a further 9,890 in the surrounding *comune* of 135 km².[2]

At Petelia, a town in Bruttium (corresponding to the modern Strongoli), a donor under Antoninus Pius bequeathed a fund of HS100,000 whose purposes included a distribution to the citizens.[3] Virgil referred to this town as 'parva Petelia'.[4] The inscription is particularly valuable because (like the Siagu inscription) it gives explicitly all the details needed to infer the number of recipients. The interest-rate was 6%, and the income thus HS6,000. Of this total, HS1,200 was to pay for a distribution for the decurions, together with the cost of the feast at which the distribution took place ('ut...distributio fiat decurionibus epulantibus...deducto ex his sumptu strationis').[5] The Augustales were to receive HS600 for the same purpose, and HS200 was to be spent on a commemorative feast ('cena parentalicia'). The residue (HS4,000) was to be spent on sportulae of HS4 per head for the citizens of either sex according to the custom of the town ('municipibus Petelinis utriusque sexus ex more loci'). This was enough to benefit 1,000 recipients. If there had been a need for many more shares in the popular distribution, the lower rate of HS2 per head might well have been chosen. Nevertheless, the number 1,000 may not exactly represent the free adult population of the town, since it is a round total from a gift whose capital is also a round total. The actual number of potential recipients could have been as high as 1,300 without this being reflected in the conventional sportula-rates. But we can only use the figures as they stand. Extrapolating from the number of adult recipients, the total free plebeian population would have been roughly 1,750. The details of another gift by the same donor allow the inference that there were 30 decurions and 20 Augustales at Petelia.[6] Adding this further total of 50 and their dependants to the recipients of

---

[1] See p.142.

[2] *Enc.it.* s.v. Sentinum; *IX Censimento* s.v. Sassoferrato (prov. Ancona).

[3] C. no.664.

[4] *Aen.* 3.402. Bibliography of Petelia *Enc.art.ant.* s.v. Petelia.

[5] 'Stratio' evidently means feast here; compare the other inscription which quotes from the will of the same donor: 'ad instrumentum tricliniorum duum...arbitrio Augustalium, quo facilius strati[o]nibus publicis obire possint' (*ILS* 6469, ll.7–10).

[6] See pp.284–5.

the popular distribution and their dependants produces an overall free population of 1,925. If the plebeian adult population were as high as the 1,300 which would still be allowed within the terms of this gift (see above), the free population as a whole would be 2,360. No restriction of the gift to the *plebs urbana* is specified, but the phrase 'ex more loci' may indicate that there was such a restriction. It does not appear to refer to the explicit inclusion of women in the distribution, since we know that women did not participate in the other distribution attested at Petelia, which took place under Trajan (C. no.815). In the census of 1951 Strongoli had a population of 6,075 in the main centre and 819 in the adjoining *comune* of 85 km².[1]

At Corfinium in the territory of the Paeligni a donor gave HS50,000 for a distribution ('divisio') to the decurions and the whole citizen body ('universus populus'), probably in the early third century A.D.[2] At 5%–6% the income would have been HS2,500–3,000. Corfinium had been a notable city under the Republic; under the Empire it is recorded as having a number of municipal organisations which might suggest that its size was not entirely negligible. There were the common 'seviri et Augustales', a college of craftsmen (fabri), a college of 'venatores', and an organisation of stage performers, the 'operae urbanae scabillarii'.[3] The present gift is so small that the population which it implies cannot be anything but low; but it should probably be interpreted in terms of lower rates of benefit rather than higher. If there were 100 decurions who received the lowest of the common rates for their class (HS8), the income remaining for popular sportulae would be enough for 425–550 shares at the most frequent of the popular rates (HS4). If the benefits were instead at the lowest attested rates for these categories of recipient, HS4 and HS2 respectively, the number of popular beneficiaries would be 1,050–1,300. The projected total free population (including the assumed 100 decurions) will be 1,925–2,275, on the first hypothesis, and 3,680–4,550 on the second. The low sportula-rates on which the higher projection is based are less well attested; and the single payment of sportulae which the donor made at the dedication of his monument contained notably high rates (decurions HS30, *seviri Augustales* HS20 and people HS8).[4] The population of the modern town ('Corfinio' since 1923, previously Pèntima) was 2,047 in the census of 1951, with 68 in the adjoining *comune* of 18 km².[5]

---

[1] *IX Censimento* s.v. Strongoli (prov. Catanzaro).
[2] C. no.673. Bibliography of Corfinium *Enc.art.ant.* s.v. Corfinium.
[3] IX p.297.
[4] C. no.763.
[5] *Enc.it.* s.v. Corfinio; *IX Censimento* s.v. Corfinio (prov. L'Aquila).

A donor at Rudiae, the birthplace of Ennius in ancient Calabria, gave a foundation of HS80,000 under Hadrian to provide a distribution at specified rates to four groups in the town, 'viscerationis nomine'.[1] The decurions were to receive HS20, the Augustales HS12, the Mercuriales HS10 and the 'populus' HS8 per man. At 5% to 6% the income of HS80,000 would be HS4,000–4,800. If there were 100 decurions, 20 Augustales, and 20 Mercuriales, the number of shares available for the people would be 195–295.[2] If the decurions numbered only 30 as at Castrimoenium and Petelia, the number of popular shares would be 370–470.[3] The total free population would thus range between 1,170–1,520 and 1,540–1,890. Judging from the small size of the town, the *ordo* may well have been no larger than that at Petelia, another minor town of southern Italy. In this case, the higher estimates of population will apply. There is no modern town on the site with which to make comparisons. Rudiae was very close to Lupiae (the modern Lecce).

A donor at Fabrateria Vetus in the territory of the Hernici gave HS25,000 in the third century A.D. to pay for an annual distribution of sportulae to the *ordo* and *populus* on his birthday.[4] Fabrateria Vetus was an obscure town under the Empire, which we might expect to be small.[5] It contained two colleges, the 'cultores antistites deae Cereris' and the 'iuvenes Herculani' whose numbers appear to have been relatively low.[6] An earlier dedication to a patron indicates the presence of non-citizen residents of the town in appreciable numbers in the second century: the 'municipes popularesque' probably denote citizens on the one hand, and owners of property resident at the town who did not hold local citizenship on the other.[7] The income of the foundation at 5%–6% would have been HS1,250–1,500. An *ordo* of 100 which received the lowest of the common

---

[1] C. no.667. 'Visceratio' here evidently means a meal, not a sacrifice, and so the formula is analogous to the gift of sportulae 'epulationis nomine' in C. no.293 (Abthugni). Cf. Seneca *Ep.* 19.10: 'Nam sine amico visceratio leonis ac lupi vita est.' Also *Digesta* 32.54. For Rudiae, IX p.6; *RE* s.v. Rudiae 1.

[2] For Augustales, see pp.284–5.

[3] See p.284.

[4] C. no.679. For Fabrateria, X p.552; *Enc.it.* s.v. Fabrateria.

[5] Cf. Nissen 2.655.

[6] The same donor gave the 'cultores antistites deae Cereris' a foundation of HS4,000 for sportulae on his birthday (C. no.708), and a distribution of sportulae of HS50 per head on a single occasion (C. no.828). It is unlikely that the size of the ephemeral outlay would have been more than one-quarter of the value of the foundation, at most. This would place the membership at a maximum of 20, since 20 shares of HS50 each cost HS1,000. Another donor gave the iuvenes Herculani a foundation of HS2,000 for sportulae, and a single distribution of HS2 per head (C. nos.721; 1040). It is unlikely that the benefit provided by the foundation would have been any higher than the sportula in the ephemeral outlay (see p.262). If it was in fact the same, the membership (at interest of 5–6%) would be 50–60.

[7] X p.552 and X 5653.

rates of benefit for decurions (HS8) would leave HS450–700 for the citizens. At HS4 per head, the most frequent popular rate, the number of popular recipients on this basis would be between 112 and 175. A smaller *ordo* of 30 decurions (as at Castrimoenium and Petelia) would mean 282–315 recipients in all and a projected total citizen population of 1,060–1,280. Falvaterra, which seems to correspond with Fabrateria Vetus, had a population of 295 in 1951, with a further 696 in the surrounding *comune* of 13 km².[1]

At Saturnia in Etruria a local magistrate gave HS8,000 in A.D. 234 for an annual distribution to the Augustales and *plebs urbana* of the town ('confreq(uentatione) et spor(tulatione)'). At the dedication of his statue he had distributed sportulae of HS4 per head to the citizens ('populus').[2] At the highest interest-rate that is likely in the absence of any explicit description (6%), the annual income of the fund would be HS480. Even at the lowest sportula-rate attested in Italy (HS1) this allows scope for only 480 recipients.[3] The Augustales however are not explicitly recorded as receiving less than HS2 per head anywhere in Italy. The maximum possible number of recipients might thus be lower than 480 (460 in all if there were as few as 20 Augustales). Adding 30–100 decurions, the total free urban population might be 1,720–1,960. But if the sportula-rate were HS2 for the plebs as well as the Augustales, the total would be only 945–1,190 inhabitants. However, the figure explicitly covers only the urban inhabitants; those living in the surrounding territory would no doubt have added substantially to the population as a whole. We know that the original colonists of Saturnia received shares of 10 iugera of land per head in 183 B.C. If the colonists numbered 2,000, as in the other two citizen colonies founded in that year,[4] the area of territory accounted for by individual assignations would be not less than 50 km², though there might have been other territory as well. The population of the sub-*comune* of Saturnia in 1951 was 526 in the centre, with 272 inhabitants in the outlying territory (whose area is probably of the order of 50 km²).[5]

None of these estimates include any allowance for slaves. It is quite clear that slave-owning was deeply rooted in Roman society, and that slaves provided a large part of the labour-force in town and country. Slave numbers must have varied according to the local concentrations of wealth sufficient to afford slaves; the ratio between free and servile

---

[1] *Enc.it.* s.v. Fabrateria; *IX Censimento* s.v. Falvaterra (prov. Frosinone).

[2] C. nos.697; 1021. For Saturnia, A. Minto *Monumenti antichi* 30 (1925) 585–702.

[3] C. nos.1049–50. The other evidence for the size of Saturnia suggests that the initial sportula would not have been sustained in the terms of the foundation (cf. p.263).

[4] Livy 39.55. Cf. W. V. Harris *Rome in Etruria & Umbria* (1971) 156.

[5] *IX Censimento* s.v. Saturnia (prov. Grosseto, comune Manciano). The average area of the 8 sub-communes in Manciano is 49 km², and the average population was 1,187 in 1951.

TABLE 7. *Estimated city-populations related to modern figures*

Town	Estimated free population	Estimated total population	Date (A.D.)	Population of modern centre (1951)	Net population of modern *comune* (1951)	Area of modern *comune* (km²)
Africa						
Oea	(22,250? +)	(28,200? +)	150/85	—	—	—
Siagu	4,000/7,000	5,000/9,000	(100/220)	—	—	—
Italy						
Spoletium VI	17,850	23,000	(69/161)	13,729	25,426	349
Comum XI	14,700/17,500	18,900/22,500	111/13	56,937	13,510	37
Pisaurum VI	9,800/18,550	12,600/23,800	(120/80)	34,647	19,466	127
Sentinum VI	2,725/5,550	3,500/7,200	88/96	3,598	9,890	135
Corfinium IV	1,925/2,375	2,480/2,820	(200/40)	2,047	68	18
Petelia III	1,925	2,480	138/61	6,075	819	85
Rudiae II	1,540/1,890	1,980/2,430	117/38	—	—	—
Fabrateria Vetus I	1,060/1,280	1,360/1,650	(200/40)	295	594	13
Saturnia VII	945/1,720	1,210/2,220	234	526	272	(c. 50?)

population was bound to vary correspondingly from town to town. For practical purposes, there is little alternative to Galen's statistic about the ratio at Pergamum in the second century A.D., where he suggests that there were as many slaves as there were male citizens.[1] This will mean increasing each of the figures for the free population as a whole by 28.6%. The results are given in the third column of Table 7.

The geographical meaning of these estimates is not always clear. We know that the gifts at Comum and Saturnia benefited only the urban population. The same may be true of the gift at Pisaurum, though the evidence is less clear. It is difficult to believe that all the inhabitants of a territory as large as 800 km² can have gathered in the town-centre to receive distributions: thus the figure for Spoletium might refer primarily to the urban area (but see below). Some other small towns besides Saturnia may have had this restriction also. The estimates for Petelia and Rudiae, rendered in terms of the average city-territories of their

[1] Galen 5.49 (Kuhn). Galen's proportion (which makes slaves roughly 22% of the total population, on the age-ratio adopted here, see above, p.264 n.4) is considerably more conservative than the proportion of 40% recently suggested for Augustan Italy (Brunt 124; 702–3). If a proportion of 40% were adopted as an average figure for slaves in imperial Italy, the final totals given here for free population and slaves combined would need to be increased by a further 29.5%, or nearly one-third (a proportion for slaves of 22.2% means adding 28.6% to the free total, whereas a proportion of 40% means adding 66.7%; 166.7 is 29.5% larger than 128.6).

regions, might produce a hypothetical population density as low as 3 inhabitants per km², if interpreted as applying to the whole city-territory.[1] Such a figure appears extremely low, even for the thinly populated south. Beloch and Brunt estimate 24–28 inhabitants per km² as an average density for Italy as a whole, while the school of Nissen and Frank would estimate an average density approaching 56 inhabitants per km².[2] Thus it may be more likely that the gifts at Petelia and Rudiae benefited only urban inhabitants, and omitted those living on the city-territory. At Corfinium, however, the use of the phrase 'universus populus' seems to imply that the whole citizen population of adult males benefited from the distribution.

Even if the majority of the figures for Italian towns apply primarily to the urban centre, comparisons with modern figures will have only limited value. Patterns of population distribution are virtually bound to have shifted as a result of the economic and political changes of the last two millennia. The centres whose inscriptions survive well enough to leave detailed evidence about antiquity will often tend to be those that have developed least in the interim. In 1951 only 41% of the working population of Italy was employed in agriculture, probably less than half the proportion in Roman Italy.

The ratios between the two main estimates for the population of Augustan Italy and the population of mainland Italy in 1951, are 1 to 3 and 1 to 6.[3] The discrepancies between the present estimates and the modern figures for corresponding urban centres (where comparison is possible) are less great. At Spoletium and Saturnia the ratio is even reversed: the proportions are 1.7 to 1 and 2.3 to 1. At Pisaurum the ratio is between 1 to 1.5 and 1 to 2.7. At Petelia the ratio is about 1 to 2.5. The ratio at Comum is between 1 to 2.5 and 1 to 3.

This configuration may throw doubts on the interpretation of some of the estimates for ancient cities. It is possible that the most extreme ratio for a large town, an estimated population for Roman Spoletium which is half as large again as the census figure for the town centre in 1951, should in fact be read as a population figure for the whole territory

---

[1] See Table in Appendix 5, showing the average land-area per town in each regio. This calculation can make no allowance for *ager publicus* or infertile territory, and it has to assume that different cities in the same regio would have territories of roughly similar size.

[2] Beloch 507, 6 million (24 inhabitants per km²); Beloch *Klio* 3 (1903) 471–90, 7–8 million (28–32 inhabitants per km²); Brunt 126, 7 million (28 inhabitants per km²); Nissen 2.118, 10 million (40 free inhabitants per km², not counting slaves); T. Frank *CP* 19 (1924) 340, 14 million (56 inhabitants per km² overall). Recent support for the Nissen–Frank view of the Augustan census-figures in T. P. Wiseman *JRS* 59 (1969) 59–75 (cf. Brunt 700, 702, 706–7).

[3] For estimates for antiquity see n.2. The population of mainland Italy in 1951 was 41,852,765 (*Enc.it.* Appendice 3.1.915).

of the city. Although in modern terms it is difficult to envisage a gathering of all the free inhabitants of an area of 800 km² in a city for the purpose of receiving a small cash-handout or a dinner, it is still possible that such gatherings did take place in antiquity.[1] Pliny speaks of a somewhat analogous assembly on his estates each year on the anniversary day of a rustic temple of Ceres, when a great crowd from the whole district gathered there to make offerings and to transact business.[2] The reversal of the ratio at Saturnia is evidently the result of the decline of the town to the standing of a village in the period since antiquity. In view of the likely size of the original colony, the figure estimated for Saturnia in the third century A.D. is quite possible. If the ratios of 1 to 2.7 at Pisaurum and 1 to 2.5 at Comum and Petelia are abnormally low, this too should probably be explained by the failure of the towns on these sites to retain the relative importance which they once possessed. (The figures for Corfinium, Fabrateria Vetus and Sentinum may refer to territory as well as to urban area, and thus cannot be subjected to direct comparison with modern data.)

Insofar as they can be used as a basis for generalisation, these deductions offer support for higher rather than lower estimates of Italian population in the Principate. But the sample is too small to be a sound guide by itself. Changes in the relative importance of towns may create powerful distortions in any general trend, which cannot be detected when the examples are so few. Nevertheless, the sample still provides a quantitative index of the relative demographic importance under the Principate of different Italian cities. Although the estimates do not include figures for any of the bigger towns of Italy (such as Mediolanum, Patavium, Aquileia, Verona, or Capua)[3] the largest figure is still as high as 23,000 (Spoletium). At the bottom of the scale are towns numbering one or two thousand inhabitants (though the figures given may not always include the population of outlying territory). Petelia, evidently small in Virgil's day, numbered less than 2,000 free inhabitants under Antoninus Pius. In the early third century, Fabrateria Vetus and perhaps Saturnia appear to have been even smaller. Whatever the territorial uncertainties, it is realistic to see the factor of difference between the size of the largest and the smallest towns as being at least 20. These variants are much greater than those envisaged in such legislation as the rescript of Antoninus Pius

---

[1] Willingness to organise popular benefits on a gigantic scale is shown by the dinner given for 40,000 citizens at Ephesus in the second or early third century (*JOAI* 26 (1930) Beibl. 57), as well as by the feasts given by the Emperor at Rome attended by senators, knights and people (cf. Martial 8.50; 5.49).

[2] *Ep.* 9.39.

[3] Cf. Strabo 5.1.6–7; 5.4.10. Ausonius *Ord.urb.nob.* 7–9. Chilver 45–58. Frank *ESAR* 5.108–20; 133–4.

determining a tariff of professional immunities, which allowed for three sizes of town, or the *senatus consultum* on gladiator prices in A.D. 177/80, which allowed for two.[1]

At Saturnia the population figure specifically refers to the *plebs urbana*. The walled area of Saturnia was about 24 hectares.[2] The estimated population is so small that it is reasonable to assume that all the urban inhabitants lived within the walls in the early third century. The density that the estimates imply is still low: between 51 and 94 inhabitants per hectare (estimated population being 1,210–2,220). This is comparable with the overall population density of Hamburg in 1890, when the population was about 570,000: 76 inhabitants per hectare. It is much lower than the density of any central zone of Hamburg corresponding in size with the area of Saturnia.[3] Some other ancient town-populations seem to have been much more thickly concentrated. At Alexandria in Egypt the free population in the later first century B.C. was over 300,000 free inhabitants.[4] As Alexandria had little effective territory of its own at this date,[5] most of the total should refer to inhabitants of the main urban area; it may be fair to assume that after allowing for slaves, the total population of the walled area would have been not less than 300,000. The walls and water-front of Alexandria enclosed an area of roughly 920 hectares.[6] The resulting density is 326 inhabitants per hectare; if the whole population (including a number of slaves corresponding with the proportion at Pergamum) lived within the walls, the density would be 420. Population estimates for Ostia and Pompeii have no basis in any ancient statistic, and can only be based on appraisal of the extensive ruins. Modern estimates give population densities for the walled area alone of 300–840 to Ostia and 230 to Pompeii.[7] The maximum estimated for Ostia is very high even in comparison with densely populated nineteenth-century cities. The densest population of any part of London in 1801 (when the population was about 960,000) was 527

---

[1] *Digesta* 27.1.6.2; *ILS* 5163, ll.47–8.

[2] Plan drawn by Pasqui (*Mem.Linc., cl.sci.mor.* 10 (1882) 140, tav.1; reproduced by Minto *Monumenti antichi* 30 (1925) 491). Nissen's unexplained estimate of the area of Saturnia as 50 hectares seems to have no value (Nissen 2.37).

[3] Weber 467–8.

[4] Diodorus 17.52.6.

[5] Cf. A. H. M. Jones *Cities of the Eastern Roman Provinces*[2] (1971) 302–5.

[6] Area from Beloch 486 (corroborated by plan in *Enc.art.ant.* s.v. Alessandria).

[7] Calza estimates the population of the walled area of Ostia (69 hectares) as 36,000, Meiggs as not more than 58,000 (Meiggs 532–4). J. E. Packer, on the basis of a detailed survey of housing types, estimates the population of the walled area of Ostia as being between 20,491 and 24,491 (*JRS* 57 (1967) 86 and *The Insulae of Imperial Ostia* (1971) (*Mem. Amer.Acad. Rome* 31) 70). Beloch estimated the population of the walled area of Pompeii (65 hectares) as 15,000 (*Atene e Roma* 1 (1898) 274).

inhabitants per hectare in Westminster. In Berlin in 1890 (when the population was about 1,480,000), the population density of the zone within 1 km of the town hall was 326 inhabitants per hectare; in the zone between 1 and 2 km from the town hall the density was 540.[1] The higher Ostian estimates are surely exaggerated, even though ancient standards may have allowed less living-space per head to slaves and members of the free proletariat than those which obtained for any significant part of the population of European capitals in the nineteenth century.

The three ancient parallels suggest densities of population in large cities which dwarf the density of the relatively small town of Saturnia. But much higher possible densities must be expected at large towns, chiefly because of the greater prevalence of multi-storey buildings. The average building-height for residential buildings at Ostia is reckoned from the remains as being between $2\frac{1}{2}$ and 4 storeys.[2] Probably most small towns would have few buildings of more than two storeys, and many of their buildings would have only one. There might also be variations in the relative area absorbed by public buildings, streets and even gardens. Furthermore, the town walls themselves were a permanent feature whose position was usually fixed once for all (most often at an early stage in the town's history); they would not normally be moved either when there was a sharp decline in population, or when there was an enormous increase in numbers.[3] Thus relationships between the walled areas of different towns can be highly deceptive about the respective numbers of inhabitants.[4] It is likely that urban population densities could vary between different ancient towns by a factor of five (as suggested by the present figures) or even more.

THE SIZE OF TOWN-ORGANISATIONS

Curiae and colleges

In the West the town-organisation which came closest to being a popular assembly was the 'curia', a plebeian association found in many African cities under the Principate.[5] No direct equivalent of the African *curia* is

---

[1] Weber 463–4; 465; 467; 468. Towns that show a much higher density in the twentieth century (New York, Singapore, Calcutta, Hong Kong) are hardly relevant (C. Clark *Population growth and land use* (1967) 340–1).

[2] Meiggs 532–4. J. E. Packer *JRS* 57 (1967) 84.

[3] For the fluctuations in urban population density that occur with different patterns of growth, cf. Weber 458–69.

[4] Beloch's attempts to gauge population in the main cities of Roman Italy by translating walled area into a number of inhabitants on the basis of a fixed density are thus misleading (*Atene e Roma* 1 (1898) 257–78). For objections, see also Chilver 51–2.

[5] The African *curia* (a club with plebeian membership) should not be confused with the *curia*, a building where the town-council met, nor with the *curia*, a name for the town-council

attested on a significant scale in other parts of the Empire, though *curiae* which may be of a similar type are known at Turris Libisonis in Sardinia, and at Lanuvium in Italy.[1] The seven organisations of 'vicani' found at Ariminum may provide a rough parallel at another Italian town. At Neapolis there were 'phretriae', numbering nine or more.[2]

In municipal charters from Italy and Spain, 'curia' is used to describe a voting division of the whole citizen population of the town.[3] The number of members of an African *curia* was substantial, but it does not appear that the African *curiae* were also assemblies of the whole citizen population.[4] At one African town, Simitthus, substantial sections of the charter of a *curia* have survived; it belongs to the reign of Commodus.[5] The document shows a series of regulations in the form of payments for office within the *curia* and fines for maladministration and breaches of etiquette. The regulations clearly recall the practice of the Italian funerary and dining clubs.[6] In both contexts interest in holding dinners and in providing for the burial of members[7] are dominant motifs. In the African *curiae* those wishing to serve as officers of the *curia* had to pay for the privilege; the same was probably true of entry to the *curia* as a member (the inscription is incomplete).[8] In the Italian clubs membership

itself which started to gain currency in the second century A.D. (cf. Pliny *Ep.* 10.80), and had become the normal usage (in place of 'ordo') by the fourth century.

[1] *ILS* 6766 (the 23 *curiae* of Turris Libisonis subscribe for a statue); *ILS* 6199 (a distribution to the *curiae* at Lanuvium and a dinner for the *curia mulierum*); 6201; 6202. Cf. A. Donati *Rivista storica dell'antichità* 1 (1971) 235-7. The *curiae* at Lanuvium seem to have been limited in size (cf. 'municipes, curiales [e]t curia...ob merita eius' *ILS* 6201). The writer no longer accepts Hirschfeld's suggestion that *ILS* 6199 (from Lanuvium) should be read as containing a reference to 'cur(i)is n(umero) XXIIII' (O. Hirschfeld *Kleine Schriften* 505 n.1). As Dessau saw, this phrase in fact denotes a payment of sportulae at a rate of HS24 ('n(ummos) XXIIII'; the alternative leaves the phrase 'viritim divisit' without an object). For the omission of the symbol HS in the notation of sums of money see also C. nos.643 + 648; 803; 1051. The 5 *curiae* at Savaria classified by Gervasio as municipal were in fact sub-divisions of a college; there were only 86 members in all in A.D. 188, and they included a number of public slaves (III 4150, see p.2555; Ruggiero 2.1394; see *RE* supp. 9.604).

A few inscriptions show the existence of *curiae* with non-Roman names in parts of Gaul, Germany and Britain. See C. B. Rüger *Epigraphische Studien* 9 (1972) 251-60.

[2] See below p.282. Kaibel *IG* 14 p.191; see C. no.1052.

[3] *ILS* 6089, 52; 55; 59; 6086, 15.

[4] For the African *curiae* as bodies of limited size, not comprehensive units of the citizens, see J. Toutain *Cités romaines de la Tunisie* (1896) 284-5; Picard *Civilisation* 28 and *BAC* n.s. 4 (1968) 223-4. For the African *curiae* instead as comprehensive divisions of the citizens, see S. Gsell *Histoire ancienne de l'Afrique du Nord* 2.232-3; M. Gervasio, Ruggiero 2.1394-8; J. Roman *Annales de la Fac. de droit d'Aix* 4 (1910) 85-123; Kotula *passim*; M. Leglay *Ant.afr.* 5 (1971) 134-5; Gascou 59. Kotula provides an up-to-date list of references to the African *curiae*. Cf. now Kotula *Eos* 60 (1972) 115-28; *Klio* 54 (1972) 227-37.

[5] *ILS* 6824, the charter of the curia Iovis, dated to A.D. 185.

[6] Cf. C. nos.431 and 1388; 429 and 1394-5; 433 and 1397.

[7] Cf. *ILS* 6845ᵃ and VIII 3298.   [8] C. nos. 430; 433; 434.

was conditional on payment of an entrance-fee.[1] Two of the Italian clubs explicitly had membership of restricted size,[2] and payment of an entry-fee is an indication in itself that membership was restricted to those willing to pay in order to join. When the African *curiae* show strong resemblances to these clubs in other respects, it is most unlikely that they can still have been a comprehensive organisation of the citizens as a whole. One of the *curiae* at Lambaesis actually contained a specialised membership (the 'curia Hadriana veteranorum leg(ionis) III Aug(ustae)').[3]

Other inscriptions explicitly show that membership of the African *curiae* was restricted. At seven towns, the 'curiae' and the 'populus' appear side by side as separate entities (Theveste, (Chaouat), Thamugadi, Thugga, Thizika, Mactar and Madauros).[4] It has been suggested that 'populus' might mean women citizens as well as men in such cases.[5] But there is no explicit evidence for the inclusion of women in distributions in the African provinces.[6] Furthermore, in one of the inscriptions, the 'curiae' receive sportulae and the 'populus' is given wine (n. 4 below). It is unlikely that women can have been intended here, since the giving of wine to women was often forbidden or restricted in the Roman

---

[1] C. nos.1391; 1382; *ILS* 7213, ll.5–8.

[2] C. nos.1382; *ILS* 7213, l.5 ('hominibus n(umero) LX sub hac condicione, ut ne plures adlegantur, quam numerus s(upra) s(criptus)').

[3] VIII 18214; 18234; *AE* 1916, 22; *AE* 1968, 646 = *Ant.afr.* 5 (1971) 133.

[4] 'Curiis quoque et Augustalibus aureos binos et populo vinum dedit' (VIII 16556 = *ILS* 6839); 'epulum curiis et universo populo dedit' (VIII 25371 = *ILS* 5472); 'curiis epulum et gymnasium populo' (*AE* 1941 46); 'curiis e[pulum et universo] populo gymnasia praestentur' (VIII 26591); 'in populum [et curia]les conlatas' (*AE* 1952, 41); '[c]uriae et p[opulus]' (*AE* 1960, 115); 'epulum curiis et gymnasium populo' (*ILAlg* 1.2130).

[5] Kotula 59 and n.34. Kotula maintains that his equation of 'populus' with men and women citizens is substantiated by an inscription from Bisica: '[d]ecuriones sportulis muneravit civesque et populos universos non solum propriae urbis verum etiam (urbium) vicinarum epulis...ministravit' (VIII 23880). But 'populi' here seems to denote non-citizen residents, who are sometimes known in Africa, as in Italy, by their technical name of *incolae* (*ILS* 6818, Sicca, 'incolae qui intra continentia coloniae nostrae aedificia morabuntur'). For the inclusion of 'incolae' in gifts and distributions together with the citizens, see C. nos.248; 1001; 1002; 1026. An objection could be raised to considering the *curiae* as bodies of restricted size, on the ground that if 'populus' could mean 'incolae' when contrasted with 'cives', it might also mean 'incolae' and not 'cives' when contrasted with 'curiae'. The inscriptions in which such juxtapositions occur would then no longer imply in themselves that the *curiae* were bodies of limited size separate from the citizens as a whole (examples in n.4 above). In fact this hypothesis is most unlikely: the usage in the Bisica inscription is abnormal, and it remains true that the rules of the *curiae* are those characteristic of colleges of limited size, while the gift-inscriptions suggest that the size of the *curiae* varied too little to indicate that they were comprehensive divisions of the citizens of each town.

[6] The appearance of women among the worshippers responsible for two cult dedications at Mactar in the late third century A.D. belongs to an entirely different context (VIII 23400–1). Women may have been included in a gift at Siagu (see p.264), but the gift does not belong to one of the standard types, and the rate of distribution is abnormally low (cf. p.81).

world.[1] This evidence implies that the African 'curiae' were a series of clubs of limited size, and that the 'populus' mentioned in these inscriptions was the remainder of the male citizens, who did not belong to the clubs.

The one concrete description that might point in the opposite direction is a statue dedication at Thubursicu Numidarum by the 'o[rdo et popul]us in cu[rias con]tributus'.[2] At first sight the formula (if correctly restored) suggests that at this town the *curiae* were comprehensive units of all the citizens, however difficult such a conclusion may be in face of explicit evidence to the contrary at other African towns. But the phrase, which is not attested in any other text, is probably an ambiguous variant on the use of 'populus' to mean the membership of a college or association. In two colleges in Italy (both second century A.D.) the body of members was called the 'populus'.[3] This usage was certainly applied to the African *curiae*. Dedications were made at Sufetula by the 'universus populus curiarum' ('the whole membership of the curiae'), and at Althiburos by the 'populus curiarum X' ('the membership of the ten curiae').[4] In the formula at Thubursicu, the phrase 'populus in curias contributus' probably has the same force, restricting 'populus' to a meaning narrower than that contained in the stock phrase 'ordo et populus' by itself. The formula apparently means 'the town-council and (those citizens) organised in curiae'. A formal assembly of all the citizens in the voting divisions adopted once each year for the election of magistrates would in any case hardly be appropriate to the voting of a single statue of a civic benefactor. In fact there are virtually no references to the municipal voting divisions called 'curiae' whose existence is known from municipal charters in Italy and Spain (p.278 n.3) other than in the charters themselves.

The evidence of gifts to the *curiae* also suggests that their size was somewhat standardised. The Italian evidence considered above shows that the size of towns varied considerably in the Roman world as it does today. If the African *curiae* were in fact comprehensive organisations of the plebs, the size of their membership should be a direct reflection of the

---

[1] M. Durry *REL* 33 (1955) 108–13. In the rules of a men's college at Rome (in A.D. 153), the female donor of a foundation included herself among the recipients of cash sportulae given from her fund, but was the only recipient who did not take part in the drinking which she had also paid for (*ILS* 7213, l.12).

[2] *ILAlg* 1.1295.

[3] See also G. C. Picard *BAC* n.s. 4 (1968) 223. *ILS* 7212, 1.27 'homines tres, qui funeris eius curam agant et rationem populo reddere debebunt sine dolo m[a]lo'; 2.2 'Si quis intestatus decesserit, is arbitrio quinq(uennalis) et populi funerabitur.' *ILS* 7213, ll.3–4: 'solarium tectum...in quo populus colleg(i)i...epuletur'; l.11: 'populo sing(ulis) (denarium) (unum)'; l.12: 'populo (vinum) s(extarios) (tres)'. The members of another college are referred to as the 'plebs' (*ILS* 7313). See also *ILS* 3 p.719.

[4] VIII 11349; *ILAf* 138. *ILS* 5783.

population of the town to which they belonged. (The number of *curiae* per town was more or less standardised at 10 or 11 per town, see below.) But in fact the amounts given for dinners for the *curiae* vary surprisingly little from one town to another. At Uthina under Hadrian HS300 per *curia* was given for a dinner repeated annually. At Theveste a single *curia* received HS288 for a dinner, and another gift probably allowed HS225 per *curia*. At Abthugni each *curia* received HS240 for a dinner. At Mactar the rate was probably HS250 per *curia*, assuming that the town had ten *curiae*. While it is conceivable that the closeness of these figures is the result of a series of coincidences, it is more likely that the resemblances point to a number of members that was relatively constant from one town to another. There is one town where the feast cost was evidently much higher, the anonymous community at Zawiet-el-Laâla, where HS5,000 was given for a feast for all the *curiae*, perhaps indicating a benefit of HS500 for each *curia*.[1]

An inscription from Thamugadi listing the members of the 'curia Commodiana' in A.D. 211/12 contains 52 names, the twelfth of which is that of the 'magister' of the *curia*.[2] The membership was evidently at least 50 per *curia* at Thuburbo Maius, where a donor in A.D. 225 gave the decurions HS4 per head and the *curiae* HS200 each;[3] the members of the *curiae* could not have received more than HS4 per head (which meant not less than 50 shares per *curia*) without subverting the normal rules of precedence. We do not know for certain that the Thamugadi *curia* was at full strength, although a serious deficit would hardly be advertised in this way. If its total indicates a normal membership in the region of 50–60 members, the level of benefit implied in the feast-provisions will be roughly HS4–HS6 per head. This compares with costs of 'epula' for members of the plebs and colleges in Italy which range between HS6 and HS2 per head;[4] at Rome the rank and file members of a college received a simple meal costing between HS4.5 and HS6.2 per head under Antoninus Pius.[5]

A membership of 60 is explicitly stated in the charter of the Rome college. A funerary club at Alburnum in Dacia had 54 members at one time. A 'collegium salutare...' at Rome had 58 members, the 'cultores collegii Silvani' at Philippi 69, and the 'ordo adlectorum scaenicorum' at Bovillae 60 members.[6] At Mustis in Africa one of the *curiae*, which may have been typical, was divided into at least three '*classes*'.[7] This

---

[1] C. nos.272; 273; 277; 276; 275; 271.
[2] *CRAI* (1947) 95 = Leschi 243–4. Cf. *BAC* n.s. 6 (1970) 187–8.
[3] C. nos.301; 308.   [4] C. nos.1079g–k.
[5] See Appendix 15 and p.140.
[6] *ILS* 7213; 7215a; VI 30983; III 633; XIV 2408.
[7] *AE* 1968, 593; 588.

recalls the division of colleges elsewhere into 'decuriae'.[1] The basic size of *decuriae* in colleges was usually 20 members or thereabouts,[2] or more rarely 10.[3] Possibly the Mustis *curiae* had 3 *'classes'* of 20 members each[4] and a total membership of 60 for each *curia*.

The number of *curiae* per town is attested as 10 at Althiburos in Byzacena and at Lambaesis in Numidia. There were 11 *curiae* per town at Thuburbo Maius in Zeugitana, at Theveste in Numidia Proconsularis, and Lepcis Magna in Tripolitania. The details of an intricate foundation given at Abthugni indicate with little doubt that there were 10 *curiae* at this town.[5] These six figures, showing three towns with 10 *curiae* and three towns with 11, are enough to suggest that 10–11 was the standard number of *curiae* per town. If membership was generally of the order of 50–60 per *curia*, the total number of members per town would have been between 500 and 660 in most cases. In small towns this would be a large proportion of the male population, at big towns quite a small proportion. Actual numbers would vary with the efficiency of the officials concerned in maintaining membership. Size might also depend on the capacity of the local plebs to afford the payments involved in being a member of a curia. As a somewhat privileged group, who were accorded a favourable place in civic distributions, the *curiae* were probably an attractive goal for the social ambitions of the small man who had little prospect of gaining membership of the town-council.

We know of the existence of *curiae* at Lanuvium in Italy in the late second or early third century, without having any clue as to their size or numbers. The presence of a 'curia mulierum' is enough to show that these *curiae* were not voting divisions of the plebs. There were also 23 *curiae* at Turris Libisonis in Sardinia. Since this town lay in a former area of Carthaginian power, it may have retained Punic influences also felt in African cities.[6]

A large-scale collegiate organisation of a non-specialised kind is also attested at Ariminum on the Adriatic coast. Ariminum had seven *vici*, whose members, the 'vicani', led a corporate existence attested by a

---

[1] See *ILS* 7314; 7238; 7320; 7352; 7235 etc. (*ILS* 3 p.719).

[2] III 4150; XIV 4569; 160; VI 9405; III 633; XI 1449; *AE* 1929, 161.

[3] VI 10396; IX 3188; VI 631; 30983. Cf. Columella *de r.r.* 1.9.7.

[4] There seem to have been roughly 20 'seniores curiae Sabinae' at Lambaesis in A.D. 222/35 (VIII 2714; each of the two surviving columns contains 7 names, and a further column is evidently missing).

[5] VIII 16472; p.283; *ILTun* 728; *Revue africaine* (1956) 310; *IRT* p.263, index IX; C. no.262 and note. There were apparently not less than 10 *curiae* at Mopthi, to judge from a dedication by the 'cultores cur.X Caelestinae' (*AE* 1942–3, 58).

[6] See p.278 n.1 above. It is difficult to see why *curiae* of the type found in Africa are virtually confined to one group of provinces and do not recur on a significant scale in any other part of the West, unless they were a specifically African, and hence Punic, phenomenon.

number of dedications. A suggestion that the *vicani* were simply the whole plebs of the town under another name[1] encounters difficulties. The 'vicani vicorum VII' took precedence over the colleges of *fabri, centonarii* and *dendrophori*, which the plebs as such would not ordinarily do. In other inscriptions of Ariminum, the 'plebs' and 'plebs urbana' are attested as such.[2] And on one occasion the seven *vici* received a funded gift in seven units of equal size, suggesting that their membership was consistent. The number of members that may be suggested is 250–300 per *vicus*. Each *vicus* received HS20,000 whose income was to provide annual sportulae for the *vicani* on the donor's birthday. At the dedication of his statue, the donor gave sportulae of HS4 to the *vicani*.[3] The gift under the terms of the foundation itself is most unlikely to have been at any higher rate; the rates below HS4 authenticated elsewhere result in numbers that are implausibly large. The implied total membership seems to be in the region of 1,750–2,100 in all.

The largest colleges of craftsmen whose size we can gauge have a membership of the order of 1,200–1,500. The colleges of *fabri* at Rome and Milan seem to have had no less than 1,200 members.[4] Perhaps the total at these cities was more, since Ravenna, a lesser town under the Principate, seems to have had a college of *fabri* with 1,100–1,500 members.[5] Normally the size of local colleges and craftsmen or traders was very much smaller.[6]

Decurions and Augustales

At three Italian towns, Cures Sabini, Veii and Canusium, the number of decurions is explicitly attested as 100.[7] There were probably also 100 decurions at Puteoli, and at Urso, Caesar's colony in Spain.[8] A small

---

[1] Cf. B. M. Levick *Roman colonies in southern Asia Minor* (1967) 77 n.3; Liebenam 229.

[2] XI 377; 418; 387.

[3] C. nos.681; 977.

[4] The Rome college had 60 decurions, and decuriae of 20 members or more (VI 1060; 10300; 9405). The college at Milan had 12 *centuriae* (ILS 6730).

[5] A total of 112–50 decurions is indicated by C. no.678; the *decuriae* would hardly have fewer than 10 members (see above p.282 nn.2–3).

[6] For totals, see Waltzing 4 *passim* (his lists do not include any tabulation of the total membership of different colleges).

[7] *ILS* 460; 6579; IX 338, cf. *ILS* 6121. An inscription from Thuburbo Maius of the reign of Commodus contains the phrase '...onib. n(umero) ccc ccc denarios sing[ulos]' (*ILAf* 266); Carcopino's recent conjecture '[epul]onib(us)' (*AE* 1964, 44) is clearly preferable to the reading '[decuri]onib(us)' once supported by the writer (*PBSR* 30 (1962) 70, whence Jones *LRE* 3.228, n.26). Other dinners for 600: Suetonius *Claud.* 32; Martial 11.65.

[8] In one decree at Puteoli 92 decurions were present; in another there were at least 70 (X 1783 = *ILS* 5919; X 8180). At Urso it required 50 decurions to discuss any proposal for the offer of the patronate of the town, but three-quarters of the decurions to discuss the offer of the patronate to a senator. Since the latter contingency was the more serious, it

town in Latium, Castrimoenium, had only 30 decurions.[1] The gifts contribute further examples of both archetypes. At Ostia two accounts of the same benefaction show that there were 110 decurions of the city in the late second century: in one version their sportulae cost HS2,200 in all, and in the other the rate is HS20 per head.[2] The intricate details of a foundation gift at Abthugni in Africa indicate a total number of decurions of 100–105.[3] At Firmum Picenum a total of approximately 100 is suggested by the terms of another foundation. The fund of HS100,000 appears to have provided sportulae of HS24 for the decurions and HS4 for their wives on two occasions each year.[4] An assumed interest-rate of 6% allows shares for 114 decurions and their wives (assuming that every man was married). A foundation for a single annual distribution of sportulae to the decurions at Sufes in Byzacena had a capital of HS50,000. At an interest-rate of 6% the sportula-rate of HS30 (three times attested for decurions in Italy) would allow 100 recipients.[5] The *ordo* is not likely to have been smaller when the gift is so large.

The second archetype, an *ordo* of 30 decurions, seems to recur at Petelia in Bruttium. Here a donor whose gifts have already been cited allowed HS600 per year for a dinner and sportulae for the Augustales, of whom there were evidently 20 at this town. He allowed the decurions HS1,200 for the same purpose.[6] The decurions are likely to have received substantially more per head, which would place their numbers at less than 40. If they numbered 30, their rate per head would be HS40, for the meal and sportula, as compared with HS30 for the Augustales. The *ordo* may have been equally small at Gor, an African civitas where a sum as small as HS240 was sufficient to provide the decurions with an *epulum*, as well as paying for public boxing displays and an oil distribution.[7]

The total number of Augustales does not appear to be stated explicitly in any inscription. But we know of the celebration at Cures Sabini of a feast at which the decurions occupied 10 *triclinia* and the *sevirales* (i.e. Augustales)[8] occupied 2 *triclinia*.[9] Since there were 9 places in the Roman *triclinium*,[10] this leads to a total of 90 places for decurions and 18 for Augustales. The *ordo* at Cures Sabini is known to have had a full member-

appears that three-quarters of the *ordo* was more than 50 members, apparently pointing to a total membership of 100 (*ILS* 6087, 97; 130).

[1] *ILS* 3475. [2] C. no.672.
[3] C. no.262 and note.
[4] C. no.662 and note.
[5] C. no.256; for the sportula-rate of HS30, see C. nos.838; 839; 842.
[6] C. no.664; see below p.285. [7] C. no.267; cf. no.701 (Capena).
[8] Cf. IX 4957; 4970; 4977; 4978.
[9] IX 4971 = *ILS* 6560.
[10] *ILS* 6087, 132; *HA Elag.* 29.3.

ship of 100;[1] the corresponding implied total for the Augustales is 20 members. At Petelia, the Augustales likewise dined in public at two *triclinia*, indicating a similar total.[2] By contrast at Puteoli, the major port in Campania, the Augustales seem to have numbered at least 200. The members were divided into two *centuriae*, called Cornelia and Petronia. (Since these units are attested two and three times respectively, there may have been no more than two altogether.[3]) At Barcino, a large city on the coast of Tarraconensis, a foundation of the reign of Trajan seems to have provided enough shares for 250 Augustales (assuming the common total of 100 decurions).[4] At Ostia two foundations for sportulae for the Augustales, whose interest-rate seems to have been 6%, provided net annual amounts of approximately HS2,900 and HS2,300 for this purpose. The smaller foundation is dated to A.D. 182, the larger to 230/40.[5] A rise in the membership of the Augustales may be indicated, since the second foundation seems to be a punctilious imitation of the first in everything except the size of its capital. Alternatively we might expect to see the effects of inflation by the 230s; but there is little evidence that the level of sportulae was higher in the mid-third century than at earlier dates.[6] The donor of the second foundation gave sportulae at HS20 per head to the Augustales at the dedication of his statue.[7] But the sportula in the foundation itself might well have been lower. If it were HS12, the next common rate below HS20, the implied membership would be between 190 in the earlier foundation, and 240 in the later. If the sportula were constant at a rate of HS20, the numbers would only be 115–145. The higher total is probably more plausible for a major port, in view of the likely total at Barcino.

The membership of the Augustales was probably well over one hundred at Spoletium, where a foundation for the *seviri Augustales*, the *compitales Larum Aug(ustorum)* and the *magistri vicorum* appears to have provided enough revenue for 300 shares.[8] At Altinum also the membership of the Augustales seems to have been not less than one hundred. A foundation of HS200,000 left income for three sportula-distributions each year, to the decurions, the *seviri* and the Augustales.[9] If the interest was 5% as would be usual for a foundation of this size,[10] and a standard *ordo* of 100 decurions received sportulae of not more than HS20 (the highest common rate), the amount remaining for the Augustales at each of the three

[1] *ILS* 460; 3702; 5670; 6559.   [2] *ILS* 6469.
[3] *EE* 8.369; x 1874; 1873; 1888; 8178.
[4] II 4511; see R. Duncan-Jones *Historia* 13 (1964) 205.
[5] C. nos.674–5 and notes.
[6] Cf. p.356 below.   [7] C. no.864a.
[8] C. no.659; see p.268 n.1 above.
[9] C. no.654.   [10] See p.134.

TABLE 8. *The number of decurions and Augustales in different cities*

Italy	Decurions	Augustales	Africa	Decurions	Augustales
Canusium	100 (+25 praetextati)	—	Abthugni	(100/105)	—
			Sufes	(100)	—
Ostia	110	(190–240)	Gor	(30?)	—
Firmum Picenum	(110?)	—			
Cures Sabini	100	18–20	Spain		
Veii	100	—	Barcino	(100?)	(250 ?)
Puteoli	(100)	200 (? +)			
Castrimoenium	30	—			
Petelia	(30)	18–20			
Altinum	—	(100?)			
Spoletium	—	(100? +)			
Reate	—	(50? +)			
Aletrium	—	(25? +			

distributions would be HS1,333. Assuming that there was as usual a differential between the sportula of the decurions and that of the Augustales, the next highest common rate of HS12 would allow enough shares for 111 members.

At Reate and Aletrium the implied totals are smaller. A donor at Reate gave HS20,000 whose income was to provide an annual dinner for the Augustales.[1] A bequest of HS10,000 provided for the same purpose at Aletrium.[2] At 5–6% the respective incomes would be HS1,200–1,000 and HS600–500. At the commonest rates of benefit for the Augustales, HS8, HS12 and HS20, the implied membership will range between 150 and 50 at Reate, and between 75 and 25 at Aletrium. Thus the minimum strength is likely to have been not less than 50 at Reate and 25 at Aletrium. (The totals are summarised in Table 8.)

At Petelia we have estimates for the number of decurions and Augustales, as well as for the population as a whole (decurions *c.* 30; Augustales *c.* 20; remaining population *c.* 2,400). These figures suggest that roughly one in eleven of the male citizens at this small town belonged either to the town-council, or to the body of Augustales. Assuming that the outlying population was not so large as to transform this ratio, the relationship may help to explain why difficulties in maintaining the number of Augustales were being felt at Petelia under Antoninus Pius.[3]

[1] C. no.683. [2] C. no.687.
[3] 'Hoc autem nomine relevati inpend(i)is facilius prosilituri hi qui ad munus Augustalit[a]tis compellentur' (*ILS* 6469, ll.24–6). Cf. *ibid.* ll.10–12 'Quod ipsum ad utilitate[m] rei p.n. pertinere existimavi, facilius subituris onus Augu[s]talitatis, dum hoc commodum ante oculos habent.'

A relatively high ratio of civic officials to town population was not peculiar to cities as small as Petelia. The town-council might number 100 instead of 30 members elsewhere, and the number of Augustales might also be larger. A town with 100 decurions and 50 Augustales would still have the same ratio of officials as at Petelia if its overall urban population were 7,300 inhabitants.

Mean averages for town-population based on estimates of the population of Italy overall are no guide to typical town-sizes. The actual range of variation in town population was very considerable, as the figures assembled above show (perhaps a factor of 20 or more). But the size of the town-council appears to have been allowed to vary with the capacity of the town only to a limited degree. Only two basic levels for the complement of decurions are known in western cities, 100 and 30 decurions.[1] This three-fold difference is very much smaller than the differences in town-size indicated by the present figures for population. The number of officials was not the only variant which determined the impact of Roman institutions on a town; the level of the payments for office was also important. In Africa, the only source of detailed information, charges for a given office could vary between different towns by a factor of 12 or 13.[2] In Italy the number of Augustales could apparently vary quite widely also. Nevertheless, the number of magistrates and decurions evidently fluctuated much less than the size of town populations. The effects of the demands of Roman civic institutions probably varied considerably from town to town, depending on the relation between the wealth and population of the town and the size and weight of the administrative superstructure. In the case of towns at which this relationship was unfavourable, shortage of candidates for the *ordo* may have been endemic.

[1] Massilia (Marseilles), with 600 councillors, had Greek institutions and is not representative of the West (Valerius Maximus 2.6.7; Strabo 4.1.5; Liebenam 229). Eastern totals: Broughton *ESAR* 4.814 (*ordo* of 80 at Parthicopolis(?) p.83 n.6). Whether or not Pomponius's statement that decurions were so called because they generally formed one-tenth of the original colonists of a new foundation is true, there is little to suggest that the permanent size of the *ordo* reflected the numerical diversity of the original bodies of colonists (*Digesta* 50.16.239.5). Numbers of colonists per town attested in the Republic include the following: 300, 1,500, 2,000, 2,500, 3,000, 3,300, 4,000, and 6,000 (J. Beloch *Italische Bund* (1880) 149–50; A. J. Toynbee *Hannibal's Legacy* (1965) 2.654–6).

[2] The charge for the *quinquennalitas* was 12.7 times higher at Carthage than at Thuburbo Maius (HS38,000 and HS3,000; C. nos.360, 364). The charge for the decurionate was 12.5 times higher at Cirta than at Muzuc (HS20,000 and HS1,600; C. nos.345, 347). The charge for the perpetual flaminate was 12 times higher at Lambaesis and Uchi Maius than at Sarra (HS12,000 and HS1,000; C. nos.365, 366, 377).

7
Government subsidies for population increase

INTRODUCTION

The opening of the second century A.D. saw the propagation of a system of government *alimenta* or public subsistence payments in Italy. They provided for the support of children in towns spread all over the Italian peninsula.[1] Boys received a cash payment of HS16 per month, girls HS12; illegitimate children received somewhat less in each case.[2] The ages of eligibility are not explicitly known. Hadrian legislated in a different context that boys should be supported until the age of 18 and girls until 14.[3] This referred to provisions for alimentary support made by private individuals, but the details may reflect the practice of the government scheme in his time. In Hadrian's own endowment for the support of children at Antinoopolis in Egypt, eligibility began within thirty days of birth.[4] The Italian *alimenta* were financed by government grants placed with landowners in the districts in which children were to be supported. Generally speaking, each landowner who accepted a loan received a sum worth about 8% of the stated value of his land, on which he had to pay the city interest of 5% per year, which formed the income from which the children were supported.[5]

It is worthwhile to consider the overall purpose of the scheme as well as its mechanism. A number of questions are controversial. It is often maintained that the landowners who took up the loans benefited by doing so, and that cheap loans were being offered as a deliberate device to encourage Italian agriculture, which would show a degree of economic

---

[1] 39 towns at which *alimenta* are attested, usually by the mention of magistrates in charge of alimentary funds, are listed by Ruggiero 1.405. The connexion between these magistrates and the imperial funds is explicit in a number of the inscriptions: *ILS* 6620; 6456; 6512; 6587. Other inscriptions not listed by Ruggiero allow 10 more towns to be added, increasing the total to 49. For details see Appendix 5.

[2] XI 1147. In a college on the via Appia near Rome the size of wine-rations depended on the rank of the recipient, varying in a ratio of 3:2:1 (*ILS* 7213).

[3] This ruling was reaffirmed by Caracalla, *Digesta* 34.1.14.1.

[4] *Aegyptus* 13 (1933) 518–22; H. I. Bell *JRS* 30 (1940) 143. In 2 private schemes eligibility began. respectively at birth and at the age of 3, *ILS* 6278; 6818.

[5] XI 1147; IX 1455. Dessau's abstracts are very selective (*ILS* 6675; 6509).

liberalism unusual for a Roman government.[1] We know little about which children benefited, or under what conditions landowners came forward, but it is possible to make some inferences from what evidence survives. The pattern of the underlying loans has puzzling features which also deserve further scrutiny.

THE NATURE OF THE EVIDENCE

Literary sources tell us little about the workings of the government *alimenta*,[2] while the frequent references to *alimenta* in the jurists are concerned with private gifts which provided subsistence for dependants of the donor.[3] But there is plentiful information about the detailed workings of the government scheme in inscriptions. The most important is the lengthy Table of Veleia, an inscription on bronze running to 674 lines, whose text is effectively complete.[4] This inscription reveals the number of children supported at the town, together with their sex and civil status, and gives elaborate details of the many landholdings on which the loans were based. The inscription describes in reverse order a small alimentary scheme at Veleia set up between A.D. 98 and 102, and a much larger second scheme established at some point between 102 and 113. Tantalising fragments of another inscription probably belong to an earlier alimentary scheme at the town, whose details remain uncertain.[5] The companion to the Table of Veleia is the earlier Table of Ligures Baebiani, a much shorter account of the government *alimenta* established at that town in A.D. 101.[6] Some of the landowners refer to an 'obligatio VIIII', apparently alluding to a different series of pledges;[7] this seems to indicate that Ligures Baebiani also received *alimenta* in at least two stages. The first of the three columns of this inscription is partly missing; as a result 80 out of a total of 246 lines are fragmentary. The amounts payable on the loans survive complete however, and the size of the overall loan at Ligures Baebiani is therefore known. The number of beneficiaries is not stated, but the approximate total can be inferred from the size of the loan.[8]

---

[1] Compare the harshness of the method employed by Domitian to encourage a shift to cereal crops a few years earlier: he ordered that half of all provincial vineyards be destroyed, and that no new areas be planted with vines in Italy (see p.35 n.4).

[2] Taken as indications about the Italian *alimenta* of the time of Trajan, the two technical details provided by literary sources are both misleading. *HA Marc.* 7.8 refers to alimentary payments in corn; while *HA Pert.* 9.3 suggests that the beneficiaries received grants at regular intervals paid from the treasury. In fact the Trajanic *alimenta* in Italy took the form of payments in money which were funded locally, not paid direct from the treasury.

[3] Cf. *Vocab.Iurisp.Rom.* s.v. alimentum.

[4] XI 1147.

[5] XI 1149, cf. 1151. See Appendix 3.

[6] IX 1455.

[7] IX 1455, 2.26; 3.14; 3.18.

[8] Probably 110 or 120 children; see Appendix 6.

We thus have abundant details of the Trajanic *alimenta* established at one town in northern Italy, and at one town in southern Italy: Veleia was in regio VIII near Placentia, Ligures Baebiani in regio II near Beneventum. Both towns were evidently small.[1] Their main inscriptions show that the rationale of the loans was similar at the two towns: loans worth roughly 8% of the estates occur in both cases, and the interest-rate seems to be identical.[2] In many cases the main Veleian loans were more complex than those at Ligures Baebiani. It is reasonable to think that the two inscriptions provide typical illustrations of the scheme as it existed in many parts of Italy. Another bronze inscription shows the town of Ferentinum in Latium granting the title of patron to a consular senator in recognition of a 'cura' which was evidently the setting up of the *alimenta* at that town.[3] Stone inscriptions from 45 more towns in Italy briefly indicate the existence of government *alimenta*, most often by the mention of a 'quaestor alimentorum'.[4] Trajan began 'alimenta' for children in Rome very early in his reign; there were 5,000 or more beneficiaries.[5] This scheme was probably in substance the metropolitan section of the Italian *alimenta*. Trajan's initiative at Rome has been construed as an addition to the 'plebs frumentaria',[6] but Pliny does not say that this was the case. It is more likely that the gift was intended as a distinct infant alimentary scheme, akin to the Italian *alimenta* although it probably took the form of a direct payment of corn.[7] An inscription from Attica which appears to be Hadrianic shows the pledging of estates belonging to private landowners on a basis which resembles that of the Italian alimentary loans.[8] This probably indicates that Hadrian gave an alimentary scheme to Athens (private donors would hardly be in a position to place their capital with other private landowners). We also know that Hadrian provided child-support arrangements at Antinoopolis, the town that he founded in Egypt.[9] There is no other evidence that the privilege of government *alimenta* was extended to the provinces. There

---

[1] Cf. Ruggiero s.v. Ligures Baebiani; *Enc.art.ant.* s.v. Velleia.

[2] The interest-rate is stated as 5% in the Table of Veleia, XI 1147; it is virtually certain that the 2½% payments listed at Ligures Baebiani are six-monthly, indicating the same 5% annual rate (see Mommsen in IX, p.129; Billeter 191–3). Veyne 1964, 172–3 and R. Andreotti *St.Vel.* 5 hold that 2½% was the annual rate.

[3] VI 1492 = *ILS* 6106; cf. XI 1147, 3.13; 3.53.

[4] See Appendix 5.

[5] Pliny gives the total as slightly below 5,000, but says that the number was growing daily (*Pan.* 28.4; 28.7).

[6] Cf. M. Durry ed. *Pline le Jeune, Panégyrique de Trajan* (1938) 235–6.

[7] Cf. O. Hirschfeld *Philologus* 29 (1870) 10.

[8] *IG* II–III² 2776; J. Day *An economic history of Athens under Roman domination* (1942) 230.

[9] P.288 n.4 above.

were a few public alimentary schemes given by private individuals in Africa and Spain; but these only parallel the similar gifts that were still being made in Italy even after the inception of the government *alimenta*.[1]

THE FOUNDING OF THE 'ALIMENTA'

A fourth-century source, the *Historia Augusta*, twice identifies the Italian *alimenta* as Trajanic in origin, and the excerpts of Cassius Dio, the Severan historian, mention the *alimenta* in their account of the reign of Trajan.[2] The three datable inscriptions that refer to the setting up of individual alimentary schemes all belong to the reign of Trajan.[3] Nevertheless, it is uncertain whether Trajan founded the institution.

According to one modern view, Domitian founded the government *alimenta*.[4] Asbach held that Pliny's mention of 'alimenta' for children in c.28 of the *Panegyric* refers to the Italian *alimenta*. The words 'nullam congiario culpam, nullam alimentis crudelitatem redemisti' evidently contrast Trajan's subsidies with those of Domitian. It should follow that Domitian also gave 'alimenta'. But the most obvious 'alimenta' mentioned in the *Panegyric* were payments of corn to the plebs at Rome, which Trajan had recently extended.[5] This leaves no clear case for thinking that Domitian had made any innovation, since his 'alimenta' need be no more than the accustomed payments to the plebs. It is not clear in any case that Pliny's reference definitely implies an innovation by Domitian. Thus on this evidence there is little basis for seeing Domitian as founder of the *alimenta*.

Another fourth-century source, Ps.-Aurelius Victor, states explicitly that Nerva began the Italian *alimenta*.[6] There is no evidence for the Italian *alimenta* on Nerva's coins,[7] but his reign was so short, only sixteen

---

[1] Africa: *ILS* 6817; 6818; 8978 (dependants only); VIII 22904. Spain: II 1174 (3 schemes at Hispalis, cf. *Historia* 13 (1964) 206–8). Italy: C. nos.637; 638 (dependants only); 641; 642; 644; 650; XI 1602.

[2] *HA Had.* 7.8 'pueris ac puellis quibus etiam Traianus alimenta detulerat'; *HA Pert.* 9.3 'alimentaria etiam compendia, quae novem annorum ex instituto Traiani debebantur'; Cassius Dio 68.5.4.

[3] IX 1455; XI 1147; VI 1492.

[4] J. Asbach *Römisches Kaisertum und Verfassung bis auf Traian* (1896) 188. Asbach's theory was accepted by Strack 1.188, and is noted by Syme 224, n.1 and K. A. Waters *AJP* 90 (1969) 404. It is rejected by Garzetti *Nerva* 70, n.2 and by Sirago 276, n.3.

[5] *Pan.* 26–8; see above, p.290 nn.5–7.

[6] *Epit. de Caes.* 12.4: 'puellas puerosque natos parentibus egestosis sumptu publico per Italiae oppida ali iussit'. For the value of this sometimes under-rated source, cf. C. P. Jones *JRS* 60 (1970) 99, n.14.

[7] The coin with the legend TUTELA ITALIAE showing Nerva with 'Italia' and two children is cited as evidence that Nerva began the *alimenta* by Hirschfeld *VW*² 212 and Garzetti

months,[1] that this may not be significant. Had Trajan's reign been equally short, it is possible that there would be no mention of the *alimenta* on his coins either: the first dated reference to the *alimenta* on Trajan's coins belongs to 103, two years after the first dated inscription describing the scheme.[2] The founding of the alimenta is not unlike innovations of Nerva's reign such as the revival of land-allotments for the plebs,[3] and the creation of a burial-fund for the people of Rome.[4] All three institutions can be seen as new types of government hand-out. Nerva also carried out a reform of one of the traditional distributions, the corn-dole at Rome; some of his coins bear the legend PLEBEI VRBANAE FRVMENTO CONSTITVTO.[5] Pliny reveals that Nerva encouraged generosity towards the community in his speeches as well as by example, and shows that his policy had some effect.[6] In a poem addressed to Nerva, Martial writes as though munificence were a prime feature of his reign: 'Largiri, praestare, breves extendere census/et dare quae faciles vix tribuere dei/ nunc licet et fas est.'[7]

Thus Ps.-Aurelius Victor's statement that Nerva began the Italian *alimenta*, although isolated, is in keeping with other evidence about Nerva's policies. It is less easy to see corroborative features in policies originated by Trajan. Granted that Nerva's brief reign was too short to allow the full growth of an institution as elaborate as the *alimenta*, later tradition might have transferred credit for originating the scheme to the successor in whose reign the *alimenta* were developed. Other memorials to Imperial generosity took their name from the Emperor under whom they were completed, not from the Emperor who began the project.[8] The official documents of the reign of Trajan which describe the setting up of units of the *alimenta* naturally refer to the *indulgentia* of Trajan, and make no allusion to any other ruler.[9] The *Historia Augusta*'s

---

Nerva 73; but Merlin showed the coin to be a probable forgery (A. Merlin *Revue numismatique* 10 (1906) 298–301; Strack 1.188, n.820; Mattingly 3.xlix).

[1] Nerva reigned from 18 September 96 to 27 (?) January 98 (Garzetti *Nerva* 31; 95).

[2] Mattingly 3.82; IX 1455.

[3] Cassius Dio 68.2.1; Pliny *Ep.* 7.31.4; *ILS* 1019. Cf. *Digesta* 47.21.3.1; Martial 12.6.9–11.

[4] *Chronica Minora* (ed. Mommsen) 1.146; A. Degrassi *Scritti vari di antichità* 1 (1962) 697–702.

[5] Mattingly 3.21, 25; Garzetti *Nerva* 69.

[6] Pliny *Ep.* 10.8.1.

[7] Martial 12.6.9–11.

[8] For example the building of the Aqua Claudia was begun by Caligula (Pliny *NH* 36.122). The 'Forum Nervae' was begun by Domitian (Garzetti *Nerva* 54).

[9] 'Indulgentia' in IX 1455 pr.; XI 1147 pr. and 7.32. At Ferentinum (*ILS* 6106) Trajan is 'indulgentissimus' and shows 'liberalitas' (ascribed instead to the alimentary commissioner by Garnsey 1968, 381; cf. H. Kloft *Liberalitas principis* (1970) 97, n.62).

ascription of the *alimenta* to Trajan leaves it uncertain who was the founder, but the balance of evidence slightly favours Nerva.[1]

It could be objected that the absence of any specific reference to the *alimenta* in Pliny's *Panegyric* delivered in A.D. 100 shows that they cannot have been in existence in the early years of Trajan's reign, and thus cannot have been founded by his predecessor. Pliny's eulogy of Trajan's character and policies in this speech is long and apparently thorough. But there is unequivocal evidence that the *alimenta* were functioning at one Italian town by A.D. 101; and there were apparently two stages in the establishing of the *alimenta* at that town.[2] The earlier of the alimentary schemes recorded at Veleia may be earlier than 101.[3] In view of the complexity of setting up the *alimenta* at any one town, it is difficult to believe that the scheme can have been unknown at the beginning of A.D. 100. Another explanation must be sought for the absence of explicit allusion to the *alimenta* in the *Panegyricus*.[4] Pliny's account of child-support arrangements in this speech concentrates on Trajan's initiative providing for 5,000 children who were evidently at Rome.[5] If the Italian *alimenta* were in process of formation at the start of A.D. 100, but had not progressed far in numerical terms, it is possible that Pliny disregarded them in his speech in favour of the more imposing example offered by the large number of children already being supported at Rome. The demographic rationale[6] behind the child-support scheme and the illustration of the Emperor's far-sightedness that this offered were more important for Pliny's purposes than the details of where the children were located. Furthermore, the main geographical viewpoint of the speech is the city of Rome, and Pliny finds no occasion for a separate discussion of Italy here or in any other context.

[1] Nerva as founder (sometimes in part on the basis of uncertain numismatic evidence, see p.291 n.7 above): Sherwin-White 572; Garzetti *Nerva* 73; Sirago 276; Stein *RE* 4.144. Trajan as founder: M. Hammond *Mem.Amer.Acad.Rome* 21 (1953) 147–51.

[2] IX 1455; cf. '*obligatio* VIIII' in 2.26; 3.14; 3.18.

[3] The Gallicanus scheme is dated to between 98 and 102. It was evidently preceded at Veleia by a scheme under the supervision of Pomponius Bassus (see Appendix 3). Since the Gallicanus scheme has a different security-quotient from the Ligures Baebiani scheme dated to 101 and the main Veleia scheme dated to 102/13 (10-fold security instead of 12½-fold), the Gallicanus scheme may have been earlier than 101 and the Bassus scheme earlier still.

[4] The Panegyric was revised after being delivered at the beginning of A.D. 100 (*Ep.* 3.18) and was evidently much expanded. But it is difficult to trace anything which definitely refers to a later date (cf. R. Syme *JRS* 28 (1938) 217–18).

[5] *Pan.* 28.4.

[6] *Pan.* 26.5; 28.5–7.

THE PURPOSE OF THE 'ALIMENTA'

At both towns of which we have detailed knowledge, the *alimenta* were evidently set up in at least two stages. Nothing is known of the first stage at Ligures Baebiani, except that it bore the cryptic title 'obligatio VIIII', and its declarations were incorporated in the main scheme at that town.[1] At Veleia, the first scheme was evidently that managed by the consular T. Pomponius Bassus, an acquaintance of the younger Pliny, whose activities are also attested much further south, at Ferentinum.[2] The details of this scheme were apparently set out in an inscription of which we have a few fragments; landowners arranged by locality declared small amounts of property, perhaps only one farm each. The loan-security may have been as low as 4-fold, although this rests on the speculative identification of another bronze fragment as referring to the Bassus scheme.[3] The number of children supported is not known. Next, at some point between 98 and 102 came a scheme managed by another consular, C. Cornelius Gallicanus, details of which are set out at the end of the main Table of Veleia.[4] The beneficiaries were 18 boys and one girl, and the relatively small capital sum required for their support, HS72,000, was distributed on 10-fold security between five landowners. This was followed, at a date between 102 and 113, by a large-scale scheme which supported 246 boys and 35 girls. The large capital sum of HS1,044,000 was distributed in loans granted on security of $12\frac{1}{2}$-fold to 45 private landowners and one city.[5] Since the grand total of the two schemes mentioned in the main Table was 300 children in all,[6] the schemes were evidently complementary, and between them reached a determined target figure.

The procedures needed to establish the *alimenta* were undoubtedly cumbersome. First the government fixed the number of beneficiaries to be supported at a particular town. Local applications for support were then invited, the offer being closed when enough eligible children had been found and the agreed total had been reached. The annual payment

---

[1] IX 1455, 2.26; 3.14; 3.18. Conceivably this phrase denoted an *obligatio* with 9 participants; the Gallicanus scheme at Veleia was confined to 5 landowners. (Mommsen saw it as the ninth allocation of funds made in Italy as a whole, IX p.128, 1.)

[2] Bassus was also a friend of Trajan's father, whom he served as legate in Asia, *ILS* 8797; full name in *ILS* 6106; XI 1147, 3.13; 3.53; Pliny *Ep.* 4.23; Sherwin-White 301; *PIR*[1] P 530.

[3] Discussed in Appendix 3.

[4] XI 1147, 7.31–60. *PIR*[2] C 1367.

[5] XI 1147, pr. and 1.1–7.30.

[6] The widespread modern notion that the number of children benefited at Veleia was less than 300 results from overlooking the Gallicanus scheme at the end of the Table (see e.g. Hirschfeld *VW*[2] 213, n.1; Bourne 58).

required to maintain the children at that town could be calculated only when the sex and civil status of all actual beneficiaries were known, since there were four different rates of benefit.[1] Next a sum twenty times larger than the required annual income was allocated, and parcelled out at a low rate among a series of local landowners. This stage required detailed enquiry into local landholdings, and was a complex process in itself. When the loans had been successfully placed, the scheme could at last begin to function. Regional supervision of the *alimenta* was carried out by senatorial and equestrian officials; but the immediate administration at any one town was in the hands of magistrates of the town, the 'quaestores alimentorum'.[2]

The *alimenta* were evidently intended to encourage a rise in the birth-rate. Pliny spoke in his *Panegyric* of Trajan's benefactions for the support of children as a source of future demographic increase and consequent prosperity: 'ex his castra, ex his tribus replebuntur, ex his quandoque nascentur quibus alimentis opus non sit'. A motion passed one or two years later by the town-council of Ferentinum in Latium described responsibility for the *alimenta* as a '(cura) qua (Imperator) aeternitati Italiae suae prospexit'.[3] Although both passages are rhetorical, there is little reason to doubt the existence of the demographic motive which they imply. ALIM(enta) ITAL(iae) appears on some of Trajan's coins; others bear the legend ITAL(ia) REST(ituta).[4]

Most modern commentators have seen in the *alimenta* the further object of providing landowners with cheap credit, as a benefit in itself.[5] Some have even regarded it as the primary purpose of the scheme. It is

[1] Boys received HS16 or HS12 per month, girls HS12 or HS10, depending on whether they were legitimate, an interesting financial discrimination (XI 1147).

[2] Local administration: Ruggiero 1.406–8. Regional administration: *Staatsrecht* 2.1079–81; Hirschfeld *VW*[2] 215–22; Pflaum 496–8. Enforcement in Italy of the *senatus consultum* about gladiatorial expenditures in A.D. 177/80 was confided to the *praefecti alimentorum* in the first instance ('praefectis alimentorum, si aderunt' *ILS* 5163, l.43).

[3] Pliny *Pan.* 28.5; *ILS* 6106. Reputed concern for 'aeternitas Italiae' on the part of the ruler was not new: cf. 'cum...totius Italiae aeternitati prospexerit', a reference to Claudius (*ILS* 6043).

[4] Direct references to the *alimenta*: Mattingly 3.82, 88, 96, 183, 184, 194, 202, 203, 206, 211, 214; Strack 1.188–9. ITAL REST: Mattingly 3.195, 203.

[5] E. Desjardins in DS 1.184; G. Kubitschek in *RE* 1.1486; Ruggiero 1.405; E. E. Bryant *Reign of Antoninus Pius* (1895) 122; Hirschfeld *VW*[2] 213–14; de Pachtere 114; A. Ashley *Eng.Hist.Review* 36 (1921) 7; B. W. Henderson *Five Roman Emperors* (1927) 215; Rostovtzeff *SEHRE*[2] 199; L. Homo *Histoire Générale* (ed. G. Glotz) 3.3.437; G. Rodenwaldt *CAH* 11.788; Mattingly 3.xliv; H. G. Ramsay *Classical Journal* 31 (1935–6) 488; R. Paribeni in *Enc.it.* 34.155; Frank *ESAR* 5.66; E. T. Salmon *History of the Roman World from 30 B.C. to A.D. 138* (1963) 270; Veyne 1958, 228; Bourne 69 ff.; R. Andreotti *St.Vel.* 6; A. Bernardi in C. M. Cipolla (ed.) *The economic decline of empires* (1970) 30. A more cautious approach is adopted by Billeter 187 ff.; R. P. Longden *CAH* 11.211–12; Sirago 287–9; A. Garzetti *L'Impero da Tiberio agli Antonini* (1960) 365.

noticeable that the Emperors of this period showed some interest in Italian land: Domitian attempted to encourage cereals at the expense of vines; Nerva made allocations from the *ager publicus* to members of the Roman plebs; while Trajan laid down that every senator who stood for office at Rome must hold one-third of his resources in Italian land.[1] The complaints of a contemporary senator about the condition of his estates[2] might imply that Italian agriculture was not in a flourishing state, and that landlords stood in need of capital.

Whether or not Pliny's Letters show that Italian agriculture as a whole was in difficulties, there is very little basis for regarding the *alimenta* as being intended to aid the landowner in addition to the children who were fed. In fact engaging money in land was the normal method of securing a permanent revenue for a perpetual foundation. This can be seen by comparing the alimentary inscriptions with the Italian private foundations whose basis is known: the majority show that the capital was invested in land. Most of these foundations are undated, but one is certainly earlier than the period of Nerva and Trajan.[3] Farming out loans to private landowners was probably the only effective means available for securing a permanent locally based revenue on a sufficient scale. Neither imperial holdings nor *ager publicus* is likely to have been disseminated widely enough at this date to have allowed the possibility of investing the imperial funds there. Furthermore the tenants who occupied such land may not always have been sufficiently prosperous to make reliable creditors. A crude index of the relative importance of different types of property (the references to adjoining properties, of which there are nearly 700) gives the following information about the district round Veleia: reckoned on the number of times properties are mentioned, land in private hands makes up 71.6%; *ager publicus* ('populus') 22.4%; land belonging to cities 5.2%; land belonging to the Emperor 0.6%.[4] Veleia need not be typical, but it is unlikely that imperial and public land was consistently present in the vicinity of most other cities in much greater amounts. In the event, neither imperial nor public land was used

---

[1] Domitian, see p.35 n.4; Nerva, see p.292 n.3 above; Trajan, Pliny *Ep.* 6.19 (cf. *HA Marcus* 11.8).

[2] For Pliny's agricultural complaints, see p.21 n.2. Pliny's grumbles about bad harvests tell us nothing about long-term trends (*Ep.* 4.6.1; 8.2; 9.16; 9.20; 9.28); and his experiment with *métayage* may be a product of Pliny's distinctive financial ingenuity (*Ep.* 9.37; cf. 7.18; 8.2). For a different view see Brockmeyer 193.

[3] *ILS* 3546 (Domitianic); 3775; 6271; 6328²; 6663; 6664; 8370; 8376; Pliny *Ep.* 7.18. Cf. Sirago 277 and n.2. We also have record of one Italian foundation whose income came from wool production, and of another vested in a house (*ILS* 5595; Pais no.181; also *ILS* 8366).

[4] xi 1147. The totals: private 499; 'populus' 156; city of Luca 26; Veleia 6; Placentia 4; Emperor 4. The 'proc(urator) vectigalior(um) [p]opul(i) R(omani) quae sunt citra Padum' was presumably concerned among other things with revenue from *ager publicus* (*ILS* 1396).

as the basis for alimentary loans as far as we know, although limited use was made of estates belonging to municipalities.

The imperial *alimenta* seem to have been directly modelled on the privately given perpetual foundations for the support of children that already existed in Italy at this date.[1] The short-term cost of making grants in the form of perpetual foundations was enormously greater than the cost of a direct annual subsidy from the treasury: twenty years' income had to be made available at once in order to form a foundation with the interest-rate of 5%. But because it was self-contained, the perpetual foundation had the advantage that it would protect the dependants from any suspension of payment in years of treasury deficit. This format also circumvented the need to transport substantial amounts of coin from Rome to towns all over Italy at regular intervals. Nevertheless, there seem to have been some units of the *alimenta* whose payments were not funded: the *Historia Augusta* states that Pertinax made up nine years of back payments, implying that some sections of the scheme depended on regular grants.[2] Units of the scheme that were founded after the time of Trajan might have had a different basis from that shown in the two Tables, although Hadrian in at least one instance was apparently able to continue the funded method of establishing new *alimenta*.[3]

Modern historians have often also assumed that the government alimentary loans were especially intended to benefit the small landowner as distinct from the large one.[4] Internal evidence argues against this view. At Veleia, the owners of estates worth less than HS50,000 were apparently ineligible for alimentary loans. More than half the loans in the main scheme went to the owners of property worth over HS100,000; the three richest participants each declared property worth more than HS1 million.[5] At Ligures Baebiani the pattern was different: more than a quarter of the participants owned property worth less than HS50,000. But Ligures Baebiani was evidently a very small town, one of several communities attributed to Beneventum;[6] the number of children supported was

---

[1] *ILS* 977, an alimentary foundation of HS400,000 set up by a senator at Atina Latii not later than the reign of Nero (cf. Hammond cited on p.293 n.1 above); XI 1602, a private alimentary foundation at Florentia which apparently belongs to the late Flavian period.

[2] *HA Pert.* 9.3. Whether this implies a breakdown of the *alimenta* under Commodus is by no means clear: the hierarchy of alimentary administrators was certainly still functioning in his reign (*HA Pert.* 4.1; *Iulian.* 2.1; Pflaum 1006 (no.178 *bis*), 1037 (no.295) 1041 (no.235)). The *alimenta* were also functioning under the Severi: x 5398.

[3] See above, p.290 n.8.

[4] See Desjardins, Kubitschek, Ruggiero, Henderson, Homo, Ramsay, Paribeni and Salmon cited in p.295 n.5 above; also G. Segré *Bullettino dell'Istituto di diritto romano* (1889) 106, and G. Salvioli *Archivio giuridico 'Filippo Serafini'* 62 (1899) 538.

[5] XI 1147 *obligationes* 13; 17; 31 (with *obligationes* 48 and 51).

[6] The other attributed communities included pagus Veianus and Caudium (Mommsen IX

apparently less than half that at Veleia,[1] though Veleia was hardly a large town. The wealthiest landowner who declared property at Ligures Baebiani was worth only HS501,000.[2] Thus the pattern at Ligures Baebiani may be an inevitable reflection of the shortage of large estates characteristic of a very small town.

At both towns there was a tendency for large farms to receive loans at a higher rate than small ones.[3] If the loans were a benefit in themselves, as is usually supposed, the loan-distribution would thus imply the opposite of particular favour towards the small landowner. But it is very doubtful whether the alimentary loans can generally have been regarded as economically beneficial by their recipients.[4] Loans given in perpetuity, as the alimentary loans almost certainly were,[5] are not the same thing as ordinary market loans, which are repayable, are available on demand, and are given for whatever period the borrower may need them. The alimentary borrower had to take up the loan at the time when the scheme was being floated, and was not in a position to return it to the lender. His commitment to pay the interest was permanent, unless he sold the estates on which the loan was pledged. If he decided to do so, he would probably find that the difference between the price which he could get and the price that the estate would have fetched if not encumbered was greater than the amount of the loan which he had received.

One of Pliny's Letters shows that a permanent charge lowered the market-value by a greater amount than the loss indicated in the amount of the charge itself.[6] When endowing his own alimentary foundation at Comum, which had a promised value of HS500,000, Pliny first made over

---

pp.133 and 198). *ILS* 6512 indicates that Ligures Corneliani was separate from Ligures Baebiani (despite *Liber coloniarum* p.235), but its site has not yet been identified (Ruggiero 4.1055).

[1] There were probably 110 or 120 children, compared with more than 300 at Veleia (Appendix 6).

[2] IX 1455, 2.29, emending to read the arithmetical total of the component valuations as suggested by Mommsen.

[3] See below, p.315. Cf. now *Nuove questioni di storia antica* (1968) 760–1 (L. C. Ruggini).

[4] Sirago saw signs of a lack of enthusiasm for the loans in the fact that dedications in gratitude for the *alimenta* always came from the recipients of *alimenta*, not from the recipients of loans, despite the fact that landowners were much better able to afford the expense of a dedication (Sirago 288–9). But it is doubtful whether wealthy landowners felt sufficient community of interest, whatever their attitude towards the loans, to club together for a statue in this way.

[5] Henzen 25; Mommsen IX p.128, 1; de Pachtere 114; Garzetti (cited above p.295 n.5) 365. Bourne's arguments for thinking the alimentary loans returnable at the request of the landowner take too little account of the administrative difficulties that would have resulted. They also fail to explain why the lists of the estates that had been pledged were published in a permanent form. Bourne 59.

[6] *Ep.* 7.18, cf. 1.8.10.

to the *actor publicus* by *mancipatio* an estate worth considerably more; he received it back charged with an annual *vectigal* or rent of HS30,000, which was to provide the city with the income for his foundation. Evidently Pliny would continue to exploit the estate himself during his lifetime, and the estate would remain in private hands in perpetuity, although the city (which remained technically the owner) would always have the right to HS30,000 of the annual income from the estate. This device was intended to protect the fund for Pliny's *alimenta* from the neglect suffered by the public lands that came under the city's direct control. Pliny congratulated himself that because the estate was worth much more than the HS500,000 whose income was represented by the annual charge of HS30,000, it could be sure of always finding an 'owner' who would work it[1] (in other words enough income would remain after the *vectigal* had been paid to make it a commercial proposition). Nevertheless, Pliny concedes that because a permanent charge had been placed on the property, its market-value ('pretium') had been lowered by rather more than the sum that he appeared to have donated.[2]

Pliny's letter shows that a perpetual charge on an estate, 'necessitas vectigalis', had the effect of lowering the estate's value by an amount greater than that suggested by the size of the charge itself. (There is no reason to think the phenomenon peculiar to Roman economic conditions.) The interest-payment was constant, whereas agricultural revenues depended on the size of each harvest. Consequently the interest might reduce the net revenue available to the landlord to insignificant proportions in a year of drought when he needed the whole of the small crop that was available. This would act as a discouragement to purchasers, who might be further discouraged by the fact that the creditor was the State. Pliny mentions elsewhere that it was difficult to find anyone who

---

[1] 'semper dominum a quo exerceatur inveniet.'

[2] 'Nec ignoro me plus aliquanto quam donasse videor erogavisse, cum pulcherrimi agri pretium necessitas vectigalis infregerit.' The alternative view (Bourne 53, cf. F. Millar *JRS* 58 (1968) 222) that Pliny's land became *ager vectigalis* and the city became effective as well as technical owner of the estate, which it would lease to a series of tenants (called by Pliny 'dominus'), is excluded by the fact that the estate was worth much more than HS500,000 ('longe pluris'). If Pliny had really ceded effective use of the estate to the city apart from his own lifetime interest, he would have been donating the whole value of the estate, not merely the HS500,000 which was the value of his gift. It is clear from the appraisal of Pliny's losses at the end of the letter (quoted above) that this is not what took place. If the estate had now effectively belonged to the city, Pliny could have no interest in its future 'pretium'. (Cf. also Sherwin-White 423.) The legal status of the land in question is left unclear; possibly the transaction represented the type of lease referred to as 'in avitum' or 'ob avitum et patritum' (*FIRA* 3, nos.114; 131a; L. Bove *Ricerche sugli 'agri vectigales'* (1960) 66–8). The list in the Table of Veleia contains much land in private ownership which carried a 'vectigal' of some kind (XI 1147, obligations 2; 3; 13; 15; 16; 19; 22; 24; 30; 31; 37; 42; 44). For private charges on property cf. *Digesta* 34.1.4.pr.; 34.1.12; 34.1.20.2; 32.27.2.

would borrow at the official rate from cities in Bithynia when they could obtain loans at the same rate from private individuals.[1] The interest-rate on the alimentary loans is a little lower than the rate mentioned as a normal return on landed investments: 5% as compared with 6%.[2] The difference may have been enough to offset the effects of the loan on the market-price of the estate in some cases; but the actual profitability of estates and the efficiency of exploitation would vary considerably between one landlord and another. It remains highly doubtful whether the alimentary loans could offer any real economic attraction to borrowers, except those who needed to be bailed out of debt (if they were eligible for loans). Thus it is unlikely that the scheme was devised in order to serve the interests of the landowners. Local banking facilities of the kind needed to guarantee an annual interest payment did not exist at Italian secondary towns;[3] the landowners were brought in to meet this deficiency. The only beneficiaries appear to have been the children whose subsistence the interest-payments guaranteed.

THE SOCIAL BASIS OF THE DISTRIBUTIONS

There is no direct evidence about the arrangements for the support of the children benefited by the *alimenta*, beyond the account in the Table of Veleia of the rates of subsidy for either sex. But the statistics about the number of beneficiaries at Veleia allow some inferences. It is unlikely that a minor town such as Veleia[4] would have had a population large enough to include at one time as many as 264 orphan boys, although this is the number of male beneficiaries listed in the Table. Furthermore, if the support of orphans had been the prime object, some arrangements for child care would be needed, yet the inscription promises nothing besides grants of money. This makes it likely that the grants were mainly intended for children who had parents to look after them. A dedication

---

[1] *Ep.* 10.54. [2] See p.133.

[3] The lack of institutional investment arrangements is illustrated in two of Pliny's Letters. It does not seem that there was any possibility of obtaining safe long-term revenue by placing funds in a bank, either at Comum or in large cities in Bithynia (*Ep.* 7.18; 10.54). Cf. *ESAR* Index s.v. Banks. At an African town a gift for annual payments was made without the capital being invested to produce revenue (no.344).

[4] Cf. *Enc.art.ant.* s.v. Velleia. Although the respective Tables suggest that Ligures Baebiani was smaller still, the physical remains of its public buildings imply that Veleia was a small community. The town was sufficiently obscure for the elder Pliny to think it necessary to identify Veleia as '(oppidum)...citra Placentiam in collibus' (*NH* 7.163–4). The remarkable longevity at Veleia of which Pliny found evidence cannot be taken at face value. On Pliny's reading of the census-returns under Vespasian, Veleia provided 6 of the 14 persons aged 110 and one of the 3 persons aged 140 listed in regio VIII as a whole! These figures appear to belong to a backward community with low literacy and low 'numeracy'.

at Asisium supports this inference: a statue of the local magistrate in charge of the *alimenta* was dedicated by the 'pueri et puellae qui ex liberalitate sacratissimi principis aliment(a) accipiunt, *consensu parentium* ex aere conlato'. Pliny's speech describing his own alimentary gift sought to explain to the childless the benefits of 'quod parentibus dabatur'. Similarly Ps.-Aurelius Victor states that Nerva's *alimenta* benefited the 'puellas puerosque natos parentibus egestosis'.[1]

Little more than 300 families[2] could have benefited from the *alimenta* at Veleia, though it is unlikely that the proletariat of the town had fewer families than this.[3] There would thus have been competition for what were in effect family allowances, and so the authorities might well have restricted the number of children from any one family who could receive payments, perhaps to the point of allowing no more than one or two beneficiaries per family. In such circumstances it would need little acuteness to grasp that a son who received the alimentary dole would add more to the household budget than a daughter, whose allowance was only 75% of the masculine rate. Thus all parents who had sons of appropriate age would presumably have applied on their behalf rather than on behalf of any daughters. The very low proportion of girls benefited at Veleia (36 out of 300 children in the two schemes of which we have details) may reflect nothing more than the proportion of families whose only children of appropriate age were girls, among the families that benefited from the scheme. The figures are certainly not a realistic indication of the sex-ratio among children that Veleian parents chose to rear; even if there was some tendency towards exposing girls at birth,[4] no race in which males were allowed to outnumber females by 7 to 1 could have survived for long. Although so few girls are recorded in the Table of Veleia, girls seem to have had a regular place in the Italian *alimenta*: at every town where there are details, the beneficiaries included both sexes.[5]

There are a number of collective dedications by the children whom the *alimenta* supported, like the text from Asisium quoted above. Five of these are dedications to Antoninus Pius and Marcus Aurelius, which overlap because one dedication to Pius is posthumous, and one to Marcus

---

[1] *ILS* 6620 = XI 5395; Pliny *Ep.* 1.8.12; *Epit. de Caes.* 12.4.

[2] The Bassus scheme (Appendix 3) is unlikely to have supported many more than the Gallicanus scheme, which had 19 beneficiaries in all. 300 is the combined total of the Gallicanus scheme and its larger successor (XI 1147 pr. 1.2 and 7.34–5).

[3] Compare the figure of roughly 2,400 deduced for Petelia under Antoninus Pius (see p.270).

[4] Cf. *POxy* 744 (A. S. Hunt, C. C. Edgar *Select Papyri* no.105); there is a high ratio of sons to daughters in the list of *circitores* and their families from Tibur in XIV 3649 (cf. *IIt* 4.1. no.238).

[5] IX 1455; 5700; XI 4351; 5395 = *ILS* 6620; XI 5956; 5957; 5989 = *ILS* 328; XIV 4003 = *ILS* 6225.

dates from before his accession.[1] One dedication is addressed to Trajan, one to L. Aelius Caesar, and one (at Asisium) to the local *quaestor alimentorum*.[2] Six of these dedications were evidently financed by the children themselves.[3] It may seem paradoxical that the recipients of imperial charity should respond by financing monuments to their benefactors. But exchanges of this kind were important in Roman munificence:[4] the recipient was expected to show tangible signs of gratitude as part of the social rapport which the gift established. Thus the urban proletariat frequently honoured its benefactors with statues.[5] The client at Rome who received a cash sportula was expected to advertise his dependence on the patron by paying morning visits as well as afternoon calls at the baths.[6] Members of a private household might erect a statue of a generous master,[7] and farm labourers might honour their overseer in the same way.[8] The alimentary dedications do not show that the children who benefited from the *alimenta* were undeserving of charity, any more than the farm dedications show that rustic slaves were well paid. A joint dedication shared among many made slight financial demands; and the price of statues was not necessarily exorbitant.[9] The cost of one statue shared among several hundred alimentary beneficiaries might be less than a month's subsistence for each contributor.[10]

Nevertheless, the Trajanic alimentary subsidies were relatively low.[11] It is unlikely that they could provide more than a subsistence diet of bread, wine, and oil. Other donors were sometimes more generous: Caelia Macrina provided 100 children of either sex at Tarracina with amounts 25% higher in the case of boys and 33% higher in the case of girls.[12] Private donors who bequeathed *alimenta* for members of their

---

[1] IX 5700; XI 5956; 5957; 6002; XIV 4003.

[2] XI 4351; 5989; 5395.

[3] IX 5700; XI 5395; 5956; 5957; 6002; XIV 4003.

[4] For the niceties of munificence cf. Seneca *de beneficiis*. Historical parallels: M. Mauss *The gift* (1954).

[5] Cf. *ILS* 904; 930a; 931; 1159; 5501; 6522; 989; 2677; 2720; 2722; 5503; 6553; 6609; 6646; 6655; 6660; 6623; 6678; 6894; 6897; 7170; 6772.

[6] Cf. Martial 3.36; 6.88; 3.7; 9.100; 8.44.

[7] *ILS* 8978, cf. 7366; VI 1747; IX 825; Petronius *Sat.* 30; X 860.

[8] *ILS* 7367–8.

[9] In Africa, the only area where information is extensive, statues could cost as little as HS2,000 or HS3,000, C. nos.189–212. For Italian prices, C. nos.491–504.

[10] Shared among 300 (the total of the two schemes in the Table of Veleia) a statue costing HS3,000 would require an individual contribution of HS10, which is less than either of the basic monthly rates for legitimate children (HS16 and HS12, XI 1147).

[11] The grants at Rome could be called a *perceptio frumentaria* (*HA Marc.* 7.8, with *ILS* 6065); it is unlikely that the Italian provisions were significantly more generous. For wheat prices at Rome, almost certainly higher than those in Italy, see Appendix 8.

[12] *ILS* 6278. See also II 1174.

household seem to have given substantially more, though as a rule they would be dealing with fewer beneficiaries. Two examples show rates of HS83 and HS85/70 per month,[1] four or five times more than the highest Trajanic rate. The differential is much greater than can be explained by the different dietary requirements of children and adults.

The low rate of benefit suggests that the Trajanic grants were intended for poor families, although we cannot tell how effectively the intention was carried out. Small grants of less than HS200 per year could not have been considered an effective inducement to the well-to-do to have children.[2] Pliny portrays the beneficiaries of the alimentary provisions at Rome as prospective recruits to the army; army privates were not an economically privileged class.[3] He also expresses the hope that the descendants of the beneficiaries may be so circumstanced that they will not need subsidy; this suggests that those who benefited were in some sense needy. Ps.-Aurelius Victor explicitly refers to the parents whose children the *alimenta* benefited as needy ('egestosi').[4] Thus modern views that depict the Italian *alimenta* as not directed towards the poor are probably misleading.[5]

THE LANDOWNERS

The lists of landowners who took alimentary loans at Veleia and Ligures Baebiani provide an interesting cross-section in terms of wealth. The 46 estates declared in the main scheme at Veleia range in value from HS1,600,000 to HS50,000, a difference of 32-fold;[6] while at Ligures Baebiani the 55 estates whose value is known ranged from HS501,000 to HS14,000, a difference of 36-fold.[7] The average valuations were HS283,500 and HS77,300, respectively. At the top of the scale there are estates large enough to qualify their owners in economic terms for membership of the Senate.[8] At the bottom are holdings so small that

---

[1] *Digesta* 34.1.20. pr.; *ILS* 2927 (see p.30 n.2).

[2] At the top of the social scale, HS200,000 per child was a derisory subvention for a senator who had children, Tac. *Ann.* 2.37–8. Cf. Pliny *Pan.* 26.5.

[3] *Pan.* 26.3; 28.5. Basic pay in the praetorian élite was probably HS4,000 and pay in the legions HS1,200 after Domitian's increase (P. A. Brunt *PBSR* 18 (1950) 71). The words 'Vixi... pauper honeste' appear on the tombstone of a praetorian soldier who served for 18 years and retired in A.D. 29 (*ILS* 2028).

[4] *Epit. de Caes.* 12.4.

[5] A. R. Hands *Charities and social aid in Greece and Rome* (1968) 114 (cf. *JRS* 59 (1969) 288). The scale of Hadrian's provision for a single town, Antinoopolis, is not necessarily a reliable basis for assessing Trajan's provision for many Italian towns.

[6] XI 1147, *oblig.* 43; 8; 29.

[7] IX 1455, 2.29; 2.36.

[8] Actual membership usually required much more than the nominal HS1 million (Cassius Dio 54.17.3) or HS1,200,000 (Suetonius *Aug.* 41.1; Cassius Dio 55.13.6). Cf. Pliny *Ep.* 10.4; Tac. *Ann.* 2.37–8; 13.34; Suetonius *Nero* 10; *Vesp.* 17.

their owners could hardly have been qualified for the town-council, if these properties were all the wealth they possessed. Some of the declarations appear to be comprehensive accounts of the landholdings of the individuals concerned.[1] The references to neighbours at Veleia show many other landowners in the neighbourhood who did not receive loans from the alimentary commissioners under the two schemes of which we have detailed record, although the last three landowners in the main series of loans declared estates which lay at Placentia, not at Veleia.[2]

The social identity of the borrowers remains obscure. Neither of the Tables reproduces marks of rank, or makes any allusion to occupation. In economic terms, many of the landowners were eligible for membership of the town-council. The only qualifying figure that we know is HS100,000 at Comum;[3] at much smaller towns such as Veleia and Ligures Baebiani, the qualification may have been less. We cannot be certain whether these towns would have had the 100 decurions attested elsewhere in Italy, at Veii and at Cures Sabini.[4] In previous discussions it has been argued in turn that the lists of names clearly indicate that some borrowers were decurions,[5] and that no borrowers were decurions.[6] Neither conclusion can be substantiated in the present state of the evidence. There is too little ancillary information about the composition of the *ordo* at either town to establish a single firm case of identity between a borrower and a member of the *ordo*.[7] But conversely, the certain exclusion from the *ordo* of some borrowers (the eight women who declared in the two schemes in the Table of Veleia, and the three who declared at Ligures Baebiani) does not show that no borrowers belonged to the *ordo*.[8]

But the character of the civic administration which was expected to administer the alimentary payments cannot be ignored. There are clear indications that the reliability of local government in Italian towns at this date was uncertain, and that the government was beginning to

---

[1] Entries in which land declared under previous schemes is referred to as being excluded from what is now pledged: XI 1147, *oblig.* 13; 16; 17; 30; 31.

[2] Lists in XI pp.229–31. XI 1147 *oblig.* 44–6.

[3] Pliny *Ep.* 1.19; cf. Petronius *Sat.* 44; Cassius Dio 72.16.3; Catullus 23.26–7. See p.243.

[4] *ILS* 460; 6579 (3.p.675). For towns with 30 decurions, see p.284.

[5] Veyne 1958, 218–19; Garnsey 1968, 375–7.

[6] R. Duncan-Jones *PBSR* 32 (1964) 134.

[7] Despite attempts to revive prosopographical arguments (Garnsey 1968, 371–7), only 2 of the 100 or so named landowners who declare properties in the two Tables bear names identical with those of known magistrates or decurions. Since neither corroborative inscription is known to belong to the period of the alimentary Tables, the coincidences do not prove anything in themselves (IX 1455, 2.47 with IX 2220 from Telesia; XI 1147, 3.87 with XI 1162 from Veleia).

[8] The exclusion from the *ordo* of other categories of borrower (*PBSR* 32 (1964) 132) is more uncertain.

exercise direct supervision over city affairs. Pliny the younger, although a devoted citizen of Comum, to which he gave large endowments, twice had to admit cases where local administration could not be trusted. He advised a would-be benefactor not to hand over either cash or property to their native town because cash may be allowed to disappear, while property will receive the same neglect as the public lands. (It is better to retain the capital in one's own hands and pay the town the income.) When Pliny wanted to provide Comum with a town schoolmaster, he decided to withhold the payment of a full salary which he could easily have made, because he knew too many cases where teachers' salaries paid from public funds had been misappropriated.[1] Municipal corruption was hardly peculiar to the Trajanic period.[2] But at this time the government took initiatives to regulate town spending through the appointment of *curatores reipublicae* in Italy, whose permission was needed for example before new buildings could be put up at public expense.[3]

We also know that Roman administration was sufficiently aware of the possibilities of corruption to restrict the financial activities of decurions in circumstances where a conflict between private interest and public responsibility was possible. Decurions were prohibited from contracting for local revenues in their own towns; and they might be prohibited from leasing town lands.[4] The administration of the alimentary funds offered an analogous problem: the local administrator who collected interest from the landlords and distributed it among the recipients of *alimenta* was inevitably a decurion of the city.[5] If the landlords from whom interest was to be collected were also decurions, or if the alimentary quaestor were himself one of those from whom interest was due, he might be under temptation to allow reduced interest payments.

If grounds were wanted for concentrating the alimentary loans outside the *ordo*, these conditions would probably have provided sound arguments for doing so. Moreover, if the loans were recognised as a potential burden by the government, the class on whom municipal burdens already impinged most heavily might have been excluded from them. We cannot tell whether these considerations were actually applied, although the

---

[1] *Ep.* 7.18; 4.13.

[2] Corruption and mismanagement of funds were probably to some extent endemic. Further contemporary illustrations of local financial inefficiency (in cities in the East) in Pliny *Ep.* 10 (see Sherwin-White 527).

[3] *ILS* 5918a shows the functioning of the *curator rei publicae* at Caere in A.D. 113: the town council has to write to the curator (who resides elsewhere, at Ameria, where he was a local magistrate, XI 4347) before it can cede land to a private donor for a new building to house the meetings of the Augustales. Ruggiero 2.1345–77; *Staatsrecht* 2.1082–4.

[4] *Digesta* 50.2.6.2; 50.8.2.1.

[5] Ruggiero s.v. Alimenta.

heavy security asked of the borrowers suggests that the *alimenta* were not conceived in a spirit of careless idealism. It still remains possible, however, that eligibility for alimentary loans was primarily construed in economic terms, not in terms of status or occupation.

THE RATIONALE OF THE ALIMENTARY LOANS

The broad outline of the loan arrangements emerges clearly from the two Tables. Loans were placed with the owners of land in the vicinity of each town; and their amounts were related to the property declared, averaging roughly 8% at Ligures Baebiani and in the main scheme at Veleia. There are several problems: were the loans farmed out on a voluntary basis? why was the rate of loan so low? and was the variation in loan-rates between one property and another in any way meaningful?

Pliny the younger indicates that a permanent charge on an estate reduced its value by an amount greater than is indicated by a capitalisation of the charge itself.[1] There is no reason to think that the alimentary borrowers, who accepted loans that were evidently permanent, were exempt from the working of this mechanism. Accepting the obligation to pay an annual charge was almost bound to prejudice the value of the estate. Nevertheless, the amount of the alimentary loans was so small (8% of the estate's value) that the impact would not have been important, at least in the short term. In contrast Pliny's own arrangement probably meant a charge that absorbed a much larger proportion of the estate's revenue: in view of what is known of Pliny's wealth,[2] it is impossible to believe that he consecrated to his *alimenta* an estate big enough to reduce the capitalisation of the rent charge to a mere 8% of the estate's value. This would have meant his making over land worth HS6 million. More probably 'longe pluris' in his description points to a total estate-size in the region of HS1 or HS1½ million, and a rent charge corresponding with 30 or 50% of the estate-value.[3] Hence this example need not argue that the financial drawbacks of accepting a loan under the terms of the Trajanic *alimenta* were very great.

In the short term these drawbacks would be offset by the presence of the cash value of the loan itself. But in the longer term, the loan would be an economic asset only if it could be reinvested permanently at a higher rate of interest.[4] Re-lending the money was almost bound to be

---

[1] See above p.299.
[2] He was probably not worth more than HS20 million or so; see p.20.
[3] For details of Pliny's transaction, see above p.299.
[4] Bourne's optimism about local opportunities for reinvestment in Italian towns is unrealistic (Bourne 69).

profitable, since private loans would normally be at rates above 5%;[1] but there is unlikely to have been sufficient demand to absorb the whole alimentary loan in this way or even a substantial part of it, granted that private loans were mainly of limited term. Reinvestment in land might not be easy to negotiate; it would depend on the state of the land-market, and the availability of adjoining estates. The smaller loans, of a few thousand sesterces, could not easily be converted into a useful addition to the working area of a farm, unless land happened to be available in very small units on an adjacent site. Furthermore, the release of relatively large sums for reinvestment in a single town would tend to lower interest-rates and raise land prices, thus making it more difficult to obtain a permanent running yield that exceeded the interest payable to the alimentary fund.

The correspondence between Pliny as governor of Bithynia and Trajan contains an exchange in which Pliny proposes to impose forced loans at 9% on the decurions of the province as a means of obtaining revenue from civic funds that cannot be invested by other means. Trajan forbids this move, saying that it is out of keeping with the spirit of his reign to impose loans on those who may find them useless. Pliny must find an interest-rate that will attract a sufficient number of borrowers.[2] It seems straightforward enough to turn to Trajan's *alimenta* and to infer that the alimentary loans must have been placed on a wholly voluntary basis. If the loans contained some economic drawbacks, as seems to have been the case, we might assume that there were enough landowners willing to make minor sacrifices to make placing the loans a feasible proposition. On the analogy of Trajan's ruling about Bithynia, 5% might have been chosen as being an interest-rate that would attract enough volunteers.

This reasoning is attractively clear-cut, and it may be enough to determine our interpretation of the basis of the loans. But the evidence from Veleia suggests a pattern imposed from above rather than the random outcome of voluntary initiative. Some declarations of property in the main scheme appear to be comprehensive accounts of all land owned by the person concerned: in all five cases where land was pledged under previous schemes as well as in the main scheme at Veleia, it is stated that the final valuation excludes the land previously pledged.[3] It is reasonable to think that if the basis of the loans were entirely volun-

---

[1] Cf. Pliny *Ep.* 9.28.5; 10.54.1 (see n.2 below); L. Breglia in *Pompeiana. Raccolta di studi per il secondo centenario degli scavi di Pompei* (1950) 52.

[2] Pliny *Ep.* 10.54–5. The rate is undoubtedly 9% (Mommsen *Hermes* 5 (1871) 132, n.2; Billeter 105), though it is often rendered as 12% (see Sherwin-White 635; Radice *Pliny* 2.231). The stated amounts of principal and interest make it clear that ἐπὶ τόκῳ ἀσσαρίων δεκαδύο ἀργυρῶν meant 9% in a Trajanic foundation at Ephesus (J. H. Oliver *Hesperia* supp. 6 (1941) 55–85 ll.301–2).

[3] XI 1147 *oblig.* 13; 16; 17; 30; 31.

tary some borrowers would wish to pledge only part of what they owned. Comparison between the two alimentary schemes in the Table of Veleia shows that the five individuals concerned in the scheme under Gallicanus include four of the five largest private landowners who took part in the much larger main scheme,[1] which involved 45 separate private landholdings. The landowners who received loans under Gallicanus were evidently selected for this purpose on the grounds of their wealth; the proportion is too high to be mere coincidence. The remaining member of the group of five largest landowners in the main scheme had also declared property in a previous scheme, the scheme under the charge of Pomponius Bassus.[2] None of the remaining 41 landowners had declared in previous schemes. At the early stage represented by the Gallicanus scheme the commissioners were evidently concerned to distribute the loans widely, among landowners who had much more land than the amounts which they pledged under these loans. In fact each of the four who also appear in the main scheme owned more than enough property to have carried all the loans in the Gallicanus scheme singlehanded. The main scheme also contained economic restrictions: no loans went to landowners with estates worth less than HS50,000. When 16, or more than one-third of the Veleian declarations fall into the range between HS80,000 and HS50,000, it is clear that there must have been numbers of smaller estates at the town.[3] At Ligures Baebiani, where the terms of eligibility were different, 21 estates below HS50,000 were pledged, with values ranging between HS48,000 and HS14,000.[4] It cannot be argued that the restriction at Veleia was accidental: the last three declarations of property in the main scheme are entirely composed of property at Placentia, which implies that suitable holdings on Veleian territory had been exhausted.[5]

The one declaration of publicly owned land at Veleia is also interesting, since the land belonged to the colony of Luca, a city some distance from Veleia, whose territory adjoined Veleian territory.[6] We know that Veleia had town land of its own: there are six references to it in the lists of neighbours in the Table.[7] But it was not pledged under either of the alimentary schemes. It is difficult to conceive that the town-council of Veleia was actually reluctant to provide support for the scheme at Veleia of a kind made available by another city. Hence it seems that the com-

[1] XI 1147 *oblig.* 31 and 48 (father and daughter, the father bequeathing the estate to his daughter before the second loan was floated); 13 and 51; 16 and 47; 30 and 49.
[2] *Oblig.* 17.
[3] See C. nos.1249–83 *passim.*
[4] C. nos.1284–1305.   [5] XI 1147, *oblig.* 44–6.
[6] Cf. XI pp. 295–6.
[7] XI 1147, 1.63; 2.104; 3.74; 4.60; 4.64; 7.39.

missioners deliberately chose the Lucan estate in preference to land belonging to Veleia, presumably for economic reasons. Its place in the list is hardly random: the account of the estate falls at the end of the forty-two declarations of Veleian land made by private borrowers, and is followed by the three private declarations from Placentia.

Finally, the total number of children supported by the two schemes listed in the Table of Veleia was exactly 300,[1] which was evidently a deliberate target figure. The fact that the government was able to work in terms of local targets of this kind, while complicating its task by asking for security as heavy as 12- or 13-fold might suggest that the task of distributing the loans was backed where necessary by compulsory powers. If the alimentary commissioners were dependent on the goodwill of the landowners for setting up the scheme, it might be thought that they would not have been so careless about giving each borrower the amount to which his land entitled him (the loan pattern is discussed below). Local willingness to take up loans was almost bound to vary from town to town, according to the impact of existing municipal burdens and the size of the propertied class.[2] It is not clear that the success of the government's plan for 'alimenta Italiae' could have been allowed to depend on a variant of this kind. Since there is no basis for the modern dual-purpose interpretation of the *alimenta* (discussed above), placing the loans with landowners evidently served the government's convenience, not the convenience of the landowners. No doubt volunteers, anxious to show their public spirit, and to receive permanent commemoration of their action, would often have been available. Where volunteers were lacking, the high security demanded would still effectively limit the financial impact of the loans on the recipients to relatively insignificant proportions.[3]

If justification for compulsory powers were needed, beyond the philanthropic purpose of the scheme, some basis existed in the known pattern of civic obligations. Even those not on the town-council were liable to perform *munera* on behalf of the city. These could include such tasks as the provision of hospitality on behalf of the town,[4] or providing

[1] pr. 2; 7.34-5.
[2] Cf. Piganiol in Veyne 1964, 178. Some Italian towns were already obtaining dispensations to impose local obligations on outsiders in the first half of the second century: Aquileia under Trajan (*ILS* 1374); Tergeste under Pius (*ILS* 6680). Claudius expected Tridentum to find the loss of inhabited territory wrongly 'attributed' to it a *gravis iniuria*, and consequently confirmed the position as it stood (*ILS* 206). The Domitianic charter of Malaca in Spain provided for the contingency of there being too few candidates to fill the local magistracies (*ILS* 6089 c.51).
[3] Cf. Veyne 1964, 173.
[4] *Digesta* 50.4.18.30; cf. *ILS* 2735.

a certain number of days' manual labour[1] (those who could afford it would send their slaves). The *munera* also included direct outlays such as the provision of fuel for the public baths, or dealing with street repairs.[2] Transport obligations were apparently imposed on local property-holders irrespective of whether they were local citizens.[3] The current magistrates were dispensed from performing these tasks.[4] The financial drain threatened by some ordinary civic *munera* was more intimidating than that posed by a permanent obligation to service a government loan at 5%. Trajan's admonition to Pliny in Bithynia refers to a proposal to coerce decurions, who were already heavily involved in municipal obligations because of their position.[5] The various financial duties of civic life were meant to be assigned equitably among those who were liable to them;[6] if the alimentary commissioners were forced to nominate the recipients of loans (as the *ordo* might be forced to nominate local office-holders)[7] they would probably look for those whose burdens were not already heavy. We know that the commissioners tended to prefer the larger landowner where there was a choice.

LOAN VARIATIONS

The two alimentary Tables show different degrees of elaboration in the determining of loan-amounts. The earlier of the two, the Table of Ligures Baebiani, contains a series of loans to individuals whose rates vary widely, between extremes as remote as 10% and 2.94% of the value of the property.[8] But these rates are exceptional and the loans in the surviving section of the Table (about one-sixth of whose details are missing) produce an average of 7.61% taken as a whole. This is quite

---

[1] *ILS* 6087, c.98; 5630; 5729; 5590; 6888; 6889; *AE* 1916, 60–1; *ILAlg* 2.3596. Cf. *Digesta* 50.4.12; Cicero *Verr.* 2.5.48.

[2] *Digesta* 50.4.1.2; *ILS* 5875 shows the neighbouring landowners contributing more than HS500,000 to the repair of an Italian trunk road under Hadrian. In *ILS* 5368 (A.D. 119) the 'possessores circa forum (pecuarium)' provide funds for road works.

[3] *Digesta* 50.4.1.1; 50.4.6.5.

[4] *Digesta* 50.4.10.

[5] Pliny *Ep.* 10.54–5.

[6] *Digesta* 50.4.3.15.

[7] *Digesta* 50.1.17.4; 50.1.18; 50.4.11. pr.; *ILS* 6089 c.51. The received text of one of Trajan's replies to Pliny, referring to Bithynia, mentions 'eos qui inviti fiunt decuriones' (*Ep.* 10.113). Sherwin-White's emendation of 'inviti' to 'invitati' (also incorporated in the recent Oxford text of Pliny's Letters) is somewhat unconvincing, cf. C. P. Jones *Phoenix* 22 (1968) 137–8; Sherwin-White 722–3. Sherwin-White contends that Pliny's request for guidance contains no reference to compulsion, and that to find any allusion to it in Trajan's reply, which is likely to deal only with the problems that Pliny specifically raised, would therefore be gratuitous. But as Jones pointed out, adlection, which Pliny mentions, may be compulsory.

[8] IX 1455, 3.23; 3.36; 2.10.

close to the average in the main scheme at Veleia of 8.01%.[1] Loans to individuals in the Gallicanus scheme at Veleia were made at a straight 10% with no variations. In the later main scheme loans followed a more complex pattern: the majority represent 8% or 8.05% of the total estate-valuation in each case.[2] But many property declarations contain a long enumeration of individual farms; these farms receive component loans which make up the aggregate loan for the estate as a whole. The loan rates here vary as widely as those in the Table of Ligures Baebiani: the extremes are 3.2% and 12.2%.[3] The amounts of the component loans and those of the aggregate loans tally throughout the Table, but the aggregate and component land-valuations often disagree. In an extreme case, the aggregate value of an estate is stated as HS77,192, but the values assigned to the farms of which the estate is composed total HS112,829, an excess of 46%.[4]

Modern scholars have explained these variations and discrepancies in different ways. Desjardins conjectured that the contradictory valuations reflected variations in the condition and profitability of the estates.[5] De Pachtere argued that they resulted from the use of out-dated sale-prices or old census-returns for the valuations, while current revenue was being used to determine the loans.[6] There are cryptic mentions of the word 'census' in an early alimentary document. But the valuations in the

---

[1] See Appendix 4. The missing loans at Ligures Baebiani may have brought the overall average closer to 8%. But the loan amounts, whose totals we can calculate throughout, show that the rate for the missing properties would need to be more than 12% in order to raise the average loan-rate to 8%. Since the highest individual rate known at Ligures Baebiani is 10% (3.23; 3.36), it is virtually certain that the average loan-rate must have fallen short of 8% at this town, though not by a wide margin.

[2] De Pachtere showed convincingly that the target loan in the main scheme at Veleia was 8.05%, calculated on the overall estate-valuation (rounded off, where the total was irregular, to the next thousand below the amount declared). The loan on an estate valued at HS53,900 was thus calculated as 8.05% of HS53,000, or HS4,266.5. The Table gives a loan figure of HS4,265, rounding the loan amount to a multiple of 5 (*oblig.* 33). Using this discovery, de Pachtere was able to emend a number of the estate valuations in the Table on the basis of the loan amounts, which appear to be reliable, since they add up to the stated total amount of the overall loan at Veleia (with an error of HS10, see p.313 n.3). But it is not clear that his more drastic substitutions are necessarily correct. There is too much residual error in the Table to make it easy to say that the loans were always accurately related to the declared valuation (de Pachtere 98 ff. and table p.100).

[3] XI 1147, 4.4; 5.91. [4] XI 1147 *oblig.* 3.

[5] E. Desjardins *De tabulis alimentariis* (1854) 51; cf. Bormann XI p.221, 2.

[6] De Pachtere assumed that an isolated declaration at Veleia which referred to estimation of value from revenue (*oblig.* 39) showed the source of the estate-valuations as a whole. In fact this is most unlikely, because the ensuing valuation was a very round figure (HS100,000) which most of the other valuations are not, and the procedure followed here seems to have been a special one, made necessary by the failure of the owner to declare the valuation herself. De Pachtere 106–10.

main alimentary schemes were not based on previous census-returns. It is clear that the landowner or his agent had to make a declaration of the current value; if the valuations had been drawn from existing census lists, there would have been no need for landlords to depute their farm-managers on the spot to enumerate properties and their values.[1] Veyne argued that the variations showed that the alimentary commissioners took as the basis for loans concealed valuations of their own which differed from the owners' valuations given in the inscriptions.[2] The two latter interpretations assume that the loan-figures are reliable, while the valuations must be distrusted. There is a fundamental implausibility in supposing that the alimentary commissioners knew the valuations to be unreliable, made other assessments of their own, and yet included the faulty details, not the true ones, in a permanent public record. Earlier investigations by the present writer suggested that the loans followed no consistent pattern of an intelligible kind, although there was a limited tendency to give loans at higher rates on the security of bigger farms.[3]

The explanation seems to be disconcertingly simple. The alimentary commissioners had to allocate a fixed sum of money and were expected to obtain a certain level of security; but they were often slovenly about parcelling the money out in loans at a consistent rate. The miniature scheme set up at Veleia under Cornelius Gallicanus was an exception; its loan-rate of 10% (which was easy to calculate) was applied consistently to the five landowners who took part. But the much bigger schemes set up at Ligures Baebiani and later at Veleia, where the commissioners were working with rates of 8% and 8.05% followed an irregular pattern. At Ligures Baebiani the commissioners usually worked in crude round totals; this is true of 86% of the loan figures. A property at this town valued at HS100,000 might receive a loan of HS10,000, 9,000 or 6,000.[4] Precise calculation was unlikely, and the resulting loan would probably have a round total even with irregular valuations. The commissioners kept sufficiently close to their prescribed limits to maintain an overall rate of loan that approximated to the intended norm;[5] but that was all. In the main scheme at Veleia, which is later and more sophisticated,

---

[1] For the mention of 'census' see Appendix 3. Cornelia Severa declared property 'in Veleiate per Primigenium ser(vum) suum et in Placentino (per) Zosimum ser(vum) suum' (XI 1147 *oblig.* 31). Other declarations through freedmen or slaves who are presumably the *actores* or *vilici* of the estates in question: IX 1455, 1.65; 2.4; 2.71; 2.74; XI 1147, *oblig.* 1; 9; 15; 16; 19; 29; 30; 35; 38; 41.

[2] Veyne 1958, 185–204; cf. Veyne 1964, 174.

[3] *PBSR* 32 (1964) 137–9. The method employed there for analysing loan-rates now seems inappropriate.

[4] See IX 1455, 3.23 and 3.36; 2.64 and 3.34; 3.69.

[5] For overall rates of loan see above pp.310–11 and 311 nn.1–2.

there was much more concern for an appearance of consistency. The third or so of properties that took the form of one or two holdings received loans at a fixed rate of 8.05% to within a close accuracy in a number of cases.[1] The remaining two-thirds each consisted of multiple declarations in whose interior loans were assigned on a basis as random as that at Ligures Baebiani; but in most cases the loan calculated on their overall valuation approximated to the standard rate.[2] The discrepancies between the stated overall valuations and the arithmetical total of the component valuations seem to result from error in stating valuations, whether by the owner or by the engraver, and from omission.[3]

The fact that an estate of a given size received a mixture of loans at different rates if composed of a number of units, but a straight 8% loan if composed of a single holding, is enough to show that loan variation was a random and not a meaningful variant. If some test of the loan-worthiness of the estates were being made, or if recourse were being had to a hidden second source of valuations, the effects would hardly have been restricted to estates which had several components, irrespective of their overall size. If loan-modulation is regarded as meaningful, there is no evident reason why the ten declarations with only one constituent valuation[4] should have been exempt from significant deviation, when the

---

[1] Taking the figures as they stand, this is true of *obligationes* 1, 7, 8, 10, 37, 43. De Pachtere's emendations contribute further examples; see p.311 n.2 above (de Pachtere, table p.100).

[2] Bormann gives a convenient résumé of all loans and valuations (though not their percentage relationships) in XI pp.223–5.

[3] It is often uncertain whether the errors occur in stating component valuations, or in totalling them. De Pachtere showed that the stated aggregate valuations sometimes contain errors (p.311 n.2). Bormann showed that in nine of the thirteen cases where there is a mention of a *vectigal*, the aggregate stated valuation is lower than the total of the component valuations (*oblig.* 2; 3; 15; 16; 19; 31; 37; 42, 44; compare 13; 22; 24; 30. XI p.222, 1). He also showed that the owners were liable to error in their declarations: where a single property is shared equally between owners who declare separately, they may assign different values to the two halves, while the fact that only a fraction is owned and not the whole farm is sometimes omitted altogether (XI p.221, 1). There are palpable errors in the valuations and loans, although the randomness of the component loans makes it difficult to be certain in identifying error. Two instances may be given: in *obligatio* 29, the engraver gives the loan figure on an estate of HS50,000 as $\overline{III}$ LXXV (3,075) instead of $\overline{IIII}$ XXV (4,025). Since the second figure converts what was otherwise a very small loan to exactly 8.05%, this emendation (noticed by de Pachtere, table p.100, though not by Bormann) is clearly correct. It has the incidental merit of increasing the arithmetical total of the aggregate loan in the main scheme (stated in the preamble as HS1,044,000) to HS1,044,010, and eliminating what was otherwise a deficiency of nearly HS1,000. Secondly, in *obligatio* 3 there is a discrepancy of more than HS35,000 between the stated total valuation and the arithmetical total of the components; one of the components is a property valued at HS70,000 which receives a loan of HS3,197, or 4.57%. If this valuation is emended to HS40,000, the loan-rate on the property concerned becomes a straight 8%, and the overall discrepancy between stated and arithmetical valuation is reduced to less than HS6,000.

[4] This category includes the largest declaration of all, the property owned by the town of

bulk of the remaining property received most of its loans at a non-modal rate.

The sporadic occurrence of exact amounts among the component loans at Veleia can usually be seen as a resort to precision in order to attain the modal loan-rate for the estate as a whole. Thus in *obligatio* 6, component loans are as follows: 25,000, 2000 and 7,206, representing rates of 9.1%, 8% and 5.8%. If the third loan had been a round figure like the others, it would not have been possible to reach the modal loan rate of 8.05% in relation to the total valuation of the estate. When a declaration was composed of as many as twenty separate units, the loans on each unit were still mainly in round figures.[1] Occasional precise calculations were needed as a corrective to stop the overall relationship between declared valuation and loan from getting out of line. Evidently the same applied at Ligures Baebiani, though more loosely. Most of the overall loans to estates here had round totals, but a few were irregular. The fact that the loan-rates which the irregular amounts embody are non-modal, although the result of more or less precise calculation,[2] arose because they were a corrective to the overall pattern of loans at Ligures Baebiani, not a corrective affecting the individual landowner. Evidently it was necessary that the loan-capital should be underwritten with overall security of 12- or 13-fold, but it did not have to be distributed consistently among the various holdings.

The allocations were apparently influenced by some tendency towards giving larger loans to bigger estates. Since this occurred at Veleia within estate-holdings, depending on whether the individual component was small or large, the practice does not appear to have been directed towards the creditworthiness of the owner. It might have had some economic motive nonetheless, since farms could change hands in the course of time, and estates might be split up at the death of their owner. Bigger holdings may have been considered a more reliable investment. But if the tendency were deliberate, we might expect it to be consistent. In fact it is not, since single-unit declarations at Veleia almost never receive more than 8.05%, even when their size exceeds that of component holdings which receive a higher rate. *Obligatio* 10 at Veleia provides a simple illustration: there are two components, a farm worth HS56,000 which receives HS5,000, or 8.9%, and a farm worth HS24,000 which receives HS1,438 or 6%. Yet the much bigger single unit worth HS108,000 that constitutes

Luca, whose net valuation was HS1,600,000 (*oblig.* 43). *Oblig.* 1; 7; 8; 29; 34 (7.93%); 38; 39; 40; 41; 43.

[1] For instance *obligatio* 13 has only two seriously irregular amounts among 24 loan-figures.

[2] IX 1455, 2.29, HS42, 440 (8.5%); 1.34 HS5,600 (6.5%); 1.40, HS4,400 (6.7%); 2.7 HS3,520 (7.05%); 3.73, HS3,560 (7.1%); 2.45, HS1,680 (8.4%).

obligatio 1 received only HS8,692 or 8.05%, being bound to the modal rate. Where it exists at all, the pattern of loan-modulation is broadly consistent: the 15 largest component valuations at Veleia received an aggregate loan of 8.56%, while the 15 smallest received 7.62%.[1] At Ligures Baebiani the corresponding statistics (for overall estate declarations) are 7.33% for the 15 largest estates and 6.83% for the 15 smallest estates.[2] However, the modulation does not represent a large variant in either case.

The main reason for the randomness of the loans can be deduced from the pattern of the loan-amounts: the predominance of round totals shows a lack of arithmetical diligence. The commissioners seem to have been inclined to do as few exact division sums as possible: at Veleia this meant only one or two such calculations for each estate, irrespective of how many component loans it received. In the Ligures Baebiani scheme, the same practice meant only a few exact calculations in the whole Table. The main determinant of variation thus appears to have been random error, probably due to lack of time, linked with a minor tendency towards concentrating capital more heavily with the larger units of exploitation.

CONCLUSION: THE SCOPE AND EFFECTIVENESS OF THE 'ALIMENTA'

There is evidence for public *alimenta* at more than fifty towns in Italy.[3] A few of the schemes were privately donated, but in most cases an allusion to a town-magistrate in charge of alimentary payments indicates the presence of the state scheme. The locations of the magistrates, and the names of the alimentary circumscriptions entrusted to procurators and prefects, indicate that there was almost no part of Italy which lacked units of the government scheme. The scheme was perhaps thus comprehensive in its geographical scope, although the rate at which the cumbersome mechanism could be established was probably so slow that the process cannot have been complete at the death of Trajan. The shortage of evidence from northern and southern Italy in comparison with central Italy, despite good epigraphic survival, almost certainly shows that the scheme never reached all Italian cities.[4] But the depth of attestation is too

---

[1] Veleia, 15 largest component valuations: XI 1147, 1.95; 2.9; 2.68; 3.5; 3.35; 3.63; 3.75; 3.77; 4.47; 4.87; 5.20; 5.43; 5.59; 5.91; 6.88; 15 smallest: 2.77; 2.63; 2.80; 2.32; 2.65; 2.60; 2.86; 4.63; 4.65; 4.100; 5.4; 5.18; 5.27; 6.9; 6.18.

[2] Ligures Baebiani, 15 largest total valuations: IX 1455, 2.29; 2.50; 3.78; 2.33; 3.27; 2.3; 3.55; 2.68; 2.64; 3.23; 3.34; 3.36; 3.69; 3.12; 1.34; 15 smallest: 2.36; 3.8; 3.50; 3.48; 3.38; 2.45; 2.16; 2.71; 3.61; 3.64; 3.44; 3.5; 2.74; 2.10; 3.10.

[3] See Appendix 5.

[4] The regional distribution of surviving references is analysed in Appendix 5.

slight to imply that the 49 examples which we know are anything approaching a complete record.[1]

The existence of heavily financed private schemes alongside a determined state initiative is a little surprising. Private schemes continued to be founded after the government *alimenta* had begun, though they are found only at major towns.[2] It is possible that Nerva or Trajan deliberately encouraged the wealthiest men of large towns to contribute their own schemes for child support, in order to be able to limit the state's efforts to the bulk of secondary towns.[3] Smaller towns would rarely have any citizen rich enough to subscribe a scheme of adequate size as a voluntary action; in these cases a state subvention was the only practical expedient. On this view, Pliny's *alimenta* at Comum should be seen as one of the generosities to which he was encouraged by the Emperor. Tarracina, whose *alimenta* were privately donated, might have received no support from the Emperor.[4] The mentions of quaestors of the *alimenta* at such towns as Ariminum, Brixia and Neapolis might also need to be explained as allusions to the administration of funds given by private benefactors.[5] There is specific evidence for magistracies charged with the management of privately subscribed endowments.[6] But not every senator was a Pliny in generosity, and large towns which did not benefit from their own citizens may have received alimentary funds from the Emperor. Some of the private schemes might have supplemented state efforts that were considered inadequate for large towns; the number of beneficiaries in known alimentary schemes is never enough to suggest that any one scheme provided for all the free infants of the town. Supplementary *alimenta* provided by private donors are specifically attested in two cases.[7]

Any view of the usefulness of the *alimenta* is bound to be speculative, and should be recognised as such. Pliny's rhetoric suggests that one purpose was to supply military recruits,[8] but surviving legionary registers reveal few Italians in the legions after Trajan's time. Recruitment of Italians to the praetorians, a relatively small body of troops, remained common.[9] But their entry into the legions in this period is attested only

---

[1] With the exception of Peltuinum and Auximum, no Italian town provides more than two documents referring to the government *alimenta*.

[2] See Appendix 5.

[3] Nerva is known to have encouraged munificence in his public addresses (Pliny *Ep.* 10.8.1).

[4] C. nos.638; 642; 644.

[5] See Appendix 5.

[6] For example the 'curator calendar(ii) pecuniae Valentini HS $\overline{DC}$' at Pisaurum (XI 6369). See *PBSR* 33 (1965) 206 n.65.

[7] C. no.637; II 1174.

[8] 'alimentisque tuis ad stipendia tua pervenirent'; 'ex his castra...replebuntur' (*Pan.* 26.3; 28.5).

[9] Cf. A. Passerini *Le coorti pretorie* (1939) 148–59.

on the smallest scale;[1] it is not clear that in ordinary circumstances the government even sought to recruit Italians. Nevertheless, it remained possible to raise new legions in Italy on the rare occasions when further units were added (2 new legions under Marcus Aurelius, 3 under Septimius Severus).[2] Population movements in Italy during the second century are not readily determined.[3] The last citizen census figure that we know belongs to the time of Claudius.[4] There are very few statistics for the population of individual towns, and none for any town at two different dates. Distribution figures give some minima, but we have the greatest difficulty in computing the population of Rome.[5] We might hope to determine whether subsistence allowances generally have the effect of encouraging population increase; but the relevance of any conclusion would depend on the degree to which the allocation of alimentary grants was equitable and impartial.

The total number of children that the *alimenta* supported was not very large, probably owing to the costly method by which the scheme was financed. Even if the scheme had extended to every town, the number supported would hardly have been more than 100,000 or 150,000, a relatively small proportion of the population of Italy, however that is estimated.[6] The economic effects of the permanent alimentary loans on Italian agriculture are likely to have been mildly unfavourable in many cases. Paradoxically the proportion of Italian farm land affected by the alimentary loans was considerably higher than the proportion of the population that benefited from the subsistence allowances: each child that the scheme supported represented underlying capital of nearly HS50,000.[7] When an

---

[1] The numbers of legionaries of known origin for the period from Hadrian to the end of the third century collected by Forni in 1953 are: Italians 17 + ; provincials 1,866 + . New evidence in an inscription from Nicopolis which revealed another 15 Italian legionaries serving in Egypt under Antoninus Pius (as well as another 118 provincials) shows that these figures rest on a fragile base. Nevertheless, there is no doubt that provincials far outnumbered Italians in the legions in the second century. The Italians listed at Nicopolis entered the legion at the time of Hadrian's Jewish war and may have been specially recruited (J. F. Gilliam *AJP* 77 (1956) 362–3). G. Forni *Il reclutamento delle legioni da Augusto a Diocleziano* (1953) 187–212; Nicopolis text in full, G. Forni and D. Manini in *Studi di storia antica in memoria di Luca de Regibus* (1969) 177–210 = *AE* 1955,238 + 1969–70, 633.

[2] J. C. Mann *Hermes* 91 (1963) 483–9.

[3] Cf. Beloch 435–43. A recent interpretation of evidence for the late Republic and Augustan period in Brunt 121–30. Cf. T. P. Wiseman *JRS* 59 (1969) 59–75.

[4] Tacitus *Ann.* 11.25 gives a total of 5,984,072 Roman citizens.

[5] Cf. F. G. Maier *Historia* 2 (1953–4) 318–51, at 321–3; J. E. Packer *JRS* 57 (1967) 87–9; Brunt 382–3.

[6] Population of Augustan Italy: 14 million (Frank *ESAR* 5.1); 7 million (Brunt 131 and 127, endorsing Beloch's later figure). There were approximately 430 towns in Italy (Beloch 391); the number of children supported by the government *alimenta* varied between *c.* 110 at Ligures Baebiani and *c.* 300 at Veleia, but may have been greater at larger centres.

[7] It took land valued at HS13,039,095 to underwrite the main scheme at Veleia, which

estate fell in value, the impact of the interest payment would become more burdensome. But the loans were proportionately so small that only estates already suffering grave deterioration would feel really serious effects.

It would be unfair to dismiss the state alimentary scheme on the ground of our ignorance of its results. State philanthropy was not a common feature of imperial policy, while the widespread munificence of private benefactors rarely had a charitable purpose.[1] The explicit intention of the *alimenta* was increase of numbers rather than relief of poverty, but if the scheme was well executed, some redistribution of wealth would have resulted. The grants were too small to benefit the well-to-do significantly, and were thus presumably intended for their inferiors.[2] While the state *alimenta* were restricted to Italy, as the corn doles were restricted to Rome, the area which they tried to benefit was a large one. The problem which the *alimenta* attempted to remedy was real. The measures of Augustus and Trajan imply that endemic reluctance to rear children pervaded the society of Rome and Italy;[3] the popular scope of the *alimenta* suggests that the rich were not the only class to be affected.

The effort attempted here must seem worthier than the monumental fantasies of the Emperors, though the total cost of the *alimenta* to the state was hardly more than that of a major building project at Rome.[4] The fact that later Emperors felt that they should add to the *alimenta*[5]

supported 281 children (XI 1147), an average of HS46,405 per child. At Ligures Baebiani, where the security was slightly heavier, the average was presumably higher, unless the sex-ratio was more equal than at Veleia (cf. Appendix 6 and p.311 n.1 above). On the lower overall population figure, 7 million (p.274 n.2, above), parity between the proportion of land and the proportion of the population affected would require an average valuation for land under exploitation in Italy of the order of HS8,000 per iugerum. This is undoubtedly far too high, cf. p.52. (The area of modern Italy is 260,381 km², *Enc.it.* 19.698, about 103 million iugera; the estimate assumes that 40% would be under exploitation, cf. Brunt 126.) Any higher population figure would entail a greater disproportion.

[1] Cf. *JRS* 59 (1969) 288.

[2] The rich needed 'ingentia praemia' to make them bring up children, Pliny *Pan.* 26.5; cf. Tac. *Ann.* 2.37–8. See also p. 303.

[3] Bourne 49–55; Brunt 558–66; Nissen 2.125–30.

[4] A contemporary criticism of government spending patterns: Philostratus *Apoll. Epist.* 54. The Domus Aurea, much of which was already built, received a supplementary grant of HS50 million towards its completion from Otho (Suetonius *Otho* 7.1; for the building, cf. J. B. Ward Perkins *Antiquity* 30 (1956) 209–19). The gilding of Domitian's Capitol cost more than HS288 million, the Aqua Marcia (built in the second century B.C.) HS180 million, and the Aqua Claudia and Anio Novus HS350 million (Plutarch *v. Public.* 15.3; Frontinus *de aq.* 1.7; Pliny *NH* 36.123). The *alimenta* at Veleia cost roughly HS1,200,000 (we do not know the size of Bassus's scheme, for which see Appendix 3); those at Ligures Baebiani HS401,800 (Appendix 4). The total cost of the *alimenta*, if equivalent to giving 400 cities schemes worth HS1 million each, would amount to HS400 million; but the number of cities concerned was probably substantially less (cf. Appendix 5).

[5] The 'pueri et puellae Ulpiani' who addressed a dedication to Trajan at Ameria in A.D. 101–2 were saluting their immediate benefactor (XI 4351). If the same is true of the other

indicates that, effective or not, the institution kept its place in the ideology of the Empire. But later endorsements of Trajanic policy need not imply much added outlay. Trajan's foundations were all self-supporting as far as we know, and should have required no further subvention, apart from salaries for the few administrators of high rank. The orders of children founded by the Antonines to commemorate events in the life of the Imperial family probably meant only some additional recipients of the corn-dole at Rome.[1] There is no evidence that these orders were extended to other towns. The *alimenta* were still functioning under the Severi,[2] but they had apparently ceased to exist by the time of Constantine.[3]

dedications by alimentary beneficiaries, we might infer that Antoninus Pius and Marcus Aurelius were active in setting up new units of the scheme in central Italy: at Cupra Montana (IX 5700); Pitinum Mergens (XI 5956–7); Sestinum (XI 6002) and Ficulea (XIV 4003). Compare the late Hadrianic dedication at Tifernum Mataurense (XI 5989).

[1] Antoninus Pius created an order of 'puellae Faustinianae' in memory of his wife (*HA Pius* 8.1, with Mattingly 4.48, 51, 235, 245; Strack 3.97). Marcus Aurelius created orders of children of either sex who would receive a *perceptio frumentaria*, as a celebration of the marriage of Lucius Verus and Lucilla (*HA Marc.* 7.8). He also set up the 'novae puellae Faustinianae' in memory of Faustina the younger (*HA Marc.* 26.6, with *ILS* 6065, a six-year-old beneficiary). The creation of further orders of 'pueri et puellae Antoniniani' and of 'pueri et puellae Mamaeani' is alleged without corroborative evidence by *HA Diad.* 2.10 and *Alex.* 57.7.

[2] X 5398. Hirschfeld *VW*² 218–20.

[3] *C.Th.* 11.27.1. Bourne 68.

APPENDICES

APPENDIX 1

Estate-sizes in Italy

ACTUAL ESTATES

There were two contrasting tendencies in large-scale Italian landownership under the early Empire. One was the aggregation of enormous single land units; the other was ownership of scattered farm holdings which were not necessarily all in one district, and might not be large individually. Although writers on agriculture such as Columella and Pliny the elder maintained that the possession of very large single units held practical disadvantages, it is doubtful whether many capitalists took their advice (Columella *de r.r.* 1.3.12; Pliny *NH* 18.35). The prevalence of scattered holdings belonging to one individual seems to have been mainly caused by the accidents of inheritance, and the chance of what land was available for purchase. There are many illustrations of the splitting of farms that occurred when an inheritance was shared, in the Table of Veleia (XI 1147, cf. XI p.221, 1).

Pliny the younger for example held land in two main blocks, one in Cisalpina near lake Como, the other in Umbria at Tifernum Tiberinum. The Comum holdings came to him from his father, his mother and other connexions there (*Ep.* 7.11.5); the estate at Tifernum almost certainly came from his uncle, the elder Pliny, whose heir he was (*Ep.* 5.8.5; see p.19). One letter shows that he saw possible advantages in further enlargement of an estate which was already very big (he was contemplating the addition of a property formerly worth HS5 million which was adjacent to his land at Tifernum worth roughly HS7 million; *Ep.* 3.19, see p.20). Although over-concentration in one area was possibly dangerous in the event of a harvest-failure, Pliny did not think this a decisive objection.

The elder Pliny's much-discussed description of great estates as being the ruin of Italy ('latifundia perdidere Italiam') seems to be in large part an expression of his dislike of cultivation by chained slaves (*NH* 18.35; cf. Mommsen *Ges.Schr.* 5.144–5). Although his argument is rambling and obscure at this point, he seems to have regarded chained slaves as a characteristic feature of the running of very large estates. This view is explicit in Seneca's vignette of the great landlord in *de ben.* 7.10.5, and it is also suggested by Columella in *de r.r.* 1.3.12; cf. Martial 9.22.4. Pliny depicts the agriculture of his time as characterised by the employment of chained slaves in one passage, and indicates shortly afterwards that modern agriculture characteristically takes the form of large estates (*NH* 18.21; 35). He repeats his attack on employing slaves from prisons almost at once, saying that their work in agriculture is totally bad, as is everything done by men without hope (*NH* 18.36). Thus Pliny evidently felt that the practice was morally repugnant, as well as economically disadvantageous. Chained slaves (variously known as *vincti*, *conpediti* or *alligati*) no doubt owed their popularity

[323]

with landlords to the fact that they could be obtained more cheaply than other agricultural slaves (a fact indicated by Pliny *Ep.* 3.19.7; see also Col. *de r.r.* 3.3.8 and Appendix 10, p.349). They were commonly ex-criminals (Pliny *NH* 18.21; 36; Col. *de r.r.* 3.3.8 with 1.9.4; cf. Apuleius *Met.* 9.12); the landlord might also relegate other slaves to the *ergastulum* as a punishment (Col. *de r.r.* 1.8.16). Cato and Columella both assume that the landlord will have some chained slaves, and Pliny, Martial and Juvenal show that they were still well known in Italy in the second century (Cato 56; Columella *de r.r.* 1.8.16; 1.9.4; 11.1.22; cf. 1.3.12; 3.3.8; Pliny *Ep.* 3.19.7; Martial 9.22.4; Juvenal 8.180; cf. Suet. *Aug.* 32; *Tib.* 8). It is doubtful whether the elder Pliny's rhetorical remark has any wider significance as an economic observation about Italian estates. Attempts to find a reasoned prescription for the agrarian well-being of Italy in Pliny's work (Martin 375 ff.) are unrealistic. It is conceivable however that Pliny regarded *latifundia* as a type of concern especially prone to rapid economic collapse, to judge from his story of Tarius Rufus (*NH* 18.37; for other views about *latifundia*, K. D. White *Bulletin of the Institute of Classical Studies* 14 (1967) 62–79). Elsewhere Pliny writes colloquially of a table valued at HS1,300,000 that the sum was enough to buy a *latifundium*. This figure is quite large; it hardly indicates that Roman *latifundia* in general were small in size (as suggested by Martin 383, who gives the figure as HS1,400,000; Pliny *NH* 13.92, cf. Seneca *de ben.* 7.9.2).

Men who attained great wealth in their own lifetime from sources other than land, such as Tarius Rufus, might be able to buy up very large single landholdings (Pliny *NH* 18.37. Cf. Pliny *NH* 18.35; Columella *de r.r.* 1.3.12; Seneca *de ben.* 7.10.5; Petronius *Sat.* 53; 48). Otherwise, the important landowner was more likely to have several farmholdings, whether in one district or in several, acquired mainly by inheritance or by marriage, but perhaps extended by purchases. (We do not know how active a land market there was in Italy: Pliny's report that the land market in Bithynia was largely static is interesting but need not be relevant, *Ep.* 10.54.) Two more landowners whose property lay in different regions appear in Pliny's circle: his mother-in-law Pompeia Celerina held property at Ocriculum, Narnia, Carsulae, Perusia and Alsium (*Ep.* 1.4.1; 6.10.1); and his wife's grandfather, L. Calpurnius Fabatus, lived at Comum and held other property at Ameria and in Campania (*Ep.* 5.11; *ILS* 2721; *Ep.* 8.20.3; 6.30.2–4). Pliny's rival at the bar, M. Aquillius Regulus, who was a wealthier man, like Pliny had landholdings in two different parts of Italy (in Umbria and Etruria; Martial 7.31; Pliny *Ep.* 2.20). A speech of Cicero provides an unusually clear instance of the fragmentation of landholdings: Cicero's client Sex. Roscius, the richest citizen of Ameria, had owned thirteen farms, mostly adjoining the Tiber, which were worth HS6 million in all (Cicero *pro Rosc.Amer.* 18–20; cf. *Digesta* 32.41.2). (Yeo's view that fragmentation of property was a deliberate device to distribute the risk of crop failure is unconvincing; most fragmentation must have resulted from the random causes mentioned above. Yeo 459; Friedlaender 1.123–4.)

Estate areas are rarely mentioned in our sources, though there are numbers of estate valuations, the majority from the two alimentary tables of Trajan's time. Two different estates of 1,000 iugera (*c.* 250 hectares) in the neighbourhood of Rome are mentioned at the end of the Republic (Cicero *Att.* 13.31; Varro *r.r.* 2.3.10). Horace refers to an estate of this size at Falerii (*Epod.* 4.11 ff.). Varro also mentions the 200 iugerum estate at Reate which belonged to a senator, Q. Axius (*r.r.* 3.2.15). One of the vineyards developed at Nomentum by Acilius Sthenelus under Nero measured 60 iugera; the figures for his other Nomentum vineyard later bought by Seneca suggest an area of about 360 iugera (*NH* 14.48–51; see p.47). It is unlikely that these figures convey any notion of the area of really large landed estates. At Leontini in Sicily, most of whose territory was farmed by citizens of other towns, the average holding in the third year of Verres' rule was roughly 1,900 iugera, allowing for fallow: there were 32 farmers for an area under wheat of 30,000 iugera (Cicero *Verr.* 2.3.113; 116; 120).

Although they are not agricultural, the game-parks whose size Varro mentions are of interest. T. Pompeius had one covering 4 square miles in Gaul (3,480 iugera; Varro *r.r.* 3.12.2, cf. Col. *de r.r.* 9.1.4). Q. Fulvius Lippinus owned a game-park of 40 iugera at Tarquinii, and a larger one at Statonia; while Q. Hortensius the orator owned a 'therotrophium' of more than 50 iugera at Laurentum (*r.r.* 3.12.1; 3.13.2; cf. Pliny *NH* 8.211; 9.173). With the exception of the Gallic estate these figures are surprisingly low.

Diodorus records that an equestrian named T. Vettius owned 400 slaves on his estates in Campania (Diodorus 36.2). The implied area of the estates, using the manning ratios from the agricultural writers, lies in the region between 2,800 iugera (Columella's vineyard ratio of 1 man to 7 iugera) and 8,800 iugera (Cato's ratio of 1 man to 22 iugera for non-managerial staff on an olive-farm; see p.327). We do not know what the main crop was, although in Campania where wine-yields were high to judge from modern figures, and cultivation was easy (cf. Columella *de r.r.* 5.4.3; Pliny *NH* 18.111), the attractions of wine-growing must often have been strong. The lower estimate of area may thus be the more probable.

Pliny's account of the spectacular bequests of C. Caecilius Isidorus in 8 B.C. offers two possible indices to the size of his estates, which were clearly enormous. The number of oxen was 7,200 (360,000 iugera of arable from the ratio in Columella *de r.r.* 2.12.7). The number of slaves was 4,116 (between 29,000 and 123,000 iugera from the ratios in the agricultural writers, see p.327–8). It is not possible to find a coherent overall estimate from these figures: there are not enough slaves to exploit the ploughing capacity as well as tending the 257,000 herd animals bequeathed by Isidorus. Conceivably the oxen worked estates run by *coloni*, although the herd-animals are more likely to have been in the hands of slaves (cf. Varro *r.r.* 2.1.26). It is clear at any rate that Isidorus owned large arable estates as well as much ranching country (Pliny *NH* 33.135).

(The estimates of farm-sizes made by Day from wine storage capacity have little value; see p.45 n.3 above.)

ESTATE-SIZES IN THE AGRICULTURAL WRITERS

Cato is almost the only writer to refer to the area of estates. At the outset of his work, he implies in a colloquial statement about the relative advantages of different types of cultivation that 100 iugera is an optimum size of holding (Cato 1.7). This is borne out in his prescription of staff and equipment needed for a vineyard, whose area is also 100 iugera (Cato 11.1). However, the olive-yard whose appointments are described is considerably bigger, 240 iugera (10.1). Columella, or rather Saserna, took as his instance of an arable-farm one with an area of 1 centuria, or 200 iugera (*de r.r.* 2.12.7; Varro *r.r.* 1.19.1).

Modern scholars have tried to add to these meagre statistics (which may be exemplary rather than descriptive). Since Varro found Cato's prescriptions irksome, and said satirically that an olive-farm of 480 iugera would not need 2 *vilici*, Varro's own estates must have been at least twice the size envisaged by Cato (*r.r.* 1.18.3; Yeo 454;

Martin 220, n.4). Secondly, since Cato allows only 14 *labra* for olive-oil for 240 iugera, whereas Columella speaks of 90 *labra*, Columella's farm must have outstripped Cato's by 90 to 14, implying that its area was more than 1,500 iugera (Cato 13.2; Col. *de r.r.* 12.52.11–12; Gummerus 77 ff. followed by Frank *ESAR* 5.171 and Yeo 454). The first point is invalid, since Varro's analysis is no more than a commonsense objection to Cato's schematism. The second breaks down because *labra* were not storage vessels, but processing vessels (Columella *de r.r.* 12.52.11–12). The oil was stored in *dolia*, of which Cato in fact prescribes 100 for the olive-farm (Columella *de r.r.* 12.52.14; Cato 11.1; 10.4). There is no figure for the number of *dolia* in Columella. The size of *labra* was not necessarily always the same, and the elaboration of olive-processing may have increased in the two centuries which divided Columella from Cato. (J. E. Skydsgaard presents similar arguments in *Analecta Romana Instituti Danici* 5 (1969) 31.)

It is conceivable that Cato took examples from details of his own estates: episodes of his work such as the description of buying an olive-mill at Suessa are circumstantial enough to look like actual transactions (22.3). It is also difficult to see what process of theoretical reasoning could produce the mass of minute numerical detail in Cato's lists of estate equipment (Cato 10–13, analysed by Hörle 238–52). But there is little indication that Columella's approach was the same; apart from brief mentions of his estates, and experiences as a wine-grower, his work contains little autobiography, and there is no figure that might indicate the size of his estates (*de r.r.* 3.3.3; 3.9.2; 3.9.6; 3.20.4; 12.20.7). As the owner of estates in three different areas, Columella must have been well-to-do; the estates were all close enough together to allow him to visit each one without difficulty, following his own precepts. They were situated at Alba, Carsioli, and Caere; his holding at Ardea disposed of some time before the date of writing belongs to the same geographical zone (3.9.2; 3.3.3). Columella is clearly thinking in terms of large units when he recommends the owner to organise slaves into *decuriae* (work-groups of 10 men), and speaks of the need to distinguish vine-dressers from ploughmen and ploughmen from ordinary farm-hands (*de r.r.* 1.9.6–8). Nevertheless, he offers no indication about maximum or optimum size, beyond his caveat against acquiring estates which are too big for the landlord to carry out his inspections (*de r.r.* 1.3.9–13). (Martin's statement that Columella has in mind an estate not larger than 2,500 hectares is based on C.'s criticism of the 'praepotentes qui possident fines gentium quos ne circumire (quoque/equis quidem) valent'. Whichever reading is adopted, this passage has no precise significance; *de r.r.* 1.3.12; Martin 349.)

APPENDIX 2

Agricultural work loads and manning ratios

The surviving agronomists are more generous with information about staffing and manpower than with details of profitability. Their information falls into two categories, one being accounts of the complement of slaves needed for different types of estate, the other, details of the number of man-days (*operae*) absorbed by different agricultural tasks. Varro was evidently conscious of the weakness of both indexes as used by his contemporaries. Rigid staffing ratios for monoculture estates of particular sizes are difficult to apply generally, when cultivation might be mixed, and when the size of the estate might be different from that of the model. And actual rates of manual work depend on the nature of the soil and quality of the crop, so that single prescriptions for each task which take no account of these variables have limited value. Varro's injunction that the owner should act empirically and adopt the practice followed in the neighbourhood of his estates, while varying it enough to see if improvements were possible, is eminently sane (*r.r.* 1.18.1–8; cf. Pliny *NH* 18.170).

The information about manning requirements is as follows. According to Cato (10.1) an olive plantation of 240 iugera will need a staff of 13, made up of an overseer (*vilicus*), a housekeeper (*vilica*), 5 labourers, 3 ploughmen, 1 mule-driver, 1 swineherd and 1 shepherd. A vineyard of 100 iugera will need a staff of 16, containing an overseer, a housekeeper, 10 labourers, 1 ploughman, 1 mule-driver, 1 willow-worker and 1 swineherd (11.1). These details show that the olive-plantation envisaged by Cato contained a larger amount of land not used for the main crop than did the vineyard. This corresponds with the fact that the planting distances prescribed for olive-groves were much wider than those for vineyards (olives at intervals of 25, 30, 50 or 60 feet, vines at intervals of 3 to 10 or 5 to 10 feet; Cato 6.1; Col. *de r.r.* 5.9.7; *de arb.* 17.3; *de r.r.* 5.3.1–9; *de arb.* 4). The two extra ploughmen and the shepherd cannot have been added to meet the needs of the staff of the oliveyard since its total number was lower than that of the staff of the vineyard. Vines were clearly much more labour-intensive, acre for acre, as implied by Columella *de r.r.* 5.8.1–2. There are three other figures for manning vineyards. Pliny says that the ratio in Italy is 10 to every 100 iugera or 1 man to every 10 iugera (*NH* 17.215). Columella's specimen calculation assumed 1 man to 7 iugera, while Saserna gives a figure of 1 man to 8 iugera (apparently for vines, Varro *r.r.* 1.18.2; Columella *de r.r.* 3.3.8). These statistics suggest rough correspondence of practice, though none is demonstrably based on dividing the number of workers on an actual vineyard into the total area. In terms of total non-managerial staff, the ratio for Cato's oliveyard is 1 man to 22 iugera.

In fact the value of Cato's vineyard figures is open to doubt, although his ratio of field workers to area is roughly corroborated by the three other writers just mentioned (Cato 11). His figures apparently assume that an estate of 100 iugera could support a staff of 16 and still produce wine as its main crop: the equipment includes the same provision for storing a crop of wheat as for the olive-yard whose staff numbers 13, '(dolia) frumentaria XX' (11.1, cf. 10.4). Elsewhere he prescribes grain rations of *c*. 50 modii annually for field workers and 36 modii for the *vilicus*, *vilica* and others (c.56). On these figures the vineyard would need to produce *c*. 720 modii of grain per year (10 rations of 50 modii, 6 of 36). Even if as much as half of the estate area were utilised for grain, the yield figure, assuming fallowing (p.49 n.5), would need to be nearly 7-fold. (Seed for 50 iugera = 250 modii, p.49 n.3 above; to achieve a net crop of 1,440 modii in alternate years, a gross yield of 1690 modii is therefore required; $1690 \div 250 = 6.86$.) A yield of 7-fold is difficult to reconcile with Columella's alleged Italian average of 4-fold; it also seems high for antiquity compared with Italian figures of 4- and 6-fold for the sixteenth and seventeenth centuries which are better authenticated (see above p.49 and n.4). If the land were not fallowed, the annual crop would still need to be almost 4-fold, as much as the Columella figure which assumed fallowing (p.49 nn.4–5 above). (Seed = 250 modii; net annual crop of 720 modii requires a gross yield of 970 modii; $970 \div 250 = 3.88$.)

Cato's figures are probably misconceived. White 395 (citing unpublished work of Brunt) also notes that there is not enough room for grain, without giving workings. It is unlikely that 'the grain was grown elsewhere' (White 395). The provision of a ploughman and grain storage facilities shows that Cato had not forgotten to think of grain; and there is every likelihood that he would have intended the estate to be self-supporting (cf. pp.37–8 above). Furthermore, if the estate were part of some larger unit, it would not require its own *vilicus* and *vilica*.

Columella gives a staffing ratio of 8 men for 200 iugera of arable, and, citing Saserna as his authority, 11 men to 200 iugera for *arbustum* (vines supported on trees, with intercultivation of other crops; *de r.r.* 2.12.7 with Varro *r.r.* 1.19.1). The manning ratios here, 1 to 25 iugera for arable and 1 to 18 iugera for *arbustum* are apparently very much lower than those for vines; but fallowing if widely practised would roughly halve the effective figure for arable; p.49 n.5. An earlier reference in Varro suggests that Columella's figure for arable manning may also have come from Saserna, a source whose credentials it is difficult to gauge from the surviving allusions (Varro *r.r.* 1.19.1; 1.2.27–8). The ploughing-rates that immediately follow this citation in Columella, which do not agree with those given later in his work (see below) might also come from Saserna. It is not clear how close the purely arable farm cultivated by slaves is to Columella's own experience: he advises the landlord to leave grain cultivation in the hands of *coloni*, unless he is able to keep an eye on the running of the farm himself (*de r.r.* 1.7.6). There are no other manning figures for arable, which is thus less well documented than the manning of vineyards.

Working-rates for both arable and vine land are given by Columella. Saserna provided at least one detail of this kind (cited by Varro, who questioned the value of such figures: *r.r.* 1.18.6); Varro gives one figure of his own (1.50.3); and Columella once refers to the unreliability of a previous statistic, whose source he does not name (*de r.r.* 11.2.82). Thus it is not clear how far Columella's plentiful details of working-rates were new to the corpus of agrarian writings as it existed in his day. Columella may have been producing conscious adaptations of previous prescriptions in the light of his own experience (cf. *de r.r.* 11.2.82), or he may have been reproducing material from elsewhere unchanged. There are discrepancies not only between figures in the *de re rustica* and those in the *de arboribus*, but also between figures given in different parts of the *de re rustica* (see below). It is more likely that they result from disagreements between different underlying sources used by Columella, than from any inability to reach consistent conclusions of his own. In his main list of working times for different crops, Columella is unable to give any details for hemp ('incertum est quantam impensam curamque desideret') or a reaping time for millet and panic ('quot operis carpantur incertum est') (*de r.r.* 2.12.6; 2.12.4). The lapses may indicate reliance on a source or sources which failed at these points.

Taking arable first, Columella gives a detailed series of prescriptions for work on different crops (*de r.r.* 2.12). (The figures for sixteen crops other than wheat are not reproduced here.) The sowing quantities named are evidently those intended for 1 iugerum of land, since the formula for *triticum* or common wheat involves 4–5 modii, which is the quantity he names elsewhere for sowing on 1 iugerum (*de r.r.* 11.2.75; 2.9.1). Columella states that sowing this quantity of *triticum* entails 4 man-days ploughing, 1 harrowing, 3 hoeing, 1 weeding and 1½ reaping, making 10½ man-days in all, to bring the wheat grown on 1 iugerum of land to the threshing floor (2.12.1). The time for reaping is given by Varro as 1 man-day instead of 1½ (*r.r.* 1.50.3), but a discrepancy with Columella's own account in a later book is more serious. There the time for ploughing becomes 6.5–3.25 man-days per iugerum, depending on whether or not the soil is difficult to work (*de r.r.* 11.2.46). Neither total agrees with the figure in book 3 of 4 man-days for ploughing. This reduces the value of Columella's detailed reckoning of the total time taken to work the land for wheat. Cutting the straw after the harvest absorbed one more man-day per iugerum, we learn in book 11 (*de r.r.* 11.2.54). Threshing-time is not stated, though it is likely to have been not less than 2–3 man-days per iugerum (cf. Cato 136, where threshing the grain increases the remuneration of the share-worker doing field maintenance and harvesting by 20% to 60%). The actual range of variation in land was of course greater than could be comprised in a simple dual formula for difficult and easy land. The younger Pliny had land at Tifernum Tiberinum in Umbria which needed up to 8 ploughings instead of the 3 allowed by Columella and Varro (Pliny *Ep.* 5.6.10; Col. *de r.r.* 11.2.46; Varro *r.r.* 1.29.2). Pliny the elder reckoned 4 ploughings as the norm for Italy, and 8 ploughings for Tuscany (*NH* 18.181).

Columella only once attempts to reconcile figures for the daily rate of work with those for work on a yearly basis. On a 200 iugerum farm (probably an example from Saserna, cf. Varro *r.r.* 1.19.1) half the land will evidently be fallow in any one year, to judge from the sowing quantities prescribed for wheat (*de r.r.* 2.12.7). Each of the two plough-teams required for this area will spend 250 days of the year in activity assignable to the main crops (though 45 days of this period are without work because of rain and holidays, and on a further 30 days after the sowing there is no work for the teams to do). The residue of 115 days in the year can be usefully spent in sowing 3-month crops, or in haulage of hay, forage or manure (*de r.r.* 2.12.7–9). No effort is made in this brief and curious passage to find work for the teams during the 30 days' rest after the sowing, although Columella elsewhere shows the customary zeal of the agrarian writers to see that his labour force is fully occupied at all times (cf. *de r.r.* 1.8.8; 2.21.3; 11.1.21; 11.1.26–7; 11.2.55). The description of the plough-teams inconsequentially follows the account of sowing quantities and working times for different crops, although it is introduced as if this mixed catalogue somehow dictated a ratio of 2 plough-teams and 8 men to 200 iugera. ('Hac consummatione operarum colligitur posse agrum ducentorum iugerum subigi duobus iugis bovum totidem bubulcis et sex mediastinis, si tamen vacet arboribus' 2.12.7.) The logic is spurious, and the citation of Saserna which comes next may point to the original author of most of these details, which seem inadequately assimilated. The generous allowance for loss of working time in the plough-team calculation (see above) also recalls Saserna, who is known to have reckoned that 13 out of 45 working days would be lost during digging operations for various reasons (Varro *r.r.* 1.18.2).

Saserna–Columella reckon 50 iugera as the working area for one plough-team (*de r.r.* 2.12.7–9; Varro *r.r.* 1.19.1). Pliny envisaged a smaller area: 40 iugera of easy soil or 30 iugera of difficult soil (*NH* 18.173). Columella returns to the subject of ploughing times in book 11, and here produces a different set of figures. Ploughing for wheat now takes 6.5–3.25 days per iugerum, instead of 4 days (as already noticed). And the ploughing capacity of 1 yoke of oxen is now expressed as a main sowing crop of 150 modii of wheat and 100 modii of legumes, instead of equal quantities of the two crops as in the earlier passage (11.2.46–7; 2.12.1; 2.12.7–8). While the total bulk sown is the same, the capacity has in fact been increased, since legumes took less ploughing time than wheat on average (2.12.8–9). The fact that there are two prescriptions, one for difficult and one for easy land, may suggest that Columella is now producing his own adaptation of traditional figures. If so, the later group of ploughing times should be the more reliable. Pliny gives some incomplete ploughing times: 1.66–3 man-days per iugerum for the first two ploughings, depending on whether the land is difficult or easy (*NH* 18.178). These figures are markedly lower than the corresponding amounts in Columella, which are 3–5 man-days. However, Pliny envisaged 4 ploughings as the norm in Italy, as compared with Columella's 3 ploughings (*NH* 18.181; also 3 in Varro *r.r.* 1.29.2). If Pliny's prescriptions were based on a considered assessment, the total time occupied may not have been very different. Pliny's allowance of a smaller ploughing area for the ox-teams (see above) is however difficult to reconcile with the ploughing-times. Another ploughing figure is mentioned in isolation: two days for the first ploughing on 1 iugerum of rich land, if the ploughing is done out of season in January when the land is still wet (*de r.r.* 11.2.8). This compares with a normal time for first ploughing of 3 days for difficult land and 2 days for easy land (11.2.46). A further figure for hoeing is also given in book 11: 1 iugerum of land sown with 3 modii of grain can easily be hoed for the second time in March taking 1 man-day (11.2.26). This slightly disagrees with the account in book 2, where the second hoeing of land sown with 4–5 modii also takes 1 man-day (2.12.1). Harrowing and digging round the trees on land planted with beans and vetch takes $1\frac{1}{2}$ man-days per iugerum (*de r.r.* 11.2.82). Here Columella states that his figure differs from that alleged by earlier writers ('antiqui'), who gave a rate of work which Columella cannot credit (1 man-day instead of $1\frac{1}{2}$). This is the only occasion on which Columella allows that the working-rates are subject to dispute.

Discrepancies again occur in Columella's accounts of working-times in the vineyard. The basic operation on which good viticulture hinged in Columella's view was thorough trenching before the vines were planted, called *pastinatio* or *repastinatio* (*de r.r.* 3.17.1). In the early *de arboribus* Columella gives trenching times for 1 iugerum of 50 man-days for a depth of $1\frac{1}{2}$–2 Roman feet on flat land, 60 man-days for a depth of 2 feet on sloping ground, and 80 man-days for a depth of 3 feet. The last total is the same in the *de re rustica*, but the remaining figures differ: here a depth of $1\frac{1}{2}$ feet takes 30 man-days; 2 feet takes 40 man-days; and $2\frac{1}{2}$ feet 50 man-days (*de arb.* 1.5–6; 4.2; *de r.r.* 11.2.17). The rate at which a furrow for planting vines (*sulcus*) can be dug is apparently faster in the later work: 1 man-day for a depth of 2½ feet, a width of 2 feet and a length of 120 feet, compared with a depth of 2 feet and length of 70 feet in the same time in the *de arboribus* (*de r.r.* 11.2.28; in *de arb.* 4.3, the width is not stated, but is not likely to exceed the depth in the absence of a specific figure). Higher man-output is also seen in the figures in the later work for digging planting-holes for vines (*scrobae*): 14 as compared with 12 holes 4 foot square in 1 man-day (*de r.r.* 11.2.28; *de arb.* 4.3). The two works agree in making 18 the number of holes measuring 3 feet square that can be dug in 1 man-day, while the *de arboribus* adds that 20 holes two feet square take the same time. Since Columella never admits discrepancies between his different estimates, it is unlikely that the variants result from conscientious re-timing of the tasks concerned. If the totals are his own (which they may not be), they are probably based on a rule-of-thumb proportioning of a basic working-rate to different requirements which was so random that it produced different results on different occasions.

The most interesting of his figures for work done in the vineyard are the timings for different maintenance operations, which cover a large part of the tasks that had to be carried out during the year. In the *de arboribus*, Columella says that for 1 iugerum of vines (those on props, not *arbustum*), it takes 5 man-days to loosen the soil (*ablaqueare*), 5 man-days to trench round the trees (*fodere*), 3 man-days to hoe (*occare*), 4 man-days to prune (*putare*), and 6 to tie up the vines (*alligare*) (*de arb.* 5.5). The total is 23 man-days per iugerum. A further statistic of 1 day's work by a boy for trimming 1 iugerum (*pampinare*) can perhaps be treated as ½ man-day, making 23½ man-days for the main operations other than grape-harvesting and vinification (*de r.r.* 11.2.44). On Columella's allowance of manpower (1 *vinitor* for 7 iugera, *de r.r.* 3.3.8) 52 man-days per iugerum were potentially available each year. The manning figures from the other writers give maxima of 44½–36½ man-days per iugerum (Cato 11.1; Pliny *NH* 17.215; Saserna *apud* Varro *r.r.* 1.18.2). If we assume that harvesting and vinification would take at least a further 7 man-days per iugerum, the supplemented total from the *de arboribus* will be 31½ man days per iugerum, which can easily be reconciled with the maximum of 52 man-days available annually.

Nevertheless, the working times are open to doubt in certain ways. In his detailed calendar of the seasons in book 11 of the *de r.r.* (for which compare the stone calendar in *ILS* 8745), Columella assigns the tasks of soil-loosening and trenching vineyards (*ablaqueatio* and *fossura*) to the period between 15 October and 31 October. If both tasks had to be fitted into this period, and if each took the 5 man-days per iugerum assigned to them by Columella in the *de arboribus* (5.5), 1 man would only be able to deal with 1½ iugera in the 17 days available, a minute fraction of the area of 7 to 10 iugera for which he would be responsible from the manning figures. Furthermore, some of the formulae for daily work (those for pruning and tying, taking 11 man-days per iugerum) were bound to depend on planting density. Columella was intermittently aware of the difficulties which such variants could cause, since the passage in the *de arboribus* (5.6) goes on to say that no prescription of working-rates for *arbustum* can be made, because of the irregularities in their planting density. (His successor Pliny nevertheless gave a rate for tying up vines in *arbustum* of 15 trees per man-day, *NH* 18.241.) Yet Columella makes no allowance for variations in the planting density of the vines on props in assessing working times, although he makes abundantly clear elsewhere that planting densities could vary drastically, by a factor of 3 or 4 (see p.53 n.1). He does not even say what density is allowed for in the working rates which he gives. Thus the guidance offered by these figures is very approximate at best.

A different statistic is offered for work on digging round trees, which are not specified as vine-supporting, and may thus be either fruit-trees or *arbustum*. It takes 1 man-day to dig round (*circumfodere*) 80 young trees, 65 middling trees, or 50 big trees (*de r.r.* 11.2.40). Cutting and shaping wood could be carried out at the rate of 100 stakes (*palus*) or 60 props (*ridica*) per man-day, Columella says (*de r.r.* 11.2.12). His last field statistic refers to hay cutting. A good worker, Columella says, can cut 1 iugerum of meadow in a day; binding 1,200 bundles of hay weighing 4 pounds each also takes 1 man-day (*de r.r.* 11.2.40; also *NH* 18.262). This second figure is quite improbable, since it would take one man 20 hours to tie this number of bundles working at the rate of 1 bundle per minute with no breaks whatever. Half or a quarter of the rate might be possible to credit.

Finally there are figures for the time taken to dress different kinds of timber. It takes 1 man-day to dress 20 square feet of oak, 25 square feet of pine, 30 square feet of elm or ash, 40 square feet of cypress, or 60 square feet of fir or poplar (*de r.r.* 11.2.13).

The reliability of the manpower figures is difficult to assess as a whole. Several writers give figures for the manning of vineyards which roughly agree with each other; and the one list of working times in the vineyard can easily be reconciled with these ratios (though, since the list is incomplete, their compatibility may be a matter of accident). However, the figures for working times are often open to doubt, not merely because of their mutual inconsistencies. They seem to have the character of ancestral prescriptions; such statistics were distrusted by Varro as being too rigid. If they were serious practical guides which Columella had tested for himself, it is difficult to see how he could fail (as he so often does) to give more than one set of figures, to allow for variations in soil or in planting arrangements. Occasionally Columella does admit the existence of variants, as in his second discussion of ploughing rates, and in his account of a formula for laying out vines. In the first case, he usefully gives two sets of figures for ploughing-times, one for difficult and one for easy soil (*de r.r.* 11.2.46). In the second, he works out in needless detail how a simple planting formula for vines should be applied to 12 different planting distances (*de r.r.* 5.3.1–9). But this spirit of adaptation is not present elsewhere, and Columella enumerates the days worked on different pursuits without either considering possible variants, or explaining to what conditions his figures apply.

The criticism brought against the Roman agronomists by Arthur Young, that they 'had no notion of registering experiments', can fairly be applied here (A. Young *A Course of Experimental Agriculture* (1770) vii). The working-rates do however illustrate the concern of the Roman *latifondista* to get as much work out of his slaves as possible. The figures were probably intended as an index with which the owner, or his *vilicus*, could organise farm schedules, and check the work output of the labour force. Whether the figures themselves could have served this purpose adequately is another matter.

(Comparisons with modern working-rates are potentially interesting, though they are bound to be somewhat speculative when the ancient figures are inconsistent or improbable. White's comparisons do not take into account the discrepancies between Columella's different versions of the same operations. One of Columella's versions of the ploughing year (*de r.r.* 2.12.7–9) is taken as the basis for assuming that vine-hands worked 250 days per year, although there is no obvious relation between the two calendars. The statement that Columella gives a total of 63 working days per year for

1 iugerum of vines is at variance with Columella's manning ratio of 1 *vinitor* to 7 iugera, which allows a maximum of 52 working days per iugerum per year (White 373; 413–14; 'The productivity of labour in Roman agriculture' *Antiquity* 39 (1965) 102–7).)

APPENDIX 3

The first alimentary scheme at Veleia

Fragments of a bronze inscription found at Veleia in the eighteenth century some years after the discovery of the main Table seem to preserve the record of another *obligatio praediorum* (XI 1149; cf. 1151). Bormann did not attempt to decide its purpose, although he noted the apparent recurrence of L. Annius Rufinus who is mentioned in the main Table, and suggested that this might be some form of preliminary document belonging to the alimentary scheme (XI 1149 commentary). It can hardly be a preliminary account of one of the known schemes at Veleia, because the remaining landowners who declare property here appear (where identifiable) to be individuals who are mentioned only as neighbours in the main inscription (see below). The fragments contain no reference to *alimenta*; but since they record the pledging of estates at a town which is known to have received *alimenta*, and since large-scale pledging of local properties was otherwise very unusual, it is safe to think that the inscription refers to alimentary loans.

One of the landowners who declared property is named as L. ANNIO RVF (XI 1149, b 4). A L(ucius) Annius Rufinus declared the third largest estate in the main scheme at Veleia (*oblig.* 17, HS1,014,090), but stated that he had already pledged land in a previous scheme under the supervision of Pomponius Bassus. One other landowner who declared property in the main scheme had also pledged land under Bassus: C. Coelius Verus, who declared the fourth largest private estate in the main scheme (*oblig.* 16, HS843,879). There is no other explicit allusion to the Bassus scheme. But the apparent allusion to Rufinus seems to indicate that the fragmentary inscription is an account of the Bassus scheme, in which Rufinus is known to have taken part. (The most acceptable alternative would be to see the fragmentary inscription as an account of re-allocations of loan funds made after the date of the main Table, as a result of subsequent changes in the ownership of property. But the declarations appear too brief and too stereotyped to fit this hypothesis.) The Bassus scheme was thus apparently located at Veleia, as Henzen concluded (Henzen 14). Bormann argued that the Bassus scheme belonged to Luca, not to Veleia (XI p.220), since Rufinus and Verus are the only landowners in the main scheme at Veleia (other than the Lucenses themselves) to declare property on the territory of Luca. But the present inscription was certainly set up at Veleia.

If this is another early alimentary scheme at Veleia, why is it not described in the main inscription in addition to the two schemes set out there? The explanation was evidently not that Bassus's scheme had lapsed by the date when the Table of Veleia was inscribed, the continued existence of his scheme being implied in the fact that Rufinus and Verus excluded from their declarations land already pledged through Bassus (XI 1147, *oblig.* 16 and 17). The details of the early Gallicanus scheme were presumably included in the main record because they had not been previously published in an inscription; this was evidently not true of the Bassus scheme. Unless details were published more than once, there would have been no need to describe the Bassus scheme in the main inscription, since the tablet whose fragments are preserved had already published its details to the town. A more important distinction might be conjectured. The main alimentary inscription describes the processes by which the 'indulgentia' of Trajan benefited Veleia. Conceivably the Bassus inscription might have done the same for Nerva. (A fragment of a posthumous dedication to Nerva survives from Veleia, XI 1173.) The pledges that this inscription records can hardly be later than the first years of Trajan.

The most intelligible fragment (XI 1149 a) consists of a list of landowners; each name, given in the ablative, is followed by the words 'PRO. FVNDO'. The remainder of the line presumably contained a valuation and an amount loaned on the security of the property. The declarations in the Table of Veleia and in the Baebian Table end with the formula 'HS(tot) IN HS(tot)', the amount of the valuation followed by the amount of the loan. At this stage in the formation of the *alimenta* it was evidently possible to declare house-property as security for loans, though in the main scheme the only eligible property was landed estates ('. . . A.l. Adepta pro domu ex p[rofessione]' XI 1149 d 5). House-property would only be revenue-producing if it were leased (cf. Pliny *Ep.* 10.70.2; C. no. 714).

The list was perhaps arranged geographically. The word PAGI appears in much larger letters than the remainder of the inscription (XI 1149, a 3), which suggests that it is an intermediate column-heading; in full the line might have read 'possessores PAGI (cuiusdam)'. The account of each landowner and his property receives only one line, which suggests that the declarations were very simple. Possibly each landlord was only expected to declare one farm; but the geographical heading may indicate that the list was arranged in order of adjacent properties, instead of grouping all properties from different parts of the city-territory under the landlord to whom they belonged, as in the later schemes. If this were so, the name of a given landlord might perhaps recur under different headings, if the list was at all extensive. The two isolated mentions of the word CENSVS (XI 1149 h) seem to refer either to valuations taken from the census-lists, or to the 'census' or fortune of particular individuals. Census information for regio VIII, the part of Italy where Veleia was situated, was compiled under Vespasian, if no more recent survey had taken place (Pliny *NH* 7.163, mentioning Veleia). The phraseology appears to exclude the possibility that the inscription itself belongs to a census register (cf. 'pro fundo' *passim* and 'dedit hac die id quod. . .' XI 1149 d).

Another bronze fragment, numbered separately by Bormann, may illustrate the procedures of the Bassus scheme, although this is extremely speculative. This fragment

(XI 1151) gives a list of figures from the right-hand margin of an inscription the rest of which has perished. The least damaged line shows a sum of money followed immediately by another sum: HS11,200 is followed by HS2,800, which is one quarter of the previous figure. HS11,200 is a possible valuation for a 'fundus' at Veleia (there are five *fundi* valued at HS12,000 or less, XI 1147, 2.77; 2.60; 4.63; 4.65; 5.4). If this fragment does belong to the Bassus scheme, it would imply that 4-fold security was being asked from the borrowers at this early stage. The Table indicates clearly that the security asked rose from 10-fold to 12½-fold between the dates of the Gallicanus scheme and the main scheme at Veleia. This fragment might suggest a progression from a still earlier security of 4-fold.

Coincidences of nomenclature between the 'Bassus' fragments and the Table of Veleia are as follows. All identifiable gentilicia can be reconciled with gentilicia in the main Table. (References to the different sections of XI 1149 are given by letter and line number only; abbreviations as in XI pp.229 ff.: *dom.* = landlord who declares property in the Table; *adf.* = neighbour mentioned in the Table; *mand.* = agent who declares property on behalf of a landlord in the Table.)

1. Possible identifications

L. ANNIO RVF b.4. See L. Annius Rufinus *dom.* XI 1147, 3.52; 6.62; *adf.* XI 1147 *passim.*

SENINO a.5. See Publicius Seninus *adf.* XI 1147, 7.26.

VERECVNDO d.6. See C. Volumnius Verecundus *adf.* XI 1147, 4.75; 4.79; 4.72; 5.88.

L. VIBIO SA b.3 (probably not Saturninus, cf. b.6). See Vibius Sabinus *mand.* XI 1147, 2.27; cf. Vibia Sabina *dom.* XI 1147, 7.57.

L. VIBVL c.4. See Vibulli fr(atres) *adf.* XI 1147, 4.60.

2. Other resemblances

A. L. ADEPTA d.5. Cf. Solonius Adeptus *adf.* XI 1147, 5.74.

M. FABIO MARCEL b.5. Cf. Fabius Firmus *adf.* XI 1147, 5.66.

SEX.GE b.7. Cf. Geminius *adf.* XI 1147, 5.80.

...ISCO a.6. Cf. e.g. Albius Priscus *adf.* XI 1147, 7.20.

MINI b.2. Cf. M. Minicius *adf.* XI 1147, 3.41; Minicius Verus *adf.* XI 1147, 2.21.

vi?BI CRASSI e.3. 12 Vibii in XI 1147; 4 Baebii (XI p.231, 3; p.230, 2).

L. VIBIO SATVRN b.6. 12 Vibii in XI 1147 (XI p.231, 3).

...VRINA a.4. Cf. P. Valerius Ligurinus *dom.* XI 1147, 1.53.

APPENDIX 4

Statistics from the alimentary tables

The statistics given here for Veleia refer only to the main scheme at that town (*obligationes* 1–46). The miniature earlier scheme was planned on a different basis of 10% loans (*obligationes* 47–52). The valuations of estates in the two Tables are listed in full in C. nos. 1197–1305, see pp. 211–15 above. (A useful regional analysis of the declarations at Veleia showing the value of the property declared in each *pagus*, together with the number of owners, neighbours, and holdings per *pagus*, is given by Chilver 160–1.)

	LIGURES BAEBIANI (A.D. 101)	VELEIA (A.D. 102/13)
Number of estates whose owners received loans	66	46
Total of overall estate-valuations	(HS4,249,000 + ; 11 valuations are missing or incomplete)	HS13,039,095
Largest estate	HS501,000	HS1,600,000
Smallest estate	HS14,000	HS50,000
Average estate size	HS77,254	HS283,458
Average size of 15 largest properties	HS164,600	HS230,813 (using only single components within larger estates)
Average loan to 15 largest properties	7.33%	8.56% (basis as above)
Average size of 15 smallest properties	HS25,066	HS15,037 (basis as above)
Average loan to 15 smallest properties	6.83%	7.62% (basis as above)
Amount of the loan	HS401,800 (complete)	HS1,044,000
Average loan per estate	HS6,087.88	HS22,695.65
Ratio of loans to estate-valuations overall	1:13.13 or 7.61% (from the 55 complete valuations)	1:12.49 or 8.01% (7.93% if component-valuations are substituted for aggregate valuations of estates having several components)

APPENDIX 5

The distribution of alimentary towns in Italy

I

10 towns can be added to the 39 listed by Ruggiero as having record of the state *alimenta*, making a total of 49; all the towns are listed in section ii below. The accepted view that an inscription recording a magistrate in charge of *alimenta* refers to the state scheme and not to a private gift appears to be correct. Although special appointments might be made to administer large sums donated to the city privately, separate private funds in the hands of Italian cities were normally identified by the name of the donor, see p.316 n.6. (Only six Italian towns are known to have received privately given *alimenta*; see section ii below.) Thus not less than 11% of the towns in Italy appear to have received units of the state scheme. There is too little epigraphic evidence overall for this low percentage to be significant in itself. (The survival rate of Italian inscriptions is probably lower than 5%, see Appendix 13.) But the distribution of the alimentary evidence in relation to town concentrations in different parts of Italy is very uneven. The pattern which it follows is effectively one of high frequency in areas adjoining Rome, and low frequency in peripheral areas to the north and south. The approximate location of the towns (apart from Lucus Feroniae, Tifernum Mataurense, Urvinum Mataurense and Ciciliano) is shown on the map in *PBSR* 32 (1964) 125.

Four central regions have a higher proportion of alimentary towns than the rest. They are regio IV, the part of central Italy bordered by Umbria, Apulia and the Adriatic (where 20.9% of the towns have record of the *alimenta*); regio VI, Umbria (where the proportion is 16.3%); regio I, Latium and Campania (13.9%); and regio VII, Etruria (12.2%). In all four regiones the number of references to the *alimenta* in proportion to the number of towns is higher than the average of 11.4%. Southern Italy by contrast, comprising Apulia, Calabria, Lucania and Bruttium (regiones II and III) has a proportion of only 7%. The far north (regiones IX, X and XI) has an even lower proportion, 5.5%. There is a difference between the four central regions and the five regions furthest from Rome of almost 5 to 2 in aggregate, in the frequency of mentions of the *alimenta* related to town numbers (the respective frequencies are 15.4% and 6.5%). The remaining central zone, Picenum (regio V) constitutes a minor exception to the pattern, with a proportion of only 8.7%. But this is hardly significant: the total is so small that the discovery of a single further alimentary inscription would be enough to make it exceed the average (see Table 9 below).

These figures strongly imply that the state *alimenta* never reached all the towns of Italy. They suggest that in practice certain parts of Italy (those nearer to Rome) were favoured over others. It is interesting that neither of the early records which provide most of our detailed knowledge of the *alimenta* comes from one of the more favoured regions: Veleia was in regio VIII, where the proportion of alimentary towns is 7.7%; and Ligures Baebiani was in regio II, where the proportion is 5.3% (the average for the eleven regiones is 11.4%). But survivals are so few that the figures for individual regiones cannot be relied on very far. It must be noticed that there were units of the state *alimenta* in regio XI, Transpadum, despite the absence of any allusion to them in the 2,000 or more inscriptions found there. Inscriptions found elsewhere record a 'procurator alimentorum per Transpadum Histriam Liburniam'; *ILS* 1347 (from Africa); 1396 (from Asia).

The rate of epigraphic survival is virtually bound to vary between different parts of a large country. In one regio of Italy (regio X) the number of inscriptions per town is as high as 234, while in another (regio III) it is as low as 23. Such contrasts may come in part from variations in town sizes: the average area per town (making no subtraction for *ager publicus* or infertile country) is 2,040 km² in regio X and 1,146 km² in regio III. But the much larger difference in the number of inscriptions per town (more than 10-fold) indicates that there were probably also variations in the rate of inscription-survival. The area-based statistics likewise show very large variations: the extremes differ by a factor of 27 (regio III with 2.0 inscriptions per 100 km², and regio I with 55 inscriptions per 100 km²).

But it is unlikely that variations in inscription-survival can account for the relatively low proportion of mentions of the *alimenta* in the more remote regions. The number of inscriptions in the four central regiones mentioned above (I, IV, VI, VII) is 83 inscriptions per town in aggregate, compared with a figure of 75 inscriptions per town in the outlying regiones (II, III, IX, X and XI). This discrepancy of 11% is hardly significant when compared with the difference of 5 to 2 in the frequency with which towns in the two areas leave record of the *alimenta*.

In the new analysis below, figures for the regional distribution of the state *alimenta* (from Ruggiero s.v. Alimenta, with 10 supplements) are collated with figures for the number of cities and for the area of regiones (from Nissen 2.3, modifying those in Beloch 431). The figures for the number of inscriptions in different regions, which are based exclusively on *CIL*, have been recalculated to take account of *CIL* XI and *CIL* XIV which were not available to Beloch (his figures in Beloch 431); they now also include the inscriptions printed under Additamenta at the end of each volume. Inscriptions from Rome, milestones, wall-inscriptions from Pompeii and Herculaneum, and inscriptions on lamps, vases, jewels, weights, tiles, amphorae, etc. are excluded. The Ostian inscriptions, of which there are over 3,000 in *CIL*, have also been omitted. They are enough to increase the total yield for Italy by almost 10%. When there is so great a disproportion between the number of inscriptions from one town and the rest, it is clear that the inclusion of evidence from that town would make the average figures less representative of the area as a whole.

TABLE 9. *The distribution of alimentary towns related to area, town concentrations and epigraphic density*

	Towns by regio (Nissen)	Towns with state *alimenta*	Towns with state *alimenta* as % of all towns in regio	Area of regiones in km² (Nissen)	Average area per town in km² (Nissen)	Inscriptions (*CIL*)
Regio I	86 (20.0%)	12	14.0	15,500 (6.2%)	180	8,523 (25.9%) [without Ostia]
Regio II	76 (17.7%)	4	5.3	25,000 (10.0%)	329	2,512 (7.6%)
Regio III	24 (5.6%)	3	12.5	27,500 (11.0%)	1,146	551 (1.7%)
Regio IV	43 (10.0%)	9	20.9	18,000 (7.2%)	419	2,895 (8.8%)
Regio V	23 (5.3%)	2	8.7	6,500 (2.6%)	283	951 (2.9%)
Regio VI	49 (11.4%)	8	16.3	10,000 (4.0%)	204	2,835 (8.6%)
Regio VII	49 (11.4%)	6	12.2	31,000 (12.4%)	633	4,624 (14.1%)
Regio VIII	26 (6.0%)	2	7.7	19,500 (7.8%)	750	1,525 (4.6%)
Regio IX	17 (4.0%)	1	5.9	14,000 (5.6%)	824	474 (1.4%)
Regio X	25 (5.8%)	2	8.0	51,000 (20.4%)	2,040	5,858 (17.8%)
Regio XI	12 (2.8%)	—	—	32,000 (12.8%)	2,667	2,159 (6.6%)
Average	39.1	4.5	11.4	22,727	581	2,991
Total	430	49	—	250,000	—	32,907

	Inscriptions per town (average)	Inscriptions per 100 km² (average)	Mentions of state *alimenta* per 10,000 km² (average)
Regio I	99	55.0	7.7
Regio II	33	10.0	1.6
Regio III	23	2.0	1.1
Regio IV	67	16.1	5.0
Regio V	41	14.6	3.1
Regio VI	58	28.3	8.0
Regio VII	94	14.9	1.9
Regio VIII	59	7.8	1.0
Regio IX	28	3.6	0.7
Regio X	234	11.5	0.4
Regio XI	180	6.7	—
Average for Italy	76	13.2	2.0

II. THE ALIMENTARY TOWNS

TABLE 10. *The alimentary towns:* (a) *The State scheme*

Ten towns have been traced independently. The remainder were listed by Ruggiero s.v. Alimenta (sometimes referring only to collections of inscriptions that are now obsolete).

Regio I

Abella	X 1208; 1216
Abellinum	X 1138
Anagnia	X 5920; 5928 = *ILS* 6264
Caiatia	X 4570; 4582
Cales?	X 3910
(Ciciliano)	[see XIV p.360] *ACSDIR* 2 (1969–70) 151–2
Ferentinum Latii	VI 1492 = *ILS* 6106
Formiae	*AE* 1927, 126–7
Fundi	X 6243
Neapolis	X 1491 = *ILS* 6456
Ostia	XIV 298; 4664
Suessula?	X 3764 = *ILS* 6341

Regio II

Compsa	IX 981
Ligures Baebiani	IX 1455 = *ILS* 6509
Sipontum?	IX 699 = *ILS* 6476
Trivicum	IX 1415

Regio III

Atina Lucaniae	X 330
Locri	X 20 = *ILS* 6465
Vibo	X 47

Regio IV

Alba Fucens	IX 3923 = *ILS* 6536
Allifae	IX 2354 = *ILS* 6512
Aufidena	IX 2807
Aufinum	IX 3384 = *ILS* 6529
Cures Sabini	IX 4976
Ficulea	XIV 4003 = *ILS* 6225
Nomentum	XIV 3941 = *ILS* 4378
Peltuinum	IX 3434; 3438
Saepinum	IX 2472 = *ILS* 6519

Regio V

Auximum	IX 5825; 5849; 5859
Cupra Montana	IX 5700

Regio VI

Ameria	XI 4351
Arna	XI 5614 = *ILS* 6621
Asisium	XI 5395 = *ILS* 6620
Pisaurum	XI 6357 = *ILS* 5057
Pitinum Mergens	XI 5956–7
Sestinum	XI 6002
Tifernum	XI 5989 = *ILS* 328
Mataurense	
Urvinum	XI 6073
Mataurense	

Regio VII

Capena	*AE* 1954, 167
Falerii	XI 3123 = *ILS* 6587
Forum Clodii	XI 7556 = *ILS* 6584
Lucus Feroniae	*RPAA* 33 (1960–1) 183, fig. 9
Nepet	XI 3211
Saturnia	XI 7265 = *ILS* 6596

Regio VIII

Ariminum	XI 416; 417 = *ILS* 6661
Veleia	XI 1147 = *ILS* 6675; XI 1149

Regio IX

Industria	V 7468 = *ILS* 6745

Regio X

Acelum?	V 8808
Brixia	V 4384

Regio XI

—	—

The alimentary towns: (b) Private alimentary schemes in Italy

Only those schemes which provided public arrangements for the support of children are listed. Restricted alimentary schemes which provided for dependants of the donor (often adults) were probably much more common (cf. *ILS* 2927; 8978; *Digesta* 34.1.1–23; 2.15.8).

Regio I		*Regio XI*	
Atina Latii	x 5056 = *ILS* 977	Comum	Pliny *Ep.* 7.18; 1.8; v 5262
Capua?	(see C. no.637 and n.)		= *ILS* 2927; cf. *AE* 1947, 65
	Fronto *ad amic.* 1.14		
Ostia	XIV 4450		
Tarracina	x 6328 = *ILS* 6278		
Regio II			
Canusium	*Epigraphica* 34 (1972) 150		
Regio VII			
Florentia	XI 1602		

APPENDIX 6

The table of Ligures Baebiani

Several points in the reconstruction of the *alimenta* depend on the size of the Baebian Table, dated to A.D. 101 (IX 1455). As it survives, this bronze inscription contains the two final columns of the list of *obligationes*, together with rather less than half of the preceding column; the amount missing is the same throughout the length of the column. Since the figures giving the interest due on each loan have survived in the right-hand margin throughout the incomplete column, the amount of every loan that it contained can be accurately inferred, by multiplying by 40 (see p.290 n.2 above). However, the estate-valuations in this column survive complete in only 5 cases out of 16 (see C. nos. 1246, 1258, 1260, 1263, 1286), and accurate restoration is impossible here, because of the shifting relationship between loans and valuations. Mommsen and Henzen, who examined the bronze in detail, both concluded that it only contained three columns in all (Henzen 62; IX 1455 commentary; Mommsen *Ges.Schr.* 5.126). Since the preamble forms a single text running the whole width of the inscription, the original width could be calculated approximately. A modern view that there were originally four columns in all (not based on scrutiny of the inscription) cannot be accepted (Veyne 1957, 83 and n.1).

The total amount of the loan farmed out for the *alimenta* at Ligures Baebiani can thus be deduced from the surviving text, since the payments of interest due on each loan survive complete in all three columns. The resulting total is HS401,800. The annual income was 5% of this, HS20,090. This total is extremely close to HS20,160, the sum required to support 60 boys and 60 girls at the Veleian rates: (HS192 × 60 = 11,520)+(HS144 × 60 = 8,640). The sum available annually falls short by HS70 in all, or 0.35%. If there were one illegitimate boy and one illegitimate girl (as at Veleia), the income required would fall to HS20,158, or HS2 less than the income actually available. (At the Veleian rates illegitimate boys received HS48 per year less than if they had been legitimate, illegitimate girls HS24 less.)

Parity of numbers between the sexes can be paralleled in privately donated alimentary schemes (*ILS* 6278 and 6818). But at Veleia the sex ratio was about 1:7 in favour of males. Although we know that girls were also supported at Ligures Baebiani (they are mentioned in the preamble), they may have been in the minority. Assuming that there was still a round number total of beneficiaries (at Veleia there were 300 in all in the Table of Veleia) the most likely total would be 110. If composed of 88 legitimate boys and 22 legitimate girls, the total income required would be HS20,064, which is only HS24 or 0.12% less than the sum actually available (HS20,090).

Thus assuming that the rates of subsidy were the same at Ligures Baebiani as at Veleia (they were the same in both of the later Veleian schemes, although the loan arrangements differed), the number of beneficiaries at Ligures Baebiani was probably either 110 or 120 children.

The size of private fortunes under
the Principate

Previous lists (overlapping with each other): Mommsen (8 items); Frank (11 items); Jones (8 items). (Mommsen *Ges.Schr.* 5.589–90; Frank *ESAR* 5.22–8; 56–8; A. H. M. Jones *Third International Conference of Economic History, Munich 1965* (1969) 3.92 n.3.)

Only fortunes of substantial size whose amount is indicated in ancient sources are included here. Invented totals such as those given by Petronius and Martial are omitted. Fortunes whose minimum size is suggested by the amount of large public gifts are likewise omitted. The fortunes in the list belonged to senators (or to members of senatorial families) with the following exceptions, marked with an asterisk below: nos. 2, 6, 7, 10 (imperial freedmen); 16 (private freedman); 14, 25–8 (provincial magnates, sometimes equestrian); 19, 22 (physicians); 23 (court poet). The largest private fortune of the Republic (excluding Sulla and Pompey) amounted to HS200 million (M. Crassus, Pliny *NH* 33.134).

1. HS400 million, Cn. Cornelius Lentulus (died A.D. 25). Seneca *de ben.* 2.27; Suetonius *Tib.* 49.1 ('census maximus fuit'). *PIR*² C 1379.
*2. HS400 million, Narcissus, freedman of Claudius (died A.D. 54), Cassius Dio 60.34. *PIR*¹ N 18.
3. (More than HS300 million, because richer than Seneca), L. Volusius Saturninus (died A.D. 56). Tacitus *Ann.* 14.56.1; 13.30.1. Cf. 3.30.1. *PIR*¹ V 661.
4. HS300 million, L. Annaeus Seneca (died A.D. 65). Tacitus *Ann.* 13.42; Cassius Dio 61.10.3. *PIR*² A 617.
5. HS300 million, Q. Vibius Crispus (died *c.* A.D. 83/93). Tacitus *Dial.* 8; cf. Martial 4.54.7. *PIR*¹ V 379.
*6. HS300 million, M. Antonius Pallas (died A.D. 62). Tacitus *Ann.* 12.53. *PIR*² A 858.
*7. (HS300–HS200 million?), C. Iulius Licinus (died after A.D. 14). Juvenal 1.109 (his wealth comparable with that of Pallas, no.6 above); Seneca *Ep.* 119.9, cf. 120.19 (his wealth comparable with that of Crassus [HS200 million, Pliny *NH* 33.134]). *PIR*² I 381.
8. The largest private fortune of the early second century A.D. was less than HS288 million. Plutarch, *v. Public.* 15.3.
9. HS280 million, private wealth of the Emperor Tacitus (before A.D. 275). *HA Tac.* 10. *PIR*² C 1036.
*10. More than HS200 million, C. Iulius Callistus (died *c.* A.D. 52). Pliny *NH* 33.134. *PIR*² I 229.
11. HS200 million, T. Clodius Eprius Marcellus (died *c.* A.D. 79). Tacitus *Dial.* 8. *PIR*² E 84.

12. HS200 million, C. Sallustius Passienus Crispus (died *c*. A.D. 46/7, Syme 328, n.12). Suetonius *v. Pass. Crisp. PIR¹* P 109 with *AE* 1924, 72.

13. HS110 million, M. Gavius Apicius (died after A.D. 28). Seneca *ad Helv.* 10.9; Martial 3.22 (HS70 million alleged). *PIR²* G 91.

*14. HS100 million, Ti. Claudius Hipparchus of Athens, grandfather of Herodes Atticus (died after A.D. 81). Suetonius *Vesp.* 13. *PIR²* C 889.

15. HS100 million, L. Tarius Rufus (31 B.C./A.D. 14). Pliny *NH* 18.37. *PIR¹* T 14.

*16. HS60 million, C. Caecilius Isidorus (died 8 B.C.). Also bequeathed 4,116 slaves and 257,000 herd animals. Pliny *NH* 33.135. *PIR²* C 50.

17. HS60 million (in part anticipated), M. Aquillius Regulus (died *c*. A.D. 105, Syme 102). Pliny *Ep.* 2.20.13. *PIR²* A 1005.

18. More than HS40 million, Lollia Paulina (died A.D. 49). Pliny *NH* 9.117–18. *PIR²* L 328.

*19. HS30 million, C. Stertinius Xenophon and Q. Stertinius (joint estate; *c*. A.D. 41/54). Pliny *NH* 29.7–8. *PIR¹* S 658; 666.

20. HS20 million, a 'moderate' fortune under Marcus Aurelius. Galen 13.636 (Kühn).

21. *c*. HS20 million, C. Plinius Caecilius Secundus (died *c*. A.D. 111/13). See pp.20–32 above. *PIR¹* P 370.

*22. Nearly HS20 million, Crinas of Massilia (*c*. A.D. 54/68). Pliny *NH* 29.9 *RE* 11.1865.

*23. HS10 million, P. Vergilius Maro (died 19 B.C.). Donatus *v. Verg.* 13; Probus *v. Verg.* 16. *PIR¹* V 279.

24. More than HS5 million, M. Calpurnius Piso (in A.D. 20). Tacitus *Ann.* 3.17. *PIR²* C 296.

*25. HS4 million, Aemilia Pudentilla of Oea (in A.D. 158/9). Apuleius *Apol.* 71; 77. *PIR²* A 425.

*26. HS4 million, C. Licinius Marinus Voconius Romanus of Saguntum (*c*. A.D. 98/100). Pliny *Ep.* 10.4.2. *PIR²* L 210.

*27. HS3 million, Herennius Rufinus of Oea (A.D. 158/9). Apuleius *Apol.* 75. *PIR²* H 123.

*28. HS2 million, L. Apuleius of Madauros (father of the novelist; *c*. A.D. 140/50). Apuleius *Apol.* 23.

29. HS1,800,000 (or more), M. Hortensius Hortalus (died after A.D. 16). Tacitus *Ann.* 2.37–8. *PIR²* H 210.

APPENDIX 8

Prices at Rome[1]

The ordinary price of wheat in first-century Italy is unlikely to have been much more than HS4 per modius (see above, p.146). Yet flour prices given by Pliny the elder ranging upwards from HS12 per modius for different grades of flour imply that normal market prices for wheat at Rome were considerably more than this. Pliny says that his figures refer to periods when prices were moderate. It has been suggested that minimum wheat-prices of HS8–HS10 per modius are implied by Pliny's figures, after compensating for milling costs (Jasny 137; 162–3; Pliny *NH* 18.90).

Other ancient sources explicitly state that prices were substantially higher at Rome than elsewhere. Martial, a Spaniard who lived in Rome for more than thirty years (Martial 12.31), justifies his nostalgia for Spain by referring to the lower cost of living there (compare *Digesta* 35.2.63.2). In Rome it is expensive to satisfy one's hunger, and food prices are ruinous, whereas in Spain one can live well on a small income (Martial 10.96: residence in Rome also requires expensive social displays such as wearing the toga every day; cf. Juvenal 3.171 ff.). High prices in the capital are reflected when Martial describes the cheapness of the 'vita municipalis': the landowner living outside Rome can obtain everything he needs without paying for it (Martial 4.66). Juvenal in turn says that at Rome one has to spend heavily in order to obtain a vile lodging, enough food for one's slaves and a modest dinner for oneself (Juvenal 3.165–7). Housing in Rome is so expensive that the annual rent of a dark abode in Rome would buy the freehold of a fine house and garden at a nearby town, Juvenal says (3.223 ff.). For high land prices and housing costs at Rome see also *PBSR* 33 (1965) 224–5; cf. p. 52 above. Later testimony to the high cost of living at Rome is provided by Apuleius (*Met.* 11.28).

The proximity of cities and of Rome in particular tended to raise prices in the neighbouring countryside. If one's farm lay near a town, barley would be too costly to allow it to be fed to sheep; in other words one should send it to market and take advantage of the high price (Columella *de r.r.* 7.3.22; cf. 7.3.13; 7.9.4; Varro *r.r.* 1.16.3). Single fruit-trees grown near Rome could produce annual crops that would fetch as much as HS2,000 (Pliny *NH* 17.8; peaches are mentioned elsewhere as the most expensive fruit, fetching up to HS30 each, *NH* 15.40). The permanent demand for luxury foods at Rome made it profitable for the owners of farms near the capital to concentrate on rearing different kinds of poultry for the table, which they could sell at enormous prices in the city (cf. Columella *de r.r.* 8.8.9–10). Varro mentions the high incomes of three villa-owners who took advantage of this demand; the villas (at Ostia, on the via Salaria, and at Alba) brought in revenues of HS50,000, HS60,000 and HS20,000 (*r.r.* 3.2.7; 3.2.14; 3.2.15; 3.2.17). Mullets could fetch as much as

HS10,000 each at Rome, wine up to HS1,000 per amphora (Suet. *Tib.* 34, cf. p.250 n.1; Pliny *NH* 14.57). Even goat's milk was costly enough at Rome to bring in HS4 from each animal per day, Varro suggests (*r.r.* 2.3.10). The Roman food market was so buoyant that it was profitable to drive geese to Rome from the other side of the Alps, and to ship farm-produce from farms in Italy 150 miles away (Pliny *NH* 10.53; Pliny *Ep.* 5.6.12; 10.8.6).

The question of wheat-prices at Rome is complicated by the fact that the government regularly issued wheat to a section of the city population free of charge. But the 'plebs frumentaria' was not the whole population of the city, cf. Fronto, van den Hout 200.4–5 (recent estimates for the late Republic in Brunt 382–3), and those not entitled to free corn presumably had to buy it at commercial rates. The government only appears to have intervened in the commercial sector of the city corn-supply in time of shortage or famine (Tac. *Ann.* 2.87; 15.39). Judging from the other evidence for commodity prices, it would not be at all surprising if the exceptional concentration of purchasing power at Rome also meant that corn-prices were normally well above those prevailing elsewhere in Italy. Pliny's figures seem to show that this was the case.

Nevertheless, wheat may not have been as expensive as Jasny's extrapolations from Pliny suggest. The collations with modern wheat prices on which Jasny relies for part of his argument are inherently spurious (Jasny 139 ff.). And his estimate of milling-costs at Rome (HS1 per modius) from ancient figures for Egypt probably places them too low, although he compensates by a factor of two to allow for differences in price-levels between the two areas (Jasny 160). In Diocletian's Edict, the price of ground millet is twice that of grain millet, volume for volume (*ESAR* 5.318 = Lauffer 98; the volume of usable wheat-flour would almost equal the volume of the grain from which it was milled, because of the greater bulk of flour; Moritz 191, Table VIII). The base-price for ordinary wheat-flour was HS12 per modius according to Pliny *NH* 18.90 (not HS10; see Jasny 162). In view of the likelihood of high charges for milling and retailing at Rome, the wheat-price with which this corresponded might be nearer to HS6 per modius than to the HS8 suggested by Jasny (Jasny 166). In assessing the actual grain price we also have to take account of the price fetched by the subsidiary milling products, *cibarium* and bran, though no figures are known (for quantities extracted, Moritz 191, Table VIII). The price which Pliny apparently indicates for the finest grade of flour (*siligo castrata*) is much higher, HS20 per modius (*NH* 18.90, with Moritz 171 n.3).

Evidence from the East also suggests that prices for grain might be substantially higher in large towns than they were outside. The normal price for wheat in the mid-fourth century at Syrian Antioch, one of the biggest towns in the Empire, was apparently double the normal price in Egypt (Julian *Misopogon* 369; Jones *LRE* 446). Cicero indicates that grain prices at Ephesus, a great city on the coast, were substantially higher than those at Philomelium, a town in central Asia Minor (*Verr.* 2.3.191). A series of inscriptions show extremely high prices for bread at Ephesus at different dates under the Principate (*Forschungen in Ephesos* 3 (1922) 102–3; *Jahresh. Öst.Arch.Inst.* 23 (1926) Beibl. 281–2; both texts also in Broughton *ESAR* 4.879–80; for some comments on the types of bread, N. Jasny *Agricultural History* 21 (1947) 190–2). Dio Chrysostom claimed that the famine price of wheat at Prusa in northern Asia Minor was no higher than the price which prevailed in some other towns when prices were at their lowest (*Or.* 46.10).

(Yeo attempts to explain the high level of Pliny's flour prices by arguing that wheat prices were exceptionally high at Rome under Vespasian because of an impending agricultural crisis later attested by Domitian's vine-edict. This is unconvincing, because the Roman grain supply was largely provided by tribute from the provinces, and would not easily reflect changes in the state of Italian agriculture. C. A. Yeo *TAPHA* 77 (1946) 244.)

APPENDIX 9

The price of land in Africa

Apuleius's figures for the wealth and possessions of a large landowner in Tripolitania under Antoninus Pius may suggest that cultivated land cost less there than the price which Columella gives for uncultivated land nearly a century earlier. (Columella *de r.r.* 3.3.8 gives a price of HS1,000 per iugerum for unprepared land which is to be turned into vineyard; he later recommends the use of uncultivated or virgin land for growing vines, 3.11.1–3; his land price appears to take in the provinces as well as Italy in 3.3.11.) Apuleius's *Apologia* can be dated to 158/9 (R. Syme *REA* 61 (1959) 310–19).

In the *Apologia* Apuleius is concerned among other things to clear himself from allegations of sorcery. Nevertheless, the dispute was ultimately concerned with property, since Apuleius's accusers included members of his wife's family who saw a large fortune threatened as a result of Pudentilla's marriage to Apuleius. Thus the size of Pudentilla's fortune and the extent of her possessions were matters of some importance for the court. Apuleius says that Pudentilla was worth HS4 million (*Apol.* 71; 77). She had a town house in Oea (the modern Tripoli) where there were 15 slaves, and a 'suburbana villa' somewhere nearby, together with a country estate more than 100 miles away, which must also have had a landlord's house (*Apol.* 43–5; 87; 44). Some part of her HS4 million was already promised to her sons (*Apol.* 71). This promise was carried out by a donation in kind after the marriage (*Apol.* 93). At Apuleius's instigation, his step-sons were given land to the value of the amount owed (assessed at a low price as an act of generosity). They were also given as an *ex gratia* advance on their eventual inheritance, further acres of very fertile land, a fine house, large quantities of corn, barley, wine, oil and other crops, together with 400 slaves, and sizeable herds of animals. Although he is concerned to depict the generosity of this gift in the most favourable light, Apuleius does not say that it impoverished Pudentilla; if she had been left with tiny revenues and few rustic slaves, the fact would not have gone unmentioned. Thus it is probably fair to assume that her original fortune included a disposable labour force not less than 600 strong (the figure may be too low).

The bulk of Pudentilla's fortune must have been invested in land. If we assume that HS3 million represents the value of her original estates (the rest being the value of the houses and slaves, and money in cash, cf. *Apol.* 87), and that at least two-thirds of her slaves would be adult agricultural slaves, the ratio of slaves to land is 400 slaves to HS3 million worth of land. The most important crops on a Tripolitanian estate are likely to have been grain and olives; Apuleius also mentions wine as a crop (see above). The manning ratios given by the agrarian writers are 1 man to 25 iugera for grain, 1 to 22 iugera for olives, 1 to 7–10 iugera for vines (Appendix 2). If grain, olives and vines existed on Pudentilla's estates in a ratio of 4:2:1, the area per man would be 19 *iugera*, from the ratios $(4 \div 25) + (2 \div 22) + (1 \div 8.75)$. If this figure has any value, it would suggest that a working force of 400 labourers would mean an area under cultivation of 8,800 iugera (assuming manning no heavier in Africa than in Italy). On this basis the implied land price for Pudentilla's estate is about HS390 per iugerum.

If a radically different interpretation of the slave-totals is adopted, it is possible to reach a higher figure, though this still falls short of the Columella price for land. If it is held (somewhat implausibly) that the total for slaves represents the whole of a population which was entirely self-reproducing, and that the only fieldworkers were adult males, a slave-total of 600 will give a figure for adult males of about 170 (cf. *JRS* 53 (1963) 87 n.24). Substituting this figure for the 400 used previously, the land-price becomes approximately HS920 per iugerum. (Neither calculation is intended as more than a rough indication of a possible order of size.)

Evidence for land prices lower than HS1,000 per iugerum is found in Egypt. Averages from papyri work out at *c*. HS140 for the first century A.D. and *c*. HS180 for the second (Appendix 16). If the cost of land in Egypt were half of that elsewhere, these figures would still point to land prices well below those suggested by Columella (see pp.48–52 above).

APPENDIX 10

Prices of slaves in Rome and Italy

Previous lists (partly overlapping): Wallon (7 items); Westermann (11 items) (H. Wallon *Histoire de l'esclavage dans l'antiquité* 2 (1879) 165–8; W. L. Westermann *The slave systems of Greek and Roman antiquity* (1955) 100–1.)

Prices from epigraphic and other historical sources are listed in section i. Prices from poets and novelists are listed in section ii. Slaves were often assumed to have a value of HS2,000 for legal purposes: VIII 23956 (Commodus); *Digesta* 4.4.31; 40.4.47;

5.2.8.17; 5.2.9. For legal valuations in the later Empire, sometimes 20 solidi, cf. *Cod. Iust.* 6.1.4; 6.43.3.1; 7.7.1.5 (S. Gsell *Mélanges Glotz* 1 (1932) 399, n.4; market prices from this period in Jones *LRE* 2.852). A *senatus consultum* in 177/80 restricted the price of condemned men (*noxii*) to HS600 (*ILS* 5163, ll.57–8).

(i) FIGURES FROM EPIGRAPHIC AND OTHER HISTORICAL SOURCES

Rome

1. HS700,000 (the highest legitimate slave price known to Pliny) paid for Daphnis (later Lutatius Daphnis), a *grammaticus*. Pliny *NH* 7.128; Suetonius *de gramm.* 3 (*c.* 86 B.C., *RE* 13.2095).

2. HS100,000 paid for a well-known prostitute by Elagabalus. *HA Elag.* 31.1 (A.D. 218/22).

3. HS100,000 each for 11 slaves of Calvisius Sabinus each of whom knew the works of one Greek poet by heart. Seneca *Ep.* 27.5–7; cf. *PIR²* C 351 (before A.D. 65).

4. HS10,000 paid as manumission price by Paris, the *pantomimus* who belonged to Domitia Lepida, aunt of Nero. *Digesta* 12.4.3.5; Tacitus *Ann.* 13.27; cf. *RE* 18.2.1536 (A.D. 56).

5. HS2,700 as the price of a cook (the HS8,000 paid for a fish is enough to purchase 3 cooks). Pliny *NH* 9.67 (before A.D. 80).

Italy

6. HS50,000 paid as manumission price by P. Decimius Merula, a doctor who held the sevirate at Asisium. XI 5400 = *ILS* 7812 (first century A.D.).

7. HS6,000–8,000 as the appropriate price for a skilled vine-dresser. Columella *de r.r.* 3.3.8 (A.D. 54/68).

8. HS4,050 paid for a male slave at Herculaneum. Tab. Herc. 61, *PP* 9 (1954) 55 (8 May A.D. 63).

9. (HS2,650) each for 2 *mancipia veterana* sold at Pompeii for HS5,300. IV 3340⁴⁹ (before A.D. 80).

10. HS2,500 paid for an adult female slave at Ravenna. *FIRA* 3 no.134 (second century A.D.).

11. HS1,400 as the sum for which a *puella* is pledged (?) at Herculaneum. Tab. Herc. 72, *PP* 9 (1954) 68, cf. 72 n. 1 (before A.D. 80).

12. HS900 paid for a male slave at Herculaneum. Tab. Herc. 59, *PP* 9 (1954) 55 [= *AE* 1952, 162 *male*] (before A.D. 80).

13. (HS725) each for 2 slave-boys, sold at Pompeii for HS1,450. IV 3340¹⁵⁴⁻⁵ + *FIRA* 3 no. 91 (A.D. 61).

14. HS600 as the sum for which a *puella* is pledged at Herculaneum. Tab. Herc. 65, *PP* 9 (1954) 64 (A.D. 54/68).

(ii) FIGURES FROM POETS AND NOVELISTS

Rome

15. Slaves purchased for HS200,000 by ostentatious millionaire 'Quintus'. Martial 3.62.

16. And for HS100,000 (see 15).

17. *Pueri* bought for HS100,000. Martial 11.70.

18. Deceased slave belonging to 'Scissa' valued at HS50,000 for tax purposes. Petronius 65.
19. HS20,000 paid for imbecilic jester (*morio*). Martial 8.13.
20. HS20,000 paid for deaf muleteer. Martial 11.38.
21. HS8,000 as the asking price for a *puer* born at Tibur or Gabii, who knows some Greek. Horace *Ep.* 2.2.2–19.
22. HS4,000 as manumission price paid by 'Hermeros'. Petronius 57.
23. HS2,000 paid by Horace for his slave 'Davus'. Horace *Sat.* 2.7.43.
24. A slave sold to pay for a 4-pound mullet fetched HS1,200. Martial 10.31.
25. HS1,200 for versatile slave bought by 'Habinnas'. Petronius 68.
26. HS1,000 reward offered for the return of the boy 'Giton'. Petronius 97.
27. HS600 bid for a *puella* 'famae non nimium bonae.../quales in media sedent Subura'. Martial 6.66.

Italy

28. HS6,000 paid for a fish by Crispinus is more than enough to purchase a fisherman. Juvenal 4.25–7; *PIR²* C 1586.

APPENDIX 11

The chronological distribution of prices in Africa and Italy

Establishing the chronology of the costs in the present sample has two purposes. It enables the costs (considered as abstract economic data) to be placed in their historical context, in relation to changes in the coinage and to changes in general economic conditions. And it serves the secondary purpose of charting the course of private munificence, a majority of these costs being derived from gifts to the community.

(*a*) Since the samples for both areas very largely come from inscriptions, their concentrations are likely to reflect the concentrations of the dated inscriptions as a whole. The main category of dated inscriptions is provided by the dedications to the Emperors. In some ways this is a crude and fallible index. Emperors who suffered *damnatio memoriae* are inevitably under-represented; while Emperors whose reigns were very short tend to be over-represented because of a tendency to put up more monuments to the ruler soon after his accession. Nevertheless, the sample of Emperor-dated inscriptions is quite large, and its ratios almost certainly indicate the broad outlines of public building as a whole and its fluctuations (see Table 11).

TABLE II. *Analysis of all African and Italian inscriptions
in* CIL *dated by Emperor*

	Africa		Italy	
Ruler	Commemorations per reign-year (average)	Commemorations (total)	Commemorations per reign-year (average)	Commemorations (total)
Octavian/ Augustus	0.05	3 (0.3%)	3.0	172 (17.4%)
Tiberius	0.3	7 (0.6%)	3.5	82 (8.3%)
Claudius	0.4	6 (0.6%)	4.2	58 (5.9%)
Nero	0.07	1 (0.1%)	1.8	24 (2.4%)
Vespasian	1.6	16 (1.5%)	5.2	52 (5.3%)
Titus	0.4	1 (0.1%)	3.5	8 (0.8%)
Domitian	0.2	3 (0.3%)	1.3	20 (2.0%)
Nerva	2.1	3 (0.3%)	17.2	25 (2.5%)
Trajan	2.1	40 (3.7%)	4.4	85 (8.6%)
Hadrian	3.6	78 (7.2%)	3.6	78 (7.9%)
Pius	5.5	122 (11.2%)	4.4	91 (9.2%)
Marcus	7.0	135 (12.4%)	2.9	56 (5.7%)
Commodus	4.8	62 (5.7%)	1.6	20 (2.0%)
Severus	14.9	262 (24.1%)	5.5	97 (9.8%)
Caracalla	41.3	252 (23.2%)	13.4	82 (8.3%)
S. Alexander	4.3	57 (5.2%)	1.1	15 (1.5%)
Gordian III	6.6	38 (3.5%)	4.2	24 (2.4%)
Total	—	1,086	—	989

Note: Percentages refer to the totals at the foot of each column.

The African totals are compiled from the index to *CIL* VIII, the Italian totals from the indexes to *CIL* V, IX, X and XI. *CIL* XIV, which is dominated by inscriptions from Ostia, has been omitted because the survival pattern from this town is not necessarily the same as that from Italy as a whole. Ostia, which has left more than 3,000 inscriptions, was closely linked in prosperity to Rome, whose size, wealth and political importance exclude it from being considered a typical Italian town. The Italian sample on which the present figures are based contains a small amount of extraneous material (about 4.5% of the total epigraphic sample), because of the presence in *CIL* V and X of inscriptions from Alpes Maritimae, Alpes Cottiae, Sardinia, Corsica and Sicily. All commemorations of living Emperors on civic monuments as well as commemorations of their relatives during their lifetime, are included in the present totals. Records on milestones, lead pipes, lamps, vases, jewels, weights, tiles, amphorae etc. are omitted. References about which the *CIL* editors are doubtful are also omitted.

The Italian sample of 989 inscriptions is almost evenly divided between the first century and the second to third centuries (inscriptions after the death of Gordian III in A.D. 244 being omitted). The African sample of 1,086 inscriptions is by contrast very heavily concentrated in the second and third centuries. In Italy 44.6% of the sample belongs to the period before the accession of Trajan in A.D. 98, whereas in Africa only 3.8% of the sample belongs to this period. The African inscriptions ascend in frequency from Trajan (2.1 per year) to Caracalla (41.3 per year) with only one break (in the reign of Commodus), probably due only to the destruction of monuments of Commodus soon after his death. The Italian inscriptions oscillate in frequency without following any clear pattern of growth or decline. The figure under Marcus Aurelius (2.9 per year) is the lowest for any reign without *damnatio* up to that point, and it might be expected to portend a long-term drop in frequency. But in Italy (as in Africa) the reigns of the early Severi at the start of the third century in fact saw an acceleration of building activity; the averages for the reigns of Severus and Caracalla are as high as any during the previous two centuries (5.5 and 13.4 per year). In both areas the number of imperial commemorations had fallen drastically by the mid-third century. In Africa the most prolific period between Gordian and Diocletian, the reigns of Valerian, Gallienus, Claudius and Aurelian, show a combined average of 2.8 per year. This is below any figure for Africa in the second century except the earliest (2.1 in the reign of Trajan).

Another index of building activity is provided by dated buildings constructed from private funds. The sample is much smaller, but it is more homogeneous, and almost certainly offers a better guide to the course of large-scale munificence than the pattern of imperial dedications as a whole.

TABLE 12. *Analysis of buildings dated by Emperor*

Ruler	Africa			Italy and remaining western provinces		
	Average frequency per year	Total		Average frequency per year	Total	
Trajan	0.3	6	(5.4%)	0.6	12	(29.2%)
Hadrian	0.6	13	(11.6%)	0.2	5	(12.2%)
Pius	0.8	18	(16.1%)	0.4	9	(22.0%)
Marcus	0.7	14	(12.5%)	0.2	4	(9.8%)
Commodus	1.2	16	(14.3%)	0.2	2	(4.9%)
Severus	1.2	21	(18.7%)⎫	0.25	6	(14.6%)
Caracalla	1.5	9	(8.0%)⎭			
S. Alexander	0.8	10	(8.9%)	0.15	2	(4.9%)
Gordian III	0.9	5	(4.5%)	0.2	1	(2.4%)
Total	—	112		—	41	

(The African evidence comes from Romanelli, *Storia*, with the following supplements: Trajan, *ILAf* 384; Hadrian, *ILAlg* 1.2082, VIII 15381; 16441; Pius, VIII 26245; *ILAf* 238; Marcus, Leschi 117; Commodus, *ILAf* 517; Severus, VIII 9015; 9320; Caracalla, *ILAlg* 1.3040; *ILTun* 718; S. Alexander, VIII 1578; 9065; 15497; 26458; Gordian III, VIII 1334. The material for Italy and the remaining western provinces comes from lists in J. C. Rockwell *Private Baustiftungen für die Stadtgemeinde auf Inschriften der Kaiserzeit im Westen des römischen Reiches* (1909) 82–3. Rockwell's lists are incomplete, and his figures are less useful than those given for Africa.

TABLE 13. *The concentrations of dated African construction costs*

	African building costs		African statue costs		African statue and building costs combined	
Vespasian	1	(2.5%)	—		1	(1.1%)
Domitian	1	(2.5%)	—		1	(1.1%)
Nerva	1	(2.5%)	—		1	(1.1%)
Trajan	2	(5.0%)	1	(1.9%)	3	(3.3%)
Hadrian	5	(12.5%)	1	(1.9%)	6	(6.5%)
Pius	4	(10.0%)	13	(25.0%)	17	(18.5%)
Marcus	6	(15.0%)	5	(9.6%)	11	(12.0%)
Commodus	4	(10.0%)	6	(11.5%)	10	(10.8%)
Severus	8	(20.0%)	21	(40.4%)	29	(31.5%)
Caracalla	4	(10.0%)	4	(7.7%)	8	(8.7%)
S. Alexander	3	(7.5%)	1	(1.9%)	4	(4.3%)
Gordian III	1	(2.5%)	—		1	(1.1%)
Total	40 (100.0%)		52 (100.0%)		92 (100.0%)	

Note : The 10 dated African construction costs later than Gordian III are omitted in order to allow direct comparison with the percentages for each reign in Tables 11 and 12. For their details see Table 15 below.

TABLE 14. *The concentrations of dated Italian foundations and sportulae*

	Italian foundations of known size		Italian distributions of sportulae of known amount	
Caligula	1	(5.0%)	—	
Claudius	—		1	(2.2%)
Nero	1	(5.0%)	—	
Vespasian	—		—	
Titus	—		—	
Domitian	1	(5.0%)	—	
Nerva	—		—	
Trajan	4	(20.0%)	1	(2.2%)
Hadrian	2	(10.0%)	4	(8.9%)
Pius	6	(30.0%)	9	(20.0%)
Marcus	3	(15.0%)	13	(28.9%)
Commodus	1	(5.0%)	8	(17.8%)
Severus	—		7	(15.6%)
Caracalla	—		1	(2.2%)
S. Alexander	1	(5.0%)	1	(2.2%)
Total	20 (100.0%)		45 (100.0%)	

TABLE 15. *The size of dated costs*

	African buildings and other large outlays				African statues			
	median	highest	lowest	total	median	highest	lowest	total
Vespasian	200,000	200,000	200,000	1	—	—	—	—
Domitian	80,000	80,000	80,000	1	—	—	—	—
Nerva	42,000	42,000	42,000	1	—	—	—	—
Trajan	20,000	90,000	10,000+	3	10,600	10,600	10,600	1
Hadrian	60,000	200,000+	50,000+	5	68,335	68,335	68,335	1
Pius	40,000	500,000	9,000+	4	5,000	12,000	800	13
Marcus	67,250	1,300,000	24,000+	6	6,000	38,000	3,000	5
Commodus	82,500	1,000,000+	6,000+	4	4,500	12,000	2,000	6
Severus	36,100	120,000	7,000+	8	4,800	50,000	1,500	21
Caracalla	100,000	696,000+	3,000+	4	6,500	12,000	4,000	4
S. Alexander	12,000	90,000	10,000	3	5,200	5,200	5,200	1
Gordian III	50,000+	50,000+	50,000+	1	—	—	—	—
Gallienus	53,750	200,000	41,200	4	—	—	—	—
Probus	28,000	28,000	28,000	3	—	—	—	—
Tacitus	—	—	—	—	16,000	16,000	16,000	1
Diocletian	205,500	350,000	61,000	2	—	—	—	—
Late third century	—	—	—	—	41,100	50,000	32,200	2

	Italian foundations				Italian sportulae			
	median	highest	lowest	total	median	highest	lowest	total
Caligula	400,000	400,000	400,000	1	—	—	—	—
Claudius	—	—	—	—	4	4	4	1
Nero	400,000	400,000	400,000	1	—	—	—	—
Vespasian	—	—	—	—	—	—	—	—
Titus	—	—	—	—	—	—	—	—
Domitian	120,000	120,000	120,000	1	—	—	—	—
Nerva	—	—	—	—	—	—	—	—
Trajan	200,000	1,866,666	4,000	3	2	4	1	3
Hadrian	48,000	80,000	16,000	2	10	20	4	7
Pius	55,000	200,000	5,000	6	7	400	4	14
Marcus	10,000	2,000,000+	5,000	3	8	100	2	29
Commodus	40,000	40,000	40,000	1	8	50	4	15
Severus	—	—	—	—	10	20	2	12
Caracalla	—	—	—	—	4	4	4	1
S. Alexander	8,000	8,000	8,000	1	4	4	4	1

Note : The number of sportulae is higher in Table 15 than in Table 14 because distributions at several different rates are counted once only in Table 14, whereas each rate is counted separately in Table 15.

References

AFRICA. *Buildings and other large outlays* Vespasian: no.3; Domitian: 7; Nerva: 402; Trajan: 324; 56; 67a; Hadrian: 281; 8; 254; 34; 12; Pius: 63; 306; 36; 69b; Marcus: 248; 45; 9;

The African figures show a pattern of ascending frequency from the time of Trajan to the time of Caracalla which is similar to the pattern in Table 11. In terms of buildings the reign of Commodus appears as a period of high frequency, with an average figure above that for any preceding reign. Commodus's reign was almost certainly a time of intensive building in Africa, a fact partly masked by the destruction of most statues of this Emperor after the *damnatio memoriae*. Buildings and their dedications were less easy to dispose of.

The figures for Italy and the other western provinces show no cumulative tendency over the second century, although the sample is so small that little can be deduced from the figures for any individual reign.

(*b*) There are relatively few dated costs (apart from the Trajanic land-valuations which have no relevance to tracing a chronology). The main categories are as follows: African building costs (48 dated examples); African statue costs (55); Italian perpetual foundations (20); Italian sportulae (45 dated distributions, with 86 individual rates). They can usefully be analysed in two ways, in terms of frequency, and in terms of size.

The African construction costs show a chronology similar to that of the records of African public buildings financed from private sources listed in Table 12. The main discrepancies occur in the reigns of Hadrian (with only 6.5% of the construction costs, but 11.6% of dated private building) and Severus (with 31.5% of the construction costs, but only 18.7% of dated private building). The 'private' building series tabulated in Table 12 is the more useful index of munificence, because it is more homogeneous and is based on a slightly larger sample. But these discrepancies between the two series suggest that the custom of specifying the cost of monuments had grown more frequent in Africa by the end of the second century.

The Italian distribution likewise points to more frequent mention of costs in the second half of the second century. But the peak occurs somewhat earlier than in Africa, where the highest concentration belongs to the reign of Septimius Severus. The Italian sportulae are most frequent under Marcus Aurelius and Commodus, while the few dated foundations show their greatest frequency under Antoninus Pius. The concentrations of both sportulae and foundations lie mainly in the second century.

10a; 11; 17; Commodus: 249; 4 & 260; 331; 71; Severus: 253 & 67; 5; 33; 13; 330; 19a; 23; 24; Caracalla: 32–250–382; 48; 6a; 26; S. Alexander: 400; 58; 60; Gordian III: 37; Gallienus: 398a; 10; 323; 64; Probus: 403; Diocletian: 2; 63a.

Statues Trajan: 138a; Hadrian: 83–4; Pius: 88 & 139; 150; 117; 133; 138; 144; 147; 170; 171; 174; 202; 90; 211; Marcus: 97; 101; 189; 167; 197; Commodus: 104; 112; 142; 168; 190; 203; Severus: 78; 98; 103; 106; 107; 108; 118; 143; 159; 160; 165; 169; 178; 179; 187 & 201; 194; 195; 87; 204; Caracalla: 102; 109; 172; 173; S. Alexander: 140; Tacitus: 99; late third century: 91, 92.

ITALY *Foundations* Caligula: 647; Nero: 650; Domitian: 658; Trajan: 638; 655; 706; Hadrian: 667; 685; Pius: 656; 663; 664; 694; 693; 702; Marcus: 637; 692; 701; Commodus: 675; S. Alexander: 697.

Sportulae Claudius: 999; Trajan: 1015; 1043; 1049; Hadrian: 867; 896; 901; 915; 943; 980; 1020; Pius: 818; 819; 820; 884; 916; 926; 954; 970; 1006; 1007; 1010; 1014; 1031; 1026; Marcus: 824; 826; 829; 849; 852; 859; 861; 870; 886; 890; 900; 905; 910; 928; 937; 941; 951; 957; 966; 972; 978; 979; 981; 998; 1009; 1012; 1018; 1032; 1042; Commodus: 830; 846; 847; 863; 873; 877; 911; 919; 920; 953; 970a; 973; 974; 1018a; 1027; Severus: 872; 874; 882; 895; 904; 907; 938; 945; 962; 1012; 1030; 1045; Caracalla: 1008; S. Alexander: 1021.

This contrasts with the pattern of Italian Imperial dedications as a whole (Table 11), based on a much larger sample, where 45% of the sample falls before the accession of Trajan. But the imperial dedications include many monuments financed by cities, instead of by private individuals.

In many cases the sample for an individual reign is too small to allow any valid average to be deduced. Because the evidence is collected from two very large areas each of which contained many cities, the averages are always a prey to local variants which may undermine any useful chronological inference. The apparently low average for African building costs in the reign of Septimius Severus, less than half of the average for the preceding reign, is obviously influenced by the fact that the evidence for this reign partly comes from small and obscure towns (they include Duamis-es-Slitnia, Verecunda, Magifa and Hr. Sidi Navi). (The towns from which the dated sample is drawn are listed in *PBSR* 30 (1962) 76–7.) It is difficult to deduce any variation either in building costs or in the generosity of donors from the two sets of African figures. The relatively large dated sample of statue costs shows a steady average between HS4,500 and HS6,500 for the eighty-year period from the accession of Antoninus Pius to the death of Caracalla (A.D. 138–217). There is no obvious trend within these limits; the sample sizes vary between extremes of 21 and 4 costs per reign. It is probably safe to infer that construction costs did not vary very greatly within this period. (The one statue-cost from the later reign of Severus Alexander, HS5,200, falls within the same limits, but little weight can be given to a single example.)

The sample of dated Italian foundations is too small to offer usable average figures for any reign. But it is noticeable that no really large foundations are dated later than the reign of Marcus Aurelius. The last large-scale Italian costed gift of any description is dated to A.D. 184 (HS100,000 or more given 'in annonam' at Reate in A.D. 184, no.1180). The proportion of the costs that are dated is so low that this need not indicate any precise threshold in itself. But there is an undoubted contrast between Italy and Africa in the fact that gifts in five figures continue in Africa throughout the third century (if sporadically), but are not attested in Italy after the Antonines. The actual value of the later African gifts is bound to have been undermined by inflation, but the contrast between the two areas remains striking nevertheless.

The sportulae likewise show a peak under the Antonines, with maxima of HS400 and HS100 per head reached under Antoninus Pius and Marcus Aurelius. The average figures remain relatively steady, between HS7 and HS10 per head, during the period of nearly a century from the accession of Hadrian to the death of Septimius Severus (A.D. 117–211). But very often the level of sportulae is recognisably dependent on the standing of the towns from which the sportulae come (cf. p.141 n.3). It is not clear that the dated sample (with 86 rates) is large enough to compensate by its size for the undoubted local variants that affected the amount of distributions.

The dated sample as a whole is useful in showing the period to which the costs derived from gifts mainly belong. In Africa this period is the second century and early third century. In Italy the second century is equally important, but the sample begins somewhat earlier, under the Julio-Claudians or Flavians, and has already declined in density by the time of the Severi. In the African costs there are suggestions of a period of broad price-stability extending through most of the second century and into the third. The Italian sportulae show averages that are no less stable for an even longer period, but gratuitous payments which did not correspond with goods or services would not necessarily respond in any linear way to fluctuations in price-levels. The disappearance of large-scale costed gifts from Italian inscriptions in the time of the Severi may indicate that Italy was by that stage feeling an inflation which had not as yet affected Africa so seriously.

APPENDIX 12

The regional distribution of prices in Africa and Italy

1. AFRICA

CATEGORIES: I Buildings; II Statues; III Tombs; altars; IV Perpetual foundations and entertainments; V Voluntary and obligatory payments to cities; VI Miscellaneous and unclassified costs.

2. ITALY

REGIONS: I Latium and Campania; II Apulia, Calabria and Hirpini; III Lucania and Bruttium; IV Sabini, Vestini, Aequi, Marsi, Paeligni, Frentani, Samnium; V Picenum; VI Umbria; VII Etruria; VIII Aemilia; IX Liguria; X Venetia and Histria; XI Transpadana.

CATEGORIES: I Building costs; II Statue costs and weights; III Tomb and burial costs; IV Perpetual foundations; V Sportulae: per capita and collective group rates; VI Games and feasts; VII–VIII Commemorative rites; funds for upkeep of monuments; IX Subsistence grain and land costs (X Funds for heating and running baths; all costs subsumed in section IV); XI Obligatory and voluntary payments to cities; XII Miscellaneous and unclassified costs; XIII Collegiate provisions.

The proportion of costs per region corresponds to some degree with the proportion of inscriptions that survive from each region. (Ratios for 33,000 Italian inscriptions are given in Appendix 5 p.339, the 3,000 inscriptions from Ostia in *CIL* being omitted.) But there are five notable cases of discrepancy: region III (5.6% of the costs listed here, but less than 1.7% of the Italian inscriptions in *CIL*); region VI (14.1% of the costs listed here, but less than 8.6% of the Italian inscriptions in *CIL*); region VII (5.5% of the costs listed here, but roughly 13% of the Italian inscriptions in *CIL*); region VIII (8.9% of the costs listed here, but less than 4.6% of the Italian inscriptions in *CIL*); region X (8.0% of the costs listed here, but roughly 16.5% of the Italian inscriptions in *CIL*). Thus in three regions, III, VI and VIII, the number of costs is well above expectation; and in two other regions, VII and X, the number is well below expectation. The preponderance in region III (Lucania and Bruttium) is explained by a large number of sportula-rates (33 of the 51 costs from this region); sportulae are also a prominent feature in region VI (Umbria) (56 out of 128 costs); the high number

TABLE 16. *The regional distribution of African costs*

Area	I		II		III		IV		V		VI		Total	
Zeugitana (PZ)	33	(37.9%)	33	(23.6%)	3	(5.5%)	26	(48.1%)	31	(44.3%)	28	(48.2%)	154	(33.2%)
Byzacena (PB)	7	(8.1%)	10	(7.1%)	1	(1.8%)	3	(5.6%)	7	(10.0%)	2	(3.5%)	30	(6.5%)
Tripolitania (PT)	8	(9.2%)	5	(3.6%)	4	(7.3%)	2	(3.7%)	2	(2.9%)	8	(13.8%)	29	(6.3%)
Numidia Proconsularis (NP)	14	(16.1%)	16	(11.4%)	2	(3.6%)	10	(18.5%)	7	(10.0%)	5	(8.6%)	54	(11.6%)
Numidia (N)	24	(27.6%)	71	(50.7%)	43	(78.2%)	8	(14.8%)	22	(31.4%)	13	(22.4%)	181	(39.0%)
Mauretania Caesariensis (MC)	—		5	(3.6%)	2	(3.6%)	5	(9.3%)	1	(1.4%)	2	(3.5%)	15	(3.2%)
Mauretania Tingitana (MT)	1	(1.1%)	—		—		—		—		—		1	(0.2%)
Total	87		140		55		54		70		58		464	

For comments on the regional distribution of African costs, see pp.67–74 above.

TABLE 17. *The regional distribution of Italian costs*

Categories	I	II	III	IV	V	VI	VII-VIII	IX	XI	XII	XIII	Total
Regio I	17 (29.8%)	29 (43.3%)	40 (43.5%)	33 (23.6%)	96 (34.7%)	13 (46.4%)	5 (35.7%)	11 (8.1%)	15 (45.5%)	5 (10.2%)	8 (40.0%)	271 (29.7%)
Regio II	2 (3.5%)	2 (3.0%)	4 (4.3%)	4 (2.9%)	18 (6.5%)	2 (7.1%)	—	57 (41.9%)	3 (9.1%)	4 (8.2%)	—	96 (10.5%)
Regio III	1 (1.8%)	3 (4.5%)	3 (3.3%)	4 (2.9%)	33 (11.9%)	—	2 (14.3%)	1 (0.7%)	4 (12.1%)	—	—	51 (5.6%)
Regio IV	4 (7.0%)	5 (7.5%)	12 (13.0%)	2 (1.4%)	18 (6.5%)	4 (14.3%)	—	5 (3.7%)	—	4 (8.2%)	12 (60.0%)	66 (7.2%)
Regio v	1 (1.8%)	—	3 (3.3%)	4 (2.9%)	13 (4.7%)	—	—	1 (0.7%)	2 (6.1%)	—	—	24 (2.6%)
Regio VI	8 (14.0%)	5 (7.5%)	9 (9.8%)	20 (14.3%)	56 (20.2%)	8 (28.6%)	1 (7.1%)	5 (3.7%)	2 (6.1%)	14 (28.6%)	—	128 (14.0%)
Regio VII	7 (12.3%)	6 (9.0%)	5 (5.4%)	5 (3.6%)	23 (8.3%)	—	—	—	3 (9.1%)	1 (2.0%)	—	50 (5.5%)
Regio VIII	—	5 (7.5%)	2 (2.2%)	12 (8.6%)	6 (2.2%)	1 (3.6%)	2 (14.3%)	51 (37.5%)	—	2 (4.1%)	—	81 (8.9%)
Regio IX	—	—	—	1 (0.7%)	—	—	—	1 (0.7%)	—	—	—	2 (0.2%)
Regio X	9 (15.8%)	8 (11.9%)	9 (9.8%)	33 (23.6%)	3 (1.1%)	—	4 (28.6%)	—	2 (6.1%)	5 (10.2%)	—	73 (8.0%)
Regio XI	5 (8.8%)	3 (4.5%)	5 (5.4%)	21 (15.0%)	2 (0.7%)	—	—	1 (0.7%)	—	9 (18.4%)	—	46 (5.0%)
Sicily	1 (1.8%)	1 (1.5%)	—	—	4 (1.4%)	—	—	—	1 (3.0%)	5 (10.2%)	—	12 (1.3%)
Alpes Mar.	—	—	—	1 (0.7%)	5 (1.8%)	—	—	—	—	—	—	6 (0.7%)
Uncertain	2 (3.5%)	—	—	—	—	—	—	3 (2.2%)	3 (3.0%)	—	—	6 (0.7%)
Total	57	67	92	140	277	28	14	136	33	49	20	913

Note: percentages refer to the total at the foot of each column.

of costs in region VIII (Aemilia) is due to the Veleian alimentary table (land-valuations provide 51 of the 81 costs from the region).

Two broad geographical tendencies are noticeable. Gifts of sportulae are almost entirely concentrated in southern and central Italy: 257 of the sportula costs come from regions I–VII and only 11 from regions VIII–XI. This seems to reflect differing social customs. Sportulae were often given to the people or to large town-organisations such as trade-colleges; and on average, town-sizes were larger in the far north of Italy than elsewhere (Strabo 5.1.12 and Chilver 45–58; cf. Appendix 4 p.338). Thus in these north Italian towns the donor of sportulae was potentially faced with a larger bill for any distributions which extended beyond the narrow circle of the town-council. The potential number of recipients may have been a discouragement to adopting the custom of indiscriminate cash handouts that existed further south.

The distribution of foundations shows a complete contrast. The heaviest concentrations are in the north, and there are few examples in the far south and south-east: 129 examples come from regions I and V–XI, but only 10 (7.2%) from regions II–IV. These three regions in the south nevertheless provide roughly 21.5% of the Italian inscriptions in *CIL*. The frequency of foundations in the north perhaps implies the existence of good investment opportunities in that part of Italy. The prosperity of towns in the north is well attested (cf. Frank *ESAR* 5.107–14).

One further geographical feature is striking: region I (Latium and Campania) which provides 29.4% of the costs overall, is the source of a much larger proportion of certain types of cost. 43.3% of the figure for statues (including statue-weights); 43.5% of the costs for tombs and burials; and 45.5% of the payments to cities come from this area.

APPENDIX 13

The rate of inscription-survival

(i) The fact that town A has left more inscriptions than town B in the same area almost never indicates in itself that A was larger, wealthier, or had a bigger population than B. In fact the maximum rate of inscription-survival is normally so low that it is quite possible for small towns that are well preserved to leave more inscriptions than large towns that have survived badly. In Africa for example, minor inland towns such as Thugga and Celtianis leave more inscriptions than much bigger coastal towns such as Hadrumetum and Leptis Minor. Regional variations in inscription-survival are also noticeable in Italy (Appendix 5 at p.338). The local rate of survival depends on a series of variables which include the proportion of the town area that has been excavated (if any); the durability of the local stone; the extent to which later generations used the Roman town as a quarry; how far continued occupation of the site has erased the Roman town from view; whether the necropolis (usually a major source of inscriptions) has been unearthed; and so on. It is clearly impossible to quantify most of these functions, least of all the extent to which the ancient town has been plundered. Consequently no general coefficient of inscription survival can be applied with confidence to any single town. Nor can the number of local inscriptions generally be used as an index (either primary or ancillary) of the relative prosperity or importance of the town. The most that can be done is to point to the causes that seem to determine the size of the local epigraphic yield, after assessing the conditions determining survival as they apply to the town in question. Even then it is difficult to reconstruct the original total number of inscriptions from the town; but it may be possible to account for an epigraphic yield that appears relatively low or relatively high.

(ii) In some ways the uncertainties are less acute in large areas, provinces rather than towns. If there is an overall sample of several hundred towns, the random variants mentioned will tend to even each other out. Any average figure can only be applied in the most general way: it will be patently inaccurate if applied to small towns that have left thousands of inscriptions, such as Thugga, and no less inaccurate if applied to town sites which are overgrown and unexcavated. There may nevertheless be some value for general purposes in trying to assess the maximum average rate of inscription-survival, despite the obvious imperfections of the means available for doing so.

A very rough estimate of the maximum likely rate of inscription-survival can be produced for one major area of the West. It is fair to assume that the African yield is one of the highest in percentage terms. Few other parts of the Empire offer the same combination of dense urban concentrations in antiquity with less heavy settlement in later periods (even when modern excavation has been equally intensive).

A calculation can be constructed as follows: Africa Proconsularis is an area whose dated inscriptions are mainly concentrated within a relatively short span of time; the inscriptions include records of an annual priesthood probably set up regularly in different parts of the area throughout this period; by dividing the number that survive into the total number of such records probably produced during this period, we reach a fraction that may indicate the rough proportion of monumental inscriptions that survive from the period. The calculation points to a maximum figure; the actual figure (insofar as it can be derived from these data) may be lower, since our information about the number of records set up annually is uncertain, and the estimate that appears justified by the pattern of surviving evidence may be too low.

The bulk of dated African inscriptions (excluding milestones) are concentrated within the period from Trajan to Gordian III (A.D. 98–244; see Appendix 11, Table 11). It is probably fair to assume that the configuration of the undated inscriptions broadly follows that of the dated material (the dated sample numbers more than a thousand inscriptions; see Appendix 11, Table 11). Thirteen holders of the annual priesthood of the province who probably belong to this period are known from inscriptions. (See R. Duncan-Jones *Epigraphische Studien* 5 (1968) 151–8; this total excludes C. Caecilius Gallus, whose priesthood is probably Flavian.) The provincial priesthood was a great honour in municipal terms; its holders were 'die Spitzen der municipalen Nobilität' (Dessau *Hermes* 45 (1910) 12). In a province with several hundred cities, the number of towns that could expect to contribute a priest of the province in any one generation was relatively small. There is little doubt that in a province as prolific of monuments as Africa every priest would thus have received official commemoration in his native town. Six of the thirteen priests whose names survive from this period are in fact known from official public dedications in their honour (VIII 11546; 12039; 14611; *ILTun* 36; *ILAlg* 1.1295; *BAC* (1951–2) 197).

The holder of the priesthood would probably receive at least one other commemoration from some other source: six of the seven remaining priests appear on monuments financed by relatives, or by other towns, or on monuments which they themselves paid for (VIII 14731; 16472; 25385; *IRT* 397; *AE* 1916, 13 and *AE* 1949, 40; VIII 2343; *BCB* 318). Thus it is likely that priests would generally have been commemorated by at least two monuments. The Thamugadi priest who has four surviving commemorations may well be atypical (see *Epigraphische Studien* 5 (1968) 157); but there is also a priest from Cuicul of whom there are two surviving records. The compensated number of commemorations (excluding two of those referring to the Thamugadi priest) is thus 15. This is to be set against a theoretical original total of 292 commemorations (2 per year for a period of 146 years), The resulting percentage is 5.1%. This is probably a maximum, since the original number of commemorations may have been higher than two per man.

The calculation has obvious weaknesses: it uses data from only thirteen sites to generalise about the amount that has been found in an area with several hundred towns. It does not apply to a very large segment of African inscriptions, the funerary texts, since the calculation is based on public monuments and only takes them into account (none of the priests is known from his tombstone). No allowance can be made for possible fluctuations in the rate of building within the period, although fluctuations are implied by the figures for imperial dedications (Appendix 11, Table 11). Nevertheless, lacking any better index, this calculation may have some value as an approximate guide.

APPENDIX 14

Criteria for dating inscriptions

In compiling the main list of costs, an attempt has been made to supplement the few explicit dating indications by the use of dating termini drawn from incidental features of inscriptions. Where such termini are used, the resulting date is given in brackets. The use of a *signum* is first attested in a dated Latin inscription in 177/80 (*ILS* 9022 from Rome; cf. R. Duncan-Jones *CP* 64 (1969) 230 and n.10). Inscriptions in which a *signum* appears have generally been dated not earlier than A.D. 180 and in certain cases not earlier than 200.

The first appearance of the Augustales in inscriptions as a collective group receiving sportulae seems to belong to the time of Trajan (cf. L. R. Taylor *TAPHA* 45 (1914) 243; R. Duncan-Jones *PBSR* 33 (1965) 304). Such distributions have been dated to after A.D. 100.

The date by which citizen names lacking a cognomen had generally died out has been taken as A.D. 100, on the basis of two lists. The album of the familia Silvani at Trebula Mutuesca (50 km from Rome on the Via Salaria) drawn up in A.D. 60 contains 78 names all of which have the cognomen (*NS* 1928, tav v. cf. nos.1377–88). In the alimentary table from the much more remote town of Veleia dated to A.D. 98/113, 4 of the 53 landowners who declared estates still have no cognomen. This suggests that the practice had become rare even in backward areas by the end of the first century A.D., and was probably extinct elsewhere at an earlier date (cf. R. Duncan-Jones *PBSR* 33 (1965) 304–5).

The archaic system of Roman numerals seems to have died out during the first century A.D. The last explicitly dated instances in the present sample belong to the reign of Nero (nos.587 and 650). In view of the shortage of dated costs in the first century, A.D. 100 has been adopted as the *terminus ante quem* (R. Duncan-Jones *PBSR* 33 (1965) 305).

The normal notation for sesterces in the earlier period, HS, begins to change to SS during the late second and third centuries. The first appearance of SS in Africa is in an inscription dated to A.D. 176/92 (no.121). The first dated Italian examples belong to A.D. 234 and 247/48 (nos.697, 841 + 1358), but there is little dated evidence from the Severan period in Italy. In Africa the new notation has been dated to after A.D. 180, in Italy to after A.D. 200. (For discussion of monetary notations in inscriptions, S. Mrozek *Eos* 57 (1967/8) 288–95.)

Résumé

(pre-100)	archaic system of numerals
(pre-100)	citizen names lacking the cognomen
(post-100)	multiple distributions involving Augustales
(post-180/200)	use of the *signum*
(post-180)	use of SS symbol in Africa
(post-200)	use of SS symbol in Italy

APPENDIX 15

The price of wine at Rome

In A.D. 153 a benefactress gave the college of Aesculapius and Hygia on the via Appia less than 2 Roman miles from Rome a capital of HS50,000. Its exclusive purpose was to provide the 60 members of the college with six distributions in which the donor would take part, four of the distributions being accompanied by a meal (VI 10234 = *ILS* 7213; cf. *AE* 1937, 161). The distributions were to be of two types, one providing cash sportulae alone for all the members, the other providing a meal for all members together with cash sportulae for the more important. The cost of the distributions was as follows (the number of 'immunes' which is not stated is estimated as 4; the other details are indicated in the inscription):

Type A: HS12 × 3 shares = 36
      HS8 × 6 (?)   = 48
      HS4 × (52) = 208
                  HS292

Type B: HS24 × 3 shares = 72   *Wine* 9 sextarii × 2 = 18
      HS16 × 6 (?)   = 96   6 × 6 (?)   = 36
  (bread) 60 × HS0.75 = 45   3 × 52   = 156
                 HS213   210 sextarii

Type A occurred twice each year and thus cost HS584 annually. Type B occurred four times, and thus cost HS852 annually, plus the cost of 840 sextarii (17.5 amphorae) of wine in all. The total cost of the provisions whose cost is known is thus HS1,436. If the interest-rate was 5% (for which there are parallels with foundations of this size) the total income would be HS2,500; at 6%, which is also paralleled, the income would be HS3,000. Thus the sum available to cover the cost of wine was probably between HS1,064 and HS1,564. The implied price is between HS61–88.5 per amphora (between HS1.27–1.84 per sextarius). The lower price may be the more credible, since the wine is not stated as being of a particular quality.

This price can be compared with the series of first-century wine prices from Pompeii and Herculaneum. These run as follows: Pompeii HS12, HS24, HS48 per amphora; Herculaneum HS24, HS36, HS48, HS54 per amphora (see p.46 n.3 above). The two Campanian tariffs consist of retail prices for wine 'by the glass' which can be no later than A.D. 79. The highest Pompeian price (HS48) is stated as being for Falernian wine; and although this inscription is colloquial enough to be doubted, the highest price in the more prosaic tariff from Herculaneum is very close

(HS54 per amphora). Hence a price of HS61–HS88 per amphora at Rome for wine whose quality is unspecified suggests that ordinary wine cost substantially more at the capital than it did in Campania. Petronius's creation Trimalchio gained his first fortune by shipping wine to Rome at a time when it was 'worth its weight in gold' (*Sat.* 76). We also know from a variety of sources that prices in general were higher at Rome than elsewhere (see Appendix 8).

Since the cost of wine was HS1.27–HS1.84 per sextarius, the amounts spent on the meal (each man receiving the same loaf costing HS0.75) would be HS4.5–6.2 for the 'populus' of the college, who received 3 sextarii of wine each; HS8.3–11.7 for the *immunes* and *curatores* who received 6 sextarii of wine each; and HS12.1–17.2 of the *quinquennalis* and 'pater collegii' who received 9 sextarii of wine each. The sportulae of the latter two groups were respectively HS16 and HS24, and so the amount which they received in cash handsomely exceeded the amount spent on their meal.

APPENDIX 16

Wheat and land prices in Egypt

An independent analysis of the lists provided by Johnson in *ESAR* 2 produces the following results.

(i) Wheat prices (*ESAR* 2.310–11). The table is based on prices dated by year or by reign, payments specified in non-standard currencies being omitted. The original prices in Egyptian drachmas per artaba have been converted into prices in sesterces per modius by multiplying by 3.33.

Period	Sample size	Median average (HS per modius)	Maximum	Minimum
18 B.C.–A.D. 14	7 prices	0.9	1.2	0.6
A.D. 14–98	10 prices	2.0	2.6	0.7
A.D. 98–192	7 prices	2.5	6.0	1.8
A.D. 193–260	3 prices	4.2	4.8	3.6

All three indices show a steady increase throughout the four periods, with the exception of the maximum, whose peak in the third period results from a famine price in the reign of Commodus.

(ii) Land prices (*ESAR* 2.150–3). The table is based on prices dated by year or by reign, payments specified in non-standard currencies being omitted. The original prices in Egyptian drachmas per aroura have been converted into sesterces per iugerum by dividing by 1.09.

Period	Sample size	Median average (HS per iugerum)	Maximum	Minimum
First century A.D.	11 prices	141	459	11
Second century	16 prices	183	612	26
Third century	8 prices	147	1101	58

The median figures for land do not show an increase; but there is a consistent rise in both maximum and minimum figures. The usefulness of the land prices is considerably reduced by the fact that values depended crucially on the quality of the land, about which the papyri in question give few indications.

APPENDIX 17

Diocletian's Price Edict and the cost of transport

S. Lauffer *Diokletians Preisedikt* (1971) gives the fullest text of the Edict, together with bibliography and brief commentary. Th. Mommsen & H. Blümner *Der Maximaltarif des Diocletian* (1893, reprinted 1958) contains a text and an extensive commentary on the sections known eighty years ago, which lack the sea-freight-rates and other categories of price. Another incomplete text, with translation by E. R. Graser, appears in *ESAR* 5.307–421, with a supplement containing sea freight-rates in *TAPHA* 71 (1940) 157–74. Our knowledge of the Edict's contents is not by any means complete, but very large sections are now known, and there is a prospect of further fragments being revealed by excavation (Lauffer gives some recent discoveries from Aphrodisias). Fragments have been found at more than thirty cities.

(i) The Edict, passed late in A.D. 301, was evidently promulgated only in the eastern part of the Empire (J. Lafaurie *CRAI* (1965) 192–210; J. & L. Robert *REG* 77 (1964) 140–1). The degree of inflation shown by the Edict's wheat-price when compared with second-century prices for wheat is of the order of 25–50-fold (see p.66 n.4 above). The Edict's long tabulation of prices and wages all of which belong to the same year makes it unique in ancient price evidence. If its figures are representative, the

Edict can provide important insight into ancient price structures which is not obtainable elsewhere. But is it a reliable source?

The Edict announces itself as an attempt to enforce price-restraint and to halt price-speculation by profiteers who were asking 4 or 8 times what was a fair price for their goods, or even more (Lauffer 95 = *ESAR* 5.314). It follows that the Edict's prices are not a description of the market rates prevailing in A.D. 301. At least in part, they are the result of a deliberate attempt to lower current prices which the government regarded as exorbitant. This is reflected in Lactantius's statement that the Edict drove goods off the market (evidently because its price-ceiling was too low to allow any profit: *de mort.pers.* 7.6, cf. A. H. M. Jones *EcHR* 5 (1952–3) 293–318 at 299). Yet despite the Edict's conservative intentions, its price-levels are enormously higher than those of the first two centuries, 25–50-fold in the case of wheat (see above). Hence the actual degree of inflation prevailing in 301 must have been greater still. There is little chance that the price-relationships of the earlier Principate could have survived such a great dislocation unaltered, even if the Edict claimed (as it does not) to be a description of current price-levels. The spectacular inflation is virtually bound to have distorted the price-relationships of a stable economy.

Prices were moving so fast by this date that the Edict's stipulations soon became quite irrelevant: for example, a papyrus of A.D. 335 gives a wheat price 63 times higher than the wheat price of the Edict (*P. Lond* 1914; other examples in Jones *loc. cit.* 308). Under conditions of such rapid price change, a market survey would not necessarily serve as an adequate base for determining acceptable levels; some of the Edict's values may be entirely theoretical. It is noticeable for instance that many of the Edict's wage-rates follow a simple and schematic pattern. The basic level of 25 denarii occurs 9 times as a daily or piece-rate, while the double level of 50 denarii occurs 16 times (Lauffer 118–24 = *ESAR* 5.337–46). Furthermore, the Edict's total disregard of regional variation (cf. Appendix 8, p.346) suggests that it cannot have been based on an appraisal of how prices stood in different parts of the Empire. If the figures are realistic in any way, they are probably closest to the price-levels of the large Eastern town from which the Edict emanated, perhaps Nicomedia; prices in the country and in small towns might have been substantially less (cf. pp.345–6). Finally, it is notable that the Edict makes no provision for differences between wholesale and retail prices, although the wholesaler who took all of what the Edict allowed was bound to drive the retailer into exceeding its limits. (For wholesale and retail prices, see p.48 n.3.)

But even if the Edict is somewhat theoretical, it is still interesting to know what price-levels the government considered appropriate at a time of dislocation. The Edict may be best regarded as an attempt to reassemble the structures and relationships of a period of more settled prices. How successful it was in doing so can only be gauged by testing the relationships that the Edict contains. What follows is a brief attempt to assess the evidence offered by the transport charges in the Edict.

(ii) The Edict is virtually our only source of information about Roman freight rates for transport by sea, and almost the only source for river and land freight rates (for costs in Cato, C. A. Yeo *TAPHA* 77 (1946) 221–44). The freight charges for sea transport give a series of sums payable per kastrensis modius for carriage between specified destinations. Not all charges are at the same rate (for example, the 4 denarii charged for transport between Africa and Gaul is exceptionally low; see also J. Rougé *Recherches sur l'organisation du commerce maritime en Méditerranée sous l'empire romain*

(1966) 370–1). A representative figure is the 16 denarii per kastrensis modius charged between Alexandria and Rome. Jones (taking the distance as 1,250 Roman miles = 1,847 km = 1,148 British miles) used this as the basis for deducing the cost of sea transport. From the Edict's price of 100 denarii per kastrensis modius of wheat, the cost for transporting wheat by sea would be 1.3% per 100 Roman miles (A. H. M. Jones *Recueils de la Société Jean Bodin* 7.2 (1955) 163). (L. Casson estimates that because of the pattern of prevailing winds the voyage from Alexandria to Rome covered a distance of 1,700 miles, whereas Rome–Alexandria meant 1,000 miles, *TAPHA* 81 (1950) 43–56 at 51.)

The Edict's prices for land transport are naturally very much higher than those for shipment by sea. The freight-charge for a 1,200 pound wagon (Roman measure) is given as 20 denarii per Roman mile (Lauffer 149 = *ESAR* 5.368). If an average type of wheat weighs 22 pounds per Italian modius (cf. Pliny *NH* 18.66) and the kastrensis modius costing 100 denarii is equal to 1–2 normal Italian modii (see p.66 n.4), the cost of transport will be 36.7–73.4% of the value of the wheat for every 100 Roman miles. Carriage by camel is 20% lower in the Edict (8 denarii for a 600-pound load); transported by this method wheat costs would increase by 29.3–58.6% per 100 Roman miles. The Edict contains no explicit cost for river transport, but an Egyptian papyrus gives the cost of transporting wheat by water roughly 13.6 Roman miles from Arsinoe to Ptolemais Hormos in A.D. 42 as a rate corresponding to 6.38% per 100 miles (BGU 802 in Johnson *ESAR* 2.407: the charge for shipping 267,897.5 artabas was 2,330 artabas; distance from *International Map of the Roman Empire* 1 : 1,000,000 'Cairo' 1934).

In England in the late fifteenth and sixteenth centuries wheat cost roughly 25% per 100 miles to transport by road (P. J. Bowden in Thirsk 612; conversion into Roman miles does not alter this figure significantly). The cost of transport by wagon given in the Edict would thus be 1½–3 times greater than the later English figure, in terms of wheat values. A substantial difference is quite plausible; Roman harnessing techniques were relatively primitive (cf. A. Burford *EcHR* 13 (1960–1) 1–18).

Taking the Diocletianic figures for sea transport and road transport by wagon, the cost ratios for the three types are sea 1, inland waterway 4.9, and road 28–56 (depending on the interpretation of the kastrensis modius). Some approximate ratios for England in the first half of the eighteenth century are as follows: sea (transatlantic shipment): 1; river: 4.7; and road: 22.6.

It is interesting that these ratios show some mutual resemblance. Nevertheless, those drawn from the Edict are not necessarily reliable. The sea transport cost is so low that the implied cost of carrying foodstuffs by water is almost negligible in relation to distances within the Mediterranean: it would take an 800 mile voyage to raise the price of wheat even by 10%, from the Diocletianic figures. Such a low cost appears unrealistic in view of what is known of the slowness and ineffectiveness of Roman shipping (cf. p.2 above). This may thus be an instance in which price discontinuities created by the disruptive inflation of the late third century (such as were posited above) led the Edict's authors to prescribe theoretical wheat costs and transport costs that were out of line with one another. Wheat prices were almost certainly more volatile than transport costs; it is possible that the wheat price in the Edict represents an exceptionally high urban level (cf. p.8 n.2). In that case, the amount by which transporting wheat by sea from a producing area increased its cost (assuming the Edict's transport costs to have validity) would normally have been greater than the Edict's figures show.

(English figures from Ralph Davis *The rise of the English shipping industry in the seventeenth and eighteenth centuries* (1962) 360, giving the freight charge for tobacco shipped by the *Diligence*, a ship of 80 tons burden, from Whitehaven to Virginia, a distance of approximately 3,400 miles, as £7 10*s* per ton in the years from 1730–40. H. J. Dyos, D. H. Aldcroft *British transport; an economic survey from the seventeenth century to the twentieth* (1969) 40 give the average cost of river and road transport in the early eighteenth century as 2½*d* and 1 shilling per ton-mile respectively.)

BIBLIOGRAPHY

The bibliography is primarily a list of works cited in the notes and Appendices. A supplementary list containing further titles appears on pp.x–xiv under Abbreviations. References to encyclopedias and other standard works are not reproduced here.

Accame, S. 'Il testamento di C. Cornelio Egriliano e l'arco di Caracalla in Tebessa' *Epigraphica* 3 (1941) 237–43

Allain, E. *Pline le Jeune et ses héritiers* 1901–2

Andrews, A. C. 'The Roman craze for surmullets' *Class. Weekly* 42 (1948–9) 186–8

Antoniadis-Bibicou, H. 'Démographie, salaires et prix à Byzance au XIe siècle' *AESC* 27 (1972) 215–46

Asbach, J. *Römisches Kaisertum und Verfassung bis auf Trajan* (1896)

Ashby, T. *The Aqueducts of ancient Rome* (1935)

Ashley, A. 'The alimenta of Nerva and his successors' *English Historical Review* 36 (1921) 5–16.

Ashtor, E. *Histoire des prix et des salaires dans l'Orient médiéval* (1969)

Aymard, A. 'Les capitalistes romains et la viticulture italienne' *AESC* 2 (1947) 257–65

Bagnani, G. 'And Passing Rich...' *Studies in honour of G. Norwood* (1952) 218–23
    'The house of Trimalchio' *AJP* 75 (1954) 16–39

Balsdon J. P. V. D. *Life and leisure in ancient Rome* (1969)

Bass, G. F. (ed.) *A History of Seafaring based on Underwater Archaeology* (1972)

Bell, H. I. 'Antinoopolis, a Hadrianic foundation in Egypt' *JRS* 30 (1940) 133–47

Beloch, J. *Der Italische Bund unter Roms Hegemonie* (1880)
    'Le città dell'Italia antica' *Atene e Roma* 1 (1898) 257–78
    'Die Bevölkerung Italiens im Altertum' *Klio* 3 (1903) 471–90

Benoit, F. *L'Afrique méditerranéenne* (1931)

Bernardi, A. 'The Economic Problems of the Roman Empire at the Time of its Decline' in C. M. Cipolla (ed.) *The Economic Decline of Empires* (1970), 16–83 [from *SDHI* 31 (1965)]

Billiard, R. *La vigne dans l'antiquité* (1913)

Blake, M. E. *Ancient Roman Construction in Italy* (1947–59)

Boethius, A. & J. B. Ward Perkins *Etruscan and Roman Architecture* (1969)

Bove, L. *Ricerche sugli 'agri vectigales'* (1960)

Bourgarel-Musso, A. 'Recherches économiques sur l'Afrique romaine' *RAf* 75 (1934) 354–414; 491–520

Bradford, J. *Ancient landscapes* (1957)

Breeze, D. J. 'Pay grades and ranks below the centurionate' *JRS* 61 (1971) 130–5

Breglia, L. 'Circolazione monetale ed aspetti di vita economica a Pompei' in [A. Maiuri ed.] *Pompeiana. Raccolta di studi per il secondo centenario degli scavi di Pompei* (1950) 41–59

Bréhaut, E. *Cato the Censor on Farming* (1933)

Broughton, T. R. S. 'The territory of Carthage' *REL* 47.2 (1969) 265–75

Brunt, P. A. 'Pay and superannuation in the Roman army' *PBSR* 18 (1950) 50–71

Burford, A. 'Heavy transport in classical antiquity' *EcHR* 13 (1960–1) 1–18

Cagiano de Azevedo, M. 'I Capitolia dell'Impero romano' *Atti Pont.Acc.Rom.Arch. Mem.* 5 (1941) 1–76

Cagnat, R. 'Les bibliothèques municipales dans l'Empire romain' *Mem.Inst.Ac.Insc.* 38 (1909) 1–26

L'Armée romaine d'Afrique[2] (1913)

'La colonie romaine de Djemila (Algérie)' *Musée belge* 27 (1923) 113–29

Callu, J.-P. *La politique monétaire des Empereurs romains de 238 à 311* (*Bibl.Ec.fr. Ath.Rome* 214) (1969)

'La fonction monétaire dans la Société romaine sous l'Empire' *Ve Congrés Int. d'Histoire Économique, Leningrad* (1970)

Calza, G. *La necropoli del Porto di Roma nell'Isola Sacra* (1940)

Caputo, G. *Il teatro di Sabratha e l'architettura teatrale africana* (1959)

Carcopino, J. *Rencontres de l'histoire et de la littérature romaines* (1963)

Casson, L. 'The Isis and her voyage' *TAPHA* 81 (1950) 43–56

Castagnoli, F. *Le ricerche sui resti della centuriazione* (1958)

Castello, C. '"Genuates" e "Viturii Langenses" nella "Sententia Minuciorum"' *Synteleia V. Arangio-Ruiz* (1964) 1124–35

Ciotti, U. 'Del coronamento degli archi quadrifronti. I' *BCAR* App.15 (1946–8) 21–42

Clark, Colin *Population Growth and land use* (1967)

Clark, C. & M. Haswell *The economics of subsistence agriculture* (1970)

Constans, L.-A. *Gigthis. Études d'histoire et d'archéologie sur un emporium de la petite Syrte* (1916) [from *NAM* 14 (1916)]

Cope, L. H. 'The Metallurgical Analysis of Roman Imperial Silver and *Aes* Coinage' in E. T. Hall & D. M. Metcalf (ed.) *Methods of chemical and metallurgical investigation of ancient coinage* (1972) 3–47

Cornwall, J. 'English population in the early sixteenth century' *EcHR* 23 (1970) 32–44

Corsetti, R. 'Sul prezzo dei grani nell'antichità classica' *Studi di storia antica pubb. da G. Beloch* 2 (1893) 65–92

Courtois, C. *Timgad, antique Thamugadi* (1951)

Les Vandales et l'Afrique (1955)

Crawford, M. H. 'Money and exchange in the Roman world' *JRS* 60 (1970) 40–8

Crema, L. *L'architettura romana* (1959) (G. B. Pighi ed. *Encic. classica* 12.1)

Crook, J. A. *Law and life of Rome* (1967)

D'Arms, J. *Romans on the Bay of Naples* (1970)

Davis, Ralph *The rise of the English shipping industry in the seventeenth and eighteenth centuries* (1962)

Davis, W. S. *The influence of wealth in ancient Rome* (1910)

Day, J. 'Agriculture in the life of Pompeii' *Yale classical studies* 3 (1932) 165–208

An economic history of Athens under Roman domination (1942)

Desjardins, E. *De tabulis alimentariis* (1854)

Dessau, H. 'Die Herkunft der Offiziere und Beamten des römischen Kaiserreiches während der ersten zwei Jahrhunderte seines Bestehens' *Hermes* 45 (1910) 1–26

Dilke, O. A. W. *The Roman land surveyors* (1971)

Dion, R. *Histoire de la vigne et du vin en France des origines au XIXe siècle* (1959)

Dobson, B. 'Legionary centurion or equestrian officer? A comparison of pay and prospects' *Ancient Society* 3 (1972) 193–207

Duckworth, G. *The nature of Roman comedy* (1952)

Duncan-Jones, R. P. 'Costs, outlays and summae honorariae from Roman Africa' *PBSR* 30 (1962) 47–115

'Wealth and munificence in Roman Africa' *PBSR* 31 (1963) 159–77

'City population in Roman Africa' *JRS* 53 (1963) 85–90

'Human numbers in towns and town-organisations of the Roman Empire: the evidence of gifts' *Historia* 13 (1964) 199–208

'The purpose and organisation of the alimenta' *PBSR* 32 (1964) 123–46

'An epigraphic survey of costs in Roman Italy' *PBSR* 33 (1965) 189–306

'The finances of the younger Pliny' *ibid.* 177–88

'Equestrian rank in the African provinces: an epigraphic survey' *PBSR* 35 (1967) 147–88

'The chronology of the priesthood of Africa Proconsularis' *Epigraphische Studien* 5 (1968) 151–8

'Praefectus Mesopotamiae et Osrhoenae' *CP* 64 (1969) 229–33

review of A. R. Hands *Charities and social aid in Greece and Rome*, *JRS* 59 (1969) 287–9

Dureau de la Malle, A. J. C. *Économie politique des Romains* (1840)

Durry, M. 'Les femmes et le vin' *REL* 33 (1955) 108–13

Dyos, H. J. & D. H. Aldcroft *British transport: an economic survey from the seventeenth century to the twentieth* (1969)

Ferguson, J. F. 'Aere conlato' *Class. Journal* 13 (1917–18) 515–20

Finley, M. I 'Technical innovation and economic progress in the ancient world' *EcHR* 18 (1965) 29–45

The ancient economy (1973)

Ford, G. B. 'The letters of Pliny the Younger as evidence of agrarian conditions in the principate of Trajan' *Helikon* 5 (1965) 381–9

Forni, G. *Il reclutamento delle legioni da Augusto a Diocleziano* (1953)

Forni, G. & D. Manini 'La base eretta a Nicopoli in onore di Antonino Pio dai veterani della legione II Traiana' in *Studi di storia antica in memoria di Luca de Regibus* (1969) 177–210

Foucher, L. *Hadrumetum* (1964)

Fraccaro, P. 'C. Herennius Capito di Teate, procurator di Livia, di Tiberio e di Gaio' in P. Fraccaro *Opuscula* 3 (1957) 263–71

Frank, T. 'Roman census statistics from 225 to 28 B.C.' *CP* 19 (1924) 329–41

'On the Export Tax of Spanish Harbors' *AJP* 57 (1936) 87–90

Frederiksen, M. W. & J. B. Ward Perkins 'The ancient road systems of the central and northern ager Faliscus. (Notes on southern Etruria 2)' *PBSR* 25 (1957) 67–208

Garnsey, P. *Social status and legal privilege in the Roman Empire* (1970)

Garzetti, A. *L'Impero da Tiberio agli Antonini* (1960)

Gauckler, P. *Enquête sur les installations hydrauliques romaines en Tunisie* (1897–1904)

Giacchero, M. 'Prezzi e salari dell'antica Roma' *Studi Romani* 18 (1970) 149–62

Gilliam, J. F. 'The veterans and praefectus castrorum of the II Traiana in A.D. 157' *AJP* 77 (1956) 359–75

Goodchild, R. G. 'Roman sites on the Tarhuna plateau of Tripolitania' *PBSR* 19 (1951) 43–77

Gordon, A. E. 'Supralineate abbreviations in Latin inscriptions' *Univ.Calif.Pub. in Class.Archaeology* 2.3 (1948) 59–132

Graindor, P. *Un Milliardaire antique: Hérode Atticus et sa famille* (1930)

Green, W. M. 'Appropriations for the games at Rome in A.D. 51' *AJP* 51 (1930) 249–50

Gsell, S. *Essai sur le règne de l'empereur Domitien* (1894)

Histoire ancienne de l'Afrique du Nord (1913–30)

'Esclaves ruraux dans l'Afrique romaine' *Mélanges G. Glotz* 1 (1932) 397–415

Hammond, M. 'A statue of Trajan represented on the Anaglypha Traiani' *Mem. Amer.Acad. in Rome* 21 (1953) 125–83

Hands, A. R. *Charities and social aid in Greece and Rome* (1968)

Hanslik, R. 'Plinius der Jüngere, II Bericht' *Anzeiger für die Altertumswissenschaft* 17 (1964) 1–16

Harris, W. V. *Rome in Etruria and Umbria* (1971)

Henderson, B. W. *Five Roman Emperors* (1927)

Hirschfeld, O. 'I Sacerdozi dei Municipii Romani nell'Africa' *Annali del Inst. di Corrisp. Archaeologica* 38 (1866) 28–77

'Die Getreideverwaltung in der römischen Kaiserzeit' *Philologus* 29 (1870) 1–96

Kleine Schriften (1913)

Homo, L. *Le Haut-Empire* (G. Glotz (ed.) *Histoire Générale* 3.3) (1933)

Hopkins, K. 'Contraception in the Roman Empire' *Comp. Studies in Society and History* 8 (1965–6) 124–51

Howard, C. L. '*Quisque* with ordinals' *Class. Quarterly* 52 (1958) 1–11

Huschke, E. *Über den Census und die Steuerverfassung der frühern römischen Kaiserzeit* (1847)

Hutchison, R. & V. H. Mottram *Food and the Principles of Dietetics*[11] (1956)

Jasny, N. 'The breads of Ephesus' *Agricultural History* 21 (1947) 190 ff.

Johnson, A. C. & L. C. West *Byzantine Egypt: economic studies* (Princeton 1949)

Jones, A. H. M. 'Egypt and Rome' in S. R. K. Glanville (ed.) *The Legacy of Egypt*[1] (1942) 283–99

'Inflation under the Roman Empire' *EcHR* ser.2.5 (1952–3) 293–318

'The cities of the Roman Empire' *Recueils de la Société Jean Bodin* 6 (1954) 135–76; 7.2 (1955) 161–94

'The origin and early history of the follis' *JRS* 49 (1959) 34–8

'The ancient Empires and the economy: Rome' *Third International Conference of Economic History, Munich 1965* (1969) 3, 81–104

Jones, A. H. M. and others *Cities of the Eastern Roman Provinces*[2] (1971)

Jones, C. P. 'Sura and Senecio' *JRS* 60 (1970) 98–104

Jones, P. J. 'Per la storia agraria italiana nel Medio Evo: lineamenti e problemi' *RSI* 76 (1964) 287–348

Judges, A. V. 'Scopi e metodi della storia dei prezzi' *RSI* 63 (1951) 162–79

Klebs, E. *Die Erzählung von Apollonius aus Tyrus* (1899)

Kloft, H. *Liberalitas Principis, Herkunft und Bedeutung. Studien zur Prinzipatsideologie* (1970)

Kohns, H. P. *Versorgungskrisen und Hungerrevolten im spätantiken Rom* (*Antiquitas* 6) (1961)

Kotula, T. 'Les principes gentis et les principes civitatis en Afrique romaine' *Eos* 55 (1965) 347–65

de Laet, S. J. *Portorium* (1949)

Lafaurie, J. 'Remarques sur les dates de quelques inscriptions du début du IVe siècle' *CRAI* (1965) 192–210

Lancel, S. 'Populus Thabarbusitanus et les gymnasia de Quintus Flavius Lappianus' *Libyca* 6 (1958) 143–51

le Bras, G. 'Les fondations privées du Haut Empire' in *Studi in onore di S. Riccobono* 3 (1936) 23–67

Leglay, M. 'Les Flaviens et l'Afrique' *MEFR* 80 (1968) 201–46

'La vie religieuse à Lambèse d'après de nouveaux documents' *Ant.afr.* 5 (1971) 125–53

Leschi, L. *Djemila, antique Cuicul* (1953)

Levick, B. M. *Roman colonies in southern Asia Minor* (1967)

Lézine, A. 'Sur la population des villes africaines' *Ant.afr.* 3 (1969) 69–82

Lilja, S. 'The singular use of *nos* in Pliny's Letters' *Eranos* 69 (1971) 89–103

Loposko, T. 'De Romanorum largitionibus privatis' (in Polish) *Meander* 17 (1962) 207–14

Lugli, G. *La tecnica edilizia romana* (1957)

Lussana, A. 'Osservazioni sulle testimonianze di munificenza privata della Gallia Cisalpina nelle iscrizioni latine' *Epigraphica* 12 (1950) 116–23

'Munificenza privata nell'Africa romana' *Epigraphica* 14 (1952) 100–13

'Contributo agli studi sulla munificenza privata in alcune regioni dell'Impero' *Epigraphica* 18 (1956) 77–93

Macmullen, R. 'Roman Imperial Building in the Provinces' *HSCP* 64 (1959) 207–35

Enemies of the Roman Order (1967)

'Market-days in the Roman Empire' *Phoenix* 24 (1970) 333–41

de Maddalena, A. 'Il mondo rurale italiano nel Cinque- e nel Seicento. (Rassegna di studi recenti)' *RSI* 76 (1964) 349–426

Magaldi, E. *Lucania romana* 1 (1947)

Maier, F. G. 'Römische Bevölkerungsgeschichte und Inschriftenstatistik' *Historia* 2 (1953–4) 318–51

Manganaro, G. 'Epigrafi frammentarie di Catania' *Kokalos* 5 (1959) 145–58

Mann, J. C. 'The raising of new legions during the Principate' *Hermes* 91 (1963) 483–9

Marec, E. *Hippone la royale* (1954)

Marmorale, E. *La questione petroniana* (1948)

Martin, R. 'Pline le Jeune et les problèmes économiques de son temps' *REA* 69 (1967) 62–97

Mauss, M. *The gift: forms and functions of exchange in archaic societies* (English edition 1954)

Mazza, M. *Lotte sociali e restaurazione autoritaria nel 3° secolo d.C.* (1970)

Melville Jones, J. R. 'Denarii, Asses and Assaria in the early Roman Empire' *Bull. Inst.Class.Stud.* 18 (1971) 99–105

Merlin, A. 'Le grand bronze de Nerva, *Tutela Italiae*' *Revue numismatique* 10 (1906) 298–301

Meunier, J. 'L'arc de Caracalla a Theveste (Tébessa)' *RAf* 82 (1938) 84–107

Mickwitz, G. *Geld und Wirtschaft im römischen Reich des vierten Jahrhunderts n.Chr.* (1932)

'Economic Rationalism in Graeco-Roman Agriculture' *English Historical Review* 52 (1937) 577–89

Millar, F. with D. Berciu, R. N. Frye *The Roman Empire and its neighbours* (1967)

Millar, F. review of A. N. Sherwin-White *The Letters of Pliny*, *JRS* 58 (1968) 218–24

Minto, A. 'Saturnia etrusca e romana. Le recenti scoperte archeologiche' *Monumenti antichi* 30 (1925) 585–702

Mommsen, Th. *De collegiis et sodaliciis Romanorum* (1843)

'Zur Lehre von der Erbeseinsetzung *ex certa re*' *Zeitschr.f.Rechtsgesch.* 7 (1868) 314–18

Mommsen, Th. & H. Blümner *Der Maximaltarif des Diocletian* (1893) (unaltered reprint 1958)

Moreno, P. 'Aspetti di vita economica nel "Satyricon"' *Istituto italiano di numismatica. Annali* 9–11 (1962–4) 53–73

Mrozek, S. 'Die Sesterz- und Denarbezeichnungen auf römischen Inschriften während des Prinzipates' *Eos* 57 (1967–8) 288–95

'Zur Frage der tutela in römischen Inschriften' *AAASH* 16 (1968) 283–8

'Quelques remarques sur les inscriptions relatives aux distributions privées de l'argent et de la nourriture dans les municipes italiens aux Ier, IIe et IIIe siècles d.n.è.' *Epigraphica* 30 (1968) 156–71

'Zur Geldfrage in den Digesten' *AAASH* 18 (1970) 353–60

'De variis in Italicis municipiis munificentiae privatae generibus' (in Polish) *Meander* 25 (1970) 15–31

'Zu den Preisen und Löhnen bei Lukian' *Eos* 59 (1971) 231–9

'*Primus omnium* sur les inscriptions des municipes italiens' *Epigraphica* 33 (1971) 60–9

Oates, D. 'The Tripolitanian Gebel. Settlement of the Roman period around Gasr-ed-Dauun' *PBSR* 21 (1953) 81–117

Oliver, J. H. *The Sacred Gerusia* (*Hesperia* supp. 6) (1941)

Oliver, J. H. & R. E. A. Palmer 'Minutes of an Act of the Roman Senate' *Hesperia* 24 (1955) 320–49

Packer, J. E. 'Housing and population in imperial Ostia and Rome' *JRS* 57 (1967) 80–9

The Insulae of Imperial Ostia (1971) (*Mem.Amer.Acad.Rome* 31)

Panciera, S. 'Miscellanea storico-epigraphica III' *Epigraphica* 29 (1967) 18–61

Paratore, E. *Il Satyricon di Petronio* (1933)

Passerini, A. *Le coorti pretorie* (1939)

Pekáry, T. 'Studien zur römischen Währungs- und Finanzgeschichte von 161 bis 235 n.Chr.' *Historia* 8 (1959) 443–89

Untersuchungen zu den römischen Reichsstrassen (*Antiquitas* 17) (1968)

Perkins, A. (ed.) *The excavations at Dura-Europos. Final report* 5 (1959)

Perry, B. E. *The Ancient Romances* (1967)

Petit, P. *La paix romaine* (1967)

Pfeiffer, H. 'The Roman library at Timgad' *Mem.Amer.Acad.Rome* 9 (1931) 157–65

Pflaum, H.-G. 'La romanisation de l'ancien territoire de la Carthage punique à la lumière des découvertes épigraphiques récentes' *Ant.afr.* 4 (1970) 75–117

Picard, G. C. '(Les curies dans l'Afrique romaine)' *BAC* n.s. 4 (1968) 223–4

Piganiol, A. *Les documents cadastraux de la colonie romaine d'Orange (Gallia supp. 16)* (1962)

Poinssot, Cl. 'Immunitas perticae Carthaginiensium' *CRAI* (1962) 55–76

Rambaldi, A. 'Nuove epigrafi romane a Spoleto' *BCAR* App.16 (1949–50) 49–60

Ramsay, H. G. 'Government relief during the Roman Empire' *Class.Journal* 31 (1936) 479–88

Rockwell, J. C. *Private Baustiftungen für die Stadtgemeinde auf Inschriften der Kaiserzeit im Westen des römischen Reiches* (1909)

Rogers, J. E. T. *A History of Agriculture and Prices in England* (1866–1902)

Roman, J. 'Notes sur l'organisation municipale de l'Afrique romaine I, Les Curies' *Annales de la Fac. de droit d'Aix* 4 (1910) 85–123

Romano, R. (ed.) *I prezzi in Europa dal XIII secolo a oggi* (1967)

Rose, K. F. C. 'Time and place in the Satyricon' *TAPHA* 93 (1962) 402–9
'Trimalchio's accountant' *CP* 62 (1967) 258–9
The date and author of the Satyricon (Mnemosyne supp.16) (1971)

Rougé, J. *Recherches sur l'organisation du commerce maritime en Méditerranée sous l'empire romain* (1966)

Rowell, H. T. 'The gladiator Petraites and the date of the Satyricon' *TAPHA* 89 (1958) 14–24

Rüger, C. B. 'Gallisch-germanische Kurien' *Epigraphische Studien* 9 (1972) 251–60

Ruggini, L. C. *Economia e società nell'Italia annonaria* (1961)
'Esperienze economiche e sociali nel mondo romano' in (anon.) *Nuove questioni di storia antica* (1968) 685–813

Russell, J. C. *Late Ancient and Mediaeval Population (Trans.Amer.Philos.Soc. 48.3)* (1958)

de Sainte Croix, G. E. M. 'Greek and Roman accounting' in A. C. Littleton, B. S. Yamey (ed.) *Studies in the history of accounting* (1956) 14–74

Salama, P. *Les Voies romaines de l'Afrique du Nord* (1951)

Salmon, E. T. *History of the Roman world from 30 B.C. to A.D. 138* (1963)

Saria, B. 'Ein Dionysosvotiv aus dem Konsulatsjahr des P. Dasumius Rusticus' *JOAI* 26 (1930) 64–74

Sartori, A. T. 'I confini del territorio di *Comum* in età romana' *ACSDIR* 1 (1967–8) 275–90

Scamuzzi, U. 'Contributo ad una obiettiva conoscenza della vita e dell'opera di Marco Valerio Marziale' *Rivista di studi classici* 14 (1966) 149–207

Schneider, A. M. *Die römischen und byzantinischen Denkmäler von Iznik-Nicaea (Istanbuler Forschungen 16)* (1943)

Scott, K. 'The significance of statues in precious metals in Emperor worship' *TAPHA* 62 (1931) 101–23

Segré, A. *Circolazione monetaria e prezzi nel mondo antico ed in particolare in Egitto* (1922)
'Note sulla storia dei cereali nell'antichità' *Aegyptus* 30 (1950) 161–97

Seston, W. 'Sur une inscription de Souk-el-Abiod' *BAC* (1946–9) 309–11

Skydsgaard, J. E. 'Nuove ricerche sulla villa rustica Romana fino all'epoca di Traiano' *Analecta Romana Instituti Danici* 5 (1969) 25–40

Slicher van Bath, B. H. *Yield ratios 810–1820 (A.A.G. Bijdragen* 10) (1963)

Spano, G. 'La tomba dell'edile C. Vestorio Prisco in Pompei' *Mem.Lincei* ser.7, 3 (1943) 237–315

Speidel, M. 'The captor of Decebalus. A new inscription from Philippi' *JRS* 60 (1970) 142–53

Sperber, D. 'Costs of living in Roman Palestine IV' *Journ.econ.soc.hist.Orient* 13 (1970) 1–15

Sullivan, J. P. *The Satyricon of Petronius* (1968)

Syme, R. review of M. Durry (ed.) *Pline, Panégyrique de Trajan, JRS* 28 (1938) 217–24

  'Proconsuls d'Afrique sous Antonin le Pieux' *REA* 61 (1959) 310–19

  'Pliny the procurator' *HSCP* 73 (1969) 201–36

Szilagyi, J. 'Prices and wages in the western provinces of the Roman Empire' *AAASH* 11 (1963) 325–89

Taylor, L. R. '*Augustales, Seviri Augustales* and *Seviri*: a Chronological Study' *TAPHA* 45 (1914) 231–53

Thouvenot, R. *Volubilis* (1949)

Tissoni, G. G. 'Nota sul patrimonio immobiliare di Plinio il giovane' *RIL* 101 (1967) 161–83

Tissot, C. J. *Géographie comparée de la province romaine d'Afrique* (1884–8)

Tourrenc, S. 'La dédicace du temple du Génie de la colonie à Timgad' *Ant.afr.*2 (1968) 197–220

Toutain, J. *Cités romaines de la Tunisie* (1895)

Toynbee, A. J. *Hannibal's Legacy* (1965)

Toynbee, J. M. C. *Art in Roman Britain* (1962)

United Nations Population studies 26 'The Aging of Populations and its economic and social implications' (1956)

Veyne, P. 'Vie de Trimalcion' *AESC* 16 (1961) 213–47

Villers, R. 'Essai sur la pollicitatio à une *res publica*' *RHDFE* 18 (1939) 1–38

de Visscher, F. 'La fondation funéraire de Iunia Libertas d'après une inscription d'Ostie' *Studi S.Solazzi* (1948) 542–53

  Le droit des tombeaux romains (1963)

Walbank, F. W. *A Commentary on Polybius* 1 (1957)

Wallon, H. *Histoire de l'esclavage dans l'antiquité* (1879)

Ward Perkins, J. B. 'Nero's Golden House' *Antiquity* 30 (1956) 209–19

Warmington, E. H. *The commerce between the Roman Empire and India* (1928)

Waters, K. A. 'Traianus Domitiani continuator' *AJP* 90 (1969) 385–405

Watson, G. R. *The Roman Soldier* (1969)

West, L. C. 'The cost of living in Roman Egypt' *CP* 11 (1916) 293–314

Westermann, W. L. *Slave systems of Greek and Roman antiquity* (1955)

White, K. D. 'Wheat-farming in Roman times' *Antiquity* 37 (1963) 207–12

  'The productivity of labour in Roman agriculture' *Antiquity* 39 (1965) 102–7

  'Latifundia' *Bull.Inst.Class.Stud.* 14 (1967) 62–79

Wiegand, Th. 'Die puteolanische Bauinschrift' *Jahrb.f.class.Phil.* Supp.Bd 20 (1894) 661–778

Winkler, A. J. *General Viticulture* (Berkeley, 1962)

Wiseman, T. P. 'The Census in the First Century B.C.' *JRS* 59 (1969) 59–75

Wittfogel, K. A. *Oriental Despotism. A Comparative Study of Total Power* (1957)

Yeo, C. A. 'Land and sea transportation in imperial Italy' *TAPHA* 77 (1946) 221–44

'The overgrazing of ranch-lands in ancient Italy' *TAPHA* 79 (1948) 275–307

Young, A. *A Course of Experimental Agriculture* (1770)

INDEX

The index contains lists of subjects, place-names, personal names and sources. Numerals in italics refer to entries in the list of costs on pp. 90-114 and 157-223. Other numerals denote page-numbers.

Chapter numbers in ancient authors, and inscription numbers have not been repeated in the index. Passages in ancient authors can be traced by means of the subject headings listed under each main author; the majority of the inscriptions used in the book are tabulated on pp. 90-114 and 157-223. Names of ancient deities and names of modern scholars are omitted from the index. Works by modern scholars are listed separately on pp. xii ff. and 370-8.